W9-AQG-803

Ethical Reflections

Develop critical thinking skills with discussion-based activities that revolve around nursing ethics.

Legal Perspectives

Promote thinking critically about legal scenarios in the discipline of nursing.

Focus for Debate

Weigh in on interesting scenarios relevant to the field of nursing and engage in ethics-related debates.

Page 4 — Chapter 1 Introduction to Ethics

approaches, and theories used in studying ethics throughout history so they can identify and analyze ethical issues and dilemmas relevant to nurses in the 21st century. Mature, ethical sensitivities are critical to ethical practice, and as Hope (2004) proposed, "we need to develop our hearts as well as our minds" (p. 6).

The Meaning of Ethics and Morals

When narrowly defined according to its original use, ethics is a branch of philosophy used to study ideal human behavior and ways of being. The approaches to ethics and the meanings of related concepts have varied over time among philosophers and ethicists. For example, Aristotle believed ideal behaviors are practices leading to the end goal of *eudaimonia*, which is synonymous with a high level of happiness or well-being; on the other hand, Immanuel Kant, an 18th-century philosopher and ethicist, believed ideal behavior is acting in accordance with one's duty. For Kant, well-being meant having the freedom to exercise autonomy (self-determination), not being used as a means to an end, being treated with dignity, and having the capability to think rationally.

As a philosophical discipline of study, ethics is a systematic approach to under-

in doing ethics. However, people sometimes allow their emotions to overtake good reasoning; when this happens, it does not provide a good foundation for ethical decisions. Evaluations generated through the practice of ethics require a balance of emotion and reason. Throughout history, people, based on their culture, have engaged in actions they believe are justifiable only to have the light of reason later show otherwise. Following a charismatic but egocentric leader such as Adolf Hitler is an example of such a practice.

> **ETHICAL REFLECTION**
>
> Consider a person who believes abortion is wrong based on the position that human life is sacred. Can this same person logically justify that the death penalty is a moral action? Discuss.

As contrasted with ethics, morals are specific beliefs, behaviors, and ways of being derived from doing ethics. One's morals are judged to be good or bad through systematic,

Page 5 — Introduction to Ethics

When people consider matters of ethics, they usually are considering matters about freedom regarding personal choices, one's obligations to other sentient beings, or judgments about human character. The term *unethical* is used to describe ethics in its negative form, for instance, when a person's character or behavior is contrary to admirable traits or the code of conduct endorsed by one's society, community, or profession. Because the word *ethics* is used when one may be referring to a situation of morals, the process-related, or *doing*, conception of ethics is sometimes overlooked today. People often use the word *ethics* when referring to a collection of actual beliefs and behaviors, thereby using the terms *ethics* and *morals* interchangeably. In this text, some effort has been made to distinguish the words *ethics* and *morals* based on their literal meanings; however, because of common uses, the terms have generally been used interchangeably.

The following features regarding the concepts of *morals* and *ethics* were adapted from Billington (2003):

- Probably the most important feature about ethics and morals is that no one can avoid making ethical decisions because social connections with others necessitates that people must consider moral and ethical actions.
- Other people are directly or indirectly involved with one's ethical decisions. Private morality does not exist.

Types of Ethical Inquiry

Ethics is categorized according to three types of inquiry or study: normative ethics, metaethics, and descriptive ethics. The first approach, normative ethics, is an attempt to decide or prescribe values, behaviors, and ways of being that are right or wrong, good or bad, admirable or dishonorable. When using the method of normative ethics, inquiries are made about how humans should behave, what ought to be done in certain situations, what type of character one should have, or the type of person one should be.

> **LEGAL PERSPECTIVE**
>
> Common law is based on customs and previously decided cases rather than on statutes.

Outcomes of normative ethics are the prescriptions derived from asking normative questions. These prescriptions include accepted moral standards and codes. One such accepted moral standard identified by Beauchamp and Childress (2019) is the common morality. The common morality consists of normative beliefs and behaviors that members of a society generally agree about and are familiar to most members of the society. These norms develop within the context of history

Page 9 — Values and Moral Reasoning

for upsetting the sociopolitical status quo. Socrates was accused of corrupting the youth of Athens who, under his tutelage, began to question traditional wisdom and religious beliefs. These accusations of corruption were based on Socrates encouraging people to think independently and question dogma generated by the ruling class. Though he was sentenced to death by the powerful, elite men within his society, Socrates refused to apologize for his beliefs and teachings. He ultimately chose to die by drinking poisonous hemlock rather than deny his values.

Plato, Socrates's student, is believed by some to have been the most outstanding philosopher to have ever lived. Plato's reasoning is based on his belief that there are two realms of reality. The first is the realm of *Forms*, which transcends time and space. According to Plato, an eternal, perfect, and unchanging ideal copy (Form) of all phenomena exists in the realm of Forms, which is beyond everyday human access. Plato believed the realm of Forms contains the essence of concepts and objects and even the essence of objects' properties. Essences exist in the realm of Forms include, for example, a perfect Form of good, redness (the color red), or a horse. In the realm of Forms, the essence of good exists as ideal Truth, and redness (a particular property of some objects, such as an apple) exists as the color red in its most perfect state. A horse in the realm of Forms is the perfect specimen of the animal that is a horse, and this perfect horse contains all the "horseness" factors that, for example, distinguish a horse from a cow. Plato considered the world of Forms to be the real world, though humans do not live in this world.

The second realm is the world of *Appearances*, which is the everyday world of imperfect, decaying, and changing phenomena; this is the world in which humans live. The purpose, or goal, of imperfect phenomena in the world of Appearances is to emulate their associated essences and perfect Forms. For example, a horse's purpose in life is to strive toward

becoming identical to the perfect specimen of a horse that exists in the world of Forms.

Plato also proposed that humans have a tripartite soul. The three parts of the soul consist of the Faculty of Reason, associated with thought and Truth, which is in one's head; the Faculty of Spirit, which expresses love, beauty, and the desire for eternal life and is in one's chest; and the Faculty of Appetite, which is an expression of human desires and emotions and is in one's gut. Plato believed the influences of these three parts of the soul exist in greater to lesser degrees in each person. Therefore, one person may be more disposed to intellectual pursuits as compared to another person who is more interested in physical pleasures.

Plato associated the tripartite soul with three classes of Greek society and one's best-suited occupation. People were believed to have an individual aptitude particularly suited to them and their purpose in society:

- Philosopher kings were associated with the Faculty of Reason and wisdom.
- Societal guardians were associated with the Faculty of Spirit and protecting others.
- Artisans and craftsmen were associated with the Faculty of Appetite and technical work.

> **FOCUS FOR DEBATE**
>
> If Florence Nightingale were alive today and she took the position that nurses represent Plato's guardian class and physicians represent the artisan class, would she be correct? Defend your answer.

Florence Nightingale, the founder of modern nursing, was a passionate student of ancient Greek philosophy. Nightingale may have aligned the function of nurses with the Faculty of Spirit (LeVasseur, 1998). Because of her education in classical Greek literature and culture and her views about nursing, LeVasseur proposed that Nightingale might have

Key Points

Review of short, bulleted summaries of key points at the end of each chapter.

may experience moral suffering and uncertainty. When passionate ethical disputes arise between nurses and physicians or when nurses are seriously concerned about the action of patients' decision-making representatives, nurses are the ones who often seek an ethics consultation. It is within the rights and duties of nurses to seek help and advice from other professionals when they experience moral uncertainty or witness unethical conduct in their work setting. This action is a part of the nurse's role as a patient advocate.

KEY POINTS

- Bioethics was born out of the rapidly expanding technical environment of the 1900s.
- The four most well-known and frequently used bioethical principles are respect for autonomy, beneficence, nonmaleficence, and justice.
- Paternalism involves an overriding of autonomy in favor of the principle of beneficence.
- Social justice emphasizes the fairness of how the benefits and burdens of society are distributed among people.
- Ethical dilemmas involve unclear choices; not clear matters of right versus wrong.
- Nurses often experience a disquieting feeling of anguish, uneasiness, or angst in their work that is consistent with what might be called moral suffering.
- It is paradoxical that patients often must trust healthcare providers to care for them before the providers show evidence that trust is warranted.
- When acting as patient advocates, nurses try to identify patients' unmet needs and help to address these needs.
- Nurses may develop good critical thinking skills by thinking about their thinking.
- It is part of a nurse's role as a patient advocate to make or suggest an ethics committee referral when indicated.

References

Agency for Healthcare Research and Quality [AHRQ] Patient Safety Network [PSNet]. (2019). *Adverse events, near misses, and errors*. https://psnet.ahrq.gov/primer /adverse-events-near-misses-and-errors
American Medical Association (AMA). (2021). *Withholding information from patients*. https://www.ama-assn.org

Buppert, C. (2017, September 18). *A major court decision: Only physicians can obtain consent*. https://www.medscape.com/viewarticle/883579
Chambliss, D. F. (1996). *Beyond caring: Hospitals, nurses, and the social organization of ethics*. University of Chicago Press.

Research Notes

Additional readings and sources are provided for further learning.

RESEARCH NOTE: TUSKEGEE SYPHILIS STUDY

During the late 1920s in the United States, syphilis rates were extremely high in some areas. The private Rosenwald Foundation teamed with the United States Public Health Service (USPHS) to begin efforts to control the disease using the drug neosalvarsan, an arsenic compound. Macon County, Alabama, particularly the town of Tuskegee, was targeted because of its high rate of syphilis, as identified through a survey. However, the Great Depression derailed the plans, and the private foundation withdrew from the work. The USPHS repeated the Rosenwald survey in Macon County and identified a syphilis rate of 22% among African American men in the county and a 62% rate of congenital syphilis cases. The natural history (progression) of syphilis had not been studied yet in the United States, and the surgeon general suggested that 399 African American men with syphilis in Tuskegee should be observed, rather than treated, and compared with a group of 200 African American men who were uninfected. The men were not told about the natural history of syphilis and were told these nontherapeutic spinal taps to provide data about the natural history of syphilis and were told these procedures were treatments for "bad blood." The men were given free meals, medical treatment for diseases other than their syphilis, and free burials. Even after penicillin was discovered in the 1940s, the men were not offered treatment. In fact, the USPHS researchers arranged to keep the uninformed study participants out of World War II because the men would be tested for syphilis, treated with penicillin, and lost from the study. The unethical research continued for 40 years, from 1932 to 1972. During the 40 years of research, an astonishing number of articles about the study were published in medical journals, and no attempt was made to hide the surreptitious terms of the research. No one intervened to stop the travesty. Finally, a medical reporter learned of the study, and the ethical issues were exposed.

After reading this chapter and researching more information on the Internet about the Tuskegee research, including the contribution of Nurse Evers, answer the following questions:

1. What were the main social issues with ethical implications involved in this study?
2. Which bioethical principles were violated by the Tuskegee study? Explain.
3. How can various ethical approaches be applied to the Tuskegee study? (Include approaches discussed in an earlier chapter 1.)
4. Discuss the role of Nurse Evers in the Tuskegee research.
5. Which procedures are in place today to prevent this type of unethical research?

Case Studies

Read and analyze real-life situations dealing with nursing ethics. Then use critical thinking skills and knowledge from the text to answer questions.

Appendix A

Case Studies

Working through the following case studies is intended to be done using this book and the American Nurses Association's (2015) *Code of Ethics for Nurses with Interpretive Statements*. Researching supplemental information also may be helpful to expand learning opportunities and provide more complete answers to questions.

Chapter 1

1-1: Which Patient's Needs Should Be Given First Priority?

Over several years, Suzie has been the nurse for 50-year-old Mrs. Gilmore, who has been frequently admitted to the oncology unit in the hospital where Suzie works. Suzie and Mrs. Gilmore have developed a close relationship based on trust and respect. During her current admission, Mrs. Gilmore's condition has been deteriorating, and she has elected to initiate a do not resuscitate (DNR) order. Today, she is experiencing agonal breathing and is nearing death. On several occasions, Mrs. Gilmore stated she is afraid of dying. She asked Suzie to promise to be with her when she dies if she is in the hospital and Suzie is working at the time. While Mrs. Gilmore's daughter is alone with her mother in the hospital room, and the daughter is frightened. While Mrs. Gilmore progresses toward imminent death, Suzie's newly postoperative oncology patient, Mr. Statten, suddenly and unexpectedly has a grand mal seizure. Suzie just met this patient when he returned from surgery earlier in the morning. Mr. Statten's wife is hysterical. As Mr. Statten's primary nurse, Suzie goes into action caring for him and notifies his physician about the seizure. Jennifer, the nursing technician working with Suzie today, comes to Suzie to figure out how to care for both of her patients. The nursing technician also has a close relationship with Mrs. Gilmore and her daughter. The wheels of Suzie's mind begin to turn trying to figure out how to care for both of her patients who need special attention as well as the other three patients she is caring for today. Suzie has a high regard for Jennifer's intellectual abilities and technician skills, but Suzie knows there are limits to what can be delegated to unlicensed, assistive personnel. It is a busy day for all the staff on the unit.

Questions

Review the chapter content.

1. What should Suzie do about caring for both her patients who need her at the same time as well as properly caring for her other three patients? What are the most ethical

SIXTH EDITION

NURSING ETHICS

Across the Curriculum and Into Practice

Welcome to

NURSING ETHICS

SIXTH EDITION

Across the Curriculum and Into Practice

The Pedagogy

Nursing Ethics: Across the Curriculum and Into Practice, Sixth Edition, drives comprehension through various strategies that meet the learning needs of students and practicing nurses while also generating enthusiasm about the topic. This interactive approach addresses different learning styles, making this the ideal text to ensure mastery of key concepts. The pedagogical aids that appear in most chapters include the following.

Objectives

These objectives provide instructors and students with a snapshot of the key information they will encounter in each chapter. They serve as a checklist to help guide and focus study.

CHAPTER 1

Introduction to Ethics

Karen L. Rich

A seed will only become a flower if it gets sun and water.

—**Louis Gottschalk**

OBJECTIVES

After reading this chapter, the reader should be able to do the following:

1. Define the terms *ethics* and *morals* and discuss philosophical uses of these terms.
2. Discuss systems of moral reasoning as they have been used throughout history.
3. Evaluate a variety of ethical theories and approaches to use in personal and professional relationships.

Introduction to Ethics

In the world today, "we are in the throes of a giant ethical leap that is essentially embracing all of humankind" (Donahue, 1996, p. 484). Scientific and technological advances, economic realities, pluralistic worldviews, and global health and social issues make it difficult for nurses to ignore the important ethical issues in the world community, their everyday lives, and their work. The Covid-19 pandemic makes this point evident for citizens of the 21st century. As controversial and sensitive ethical issues continue to challenge nurses and other healthcare professionals, many professionals have begun to develop an appreciation for traditional philosophies of ethics and the diverse viewpoints of others.

Ethical directives are not always clear, and people sometimes disagree about what is right and wrong, for example, what we owe our fellow humans. These factors lead some people to believe ethics can be based merely on personal opinions. However, if nurses are to enter the global dialogue about ethics, they must do more than practice ethics based simply on their personal opinions, their intuition, or the unexamined beliefs proposed by other people. It is important for nurses to have a basic understanding of the concepts, principles,

3

SIXTH EDITION

NURSING ETHICS

Across the Curriculum and Into Practice

Janie Butts, PhD, RN
Professor Emeritus of Nursing
The University of Southern Mississippi School of Nursing

Karen L. Rich, MN, PhD, RN
Associate Professor, Retired
The University of Southern Mississippi School of Nursing

JONES & BARTLETT
LEARNING

World Headquarters
Jones & Bartlett Learning
25 Mall Road
Burlington, MA 01803
978-443-5000
info@jblearning.com
www.jblearning.com

Jones & Bartlett Learning books and products are available through most bookstores and online booksellers. To contact Jones & Bartlett Learning directly, call 800-832-0034, fax 978-443-8000, or visit our website, www.jblearning.com.

25934-6

Production Credits
Vice President, Product Management: Marisa R. Urbano
Vice President, Content Strategy and Implementation: Christine Emerton
Director, Product Management: Matthew Kane
Product Manager: Joanna Gallant
Director, Content Management: Donna Gridley
Manager, Content Strategy: Carolyn Pershouse
Content Strategist: Christina Freitas
Content Coordinator: Samantha Gillespie
Director, Project Management and Content Services: Karen Scott
Manager, Project Management: Jackie Reynen
Project Manager: Roberta Sherman
Senior Digital Project Specialist: Angela Dooley
Director, Marketing: Andrea DeFronzo
Senior Product Marketing Manager: Lindsay White
Content Services Manager: Colleen Lamy
VP, Manufacturing and Inventory Control: Therese Connell
Product Fulfillment Manager: Wendy Kilborn
Composition: S4Carlisle Publishing Services
Project Management: S4Carlisle Publishing Services
Cover Design: Michael O'Donnell
Senior Media Development Editor: Troy Liston
Rights & Permissions Manager: John Rusk
Rights Specialist: Maria Leon Maimone
Cover & Title Page Image: © Seller 1234/Shutterstock
Printing and Binding: LSC Communications

Library of Congress Cataloging-in-Publication Data

Names: Butts, Janie B., author. | Rich, Karen L., author.
Title: Nursing ethics : across the curriculum and into practice / Janie B. Butts, Karen L. Rich.
Description: Sixth edition. | Burlington, MA : Jones & Bartlett Learning, [2023] | Includes bibliographical references and index.
Identifiers: LCCN 2022011967 | ISBN 9781284259247 (paperback)
Subjects: MESH: Ethics, Nursing | Nurse-Patient Relations--ethics
Classification: LCC RT85 .B78 2023 | NLM WY 85 | DDC 174.2--dc23/eng20220519
LC record available at https://lccn.loc.gov/2022011967

6048

Printed in the United States of America
26 25 24 23 22   10 9 8 7 6 5 4 3 2 1

Brief Contents

Contents

**Chapter 3   Ethics in Professional
             Nursing Practice 67**

**PART II   Nursing Ethics Across
          the Life Span   105**

**Chapter 4   Reproductive Issues
             and Nursing Ethics 107**

Preface

Rules and theories matter little without the formation of good character.

We are honored by our book's popularity among nurse educators, students, and other nurses. Our highest compliments came from two users of the previous editions: "I have never found anyone who said it better than Butts and Rich" and "You provide one of the best and most accessible overviews for students of how the common 4-principles framework can be both sensitive to many of the issues that care ethics raises and compatible with the development of particular ethical competencies in nursing practice." We hope readers will find the *Sixth Edition* an even better resource for teaching and learning nursing ethics.

The profession of nursing is experiencing one of the most important eras in its history. Although nurses are experiencing new and unique difficulties in their practice, they have more autonomy than ever before. With autonomy comes responsibility. For the front cover, we chose a picture focused on Zen rocks precariously balanced. The rocks stand before what we believe symbolizes a swampy low ground like the ground described by Schön (1987), which is described in Chapter 2. Nurses work in a world of ethical dilemmas with frustrating and heart-breaking conditions. However, we believe they need to aim toward maintaining equanimity, meaning maintaining an evenness of temperament particularly in difficult circumstances. We hope the content in our book will help nurses and students cultivate equanimity and the virtues needed to bring a healthy moral climate to their practice.

▶ American Association of Colleges of Nursing Recommendations in 2021

The American Association of Colleges of Nursing's (AACN's) *The Essentials: Core Competencies for Professional Nursing* Education (2021) recommends an inclusion of a comprehensive range of nursing ethics and ethical decision-making strategies in nursing curricula. The AACN's (2021) view of ethics is embedded throughout the Essentials document with a global idea of transforming nursing to a new social order for the goal of advancing the discipline of nursing. The AACN stated:

> A new social order may be necessary in which scientists, theorists, and practitioners work together to address questions related to the interplay of big data and nursing theory. Nursing graduates . . . must be well-prepared to think ethically, conceptually, and theoretically to better inform nursing care. Students must not only be introduced to the knowledge and values of the discipline, but they must be guided to practice from a disciplinary perspective—by seeing patients through the lens of wholeness and interconnectedness . . . (p. 3)

Several concepts are "interrelated and interwoven within the domains and competencies" of the Essentials document to make up the foundation for student learning (AACN, 2021, p. 12). One of those interrelated concepts is ethics. The AACN posed the question, "Can you imagine having a conversation about population health [for instance] without considering ethics and health policy?" (p. 12).

Principles of ethics in medical and health care include autonomy, beneficence, nonmaleficence, and justice. The application of these principles steers students and nurses to make sound moral choices in practice. The AACN integrated ethics into its domains, competencies, and sub-competencies for entry-level professional nursing education and advanced-level nursing education. AACN's entry-level ethical competencies pertaining to our book include:

Domain 1, Sub-Competency 1.2e	Demonstrate ethical decision making
Domain 3, Sub-Competency 3.1i	Identify ethical principles to protect the health and safety of diverse populations.
Domain 9, Sub-Competencies 9.1a, 91c, and 9.1e	9.1a-Apply principles of professional nursing ethics and human rights in patient care and professional situations. 9.1c-Demonstrate ethical behaviors in practice. 9.1e-Report unethical behaviors when observed.
Domain 9, Sub-Competency 9.2c	Demonstrate empathy to the individual's life experience.
Domain 9, Sub-Competency 9.5d	Demonstrate ethical comportment and moral courage in decision making and actions.

Some of the moral issues nurses encounter daily leave nurses to manage ethical decisions and actions in a swampy low ground of uncertainties. When nurses become bogged down in ethical situations, such as global pandemics, death, abortion, or saving premature infants, nurses will most likely experience moral distress. Nurses must be prepared to attach their own meanings to life and death. Nursing students and practicing nurse clinicians need to acquire foundational knowledge about ethics, ethical reasoning, and decision-making strategies to prepare them for the ethical issues they will encounter daily. Included in this book are decision-making approaches and models, rationale for decisions, and various topics about ethical patient care.

▶ *NCLEX-RN® Test Plan* for 2019

The National Council of State Boards of Nursing's 2019 *NCLEX-RN® Test Plan* applies the goal of nursing care, which is "preventing illness and potential complications; protecting, promoting, restoring, and facilitating comfort, health and dignity in dying" (p. 4). Examples of the integration of ethics into the test plan include the following:

- *NCLEX-RN Test Plan:* **Safe and Effective Care Environment**—Ethical Practice (pp. 8-12)
  - Recognizing ethical dilemmas and taking appropriate action
  - Inform others (clients, staff) of ethical issues affecting client care
  - Use the ANA Code of Ethics (2015) consistently as a guideline for practice
  - Evaluate outcomes to promote continued improvement of ethical practice
- *NCLEX-RN Test Plan:* **Psychosocial Integrity (p. 21-25)**
  - End-of-life care includes client coping, identifying client needs, recognizing the need for support, assisting in resolution of end-of-life issues,

and providing end-of-life care and education

- Grief and loss includes providing care for clients with grief or loss, supporting anticipatory grieving, informing client of expected reactions to grief or loss, providing resources for adjusting to grief or loss, and evaluating coping and fears
- Religious and spiritual influences on health includes identifying client emotional and spiritual issues and needs, assessing factors affecting care, assessing and planning emotional and spiritual needs, evaluating if the client's spiritual needs are met

Purposes and Readership

We have four purposes for this book. First, we wanted to provide a nursing ethics book that covers a wide array of ethical issues in nursing. We included bioethical issues nurses encounter every day—the ones Fry and Veatch (2000) stated are the "flesh and blood" issues (p. 1)—but we also covered issues from a humanistic perspective. In the body of the text, we included theoretical foundations, the most current scholarly literature and clinical evidence, related news briefs, research notes, ethical reflections, and legal perspectives surrounding ethics topics.

Second, a prominent feature of this book is its "across the curriculum" format for undergraduate nursing students. The book can be used as a supplementary textbook in each nursing course. We believe that if ethical concepts and bioethical issues are integrated in the beginning of nursing programs and throughout curricula, students will become more mindful of the myriad of ethical challenges they will face in practice and then become habituated to resolving conflicts ethically. Ultimately, we believe nurses with knowledge of ethics will want to find ways to participate in the large-scale bioethical deliberations and

decision making regarding their patients' and families' life and death issues.

As a third purpose, RN to BSN students also can use this book in their curricula, especially in ethics, professional development, or leadership courses. Even though RN to BSN students bring a wealth of real flesh-and-blood experiences with them to share in the classroom, they often return to school without substantial exposure to ethics classes or ethical content.

The last part of the book's title, "Into Practice," is related to the book's fourth purpose. Nurses' work *is* nursing ethics. The content of the book will stimulate the moral imagination of nurses so they can integrate ethical principles, theories, and decision-making skills into their everyday practice.

Comments and Feedback

We are dedicated to making this book the one that will meet your needs for the future. We are interested in your comments about the book. Please email us at Janie Butts at jbbdsn1998@ gmail.com or Karen Rich at karenrich11470@ gmail.com with feedback or questions concerning the book, questions about ethics, or any questions you may have regarding the case studies in Appendix A or the multiple choice questions in the instructor's materials. We continue to appreciate your positive support!

References

American Association of Colleges of Nursing. (2021, April 6). *The essentials: Core competencies for professional nursing education.* https://www.aacn nursing.org/Portals/42/AcademicNursing/pdf /Essentials-2021.pdf

Fry, S. T., & Veatch, R. M. (2000). *Case studies in nursing ethics* (2nd ed.). Jones and Bartlett.

National Council of State Boards of Nursing. (2019). *NCLEX-RN® detailed test plan for 2019.* https://www .ncsbn.org/2019_RN_TestPlan-English.pdf

PART I

Theories and Concepts

CHAPTER 1

Introduction to Ethics

Karen L. Rich

A seed will only become a flower if it gets sun and water.

—**Louis Gottschalk**

OBJECTIVES

After reading this chapter, the reader should be able to do the following:

1. Define the terms *ethics* and *morals* and discuss philosophical uses of these terms.
2. Discuss systems of moral reasoning as they have been used throughout history.
3. Evaluate a variety of ethical theories and approaches to use in personal and professional relationships.

▶ Introduction to Ethics

In the world today, "we are in the throes of a giant ethical leap that is essentially embracing all of humankind" (Donahue, 1996, p. 484). Scientific and technological advances, economic realities, pluralistic worldviews, and global health and social issues make it difficult for nurses to ignore the important ethical issues in the world community, their everyday lives, and their work. The Covid-19 pandemic makes this point evident for citizens of the 21st century. As controversial and sensitive ethical issues continue to challenge nurses and other healthcare professionals, many professionals have begun to develop an appreciation for traditional philosophies of ethics and the diverse viewpoints of others.

Ethical directives are not always clear, and people sometimes disagree about what is right and wrong, for example, what we owe our fellow humans. These factors lead some people to believe ethics can be based merely on personal opinions. However, if nurses are to enter the global dialogue about ethics, they must do more than practice ethics based simply on their personal opinions, their intuition, or the unexamined beliefs proposed by other people. It is important for nurses to have a basic understanding of the concepts, principles, approaches, and theories used in studying ethics throughout history so they can identify and analyze ethical issues and dilemmas relevant to nurses in the 21st century. Mature, ethical sensitivities are critical to ethical practice, and as Hope (2004) proposed, "we need to develop our hearts as well as our minds" (p. 6).

The Meaning of Ethics and Morals

When narrowly defined according to its original use, ethics is a branch of philosophy used to study ideal human behavior and ways of being. The approaches to ethics and the meanings of related concepts have varied over time among philosophers and ethicists. For example, Aristotle believed ideal behaviors are practices leading to the end goal of **eudaimonia**, which is synonymous with a high level of happiness or well-being; on the other hand, Immanuel Kant, an 18th-century philosopher and ethicist, believed ideal behavior is acting in accordance with one's duty. For Kant, well-being meant having the freedom to exercise autonomy (self-determination), not being used as a means to an end, being treated with dignity, and having the capability to think rationally.

As a philosophical discipline of study, **ethics** is a systematic approach to understanding, analyzing, and distinguishing matters of right and wrong, good and bad, and admirable and dishonorable as they relate to the well-being of and the relationships among sentient beings. Today with global warming, even relationships between people and their environment have entered the realm of ethics. Ethical determinations are applied using theories, approaches, and codes of conduct, such as codes developed for professions and religions. Ethics is an active process rather than a static condition, so some ethicists use the expression *doing ethics*. When people are doing ethics, they need to support their beliefs and assertions with sound reasoning rather than with strong opinions.

Feelings and emotions are a normal part of everyday life and can play a legitimate role in doing ethics. However, people sometimes allow their emotions to overtake good reasoning; when this happens, it does not provide a good foundation for ethical decisions. Evaluations generated through the practice of ethics require a balance of emotion and reason. Throughout history, people, based on their culture, have engaged in actions they believe are justifiable only to have the light of reason later show otherwise. Following a charismatic but egocentric leader such as Adolf Hitler is an example of such a practice.

ETHICAL REFLECTION

Consider a person who believes abortion is wrong based on the position that human life is sacred. Can this same person logically justify that the death penalty is a moral action? Discuss.

As contrasted with ethics, **morals** are specific beliefs, behaviors, and ways of being derived from doing ethics. One's morals are judged to be good or bad through systematic, ethical analysis. The reverse of morality is *immorality*, which means a person's behavior is in opposition to accepted social, cultural, or professional ethical standards and principles; examples of immorality include dishonesty, fraud, murder, and sexually abusive acts. *Amoral* is a term used to refer to actions normally judged as immoral, but the actions are done with a lack of concern for good character, one's duty, or the consequences. For example, murder is immoral, but if a person commits murder with absolutely no sense of remorse or maybe even with a sense of pleasure, the person is acting in an amoral way. Acts are *nonmoral* if moral standards essentially do not apply to the acts; for example, choosing between cereal or toast and jam for breakfast is a nonmoral decision.

When people consider matters of ethics, they usually are considering matters about freedom regarding personal choices, one's obligations to other sentient beings, or judgments about human character. The term *unethical* is used to describe ethics in its negative form, for instance, when a person's character or behavior is contrary to admirable traits or the code of conduct endorsed by one's society, community, or profession. Because the word *ethics* is used when one may be referring to a situation of morals, the process-related, or *doing*, conception of ethics is sometimes overlooked today. People often use the word *ethics* when referring to a collection of actual beliefs and behaviors, thereby using the terms *ethics* and *morals* interchangeably. In this text, some effort has been made to distinguish the words *ethics* and *morals* based on their literal meanings; however, because of common uses, the terms have generally been used interchangeably.

The following features regarding the concepts of *morals* and *ethics* were adapted from Billington (2003):

- Probably the most important feature about ethics and morals is that no one can avoid making ethical decisions because social connections with others necessitates that people must consider moral and ethical actions.
- Other people are directly or indirectly involved with one's ethical decisions. Private morality does not exist.
- Ethical decisions matter because one person's decisions often affect someone else's life, self-esteem, or happiness.
- It is difficult to reach definite conclusions or resolutions in ethical debates.
- In the area of morals and ethics, people cannot exercise ethical judgments without being given a choice; in other words, a necessity for making a sound ethical judgment is being able to choose an option from among several choices.
- People use moral reasoning to make ethical judgments or to discover right actions.

Types of Ethical Inquiry

Ethics is categorized according to three types of inquiry or study: normative ethics, meta-ethics, and descriptive ethics. The first approach, **normative ethics**, is an attempt to decide or prescribe values, behaviors, and ways of being that are right or wrong, good or bad, admirable or dishonorable. When using the method of normative ethics, inquiries are made about how humans should behave, what ought to be done in certain situations, what type of character one should have, or the type of person one should be.

LEGAL PERSPECTIVE

Common law is based on customs and previously decided cases rather than on statutes.

Outcomes of normative ethics are the prescriptions derived from asking normative questions. These prescriptions include accepted moral standards and codes. One such accepted moral standard identified by Beauchamp and Childress (2019) is the common morality. The **common morality** consists of normative beliefs and behaviors that members of a society generally agree about and are familiar to most members of the society. These norms develop within the context of history and form a "a stable societal compact" (p. 3) about how people should behave. Because it forms what can be thought of as a universal morality with a wide scope, the common morality provides society with a framework of ethical stability. The common morality contains rules of obligation, character traits, and common moral ideals. The beliefs that it is moral to tell the truth, exhibit loving-kindness, and be charitable are part of the common morality, whereas abortion is not a part of the common morality because of the many varying positions about its rightness or wrongness.

Gert and colleagues (2006) contended that many people mistakenly believe there is little agreement about moral matters, whereas, controversial issues are the focus of only a small part of ethical decision making.

Particular nonuniversal moralities adhered to by specific groups can be distinguished from the common morality (Beauchamp & Childress, 2019). Particular moralities, such as those based on a certain ethical theory or approach (see those discussed later in this chapter) or a profession's moral norms and codes, are heavily content laden and specific rather than general in nature. Yet these nonuniversal moralities generally are consistent with socially sanctioned beliefs falling under a common morality. The *Code of Ethics for Nurses with Interpretive Statements* (American Nurses Association, 2015) is a specific morality for professional nurses in the United States. A normative belief posited in the *Code* is that nurses ought to be compassionate; that is, nurses should work to relieve suffering. Nurses have specific obligations that are different from the obligations of other people. As risks and dangers for nurses become more complex, the profession's morality must evolve and be continually reexamined. Nurses might ask themselves these normative questions: Do I have an obligation to endanger my life and the life of my family members by working during a dangerous pandemic? Do I have an obligation to stay at work in a hospital during a category 5 hurricane rather than evacuating with my family? The answers to these questions may generate strong emotions, confusion, or feelings of guilt.

LEGAL PERSPECTIVE

Some actions may be legal, but people do not agree that the actions are moral. Research and debate issues such as the following:

- Breaking promises
- Palliative or terminal sedation

The focus of **metaethics**, which means *about ethics*, is not an inquiry about what ought to be done or which behaviors should be prescribed. Instead, metaethics is concerned with understanding the language of morality through an analysis of the meaning of ethically related concepts and theories, such as the meaning of *good*, *happiness*, and *virtuous character*. For example, a nurse who is actively engaged in a metaethical analysis might try to determine the meaning of a *good* nurse–patient relationship.

Descriptive ethics is often referred to as a scientific rather than a philosophical ethical inquiry. It is an approach used when researchers or ethicists want to describe what people think about morality or when they want to describe how people behave, that is, their morals. Professional moral values and behaviors can be described through nursing research. An example of descriptive ethics is research that identifies nurses' attitudes regarding telling patients the truth about their terminal illnesses.

Ethical Perspectives

Though it may seem somewhat contrary to the contention that there is an understandable common morality, ethical thinking, valuing, and reasoning are believed to fall somewhere along a continuum between two opposing views: ethical relativism and ethical objectivism. After reading the following discussion about ethical perspectives, it probably will seem sensible to reflect on the meaning of philosophy and why ethics is a philosophical pursuit. Ethical issues and discussions frequently have blurred edges. They do not fit into a circumscribed mold. However, this does not make doing ethics merely an opinion-based endeavor, though one can reasonably argue that extremes of ethical relativism come close.

Ethical Relativism

Ethical relativism is the belief that it is acceptable for ethics and morality to differ among persons or societies. There are two types of ethical relativism: ethical subjectivism and cultural relativism (Brannigan & Boss, 2001). People who subscribe to a belief in **ethical subjectivism** believe "individuals create their own morality [and] there are no objective moral truths—only individual opinions" (p. 7). People's beliefs about actions being right or wrong or good or bad depend on how people feel about actions rather than on substantive reason or systematic ethical analysis. What one person believes to be wrong might not be viewed as wrong by one's neighbors, depending on variations in how people justify their beliefs and feelings. These differences are acceptable to ethical subjectivists.

Ethical subjectivism has been distinguished from cultural relativism. Pence (2000) defined **cultural relativism** as "the ethical theory that moral evaluation is rooted in and cannot be separated from the experience, beliefs, and behaviors of a particular culture, and hence, that what is wrong in one culture may not be so in another" (p. 12). People who are opposed to cultural relativism argue that when it is practiced according to its extreme or literal meaning, this type of thinking can be dangerous because it theoretically may support relativists' exploitative or hurtful actions (Brannigan & Boss, 2001). An example of cultural relativism is the belief that the act of female circumcision, sometimes called female genital mutilation, is a moral practice. Though not considered to be a religious ritual, this act is considered ethically acceptable by some groups in countries with a Muslim or an Egyptian Pharaonic heritage. In most countries and cultures, however, it is a grave violation in accordance with the United Nations' Declaration of Human Rights.

Ethical Objectivism

Ethical objectivism is the belief that universal, or objective, moral principles exist. Many philosophers and healthcare ethicists hold this view, at least to some degree, because

they strictly or loosely adhere to a specific approach in determining what is good. Examples of objectivist ethical theories and approaches are deontology, utilitarianism, and natural law theory, which are discussed later in this chapter. Though some ethicists believe these theories or approaches are mutually exclusive, theories and approaches often overlap when used in practice. "Moral judgment is a whole into which we must fit principles, character and intentions, cultural values, circumstances, and consequences" (Brannigan & Boss, 2001, p. 23).

ETHICAL REFLECTION

Where does your personal worldview fall on the continuum between ethical relativism and ethical objectivism? Defend your position.

▶ Values and Moral Reasoning

Because ethics falls within the abstract discipline of philosophy, ethics involves many perspectives of what people value as meaningful and good in their lives. A **value** is something of worth or highly regarded. Values refer to one's evaluative judgments about what one believes is good or makes something desirable. The things people esteem to be *good* influence how personal character develops and people think and subsequently behave. Professional values are outlined in professional codes. A fundamental position in the American Nurses Association's (2015) *Code of Ethics for Nurses with Interpretive Statements* is that professional and personal values must be integrated. Values and moral reasoning in nursing fall under the domain of normative ethics; that is, professional values contained in the *Code* guide nurses in how they ought to be and behave.

Reasoning is the use of abstract thought processes to think creatively, answer questions, solve problems, and formulate strategies for one's actions and desired ways of being. When people participate in reasoning, they do not merely accept the unexamined beliefs and ideas of other people. Reasoning involves thinking for oneself to determine if one's conclusions are based on good or logical foundations. More specifically, **moral reasoning** pertains to reasoning focused on moral or ethical issues. Moral reasoning for nurses usually occurs in the context of day-to-day relationships between nurses and the recipients of their care and between nurses and their co-workers and others within organizations.

Different values, worldviews, and ways of moral reasoning have evolved throughout history and had different points of emphasis in various historical periods. Regarding some approaches to reasoning about moral issues, what was old becomes new again, as in the case of the renewed popularity of virtue ethics, or the concept of reasoning as would be practiced by a person with good character.

Ancient Greece

In Western history, much of what is known about formal moral reasoning began with the ancient Greeks, especially with the philosophers Socrates (ca. 469–399 BCE), Plato (ca. 429–347 BCE), and Aristotle (384–322 BCE). Though there are no primary texts of the teachings of Socrates (what we have of his teachings were recorded by Plato), it is known that Socrates was an avid promoter of moral reasoning and critical thinking among the citizens of Athens. Socrates is credited with the statement "the unexamined life is not worth living," and he developed a method of reasoning called Socratic questioning, or the Socratic method, which is still used today.

In using his method of inspiring open-mindedness and critical thinking, Socrates posed challenging questions and then would ask another question about the answers he received. A goal of participating in a Socratic dialogue is to investigate the accuracy, clarity, and value of one's intellectual positions and beliefs. An example of his method of questioning is as follows:

> Socrates: Why should a nurse study ethics?
> Nurse: To be a good nurse.
> Socrates: What is a good nurse?
> Nurse: It means my patients are well taken care of.
> Socrates: How do you know your patients are well taken care of?

This line of questioning should continue until the concepts and positions stemming from the original question are thoroughly explored. Socratic questioning does not mean one ends up with a final answer; however, this form of discussion encourages people to continually expand their thinking in critical and reflective ways.

ETHICAL REFLECTION

In a senior nursing ethics class, my students wanted to "go Greek" for a Socratic dialogue session. Some students dressed in a toga, they brought Greek food to school, we sat on blankets, had a picnic, and engaged in Socratic dialogues under the oak trees on campus. We had a great time! In small groups, begin a Socratic dialogue with classmates or colleagues. Develop your own questions or use the following examples. A Socratic dialogue should be civil, nonthreatening, and supportive of learning; it is not a means to belittle people who have beliefs different from one's own. After your dialogue, share your understandings with other groups.

- What does *caring* mean in nursing?
- What does *competence* mean in nursing?
- What is *academic integrity*?

Socrates had many friends and allies who believed in his philosophy and teachings. In fact, Socrates was such a successful and well-known teacher of philosophy and moral reasoning in Athens that he was put to death for upsetting the sociopolitical status quo. Socrates was accused of corrupting the youth of Athens who, under his tutelage, began to question traditional wisdom and religious beliefs. These accusations of corruption were based on Socrates encouraging people to think independently and question dogma generated by the ruling class. Though he was sentenced to death by the powerful, elite men within his society, Socrates refused to apologize for his beliefs and teachings. He ultimately chose to die by drinking poisonous hemlock rather than deny his values.

Plato, Socrates's student, is believed by some to have been the most outstanding philosopher to have ever lived. Plato's reasoning is based on his belief that there are two realms of reality. The first is the realm of *Forms*, which transcends time and space. According to Plato, an eternal, perfect, and unchanging ideal copy (Form) of all phenomena exists in the realm of Forms, which is beyond everyday human access. Plato believed the realm of Forms contains the essence of concepts and objects and even the essence of objects' properties. Essences existing in the realm of Forms include, for example, a perfect Form of good, redness (the color red), or a horse. In the realm of Forms, the essence of good exists as ideal Truth, and redness (a particular property of some objects, such as an apple) exists as the color red in its most perfect state. A horse in the realm of Forms is the perfect specimen of the animal that is a horse, and this perfect horse contains all the "horseness" factors that, for example, distinguish a horse from a cow. Plato considered the world of Forms to be the real world, though humans do not live in this world.

The second realm is the world of *Appearances*, which is the everyday world of imperfect, decaying, and changing phenomena; this is the world in which humans live. The purpose, or goal, of imperfect phenomena in the world of Appearances is to emulate their associated essences and perfect Forms. For example, a horse's purpose in life is to strive toward becoming identical to the perfect specimen of a horse that exists in the world of Forms.

Plato also proposed that humans have a tripartite soul. The three parts of the soul consist of the Faculty of Reason, associated with thought and Truth, which is in one's head; the Faculty of Spirit, which expresses love, beauty, and the desire for eternal life and is in one's chest; and the Faculty of Appetite, which is an expression of human desires and emotions and is in one's gut. Plato believed the influences of these three parts of the soul exist in greater to lesser degrees in each person. Therefore, one person may be more disposed to intellectual pursuits as compared to another person who is more interested in physical pleasures.

Plato associated the tripartite soul with three classes of Greek society and one's best-suited occupation. People were believed to have an individual aptitude particularly suited to them and their purpose in society:

- Philosopher kings were associated with the Faculty of Reason and wisdom.
- Societal guardians were associated with the Faculty of Spirit and protecting others.
- Artisans and craftsmen were associated with the Faculty of Appetite and technical work.

FOCUS FOR DEBATE

If Florence Nightingale were alive today and she took the position that nurses represent Plato's guardian class and physicians represent the artisan class, would she be correct? Defend your answer.

Florence Nightingale, the founder of modern nursing, was a passionate student of ancient Greek philosophy. Nightingale may have aligned the function of nurses with the Faculty of Spirit (LeVasseur, 1998). Because of her education in classical Greek literature and culture and her views about nursing, LeVasseur proposed that Nightingale might have compared her purpose as a nurse with the role of a societal guardian. In contrast, early physicians, whose profession developed through apprenticeship guilds, which emphasized technical practices, might be compared to the artisan class.

One of Plato's most famous stories about reasoning is his allegory of the cave. In this story, a group of people lived their lives chained to the floor of a cave. Behind them burned a fire that cast shadows of people moving on the wall in front of the people who were chained. The chained prisoners believed the shadows were real people. When one of the prisoners was freed from his chains, he left the cave. First, he was blinded by the brightness of the sun. After his sight adjusted to the light, he saw objects he realized were more real than the shadows within the cave. The freed person returned to the cave to encourage the other prisoners to break their chains and enter the more expansive world of reality. The meaning of this story has been interpreted in many ways. Whatever Plato's intended meaning, the story does prompt people to think about the problems that result when they remain chained by their closed minds and flawed reasoning.

Plato's student Aristotle developed science, logic, and ethics to world-altering proportions. Though he was influenced by Plato, Aristotle took a more practical approach to reasoning than believing in an otherworldly realm of ideal Forms. He was guided in his reasoning by his belief in the importance of empirical inquiry. He also believed all things have a purpose, or end goal (*telos*), like Plato's proposition that the goal of all things is to strive to resemble their perfect Form. In *Nicomachean Ethics*, Aristotle (trans. 2002) discussed practical wisdom (**phronesis**) as being necessary for deliberation about what is good and advantageous if people want to move toward their human purpose, or desired end goal, of happiness or well-being (*eudaimonia*). Aristotle believed a person needs education to cultivate *phronesis* to achieve intellectual excellence.

ETHICAL REFLECTION

Compare Plato's allegory of the cave to critical thinking in nursing. Think of a few personal examples when you were chained in the cave. What were the circumstances? What were the outcomes? What made a difference in your thinking?

Aristotle's conception of *phronesis* is like Plato's conception of the virtue of prudence. Wisdom is focused on the good achieved from being wise, which means one knows how to act in a particular situation, deliberates well, and has a disposition embodying excellence of character. Therefore, in ancient Greece, prudence is more than simply having good intentions or meaning well; it is knowing what to do and how to be but also involves transforming knowledge into well-reasoned actions. Aristotle believed people are social beings whose reasoning should lead them to be good citizens and friends and to act in moderate ways.

The Middle Ages

After the Roman Empire was divided by barbarians and the Roman Emperor Romulus was dethroned (ca. 476 CE), the golden age of intellectualism and cultural progress in Western Europe ended. The next historical period was the Middle, or Dark, Ages, which lasted until about 1500 CE. In the gap left by the failed political system of Rome, Christianity became the dominant religion in Western Europe as the Catholic Church took on the powerful role of educating European people. Christianity is a monotheistic (one God) revelatory religion, whereas ancient Greek philosophy was based on the use of reason and polytheism (many gods). Because Greek philosophy was believed to be heretical, its examination was discouraged during the church-dominated Middle Ages. However, it is interesting that two Catholic saints, Augustine and Aquinas, who provided the major ethical influence during the Middle Ages, were both influenced by the ancient Greeks.

Saint Augustine (354–430 CE) is often considered to be the Plato of the Middle Ages. Though Augustine was a Christian and Plato was a non-Christian, Augustine's belief in a heavenly place of unchanging moral truths is like Plato's belief in the realm of ideal Forms. Augustine believed these Truths are imprinted by God on the soul of each human being. According to Augustine, one has a duty to love God, and moral reasoning should direct one's senses in accordance with that duty; being subject to this obligation is what leads to moral perfection. Generally, Saint Augustine believed in the existence of only good, like how the essence of good would exist if it were an ideal Form. Therefore, evil is present only when good is missing or has in some way been perverted from its existence as an ideal Truth.

Augustine was 56 years old during the fall of the Roman Empire. In one of his most famous writings, *The City of God*, Augustine used the fall of the Roman Empire to explain a philosophy sometimes compared to Plato's conception of the worlds of Forms and Appearances. People who live according to the spirit live in the City of God (world of perfection/Forms), whereas people who live according to the flesh live in the City of Man (world of imperfection/Appearances). To move away from evil, one must have the grace of God. Augustine viewed humans as finite beings who must have the divine aid of grace to bridge the gap required to have a relationship with the infinite being of God.

The Crusades influenced Europe's exodus from the Dark Ages. When Christians entered Islamic lands, such as Spain, Portugal, and North Africa, they were reintroduced to intellectualism, including texts of the ancient Greeks, especially Aristotle. The moral teachings of Saint Thomas Aquinas (1224–1274) are sometimes viewed as a Christianized version of Aristotle's ethical teachings. Aquinas tried to reconcile Aristotle's teachings with the teachings of the Catholic Church. Like Aristotle, Aquinas believed people have a desirable end goal, or purpose, and developing excellences of character (virtues) leads to human happiness and good moral reasoning. Aristotle's non-Christian moral philosophy is based on humans moving toward an end goal, or dynamic state, of *eudaimonia* (happiness or well-being) through the cultivation of excellent intellect and moral character.

Aquinas expanded Aristotle's conception of the end goal of perfect happiness and grounded the requirements for happiness in the knowledge and love of God and Christian virtues. Aquinas replaced Aristotle's emphasis on the virtue of pride with an emphasis on the virtue of humility. Aristotle believed pride is an important characteristic of independent, strong men, whereas Aquinas valued the characteristic of humility because it represented to him one's need to depend on the benevolence of God. In addition to virtue ethics, Aquinas is associated with a belief in reasoning according to the natural law theory of ethics. Both ethical approaches are covered later in this chapter.

Modern Philosophy and the Age of Enlightenment

The period of modern philosophy began when the Catholic Church, the major intellectual force during the Middle Ages, began to have a diminishing influence within society while the influence of science began to increase. The scientific revolution began in 1543, when Copernicus discovered that the Earth and humans are not the center of the universe, but this revolution did not rapidly advance until the 17th century, when Kepler and Galileo moved scientific debates to the forefront of society.

With these changes came a new freedom in human moral reasoning based on people being autonomous, rational-thinking creatures rather than primarily being influenced and controlled by Church dogma and rules. During the 18th-century Enlightenment era, humans believed they were coming out of the darkness of the Middle (Dark) Ages into the light of true knowledge.

Some scientists and philosophers were bold enough to believe humans could ultimately be perfected and all knowledge would be discovered. As the belief in empirical science grew, a new way of thinking was ushered in that compared both the universe and people to machines. Many scientists and philosophers believed the world, along with its inhabitants, could be reduced through analyses into their component parts. These reductionists hoped that after most or all knowledge was discovered, the universe and human behavior could be predicted and controlled. People still demonstrate evidence of this way of thinking in health care today when *cure* is highly valued over *care* and uncertainty is believed to be something that can or should be eliminated in health and illness. A **mechanistic approach** is one that focuses on fixing problems as if one is fixing a machine, as contrasted to a humanistic, or holistic, approach, in which one readily acknowledges that well-being and health occur along a complex continuum and some situations and health problems cannot be predicted, fixed, or cured.

ETHICAL REFLECTION

Identify examples of mechanistic practices in health care today.

During the 18th century, David Hume (1711–1776) proposed an important idea about moral reasoning. Hume argued there is a distinction between facts and values when moral reasoning is practiced. This *fact/value distinction* also has been called the *is/ought gap*. A skeptic, Hume suggested a person should not acknowledge a fact and then make a value judgment based on that fact, because one logically cannot take a fact of what *is* and then determine an ethical judgment of what *ought to be*. If Hume's position is accepted as

valid, people should not make assumptions such as the following: (1) if all dogs have fleas (assuming this is a known fact) and (2) Sara is a dog (a fact), then (3) Sara ought not to be allowed to sleep on the sofa because having fleas on the sofa is a bad thing (a value statement). According to people who believe in the truth of the fact/value distinction, the chance of Sara spreading her fleas to the sofa might be a fact if she sleeps on it but determining that having fleas on the sofa is a bad thing is based on only one's values or feelings.

Postmodern Era

After the scientific hegemony of the Enlightenment era, some people began to question whether a single-minded allegiance to science was creating problems for human societies. Postmodernism often is considered to have begun around 1950, after the end of World War II. However, some people trace its beginnings back to German philosopher Friedrich Nietzsche in the late 1800s. Pence (2000) defined *postmodernism* as "a modern movement in philosophy and the humanities that rejects the optimistic view that science and reason will improve humanity; it rejects the notion of sustained progress through reason and the scientific method" (p. 43). The postmodern mind is formed by a pluralistic view, or a diversity of intellectual and cultural influences. People who live according to a postmodern philosophy acknowledge that reality is constantly changing, and scientific investigations cannot provide one grand theory or correct view of an absolute Truth that can guide human behavior, relationships, and life. Human knowledge is thought instead to be shaped by multiple factors, with storytelling and narrative analysis being viewed as core components of knowledge development.

Care-Based Versus Justice-Based Reasoning

A care approach to moral reasoning often is associated with a feminine way of thinking, and a cure approach usually is associated with a masculine, Enlightenment-era way of thinking. In 1981, Lawrence Kohlberg, a psychologist, reported his landmark research about moral reasoning based on 84 boys he had studied for more than 20 years. Based on the work of Jean Piaget, Kohlberg defined six stages of moral development ranging from childhood to adulthood. Interestingly, Kohlberg did not include any women in his research, but he expected to use his six-stage scale to measure moral development in both males and females.

When the scale was applied to women, they seemed to score at only the third stage of the sequence, a stage in which Kohlberg described morality in terms of interpersonal relationships and helping others. Kohlberg viewed the third stage of development as deficient in regard to mature moral reasoning. Because of Kohlberg's exclusion of females in his research and his negative view of this third stage, Carol Gilligan, one of Kohlberg's associates, raised the concern of gender bias. Gilligan, in turn, published an influential book in 1982, *In a Different Voice*, in which she argued that women's moral reasoning is different but not deficient. The distinction usually made between moral reasoning as it is suggested by Kohlberg and Gilligan is that Kohlberg's is a male-oriented ethic of justice and Gilligan's is a more feminine ethic of care (covered later in this chapter).

Learning from History

Often, it is only in hindsight that people can analyze a historical era in which there is a converging of norms and beliefs held in high esteem or valued by large groups within a society. Like the overlapping approaches used by some ethical objectivists, the influences of historical eras also build upon and are integrated with each other and often are hard to separate. Christians still base much of their ethical reasoning on the philosophy generated during the Middle Ages. At the same time, it is evident that individualistic ways of thinking that were

popular during the Enlightenment remain popular today in Western societies because autonomy (self-direction) is so highly valued. Because varied historical influences have affected moral reasoning, there is a pattern of rich and interesting values, perspectives, and practices evident in today's globally connected world.

Ethical Theories and Approaches

Normative ethical theories and approaches function as moral guides to answer the questions "What ought I do or not do?" and "How should I be?" A theory can provide individuals with guidance in moral thinking and reasoning as well as justification for moral actions. The following theories and approaches are not all inclusive, but they represent some of the most popular.

Western Ethics

Religion and Western Ethics

A discussion of Western ethics systems likely prompts some people to want to include monotheistic Western religious traditions, such as Judaism, Christianity, and Islam. Morality in each of these religions is based on sacred texts—the first five books of the Old Testament of the Bible (Torah) in Judaism, the Old and especially the New Testament of the Bible in Christianity, and the Qur'an (Koran) given by Allah to the Prophet Muhammad in Islam. Pleasing God, according to sacred laws and traditions, dominates prescribed moral behavior in each of these religious groups. In addition to sacred scripture, there are historical figures who heavily influenced religious ethical systems, for example, the Catholic saints Augustine and Aquinas and the medieval Jewish philosopher Maimonides.

The politically, socially, and intellectually focused ancient Greeks provided the most developed system of ethics in the Western world until the Middle Ages when religious doctrine became the primary focus. Then, as people moved into the Enlightenment period and again viewed human intellect as being trustworthy for providing moral guidance, secular systems of ethics overtook religious systems. Today, among many people, the lines between sacred and secular ethics are blurred. It is a key point of understanding ethics; however, that in a post-Enlightenment world, ethics falls under the umbrella of philosophy rather than religion. The ethical systems discussed in this chapter are those considered to be classic theories and approaches in Western ethical philosophy, though some of them do stem from religious traditions.

FOCUS FOR DEBATE

Does a person need to be religious to be moral? For example, can an atheist be moral? Can or should ethics be separated from religion? Defend your positions.

Virtue Ethics

Watch your thoughts; they become words.
Watch your words; they become actions.
Watch your actions; they become habits.
Watch your habits; they become character.
Watch your character; it becomes your destiny

—Frank Outlaw

Rather than centering on what is right or wrong in terms of one's duties or the consequences of one's actions, the excellence of one's character and considerations of what sort of person one wants or ought to be are emphasized in **virtue ethics**. Since the time of Plato and Aristotle, virtues, called *arête* in Greek, have referred to excellences regarding people or objects being the best they can be in accordance with their purpose. As the ancient Greeks originally conceived the concept, even an inanimate object can have virtue. For example, the purpose of a knife is to cut, so *arête* regarding a knife means the knife has a sharp edge and cuts very well. If one needs the services of a knife, it is probably safe to assume a knife that exhibits excellence in cutting would be the type of knife one would want to use; most people want to use a knife that accomplishes its purpose in the best way possible.

For humans, virtue ethics addresses the question "What sort of person must I be to be an excellent person?" rather than "What is my duty?" **Virtues** for humans are habitual, though not routinized, excellent traits intentionally developed throughout one's life. Annas (2011) outlined a description of how to spot virtue. Regarding a person, a virtue is a "lasting feature" (loc. 138); it is "active" and develops "through selective response to circumstances" (loc. 142). Virtue "persists through challenges and difficulties, and it is strengthened or weakened by . . . responses" (loc. 142). "A virtue is also a reliable disposition . . . it is no accident" (loc. 146).

A person of virtue, consistent with Aristotle's way of thinking, is a person who is an excellent friend to other people, an excellent thinker, and an excellent citizen of a community. Aristotle's (trans. 2002) approach to virtue ethics is grounded in two categories of excellence: intellectual virtues and character (moral) virtues. According to Aristotle, "the intellectual sort [of virtue] mostly . . . comes into existence and increases as a result of teaching (which is why it requires experience and time), whereas excellence of character results from habituation" (p. 111). The habituation Aristotle had in mind is an intelligent, mindful attention to excellent habits rather than a thoughtless routinization of behaviors.

Though Aristotle (trans. 2002) divided virtues into two kinds—those of the intellect and those of character—the two categories of virtues cannot be distinctly separated. Aristotle proposed "it is not possible to possess excellence in the primary sense [that is, having excellence of character] without wisdom, nor to be wise without excellence of character" (p. 189).

Aristotle realized good things taken to an extreme could become bad. He therefore proposed a Golden Mean. Most virtues are considered to exist as a moderate way of being between two kinds of vices or faults: the extremes of excess at one end and deficiency at the other end. For instance, Aristotle named courage as a virtue, but the extremes of rashness (too much of the virtue) at one end of a continuum and cowardice (too little of the virtue) at the other end of the same continuum are its related vices. Another example is the virtue of truthfulness, which is the mean between boastfulness (too much) and self-deprecation (too little). The mean for each virtue is unique for each type of virtue and situation; in other words, the mean is not a mathematical average.

Other examples of virtues include benevolence, compassion, fidelity, generosity, and patience. Plato designated the four virtues of prudence (wisdom), fortitude (courage), temperance (moderation), and justice as cardinal virtues, meaning all other virtues hinge on these four primary virtues. Prudence corresponds to Plato's idea of the Faculty of Reason, fortitude corresponds to the Faculty of Spirit, and temperance corresponds to the Faculty of Appetite; the virtue of justice is an umbrella virtue encompassing and tying together the other three.

The ancient Greeks are most frequently associated with virtue ethics, but other philosophers and ethicists also have proposed views about virtues. The Scottish philosopher David Hume (1711–1776) and the German philosopher Friedrich Nietzsche (1844–1900) each proposed an interesting philosophy of virtue ethics that differs from the philosophies of the Greeks, though Hume's and Nietzsche's are not the only other approaches to virtue ethics.

Hume, whose approach is used by some feminist philosophers, believed virtues flow from a natural human tendency to be sympathetic or benevolent toward other people. Virtues are human character traits admired by most people and judged to be generally pleasing as well as being useful to other people, useful to oneself, or useful to both other people and to oneself. Because of Hume's focus on the *usefulness* of virtues, his approach to ethics is also associated with utilitarianism, which is discussed later in this chapter. Hume's philosophy of ethics is based on emotion as the primary human motivator for admirable behavior rather than motivation by reason. However, Hume did not propose that ethics is based merely on opinion. Virtuous behavior is validated by the consensus of members of communities according to what is useful for a community's well-being.

A different and more radical view of virtue ethics is based on the philosophy of Nietzsche. Rather than viewing people as caring, sympathetic beings, Nietzsche proposed the best character for people to cultivate is grounded in a *will to power*. Nietzsche believed the will to power rightly should motivate people to achieve dominance in the world. Nietzsche praised strength as virtuous, whereas so-called feminine virtues, such as caring and kindness, he considered to be signs of weakness. This means, according to Nietzsche, that virtue is consistent with hierarchical power or power over other people, which makes the Christian virtue of humility a vice. It is believed another German, Adolf

ETHICAL REFLECTION

Partner with a colleague, and list several real-life examples related to each line of the quotation at the beginning of the "Virtue Ethics" section.

Hitler, adopted the philosophy of Nietzsche as his worldview. Though Nietzsche is a well-known and important person in the history of philosophy, his approach to virtue ethics has little place in nursing ethics.

Although virtue ethics is popular again today, over the years interest in this ethical approach experienced a significant decline among Western philosophers and nurses (MacIntyre, 1984; Tschudin, 2003). Many Western philosophers lost interest in the virtues when they became entrenched in the schools of thought popularized during the Enlightenment era that emphasized individualism and autonomy (MacIntyre, 1984).

Over time, nurses concluded it was not helpful professionally to follow the tradition of Florence Nightingale because her view of virtues in nursing includes a virtue of obedience (Sellman, 1997). However, Nightingale's valuing of obedience needs to be viewed within the context of the time in which she lived. Also, Nightingale's liberal education in Greek philosophy may have influenced her use of the virtue of obedience to reflect her belief in the value of practical wisdom as conceived by Aristotle (LeVasseur, 1998; Sellman, 1997). In connecting obedience to practical wisdom, some nurses now understand Nightingale's conception as approaching something akin to intelligent obedience rather than a subservient allegiance of nurses to physicians.

FOCUS FOR DEBATE

Can a limited set of virtues be identified as essential for members of the nursing profession? Which virtues are most important in nursing? Search the American Nurses Association's (2015) *Code of Ethics for Nurses with Interpretive Statements* and identify a list of virtues discussed directly or indirectly in the document. Remember, virtues are excellent qualities of character.

Natural Law Theory

There is in fact a true law—namely, right reason—which is in accordance with nature, applies to all men, and is unchangeable and eternal. By its commands this law summons men to the performance of their duties; by its prohibitions it restrains them from doing wrong.

—Marcus Tullius Cicero,
The Republic (51 BCE)

Natural law theory has a long and varied history, dating back to the work of the ancient Greeks. In fact, natural law theory is complex, and attempting to present its essence would be to oversimplify the theory (Buckle, 1993). Even the terms *nature* and *natural* are ambiguous.

Aristotle's conception of natural law theory is a universal type of justice grounded in the laws of nature rather than human law. Most modern versions of natural law theory have their basis in the religious philosophy of Saint Thomas Aquinas. Remember, Aquinas has been compared to Aristotle. Because Aquinas believed God created everything and implanted all things with purpose and order in concert with His will, he deduced that people could investigate nature and find God's expectations there. Consequently, people who use natural law theory contend the rightness of actions is self-evident because morality is inherently implanted in the order of nature and not revealed through customs and preferences. Today, natural law theory is the basis for religious prohibitions against acts some people consider *unnatural*, such as homosexuality and the use of birth control.

Though natural law theory and divine command theory sometimes are confused, they have a fundamental difference. According to divine command theory, an action is good because a divine being, such as God, commands it, whereas with natural law theory, a divine being commands an action because it is moral irrespective of said divine being.

Deontology

Deontology, literally the *study of duty*, is an approach to ethics focused on duties and rules. The most influential philosopher associated with the deontological way of thinking was Immanuel Kant (1724–1804). Kant defined a person as a rational, autonomous (self-directed) being with the ability to know universal, objective moral laws and the freedom to decide to act morally. **Kantian deontology** prescribes that each rational being is ethically bound to act only from a sense of duty; when deciding how to act, the consequences of one's actions are irrelevant.

According to Kant, it is only through dutiful actions that people can be moral. Even when individuals do not want to act from duty, Kant believed they are ethically bound to do so. In fact, Kant asserted that having one's actions motivated by duty is superior to acting from a motivation of love. Because rational choice is within one's control as compared to one's tenuous control over personal emotions, Kant was convinced that only reason, not emotion, is sufficient to lead a person to moral actions.

Kant believed people are ends in themselves and should be treated accordingly. Each autonomous, self-directed person has dignity and is due respect, and one should never act in ways that involve using other people as a means to one's personal ends. In fact, when people use others as a means to an end, even if they believe they are attempting to reach ethical goals, Kant believed people could be harmed. An example of this today is the failure to obtain informed consent from a research participant even when the researcher steadfastly believes the research will be beneficial to the participant.

Kant identified rules to guide people in thinking about their obligations. He drew a distinction between two types of duties or obligations: the hypothetical imperative and the categorical imperative. Hypothetical imperatives are optional duties, or rules, people ought to observe or follow if certain ends are to be achieved. Hypothetical imperatives are sometimes called *if–then imperatives*, which means they involve conditional, or optional, actions; for instance, if I want to become a nurse, then I must study during nursing school.

Where moral actions are concerned, Kant believed duties and laws are absolute and unconditional. Kant proposed that people ought to follow a universal, unconditional framework of maxims, or rules, as a guide to know the rightness of actions and one's moral duties. He called these absolute and unconditional duties **categorical imperatives**. When deciding about matters of ethics, one should act according to a categorical imperative and ask the question "If I perform this action, could I will that it should become a universal law for everyone to act in the same way?" No action can ever be judged as right, according to Kant, if it is not reasonable that the action could be used as a binding, ethical law for all people. For example, Kant's ethics imposes the categorical imperative that one should never tell a lie because a person cannot rationally wish

---

that all people should be able to pick and choose when they have permission not to be truthful. Another example of a categorical imperative is that suicide is never acceptable. A person, when committing suicide, should not rationally wish that all people should feel free to commit suicide, or the world would become chaotic.

Consequentialism

Consequentialists, as distinguished from deontologists, *do* consider consequences to be an important indication of the moral value of one's actions. Utilitarianism is the most well-known consequentialist theory of ethics. Utilitarianism means actions are judged by their utility; that is, they are evaluated according to the usefulness of their consequences (see Hume above). When people use the theory of **utilitarianism** as the basis for ethical behavior, they attempt to promote the greatest good (happiness or pleasure) and to produce the least amount of harm (unhappiness, suffering, or pain) possible in a situation. In other words, utilitarians believe it is useful to society to achieve the greatest good for the greatest number of people who may be affected by an action.

British philosopher Jeremy Bentham (1748–1832), a contemporary and associate of Florence Nightingale's father, was an early promoter of the principle of utilitarianism. During Bentham's life, British society functioned according to aristocratic privilege. Low income people were mistreated by people in the upper classes and given no choice other than to work long hours in deplorable conditions. Think about the workhouses discussed in Dickens' *A Christmas Carol*. Bentham tried to develop a theory to achieve a fair distribution of pleasure among all British citizens. He went so far as to develop a systematic decision-making method using mathematical calculations. Bentham's method was designed to determine ways to allocate pleasure and diminish pain by using the measures of intensity and duration. This

approach to utilitarianism has been criticized because Bentham equated all types of pleasure as being equal.

John Stuart Mill (1806–1873), another Englishman, challenged Bentham's views. Mill clearly pointed out that experiences of pleasure and happiness do have different qualities and different situations do not necessarily produce equal consequences. For example, Mill stated that higher intellectual pleasures may be differentiated from lower physical pleasures. The higher pleasures, such as enjoying a work of art or reading a good book, are considered better because only human beings, not other animals, possess the mental faculties to enjoy this higher level of happiness.

According to Mill, happiness and pleasure are measured by quality and not quantity (duration or intensity). In making these distinctions between higher and lower levels of happiness and pleasure, Mill's philosophy is focused more on ethics than politics and social utility.

Mill believed communities usually agree about what is good and things that best promote the well-being of most people. An example of an application of Mill's utilitarianism is the use of mandatory vaccination laws, which rose to the forefront during the Covid-19 pandemic—individual liberties are limited so the larger society is protected from diseases, and the consequence is that people are happier because they are free of diseases. People who use Mill's form of utilitarian theory often can use widely supported traditions to guide them in deciding about rules and behaviors that probably will produce the best consequences for the most people, such as the maxim that stealing is wrong. Through experience, humans generally have identified behaviors that produce the most happiness or unhappiness for society.

Over time, people who subscribe to a theory of utilitarianism have divided themselves into subgroups. Two main types of utilitarianism have developed over the years: rule utilitarianism and act utilitarianism. **Rule utilitarians** believe there are certain rules—such as do not kill, do not break promises, and do not lie—that, when followed, usually create the best consequences for the most people. Based on this definition, someone might ask, "What is the difference between rule utilitarianism and deontology?" The answer is that all utilitarian theories of ethics, whether based on rules or individual actions, are predicated on achieving good consequences for the most people. Deontologists, on the other hand, make decisions based on right duty rather than on right consequences.

Act utilitarians believe each action in a particular circumstance should be chosen based on its likely good consequences rather than on following an inherently moral, universal rule. The utility of each action in achieving the most happiness is the aim of act utilitarians, whereas rule utilitarians are willing to accept causing more suffering than happiness in a particular situation to avoid violating a generalized rule. For example, promise breaking is permitted according to act utilitarianism if the consequences of the action (breaking a promise) cause more happiness than suffering in a particular situation. In the same situation, a rule utilitarian would say a promise should be upheld because, in most cases, promise keeping causes more happiness than suffering.

LEGAL PERSPECTIVE

Conduct a search about the theory of utilitarianism; infectious diseases, such as Covid-19 and *Mycobacterium tuberculosis*; and the law. Discuss your findings.

Prima Facie Rights

The term **prima facie** means on one's first impression, or on the face of things; that is, something is accepted as correct until or unless it is shown to be otherwise. For example, promise keeping is considered an accepted ethical rule. However, if a nurse promised her spouse that she would be on time for dinner, but as she was about to leave the hospital, she was told the nurse replacing her would be late for work, it is expected that the nurse would break her promise to be on time for dinner so she could attend to her patients until the other nurse arrives.

Prima facie ethics is associated with the philosopher Sir William David Ross (1877–1971) and his 1930 book, *The Right and the Good*. Ross is called an ethical intuitionist because he believed certain things are intrinsically good and self-evidently true. Ross understood ethics to suggest that certain acts are prima facie good—keeping promises, repaying kindnesses, helping others, and preventing distress. However, when these prima facie good actions conflict, one must decide where one's actual duty lies. Ross conceded that human knowledge is imperfect and the best people can expect to do is use their imperfect knowledge to assess the context of each situation and make an informed judgment, although they are uncertain about the correctness of their choices. Ross's approach to ethics has quite a bit of relevance for nurses who frequently must make quick determinations of how to prioritize important actions that might cause distress for one person while helping another.

Principlism

Principles are rule-based criteria for conduct that naturally flow from the identification of obligations and duties. Consequently, the theory of deontology is a forerunner of the approach of principlism. Principles usually are reducible to concepts or statements, such as the principle of beneficence or respect for a person's autonomy. Often, principles are used as the basis for ethically related documents, such as documents reflecting positions about human rights. Examples of principle-based documents include the American Hospital Association's (2003) *The Patient Care Partnership* and the Universal Declaration of Human Rights, formulated in 1948 by the United Nations. Principlism probably is the most used ethical approach to health care. It is discussed in more detail in a later chapter 2.

Casuistry

Casuistry is an approach to ethics grounded in Judeo-Christian history. When people use **casuistry**, they make decisions inductively based on individual cases. The analysis and evaluation of strongly similar or outstanding cases (i.e., paradigm cases) provides guidance in ethical decision making. A paradigm case is a benchmark, or landmark, case against which decisions in similar cases are compared and that provides guidance in similar cases.

When people use casuistry, their ethical decision making begins as an inductive, bottom-up approach in considering the details of specific cases rather than beginning from the top down and applying absolute rules and principles. Long ago, Jewish people often tried to sort out the relevance of sacred laws in specific situations in ways that were practical and case based rather than absolute and inflexibly rule based. In Catholic history, the practice of people individually confessing their sins to priests to receive absolution reflects the use of casuistry. Based on the confessing person's specific case (i.e., the circumstances surrounding the sins), a person receives from the priest a personal penance that is required for absolution.

LEGAL PERSPECTIVE

Search the internet for information on the 1986 Florida legal case *Corbett v. D'Alessandro*. How is the final legal decision in this case related to the ethical approach of casuistry and the later case of *Schindler v. Schiavo*?

With principlism, casuistry is used in healthcare decision making even though most providers do not know the name of the approach. Casuistry is often the method used

by healthcare ethics committees to analyze the ethical issues surrounding specific patient cases. The Four Topics Method of ethical decision making is based on a casuistry approach (see discussion in a later chapter 2).

Narrative Ethics

Narrative ethics is associated with postmodernism, which was discussed in this chapter; and because it is a story-based approach, narrative ethics has similarities to casuistry. Also, according to one of the foremost modern-day virtue ethicists, Alasdair MacIntyre, narrative thinking and virtue ethics are closely connected. Both narrative ethics and virtue ethics are firmly embedded in human relationships. MacIntyre (1984) proposed that a human is "essentially a story-telling animal;" a person is "a teller of stories that aspire to truth" (p. 216). Narratives, such as novels and literary stories, change us in remarkable ways (Murray, 1997). From childhood, most people obtain moral education about character development from stories, such as fairy tales and fables (see **BOX 1-1**). When using a **narrative approach to ethics**, nurses are open to learning from a storied, nuanced view of life; that is, they are sensitive to how personal and community stories evolve, are constructed, and can be changed. Narratives are stories being lived, read, watched, heard, discussed, analyzed, or compared.

Narratives are context or situation bound. For people to decide what they should do in particular circumstances, they may first identify how their moral character and actions fit within the greater stories of their culture. People are situated within their personal life narratives, and their stories intersect with and are interwoven into the narratives of other people with whom they interact. Nurses who use narrative ethics are aware that there is more to a patient's story than is known or discussed among healthcare providers. People are not solitary creatures, and as they interact with other people and their environment, they must

BOX 1-1 Narrative Learning

1. Divide into small groups.
2. Choose a children's book from the list below or another similar type of short children's book.
3. Read the book, and as a group, apply the book's message(s) to nursing practice and ethics.
4. Share your application with other groups. You might want to develop a creative display or activity to help illustrate your points.

Books:
- *The Little Engine That Could* (Original Classic Edition)
- *The Juice Box Bully*
- *Have You Filled a Bucket Today?*
- *Lacey Walker Nonstop Talker*
- *The Fall of Freddie the Leaf*
- *What If Everybody Did That?*
- *Thanks for the Feedback, I Think*
- *Stone Soup*
- *Old Turtle*
- *The Three Questions*

ETHICAL REFLECTION

Discuss several specific stories in books and movies that have affected your moral views or made an impact on your way of thinking ethically. What are the themes and symbols used in the stories?

make choices about what they believe and how they will act. They create their own stories.

When using a narrative approach to ethics, nurses realize that individual human stories are being constantly constructed in relation to the stories of a greater community of people. In nursing, a good example of narrative ethics involves nurses with sensitive awareness encountering each patient's unfolding life story in everyday practice. These nurses know that their actions while caring for patients influence the unfolding stories of those patients

in both large and small ways. A "narrative approach to bioethics focuses on the patients themselves: these are the moral agents who enact choices" (Charon & Montello, 2002, p. xi). In narrative ethics, patients' and nurses' stories matter; however, no one story should be accepted without critical reflection.

Critical Theory

Critical theory, sometimes referred to as critical social theory, is a broad term identifying theories and worldviews addressing the domination perpetrated by specific powerful groups of people and the resulting oppression of other specific groups of people. This theory has been included in this book since the first edition. However, the theory has become controversial. There are a number of critical theories included under one broad heading. In citing the group of German philosophers who originated the concept of critical theory, Bohman (2005) stated critical theories can be distinguished from traditional theories because the purpose of critical theories is to promote human emancipation. Specifically, the purpose of using critical theories is "to liberate human beings from the circumstances that enslave them" (Horkheimer, as cited in Bohman, 2005, para. 1). According to Brookfield (2005), there are three core assumptions in critical theory that explain how the world is organized:

1. That apparently open, Western democracies are actually highly unequal societies in which economic inequity, racism, and class discrimination are empirical realities.
2. That the way this state of affairs is reproduced and seems to be normal, natural, and inevitable (thereby heading off potential challenges to the system) is through the dissemination of dominant ideology.
3. That critical theory attempts to understand this state of affairs as a necessary prelude to changing it (p. viii).

One critical theory widely used by nurses is a feminist approach to ethics. Under this broad feminist approach is the ethic of care originating from the Gilligan–Kohlberg debate discussed earlier in this chapter.

Feminist Ethics

According to Tong (1997), "to a greater or lesser degree, all feminist approaches to ethics are filtered through the lens of gender" (p. 37). This means feminist ethics is specifically focused on evaluating ethically related situations in terms of how these situations affect women. The concept of feminist ethics tends to have a political connotation and addresses the patterns of women's oppression as this oppression is perpetrated by dominant social groups, especially socially powerful men.

Ethic of Care. An ethic of care is grounded in the moral experiences of women and feminist ethics. It evolved into an approach to ethics that gained popularity because of the Gilligan–Kohlberg debate about the differences in women's and men's approaches to moral reasoning. Rather than being based on duty, fairness, impartiality, or objective principles (ethic of justice) like the values popularized during the Enlightenment era, an **ethic of care** emphasizes the importance of traditionally feminine traits, such as love, compassion, sympathy, and concern about human well-being. The natural partiality in how people care more about some people than others is acknowledged as acceptable in an ethic of care. Also, the role of emotions in moral reasoning and behavior is accepted as a necessary and natural complement to rational thinking. This position distinguishes an ethic of care from an ethic of justice and duty-based ethics that emphasize the preeminence of reason and minimize the importance of emotion in guiding moral reasoning and the moral nature of one's relationships.

Eastern Ethics

Ethics in Asian societies has similarities to and important differences from Western ethics. In both cultures, ethics often is intertwined with spiritual or religious thinking. However, from a traditional Eastern ethics perspective, societal and spiritual philosophies and beliefs are essentially seamless. Eastern ethics and philosophies may be spiritual but are not necessarily religious in nature as many Westerners believe them to be. For example, Buddhism is not really a religion. It also should be kept in mind that Westernization of Eastern people has changed Asian cultures and ways of being. Both traditional Eastern and Western philosophies of ethics examine human nature and what is needed for people to move toward well-being. However, some of the differences in the two cultural systems are quite interesting and distinct.

Whereas the goal of Western ethics is generally for people to understand themselves personally, the goal of Eastern ethics often is to understand universal interconnections, be liberated from the self, or understand that people really do not consist of a self at all (Zeuschner, 2001). Ethics viewed from Christian or other theological perspectives tends to be based on a belief in human flaws that require an intermediary (God) to transcend these imperfections. Eastern ethical systems usually are focused on individuals' innate but unrecognized perfection and the ability to transcend earthly suffering and dissatisfaction through one's own abilities. Therefore, Eastern ethics is not imposed from outside of a person but instead is imposed from within oneself. Eastern ethics tends to be a discipline of training the mind and includes the concept that unethical behavior leads to karmic results (i.e., the quality of one's actions results in fair consequences according to the universal law of cause and effect). The four largest Eastern ethical systems, which contain myriad variations and now exist in a number of countries, are Indian ethics (Hinduism and Buddhism) and Chinese ethics (Taoism and Confucianism).

Indian Ethics

Hinduism. Hinduism is an ancient ethical system. It originated with writings called the Vedas (ca. 2000 to 1000 BCE), which include magical, religious, and philosophical teachings that existed long before the well-known ethical philosophy of the ancient Greeks. The main emphasis in Hindu ethics is cosmic unity. Because of reincarnation, people are stuck in *maya*, an illusory, every day, impermanent experience. The quality of one's past actions, *karma*, influences one's present existence and future incarnations or rebirths. Therefore, people need to improve the goodness of their actions, which will subsequently improve their karma. Liberation, *moksha*, means the soul of each person is no longer reincarnated but becomes one with the desirable cosmic or universal self, *atman*, and the absolute reality of *Brahman*.

Buddhism. There is no universal self according to Buddhism. In fact, there is no self at all! The historical Buddha, Siddhartha Gautama (6th century BCE) was a Hindu prince. Because Siddhartha's father wanted to prevent the fulfillment of a prophecy that Siddhartha might become a spiritual teacher, he tried to shield his son from the world outside his palace. However, Siddhartha left the confinement of his palace and saw in his fellow human beings the suffering associated with sickness, old age, and death. He decided to devote his life to understanding and ending suffering.

In Buddhism, there is no creator God, and, as previously indicated, Buddhism is a philosophy rather than a religion. The Buddha's core teachings, the teachings that all Buddhist sects profess, are called the Four Noble Truths. The First Noble Truth is that unsatisfactoriness or suffering (*dukkha*) exists as a part of all forms of existence. This suffering goes beyond the common Western notion of physical or mental misery; suffering in a Buddhist sense arises when people are ego centered and cling to their impermanent existence and impermanent things. Suffering is emphasized in Buddhism not to suggest a negative outlook toward life but instead as a realistic assessment of the human condition. The Second and Third Noble Truths suggest that the cause of suffering is attachment (clinging or craving) to impermanent things and suffering can be transcended (enlightenment). The Fourth Noble Truth contains the path for transforming suffering into enlightenment or liberation. This path is called the Eightfold Path, and it is composed of eight right practices: Right View, Right Thinking, Right Mindfulness, Right Speech, Right Action, Right Diligence, Right Concentration, and Right Livelihood.

- Explore the practice of Right Livelihood as it is conceived within the Eightfold Path.
- Discuss and explain if and how this practice can be related to the practice of nursing.

The Buddhist *Avatamsaka Sutra* contains a story about how all perceiving, thinking beings are connected, similar to a universal community. The story is about the heavenly net of the god Indra. "In the heaven of Indra, there is said to be a network of pearls, so arranged that if you look at one you see all the others reflected in it. In the same way each object in the world is not merely itself but involves every other object and in fact is everything else. In every particle of dust there is present Buddhas without number" (*Japanese Buddhism* by Sir Charles Eliot © 2000, Psychology Press [Taylor & Francis]).

How is the story about the net of Indra related to ethics?

Because of the central place of virtues in Buddhist philosophy, one interpretation of Buddhist ethics is to identify Buddhism as an ethic of virtue. There are four virtues singled out by Buddhists as being immeasurable because, when these virtues are cultivated, it is believed they will grow in a way that can encompass and transform the whole world. The Four Immeasurable Virtues are compassion (*karuna*), loving-kindness (*metta*), sympathetic joy (*mudita*), and equanimity (*upekkha*).

Chinese Ethics

The two most influential Chinese ethical systems were developed between 600 and 200 BCE during a time of social chaos in China. The two systems are Taoism and Confucianism.

Taoism. The beginning of Taoism is attributed to Lao-Tzu (ca. 571 BCE), who wrote the Taoist guide to life, the *Tao Te Ching*. The word *tao* is translated to English as *way* or *path*, meaning the natural order or harmony of all things. Like Buddhists, Taoists do not believe in a creator God. Instead, Taoists have a very simple perspective toward reality—the purpose of humans and the purpose of nature cannot be separated. Based on the cyclic nature of life observed by ancient Chinese farmers, Taoist philosophy underscores the flux and balance of nature through *yin* (dark) and *yang* (light) elements. Living well or ethically is living authentically, simply, and unselfishly in harmony and oneness with nature.

Confucianism. K'ung Fu-tzu (551–479 BCE), who was later called Confucius by Christians visiting China, originated the Confucian ethical system. The teachings of Confucian ethics are generally contained in the moral maxims and sayings attributed to K'ung Fu-tzu along with the later writings of his followers. Confucian ethics is a social system described through the concepts of *li* and *yi* (Zeuschner, 2001). Li provides guidance regarding social order and how humans should relate to one another, including rules of etiquette, such as proper greetings and social rituals. Yi emphasizes the importance of one's motivations toward achieving rightness rather than emphasizing consequences. Sincerity, teamwork, and balance are critically important to ethical behavior. The primary virtue of Confucian ethics is *jen*, which is translated to English as benevolence or human goodness. Overall, Confucianism is a communitarian ethical system in which social goals, the good of society, and the importance of human relationships are valued.

KEY POINTS

- Ethics refers to the analysis of matters of right and wrong, whereas morals refer to actual beliefs and behaviors. However, the terms often are used interchangeably.
- Values refer to judgments about what one believes is good or makes something desirable. Values influence how a person's character develops and people think and subsequently behave.
- Normative ethics is an attempt to decide or prescribe values, behaviors, and ways of being that are right or wrong, good or bad, admirable or dishonorable. When doing normative ethics, people ask questions such as "How ought humans behave?" "What should I do?" and "What sort of person should I be?"
- Ethical thinking, valuing, and reasoning generally fall along a continuum between ethical relativism and ethical objectivism.
- The study of values and ways of moral reasoning throughout history can be useful for people living in the 21st century. Specific values and ways of moral reasoning tend to overlap and converge over time.
- Virtue ethics emphasizes the excellence of one's character.
- Deontological ethics emphasizes one's duty rather than the consequences of one's actions.
- Utilitarian ethics emphasizes the consequences of one's actions in regard to achieving the most good for the most people affected by a rule or action.
- Eastern philosophies and systems of ethics often are inseparable.

References

American Hospital Association. (2003). *The patient care partnership: Understanding expectations, rights, and responsibilities.*

American Nurses Association. (2015). *Code of ethics for nurses with interpretive statements.*

Annas, J. (2011). *Intelligent virtue* [Kindle version]. Oxford University Press.

Aristotle. (2002). *Nichomachean ethics* (C. Rowe, Trans.). Oxford University Press.

Beauchamp, T. L., & Childress, J. F. (2019). *Principles of biomedical ethics* (8th ed.). Oxford University Press.

Billington, R. (2003). *Living philosophy: An introduction to moral thought* (3rd ed.). Routledge.

Bohman, J. (2005). Critical theory. https://www.academia.edu/6857288/_Act_Naturally_Say_What_

Brannigan, M. C., & Boss, J. A. (2001). *Healthcare ethics in a diverse society.* Mayfield.

Brookfield, S. D. (2005). *The power of critical theory: Liberating adult learning and teaching.* Jossey-Bass.

Buckle, S. (1993). Natural law. In P. Singer (Ed.), *A companion to ethics* (pp. 161–174). Blackwell.

Charon, R., & Montello, M. (2002). Introduction: The practice of narrative ethics. In R. Charon & M. Montello (Eds.), *Stories matter* (pp. ix–xii). Routledge.

Donahue, M. P. (1996). *Nursing the finest art: An illustrated history* (2nd ed.). Mosby.

Gert, B., Culver, C. M., & Clouser, K. D. (2006). *Bioethics: A systematic approach* (2nd ed.). Oxford University Press.

Gilligan, C. (1982). *In a different voice: Psychological theory and women's development.* Harvard University Press.

Hope, T. (2004). *Medical ethics: A very short introduction.* Oxford University Press.

Kohlberg, L. (1981). *The philosophy of moral development moral stages and the idea of justice.* Harper & Row.

LeVasseur, J. (1998). Plato, Nightingale, and contemporary nursing. *Image: Journal of Nursing Scholarship, 30*(3), 281–285.

MacIntyre, A. (1984). *After virtue: A study of moral theory* (2nd ed.). University of Notre Dame Press.

Murray, T. H. (1997). What do we mean by "narrative ethics"? *Medical Humanities Review, 11*(2), 44–57.

Pence, G. (2000). *A dictionary of common philosophical terms.* McGraw-Hill.

Ross, W. D. (2002). *The right and the good.* Oxford University Press. (Original work published 1930)

Sellman, D. (1997). The virtues in the moral education of nurses: Florence Nightingale revisited. *Nursing Ethics, 4*(1), 3–11.

Tong, R. (1997). *Feminist approaches to bioethics: Theoretical reflections and practical applications.* Westview Press.

Tschudin, V. (Ed.). (2003). *Approaches to ethics: Nursing beyond boundaries.* Butterworth-Heinemann.

Zeuschner, R. B. (2001). *Classical ethics East and West: Ethics from a comparative perspective.* McGraw-Hill.

CHAPTER 2

Introduction to Bioethics and Ethical Decision Making

Karen L. Rich

The tiniest hair casts a shadow.

—**Johann Wolfgang von Goethe**, German poet and dramatist (1749–1832)

OBJECTIVES

After reading this chapter, the reader should be able to do the following:

1. Discuss the history of bioethics.
2. Use the approach of ethical principlism in nursing practice.
3. Analyze bioethical issues in practice and from media.
4. Identify criteria that define an ethical dilemma.
5. Consider how critical thinking is used in ethical nursing practice.
6. Use selected models of reflection and decision making in ethical nursing practice.

Introduction to Bioethics

The terms **bioethics** and **healthcare ethics** sometimes are used interchangeably. Bioethics, born out of the rapidly expanding technical environment of the 1900s, is a specific domain of ethics focused on moral issues in the field of health care (see **BOX 2-1**). During World War II President Franklin D. Roosevelt assembled a committee to improve medical scientists' coordination in addressing the medical needs of the military (Jonsen, 2000). As often happens with wartime research and advancements, the work aimed at addressing military needs also affected civilian sectors, such as the field of medicine.

Between 1945 and 1965, antibiotic, antihypertensive, antipsychotic, and cancer drugs came into common

BOX 2-1 Early Events in Bioethics

August 19, 1947: The Nuremberg trials of Nazi doctors who conducted heinous medical experiments during World War II began.

April 25, 1953: Watson and Crick published a one-page paper about DNA.

December 23, 1954: The first renal transplant was performed.

March 9, 1960: Chronic hemodialysis was first used.

December 3, 1967: The first heart transplant was done by Dr. Christiaan Barnard.

August 5, 1968: The definition of brain death was developed by an ad hoc committee at Harvard Medical School.

July 26, 1972: Revelations appeared about the unethical Tuskegee syphilis research.

January 22, 1973: The landmark *Roe v. Wade* case was decided.

April 14, 1975: A comatose Karen Ann Quinlan was brought to Newton Memorial Hospital; she became the basis of a landmark legal case about the removal of life support.

July 25, 1978: Baby Louise Brown was born. She was the first test-tube baby.

Spring 1982: Baby Doe became the basis of a landmark case that resulted in legal and ethical directives about the treatment of impaired neonates.

December 1982: The first artificial heart was implanted into the body of Barney Clark, who lived 112 days after the implant.

April 11, 1983: *Newsweek* published a story about a mysterious disease called AIDS that was at epidemic levels.

Data from Jonsen, A. R. (2000). *A short history of medical ethics.* Oxford University Press, pp. 99–114.

medical use; surgery entered the heart and the brain; organ transplantation was initiated; and life-sustaining mechanical devices, the dialysis machine, the pacemaker, and the ventilator were invented. (Jonsen, 2000, p. 99)

However, with these advances also came increased responsibility and distress among healthcare professionals. Patients who would have died in the past began to have a lingering, suffering existence. Healthcare professionals were faced with trying to decide how to allocate newly developed, scarce medical resources. During the 1950s, scientists and medical professionals began meeting to discuss these confusing problems. Eventually healthcare policies and laws were enacted to address questions of who lives, who dies, and who decides. A new field of study was developed called *bioethics*, a term that first appeared in the literature in 1969 (Jonsen, 1998, 2000, 2005).

Ethical Principles

Because shocking information surfaced about serious ethical lapses, such as the heinous World War II Nazi medical experiments in Europe and the unethical Tuskegee research in the United States, societies around the world became particularly conscious of ethical pitfalls in conducting biomedical and behavioral research. In the United States, the National Research Act became law in 1974, and a commission was created to outline principles that must be used during research involving human subjects (National Commission for the Protection of Human Subjects of Biomedical and Behavioral Research, 1979). In 1976, to carry out its charge, the commission held an intensive 4-day meeting at the Belmont Conference Center at the Smithsonian Institute. Thereafter, discussions continued until 1978, when the commission released its report called the *Belmont Report*.

The report outlined three basic principles for all human subjects research: respect for persons, beneficence, and justice (National Commission for the Protection of Human Subjects of Biomedical and Behavioral Research, 1979). The principle of beneficence, as set forth in the *Belmont Report*, is the rule to do good. However, the description

RESEARCH NOTE: TUSKEGEE SYPHILIS STUDY

During the late 1920s in the United States, syphilis rates were extremely high in some areas. The private Rosenwald Foundation teamed with the United States Public Health Service (USPHS) to begin efforts to control the disease using the drug neosalvarsan, an arsenic compound. Macon County, Alabama, particularly the town of Tuskegee, was targeted because of its high rate of syphilis, as identified through a survey. However, the Great Depression derailed the plans, and the private foundation withdrew from the work. The USPHS repeated the Rosenwald survey in Macon County and identified a syphilis rate of 22% among African American men in the county and a 62% rate of congenital syphilis cases. The natural history (progression) of syphilis had not been studied yet in the United States, and the surgeon general suggested that 399 African American men with syphilis in Tuskegee should be observed, rather than treated, and compared with a group of 200 African American men who were uninfected. The men were not told about the details of their disease. They underwent painful, nontherapeutic spinal taps to provide data about the natural history of syphilis and were told these procedures were treatments for "bad blood." The men were given free meals, medical treatment for diseases other than their syphilis, and free burials. Even after penicillin was discovered in the 1940s, the men were not offered treatment. In fact, the USPHS researchers arranged to keep the uninformed study participants out of World War II because the men would be tested for syphilis, treated with penicillin, and lost from the study. The unethical research continued for 40 years, from 1932 to 1972. During the 40 years of research, an astonishing number of articles about the study were published in medical journals, and no attempt was made to hide the surreptitious terms of the research. No one intervened to stop the travesty. Finally, a medical reporter learned of the study, and the ethical issues were exposed.

After reading this chapter and researching more information on the Internet about the Tuskegee research, including the contribution of Nurse Evers, answer the following questions:

1. What were the main social issues with ethical implications involved in this study?
2. Which bioethical principles were violated by the Tuskegee study? Explain.
3. How can various ethical approaches be applied to the Tuskegee study? (Include approaches discussed in an earlier chapter 1.)
4. Discuss the role of Nurse Evers in the Tuskegee research.
5. Which procedures are in place today to prevent this type of unethical research?

of beneficence also included the rule now commonly known as the principle of nonmaleficence, that is, to do no harm. The report contained guidelines regarding how to apply the principles in research through informed consent, the assessment of risks and benefits to research participants, and the selection of research participants.

In 1979, as an outgrowth of the *Belmont Report*, Beauchamp and Childress published the first edition of their book *Principles of Biomedical Ethics*, which featured four bioethical principles: autonomy, nonmaleficence, beneficence, and justice. Currently, the book is in its eighth edition published in 2019, and the principle of autonomy is described as respect for autonomy.

Doing ethics based on the use of principles—that is, ethical **principlism**—does not involve the use of a theory or a formal decision-making model; rather, ethical principles provide guidelines to make justified moral decisions and evaluate the morality of actions. Ideally, when using the approach of principlism, no one principle should automatically be assumed to be superior to the other principles (Beauchamp & Childress, 2019). Each principle is prima facie binding.

Some people have criticized the use of ethical principlism because they believe it is a top-down approach that does not include allowances for the context of individual cases and stories. Critics contend that simply applying principles when making ethical determinations results in a linear way of doing ethics; that is, the fine nuances present in relationship-based situations are not considered adequately. Nevertheless, the approach of ethical principlism using the four principles outlined by Beauchamp and Childress (2019) has become one of the most popular tools used today for analyzing and resolving bioethical problems.

▶ Autonomy

Autonomy is the freedom and ability to act in a self-determined manner. It represents the right of a rational person to express personal decisions independent of outside interference and to have these decisions honored. It can be argued that autonomy occupies a central place in Western healthcare ethics because of the popularity of the Enlightenment-era philosophy of Immanuel Kant. However, it is noteworthy that autonomy is not emphasized in an ethic of care and virtue ethics and these also are popular approaches to ethics today.

The principle of autonomy sometimes is described as respect for autonomy (Beauchamp & Childress, 2019). In the domain of health care, respecting a patient's autonomy includes obtaining informed consent for treatment; facilitating and supporting patients' choices regarding treatment options; allowing patients to refuse treatments; disclosing comprehensive and truthful information, diagnoses, and treatment options to patients so that they can make informed decisions; and maintaining privacy and confidentiality. Respecting autonomy also is important in less obvious situations, such as allowing home care patients to choose a tub bath versus a shower when it is safe to do so and allowing an elderly long-term care resident to choose her favorite foods when they are medically prescribed. In fact, if the elder is competent and has been properly informed about the risks, she has the right to choose to eat foods that are not medically prescribed. Restrictions on an individual's autonomy may occur in cases when a person presents a potential threat for harming others, such as exposing other people to communicable diseases or committing acts of violence; people generally lose the right to exercise autonomy or self-determination in such instances.

FOCUS FOR DEBATE

- Discuss autonomy as it relates to contentious issues among the general public, such as vaccinations and mask-wearing, arising during the Covid-19 pandemic. Defend your views about these issues.

Respecting patients' autonomy is important, but it also is important for nurses to receive respect for their professional autonomy. In considering how the language nurses choose defines the profession's place in health care, Munhall (2012) used the word autonomy (*auto-no-my*) as an example. She reflected on how infants and children first begin to express themselves through nonverbal signs, such as laughing, crying, and pouting, but by the time

FOCUS FOR DEBATE

- During a pandemic, is it ethical for nurses to say "no" to getting themselves vaccinated? Defend your position.
- During a pandemic, is it ethical for nurses to say "no" to wearing a face mask during their work? Outside of their work? Defend your position(s).

children reach the age of 2 years, they usually "have learned to treasure the word *no*" (p. 40). Munhall calls the word *no* "one of the most important words in any language" (p. 40). Being willing and able to reasonably say *no* is part of exercising one's autonomy.

Informed Consent

Informed consent regarding a patient's treatment is a legal and ethical issue of autonomy. At the heart of **informed consent** is respecting a person's autonomy to make personal choices based on the appropriate appraisal of information about the actual or potential circumstances of a situation. Though all conceptions of informed consent must contain the same basic elements, people present the description of these elements differently. Beauchamp and Childress (2019) outlined informed consent according to seven elements (see **BOX 2-2**).

Dempski (2009) presented three basic elements that are necessary for informed consent to occur:

1. Receipt of information: This includes receiving a description of the procedure, information about the risks and benefits of having or not having the treatment, reasonable

---

BOX 2-2 Elements of Informed Consent

I. Threshold elements (preconditions)
   1. Competence (ability to understand and decide)
   2. Voluntariness (in deciding)
II. Information elements
   3. Disclosure (of material information)
   4. Recommendation (of a plan)
   5. Understanding (of 3 and 4)
III. Consent elements
   6. Decision (in favor of a plan)
   7. Authorization (of the chosen plan)

Data from Beauchamp, T. L., & Childress, J. F. (2019). *Principles of biomedical ethics* (8th ed.). Oxford University Press, p. 122.

---

alternatives to the treatment, probabilities about outcomes, and "the credentials of the person who will perform the treatment" (Dempski, 2009, p. 78). Because it is too demanding to inform a patient of every possible risk or benefit involved with every treatment or procedure, the obligation is to inform the person about the information a reasonable person would want and need to know. Information should be tailored specifically to a person's personal circumstances, including providing information in the person's spoken language.

2. Consent for the treatment must be voluntary: A person should not be under any influence or coerced to provide consent. This means patients should not be asked to sign a consent form when they are under the influence of mind-altering medications, such as narcotics. Depending on the circumstances, such as the riskiness of the procedure, consent may be verbalized, written, or implied by behavior. The more risky the procedure, the more stringent the documentation of the consent should be. Silence does not convey consent when a reasonable person would normally offer another sign of agreement.

3. Persons must be competent: Persons must be able to communicate consent and to understand the information provided to them. If a person's condition warrants transferring decision-making authority to a surrogate, informed consent obligations must be met with the surrogate.

It is neither ethical nor legal for a nurse to be responsible for obtaining informed consent for procedures performed by a physician

(Dempski, 2009). In discussing a lawsuit, nurse and healthcare attorney Carolyn Buppert (2017) reported that some physicians try to delegate informed consent to other healthcare clinicians, such as nurses, nurse practitioners, and physician assistants. In 2017, the Pennsylvania Supreme Court ruled on a lawsuit involving informed consent obtained partially between a patient and a physician assistant and partially between the patient and her physician. The Pennsylvania court upheld a state law that informed consent is a physician's responsibility. Nurses may need to display the virtue of courage if physicians attempt to delegate the total responsibility to them. Though both nurses and physicians in some circumstances may believe nurses are well versed in assuring that the elements of informed consent are met for medical or surgical invasive treatments or procedures performed by a physician, nurses must refrain from accepting this responsibility.

LEGAL PERSPECTIVE

Though they may participate in obtaining a patient's signature, nurses should not obtain informed consent for a provider who will perform a patient's invasive procedure. However, nurses may be legally liable if they know or should have known informed consent was not obtained and they do not appropriately notify providers or supervisors about this deficiency.

On the other hand, it is certainly within a nurse's domain of responsibility to help identify a suitable person to provide informed consent if a patient is not competent; to verify that a patient understands the information communicated by the professional performing the procedure, including helping to secure interpreters or appropriate information for the patient in the patient's spoken language; and to notify appropriate parties if the nurse knows a patient has not given informed consent for a

procedure or treatment. In fact, it is ethically incumbent upon nurses to facilitate patients' opportunities to give informed consent. The bottom line is that informed consent is a collaborative process among healthcare professionals and patients.

LEGAL PERSPECTIVE

Assault and battery are two legal terms describing offenses against a person. Both terms are relevant to the ethical requirement of informed consent. **Assault** is the *threat* of harm; for example, someone commits assault if he or she acts or talks in a way that causes another person to feel apprehension about his or her physical safety. **Battery** consists of one person *offensively touching* another person without the person's consent.

Advanced practice nurses are legally and ethically obligated to obtain informed consent before performing risky or invasive treatments or procedures within their scope of practice. In everyday situations, all nurses are required to explain nursing treatments and procedures to patients before performing them. Nursing procedures do not need to meet all the requirements of informed consent if procedures are not risky or invasive (Dempski, 2009). If a patient understands a treatment or procedure and allows the nurse to begin the nursing care, consent has been *implied*. A competent person may convey implied consent when the person participates in or cooperates with an action without explicitly verbalizing consent or formally signing a consent form. Implied consent often is used for low to essentially nonrisky procedures. Healthcare providers need to know when implied consent is acceptable and full informed consent must be obtained. Nurses should keep a heightened awareness to assure that the person is competent to consent to an intervention and does not feel intimidated or coerced into consenting to a procedure performed by the nurse or any other healthcare worker.

When treatments and procedures that normally require consent need to be performed in an emergency, informed consent should be obtained from the patient if possible. If this is not possible, informed consent should be obtained from the patient's next of kin or surrogate. When reasonable efforts have been made to obtain informed consent, but no one is competent or available to provide the consent or time does not allow for informed consent because of the threat of death and/or disability, it is permissible to proceed with treatments and procedures without informed consent. However, it is important to keep in mind the four main elements that justify a malpractice suit (see **BOX 2-3**) and what a reasonable healthcare professional would do in a situation. The four elements of malpractice are evaluated in all malpractice cases.

BOX 2-3 Four Elements of Malpractice

1. The professional must have a duty to the patient.
2. The professional must have breached that duty.
3. The patient must experience harm or damages.
4. The patient's harm or damages must be directly connected to the professional's negligence. This fourth element involves a situation in which 100% of harm or damages are attributed to the professional's negligent action or maybe only a partial amount is attributed to the action of the professional. For example, the patient also may have contributed to the harm or damages (i.e., contributory negligence).

To decide about malpractice, expert witnesses are used to determine what a similar healthcare professional would do or would have done in a situation like the case at the center of the lawsuit.

Intentional Nondisclosure

In the past, medical and nursing patient care errors were something to be swept under the rug, and care was taken to avoid patient discovery of these errors. However, in the 1990s, when healthcare leaders realized that huge numbers of patients, as many as 98,000 per year, were dying from medical errors, the Institute of Medicine (IOM) began a project to analyze medical errors and try to reduce them. One outcome of the project is the book *To Err Is Human: Building a Safer Health Care System* (IOM, 2000). The IOM project committee determined that to err really is human and good people working within unsafe systems make the most errors.

Based on the IOM's work, it is now expected that errors involving serious, preventable adverse events be reported to patients and through other organizational reporting systems, and possibly external reporting systems, on a mandatory basis (IOM, 2000). This should be easy to understand from an ethics standpoint but reporting *near misses* has been more controversial (Lo, 2009). A near miss is "any event that could have had adverse consequences but did not and was indistinguishable from fully fledged adverse events in all but outcome" (Agency for Healthcare Research and Quality [AHRQ] Patient Safety Network [PSNet], 2019, para. 7). A near miss is like what people commonly think of as a "close call" (para. 7). A patient could have been harmed but was not harmed because of "early detection or sheer luck" (para. 7). An example provided by PSNet is a nurse trying to administer medications to the wrong patient. The patient notices that the medications are not correct for him and harm is avoided. If the patient had been less aware of his correct medications, harm may have occurred.

Some professionals tend to avoid telling patients about near-miss errors because no harm was done to the patient, but ethicists recommend disclosure of these events. Being honest and forthright with patients promotes trust, and secrecy is unethical (Jonsen et al., 2022). In addition to the direct ethical implications of being honest with patients, much can be learned from investigating the root causes of near-miss errors. Trying to prevent errors is an ethical issue unto itself, which falls under the principle of nonmaleficence (see discussion of this principle later in this chapter).

Intentionally withholding information from a patient or surrogate is legal in emergency situations, as previously discussed, or when patients waive their right to be informed. Respecting a patient's right *not* to be informed is especially important in delivering culturally sensitive care because a person not wanting to know about serious illnesses is sometimes culturally based. Other, more legally and ethically controversial circumstances of intentionally not disclosing relevant information to a patient involve three healthcare circumstances (Beauchamp & Childress, 2019). The first circumstance falls under therapeutic privilege. The second relates to therapeutically using placebos. The third involves withholding information from research subjects to protect the integrity of the research.

By invoking **therapeutic privilege**, physicians were traditionally supported in withholding information from patients if physicians, based on their sound medical judgment, believed "divulging the information would potentially harm a depressed, emotionally drained, or unstable patient" (Beauchamp & Childress, 2019, p. 126). This exception in communication is controversial today. Standards about what constitutes therapeutic privilege have differed among legal jurisdictions with standards ranging from withholding information if a physician believes the information would have *any* negative effect on the patient's health to withholding information only if divulging it is likely to have a *serious* effect. The American Medical Association's (AMA, 2021) current opinion statement, included as part of the AMA's ethics code, indicates that "except in emergency situations in which a patient is incapable of making an informed decision, withholding information without the patient's knowledge or consent is ethically unacceptable" (para. 2). The AMA's opinion statement clearly directs physicians to be honest and open with patients about their healthcare status unless a patient has asked not to be informed or the situation is an emergency. A physician does have the leeway in some circumstances, however, to delay telling patients pertinent facts about their condition until the time is deemed safe and appropriate to do so. Disclosure should be delivered in a way that meets the patient's needs and according to an explicit plan to be honest with the patient.

LEGAL PERSPECTIVE

Research the landmark legal case *Canterbury v. Spence* (464 F.2d 772, 782 D.C. Cir. 1972).

- What does it mean to be a *landmark* case?
- What were the bioethical issues involved in the case?
- What was the case outcome?

Placebos, when used therapeutically, are inactive substances given to a patient to induce a positive health outcome through the patient's belief that the inert substance really carries some beneficial power. The patient is unaware that the substance (placebo) is inactive. It is interesting that at least one study has shown placebos can have a positive effect in most patients even when the patients know they are receiving an inert pill (Scuderi, 2011) and this finding is supported by Jonsen and colleagues (2022). Proponents of using placebos say the action is covered under a patient's general consent to treatment, though the consent is not really informed. However, there is a consensus that the therapeutic use of placebos is unethical (Jonsen et al., 2022) because it violates a patient's autonomy and can seriously damage trust between patients and healthcare professionals. The use of placebos is ethical when used properly during experimental research. Participants in a research control group often are given a placebo so they can be compared to an experimental group receiving the treatment being studied. Research participants are fully informed that they may receive a placebo rather than the actual treatment.

Strict rules apply to research studies requiring that research subjects be protected from manipulation and personal risks. Thus, informed consent in research has stringent requirements. Withholding information from research subjects should never be undertaken lightly. Intentional nondisclosure sometimes is allowed only if the research is relatively risk free to the participants and the nature of the research is behavioral or psychological and disclosure might seriously skew the outcomes of the research.

Patient Self-Determination Act

The Omnibus Reconciliation Act of 1990 (OBRA-90) advance directives provisions are usually referred to as the Patient Self-Determination Act (PSDA). This act passed by the U.S. Congress in 1990 is the first federal statute designed to facilitate a patient's autonomy through the knowledge and use of advance directives. Healthcare providers and organizations must provide written information to adult patients regarding state laws covering the right to make healthcare decisions, refuse or withdraw treatments, and write advance directives (See Appendix C for sample advance directives in Mississippi). One of the underlying aims of the PSDA is to increase meaningful dialogue about patients' rights to make autonomous choices about receiving or not receiving health care.

It is important that dialogue about end-of-life decisions and options is not lost in organizational admission processes and paperwork or in other ways. Nurses provide the vital communication link between the patient's wishes, the paperwork, and the provider. When an appropriate opportunity arises, nurses need to take an active role in increasing their dialogue with patients regarding patients' rights and

end-of-life decisions. In addition to responding to the direct questions patients and families ask about advance directives and end-of-life options, nurses would do well to listen to and observe patients' subtle cues that signal their anxiety and uncertainty about end-of-life care. A good example of compassionate care is when nurses actively listen to patients and try to alleviate patients' uncertainty and fears regarding end-of-life decision making.

The Health Insurance Portability and Accountability Act of 1996 (HIPAA) Privacy and Security Rules

"Within HHS [Health and Human Services], the Office for Civil Rights (OCR) has responsibility for enforcing the [HIPAA] Privacy and Security Rules with voluntary compliance activities and civil money penalties" (U.S. Department of Health and Human Services [HHS], 2013, para. 2). The HIPAA Privacy Rule is a federal regulation designed to protect people from indiscriminate disclosure of their personal health information while supporting dissemination of information needed to achieve high quality health care. It also gives patients the right to review their medical records. The intent of the rule is to ensure privacy while facilitating the flow of information necessary to meet the needs of patients. "The Privacy Rule protects all *'individually identifiable health information'* held or transmitted by a covered entity or its business associate, in any form or media, whether electronic, paper, or oral. The Privacy Rule calls this information 'protected health information (PHI)'" (45 C.F.R. § 160.103, as cited in HHS, 2013, para. 14).

The Security Rule of the HIPAA act operationalizes the Privacy Rules. The Security Rule includes standards addressing privacy safeguards for electronic protected health information (HHS, 2020). The rule is designed to "ensure the confidentiality, integrity, and security of electronic protected health information" (para. 1).

All patient-identifiable protected health information is to be kept private unless it is being used for patient care; a patient agrees to a release; or it is released according to legitimate, limited situations covered by the act. It is incumbent on all healthcare professionals to be familiar with the content of the act. See **BOX 2-4** for healthcare professionals' frequently asked questions about HIPAA. Special topics in information privacy addressed by the Department of HHS (2021) include the following issues, which can be explored via the link provided in this chapter's references:

- HIPAA and Covid-19
- Updated joint guidance on application of HIPAA and FERPA to student health records
- Mental health and substance use disorders
- Research
- Public health
- Emergency situations: Preparedness, planning, and response
- Health information technology
- HIPAA and health apps

BOX 2-4 How Well Do You Know HIPAA?

1. How are covered entities expected to determine what is the minimum necessary information that can be used, disclosed, or requested for a particular purpose?
2. What is the difference between "consent" and "authorization" under the HIPAA Privacy Rule?
3. Can my healthcare provider discuss my health information with an interpreter?
4. Must a healthcare provider or other covered entity obtain permission from a patient prior to notifying public health authorities of the occurrence of a reportable disease?
5. Can the phone number of a patient's room be released as part of the facility directory?
6. What is telehealth?
7. If an individual instructs a covered healthcare provider that he does not want the provider to discuss his medical conditions or treatment with his family members, can the covered entity share such information with family members after the individual has died?
8. Does the HIPAA Privacy Rule permit covered entities to disclose protected health information, without individuals' authorization, to public officials responding to a bioterrorism threat or other public health emergency?
9. May a doctor or hospital disclose protected health information to a person or entity that can assist in notifying a patient's family member of the patient's location and health condition?
10. If I am unconscious or not around, can my healthcare provider still share or discuss my health information with my family, friends, or others involved in my care or payment for my care?
11. Does the HIPAA Privacy Rule permit a doctor to discuss a patient's health status, treatment, or payment arrangements with a person who is not married to the patient or is otherwise not recognized as a relative of the patient under applicable law (e.g., state law)?
12. Does FERPA or HIPAA apply to records on students at health clinics run by postsecondary institutions?
13. May physicians' offices use patient sign-in sheets or call out the names of their patients in their waiting rooms?
14. How do I know if a state law is "more stringent" than the HIPAA Privacy Rule?
15. May a hospital or other covered entity notify a patient's family member or other person that the patient is at their facility?

Find complete answers at *HIPAA FAQ for Professionals*, HHS (2017), https://www.hhs.gov/hipaa/for-professionals/faq/index.html

Nonmaleficence

Nonmaleficence is the principle used to communicate the obligation to do no harm. Emphasizing the importance of this principle is as old as organized medical practice. Healthcare professionals have historically been encouraged to do good (beneficence), but if for some reason they cannot do good, they are required to at least do no harm. Because of the two sides of the same coin connotation between these two principles, some people consider them to be essentially one and the same. However, many ethicists, including Beauchamp and Childress (2019), do make a distinction.

Nonmaleficence is the maxim or norm that "one ought not to inflict evil or harm" (Beauchamp & Childress, 2019, p. 157), whereas beneficence includes the following three norms: "one ought to prevent evil or harm, one ought to remove evil or harm, [and] one ought to do or promote good" (p. 157). As evidenced by these maxims, beneficence involves action to help someone, and nonmaleficence requires "*intentional avoidance* of actions that cause harm" (p. 157). In addition to violating the maxim to not intentionally harm another person, some of the issues and concepts Beauchamp and Childress list as frequently requiring the obligation of nonmaleficence are included in **BOX 2-5**.

LEGAL PERSPECTIVE

Negligence: Failure to render reasonable care, which results in damages or injury.

Malpractice: A negligent act by a professional, usually someone licensed. See the four elements of malpractice in Box 2-3.

Best practice and due care standards are adopted by professional organizations and regulatory agencies to minimize harm to patients. Regulatory agencies develop oversight procedures to ensure that healthcare providers

---

BOX 2-5 Issues and Concepts Associated with the Principle of Nonmaleficence

- Harm—Something that goes against someone's interests. Note, sometimes harm is justified, for example, a leg amputation due to gangrene.
- Negligence and Due Care—Failure to render reasonable care.
- Nontreatment Decisions—
  - Withholding and withdrawing care
  - Decisions about whether to render medical treatments, including artificial nutrition and hydrations
- The Rule of Double Effect
- Optional Treatments and Obligatory Treatments
- Quality of Life Judgments
- Killing or Letting Die
- Slippery Slope Arguments

Summary from Beauchamp, T. L., & Childress, J. F. (2019). *Principles of biomedical ethics* (8th ed.). Oxford University Press.

---

maintain the competence and skills needed to properly care for patients. Nonmaleficence has a wide scope of implications in health care, including the need to avoid negligent care and harm when deciding whether to provide or withhold or withdraw treatment and considerations about rendering extraordinary or heroic treatment.

The Case of RaDonda Vaught: First, Do No Harm

The following information about RaDonda Vaught's criminal case has been compiled from multiple Internet sources, including Kelman's (2022, March 27) timeline in the *Tennessean*, a legal discovery document for the *State of Tennessee vs. RaDonda L. Vaught* (2019, March 27), Tennessee Board of Nursing (2019, September 27) documentation, an anonymous complaint (intake number TN00045852) filed with the Department of Health and Human

Services Centers for Medicare and Medicaid Services (DHHS, CMS, 2018, October 13), a statement of deficiencies and plan of correction from Vanderbilt University Medical Center (VUMC) (DHHS, CMS, 2018, November 16), letters sent by the State of Tennessee Department of Health Division of Health Licenses and Regulation Office of Investigations (Welch, 2018, October 23) to Vaught and a Ms. Dubree, a joint *Statement in Response to the Conviction of Nurse RaDonda Vaught* published by the American Nurses Association (ANA) and the Tennessee Nurses Association (TNA) (2022, March 25), copyright free articles published about the case by *Kaiser Health News* (Kelman, 2022, March 22; Kelman, 2022, March 24; Kelman, 2022, March 25; Kelman & Norman, 2022, April 5), and an article published in the *Vanderbilt Hustler* (Oung, 2022, March 31). This case certainly is a landmark case in nursing and health care. An expanded outline of the case is covered here in detail and a related case study is included in Appendix A. The case study provides an opportunity for readers to consider their own interpretation of the case and apply ethical and legal principles. Note, there are some discrepancies in the plethora of information about the case. For example, the medication dispensing machine is called an Acudose in some sources and a Pyxis in other sources. Even the date that Vaught began working at VUMC varies by source.

Date of Incident

The medication error at the heart of this case occurred on **December 26, 2017**.

Relevant Background Information

- RaDonda Vaught, the defendant, was granted a registered nurse (RN) license in the state of Tennessee (TN) on February 13, 2015.
- In November 2015, Vaught began working as a "help all" nurse for the Neuro Intensive Care Unit (NICU), the stepdown, and the sixth floor nursing units at Vanderbilt University Medical Center (VUMC). It seems that her main duties were in the NICU and on the stepdown unit.

The patient who died as a result of Vaught's error, i.e., the victim, was Charlene Murphey, aged 75, who was admitted to VUMC on December 24, 2017, with a diagnosis of subdural hematoma. The patient was being prepared for hospital discharge when she received the fatal medication administered by Vaught.

On December 5, 2018, almost one year after her error, Vaught was interviewed by TN Bureau of Investigation (TBI) personnel. Vaught provided the following background information:

- Vaught said she was comfortable with the "help all" nurse job.
- She worked December 25 and 26, 2017, on the 7:00 a.m. to 7:00 p.m. shift. The error occurred on December 26, 2017.
- Vaught denied being overtired on the day of the incident. She also denied that the Neuro Intensive Care Unit (NICU) was understaffed.
- A new orientee was working with Vaught on the day of the error, but Vaught testified to TBI that she was comfortable having the orientee work with her.

Events on the Day of the Medication Error: December 26, 2017

- Murphey was taken to the radiology department to have a Positron Emission Tomography (PET) scan.
- The patient was alert and oriented when she arrived for the scan. However, she told the radiology tech that she was anxious and claustrophobic.
- The radiology tech conveyed this information to Murphey's primary nurse (not

Vaught) who obtained a verbal order for 1 mg of Versed to be administered intravenously before the scan.

Murphey's primary nurse asked Vaught (the help all nurse) to administer the Versed.

The order for Versed was entered into Murphey's medical record on December 26, 2017, at 2:47 p.m. The pharmacy verified the order for Versed at 2:49 p.m. When Vaught went to the Acudose (or Pyxis) system at 2:59 p.m., she did not find the order in the patient's profile. She checked the Medication Administration Record (MAR) in a different computer and saw the order. Since the order was not in the dispensing device's patient profile, Vaught overrode the system and typed in "VE" to search for the Versed. She selected the first medication from the list that began with the letters VE, which was vecuronium bromide. Versed was listed in the dispensing system by its generic name midazolam. Vaught told the TBI interviewers that she could not remember the reason she entered into the dispensing system to account for the override.

According to Vaught,

- She looked at the back of the vial but not the front of the vial. Note, the cap of the vecuronium vial includes a warning. See picture.
- She recognized that the medication needed to be reconstituted.
- She and her orientee took the medication to the radiology department.

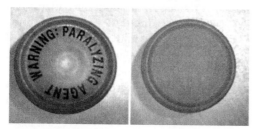

- She located Murphey and verified Murphey's identity.
- She reconstituted the vecuronium and administered 1 mg to Murphey.
- She could not find a computer to scan the medication administration. The medication administration was never scanned.
- After administering the medication, she left the patient with the radiology technician.

After the scan (about 20–30 minutes), Murphey was identified as being unconscious. Cardiopulmonary resuscitation (CPR) was initiated, and the patient was placed on a ventilator.

When the patient arrived back at the NICU, Vaught informed a physician and a nurse practitioner that she had administered vecuronium to Murphey. Vaught told TBI personnel that their response was "I'm so sorry." Note, details were not found that indicated how Vaught knew at this point that she had administered the incorrect medication other than the fact that the patient was unconscious.

The patient was diagnosed with brain death, was removed from the ventilator, and expired within 12 hours after the vecuronium administration.

Vaught's Work Repercussions

Vaught received a termination letter dated January 3, 2018, from VUMC. Termination was based on her failure to "validate the five rights of medication administration." She was not eligible for rehire.

Thus, Vaught worked at VUMC from November 2015 to January 2018.

After Vaught was fired by VUMC, she began working as a "throughput coordinator" at TriStar Centennial Medical Center in Nashville. Her position was nonclinical but did require a nursing license.

The Cover-up

- Vaught later told TBI investigators that after the patient returned to the NICU from the PET scan, the unit manager advised Vaught not to scan the medication; the MAR would note it.
- After Murphey's death, two VUMC neurologists report Murphey's death to the Davidson County Medical Examiner without mentioning the medication error, that is, they did not mention that the patient had received vecuronium instead of Versed. The patient's death was deemed to be natural and due to a brain bleed. No investigation was done by the medical examiner since inaccurate information was received.
- VUMC personnel did not report the fatal error to government agencies or the public. It was not reported, as required by law, to either state or federal officials. It also was not reported to the Joint Commission, which accredits VUMC. Death as a result of a medication error is considered to be a sentinel event.
- VUMC negotiated an out-of-court monetary settlement with Murphey's family. The settlement stipulated that the family could not speak publicly about the patient's death or the medication error.
- Someone anonymously reported the medication error and Murphey's death to the DHHS CMS and to the TN Department of Health. The TN Department of Health alerted the TN Bureau of Investigation. The DHHS CMS intake report dated October 3, 2018, is available online.
- The TN Department of Health, which oversees licensing of healthcare professionals, decided not to pursue disciplinary action against Vaught based on the anonymous complaint. Letters dated October 23, 2018, which were sent to Vaught and a Ms. Dubree indicated that Vaught's case had been investigated, but it was determined that the nurse had not violated professional rules and statutes.
- Because of the anonymous complaint, CMS made a surprise visit to VUMC. An investigation regarding the complaint was conducted from October 31, 2018, until November 8, 2018. The facts of the complaint were confirmed by CMS during the investigation. VUMC was threatened with losing Medicare payments, but instead, the hospital was allowed to respond with a plan of correction to satisfy CMS. VUMC would not release the plan of correction to the public, but it was obtained by *The Tennessean* through a public records request.
- The public learned of the incident surrounding Murphey's death in late November 2018.

TN Bureau of Investigation Report

- Vaught was interviewed by two investigators at TBI on December 5, 2018.
- Vaught voluntarily waived her constitutional rights during the interview.
- Vaught provided her recall of what happened surrounding the events of the medication error. She admitted her error.
- Regarding her medication error, Vaught admitted the following:
  - She had administered Versed before, but she had never administered vecuronium bromide.
  - She was distracted by talking to her orientee nurse about the patient's test that was to be done. She admitted that she should have been focused on dispensing and administering the medication.
  - She should not have overridden the medication system, even though it was a common practice at the facility. Vaught admitted that her override was not urgent since the order for Versed was not an emergency.

- She thought it was "a little odd" that she had to reconstitute the medication.
- She did not remember anything on the vecuronium vial to alert her to the fact that the medication was not Versed, though she also said she should have recognized that she was not preparing to administer Versed (see image on page 39).
- Vaught said she should have called the pharmacy to check the order for the Versed.
- She described her thinking: "I probably just killed a patient;" "What did I do to this patient if I didn't kill her?;" "What kind of life changing things did I just put this patient and her family through?;" "It's a horrible situation."
- She used an expletive to describe what she had done.

After Exposure of the Medication Error

On February 4, 2019, Vaught was arrested based on a criminal indictment and charged with reckless homicide in violation of Tenn. Code Ann. §39-13-25, which is a class D felony. She also was charged with knowing physical abuse or gross neglect of an impaired adult in violation of Tenn. Code Ann. §71-6-119. This is when Vaught was publicly identified for the first time in connection with the incident.

On February 5, 2019, VUMC officials finally admitted they provided a settlement to Murphey's family, they failed to report the death to state regulators, and their response to the incident was "too limited." VUMC officials met with the TN Board of Licensing Health Care Facilities, but VUMC received no disciplinary action.

Vaught stated in a GoFundMe post on February 8, 2019, that people believed it

is dangerous to indict and incarcerate a nurse for a medical error.

Vaught entered a plea of not guilty on February 20, 2019, when she first appeared in court for her criminal case. Several dozen nurses who were not from TN showed up to give support to Vaught. Vaught's attorney cast blame on VUMC for the systematic problems with the medication dispensing units.

The Nashville Medical Examiner changed the cause of Murphey's death to accidental.

On September 27, 2019, the TN Department of Health and Board of Nursing reversed its decision that Vaught's error did not warrant disciplinary actions. According to Kelman (2022, March 27), the Board gave no reason for the reversal. In addition to noting that Vaught violated the five rights of medication administration, the Tennessee Board of Nursing (2019, September 27) noted in its document, *Notice of Hearing and Charges and Memorandum for Assessment of Civil Penalties,* that Vaught did not stay with the patient after administering the medication, she failed to monitor the patient, and she failed to document administering the vecuronium in the patient's record. The formal alleged violations that constituted grounds for discipline were cited verbatim as:

- Is guilty of unprofessional conduct,
- Failure to maintain a record for each patient which accurately reflects the nursing problems and interventions for the patient and/or failure to maintain a record for each patient which accurately reflects the name and title of the nurse providing care, and
- Abandoning or neglecting a patient requiring nursing care (p. 4).

A full hearing with the Board of Nursing was set for November 20, 2019. Vaught's penalty was scheduled to be set at that hearing. Vaught was still working at Centennial Medical Center at the time the Board notified her there would be a Board hearing. She continued to work at her job thereafter.

- A legal fight ensued about whether the Board of Nursing's disciplinary hearing should be held before or after the criminal trial.
- In the spring of 2020, the COVID-19 pandemic caused both the disciplinary and criminal proceedings to be postponed.
- On July 22, 2021, Vaught's Board of Nursing disciplinary hearing began.
- At the hearing, Vaught admitted her error and accepted fault. However, she and her attorney exposed problems in the VUMC healthcare system and accused VUMC of contributing to Vaught's error.
- During the Board of Nursing hearing, the following points were included in Vaught's and her attorney's accusations of VUMC's contribution to the error:
    - At the time of the error, VUMC was having communication problems between electronic health records, medication dispensing units, and the hospital's pharmacy.
    - Medication access was delayed, and hospital personnel were allowed to override safeguards as a short-term workaround.
    - Vaught reported that overriding the medication dispensing system was an everyday practice. Overrides were even needed to obtain intravenous fluids.
- On July 23, 2021, the TN Board of Nursing revoked Vaught's nursing license. Though the Board members seemed sympathetic to Vaught, one member said that "mistakes have consequences."
- Jury selection began on March 21, 2022, for Vaught's criminal trial.
- After about 4 hours of deliberation, the jury delivered the verdict on March 25, 2022, that Vaught was guilty of criminally negligent homicide and abuse of an impaired adult. She was acquitted of reckless homicide. Her charge of negligent homicide is a lesser charge.

- Vaught faced up to 6 years in prison for neglect and up to 2 years in prison for negligent homicide. She was sentenced on May 13, 2022. Though she could have received the harsher sentence, she was granted a judicial diversion. She was given three years probation with the opportunity to have her record expunged at the end of the probation.

Other Information to Consider

- Errors committed by healthcare professionals usually are handled civilly with monetary penalties and through licensing board disciplinary procedures rather than as criminal acts.
- Vaught reported that within 3 days, Murphey's care involved at least 20 overrides of the medication dispensing unit.
- A VUMC pharmacy medication safety officer testified at Vaught's trial that there were technical problems with the medication dispensing units in 2017, but these problems were resolved weeks before Vaught retrieved the incorrect medication.
- Vecuronium is a very dangerous drug to override.
- Vaught's case is "every nurse's nightmare."
- The prosecutor at Vaught's trial compared her to a drunk driver who killed a bystander. He said it was like she was driving with her eyes closed.
- The ANA and TNA contended that the case was a criminalization of honest reporting of an error. Organizational representatives argued that it is unrealistic to believe that mistakes will not happen and that systems will not fail. They proposed that the *Vaught* verdict would further negatively impact the nursing profession that already is strained.
- The *Vaught* case legally could be precedent-setting for healthcare professionals.
- Healthcare professionals have tried to move toward a "just culture," in which medical and nursing errors are properly

analyzed and systems are changed to prevent the same errors in the future. A just culture moves away from personal blame and cover-ups. The *RaDonda Vaught* case could disrupt the cultivation of a just culture.

- The circumstances of the case appear to show that VUMC attempted a cover-up of the incident. Vaught admitted her error.
- The following information was taken from a *Vanderbilt Hustler* article authored by Katherine Oung, the forum's Deputy News Editor (2022, March 31). The *Vanderbilt Hustler* is a news forum for Vanderbilt University and students.
  - Comments from the Davidson County District Attorney: "Multiple health care professionals were on the jury...The jury felt this level of care was so far below the proper standard of a reasonable and prudent nurse that the verdict was justified" (para. 3).
  - A former editor-in-chief of the *American Journal of Nursing*, Maureen Shawn Kennedy, was interviewed for the article. Kennedy called Vaught's error "horrendous," but she stated she did not believe jail time was warranted. She indicated that she believed this trial will be precedent-setting.
  - VUMC personnel would not comment to Oung about Vaught's criminal proceedings.
  - The article notes that the Davidson Count District Attorney's office denies that the verdict is precedent-setting.

Futility

The issues and concepts included in Box 2-5 often are associated with end-of-life care. Violating the principle of nonmaleficence may involve issues of medical futility. Though it sometimes is difficult to accurately predict the outcomes of all interventions, **futile treatments** are treatments a healthcare provider, when using good clinical judgment, does not believe will provide a beneficial outcome for a patient. Consequently, these treatments may instead cause harm to a patient, such as a patient having to endure a slow and painful death that may have otherwise occurred in a quicker and more natural or humane manner. Clinical judgments usually are made in the face of uncertainty (Jonsen et al., 2022), even though medical probabilities often are fairly clear.

Healthcare professionals are not ethically bound to deliver futile treatments. A simplistic example follows: A patient or surrogate cannot legitimately demand that a provider administer an antibiotic to a patient to treat a virus. Antibiotics are not biologically plausible treatments for viruses. Hence, the treatment would be futile, or ineffective. Antibiotic treatment involves risks to patients as well as to the public through the development of drug resistance when antibiotics are used inappropriately. This example is easy to understand, but as the complexity of potentially futile treatments increases, the likelihood of needing to navigate confusing situations with ethical and legal pitfalls also increases. Cases of potential futility that involve differing recommendations between healthcare providers or healthcare providers and/or patients and families should be referred to and discussed by ethics committees. Often, when the potential patient outcomes

LEGAL PERSPECTIVE

- Research laws about healthcare professionals discontinuing ventilator support for a patient in the presence of brain death.
- Discuss ethical issues and outcomes when a family does not voluntarily accept withdrawing ventilation in such cases. Provide specific cases to illustrate your findings.

are obscure, ethics committees err on the side of recommending the treatment desired by the patient and/or family, especially to avoid legal repercussions and maintain the goodwill of the family and the larger community.

Rule of Double Effect

The **rule, or doctrine, of double effect** is mentioned in Box 2-5. This doctrine is attributed to the Medieval saint Thomas Aquinas (1224–1274) from his book *Summa Theologica* (Aquinas, 1947). Aquinas opposed saint Augustine's earlier position that it is unjust for a person to kill another person in self-defense. Details of both arguments can be found in *Summa Theologica*, but Aquinas's basic premise for justifying killing in self-defense is that an act can have two effects—one effect is the intended effect (self-defense) and the other effect is "beside the intention" (killing another person during self-defense actions) (Question 64, Article 7). Aquinas argued that moral acts are judged on what is intended, not what is accidental. He further stipulated that the person acting in self-defense should use force only in proportion to what is needed for one's personal defense and that it should not be done with "private animosity" (Question 64, Article 7).

In health care, performing some actions may have two potential outcomes. One is the intended good outcome, but to achieve the good outcome, a second, less acceptable outcome also might be foreseen to occur. In these situations, one must gauge and balance actions according to their good, intended effects as compared to their possible harmful, adverse effects. For example, although research has shown that giving morphine in regular, increasing increments for pain or respiratory distress at the end of life rarely causes complete cessation of respirations, it is possible for respiratory arrest to occur in this type of situation. It is legal and ethical for healthcare professionals to treat pain and respiratory distress, particularly at the end of life, with increasing increments of morphine even though it is

foreseen that cessation of respirations *may* occur. "The nurse should provide interventions to relieve pain and other symptoms in the dying patient consistent with palliative care practice standards and may not act with the sole intent to end life" (American Nurses Association [ANA], 2015, p. 3). The terms *killing* and *letting die* raise issues of legality, ethics, homicide, suicide, euthanasia, acts of commission and omission, and active–passive distinctions, which are beyond the scope of this chapter.

ETHICAL REFLECTION

Research examples of using the rule of double effect in health care. Debate the ethics of these examples.

Slippery Slope Arguments

Often, a **slippery slope argument** is a metaphor used as a "beware the Ides of March" warning with no justification or formal, logical evidence to back it up (Ryan, 1998, p. 341). A slippery slope situation is one that may be morally acceptable when the current, primary event is being discussed or practiced but later could hypothetically slip toward a morally unacceptable situation. A slippery slope situation is somewhat like a runaway horse that cannot be stopped after the barn door is left open. People using a slippery slope argument tend to believe the old saying that when people are given an inch, they eventually may take a mile. Because it is argued that harm may be inflicted if the restraints on a particular practice are removed, sometimes, the concept of the slippery slope is considered to fall under the principle of nonmaleficence.

Slippery slope arguments may move toward illogical extremes. Therefore, people who are afraid of a dangerous slide to the bottom of the slope on certain issues need to find evidence justifying their arguments rather than trying to form public opinions and policies based only on alarmist comparisons. One example of a slippery slope debate occurred with the legalization of physician-assisted suicide (PAS), such as the acts legalized by the Oregon Death with Dignity Act. Proponents of the slippery slope argument say allowing PAS (now also known as physician assisted death or medical aid in dying), which involves a patient's voluntary decision and self-administration of lethal drugs in well-defined circumstances, may or may not in itself be morally wrong. However, slippery slope proponents argue the widespread legalization of PAS may lead to the eventual legalization of nonvoluntary practices of euthanasia. The Oregon Death with Dignity Act was passed in October 1997, and as of 2022, no slide toward the legalization of nonvoluntary euthanasia has occurred in the United States even though other states also have legalized PAS or physician-assisted death (PAD). Opponents of slippery slope arguments believe people proposing these arguments mistrust people's abilities to make definitive distinctions between moral/legal and immoral/illegal issues and exercise appropriate societal controls.

FOCUS FOR DEBATE

Though the procedure currently is illegal in the United States, other countries, such as the United Kingdom and Ukraine, have allowed in vitro fertilization using the DNA from three people to prevent mitochondrial diseases in babies.

1. Search the Internet and check the status of the ethical positions and laws regarding three-parent babies.
2. Is this type of procedure a slippery slope issue? Why or why not?

▶ Beneficence

The principle of beneficence consists of "acts or qualities of mercy, kindness, friendship, generosity, charity and the like" (Beauchamp &

BOX 2-6   Rules of Beneficence

1. Protect and defend the rights of others.
2. Prevent harm from occurring to others.
3. Remove conditions that will cause harm to others.
4. Help persons with disabilities.
5. Rescue persons in danger.

Data from Beauchamp, T. L., & Childress, J. F. (2019). *Principles of biomedical ethics* (8th ed.). Oxford University Press, p. 219.

Childress, 2019, p. 217). **Beneficence** means people take actions to benefit and promote the welfare of other people. Examples of moral rules and obligations underlying the principle of beneficence are listed in **BOX 2-6**.

Whereas people are obligated to act in a nonmaleficent manner toward all people—that is, not to harm anyone—there are limits to beneficence or the benefits people are expected to bestow on other people. Generally, people act more beneficently toward people whom they personally know or love rather than toward people not personally known to them, though this certainly is not always the case.

Because of professional standards and social contracts, physicians and nurses have a responsibility to be beneficent in their work. Nurses are directed in Provision 2.1 of the *Code of Ethics for Nurses with Interpretive Statements* (ANA, 2015) to have their patients' interests and well-being as their primary concern. Therefore, though sometimes there are limits to the good nurses can do, nurses have a more stringent obligation to act according to the principle of beneficence than does the general public. Doing good toward and facilitating the well-being of one's patients is an integral part of being a moral nurse.

The Latin term *supererogation* "refers to the act of paying out more than is required or demanded" (Heyd, 1982, p.1). It sometimes is considered in conjunction with saintliness or a person being a hero (Urmson, 1958).

In his 1982 book *Supererogation*, Heyd outlined a theory of supererogation as being separate from other moral theories. He proposed four conditions that define supererogation.

An act is supererogatory if and only if:

1. It is neither obligatory nor forbidden.
2. Its omission is not wrong—and does not deserve sanction or criticism—either formal or informal.
3. It is morally good, both by virtue of its (intended) consequences and by virtue of its intrinsic value (being beyond duty).
4. It is done voluntarily for the sake of someone else's good and is thus meritorious (p. 115).

The bottom line is deciding what the limits of a person's or group's duties are and how beneficent they should be. Nurses need to be aware of particular issues of supererogation. One issue to analyze is current guidance by the ANA at a given point in time. The ANA provides position statements covering issues such as nurses' obligations when they themselves may be at risk of harm from the patient care they provide.

Paternalism

Occasionally, healthcare professionals may experience ethical conflicts when confronted with having to make a choice between respecting a patient's right to self-determination (autonomy) and doing what is good for a patient's well-being (beneficence). Sometimes, healthcare professionals believe they, not their patients, know what is in a patient's best interest. In these situations, healthcare professionals may be tempted to act in ways they believe promote a patient's well-being (beneficence) when the actions actually are a violation of a patient's right to exercise self-determination (autonomy). The deliberate overriding of a patient's opportunity to exercise autonomy because of a perceived obligation of beneficence is called **paternalism**. The word reflects its

roots in fatherly or male (paternal) hierarchical relationships, governance, and care. When pondering paternalism, one might think of the title of the 1954 television show *Father Knows Best*.

If a nurse avoids telling a patient that her blood pressure is elevated because the nurse believes this information will upset the patient and consequently further elevate her blood pressure, this is an example of paternalism. A more ethical approach to the patient's care is to unexcitedly give the patient truthful information while helping her remain calm and educating her about successful ways to manage her blood pressure.

Two types of paternalism are listed in **BOX 2-7**. Although paternalism once was a common practice among healthcare professionals, in general, healthcare professionals are discouraged from using it today. Paternalism is still a common practice in certain situations and among people of some cultures who, for example, believe people with authority, such as physicians or male family members, should be allowed to make decisions in the best interests of patients and patients should not be given bad news, such as a terminal diagnosis.

FOCUS FOR DEBATE

Motorcycle helmet laws vary among states from no law to a law based on age or a law for all riders. Should it be legal to mandate that motorcycle riders wear a helmet if they do not want to wear one? Is it ethical? Consider: A person who is not wearing a helmet and is injured on a motorcycle might incur costly health care. Persons incurring such costs may theoretically increase the cost of health care for other people.

Second Victim Phenomenon

A situation when the principle of beneficence is needed, which may not often be recognized

BOX 2-7 Types of Paternalism

- Soft paternalism: The use of paternalism to protect persons from their own nonvoluntary conduct. People justify its acceptance when a person may be unable to make reasonable, autonomous decisions. Examples of when soft paternalism is used include situations involving depression, dementia, substance abuse, and addiction.

- Hard paternalism: "Interventions intended to prevent or mitigate harm to or to benefit a person, even though the person's risky choices and actions are informed, voluntary, and autonomous" (Beauchamp & Childress, 2019, p. 233).

According to Beauchamp and Childress (2013), the following is a summary of justifiable reasons to practice hard paternalism:

1. A patient is at risk of a significant, preventable harm or failure to receive a benefit.
2. The paternalistic action will probably prevent the harm or secure the benefit.
3. The prevention of harm to the patient outweighs risks to the patient of the action taken.
4. There is no morally better alternative.
5. The least autonomy-restrictive alternative that will prevent the harm or secure the benefit is adopted (p. 238).

Data from Beauchamp, T. L., & Childress, J. F. (2019). *Principles of biomedical ethics* (8th ed.). Oxford University Press.

but should be discussed more often, involves the *second victim phenomenon*. As discussed earlier in this chapter, the IOM began a project in the 1990s to study and reduce the plethora of healthcare errors. Findings from the project revealed that well-intentioned professionals in the midst of flawed processes and communication systems make many preventable errors. Real people are involved in these flawed healthcare systems, and errors committed by these people take a personal toll on them (Scott, 2011).

A physician, Albert Wu (2000), coined the term *second victim* in an editorial in the *British Medical Journal*. He provided an example of a medical resident who made a serious error in interpreting a patient's electrocardiogram, and the resident consequently was labeled as being incompetent. Wu lamented the fact that physicians are the victims of "an expectation of perfection" (p. 726). He proposed that healthcare professionals, including nurses and pharmacists, who make mistakes are the "second victims" along with patients who are the "first and obvious victims of medical mistakes" (p. 726). Though Wu did not directly mention the principle of beneficence (doing good) or the virtue of benevolence (being kind), he did advocate that second victims need help from their colleagues to navigate the "grieving process" that occurs after one makes a serious mistake (p. 727). Two well-publicized cases of the second victim phenomenon center on nurses Julie Thao and Kimberly Hiatt. Mistakes made by these nurses resulted in patient deaths and tragic outcomes for the nurses, especially in the case of Hiatt.

ETHICAL REFLECTION

1. Search the Internet and learn about the cases of nurses Julie Thao and Kimberly Hiatt.
2. List and discuss lessons that you and all healthcare professionals can learn from these two cases.
3. Describe how the principle of beneficence and the virtue of benevolence could be applied to these cases.
4. In addition to benevolence, which other virtues exhibited by their colleagues might have helped Thao and Hiatt?
5. Discuss personal virtues that might be helpful to second victims themselves in navigating the grieving process.

▶ Justice

Justice, as a principle in healthcare ethics, refers to fairness; treating people equally and without prejudice; and the equitable distribution of benefits and burdens, including assuring fairness in biomedical research. Most of the time, difficult healthcare resource allocation decisions are based on attempts to answer questions regarding who has a right to health care, how much health care a person is entitled to, and who will pay for healthcare costs. Remember, however, that justice is one of Plato's cardinal virtues (see an earlier chapter 1). This means that justice is a broad concept in the field of ethics and considered to be both a principle and a virtue.

Social Justice

Distributive justice refers to the fair allocation of resources, whereas **social justice** represents the position that benefits and burdens should be distributed fairly among members of a society or, ideally, that all people in a society should have the same rights, benefits, and opportunities. The mission to define and attain some measure of social justice is an ongoing and difficult activity for the world community. One only needs to think about the obligations

---

FOCUS FOR DEBATE

Debate the following issues as they relate to obligations of beneficence. What should be the limits of beneficence in these cases?

- Rescuing a person who is drowning. What if the person is drowning in dangerous rapidly flowing water?
- Alleviating global poverty.
- Working as a nurse during a highly lethal pandemic when a vaccination is unavailable and protective equipment is limited.
- Defending the rights of immigrants.

---

of beneficence to identify how these two principles are related. For example, what are the limits of the obligation that people must do good in distributing their assets to help others?

An analysis of social justice mostly has been used to evaluate the powers of competing social systems and the application of regulatory principles on an impartial basis. Theories of social justice differ to some extent, but most of the theories are based on the notion that justice is related to fair treatment and similar cases should be treated in similar ways. People who take a communitarian approach to social justice will seek the common good of the community rather than maximizing individual benefits and freedoms. If people think beyond borders in promoting social justice, they consider how basic health care for all people can be provided and what can be done to prevent social injustice worldwide, such as ways to alleviate poverty, hunger, and abuse.

In his book, *A Theory of Justice*, John Rawls (1971) proposed that fairness and equality be evaluated under a **veil of ignorance**. This concept means that if people had a veil to shield themselves from their own or others' economic, social, and class standing, each person would be likely to make justice-based decisions from a position free of biases. Consequently, each person would view the distribution of resources in impartial ways. Under the veil, people would view social conditions neutrally because they would not know what their own position might be when the veil is lifted. This not knowing, or ignorance, of persons about their own social position means they would be unable to gain any type of advantage for themselves by their choices. Rawls advocated two principles of equality and justice: (1) everyone should be given equal liberty regardless of their adversities and (2) differences among people should be recognized by making sure the least-advantaged people are given opportunities for improvement.

In 1974, Robert Nozick presented the idea of an entitlement system in his book *Anarchy, State, and Utopia*. He proposed that individuals should be entitled to health care and the benefits of insurance only if they are able to pay for these benefits. Nozick emphasized a system of **libertarianism**, meaning justice and fairness are based on rewarding only those people who contribute to the system in proportion to their contributions. People who cannot afford health insurance are disadvantaged if Nozick's entitlement theory is used as a philosophy of social justice.

FOCUS FOR DEBATE

Is it ethical to ration health care to stretch healthcare dollars? Consider the different ways rationing criteria could be established; examples include age, income, social status, and diagnosis and treatment.

In his book, *Just Health Care*, Norman Daniels (1985) used the basis of Rawls's concept of justice and suggested a liberty principle. Daniels advocated national healthcare reform and proposed that every person should have equal access to health care and reasonable access to healthcare services. Daniels suggested there should be critical standards for a fair and equitable healthcare system, and he provided points of reference, or benchmarks, for this application of fairness in the implementation and development of national healthcare reform.

The Patient Protection and Affordable Care Act

Signed into law by President Obama on March 23, 2010, the Affordable Care Act (ACA) was intended to enact comprehensive healthcare reform in the United States, including improving quality and lowering healthcare costs and providing greater access to health care and new consumer protections. The ACA is intended to put members of the American public in charge of their own health care. For a good overview of information about the law, the insurance marketplace created by the law, prevention and wellness benefits, and facts and features of the law, visit the HHS.gov website: About the Affordable Care Act.

Before the enactment of the ACA, the long-standing U.S. healthcare system was based on a philosophy of market justice, that is, distributing health care as an economic good rather than a social good. The changing U.S. philosophy related to the distribution of health care has prompted a battle between people who tend to be libertarians (concerned about individual freedoms) and people who tend to be communitarians (concerned about the common good). Pence (2015) outlined some of the main issues, questions, and positions regarding the ACA:

- Does the ACA provide better efficiency in providing health care, or will the system be bogged down in federal bureaucracy? Medicare, Medicaid, and the Veterans Administration system are cited as success stories, even though each agency has generated both quality and economic concerns. Overall, these federal programs have provided fairly comprehensive health care for large numbers of people and have yet to go broke, as people have feared. On the negative side, historically the federal government is not known for being efficient. The Internet provides a plethora of information about wasteful federal expenditures.
- Does the ACA make medicine rational? On the positive side, the ACA is an effort to control costs, equalize coverage, and make health care a moral endeavor. People against the act say, "the more we move to perfect equality, the more individual liberty vanishes" (Pence, 2015, p. 347). Another point of contention is whether the better availability of health care prompts more people to use resources indiscriminately rather than rationally. This concern

is founded somewhat on a slippery slope argument. This position should rely on research data.

- Is health care a right or a privilege? Many people in the United States consider Medicare coverage to be a right. It is interesting that some of these same people are against a move toward universal coverage under the ACA. Rawls (1971) contended that justice is consistent with fairness within social structures. Health care falls within the American social structure; thus, on the surface of things, it is a right for all citizens. Recall from earlier in this chapter that Rawls's veil of ignorance is a test of how to determine what is just and unjust in an unbiased way. One can ponder, under the veil, how many people would choose to be without basic healthcare coverage when the veil is lifted. Libertarians who are against the ACA contend that:

America was founded on *negative rights of noninterference*: rights to be left alone, to pursue happiness, and to think, speak, assemble, and worship without interference from government. Such "freedom from" differs dramatically from "freedom to." The latter is a *positive right to some service* from others, that is, an entitlement. (Pence, 2015, p. 347)

One of the conundrums underlying this point of debate is whether minimum or basic health care can be defined at all to determine how far one's rights should be extended. Does the ACA generate a situation of intergenerational injustice? People who oppose the ACA say young generations will be enslaved by taxes to pay for health care for older Americans. People in favor of the ACA say many young people are "free riders" (Pence, 2015, p. 354) of the system and some type of means testing process can be used for more financially secure seniors to pay more for coverage.

FOCUS FOR DEBATE

Take the points of debate offered by Pence and investigate the issues further. Organize and engage in evidence-based debates around these issues and other ACA issues in the literature and on the Internet. Examples for debate include the following questions, but there are other issues that can be debated:

- Is supporting versus not supporting the ACA a matter of ethics?
- Is the social structure of America based on negative or positive rights? Which type of rights supports a more ethical social structure?
- Is health care a right or a privilege?
- Can minimum or basic health care be defined?
- Does the ACA provide a more efficient system of health care?
- Does the ACA set up a situation of intergenerational injustice?
- Does Rawls's veil of ignorance provide a good rationale for why people should support the ACA?
- Does the widespread availability of health care lead to a waste of scarce resources (i.e., can Americans be trusted to use good judgment in how resources are used)?

LEGAL PERSPECTIVE

After passage of the ACA, some politicians engaged in a prolonged attempt to repeal the act or delay implementation based on the premise that the law is unconstitutional; that is, the federal government cannot mandate individuals to purchase health insurance. After the election of President Trump, in December 2017, the individual mandate for insurance was repealed beginning in 2019 by the Tax Cuts and Jobs Act of 2017. Senator Orrin Hatch indicated this repeal started the end of the ObamaCare (i.e., the ACA) era. However, the constitutionality of the ACA was upheld by the U.S. Supreme Court in 2021.

Professional–Patient Relationships

The quality of patient care rendered by healthcare professionals and patients' satisfaction with health care often depend on harmonious relationships between professionals and patients and among the members of professions themselves. If healthcare professionals view life as a web of interrelationships, all their relationships potentially can affect the well-being of patients.

Unavoidable Trust

When patients enter the healthcare system, they usually are entering a foreign and frightening environment (Chambliss, 1996; Zaner, 1991). Intimate conversations and activities, such as being touched and probed, that normally do not occur between strangers are commonplace between healthcare professionals and patients. Patients frequently are stripped of their clothes, subjected to sitting alone in cold and barren rooms, and made to wait anxiously for frightening news regarding the continuation of their very being. When patients need help from healthcare professionals, they frequently feel a sense of vulnerability and uncertainty. The tension patients feel when accessing health care is heightened by the need for what Zaner called **unavoidable trust**. In most cases, when they need care, patients have no option but to trust nurses and other healthcare professionals.

ETHICAL REFLECTION

Suggest nursing actions to decrease patients' uncomfortable feelings when they are experiencing unavoidable trust.

This unavoidable trust creates an asymmetrical, or uneven, power structure in relationships between professionals and patients

and the patients' families (Zaner, 1991). Nurses' responsiveness to this trust needs to include the promise to be the most excellent nurses they can be. According to Zaner, healthcare professionals must promise "not only to take care of, but to care for the patient and family—to be candid, sensitive, attentive, and never to abandon them" (p. 54). It is paradoxical that trust is necessary *before* health care is rendered, but it can be evaluated in terms of whether the trust was warranted only *after* care is rendered. To practice ethically, nurses must never take for granted the fragility of patients' trust.

ETHICAL REFLECTION

On the Internet, find the poem "The Operation" by Anne Sexton. Read the poem reflectively, and do the following:

1. Analyze the story, symbolism, and feelings conveyed by Sexton in the poem; discuss and provide specific examples.
2. Discuss your perception of the quality of healthcare provider–patient relationships reflected in the poem; provide specific examples.

Human Dignity

In the first provision of the *Code of Ethics for Nurses with Interpretive Statements*, the ANA (2015) included the standard that a nurse must have "respect for human dignity" (p. 1). Typically, people refer to maintaining dignity regarding the circumstances of how people look, behave, and express themselves when they are being watched by others or are ill, aging, or dying; in circumstances of how people respect themselves and are respected by others; and in the honor accorded to the privacy of one's body, emotions, and personhood. Nurses are charged with protecting a person's dignity during all nursing care, and often a patient's nurse is the primary person who guards a patient's dignity during medical procedures.

Healthcare settings can be scenes of professionals rushing through treatments so they can efficiently move on to the next patient and job to be done. Nurses have many opportunities to be mindful of the person who is the patient: a person who wants to be respected.

Shotton and Seedhouse (1998) said the term *dignity* has been used in vague ways. They characterized dignity as persons being in a position to use their capabilities and proposed that a person has dignity "if he or she is in a situation where his or her capabilities can be effectively applied" (p. 249). For example, a nurse can enhance dignity when caring for an elderly person by assessing the elder's priorities and determining what the elder has been capable of doing in the past and is capable of doing and wants to do in the present.

A lack or loss of capability is frequently an issue for consideration when caring for patients such as children, elders, and persons who are physically and mentally disabled. Having absent or diminished capabilities is consistent with what MacIntyre (1999) referred to in his discussion of human vulnerability. According to MacIntyre, people generally progress from a point of vulnerability in infancy to achieving varying levels of independent, practical reasoning as they mature. However, all people, including nurses, would do well to realize that all persons have been or will be vulnerable at some point in their lives. Taking a "there but for the grace of God go I" stance may prompt nurses to develop what MacIntyre called the virtues of acknowledged dependence. These virtues include *just generosity, misericordia,* and *truthfulness* and are exercised in communities of giving and receiving. Just generosity is a form of giving generously without keeping score of who gives or receives the most, *misericordia* is a Latin word that signifies giving without prejudice based on urgent need, and truthfulness involves not being deceptive. Nurses who cultivate these three virtues, or excellences of character, can move toward preserving patients' dignity and working for the common good of a community.

Patient Advocacy

Nurses acting from a point of patient advocacy try to identify unmet patient needs and then follow up to address the needs appropriately (Jameton, 1984). Advocacy, as opposed to advice, involves the nurse moving from the patient to the healthcare system rather than moving from the nurse values to the patient. The concept of advocacy has been a part of the ethics codes of the International Council of Nurses (ICN) and the ANA since the 1970s (Winslow, 1988). In the *Code of Ethics for Nurses with Interpretive Statements*, the ANA (2015) continues to support patient advocacy by elaborating on the "primacy of the patient's interest" (p. 5) and requiring nurses to work collaboratively with others to attain the goal of addressing the healthcare needs of patients and the public. Nurses are called upon to ensure that all appropriate parties are involved in patient care decisions, patients are provided with the information needed to make informed decisions, and collaboration is used to increase the accessibility and availability of health care to all patients who need it. The ICN (2021), in its *Code of Ethics for Nurses*, affirms that "nurses are patient advocates and they maintain a practice culture that promotes ethical behavior and open dialogue" (p. 12).

▶ Moral Suffering

Many times, healthcare professionals experience a disquieting feeling of anguish, uneasiness, or angst that can be called **moral suffering**. Suffering in a moral sense has similarities to the Buddhist concept of *dukkha*, a Sanskrit word translated as suffering. *Dukkha* "includes the idea that life is impermanent and is experienced as unsatisfactory and imperfect" (Sheng-yen, 1999, p. 37). The concept of *dukkha* evolved from the historical Buddha's belief that the human conditions of birth, sickness, old age, and death involve suffering and *are* suffering. Nurses confront these human conditions every day. Not recognizing, and in turn struggling against, the reality that impermanence, or the changing and passing away of all things, is inherent to human life, the world, and all objects is a cause of suffering.

Moral suffering can be experienced when nurses attempt to sort out their emotions when they find themselves in imperfect situations that are morally unsatisfactory or forces beyond their control prevent them from positively influencing or changing unsatisfactory moral situations. Suffering occurs because nurses believe situations must be changed or fixed to bring well-being to themselves and others or to alleviate the suffering of themselves and others.

Moral suffering may arise, for example, from disagreements with imperfect institutional policies, such as an on-call policy or work schedule the nurse believes does not allow relaxation time for the nurse's psychological well-being. Nurses also may disagree with physicians' orders that the nurses believe are not in patients' best interests, or they may disagree with the way a family treats a patient or makes patient care decisions. Moral suffering can result when a nurse is with a patient when the patient receives a terminal diagnosis or when a nurse's compassion is aroused when caring for a severely impaired neonate or an elder who is suffering, and life-sustaining care is either prolonged or withdrawn. These are but a few examples of the many types of encounters nurses may have with moral suffering.

Another important, but often unacknowledged, source of moral suffering may occur when nurses freely choose to act in ways they, themselves, would not defend as being morally commendable if the actions were honestly analyzed. For example, a difficult situation that may cause moral suffering for a nurse would be covering up a patient care error made by herself or himself or a valued nurse friend. On the other hand, nurses may experience moral suffering when they act virtuously and courageously by doing what they believe is morally right despite anticipated disturbing

consequences. Sometimes, doing the right thing or acting as a virtuous person would act is hard, but it is incumbent upon nurses to habitually act in virtuous ways, that is, to exhibit habits of excellent character.

The Dalai Lama (1999) proposed that how people are affected by suffering is often a matter of choice or personal perspective. Some people view suffering as something to accept and transform if possible. Causes may lead toward certain effects, and nurses are often able to change the circumstances or conditions of events so positive effects occur. Nurses can choose and cultivate their perspectives, attitudes, and emotions in ways that lead toward happiness and well-being even in the face of suffering.

ETHICAL REFLECTION

- Have you experienced moral suffering during your work as a nurse or student nurse? Describe it.
- How can this experience help you grow as a kind person and nurse?

The Buddha was reported to have said, "Because the world is sick, I am sick. Because people suffer, I have to suffer" (Hanh, 1998, p. 3). However, in the Four Noble Truths, the Buddha postulated that the cessation of suffering can be a reality through the Eightfold Path of eight right ways of thinking, acting, and being, sometimes grouped under the three general categories of wisdom, morality, and meditation. In other words, suffering can be transformed. When nurses or other healthcare professionals react to situations with fear, bitterness, and anxiety, it is important to remember that wisdom and inner strength are often increased most during times of the greatest difficulty. Thich Nhat Hanh (1998) wisely stated, "without suffering, you cannot grow" (p. 5). Therefore, nurses can learn to take their disquieting experiences of moral anguish and uneasiness—that is, moral suffering—and transform them into experiences that lead to well-being.

Ethical Dilemmas

An **ethical dilemma** is a situation in which an individual is compelled to choose between two actions that will affect the welfare of a sentient being and both actions are reasonably justified as being good, neither action is readily justified as being good, or the goodness of the actions is uncertain. One action must be chosen, thereby generating a quandary for the person or group who is burdened with the choice.

Kidder (1995) focused on one characteristic of an ethical dilemma when he described the heart of an ethical dilemma as "the ethics of right versus right" (p. 13). Though the best choice about two right actions is not always self-evident, according to Kidder, right versus right choices clearly can be distinguished from right versus wrong choices. Right versus right choices are nearer to common societal and personal values, whereas the closer one analyzes right versus wrong choices, "the more they begin to smell" (p. 17). He proposed that people generally can judge wrong choices according to three criteria: violation of the law, departure from the truth, and deviation from moral rectitude. Of course, the selection and meaning of these three criteria can be a matter of debate.

When a person is facing a real ethical dilemma, often, none of the available options feel right. Both choices may feel wrong. For a daughter trying to decide whether to withdraw life support from her 88-year-old mother, it may feel wrong not to try to save her mother's life but allowing her mother to suffer in a futile medical condition probably will also feel wrong. On the other hand, for a healthcare professional considering this same case, there may be no real dilemma involved—the healthcare professional may see clearly that the right choice is to withhold or withdraw life support.

Considering the preceding explanations, it is important to note that the words *ethical dilemma* often are used loosely and inappropriately. Weston (2011) stated, "today you can hardly even mention the word 'moral' without 'dilemma' coming up in the next sentence, if it waits that long" (p. 99). He called an ethical dilemma "a very special thing" (p. 99), contending that often, when people believe they face a dilemma, they are facing a "false dilemma"; the person needs only to work on identifying "new possibilities or reframing the problem itself" (p. 99) to solve the problem. As an example, he presented the classic case of the Heinz dilemma used by Lawrence Kohlberg in his research. The story is about Heinz, whose wife is dying of cancer. She needs a particular drug to save her life. The pharmacist who makes the drug charges much more than it costs him to make it. The cost is way beyond what Heinz can afford to pay. Heinz tries to borrow the money needed but is not successful. He asks the pharmacist to sell him the drug at a lower cost, but the pharmacist refuses his request. Finally, Heinz robs the pharmacy to obtain the drug. The question is whether Heinz should have committed the robbery. Did Heinz face a dilemma? Weston discussed the Heinz dilemma with his students, and they generated some very creative ways of approaching the problem that did not involve robbing the pharmacy.

Introduction to Critical Thinking and Ethical Decision Making

In healthcare and nursing practice, moral matters are so prevalent that nurses often do not even realize they are faced with minute-to-minute opportunities to make ethical decisions (Chambliss, 1996; Kelly, 2000). It is vitally important that nurses have the analytical thinking ability and skills to respond to many of the everyday decisions that must be made. Listening attentively to other people, including patients, and not developing hasty conclusions are essential skills for nurses to conduct reasoned, ethical analyses. Personal values, professional values and competencies, ethical principles, and ethical theories and approaches are variables to consider when a moral decision is made. Pondering the questions "What is the right thing to do?" and "What ought I do in this circumstance?" is an ever-present normative consideration in nursing.

Critical Thinking

The concept of critical thinking is used quite liberally today in nursing. Many nurses probably have a general idea about the meaning of the concept, but they may not be able to clearly articulate answers to questions about its meaning. Examples of such questions include the following: Specifically, what is critical thinking? Are critical thinking and problem-solving interchangeable concepts? If not, what distinguishes them? Can critical thinking skills be learned, or does critical thinking occur naturally? If the skill can be learned, how does one become a critical thinker? Is there a difference between doing critical thinking and reasoning?

Socrates's method of teaching and questioning, covered in an earlier chapter 1, is one of the oldest systems of critical thinking. In modern times, the American philosopher John Dewey (1859–1952) is considered one of the early proponents of critical thinking. In his book *How We Think*, Dewey (1910/1997) summarized reflective thought as:

> active, persistent, and careful consideration of any belief or supposed form of knowledge in light of the grounds that support it, and the further conclusions to which it tends. . . . Once begun it is a conscious and voluntary effort to establish belief upon a firm basis of reasons. (p. 6)

Paul and Elder (2006), directors of the Foundation for Critical Thinking, defined critical thinking as "the art of analyzing and evaluating thinking with a view to improving it" (p. 4). They proposed that critical thinkers have certain characteristics:

- They ask clear, pertinent questions and identify key problems.
- They analyze and interpret relevant information by using abstract thinking.
- They can generate reasonable conclusions and solutions that are tested according to sensible criteria and standards.
- They remain open minded and consider alternative thought systems.
- They solve complex problems by effectively communicating with other people.

The process of **critical thinking** is summarized by Paul and Elder (2006) as "self-directed, self-disciplined, self-monitored, and self-corrective thinking [that] requires rigorous standards of excellence and mindful command of their use" (p. 4). Fisher (2001) described the basic way to develop critical thinking skills as simply "thinking about one's thinking" (p. 5).

Moral Imagination

[Persons], to be greatly good, must imagine intensely and comprehensively; [they] must put [themselves] in the place of another and of many others. . . . The great instrument of moral good is the imagination.

—**Percy Bysshe Shelley**, *Defense of Poetry*

The foundation underlying the concept of moral imagination, an artistic or aesthetic approach to ethics, is based on the philosophy of John Dewey. Imagination, as Dewey proposed it, is "the capacity to concretely perceive what is before us in light of what could be" (as cited in Fesmire, 2003, p. 65). Dewey (1934) stated imagination "is a way of seeing and feeling things as they compose an integral whole" (p. 267). **Moral imagination** is moral decision making through reflection involving "empathetic projection" and "creatively tapping a situation's possibilities" (Fesmire, 2003, p. 65). It involves moral awareness and decision making that goes beyond the mere application of standardized ethical meanings, decision-making models, and bioethical principles to real-life situations.

ETHICAL REFLECTION

Perform a written self-analysis of your critical thinking skills. What are your strengths? In what ways do you need to improve? Be specific with your analysis.

The use of empathetic projection helps nurses be responsive to patients' feelings, attitudes, and values. To creatively reflect on a situation's possibilities helps prevent nurses from becoming stuck in their daily routines and instead encourages them to look for new and different possibilities in problem solving and decision making that go beyond mere habitual behaviors. Although Aristotle taught that habit is the way people cultivate moral virtues, Dewey (1922/1988) cautioned that mindless habits can be "blinders that confine the eyes of mind to the road ahead" (p. 121). Dewey proposed that habit should be combined with intellectual impulse:

> Habits by themselves are too organized, too insistent and determinate to need to indulge in inquiry or imagination. And impulses are too chaotic, tumultuous and confused to be able to know even if they wanted to. . . . A certain delicate combination of habit and impulse is requisite for observation, memory and judgment. (p. 124)

Dewey (1910/1997) provided an example of a physician trying to identify a patient's diagnosis without proper reflection:

> Imagine a doctor being called in to prescribe for a patient. The patient tells him some things that are wrong; his experienced eye, at a glance, takes in other signs of a certain disease. But if he permits the suggestion of this special disease to take possession prematurely of his mind, to become an accepted conclusion, his scientific thinking is by that much cut short. A large part of his technique, as a skilled practitioner, is to prevent the acceptance of the first suggestions that arise; even, indeed, to postpone the occurrence of any very definite suggestions till the trouble—the nature of the problem—has been thoroughly explored. In the case of a physician this proceeding is known as a diagnosis, but a similar inspection is required in every novel and complicated situation to prevent rushing to a conclusion. (p. 74)

Although Dewey's example is about an individual physician–patient clinical encounter, the example also is applicable for illustrating the dangers of rushing to conclusions in the moral practice of the art and science of nursing with individuals, families, communities, and populations. The following story provides an example of a nurse not using moral imagination. A young public health nurse moves from a large city to a rural town and begins working as the occupational health nurse at a local factory. The nurse notices that many workers at the factory have developed lung cancer. He immediately assumes the workers have been exposed to some type of environmental pollution at the factory and the factory owners are morally irresponsible people. The nurse discusses his assessment with his immediate supervisor and an official at the district health department. Upon further assessment, the nurse finds data showing the factory's environmental pollution is unusually low. However, the nurse does learn that radon levels are particularly high in homes in the area and a large percentage of the factory workers smoke cigarettes. The nurse plans interventions to increase home radon testing and reduce smoking among employees.

In the following example, a home health nurse uses moral imagination. The nurse visits Mrs. Smith, a homebound patient diagnosed with congestive heart failure. The patient tells the nurse she has difficulty affording her medications and she does not buy the low-sodium foods the nurse recommends because the fresh foods are too expensive. However, the patient's television set broke, and she bought a new, moderately priced television she is usually watching when the nurse visits. The home health aide who visits the patient tells the nurse, "No wonder Mrs. Smith can't afford her medications—she spent her money on a television." Rather than judging the patient, the nurse uses her moral imagination to try to empathetically envision what it must be like to be Mrs. Smith—homebound, consistently short of breath, and usually alone. The nurse decides Mrs. Smith's television may have been money well spent in terms of the patient's quality of life. With Mrs. Smith's physician and social

worker, the nurse explores ways to help the patient obtain her medications. The nurse also works patiently with Mrs. Smith to try to develop a healthy meal plan that is affordable for her. Finally, the nurse engages in a constructive, nonthreatening discussion with the home health aide about why negative judgments and conclusions should be carefully considered. She is a mentor to the aide and teaches her about moral imagination.

Dewey (1910/1997) seemed to be trying to make the point that critical thinking and moral imagination require suspended judgment until problems and situations are fully explored and reflected upon. Moral imagination includes engaging in frequent considerations of "what if?" regarding day-to-day life events and novel situations. In a public interview on July 22, 2004, immediately after the U.S. Congress released the *9/11 Commission Report*, former New Jersey governor and 9/11 Commission chairman Thomas Kean made a statement regarding the findings about the probable causes of the failure to prevent the terrorist attacks on September 11, 2001. The commission concluded, above all, that there was a "failure of imagination" (Mondics, 2004, p. A4).

An important role for nurses is to provide leadership and help create healthy communities through individual-, family-, and population-based assessments and program planning, implementation, and evaluation. When assuming this key leadership role, nurses continually make choices and decisions that may affect the well-being of both individuals and populations.

FOCUS FOR DEBATE

- Do members of the nursing profession have an imbalanced focus on the caring nature of nursing, thus minimizing a focus on nurses' scientific knowledge and thereby hurting nursing's public image?
- Do you believe public impressions of the profession have changed in the last decade? Support your answer.

Opinions should not be formed hastily, nor should actions be taken without nurses cultivating and using their moral imaginations.

The High, Hard Ground and the Swampy, Low Ground

It is generally agreed that nursing is based on the dual elements of art and science. Schön (1987) postulated that professional decision points sometimes arise when there is tension between how to attend to knowledge based on technical, scientific foundations and indeterminate issues that lie beyond scientific laws. Schön (1987) described this tension as follows:

> In the varied topography of professional practice, there is a high, hard ground overlooking a swamp. On the high ground, manageable problems lend themselves to solution through the application of research-based theory and technique. In the swampy lowland, messy, confusing problems defy technical solutions. The irony of this situation is that the problems of the high ground tend to be relatively unimportant to individuals or society at large, however great their technical interest may be, while in the swamp lie the problems of greatest human concern. The practitioner must choose. (p. 3)

Gordon and Nelson (2006) argued that nursing has suffered by not emphasizing the profession's scientific basis and the specialized skills required for nursing practice. These authors proposed the professional advancement of nursing has been hurt by nurses and others (including general members of society) focusing too much on the virtues of nurses and the caring nature of the profession, essentially the art of nursing:

> Although much has changed for professional women in the twentieth century, nurses continue to rely on religious, moral, and sentimental symbols and rhetoric—images of hearts, angels, touching hands, and appeals based on diffuse references to closeness, intimacy, and making a difference. . . . When repeated in recruitment brochures and campaigns, appeals to virtue are unlikely to help people understand what nurses really do and how much knowledge and skill they need to do it. (pp. 26–27)

Reflective Practice

Schön (1987) distinguished reflection-*on*-action from reflection-*in*-action. Reflection-on-action involves looking back on one's actions, whereas reflection-in-action involves stopping to think about what one is choosing and doing before and during one's actions. In considering the value of reflection-in-action, Schön (1987) stated, "in an action present—a period of time, variable with the context, during which we can still make a difference to the situation at hand—our thinking serves to reshape what we are doing while we are doing it" (p. 26). Mindful reflection while we are still able to make choices about our behaviors is preferable to looking backward. However, as the saying goes, hindsight is 20/20, so there is certainly learning that can occur from hindsight.

Because ethics is an active process of doing, reflection in any form is crucial to the practice of ethics. Making justified ethical decisions requires healthcare professionals to know themselves and their motives, ask good questions, challenge the status quo, and be continual learners (see **BOX 2-8**). There is no one model of reflection and decision making that can provide healthcare professionals with an algorithm for ethical practice. However, there are models professionals can use to improve their skills of reflection and decision making during their practice. The Five Rs Approach, discussed here, is one such model.

ETHICAL REFLECTION

Use the Gibbs' Cycle (**FIGURE 2-1**), and reflect on a challenging, personal, ethical situation that occurred during your nursing practice or personal life.

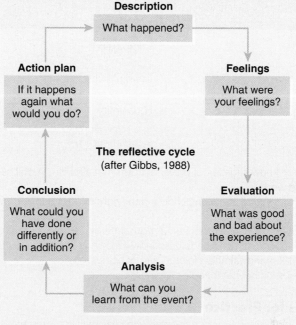

FIGURE 2-1 Gibbs' Reflective Cycle.

Courtesy of Graham Gibbs. (1988). *Learning by doing: A guide to teaching and learning methods*. Oxford Polytechnic.

BOX 2-8 The Five Rs Approach to Ethical Nursing Practice

1. **Read** and learn about ethical philosophies, approaches, and the ANA's *Code of Ethics for Nurses*. Insight and practical wisdom are best developed through effort and concentration.

2. **Reflect** mindfully on one's egocentric attachments—values, intentions, motivations, and attitudes. Members of moral communities are socially engaged and focus on the common good. This includes having good insight regarding life events, cultivating and using practical wisdom, and being generous and socially just.

3. **Recognize** ethical bifurcation (decision) points, whether they are obvious or obscure. Because of indifference or avoidance, nurses may miss both small and substantial opportunities to help alleviate human suffering in its different forms.

4. **Resolve** to develop and practice intellectual and moral virtues. Knowing ethical codes, rules, duties, and principles means little without being combined with a nurse's good character.

(continues)

BOX 2-8 The Five Rs Approach to Ethical Nursing Practice *(continued)*

5. **Respond** to persons and situations deliberately and habitually with intellectual and moral virtues. Nurses have a choice about their character development and actions.

Intellectual virtues	Moral virtues
Insight	Compassion
Practical wisdom	Loving-kindness
	Equanimity
	Sympathetic joy

Insight: Awareness and knowledge about universal truths that affect the moral nature of nurses' day-to-day life and work

Practical wisdom: Deliberating about and choosing the right things to do and ways to be that lead to good ends

Compassion: The desire to separate other beings from suffering

Loving-kindness: The desire to bring happiness and well-being to oneself and other beings

Equanimity: An evenness and calmness in one's way of being; balance

Sympathetic joy: Rejoicing in other people's happiness

Considerations for Practice

- Trying to apply generic algorithms or principles when navigating substantial ethical situations does not adequately allow for variations in life narratives and contexts.
- Living according to a philosophy of ethics must be a way of being for nurses before they encounter critical ethical bifurcation points.

The Four Topics Approach to Ethical Decision Making

Jonsen and colleagues' (2022) Four Topics Method for ethical analysis is a practical approach for nurses and other healthcare professionals. The nurse or team begins with relevant facts about a particular case and moves toward a resolution through a structured analysis. In healthcare settings, ethics committees often resolve ethical problems and answer ethical questions by using a case-based, or bottom-up, inductive, casuistry approach. The Four Topics Method, sometimes called the Four Box Approach (**TABLE 2-1**) is found in the book *Clinical Ethics: A Practical Approach to Ethical Decisions in Clinical Medicine* (Jonsen et al., 2022).

This case-based approach allows healthcare professionals to construct the facts of a case in a structured format that facilitates critical thinking about ethical problems. Cases are analyzed according to four topics: "medical indications, preferences of patients, quality of life, and contextual features" (Jonsen et al., 2022, p. 8). Nurses and other healthcare professionals on the team gather information to answer the

TABLE 2-1 Four Topics Method for Analysis of Clinical Ethics Cases

Medical Indications

The Principles of Beneficence and Nonmaleficence

1. What is the patient's medical problem? Is the problem acute? Chronic? Critical? Reversible? Emergent? Terminal?
2. What are the goals of treatment?
3. In what circumstances are medical treatments not indicated?
4. What are the probabilities of success of various treatment options?
5. In sum, how can this patient be benefited by medical and nursing care, and how can harm be avoided?

Preferences of Patient

The Principle of Respect for Autonomy

1. Has the patient been informed of benefits and risks of diagnostic and treatment recommendations, understood this information, and given consent?
2. Is the patient mentally capable, and legally competent, and is there evidence of incapacity?
3. If mentally capable, what preferences about treatment is the patient stating?
4. If incapacitated, has the patient expressed prior preferences?
5. Who is the appropriate surrogate to make decisions for the incapacitated patient? What standards should govern the surrogate's decisions?
6. Is the patient unwilling or unable to cooperate with medical treatment? If so, why?

Quality of Life

The Principles of Beneficence and Nonmaleficence and Respect for Autonomy

1. What are the prospects, with or without treatment, for a return to normal life and what physical, mental, and social deficits might the patient experience even if treatment succeeds?
2. On what grounds can anyone judge that some quality of life would be undesirable for a patient who cannot make or express such a judgment?
3. Are there biases that might prejudice the provider's evaluation of the patient's quality of life?
4. What ethical issues arise concerning improving or enhancing a patient's quality of life?
5. Do quality-of-life assessments raise any questions that might contribute to a change of treatment plan, such as forgoing life-sustaining treatment?
6. Are there plans to provide pain relief and provide comfort after a decision has been made to forgo life-sustaining interventions?
7. Is medically assisted dying ethically or legally permissible?
8. What is the legal and ethical status of suicide?

Contextual Features

The Principles of Justice and Fairness

1. Are there professional, interprofessional, or business interests that might create conflicts of interest in the clinical treatment of patients?

(continues)

TABLE 2-1 Four Topics Method for Analysis of Clinical Ethics Cases *(continued)*

2. Are there parties other than clinician and patient, such as family members, who have a legitimate interest in clinical decisions?
3. What are the limits imposed on patient confidentiality by the legitimate interests of third parties?
4. Are there financial factors that create conflicts of interest in clinical decisions?
5. Are there problems of allocation of resources that affect clinical decisions?
6. Are there religious factors that might influence clinical decisions?
7. What are the legal issues that might affect clinical decisions?
8. Are there considerations of clinical research and medical education that affect clinical decisions?
9. Are there considerations of public health and safety that affect clinical decisions?
10. Does institutional affiliation create conflicts of interest that might influence clinical decisions?

questions in each of the four boxes. The Four Topics Method facilitates dialogue between the patient–family/surrogate dyad and members of the healthcare ethics team or committee. By following the outline of the questions, healthcare providers can inspect and evaluate the full scope of the patient's situation and the central ethical conflicts. After the ethics team has gathered the facts of a case, an analysis is conducted. Each case is unique and should be considered as such, but the subject matter of particular situations often involves common threads with other ethically and legally accepted precedents, such as landmark cases that involve withdrawing or withholding treatment. Though each case analysis begins with facts, the four fundamental principles—autonomy, beneficence, nonmaleficence, and justice—along with the Four Topics Method are considered together as the process and resolution take place (Jonsen et al., 2022). In Table 2-1, each box includes principles appropriate for each of the four topics. To see an analysis of a specific case, go to the University of Washington Department of Bioethics and Humanities website under "Bioethics Tools."

Frustration, anger, and other intense emotional conflicts may occur among healthcare professionals or between healthcare professionals and the patient or the patient's surrogates. Unpleasant verbal exchanges and

ETHICAL REFLECTION

Civility involves treating others with courtesy and kindness, whereas incivility is consistent with exhibiting rudeness and disrespect. Incivility seems to be pervasive in society today. Acting with incivility involves a decision. Sometimes, people develop such an ingrained habit of acting without civility that being rude and disrespectful to others seems to be automatic. Using the five Rs of ethical nursing practice model in Box 2-8, consider ways that incivility among nurses and nursing students can be reduced.

hurt feelings can result. Openness and sensitivity toward other healthcare professionals, patients, and family members are essential behaviors for nurses during these times. As information is exchanged and conversations take place, nurses need to maintain an attitude of respect as a top priority. If respect and sensitivity are maintained, lines of communication more likely will remain open.

The Healthcare Team

When patients and families are experiencing distress and suffering, often it is during times when decisions need to be made about risky procedures or end-of-life care. Family members may want medical treatment for their loved one, whereas physicians and nurses may be explaining to the family that to continue treatment most likely would be nonbeneficial or futile for the patient. When patients are weakened by disease and illness and family members are reacting to their loved one's suffering, decisions regarding care and treatment become challenging for everyone concerned.

In caring for patients and interacting with their families, nurses sometimes find themselves caught in the middle of conflicts. Though nurses frequently make ethical decisions independently, they also act as an integral part of the larger team of decision makers. Many problematic bioethical decisions will not be made unilaterally—not by physicians, nurses, or any other single person. By participating in reflective dialogues with other professionals and healthcare personnel, nurses often are part of a larger team approach to ethical analysis. When a team is formally assembled and composed of preselected members who come together regularly to discuss ethical issues within an organization, the team is called an ethics committee. An organization's ethics committee usually consists of physicians, nurses, an on-staff chaplain, a social worker, a representative of the organization's administrative staff, possibly a legal representative, local community representatives, and others drafted by the team. Also, the involved patient, the patient's family, or a surrogate decision maker may meet with one or more committee members. See **BOX 2-9** for examples of the goals of an ethics committee.

Members of the healthcare team may question the decision-making capacity of the patient or family, and the patient's or family's decisions may conflict with the physician's or healthcare team's recommendations regarding treatment. Sometimes, a genuine ethical dilemma arises in a patient's care, difficult decisions must be made, difficult and unpleasant situations must be navigated, or no surrogate can be located to help make decisions for an

---

BOX 2-9　Goals of an Ethics Committee

- Provide support by providing guidance to patients, families, and decision makers.
- Review cases, as requested, when there are conflicts in basic values.
- Assist in clarifying situations that are ethical, legal, or religious in nature that extend beyond the scope of daily practice.
- Help clarify issues, discuss alternatives, and suggest compromises.
- Promote the rights of patients.
- Assist the patient and family, as appropriate, in coming to consensus with the options that best meet the patient's care needs.
- Promote fair policies and procedures that maximize the likelihood of achieving good, patient-centered outcomes.
- Enhance the ethical tenor of both healthcare organizations and professionals.

---

incompetent patient. When these situations emerge, a team approach to decision making is helpful and in accordance with the IOM's (2003) call for healthcare professionals to work in interdisciplinary teams by cooperating, collaborating, communicating, and integrating care "to ensure that care is continuous and reliable" (p. 4).

At times, nurses do not agree with physicians', family members', or surrogates' decisions regarding treatment and subsequently

---

ETHICAL REFLECTION

In class or on your own, watch the HBO movie *Wit* starring Emma Thompson.

1. Apply as many concepts to the movie as you can from what you have read about and learned in this chapter and an earlier chapter 1.
2. Discuss your reflections with your peers in a classroom setting.

may experience moral suffering and uncertainty. When passionate ethical disputes arise between nurses and physicians or when nurses are seriously concerned about the action of patients' decision-making representatives, nurses are the ones who often seek an ethics consultation. It is within the rights and duties of nurses to seek help and advice from other professionals when they experience moral uncertainty or witness unethical conduct in their work setting. This action is a part of the nurse's role as a patient advocate.

KEY POINTS

- Bioethics was born out of the rapidly expanding technical environment of the 1900s.
- The four most well-known and frequently used bioethical principles are respect for autonomy, beneficence, nonmaleficence, and justice.
- Paternalism involves an overriding of autonomy in favor of the principle of beneficence.
- Social justice emphasizes the fairness of how the benefits and burdens of society are distributed among people.
- Ethical dilemmas involve unclear choices; not clear matters of right versus wrong.
- Nurses often experience a disquieting feeling of anguish, uneasiness, or angst in their work that is consistent with what might be called moral suffering.
- It is paradoxical that patients often must trust healthcare providers to care for them before the providers show evidence that trust is warranted.
- When acting as patient advocates, nurses try to identify patients' unmet needs and help to address these needs.
- Nurses may develop good critical thinking skills by thinking about their thinking.
- It is part of a nurse's role as a patient advocate to make or suggest an ethics committee referral when indicated.

References

Agency for Healthcare Research and Quality [AHRQ] Patient Safety Network [PSNet]. (2019). *Adverse events, near misses, and errors*. https://psnet.ahrq.gov/primer /adverse-events-near-misses-and-errors

American Medical Association (AMA). (2021). *Withholding information from patients*. https://www.ama-assn.org /delivering-care/ethics/withholding-information -patients

American Nurses Association (ANA). (2015). *Code of ethics for nurses with interpretive statements*.

American Nurses Association and Tennessee Nurses Association. (2022, March 25). Statement in response to the conviction of nurse RaDonda Vaught. https://www .nursingworld.org/news/news-releases/2022-news -releases/statement-in-response-to-the-conviction-of -nurse-radonda-vaught/

Aquinas, T. (1947). *Summa theologica* (Benzinger Bros. Edition). (Fathers of the English Dominican Province, Trans.). https://www.ccel.org/a/aquinas/summa/SS /SS064.html#SSQ64OUTP1

Beauchamp, T. L., & Childress, J. F. (2019). *Principles of biomedical ethics* (8th ed.). Oxford University Press.

Buppert, C. (2017, September 18). *A major court decision: Only physicians can obtain consent*. https://www .medscape.com/viewarticle/885579

Chambliss, D. F. (1996). *Beyond caring: Hospitals, nurses, and the social organization of ethics*. University of Chicago Press.

Dalai Lama. (1999). *Ethics for the new millennium*. Riverhead Books.

Daniels, N. (1985). *Just health care*. Cambridge University Press.

Dempski, K. (2009). Informed consent. In S. J. Westrick & K. Dempski (Eds.), *Essentials of nursing law and ethics* (pp. 77–83). Jones and Bartlett Publishers.

Department of Health and Human Services Centers for Medicare and Medicaid Services (DHHS, CMS), 2018, October 13). Intake information number TN00045852. https://www.documentcloud.org/documents /6542003-CMS-Complaint-Intake.html

Department of Health and Human Services Centers for Medicare and Medicaid Services (DHHS, CMS), 2018, November 16). Statement of deficiencies and plan of correction. https://www.documentcloud.org

/documents/6535181-Vanderbilt-Corrective-Plan.html

Dewey, J. (1934). *Art as experience*. Perigee Books.

Dewey, J. (1988). *Human nature and conduct: The middle works, 1899–1924* (Vol. 14) (J. A. Boydston & P. Baysinger, Eds.). Southern Illinois University Press. (Original work published 1922)

Dewey, J. (1997). *How we think*. Dover. (Original work published 1910)

Fesmire, S. (2003). *John Dewey and moral imagination: Pragmatics in ethics*. Indiana University Press.

Fisher, A. (2001). *Critical thinking: An introduction*. Cambridge University Press.

Gibbs, G. (1988). *Learning by doing: A guide to teaching and learning methods*. Oxford Polytechnic.

Gordon, S., & Nelson, S. (2006). Moving beyond the virtue script in nursing. In S. Nelson & S. Gordon (Eds.), *The complexities of care: Nursing reconsidered* (pp. 13–29). Cornell University Press.

Hanh, T. N. (1998). *The heart of the Buddha's teaching: Transforming suffering into peace, joy, and liberation*. Broadway Books.

Heyd, D. (1982). *Cambridge studies in philosophy: Supererogation*. Cambridge University Press.

Institute of Medicine (IOM). (2000). *To err is human: Building a safer health care system*. National Academy Press.

Institute of Medicine (IOM). (2003). *Health professions education: A bridge to quality*. National Academies Press.

International Council of Nurses (ICN). (2021). *The ICN code of ethics for nurses* [PDF file]. https://www.icn.ch/system/files/2021-10/ICN_Code-of-Ethics_EN_Web_0.pdf

Jameton, A. (1984). *Nursing practice: The ethical issues*. Prentice-Hall.

Jonsen, A. R. (1998). *The birth of bioethics*. Oxford University Press.

Jonsen, A. R. (2000). *A short history of medical ethics*. Oxford University Press.

Jonsen, A. R. (2005). *Bioethics beyond the headlines: Who lives? Who dies? Who decides?* Rowman & Littlefield.

Jonsen, A. R., Siegler, M., & Winslade, W. J. (2022). *Clinical ethics: A practical approach to ethical decisions in clinical medicine* (9th ed.) [Kindle Book]. McGraw-Hill.

Kelly, C. (2000). *Nurses' moral practice: Investing and discounting self*. Sigma Theta Tau International Center Nursing Press.

Kelman, B. (2022, March 22). As nurse faces prison for a deadly error, her colleagues worry: Could I be next? *Kaiser Health News*. https://khn.org/news/article/radonda-vaught-nurse-error-medication-dispenser-homicide-trial-tennessee/view/republish/

Kelman, B. (2022, March 24). In nurse's trial, investigator says hospital bears 'heavy' responsibility for patient death. *Kaiser Health News*. https://khn.org/news/article/radonda-vaught-fatal-drug-error-vanderbilt-hospital-responsibility/view/republish/

Kelman, B. (2022, March 25). Nurse convicted of neglect and negligent homicide for fatal drug error. *Kaiser Health News*. https://khn.org/news/article/radonda-vaught-nurse-drug-error-vanderbilt-guilty-verdict/view/republish/

Kelman, B. (2022, March 27). The RaDonda Vaught trial has ended. This timeline will help with the confusing case. *Tennessean*. https://www.tennessean.com/story/news/health/2020/03/03/vanderbilt-nurse-radonda-vaught-arrested-reckless-homicide-vecuronium-error/4826562002/

Kelman, B., & Norman, H. (2022, April 5). Why nurses are raging and quitting after the RaDonda Vaught verdict. *Kaiser Health News*. https://khn.org/news/article/nurses-react-radonda-vaught-verdict-conviction/view/republish/

Kidder, R. M. (1995). *How good people make tough choices: Resolving the dilemmas of ethical living*. Quill.

Lo, B. (2009). *Resolving ethical dilemmas: A guide for clinicians* (4th ed.). Wolters Kluwer.

MacIntyre, A. (1999). *Dependent rational animals: Why human beings need the virtues*. Open Court.

Mondics, C. (2004, July 23). 9/11 report details failure. *The Sun Herald*, pp. A1, A4.

Munhall, P. L. (2012). *Nursing research: A qualitative perspective* (5th ed.). Jones & Bartlett Learning.

National Commission for the Protection of Human Subjects of Biomedical and Behavioral Research. (1979). *The Belmont report* [PDF file]. https://www.hhs.gov/ohrp/sites/default/files/the-belmont-report-508c_FINAL.pdf

Nozick, R. (1974). *Anarchy, state, and utopia*. Basic Books.

Omnibus Reconciliation Act of 1990 (OBRA-90), P.L. 105-108, advanced directives provisions, §§4206 & 4751 (1990).

Oung, K. (2022, March 31). Former Vanderbilt nurse RaDonda Vaught found guilty for death of patient by accidental injection. *The Vanderbilt Hustler*. https://vanderbilthustler.com/47301/featured/former-vumc-nurse-radonda-vaught-found-guilty-for-death-of-patient-by-accidental-injection/?print=true

Paul, R., & Elder, L. (2006). *The miniature guide to critical thinking concepts and tools* (4th ed.). Foundation for Critical Thinking.

Pence, G. E. (2015). *Medical ethics: Accounts of groundbreaking cases* (7th ed.). McGraw-Hill.

Rawls, J. (1971). *A theory of justice*. Harvard University Press.

Ryan, C. J. (1998). Pulling up the runaway: The effect of new evidence on euthanasia's slippery slope. *Journal of Medical Ethics, 24*, 341–344.

Schön, D. A. (1987). *Educating the reflective practitioner*. Jossey-Bass.

Scott, S. D. (2011). *The second victim phenomenon: A harsh reality of health care professions.* https://psnet.ahrq.gov/perspective/second-victim-phenomenon-harsh-reality-health-care-professions

Scuderi, B. M. (2011, February 21). *Placebos found to have positive effects.* https://www.thecrimson.com/article/2011/2/21/study-placebos-group-medicine/

Sheng-yen, M. (1999). *Subtle wisdom: Understanding suffering, cultivating compassion through Ch'an Buddhism.* Doubleday.

Shotton, L., & Seedhouse, D. (1998). Practical dignity in caring. *Nursing Ethics, 5*(3), 246–255.

State of Tennessee vs RaDonda L. Vaught. Case No. 2019-A-76. (2019, March 27). https://www.documentcloud.org/documents/6785652-RaDonda-Vaught-DA-Discovery.html

Tennessee Board of Nursing (2019, September 27). Notice of Hearing and charges and memorandum for assessment of civil penalties. https://www.documentcloud.org/documents/6483588-Vaught-RaDonda-NOC-9-27-19.html

Urmson, J.O. (1958). Saints and heroes. In A.I. Melden (Ed.), *Essays in moral philosophy* (pp. 198–216). University of Washington Press.

U.S. Department of Health and Human Services (HHS). (2017). *HIPAA FAQs for professionals.* https://www.hhs.gov/hipaa/for-professionals/faq/index.html

U.S. Department of Health and Human Services (HHS). (2021). *Special topics in health information privacy.* https://www.hhs.gov/hipaa/for-professionals/special-topics/index.html

U.S. Department of Health and Human Services (HHS). (2013). *Summary of the HIPAA security rule.* https://www.hhs.gov/hipaa/for-professionals/security/laws-regulations/index.html

U.S. Department of Health and Human Services (HHS). (2020). *The security rule.* https://www.hhs.gov/hipaa/for-professionals/security/index.html

Welch, A. (2018, October 23). Letters to Ms. Dubree and RaDonda Vaught. https://www.documentcloud.org/documents/6785898-RaDonda-Vaught-Letters.html

Weston, A. (2011). *A practical companion to ethics* (4th ed.). Oxford University Press.

Winslow, G. (1988). From loyalty to advocacy: A new metaphor for nursing. In J. C. Callahan (Ed.), *Ethical issues in professional life* (pp. 95–105). Oxford University Press.

Wu, A. W. (2000). Medical error: The second victim, the doctor who makes the mistake needs help too. *British Medical Journal, 320,* 726–727.

Zaner, R. M. (1991). The phenomenon of trust and the patient-physician relationship. In E. D. Pellegrino, R. M. Veatch, & J. P. Langan (Eds.), *Ethics, trust, and the professions: Philosophical and cultural aspects* (pp.45–67). Georgetown University Press.

CHAPTER 3

Ethics in Professional Nursing Practice

Janie B. Butts

OBJECTIVES

After reading this chapter, the reader should be able to do the following:

1. Differentiate nursing ethics from medical ethics and bioethics.
2. Delineate key historical events that led to the development of the current codes of ethics for the American Nurses Association (ANA) and International Council of Nurses (ICN).
3. Explore professional nursing boundaries and ways nurses cross those boundaries.
4. Review the concept of nursing as praxis.
5. Propose scenarios that require a stench test before the nurse can make an ethical decision.
6. Summarize the three major nursing ethical competencies: moral integrity, communication, and concern.
7. Discriminate among the ethical competencies that comprise each major ethical competency: (1) moral integrity: honesty, truthfulness and truthtelling, benevolence, wisdom, and moral courage; (2) communication: mindfulness and effective listening; and (3) concern: advocacy, power, and culturally sensitive care.
8. Contrast moral distress from moral integrity.
9. Recall ways to discern when a nurse fits Aristotle's description of the truthful sort.
10. Define truthtelling in relation to three ethical frameworks: deontology, utilitarianism, and virtue ethics.
11. Examine the nursing ethical implications involved when a physician, through exercising therapeutic privilege, does not disclose the whole truth to a patient who is in the process of dying with cancer.
12. Create scenarios that would prompt a nurse to respond with moral courage.
13. Describe the connection in communication between mindfulness and effective listening.

(continues)

14. Relate patient advocacy, power, and the provision of culturally sensitive care to nurses' everyday ethical work.
15. Characterize two types of relationships: the nurse–physician relationship and the nurse–nurse relationship.
16. Explain how nurse recipients of horizontal violence progress to the walking wounded and then transform to the wounded healer.
17. Evaluate nurses' use of social networking in terms of the A[NA guidelines for professional, ethical conduct.
18. Imagine an incident of social media use in which a nurse violated the ANA *Code of Ethics for Nurses with Interpretive Statements.*

Introduction to Nursing Ethics

Nursing professionals from the very early years constructed the meaning of nursing around ethics and ethical ways of caring, knowing, and acting. The meaning and scope of nursing ethics expanded as a result of unique nursing issues, but the road to a greater nursing voice has been difficult. Bioethical issues are relevant to nurses' work in everyday practice, yet in matters of bioethics nurses are not always autonomous decision makers.

During the birth of bioethics from 1947 to the 1970s, nurses' voices were left out of the dialogue of ethics. Complex ethical issues in medicine prompted in-depth medical ethics discourse among physicians, philosophers, and theologians. Pinch (2009) noted that

> mainstream ethics was slow to recognize and include the voices of nurses as both scholars and practitioners who faced innumerable dilemmas in health care . . . [but] this lack of widespread acknowledgement did not mean that the profession of nursing failed to address ethical issues in practice. (pp. 238–239)

Nurses began to place emphasis on particular ethical issues that stemmed from complicated bioethics, such as pain and suffering, relationships, and advocacy. In fact, nurses led the way in the 1980s in conducting empirical research on ethical issues (Pinch, 2009). These initiatives strengthened nursing's role in bioethics.

Today, nurses in all roles engage in ethical decision making and behaviors arising from morality, relationships, and conduct issues surrounding patient care and in relationships with each other and other healthcare professionals. Some experts support the view that nursing ethics is distinctive from bioethics in other disciplines (Fry et al., 2011; Holm, 2006; Volker, 2003; Wright & Brajtman, 2011). Additional views indicate everyday ethical practice in nursing as being situated within an interdisciplinary team.

Johnstone's (2008) definition of nursing ethics is consistent with the perception of a strong connection between nursing ethics and nursing theory, which distinguishes nursing ethics from other areas of healthcare ethics. Johnstone (2008) defined **nursing ethics** as "the examination of all kinds of ethical and bioethical issues from the perspective of nursing theory and practice, which in turn rest on the agreed core concepts of nursing, namely: person, culture, care, health, healing, environment and nursing itself" (p. 16).

The nursing profession embraces all the roles that characterize nursing whether or not in practice. Nursing ethics permeates all those nursing roles. Nurses' professional relationships in patient care and within the healthcare team bring about ethical issues that are unique to nursing.

Effective **praxis in nursing** requires that nurses make morally good decisions, with indistinguishable means and ends to follow through with those decisions; nursing as praxis means ethics is embedded in practice and all activities of nursing. For everyday ethical decision making in work roles, nurses should begin by first referring to the *Code of Ethics for Nurses with Interpretive Statements* (American Nurses Association [ANA], 2015) as a nonnegotiable guide for ethics and then as needed, branching out for more support to other literature and experts on the topic. Taking an ethical stance is always about justifying the chosen position by backing it up with support from codes of ethics, moral experts, and the premium and original literature on ethical topics; this position is threaded throughout this text. Moral philosophers argue in a highly complex structure in venues such as moral philosophy articles or verbally for and against various issues. As nurses, it is not plausible to come to a strong, justified position about an ethical dilemma or issue without substantially more in-depth reading and wide-ranging consideration of the historical arguments within the moral philosophy and bioethical literature.

For good ethical decision making through praxis, nurses must be sensitive enough to recognize when they are facing everyday work that could have obscure or uncomfortable ethical issues. Obscurities can also occur when nurses, such as novice graduates, feel extreme pressure to conform to a hospital administrator's less than morally desirable decision over an action that would sustain the nurse's own moral integrity.

RESEARCH NOTE: LAABS'S STUDY ON NEW GRADUATES' PERCEPTIONS OF MORAL INTEGRITY

In 2011 Laabs explored how newly graduated baccalaureate-prepared nurses perceive moral integrity and how prepared they feel to manage challenges. The new graduates described a person with moral integrity as a person practicing virtue ethics, "acting like, becoming, and being a certain kind of person who was honest, trustworthy, consistently doing and standing up for what is right, despite the consequences," but paradoxically, they also perceived the expectations of administrators were for nurses "to set aside their values and beliefs and do what others ask, even if this would mean acting contrary to their conscience" (p. 431). These confounding statements form a level of dissonance, which leads to moral distress and burnout. The ethical challenge for new nurses is to learn how to maintain moral integrity and preserve mutual respect in an environment that trivializes and discounts nurses' work as an important contribution to care. Nurses who act contrary to their own values and beliefs to do what another person asks of them without questioning are at risk of becoming morally desensitized to their own conscience. Some nurses actually begin to think they will never be the kind of ideal, moral nurse they aspired to be.

Data from Laabs, C. (2011). Perceptions of moral integrity: Contradictions in need of explanation. *Nursing Ethics, 18*(3), 431–444.

ETHICAL REFECTION

Millikin (2018) emphasized that before nurses can make sound ethical decisions for their actions, they first must have an ethical awareness of every one of their potential nursing actions and their consequences. In other words, all nursing actions, no matter how trivial they seem, could be associated with ethical decision making for their patients. An awareness of this ethical environment will prompt nurses to be more confident in patient decision making.

ETHICAL REFLECTION

Kidder (1995) introduced nine checkpoints for ethical decision making. In his checkpoint for right versus wrong issues, he provided four ways for people to test for actions of wrongdoing. One way is the **intuition test**, also known as the **stench test**. Some actions or solutions do not pass a nurse's stench test. Nurses should test the stench by first asking this question: Does the intended action have a smell of moral wrongdoing, such as feeling not quite right, feeling wrong or uncomfortable, having an air of corruption, or making one cringe? If the answer is yes, nurses probably should not engage in the action. Nurses will develop a more intense moral sensitivity when they regularly practice ways to test for wrongdoing by way of intuition, or the gut.

FOCUS FOR DEBATE: TESTING FOR STENCH—SHOULD YOU SET ASIDE YOUR OWN BELIEFS AND VALUES?

Form two groups for a live or online classroom. Each group will provide a stance to the following question: Should you set aside your own beliefs and moral integrity values to carry out an action requested by an administrator? Suppose a transporter and an EMT dropped an unconscious patient to the floor during a transfer back to the nursing home. Deb, a new registered nurse in charge of this patient's care, witnessed the incident. A hospital nursing administrator under extreme pressure for meeting safety performance benchmarks asked the nurse *not* to document the patient fall or file an incident report.

In your opinion, does this request pass the stench test? There are definite safety implications in this scenario, but putting aside the legal aspect for a moment, consider the ethical issues of truth versus deception, truth to self versus loyalty to the organization, or promoting good versus doing harm.

- One group will take the side favoring the nurse standing up for what she values as the moral and right thing to do, no matter what the outcome is.
- The other group will take the side of the administrator.

The members of each group will discuss the ethical issues. Spokespersons for each group will present and argue the group's position. The groups should constructively argue while discussing the ethical issues arising from the positions. Apply an ethical theory or framework for your justification. Get creative with your stance and rationale.

Professional Codes of Ethics in Nursing

Professional nursing education began in the 1800s in England at Florence Nightingale's school with a focus on profession-shaping ethical precepts and values. By the end of the 1800s, modern nursing had been established, and ethics was becoming a discussion topic in nursing. First, The Nightingale Pledge of 1893 was written under the chairmanship of a Detroit nursing school principal, Lystra Gretter, to establish nursing as an art and a science. Six years later, in 1899, the International Council of Nurses (ICN) established its own organization and was later a pioneer in developing a code of ethics for nurses worldwide.

At the turn of the 20th century, Isabel Hampton Robb, an American nurse leader, wrote the first book on nursing ethics, titled *Nursing Ethics: For Hospital and Private Use* (1900/1916). In Robb's book, the titles of the chapters were descriptive of the times and moral milieu, such as the chapters titled "The Probationer," "Uniform," "Night-Duty," and "The Care of the Patient," which addressed nurse–physician, nurse–nurse, and nurse–public relationships.

The focus in the code was initially on expectations by physicians, which likely is because many male physicians usually trained nurses in the Nightingale era. Nurses' technical training and obedience to physicians remained at the forefront of nursing responsibilities into the 1960s. For example, the ICN *Code of Ethics for Nurses* reflected technical training and obedience to physicians as late as 1965. By 1973, the ICN code shifted from a focus on obedience to physicians to a focus on patient needs, where it remains to this day.

ANA Code of Ethics for Nurses

In 1926 the *American Journal of Nursing* (*AJN*) published "A Suggested Code" by the ANA, but the code was never adopted. In 1940, *AJN* published "A Tentative Code," but again it was never adopted (Davis et al., 2010). The ANA adopted its first official code in 1950. Three more code revisions occurred before the creation and addition of the interpretative statements in 1976. The ANA added the word *ethics* to the publication of the 2001 code. The seventh edition, published in 2015, is the latest revision.

The ANA outlined nine nonnegotiable provisions, each with interpretive statements for illustration of detailed narratives for ethical decision making in clinical practice, education, research, administration, and self-development. Deontology and normative ethics largely serve as the basis for the code. Although they are detailed enough to guide decision making on a wide range of topics, the interpretive statements are not inclusive enough to predict every single ethical decision or action in the process of nurses carrying out their roles. A clear patient focus in the code obliges nurses to remain attentive and loyal to all patients in their care, but nurses must also be watchful for ethical issues

and conflicts of interest that could lead to potentially negative decisions in care and relationships with patients. Politics in institutions and cost-cutting strategic plans are among other negative forces in today's environment.

The ANA (2015) explored a variety of topics in the code: (1) respect for autonomy, (2) relationships, (3) patients' interests, (4) collaboration, (5) privacy, (6) competent practice, (7) accountability and delegation, (8) self-preservation, (9) environment and moral obligation, (10) contributions to the nursing profession, (11) human rights, and (12) articulation of professional codes by organizations. The interpretative statements illustrate many moral situations. For example, Provision 6 illustrates wisdom, honesty, and courage as essential virtues to produce an image of a morally good nurse. When these virtues are habitually practiced, they promote the values of human dignity, well-being, respect, health, and independence. These values reflect what is important for the nurse personally and for patients. Notable in the code is the reference to moral respect for all human beings, including the respect of nurses for themselves.

ETHICAL REFLECTION: CODE OF ETHICS APPLICATION

- In the *Code of Ethics for Nurses with Interpretive Statements*, the ANA (2015) currently emphasizes the word *patient* instead of the word *client* in referring to recipients of nursing care. Do you agree? Please explain your rationale.
- Take a few minutes to review a copy of the ANA *Code of Ethics for Nurses with Interpretive Statements*.
- After reviewing the interpretive statements in the code, create and discuss some random, brief ethical issues on how nurses justify their actions using the following bioethical principles: autonomy, beneficence, nonmaleficence, and justice.

Another feature of the code is the emphasis on wholeness of character and preservation of self-integrity. **Wholeness of character** relates to nurses' professional relationships with patients and a recognition of the values within the nursing profession, one's own authentic moral values, integration of these belief systems, and expressing them appropriately. **Personal integrity** involves nurses' extending attention and care to their own requisite needs. Many times, nurses who do not regard themselves as worthy of care cannot give comprehensive care to others. Recognizing the dignity of oneself and each patient is essential to providing a morally enhanced level of care.

ICN Code of Ethics for Nurses

In 1953 the ICN adopted its first code of ethics for nurses (see Appendix B for the newest 2021 edition of ICN *Code of Ethics for Nurses*). In the 2021 ICN code, many substantive changes exist. The code is a globally accepted document for ethical practice in nursing. Since 1953, nurses in many countries have adapted the ICN code. The fundamental responsibilities of promoting health, preventing illness, restoring health, and alleviating suffering emanate from the role of nursing. The 2021 current code serves as a statement of nursing ethical values and professional standards that help define ethical nursing practice and guide nurses in everyday practice. The ICN presented a 4-element framework for guiding ethical practice: nurses and patients or people requiring care, nurses and practice, nurses and the profession, and nurses and global health. Similar to the ANA code, the elements in the ICN code form a deontological, normative ethics framework for nurses to internalize before using it as a guide for nursing conduct in practice, education, research, and leadership.

Common Threads Between the ANA and ICN Codes

Common threads exist between the nine provisions of the ANA code (2015) and the four elements of the ICN code (2021). The codes, which apply to all nurses in all settings and roles, are nonnegotiable, ethical nursing standards with a focus on professional values, people, relationships, and professional ideals. Both codes share principles such as virtues, respect, privacy, equality, health, and advocacy.

Nurses should protect the moral space, which is the space where nurses give patient care and uphold the nurse–patient agreement on an individual and a collective basis. Protecting the moral space of patients necessitates that nurses provide compassionate care by endorsing the principles of autonomy, beneficence, nonmaleficence, and justice. Within the codes, nursing responsibilities include promoting and restoring health and preventing illness, but a significant emphasis for nurses is to alleviate suffering of patients who experience varying degrees of physical, psychological, and spiritual suffering.

Professional Boundaries in Nursing

Professional, ethical codes serve as useful, systematic, normative guidelines for directing and shaping behavior. The ANA and ICN codes apply to all nurses regardless of their roles, although no code can provide a complete and absolute set of rules free of conflict and ambiguity, which has been a rationale often cited in favor of the use of virtue ethics as a better approach to ethics than normative ethical conduct codes (Beauchamp & Childress, 2019).

Some people believe that nurses who are without a virtuous character cannot be depended on to act in good or moral ways, even with a professional code as a guide. In the 30th anniversary issue of the *Journal of Advanced Nursing*, the editors reprinted a 1996 article by Esterhuizen (2006), titled "Is the Professional Code Still the Cornerstone of Clinical Nursing Practice?" and the journal solicited comments from three contributors for the reprinted article. This information is most relevant today.

One respondent, Tschudin (2006), agreed with Esterhuizen that nurses lack opportunities for full autonomy in moral decision making. Nurses have an abundant ground to engage in moral decisions, but they still do not have enough opportunity to participate. In the uncertain and slowly changing moral landscape, nurses often wonder about the benefit of codes of ethics. Tschudin's key message was that when virtuous nurses experience full autonomy and accountability, they have an internal moral compass to guide their practice, and do not necessarily need a code of ethics for guidance.

However one perceives the value of codes of ethics for nurses, they still serve as mandates for accountability in all roles of nursing, whether or not in practice. **Professional boundaries** are limits that protect the space between the nurse's professional power and the patient's vulnerabilities. Boundaries facilitate a safe connection because they give each person in the relationship a sense of legitimate control, whether the relationships are between a nurse and a patient, a nurse and a physician, a nurse and an administrator, or a nurse and a nurse. The National Council of State Boards of Nursing (NCSBN, 2018a) explained the power of a nurse as follows:

> The power of the nurse comes from the nurse's professional position and access to sensitive personal information. The difference in personal information the nurse knows about the patient versus personal information the patient knows about the nurse creates an imbalance in the nurse-patient relationship. Nurses should make every effort to respect the power imbalance and ensure a patient-centered relationship. (para. 2, p. 4)

The blurring of boundaries between persons in a relationship is often subtle and unrecognizable at first. Even so, two distinct types of departures from professional boundaries occur (NCSBN, 2018a). The first type of departure is **boundary violations**, which are actions that do not promote the best interest of another person in a relationship and pose a potential risk, harm, or exploitation to that person in the relationship. Boundary violations widely vary, from misuse of power, betrayal of trust, disrespect, and excessive personal disclosure to more severe forms, such as misuse of social media, sexual misconduct, and exploitation. The second type of departure, **boundary crossings**, is a short-lived, usually harmless, variation of the care, which occurs during a unique intervention and will not necessarily happen again. The ANA (2015) included numerous boundary issues in its code of ethics. Social media boundary issues are presented later in this chapter in the section on social media.

The obvious question is how nurses know when they have crossed or violated a professional boundary. In 2003, Maes asked oncology nurses this question. Years later, some of their responses are still relevant for today's nurses. Maes observed that the line in the sand is blurry.

In addition to the ethical guidelines in the code of ethics, nurses also must follow the board of nursing's legal regulations and standards for practice in their particular state of residence. Every country has its own code of ethics, and each state and country has a set of legal rules and regulations for nursing practice. Each state board of nursing is "responsible for enforcing the nurse practice act to promote safe and competent care" (NCSBN, 2018c, p. 2). Violations can result in voluntary surrender, suspension, or revocation of a nurse's license and prohibition from practice. The boards of nursing function not to protect nurses but to protect the public and ensure safe and competent patient care. Refer to state boards of nursing websites for examples of how boundary violations result in the suspension or revocation of a nurse's license.

The ANA *Code of Ethics for Nurses with Interpretative Statements* (2015) specified professional boundaries and moral obligations for clinical practice. Moral obligations include (1) respecting patients' dignity, (2) right to self-determination, (3) delegating tasks appropriately, (4) practicing good judgment, (5) accepting accountability in practice, (6) alleviating suffering, (7) being attentive to patients' interests, and (8) working with the nurse practice acts and nursing standards of practice. Professional practice boundaries include (1) maintaining authenticity in all relationships with others, such as nurse–nurse relationships, nurse–physician relationships, nurse–patient relationships, and multidisciplinary collaboration, and (2) addressing and evaluating issues of impaired practice; fraternizing inappropriately with patients or others; accepting inappropriate gifts from patients and families; confidentiality and privacy violations; and unhealthy, unsafe, illegal, or unethical environments. In the code, the ANA (2015) also offered self-care and self-development boundaries and obligations.

Boundary violations, if reported to the licensure state board of nursing, could likely result in reprimand, probation, suspension, revocation, and other disciplinary actions of the nurse's license. Violations of the nurse practice act include one or more of these nursing behaviors: (1) impairment of and/or stealing drugs or alcohol; (2) nursing actions that are not in nurse's scope of practice; (3) falsification of records; (4) boundary violations, such as sexual or other physical abuse; (5) nonadherence of the nursing practice standard of care; and (6) criminal acts (NCSBN, 2018c).

Harmful, unsafe, and incompetent care violations sometimes are also recognized as legal negligence or malpractice lawsuits (Reising, 2007). If patients or families file legal suits of negligence or malpractice in a civil court against a nurse, the plaintiff's lawyer must prove injury or harm to the plaintiff as a result of the nurse's negligence or malpractice. **Negligence** is failure of the nurse to give care as a reasonably prudent and careful person would give under similar circumstances. **Malpractice** is breach of duty, improper or unethical conduct, or unreasonable lack of skill by a nurse or other professional that results in damages.

RESEARCH NOTE AND LEGAL PERSPECTIVE: NURSING MALPRACTICE—STATISTICS AND REASONS FOR CASES

Miller and Zois (2021) are attorneys at law who maintain statistics on nursing malpractice in the United States. More than 75% of all nursing malpractice cases occur in hospitals. The clinical departments that result in the most nursing litigation include high risk areas in the order listed: (1) labor and delivery, (2) surgery, (3) medical, (4) emergency, (5) pediatric, (6) recovery, and (7) psychiatric. Reasons for the claims and the percentages of all claims were:

- Negligent communication accounted for 47%.
- Medication errors accounted for 19–20%.
- Negligent intervention accounted approximately 16–17%.
- Negligent assessment accounted for approximately 14%.
- Other claims were environmental safety, failure to seek help when doctor care was inadequate, and other.

Data from Miller, R., & Zois, L. (2021). Nursing malpractice statistics. Justia Law Firm: Baltimore, MD. https://www.millerandzois.com/nurse-malpractice-statistics.html

> ### ETHICAL REFLECTION: HOW DO NURSES KNOW WHEN THEY HAVE CROSSED A PROFESSIONAL BOUNDARY?
>
> Maes (2003) interviewed several oncology nurses to ask them how they know when they have crossed a professional boundary. Their comments are provided in the following list. All of these nurses discussed the difficulty of trying not to cross boundaries.
>
> - Emily Stacy, a hospice nurse, stated, "One danger sign could be when you 'dump' your own problems and stressors on patients or their family members because you feel close to them" (p. 4).
> - Jane Hawksley, a nurse manager, added, "New nurses have not developed their own boundaries yet; this can lead to a slippery slope of sympathy versus empathy, making crossing the line easy to do. Usually, the red flag is there . . . [so] be aware of your internal responses, and if in doubt at all, check it out because these responses are a red flag that need to be understood" (pp. 5–6).
> - Barb Henry, a psychiatric nurse practitioner, provided a description of dumping problems on patients: "My job is to help patients deal with their 'black clouds.' On one visit, I was carrying around my own black cloud and was really focused on it. The patient innocently asked me a question related to the issue, and I ended up sharing my black cloud. . . . The boundary line is difficult to maintain" (pp. 4–5).

Reproduced from Maes, S. (2003, August). How do you know when professional boundaries have been crossed? *Oncology Nursing Society, 18*(8), 3–5.

Ideal Nursing Ethical Competencies

The ethical competencies identified in this section tend to be interrelated in meaning, yet each competency has a degree of distinctiveness. Together, they characterize a well-defined, ideal nurse. This section comprises 13 competencies divided into 3 major categories: (1) moral integrity: honesty, truthfulness and truthtelling, benevolence, wisdom, and moral courage; (2) communication: mindfulness and effective listening; and (3) concern: advocacy, power, and culturally sensitive care.

Moral Integrity

The foremost ethical competency is moral integrity, a virtue often considered the fiber of all other virtues. Most of the time when people speak of a person's moral integrity, they are referring to the quality and wholeness of character, which is why some people believe moral integrity is necessary to realize full human flourishing. Plante (2004) stated that although no one is mistake free, people with moral integrity follow a moral compass and usually do not vary by appeals to act immorally. A person with moral integrity manifests a number of virtues. Presented in this section are five of those virtues: honesty, truthfulness and truthtelling, benevolence, wisdom, and moral courage. Moral distress is also presented in this section, not as a virtue, but as a problem related to nurses feeling constrained by their workplace to follow a path of moral integrity in their actions.

People with moral integrity pursue a moral purpose in life, understand their moral obligations in the community, and are committed to following through regardless of constraints imposed on them by their workplace policies. In Laabs's (2011) qualitative study, nurses described **moral integrity** as a "state of being, acting like, and becoming a certain kind of person. This person is honest, trustworthy, consistently doing the right thing and standing up for what is right despite the consequences" (p. 433).

LEGAL PERSPECTIVE: CATEGORIES OF NEGLIGENCE THAT LEAD TO MALPRACTICE LAWSUITS

Nurses increasingly are named defendants in malpractice lawsuits. From 1998 to 2001, the number of payments for nursing malpractice lawsuits increased from 253 to 413. Even though nursing educators have made strides in educating nursing students about legal responsibilities, safe care and actions, and limitations, Croke (2003) argued there are no signs of a decrease in malpractice suits because of numerous factors, including the following: (1) delegating too much and inappropriately, (2) discharging patients too soon, (3) nursing shortages and hospital downsizing, (4) increasing responsibility and autonomy of nurses, and (5) patients being more informed and families having higher expectations for safe care.

Data from Croke, E. M. (2003). Nurses, negligence, and malpractice: Continuing education. *American Journal of Nursing, 103*(9), 54–63.

Features of moral integrity include good character, intent, and performance. Said another way, nurses of good character consistently use their intellectual ability and moral propensity accompanied by pragmatic application to execute good and right actions.

Moral Distress

Nurses' work involves hard moral choices that sometimes result in moral distress, which includes emotional and physical exhaustion and suffering, painful ambiguity, contradiction, frustration, anger, guilt, and an avoidance of patients. Moral distress occurs when nurses experience varying degrees of compromised moral integrity. Jameton (1984) popularized and defined the term **moral distress** as being "when one knows the right thing to do, but institutional constraints make it nearly impossible to pursue the right course of action" (p. 6). Since Jameton's initial work, authors have continued to research and develop the conception of moral distress.

Nurses are susceptible to moral distress when they feel pressure to do something that conflicts with their values, such as falsifying records, deceiving patients, or being subjected to verbal abuse from others. Moral distress is an internal experience characterized by feelings opposite to that of maintaining a sense of moral integrity. In its Position Statement, the American Association of Critical-Care Nurses (AACN, 2020a) emphasized that some complicated issues become discounted or go unnoticed, for whatever reasons, by the leaders in healthcare settings, often to the point of detrimental consequences to nurses. Additionally, nurses sometimes have multiple organizational policy and physician patient treatment expectations that interfere with nurses' proclivity to intervene with moral integrity.

During a crisis, nurses experience moral distress even more severely and frequently than usual (AACN, 2021). For example, the Covid-19 pandemic has resulted in never-before-seen ethical challenges in this era for nurses giving care to those patients. Some of the challenges for nurses include three main categories identified by Morley and colleagues (2020):

- Nurse safety: Nurses risking their own health when severe shortages of personal protective equipment (PPE) exist.
- Resources: Nurses trying to give sufficient care to patients as they allocate how shortages or nonavailability of lifesaving therapies, such as ventilators, will be distributed and giving care with insufficient nurse-to-patient staffing ratios.
- Relationships: Nurses enforcing a very limited hospital visitation policy for patients' families and facing dying patients in complete isolation without the physical presence of their loved ones.

In a healthcare system that is often burdened with system demands, treatment options, constraints of politics, self-serving groups or interests, and organizational bureaucracy, threats to moral integrity can be a serious pit-fall for nurses. Research has indicated that these burdens have a strong effect on the degree of nurses' moral distress (Redman & Fry, 2000). Numerous scholars have linked moral distress to incompetent or poor care, unsafe or inade-quate staffing, overwork, cost constraints, inef-fective policy, futile care, unsuccessful advocacy, the current definition of brain death, objectifi-cation of patients, and unrealistic hope (Corley, 2002; Corley et al., 2005; McCue, 2011; Pendry, 2007; Schluter et al., 2008).

Leaders of nursing continue to search for strategies to reduce moral distress and pro-mote healthy work environments. In its Po-sition Statement, the AACN (2020a) strongly recommended strategies for healthcare insti-tutions and for nurses. For healthcare orga-nizations, "every institution must implement readily accessible resources to identify and mitigate the harmful effects of moral distress" (p. 1). The AACN Position Statement includes 9 must do recommendations for healthcare organizations. For nurses, they "must not hes-itate to seek professional ethical support and other types of counseling when experiencing moral distress…." (p. 1). There are 6 must do recommendations listed for nurses.

Following the Position Statement, the AACN (2020b) published a freely download-able tool titled *Address and Recognize Moral Distress*, which is a concise way for nurses to identify moral distress. The web address for this free tool is https://www.aacn.org/~ /media/aacn-website/clincial-resources/moral -distress/recognizing-addressing-moral-distress -quick-reference-guide.pdf Four major compo-nents comprise this tool (AACN, 2021):

- Determine what you are experiencing.
- Gauge the severity of your distress.
- Identify causes and constraints.
- Take action to help you move forward, which includes selecting resources.

Preventing moral distress requires nurses to recognize all environmental dynamics and decisions that could lead to moral distress. An environment of good communication and re-spect for others is essential for decreasing the likelihood of experiencing moral distress.

Honesty

A virtue of moral integrity is the ethical com-petency of honesty. Nurses continue to rank highest in the annual Gallup poll on honesty and ethics. In the 2019 Gallup poll, 85% of people rated nurses as the most honest and ethical professionals. Nurses have earned this trust because of their commitment and loyalty to their patients. According to Laabs (2011), nurses identify honesty as important for three reasons: (1) honesty is a prerequisite for good care, (2) dishonesty is always exposed in the end, and (3) nurses are expected to be honest.

In a phenomenological study of nurses on honesty in palliative care, nurses sometimes had difficulty defining honesty (Erichsen et al., 2010). In an attempt to clarify their percep-tions of honesty, they often defined lying or dishonesty as being sharp contrasts to honesty. Nurses perceived honesty as a virtue related to facts, metaphors, ethics, and communication and truthtelling as a palpable feature in trust-ing relationships.

Honesty, in simple terms, is being "real, genuine, authentic, and bona fide" (Bennett, 1993, p. 597). Honesty is more than just telling the truth; it is the substance of human relation-ships. Honesty in relationships equips people with the ability to place emphasis on resolve and action to achieve a just society. People with a mature level of honesty dig for truth in a rational, methodical, and diligent way while placing bits of truths into perspective and pru-dently searching for the missing truths before addressing the issue. In other words, honesty is a well-thought-out and well-rehearsed behav-ior that represents commitment and integrity.

There are many ways that nurses portray honesty, such as staying true to their word. Nurses must stay committed to their promises to patients and follow through with appropri-ate behaviors, such as returning to patients' hospital rooms as promised to help them with certain tasks. If nurses do not follow through with their commitments, trust may be broken, and patients potentially will see those nurses as dishonest or untrustworthy.

Honesty is also about being honest with one's self. Nurses need to establish a routine checkpoint system of ongoing self-evaluation to retain and improve honesty in actions and relationships with patients and others. For example, if a nurse is in the process of administering medications and a pill falls on the hospital floor, would the nurse be justified in wiping it off and placing it back in the cup if no one was there to see the action? Nurses might be tempted to wipe off the pill and administer it just to keep from completing a required form for a replacement medication, but if nurses evaluate their situations and make decisions based on always being honest with oneself, it is more likely they will make rational, trustworthy decisions regarding the care of patients.

Truthfulness and Truthtelling

The next virtue of moral integrity is the ethical competency of truthfulness. Aristotle identified 12 excellences of character, or virtues, in his book *Nicomachean Ethics* (Rowe & Broadie, 2002). A virtue is an intermediate state between two extremes: excessiveness and deficiency. Truthfulness, then, is the intermediate state between imposture (excessiveness) and self-deprecation (deficiency). Truthfulness is being genuine in all words and deeds and is never false or phony. A truthful person speaks in a way that symbolizes who the person really is. Aristotle explained his view of a truthful person as being *the truthful sort.*

Based on the principle of veracity, truthfulness is what we say and how we say it. **Truthfulness**, translated to *truthtelling* in the healthcare environment, means nurses are usually ethically obligated to tell the truth and are not intentionally to deceive or mislead patients, which relates to the authentic, not fake,

person in the context of Aristotle's truthful sort. Because of the emphasis in the Western world on patients' right to know about their personal health care, truthtelling has become the basis for most relationships between healthcare professionals and patients (Beauchamp & Childress, 2019). In the older, traditional approach, disclosure or truthtelling was a beneficent or paternalistic approach with actions based on answers to questions such as "What is best for my patient to know?"

Today, the ethical question to ask is "Are there ever circumstances when nurses should be morally excused from telling the truth to their patients?" The levels of disclosure in health care and the cultural viewpoints on truthtelling create too much fogginess for a clear line of distinction between nurses telling or not telling the truth. The ANA *Code of Ethics for Nurses with Interpretive Statements* (2015) obligates nurses to be honest in matters involving patients and themselves and to express a moral point of view when they are alert to any unethical practices.

In some Western cultures, such as in the United States, autonomy is so valued that withholding information is unacceptable. Under this same autonomy principle, it is assumed patients also have a right *not* to know their medical history if they so desire. Some cultures, such as those in some Eastern countries, do not prize autonomy in this same way; the head of the family or the elders usually decide how much and what information needs to be disclosed to the family member as patient.

Withholding Information from Patients

The current American Medical Association's (AMA) *Code of Medical Ethics* view is in Opinion 2.1.3, "Withholding Information from Patients" (2018). This opinion is different from the AMA's 2006 Opinion 8.082 on the definition of withholding information from patients, which is often referred to as therapeutic privilege (AMA, 2012). In the current opinion, the

AMA emphasized that withholding information without the patient's knowledge or consent is ethically unacceptable except in emergency situations when the patient is unable to make an informed decision. Once the emergency is over, the AMA emphasized the importance of disclosure to the patient. Working within this opinion enables physicians to disclose truthful information, but when necessary, they may disclose small portions of truthful information to patients over time until all of the information has been disclosed.

Physicians and nurses are obliged to communicate truthfully in a manner that preserves the patient's respect for autonomy. Physicians and nurses should base their opinion on the facts gathered from the patient's records and their interactions with the patient, family, and other healthcare professionals. Truthtelling by physicians and nurses is beneficial for patients, especially when they are in advanced stages of a diagnosis (Loprinzi et al., 2010). With the full knowledge of the disease process, patients will make fully informed decisions, be prepared for the outcomes, have more meaningful dialogue with family members, and make the most of meaningful events during their remaining life. Nurses have a difficult decision to make, especially when a patient wants to know the full truth and physicians have found it necessary to disclose portions of the truth over a span of time. Nurses must evaluate each situation carefully with wisdom and contemplation to develop a clear understanding of the transpired communication between the physician, patient, and family members.

An excellent example of truthtelling is from the play *Wit* by Margaret Edson, winner of the 1998 Pulitzer Prize. The play was published as a book in 1999 and then made into an HBO Home Movie in 2001; it is available for purchase. Susie Monahan, the registered nurse caring for Vivian Bearing, decided to tell the truth to and be forthright with a patient despite a few physicians who chose not to do so.

Benevolence

The ethical competency of benevolence is another virtue of moral integrity. **Benevolence** is a "morally valuable character trait—or virtue—of being disposed to act to benefit others" (Beauchamp, 2019, Part 1, para. 2). Some people believe benevolence surpasses the act of compassion. Confucianists place a high priority on human character, or virtuous conduct. They view benevolence as the highest-ranking, perfect virtue with the greatest degree of influence; the ideal morality is for benevolence to prevail in the world (Hwang, 2001). Altruistic, kindhearted, caring, courteous, and warmhearted are characterizations of a benevolent person; also, in definitions of compassionate care, kindness and benevolence, among other descriptors, are common.

The bioethical principle of beneficence and the virtue of benevolence are similar, but they are not necessarily connected. Benevolence refers to the propensity and desire to act to benefit others, which often prompts beneficent acts. Throughout nursing's history, nurses have placed a high importance on benevolence, or kindness. Pearce (1975), a past nursing tutor and author of the 1937 edition and many subsequent editions of *A General Textbook of Nursing*, described a benevolent scenario that is relevant today:

> Nurses soon learn to realize the value of a pleasing professional approach and the occasional glance in passing, nod of the head or smile takes no time and makes a valuable contribution to good relationships. Communication need not always be verbal, and the nurse by the exercise of her skills can convey sympathy and assurance to a patient who may be too weary or ill to listen to much conversation. (p. 4)

More than two decades ago, but still relevant today, Lutzén and Nordin (1993) found in their research that nurses described benevolence as a central motivating factor in nursing decision making and actions.

ETHICAL REFLECTION: A WOMAN WITH UTERINE CANCER

You are the nurse caring for a woman scheduled for a hysterectomy because of uterine cancer. The community knows her surgeon as having a bad surgical record in general but especially in performing hysterectomies. The woman previously heard gossip to this effect and asks you about it before her surgery because she is apprehensive about using the surgeon. You know at least one legal suit has been filed against the surgeon because you personally know the woman involved in a case of a botched hysterectomy.

Your choices are as follows: (1) you could be brutally honest and truthful with your preoperative patient, (2) you could be part truthful by giving the correct information on certain pieces of the gossip to clarify misconceptions but remaining silent on other parts of the gossip you know could be damaging, or (3) you could be totally untruthful by remaining silent or telling the patient you have heard nothing.

- Discuss these options and any other ideas you may have regarding this case. As a nurse who wants to be committed to an ethical nursing practice, what actions might you consider in this difficult circumstance? Be as objective as possible.
- Now that you have determined possible actions, please justify these actions by applying either Kant's deontological theory, utilitarian theory, or a virtue ethics approach.
- Describe the major differences and any similarities among these three frameworks (deontology, utilitarianism, and virtue ethics).
- Other than simply telling the truth verbally to patients and others, how else can you display your honesty and truthful sort in ethical nursing practice? Imagine how you would portray honesty in different settings and situations, such as patient care and family relationships, documentation, safe care, and relationships with coworkers and administrators, while taking into consideration the moral obligations delineated in the ANA *Code of Ethics for Nurses with Interpretive Statements*.

ETHICAL REFLECTION: A CASE OF TRUTHTELLING

Susie Monahan, in the book and movie *Wit*, was a registered nurse caring for Vivian Bearing, a patient who was dying of cancer, at a large research hospital. Vivian was getting large doses of cancer chemotherapy without any success of remission. In fact, the cancer was progressing at an alarming rate. She was near death, but the research physicians wanted to challenge her body with chemotherapy for as long as possible to observe the outcome effects. Everyone on the staff had been cold, indifferent, and technically minded, and no one had shown any concern for Vivian except for Susie. Vivian had not been informed about the chemotherapy failure, her prognosis, or the likelihood of her dying. One night, Susie found Vivian crying and in a state of panic. Susie first helped to calm her, and then she shared a popsicle with Vivian at the bedside while she disclosed the full truth to Vivian about her chemotherapy, her prognosis, her choices between Code Blue or DNR, and her imminent death. Susie affectionately explained,

> You can be "full code," which means that if your heart stops, they'll call a Code Blue and the code team will come and resuscitate you and take you to Intensive Care until you stabilize again. Or you can be "Do Not Resuscitate," so if your heart stops we'll . . . well, we'll just let it. You'll be "NR." You can think about it, but I wanted to present both choices. (Edson, 1999, p. 67)

> Susie felt an urge to be truthful and honest. By demonstrating respect for Vivian, Susie was showing her capacity to be human.

Data from Edson, M. (1999). *Wit*. Faber & Faber.

RESEARCH NOTE: BENEVOLENCE AS A CENTRAL MORAL CONCEPT—A GROUNDED THEORY APPROACH TO RESEARCH

Lutzén and Nordin (1993) used a grounded theory research design to explore moral decision making in psychiatric nursing practice. Fourteen seasoned nurses from Sweden participated in the study by way of interviews. After transcribing and coding the data into several categories, Lutzén and Nordin discovered that benevolence was a category with important merit because nurses characterized it as a central motivating factor for making everyday decisions with and for the patients. The researchers placed descriptions such as "have always loved other people," "being close to," and "being really close to a patient, to share his sorrow" within the category of benevolence.

Data from Lutzén, K., & Nordin, C. (1993). Benevolence, a central moral concept derived from a grounded theory study of nursing decision making in psychiatric settings. *Journal of Advanced Nursing, 18,* 1106–1111.

The foundational concepts of nursing include doing good, promoting acts to benefit others, and preventing harm or doing no harm. Nurses who use benevolence as a central motivating factor do not just perform acts of kindness in a haphazard fashion when the opportunity arises; they seek out ways to perform acts of kindness rather than only recognizing ways to do good.

Wisdom

Another virtue of moral integrity is the ethical competence of **wisdom**, often called practical wisdom, and it requires calculated intellectual ability, contemplation, deliberation, and efforts to achieve a worthy goal. Aristotle believed wisdom is an excellence of genuine quality that develops with intellectual accomplishment, or *sophia*, and practical expertise, or *phronesis* (Broadie, 2002). People are said to be wise if they successfully calculate ways to reach a worthy goal or end. The ultimate goal of happiness comes only from exercising rational and intellectual thinking, which is a product of wisdom and contemplation. Aristotle considered good deliberation as a necessary, mindful process toward reaching a worthy end or goal. He said, "So in fact the description 'wise' belongs in general to the person who is good at deliberation. . . . Nobody deliberates about what things cannot be otherwise, or

about things he has no possibility of doing" (Rowe & Broadie, 2002, p. 180).

Aristotle's viewpoint, in summary, is people cannot achieve their worthy goals or ends or be considered wise unless they develop both features that compose the virtue of wisdom, and then, only through a significant amount of deliberation and contemplation. As previously stated, the two features of wisdom are intellectual accomplishment and practical expertise.

Aristotle's conception of wisdom fits with nursing and medical practice. Pellegrino and Thomasma (1993), who were both prototypical medical philosophers, cited **phronesis** (practical wisdom) as medicine's indispensable virtue, and they also discussed the virtue of **prudence** (wisdom) as a necessary extension to *phronesis* in order to help people "discern, at this moment, in this situation, what action, given the uncertainties of human cognition, will most closely approximate the right and the good" (p. 85).

People with prudence have the feature of intellectual accomplishment *and* the proclivity to seek the right and the good. Nurses must also develop this combination. **Clinical wisdom** is sometimes cited to describe the necessary combination of prudence and practical wisdom. Benner and colleagues (1999) described this type of connection as clinical judgment and clinical comportment, both of which require nurses to continually reflect upon the present situation in terms of the "immediate past condition of the patient" (p. 10). Clinical judgment and clinical comportment encompass six areas that serve as a guide for active reflection in nursing practice: "(1) reasoning-in-transition; (2) skilled know-how; (3) response-based practice; (4) agency; (5) perceptual acuity and the skill of involvement; and (6) the links between clinical and ethical reasoning" (p. 10).

Moral Courage

The next virtue of moral integrity is the ethical competence of moral courage, which is highly valued and seems to be inherent in nursing. Nurses with **moral courage** stand up for or act upon ethical principles to do what is right, even when those actions entail constraints or forces to do otherwise. Moral courage turns into noticeable actions. If nurses have the courage to do what they believe is the right thing in a particular situation, they make a personal sacrifice by possibly standing alone, but they will feel a sense of peace in their decision. If nurses are in risky ethical situations, they need moral courage to act according to their core values, beliefs, or moral conscience. For nurses to act with moral courage means they choose the ethically right decision, even when under intense pressure by administrators, coworkers, and physicians. Refer to the boxes in the first few pages of this chapter to imagine ways that nurses could practice moral courage.

Over the past several years, Lachman has published several articles on the topic of moral courage. In 2010, she reviewed the nurse's obligations and moral courage in terms of do-not-resuscitate (DNR) orders for end-of-life decision making while considering the research by Sulmasy et al. (2008) on beliefs and attitudes

---

RESEARCH NOTE: NURSES AND PHYSICIANS ON DNR ORDERS

Sulmasy et al. (2008) surveyed more than 500 medical house staff, medical internists, and staff nurses working on medical units at teaching hospitals in the New York City area to examine and compare (1) their beliefs, attitudes, and confidence about DNR orders; (2) the role of nurses in discussions with patients and families about DNR orders; and (3) perceived confidence level in their ability to discuss DNR orders with patients and families. As of 2008, the small number of studies on this topic revealed that nurses play an important role in discussions with patients and families regarding DNR orders but, in reality, physicians are largely the ones who initiate and discuss DNR orders with patients and families. Nurses often view themselves as responsible yet powerless and uncertain about discussions with patients and families (Stenburg, 1988, as cited in Sulmasy et al., 2008). Sulmasy and colleagues' comparison findings among three groups about their roles in DNR orders indicated the following:

- Nurses found it less difficult, but more rewarding, than the two groups of physicians to discuss DNR orders with patients and families.
- Nurses reported they were not consulted very often about the evolvement of the process of end-of-life patient decisions and DNR orders.
- Nurses reported a more positive attitude about DNR discussions than did the two groups of physicians.
- Nurses were much more likely to believe it was not their place to recommend or initiate DNR orders than did the two groups of physicians.

Sulmasy and colleagues posed some ethical questions for reflection: (1) Why are staff nurses not permitted, most of the time, to initiate DNR orders? (2) What is the proper division and line of responsibilities between physicians and nurses in the care of patients during the end-of-life process? (3) What policy on responsibilities of DNR orders would best benefit patients and families?

Data from Sulmasy. D. P., He, M. K., McAuley, R., & Ury, W. A. (2008). Beliefs and attitudes of nurses and physicians about do not resuscitate orders and who should speak to patients and families about them. *Critical Care Medicine, 36*(6), 1817–1822.

of nurses and physicians about DNR orders. Because nurses have a very close proximity to patients, they need active involvement in decision making for end-of-life decisions, such as DNR orders (Lachman, 2010). In 2012, the ANA published a new position statement to reiterate the importance of nurses' involvement in patients' end-of-life decisions and DNR orders.

Nurses often feel apprehensive regarding uncertainty in outcomes, even when they have a high degree of certainty that they are doing the right thing. Other than end-of-life decision making, other examples of having moral courage are as follows: (1) confronting or reporting a peer who is stealing and using drugs at work; (2) confronting a physician who ordered questionable treatments not within the reasonable standard of care; (3) confronting an administrator regarding unsafe practices or staffing patterns; (4) standing against peers who are planning an emotionally hurtful action toward another peer; and (5) reporting another nurse for exploitation of a patient or family member, such as when a nurse posts a picture or a story of a patient on a social networking site.

RESEARCH NOTE: MORAL COURAGE IN UNDERGRADUATE NURSING STUDENTS

In a qualitative approach, Bickoff and colleagues (2017) reviewed 15 research papers to explore factors that facilitated or inhibited undergraduate nursing students' decisions to exhibit moral courage by speaking up or intervening when they encountered poor practice. The researchers found that undergraduate nursing students understand their moral obligation but they often do not speak up or intervene when they see poor practice. Instead, many keep quiet and become bystanders, or they are active participants only to a degree.

Data from Bickoff, L., Sinclair, P. M., & Levett-Jones, T. (2017). Moral courage in undergraduate nursing students: A literature review. *Collegian, 24*, 71-83.

FOCUS FOR DEBATE: IS MORAL COURAGE NECESSARY FOR NURSES?

Sulmasy and colleagues (2008) raised some significant questions for ongoing reflection and interprofessional dialogue. Since the time of this study and others, the ANA recognized the need to refresh its statement on end-of-life decisions and DNR orders in 2012 and in 2016 on patient end-of-life decisions and DNR orders. Nurses continue to experience considerable difficulties and moral distress about patient decisions about end-of-life and DNR orders possibly because of their own moral conflicts with the decisions or restrictions in their involvement in the decision-making process.

Is moral courage necessary? If so, how much and in what contexts and circumstances? The ANA's two position statements on end-of-life scenarios (2012, 2016) indicated the need for nurses to meet their ethical obligations by providing support and participating more actively in patient and family end-of-life decisions, including DNR orders, but only when those actions do not violate the principle of nonmaleficence.

Apply the same guidelines to this debate as you did for previous debates in this chapter. Before you formulate your position, refer to Sulmasy and colleagues (2008) and the ANA's two position statements on end of life (2012, 2016). Then, conduct an Internet and database search to discover other strategies and creative ways to practice moral courage.

Defend your position on the following questions:

- In what ways can nurses practice moral courage regarding patient and family discussions of end-of-life decisions and DNR orders? To answer this question, also consider the following: To what extent should the nurse be involved in initiating end-of-life decisions and DNR orders? Is it the nurse's place to recommend or not recommend a DNR order?
- Discuss some strategies and creative ideas for practicing moral courage in other circumstances.

Although a potential threat exists for physical harm, it is more likely that threats will materialize in the form of "humiliation, rejection, ridicule, unemployment, and loss of social standing" (Lachman, 2007, p. 131). Nurses can facilitate having moral courage in two ways during threatening situations. Nurses would probably regret any careless and hasty reactions, or even nonreactions or silence, on their part, so they must first try to soothe inner feelings that could trigger these behaviors. Self-talk, relaxation techniques, and moral reasoning to process information while pushing out negative thoughts are ways for nurses to keep calm in the face of a confrontation involving moral courage. Second, nurses must assess the whole scenario while identifying the risks and benefits involved in standing alone (Lachman, 2007).

Communication

The next ethical competency is communication. There is a long trail of research on nurse–physician, nurse–nurse, and nurse–patient relationships related to ethical and unethical communication. Refer to sections later in this chapter on nurse–physician and nurse–nurse relationships for a discussion of a few studies.

Communication means to impart or exchange information in meaningful, clearly understood ways between the communicators. Effective communication nurtures relationships and is fundamental to nursing; it therefore engages nurses to express messages clearly and understand the meaning of what is being communicated. To be effective, nurses must reside in a state of mindfulness and be effective listeners. Both parts of communication are integral for effective communication.

Mindfulness

Important to the ethical competency of communication is mindfulness, which in the past few decades has gained significant meaning and implications for nursing and other healthcare fields. The term *mindfulness* traces back to Eastern Buddhist philosophy as one element of the Noble Eightfold Path. When Jon Kabat-Zinn began teaching mindfulness training in 1979 at the University of Massachusetts Medical School and founded the Mindfulness-Based Stress Reduction Program, the American and other Western healthcare systems embraced the concept and expanded research-based knowledge, especially in secular practice (Center for Mindfulness, 2014; Greater Good, 2014).

Mindfulness is the degree of quality that requires "paying attention in a particular way: on purpose, in the present moment, and nonjudgmentally" (Kabat-Zinn, 2009, p. 4). This definition indicates that mindful people are engaged and attentive in their activities or roles by continuously analyzing, categorizing, and distinguishing data. People with expertise and specialized skills, such as nurses, physicians, and others, need mindfulness on a minute-by-minute basis for providing safe and competent care and building good and positive relationships with patients, other nurses, and physicians.

Even with mindfulness as a critical requirement of communication in the workplace, healthcare professionals are susceptible to in-and-out moments of mindlessness, which is the opposite of mindfulness. **Mindlessness** is a state of unawareness and not focusing, similar to functioning in autopilot mode. The moments of mindlessness can potentially increase in duration, and over a long period, people thoughtlessly begin ruling out their full range of options in everyday life and work. People in perpetually mindless states find themselves trapped in a state of unawareness without any regard to expanding choices and views in different contexts or cultures. Eventually, they are stuck in habits of not seeing (Kabat-Zinn, 2009).

The benefits of mindfulness exercises and training are numerous, and research supports its value and therapeutic benefits. The following examples are some of the benefits:

- Reduces stress, negative emotions, and depression
- Enhances healthier living and eating and an overall sense of quality of life
- Enhances attention skills and focusing
- Enhances communication skills
- Promotes more positive relationships
- Increases memory and learning capacity
- Increases the ability for a deeper type of empathy, compassion, serenity, and altruism
- Increases the immune system's ability to fight off disease

The focus of this section is the benefits of mindfulness in communication. A body of research exists on the connection between communication and mindfulness. Mindfulness enriches the moral quality of the interactions between nurses and patients, nurses and physicians, and nurses and other nurses. Effective communication facilitates nurses' ethical behavior in work, that is, to provide ethical care to achieve better patient outcomes. Mindful nurses pay close attention to their attitudes and find ethical ways to interact and behave. When nurses intentionally focus on the present moment, the present problems and issues, and the present surroundings and interactions, all in a nonjudgmental way, they reduce their own stress and expand their vision of care to a wider choice of options to effect improved patient outcomes.

Mindfulness exercises promote nurses' ability to focus and stay alert to the details of decision making and patient care. In a booklet published by the ANA, titled *Mindfulness and You: Being Present in Nursing Practice*, Bazarko (2014) emphasized the need for nurses to practice mindfulness and take care of themselves and thus provide safe patient care. In the booklet are examples of mind–body therapies, strategies for improving the mind–body connection, and a guide for a mindfulness journey.

Formal meditation is one primary way to cultivate mindfulness. However, in a video called "The Stars of Our Own Movie" (Greater Good, 2010), Kabat-Zinn emphasized that mindfulness is not just about sitting in the lotus position; it is more about living life as if life is genuinely worth living, moment by moment.

Some ways to begin brief daily mindfulness exercises are as follows (Greater Good, 2014, How Do I Cultivate It?):

- Pay close attention to your breathing, especially when you're feeling intense emotions.
- Notice—really notice—what you're sensing in a given moment, the sights, sounds, and smells that ordinarily slip by without reaching your conscious awareness.
- Recognize that your thoughts and emotions are fleeting and do not define you, an insight that can free you from negative thought patterns.
- Tune in to your body's physical sensations, from the water hitting your skin in the shower to the way your body rests in your office chair (para. 2).

ETHICAL REFLECTION: KABAT-ZINN'S VIEW OF BEING TRULY IN TOUCH

To allow ourselves to be truly in touch with where we already are, no matter where that is, we have got to pause in our experience long enough to let the present moment sink in; long enough to actually feel the present moment, to see it in its fullness, to hold it in awareness and thereby come to know and understand it better. Only then, can we accept the truth of this moment of our life, learn from it, and move on. (Kabat-Zinn, 2009, pp. xiii–xiv)

Reproduced from Kabat-Zinn, J. (2005). Introduction. *Wherever you go, there you are: Mindfulness meditation in everyday life.* Hyperion, pp. xiii-xiv. Reprinted by permission.

Effective Listening

Effective listening is the other essential feature of the ethical competency of communication. A state of mindfulness must be present for a person to effectively listen. Without attention and a strong focus, listeners cannot respond appropriately no matter how well-meaning a person's intention of listening is. As previously mentioned, people often experience in-and-out awareness moments as distractions, and wandering-off moments trickle through the mind.

Effective listening means the communicators in the exchange will comprehend the active information and then form a mutual understanding of the essence of the dialogue (Johnson, 2012). The mutual understanding compels the listeners to repeat the message to clarify facts and other details. When nurses earnestly listen, they listen with extreme thinking power because they must show a nonjudgmental interest in what the speaker is saying, absorb the information, and provide nonverbal cues and verbal feedback to signal an understanding of the message to the speaker. Why is effective listening so important to nurses? The foremost reason is that nurses have a moral obligation to provide competent care and build positive work relationships to promote better patient outcomes. Nurses will not give competent care if their minds are wandering. They risk misinterpreting facts, physician's orders, or patient interactions.

Concern

Concern is the last major ethical competency. The competency of **concern** means that nurses feel a sense of responsibility to think about the scope of care important for their patients; sometimes a sense of worrying about the health or illness of patients prompts nurses to action. Being an advocate, using power, and giving culturally sensitive care compose the ethical competency of concern for patients.

Advocacy

A general definition of **advocacy** is pleading in favor of or supporting a case, person, group, or cause, but many variations on the definition of advocacy exist. Related to professional nursing ethics, Bu and Jezewski (2006) found three central characteristics of **patient advocacy** in their concept analysis:

- Safeguarding patients' autonomy
- Acting on behalf of patients
- Championing social justice in the provision of health care (p. 104)

Patient advocacy, an essential element of ethical nursing practice, requires nurses to embrace the promotion of well-being and uphold the rights and interests of their patients (Vaartio et al., 2006).

The ANA (2015) did not explicitly define the terms *advocacy* or *patient advocacy* in the *Code of Ethics for Nurses with Interpretive Statements*, although advocating for the patient is an expectation as evidenced by Provision 3 of the code: "The nurse promotes, advocates for, and protects the rights, health, and safety of the patient" (ANA, 2015, p. 9). The ANA (2015) also provided some examples of nursing advocacy obligations. Nurses may (a) advocate to provide environments with sufficient physical privacy (Provision 3.1); (b) advocate when participants decline to participate or withdraw from research before its completion (Provision 3.2); (c) advocate for assistance, treatment, and access to fair institutional and legal processes (Provision 3.6); and (d) participate as advocates or representatives in civic activities (Provision 7.3).

These examples translate to nurses functioning as advocates for patients and their rights; for public social justice issues of health care, policy, and economics; and for each other. In matters of patient care, nurses are in ideal positions for patient advocacy. Nurses can clarify and discuss with patients their rights, health goals, treatment issues, and potential outcomes, but they must realize some of the barriers to advocacy. These barriers arise as shadows from unresolved issues.

ETHICAL REFLECTION: BARRIERS TO NURSING ADVOCACY

Hanks (2007) identified barriers to nursing advocacy based on findings from existing literature:

- Conflicts of interest between the nurse's moral obligation to the patient and the nurse's sense of duty to the institution
- Institutional constraints
- Lack of education and time
- Threats of punishment
- Gender-specific, historical, critical social barrier related to nurses' expectations of a subservient duty to medical doctors

Data from Hanks, R. G. (2007). Barriers to nursing advocacy: A concept analysis. *Nursing Forum, 42*(4), 171–177.

Hamric (2000) offered excellent ways for nurses to boost their patient advocacy skills: (1) nursing educators need to convert basic ethics education to real-life application and action, (2) practicing nurses need to continue their education on the ethical imperatives of advocacy, and (3) institutions need to review their incentives to promote patient advocacy. Butts (2011) created the acronym PRISMS as a reminder of strategies to promote patient advocacy.

ETHICAL REFLECTION: PRISMS

PRISMS is an acronym for key action verbs that describe strategies to promote patient advocacy:

P: Persuade
R: Respect
I: Intercede
S: Safeguard
M: Monitor
S: Support

Butts, J. B. (2011). *PRISMS—An acronym for key action verbs for strategies to promote patient advocacy.* Personal Collection. Ellisville, MS, copyright 2011.

Power

By definition, **power** means a person or group has influence in an effective way over others—power results in action. Nurses with power have the ability to influence persons, groups, or communities. Nurses who are ingrained with the ideals of **socialized power** seek goals to benefit others with intent to avoid harm or negative effects—an indication of the principles of beneficence, nonmaleficence, and justice at work. Goals of social benefit to others are often accomplished through global and national efforts or efforts of members of large service or state organizations. Individual volunteer organizational work by nurses contributes toward efforts of shared goals within larger organizations and smaller shared goals for individuals and communities.

Nurses and patients together form a powerful entity because of evolving paradigm shifts in clinical, political, and organizational power (Hakesley-Brown & Malone, 2007). In the past, nurses facilitated patients' emancipation from a paternalistic form of care to today's autonomous decision makers seeking quality care. Because nurses participate in and direct activities involving patient care, they are in powerful positions to improve quality in patient care and oversee professional nursing practice standards. Nurses continue to take advantage of their empowerment as a profession to control the content of their practice, the context of their practice, and their competence in practice.

Ponte and colleagues (2007) interviewed nursing leaders from six organizations to understand the concept of power from the leaders' perspectives on ways nurses can acquire power and leaders demonstrate power in practice and in work. According to the leader participants in the study, power lies within *each nurse* who engages in patient care and in other roles, such as in organizations, with colleagues, and within the nursing profession as a whole. As nurses develop knowledge and expertise in practice from multiple domains, they integrate and use their power in a "collaborative, interdisciplinary effort focused solely on the patients and families that the nurse and care team serve and with whom they partner" (Ponte et al., 2007, Characteristics of Nursing Power section, para. 1).

Eight properties of a powerful professional practice can serve as a foundation for current and future power in nursing (Ponte et al., 2007). These eight practices include nurses (1) acknowledge their role in patient and family care; (2) commit to continuous educational activities on skills and evidence-based practice; (3) exhibit professionalism and be conscious of presence in all activities; (4) value collaboration with other professionals in nursing and other disciplines; (5) position themselves to influence decisions and allocate resources; (6) develop good character and a sought-after perspective by being inspirational, compassionate, and credible; (7) recognize that nurse leaders should pave the way for nurses' voices to be heard and help novice nurses become powerful professionals; and (8) evaluate the power of nursing and nursing department organizations by analyzing the mission, values, and commitment of the organization.

Culturally Sensitive Care

Culture refers to "integrated patterns of human behavior that include the language,

---

ETHICAL REFLECTION: TWO LEVELS OF POWER

There are a variety of ways in which power is abusive, coercive, or not used at all. In fact, nurses who do not use their power for the good of a situation are ineffective. The following two examples of power represent one on a smaller scale and one on a larger scale.

Power on a Smaller Scale

Ms. Gomez's liver cancer is inoperable and incurable. She is unaware of her diagnosis and prognosis, but she realizes she is experiencing abdominal pain that she described as level 8 on a 10-point scale. Everyone working in the oncology unit is involved in her care and is aware of her diagnosis. For a few days, the nurses have been observing Ms. Gomez's continued edginess and irritability as they interact with her. Ms. Gomez senses something is terribly wrong and begins to panic when physicians gather in her room during clinical rounds and talk medical jargon about her "case" in front of her. Ms. Gomez experienced an acute anxiety reaction. The outcome of this situation could have been better managed if her nurse had discussed the situation with the physicians beforehand and tried to convince them to discuss her case somewhere else or politely asked them to explain Mrs. Gomez's diagnosis and prognosis to her. Had the nurse exerted a noncoercive power over this situation, the outcome would have been averted.

Identify some specific strategies the nurse can use to establish, on a small-scale or unit level, policies about clinical rounds or disclosure to patients?

Power on a Larger Scale

Nurse Mary works at a hospice located in a coastal region and has six patients in her care. The National Weather Service forecasted several potential life-threatening hurricanes for her region during the next few weeks. Most of her patients are financially challenged. Mary has choices to make: (1) she could do nothing and let nature take its course; (2) she could educate her patients and families on ways to prepare for a disaster; or (3) she could educate her patients and families on disaster preparedness and use her power to help low income, homebound patients—not just her patients—in the community to prepare for the disaster. One way for Mary to exercise her power immediately on a large, community-wide scale is to have an immediate fund-raiser and supply drive and then work with agencies, such as the American Red Cross, to recruit community or nurse volunteers for distributing the supplies, handing out disaster preparedness information, and verbally educating the families.

What other strategies could Mary implement?

thoughts, communications, actions, customs, beliefs, values, and/or institutions of racial, ethnic, religious, and/or social groups" (Lipson & Dibble, 2005, p. xi). Giving culturally sensitive care is a core element in closing the gap on health disparities. **Culturally sensitive care** means nurses must first have a basic knowledge of culturally diverse customs and then demonstrate constructive attitudes based on learned knowledge (Spector, 2016). A culturally competent nurse or healthcare provider of care

> develops an awareness of his or her existence, sensations, thoughts, and environment without letting these factors have an undue effect on those for whom care is provided. Cultural competence is the adaptation of care in a manner that is consistent with the culture of the client and is therefore a conscious process and nonlinear. (Purnell, 2002, p. 193)

The process of nurses getting to know themselves and their values, beliefs, and moral compass is fundamental to providing culturally competent care (Purnell, 2017). Without some degree of cultural knowledge, nurses cannot possibly provide ethical care; for example, relationships with others cannot develop into a trusting, respectful exchange.

Lipson and Dibble's (2005) trademarked acronym, ASK (awareness, sensitivity, and knowledge), can be used by nurses to approach patients from various cultures. The many cultures in the United States differ in their beliefs about health, illness, pain, suffering, birth, parenting, death, dying, health care, communication, and truth, among others. Nurses need to conduct a quick assessment of cultural diversity needs (Lipson & Dibble, 2005). The following cultural assessment is an easy and quick approach based on ASK:

1. What is the patient's ethnic affiliation?
2. Who are the patient's major support persons and where do they live?
3. With whom should we speak about the patient's health or illness?
4. What are the patient's primary and secondary languages and speaking and reading abilities?
5. What is the patient's economic situation? Is income adequate to meet the patient's and family's need? (Lipson & Dibble, 2005, p. xiii)

Nurses' genuine attention to cultural diversity and the diversity within each culture promotes ethically competent care, which is essential in everyday nursing practice. In addition, nurses

ETHICAL REFLECTION: ETHICAL COMPETENCIES OF NURSES—TEST YOUR MORAL GROUNDING!

Thus far, you have learned about the ethical competencies that define an ideal nurse. The codes of ethics and the ethical competencies serve as a foundation for nurses to develop moral grounding for professional practice, education, research, and leadership.

Test your personal moral grounding! List the ethical competencies of a nurse, and write down how these competencies will relate to your ethical nursing practice. Briefly imagine or discuss an ethical situation that could arise with regard to each competency, and then give a corresponding resolution.

Moral integrity:

- Honesty
- Truthfulness and truthtelling
- Benevolence
- Wisdom
- Moral courage

Communication:

- Mindfulness
- Effective listening

Concern:

- Advocacy
- Power
- Culturally sensitive care

must increase their knowledge when caring for culturally diverse patients. Provision 1 of the *Code of Ethics for Nurses with Interpretive Statements* (ANA, 2015) compels nurses to care for persons regardless of social or economic status, personal attributes, or nature of health problems. If nurses uphold Provision 1, they plausibly will provide culturally sensitive care.

In this section, you have read about selected nursing ethical competencies: (1) moral integrity—honesty, truthtelling, benevolence, wisdom, and moral courage; (2) communication—mindfulness and effective listening; and (3) concern—advocacy, power, and culturally sensitive care. Refer to the following boxes to test your moral grounding.

FOCUS FOR DEBATE: ETHICAL COMPETENCIES—TEST YOUR MORAL GROUNDING! IS IT OK FOR A STUDENT TO CHEAT?

Gilda, a nursing student, discovered a website that provides fee-for-service tests with answers and rationales, based on test banks from older editions of books. The legality and ethicality of the company's business are questionable, but Gilda has an upcoming exam in her health assessment class and does not have time to study because of family issues. The company's website advertises test customization for any subject matter. Without much forethought, Gilda ordered a customized test, and the company sent her digital access to it. Gilda studied the questions and answers. While she was taking the actual course exam, however, she realized that some of the questions were either very different or had variations of the wording in the purchased test, but a few questions were similar. She was happy to see a score of 82 on her course exam.

Explore the following questions to test your moral grounding. Consider a live or online classroom debate for this exercise with two or more groups of students.

- Before you continue with this activity, analyze your moral grounding. Write down basic morals you value in your personal life and what you will or currently value as a nursing professional. Where do you stand?
- Is Gilda's action considered cheating or academically dishonest by your college or university standards? Why or why not? Please explain.
- When you violate the academic integrity policy of your college or university, what can happen if you are caught? Please explain your rationale.
- Do you believe Gilda considered the action to be a necessary means to a necessary end? When answering, explore all options and consequences from the perspective of utilitarian theory.

(The story continues.)

Gilda discovered another nursing student who had difficulty passing tests. She approached the student and explained about finding the company that sells tests, but the student had uncomfortable feelings about ordering a test. The student discussed the issue with a couple of her friends from nursing school to seek their guidance. Those students told the professor about Gilda's action and the test company. Gilda was caught by such surprise when the professor approached her to verify the story that she was too nervous not to admit her actions. She rationalized it by explaining her lack of time and the family issues; then, she pleaded with the professor to overlook this one incident and said she would never cheat again. Based on the academic integrity policy, however, Gilda failed her course and was dismissed from the program.

- What was an alternative action for Gilda? Derive your explanation from any of the ethical theories or approaches, such as utilitarian theory, Kant's deontology framework, or a virtue ethics approach.
- What are a couple of academically dishonest scenarios? How do these examples compare to Gilda's action?

Nursing Professional Relationships

Nurse–Physician Relationships

In centuries past and even today, women have experienced oppression related to inequity issues and hierarchical relationships, such as in political structures and doctrines and in certain religious orders. History reveals a significant degree of women's oppression. From the 1300s to the 1600s, women who claimed to be healers were burned at the stake after accusations of witchery (Ehrenreich & English, 1973). Other events also gave rise to oppression of women during that same time. By the early 20th century, Florence Nightingale's work in the 1800s helped move nurses to a more respected, notable standing, but some people continued to think of women in general as functioning only in domestic roles. Nurses, to varying degrees, have been working since then to overcome this perception.

Stein (1967), a physician, identified a type of relationship between physicians and nurses that he called the **doctor–nurse game**. The game originated from a hierarchical relationship, with doctors being in the superior position. The hallmark of the game is the avoidance of open disagreement between the disciplines. Avoidance of conflict is achieved when an experienced nurse cautiously offers suggestions in such a way to keep the physician from perceiving that consultative advice is coming from a nurse. In the past, student nurses were educated about the rules of the game while attending nursing school. Over many years, others have acknowledged the historical accuracy of Stein's characterization of doctor–nurse relationships (Fry & Johnstone, 2002; Jameton, 1984; Kelly, 2000).

Stein and colleagues (1990) revisited the doctor–nurse game concept 23 years after Stein first coined the phrase. Nurses unilaterally had decided to stop playing the game. Some of the reasons for this change and the ways change was accomplished involved nurses engaging in more dialogue rather than gamesmanship, the profession's goal of equal partnership status with other healthcare professionals, the alignment of nurses with the civil rights and women's movements, the increased percentage of nurses who achieved higher education, and collaboration between nurses and physicians on projects. In the process of abandoning the game, many nurses took a less than togetherness approach toward physicians.

Some nurses believe an adversarial fight needs to continue to establish nursing as an autonomous profession. Nurses' reports and opinions of strained relationships between nurses and physicians have steadily appeared in the literature in many countries, despite efforts by some nurses to have friendlier relationships with physicians. Reported reasons for the strained relationships include the following: (1) the hierarchical way ethical care decisions are made, both institutional system decisions and physician decisions; (2) competency and quality-of-care conflicts; and (3) lack of communication.

Other researchers echoed Malloy and colleagues' (2009) findings of nurses' perceptions of inequality with physicians. Churchman and Doherty (2010) found that solutions to address inequality with physicians are complex and do not exist universally because certain factors contribute to the challenge of finding answers: nurses (1) are discouraged from confronting physicians in everyday practice, (2) fear conflict and aggression by physicians, and (3) fear having their views disregarded. Institutional hierarchy continues to be a source for unequal rewards and power between nurses and physicians.

Nurse–Nurse Relationships

In the provisions of its *Code of Ethics for Nurses with Interpretive Statements*, the ANA (2015) characterized various ways nurses demonstrate their primary responsibility to their patients, families, and communities. Some

RESEARCH NOTE: QUALITATIVE FOCUS GROUP STUDY ON AN ORGANIZATIONAL CULTURE

Forty-two nurses from a variety of settings in four nations (Canada, Ireland, Australia, and South Korea) participated in Malloy and colleagues' (2009) qualitative focus group study to express their opinions on dilemmas and decisions in the everyday care of elders with dementia as well as to identify how end-of-life decisions are made. The researchers extracted four themes in conjunction with an *unexpected* finding that nurses from all countries consistently voiced strained and powerless hierarchical relationships with some physicians:

- The first theme arose because of two philosophies: care (nurses) versus treatment (physicians) was a source of tension between nurses and physicians on end-of-life decisions.
- The second theme was a constrained obligation in terms of the nurse–physician hierarchy, established protocol, and the way decisions were made.
- Third, nurses perceived physicians, patients, families, and the system as silencing the nurse's voice; they also believed themselves to be unequal participants in the care of patients largely because of the system.
- The fourth theme was a lack of respect for the profession of nursing from other professionals.

Data from Malloy, D. C., Hadjistavropoulos, T., McCarthy, E. F., Evans, R. J., Zakus, D. H., Park, I., . . . Williams, J. (2009). Culture and organizational climate: Nurses' insights into their relationship with physicians. *Nursing Ethics, 16*(6), 719–733.

key indicators in the code illustrate this responsibility, such as having compassion for patients, showing respect to patients and each other, collaborating with other healthcare professionals, protecting the rights and safety of patients, advocating for patients and their families, and caring for and preserving the integrity of oneself and others. Patient and family relationships are important, but good relationships with other nurses and other healthcare professionals are necessary for the successful follow-through of the responsibility to patients.

Nurses often treat other nurses in hurtful ways through what some people have called lateral, or horizontal, violence (Christie & Jones, 2013; Kelly, 2000; McKenna et al., 2003; Thomas, 2009). **Horizontal violence**, also known as **workplace bullying**, involves interpersonal conflict, harassment, intimidation, harsh criticism, sabotage, and abuse among nurses. It may occur because nurses feel oppressed by other dominant groups, such as physicians or institutional administrators;

subsequently, nurses turn their anger toward each other.

Acts of horizontal violence often occur subtly. The behaviors repeat and escalate over a long period of time. Some nurses characterize violence that is perpetrated by nurses against other nurses who excel and succeed as the **tall poppy syndrome** (Kelly, 2000). The perpetrators feel they need an outlet for their pent-up anger, so they cut down the tall poppies (nurses) who outshine them. This type of behavior creates an ostracizing nursing culture that discourages individual success and recognition. The term *tall poppy syndrome* was popularized in Australia and New Zealand, where it is used as a derogatory reference, but the concept originates from Greek and Roman philosophers and writers.

Thomas studied the causes and consequences of nurses' stress and anger. Nurses voiced horizontal and vertical violence as common sources of stress. "One of the most disturbing aspects of our research data on nurses' anger is the vehemence of their anger

RESEARCH NOTE: QUALITATIVE STUDY OF THE INTERPROFESSIONAL NURSE–PHYSICIAN RELATIONSHIP

Pullon's (2008) qualitative study of 18 nurses and physicians in primary care settings from New Zealand is an example of research on features that build an interprofessional nurse–physician relationship. Pullon identified certain extrinsic and intrinsic factors of this relationship, but the article is focused only on the intrinsic nature of individual interprofessional relationships. Demonstrated professional competence, which is a key feature of interprofessional relationships, served as the foundation of respect for each other and in turn formed a level of trust calculated over time with reliable and consistent behavior. The findings were as follows:

- Nurses and physicians identified their professional groups as distinct but complementary.
- Nurses described the formation and maintenance of quality professional relationships with patients and others as the heart of their professional work and teamwork as one means for achieving those relationships.
- Physicians depicted the physician–patient relationship as the crux of their practice but only in the context of consultation.
- Nurses and physicians both unveiled several shared values and attitudes: (1) the provision of continuity of care; (2) the ability to cope with unpredictable and demanding care; (3) the importance of working together and building a relationship; and (4) the significance of professional competence, mutual respect for each other, and trust in an ongoing relationship but with the realization that trust could be broken quickly in the early stages of a trustworthy relationship.

Data from Pullon, S. (2008). Competence, respect, and trust: Key features of successful interprofessional nurse-doctor relationships. *Journal of Interprofessional Care, 22*(2), 133–147.

at each other" (Thomas, 2009, p. 98). The findings indicated the following common characteristics of horizontal violence:

- Subtle nonverbal behaviors, such as rolling eyes, raising eyebrows, or giving a cold shoulder
- Sarcasm, snide remarks, rudeness
- Undermining or sabotaging
- Withholding needed information or assistance
- Passive–aggressive (behind-the-back) actions
- Spreading rumors and destructive gossip
- False accusations, scapegoating, blaming (p. 98)

Horizontal Violence and Wounded Healers

Horizontal violence, or workplace bullying, in nursing is counterproductive for the profession. Nurses experience a significant level of horizontal violence, sometimes more so than in other helping professions. These long-term emotional effects can compromise patient safety and the nurses' ability to practice proficiently (Thomas, 2009). If stress and traumatic feelings are not managed properly, the unrecognized and unmanaged effects lead to unproductive coping and unresolved issues; traumatized nurses will function as the **walking wounded** (Christie & Jones, 2013). Soon, others will observe that the walking wounded have difficulty in professional and personal relationships with other people.

Healing can occur. The first step in healing is recognizing the effects of the trauma. Deep self-awareness is necessary for grasping some personal meaning (Conti-O'Hare, 2002). This awareness enables wounded nurses to initiate work toward improving their coping mechanisms. Only then can nurses begin transforming and transcending their wounds toward healing, thus becoming wounded healers.

Wounded healers are informed by their own traumatic and difficult experiences that occur in the process of their everyday work, but they also transform their raw wounds to a healed scar that enables a better understanding of others' pain. In essence, a wounded healer has a rich sense of empathy for others because of past personal wounds (Groesbeck, 1975). The process of healing takes time and requires a strong desire to develop as a wounded healer. "Woundedness lies on a continuum, and the wounded healer paradigm focuses not on the degree of woundedness but on the ability to draw on woundedness in the service of healing" (Zerubavel & Wright, 2012, p. 482).

Improving Nurse–Nurse Relationships

Safeguarding patients and patient care is a moral priority, and positive nurse–nurse relationships promote the moral climate necessary for safe and competent care. Sometimes, nurses or nursing leaders must take unpleasant, but not spiteful, action with regard to nursing behaviors and the protection of patients. Nurses serve as advocates when they take appropriate action to protect patients from unethical, illegal, incompetent, or impaired behaviors of other nurses (ANA, 2015). For nurses who become aware of these behaviors, appropriate actions involve reviewing policies; seeking guidance from administrators in the chain of command; documenting the occurrences; and approaching the offending nurse in a constructive, compassionate manner. Gossip, condescension, or unproductive derogatory talk are negative tactics that do not help but rather serve only to damage reputations and relationships.

Nurses can strengthen a sense of community within the profession by working to heal the disharmony and transform their anger to support other nurses' accomplishments rather than treating them as tall poppies that must be cut down. Individual nurses need to self-reflect at the end of the workday by examining their actions and the dialogue they had with others. All nurses—those who follow through with daily self-reflection and those who do not—need to "make a commitment to supportive colleagueship" and "refuse to get caught up in workplace negativism" (Thomas, 2009, p. 109).

▶ Nurses and Social Media

Many people who use the Internet have already experienced, to some degree, the consequences of unethical or illegal behavior, such as being the target of someone else's devious actions. The digital age has brought about new levels of public exploitation to many people. Computers strongly influence our personal and professional lives every day. Because of this influence, nurses and nursing students need to understand the potential for unethical and illegal behaviors.

Moral Spaces and Blurred Lines

The risk for crossing professional boundaries increases as lines and moral spaces become blurred in nursing practice. Blurred-lined behaviors and obvious line crossings involve an invasion of the moral spaces of others and possibly a violation of their privacy. What nurses could view as a flippant or innocent social media comment may be perceived by others as vulgar, inflammatory, or threatening. Whether the nurse remarked as a joke or an intentional display of hostility, the comment can quickly transform from mere opinion to fact-based information.

Moral space is defined as "what we live in . . . any space formed from the relationships between natural and social objects, agents and events that protect or establish either the conditions for, or the realization of, some vision of the good life, or the good, in life" (Turnbull,

2003, p. 4). Respect for one another's moral spaces takes a serious commitment by those who use the Internet. Dozens of ethical codes of conduct exist for users of the Internet, but no matter how many codes exist or what populations they serve, the codes are of no use if they are not practiced consistently or people lack moral integrity. Nurses and nursing students must remain devoted to respecting human beings in all interactions and actions, including all features of social networking. Violations of the principle of autonomy generally involve matters of respect for human beings, self-determination, trustworthiness, confidentiality, and privacy. Violations of the principle of nonmaleficence in social media exchanges include intentional and hurtful remarks that could result in perceived or actual harm to the recipients.

Social Media, Email, and Cell Phones

Social media are a collection of online platforms and tools that enable collaborative community-based exchanges among people. People share information, profiles, and opinions to promote conversations between one another or to market certain products. Nurses routinely use social media to befriend others who have common interests or keep in touch with friends. Facebook, Twitter, Snapchat, Instagram, Google+, YouTube, TikTok, and other social media sites along with email and cell phones are essential communication tools for healthcare professionals, just as they are for others. Their usefulness has both benefits and perils.

Benefits of Using Social Media

For nurses, the positive side of social media is that they provide minute-to-minute information and allow nurses to share knowledge and build professional relationships. Social networks "provide unparalleled opportunities for

rapid knowledge exchange and dissemination among many people" (ANA, 2011, p. 3).

In 2011, several key nursing and physician professional organizations published statements or booklets about the use of social media. The ANA published a booklet titled *ANA's Principles of Social Networking and the Nurse: Guidance for Registered Nurses* (2011). Three ANA documents provided a foundation for the development of the social networking principles: (1) *Code of Ethics for Nurses with Interpretive Statements* (2015), (2) *Nursing: Scope and Standards of Practice* (2010a), and (3) *Nursing's Social Policy Statement: The Essence of the Profession* (2010b). The NCSBN also published a booklet titled *A Nurse's Guide to the Use of Social Media* (2018b).

Physicians also see value in the use of social networks for taking care of routine work, such as refilling prescriptions, answering questions, and sharing informational websites. In 2011, the AMA issued an opinion that echoes support for the use of social media to allow "personal expression, enable individual physicians to have a professional presence online, foster collegiality and camaraderie within the profession, [and] provide opportunity to widely disseminate public health messages" (2011, para. 1).

Perils of Using Social Media

Refer to the previous section titled "Moral Spaces and Blurred Lines" for a discussion of nurses who post comments on social media sites. It illustrates how just one message can have long-standing negative effects. One of the foremost perils of using social media is the risk for violation of patient privacy and confidentiality. In fact, posting *any* work-related information is a legal and ethical violation of privacy, including the identification of and providing information about patients, employers, administrators, coworkers, and others. In situations involving patients, the Privacy Rule of the Health Insurance Portability and Accountability Act (HIPAA) (U.S. Department of Health and Human Services [HHS], 1996) gives patients legal privacy protection. The *Code of Ethics for Nurses with Interpretive Statements*, Provision 3.1, illustrates the ethical aspect of privacy:

> Privacy is the right to control access to, and disclosure or nondisclosure of, information pertaining to oneself and to control the circumstances, timing, and extent to which information may be disclosed. Nurses safeguard the right to privacy for individuals, families, and communities. . . . Confidentiality pertains to the nondisclosure of personal information that has been communicated within the nurse-patient relationship. (ANA, 2015, p. 9)

Employers and other leaders sometimes label the behavior as unprofessional or illegal and also as complicated and uncertain. The growing number of employee violations is pushing employers to reinforce old policies and enforce new ones by initiating disciplinary courses of action against personnel who engage in inappropriate behaviors on social network sites and cell phones.

However, the question remains whether nurses can befriend patients and interact with them on social media without violating HIPAA's Privacy Rule. Buppert (2018) asked that question and provided some options for nurses when considering whether friendship with patients or patient groups is ethically and legally acceptable. First, if nurses or other healthcare professionals feel they must continually be on guard about what they say, they need to examine whether they should befriend patients. Second, nurses have an option of setting a personal rule to avoid befriending patients. Third, nurses can post a disclaimer to communicate that their posts are not considered official advice. Fourth, nurses should avoid any posts about duty-of-care statements, considering that legal issues could potentially arise.

If nurses and other healthcare professionals follow their codes of ethics and current hospital policies, new policies on social networking and cell phone use would not be necessary. Today, most employers, educational institutions, and professional organizations have initiated a position or policy on the use of social media because employees are increasingly using the media to complain about employers, coworkers, or even patients and families.

LEGAL PERSPECTIVE: HIPAA, THE PRIVACY RULE, AND PROTECTED HEALTH INFORMATION

The Privacy Rule in HIPAA legally protects patient health information in any form, whether electronic, paper, or oral (HHS, 1996, 2003). The public nature of any social or electronic communication poses ethical and legal problems, such as violations of the HIPAA Privacy Rule. Issues arise when nurses, physicians, and patients share information that identifies the person's past, present, or future physical or mental condition; the type of health care received or considered; or past, present, or future payment for healthcare services.

Data from U.S. Department of Health and Human Services (HHS). (2003). *Summary of the HIPAA privacy rule.* https://www.hhs.gov/hipaa/for-professionals/privacy/laws-regulations/index.html

Actual Cases of Violations

The potential exists for many violations in social media, email, and cell phones in both nurses' everyday work and their personal lives. The following real-life case has been published in many articles and was a nationally publicized incident (NCSBN, 2011).

In an alarming story, nurses were suspected of patient exploitation and violations of confidentiality and privacy. The incident occurred in 2010 at Tri-City Medical Center in Oceanside, California. The medical center fired five nurses and disciplined a sixth nurse for violating confidentiality. According to a spokesperson at the medical center, there was enough substantial information to warrant the firings of the five nurses because they had discussed patient cases on Facebook ("Five Nurses Fired," 2010).

In the other social media case, the Louisiana State Board of Nursing filed complaints against three nurses at the St. Tammany Parish Hospital emergency room after discovering abhorrent patient mistreatment. Lee Zurik (2012), an investigator for Fox 8 Live WVUE-TV, reported the story. Reba Campbell, an emergency room technician, reported nurses for allegedly exploiting, making fun of, and taking cell phone pictures of unconscious patients on at least two separate occasions. One case involved an overweight man who overdosed on pain and anxiety medications. According to Zurik (2012), Campbell stated the following:

> Clancy [one of the three reported nurses] the other nurse walks in and puts these glasses on the patient and starts to make fun of him. That wasn't funny enough, so they took charcoal that we dumped down his throat and painted his face like a football player and said, "Welcome to St. Tammany Parish Hospital ER. This is your initiation for trying to kill yourself." (Zurik, para. 5)

ETHICAL REFLECTION: A CASE OF EMAIL FORWARDING

Sally, a nurse employed at a large long-term care facility, arrived at work to find a strange email from the previous night shift on her laptop. The source was unknown. Attached to the email was a photo of an elderly female wearing a gown, bending over, with an exposed backside. Sally asked the other day-shift staff members about the email and photo, and some of them confirmed they had received it on their office computers. No one knew anything about the source of the email or the identity of the woman in the photo, although the background appeared to be a patient room at the facility. In an effort to find out whether any of the staff knew who sent the email, Sally forwarded it to the computers and cell phones of several staff members, who later stated they had not seen the previous email. Some staff members were concerned, but others found it amusing and were laughing about it. Someone initiated a betting pool to guess the identity of the patient. At least one staff person posted the photo on her blog. By midday, the director of nursing had become aware of the photo and began an investigation because the organization was very concerned about the patient's rights. The local media also became aware of the matter, and law enforcement was called to investigate whether any crimes involving sexual exploitation had been committed. After a large amount of media coverage and the identification of a few people engaged in the behavior, the administrator placed several staff members on administrative leave and reported the incident to the state board of nursing. The board investigated the reported nurses to determine if federal regulations pertaining to exploitation of vulnerable adults were violated. No one ever discovered the originator of the email and photo. After administrators identified the patient, her family threatened to sue the facility and all the involved staff. When the NCSBN (2011) white paper to guide nurses on the use of social media was published, the board of nursing complaint was pending.

This scenario reflects the importance for nurses to consider their actions carefully. The nurses had a duty to immediately report the incident to their supervisor to protect patient privacy and maintain professionalism. Instead, the situation escalated to involve the board of nursing, the prosecutor, and the national media. The family experienced a high degree of humiliation, and the organization faced possible legal consequences and embarrassment by the national media focus.

Data from Data from National Council of State Boards of Nursing (NCSBN). (2011). *White paper: A nurse's guide to the use of social media.* https://www.ncsbn.org/Social_Media.pdf

Thomas (2009) conducted research by interviewing nurses across the United States to find meaning in their layers of stress and anger over unethical, harmful, and dehumanizing treatment of patients as part of a larger study to uncover reasons for nurses' stress and anger. One of the themes discovered was "I feel morally sick." Nurses described mistreatment and disregard of patients. They found the real-life observations repugnant; they felt physically sick, disgusted, and nauseated, and they believed they were powerless to do anything about those abhorrent situations. Thomas's interpretation of the narratives was that the nurses were experiencing a significant amount of moral distress and the effects of moral residue because of their layers of stress and anger. Refer to the previous moral distress and walking wounded discussions in this chapter.

The nurses' narratives in Thomas's study were depictions of their real-life experiences and feelings about stories that were not necessarily related to social networking. Unethical and illegal events have always been described and exposed by concerned healthcare personnel, but the digital age has brought new levels of public exploitation to many patients and families. Sadly, social networking potentially could be a means for nurses to express frustrations about their workplace, coworkers, and patients and their families, but no matter what reasons exist for sharing and divulging information, nurses who do so violate professional boundaries and most likely will be fired or disciplined and will have their license suspended or revoked. Sharing any privileged information amounts to illegal, inappropriate, and unethical violations. Many nurses and physicians are seeing these concerns as a valid worry and are taking action collectively through professional organizations and healthcare organizations.

Strategies for Using Social Media

Using social media in an appropriate manner is generally not harmful and without malicious intent. Adopting an attitude to keep social media use appropriate will serve as a reminder to be mindful of ethical and legal implications of social media wrongdoing and a commitment to the code. Refer to this chapter's section on the ethical competency of mindfulness. Mindfulness in communication means having a keen awareness of the present moment and its surroundings, including the facts, interactions, activities, and processing of information, which suggests that mindfulness is a key element to suitable social media communication.

The ANA (2011) published six principles of social networking for nurses. Where patients, nurses, and all surrounding issues are concerned in health care, the commitments of privacy and confidentiality serve as the foundation for all six principles of social networking.

Internet-based applications have changed the way people categorize, process, organize, and store information. In most of the codes of ethics for nurses, including the ANA code, there are explicit discussions about nurses maintaining respect, confidentiality, and privacy; those same concepts are applicable to social networking, emailing, and cell phone use. Social media and other electronic media can be instrumental in building relationships and sharing worthwhile information, but nurses must follow the ethical guidelines within the codes of ethics and the legal regulations in the applicable states and countries.

Nurses and physicians are role models for other healthcare professionals, whether or not they want this role. Nurse role models are present in every area of nursing, including practice, education, research, and administration. Nursing newcomers emulate the conduct of the role models, both the positive and negative behaviors. It is imperative that existing nurses influence new nurses and other personnel in a positive manner.

KEY POINTS

- Nursing ethics is defined as the examination of all kinds of ethical and bioethical issues from the perspectives of nursing theory and practice.
- Nursing as praxis means that nurses make morally good decisions, with indistinguishable means and ends to follow through with those decisions. The central point is to maintain an ethical practice.
- To practice nursing ethically, nurses must be sensitive enough to recognize when they are facing seemingly obscure ethical issues.
- Administrators, physicians, or patients may occasionally request that nurses carry out actions that seem morally undesirable. Making a nursing decision whether to carry out this action will require further scrutiny, such as using the stench test.
- The ANA outlined nine moral provisions with nonnegotiable obligations for nurses. Detailed guidelines with interpretive statements of each provision accompany the nine provisions.
- A clear patient focus in the code obliges nurses to remain attentive and loyal to all patients in their care and also to be watchful for ethical issues and conflicts of issues that could lead to potential negative effects.
- Common themes between the ANA and ICN codes include provision of compassionate care and alleviation of suffering, with an endorsement of the bioethical principles of autonomy, beneficence, nonmaleficence, and justice.
- Professional boundaries are limits that protect the space between the nurse's professional power and the patient's vulnerabilities.
- Boundaries give each person in the relationship a sense of legitimate control, whether the relationships are between a nurse and a patient, a nurse and a physician, a nurse and an administrator, or a nurse and a nurse.
- Boundary violations are boundary departures that pose potential harm or exploitation and do not promote the best interest of another in the relationship.
- Boundary crossings are short-lived, usually harmless, departures of unique nursing interventions.
- In addition to the ethical guidelines from the code of ethics, nurses must also follow the board of nursing's legal regulations and standards for practice in the nurse's state of residence. Violations can result in reprimand, voluntary surrender, suspension, revocation, or other disciplinary actions of the nurse's license, thus prohibiting the nurse from practicing. The boards of nursing function not to protect nurses but to protect the public and ensure safe and competent care.
- If patients or their families file legal suits of negligence or malpractice in a civil court against a nurse, the plaintiff's lawyer must prove injury or harm to the plaintiff as a result of the nurse's negligence or malpractice.
- Thirteen interrelated ethical competencies, divided into three major competency areas, combine to form a well-defined, ideal nurse. The ethical competency areas are as follows: (1) moral integrity—honesty, truthfulness, benevolence, wisdom, and moral courage; (2) communication—mindfulness and effective listening; and (3) concern—advocacy, power, and culturally sensitive care.
- Nurses with moral integrity act consistently within their personal and professional values.
- Nurses experience moral distress when institutional constraints prevent them from acting in a way that is consistent with their personal and professional composite of moral integrity.
- Nursing involves hard moral choices that sometimes cause moral distress, resulting in emotional and physical suffering, painful ambiguity, contradiction, frustration, anger, guilt, and avoidance of patients.
- Research reveals a link between moral distress and the concepts of incompetent or poor care, unsafe or inadequate staffing, overwork, cost constraints, ineffective policy, futile care, unsuccessful advocacy, the current definition of brain death, objectification of patients, and unrealistic hope.

(continues)

KEY POINTS (continued)

- Truthtelling means nurses should not intentionally deceive or mislead patients. No matter how disappointing the news will be to patients and their families, nurses must evaluate the situation carefully with wisdom and contemplation before making any decision on the degree of information disclosure.
- Benevolent nurses will seek out ways to perform acts of kindness rather than only recognizing ways to do good.
- Aristotle viewed wisdom as an excellence that develops with intellectual accomplishment and practical expertise. Having wisdom, or practical wisdom, requires that nurses engage in a calculated intellectual ability, contemplation, deliberation, and effort to achieve a worthy goal.
- When nurses have the moral courage to do what they believe is the right thing in a particular situation, they make a personal sacrifice of possibly standing alone, but they will feel a sense of peace in their decision.
- Nurses must reside in a state of mindfulness and be effective listeners to develop good communication skills.
- Mindfulness requires paying attention in a particular way—on purpose, in the present moment, and nonjudgmentally.
- Effective listening means the communicators comprehend the actively exchanged information and then form a mutual understanding of the essence of the dialogue.
- Concern means nurses feel a sense of responsibility to think about the scope of care that is important for their patients; sometimes, a sense of worrying about the health or illness of patients prompts nurses to action.
- Patient advocacy, a competency of ethical nursing practice, requires nurses to embrace the promotion of well-being and to uphold the rights and interests of their patients.
- Nurses who are ingrained with the ideals of socialized power strive to benefit others with the intent to avoid harm or negative effects.
- Nurses' genuine attention to cultural diversity and the diversity within each culture promotes ethically competent care, which is essential in everyday nursing practice.
- Successful nurse–physician relationships require a mutual presence of three essential features: competence, respect, and trust. Reasons for strained nurse–physician relationships include the hierarchical way ethical care decisions are made, competency and quality-of-care conflicts, and lack of communication.
- Nurses often treat other nurses in hurtful ways. Many refer to this hurtful treatment as tall poppy syndrome or horizontal violence, but more recently it is referred to as workplace bullying, which involves interpersonal conflict, harassment, intimidation, harsh criticism, sabotage, and abuse.
- If nurses' stress and traumatic feelings are not managed properly, the effects will lead to unproductive coping and unresolved issues. These traumatized nurses will function as the walking wounded.
- Wounded healers are informed by their own traumatic and difficult experiences that occur in the process of their everyday work, and they transform their raw wounds to a healed scar that enables a better understanding of others' pain.
- Nurses can strengthen a sense of community within the profession by working to heal the disharmony and transform their anger to support nurses' accomplishments rather than treating them as tall poppies that must be cut down.
- Nurses and physicians value their ability to use social media to retrieve minute-to-minute information, share knowledge, and build professional relationships. The use of social media has many benefits and also numerous perils.

- Social networking invokes questions of confidentiality and privacy when nurses, physicians, and patients share information with each other. The public nature of social communication poses ethical and legal problems, and solutions are usually unclear.
- Blurred-line behaviors and definite crossings occur as a result of the use of social media when it invades the moral spaces of others and violates their privacy. What nurses could view as a flippant or innocent social media comment may be perceived by others as vulgar, inflammatory, or threatening.
- The growing number of employee violations worldwide that arise from social media are pushing employers to initiate disciplinary courses of action against their personnel and enforce new policies to prevent inappropriate behaviors.

References

American Association of Critical-Care Nurses (AACN). (2020a, March). *AACN position statement: Moral distress in times of crisis.* https://www.aacn.org/~/media/aacn-website/policy-and-advocacy/stat-20_position-statement_moral-distress.pdf?la=en

American Association of Critical-Care Nurses. (2020b, July). *Recognize and address moral distress.* https://www.aacn.org/~/media/aacn-website/clincial-resources/moral-distress/recognizing-addressing-moral-distress-quick-reference-guide.pdf

American Association of Critical-Care Nurses. (2021). *Resources for moral distress.* https://www.aacn.org/clinical-resources/moral-distress#

American Medical Association (AMA). (2011). *Opinion 9.124: Professionalism in the use of social media.* https://journalofethics.ama-assn.org/article/ama-code-medical-ethics-opinions-confidentiality-patient-information/2011-07

American Medical Association (AMA). (2012). Virtual mentor: The code says: The AMA *Code of Medical Ethics'* Opinions on Informing Patients. *American Medical Association Journal of Ethics, 14*(7), 555–556. https://journalofethics.ama-assn.org/article/ama-code-medical-ethics-opinions-informing-patients/2012-07

American Medical Association (AMA). (2018). *Withholding information from patients: Code of medical ethics opinion 2.1.3.* https://www.ama-assn.org/delivering-care/ethics/withholding-information-patients

American Nurses Association (ANA). (2010a). *Nursing: Scope and standards of practice* (2nd ed.).

American Nurses Association (ANA). (2010b). *Nursing's social policy statement: The essence of the profession* (3rd ed.).

American Nurses Association (ANA). (2011). *ANA's principles for social networking and the nurse: Guidance for registered nurses.* https://www.nursingworld.org/~4af4f2/globalassets/docs/ana/ethics/social-networking.pdf

American Nurses Association (ANA). (2012). *Position statement: Nursing care and do not resuscitate (DNR) and allow natural death (AND) decisions.* https://www.nursingworld.org/~4af287/globalassets/docs/ana/ethics/ps_nursing-care-and-do-not-resuscitate--allow-natural-death.pdf

American Nurses Association (ANA). (2015). *Code of ethics for nurses with interpretive statements.*

American Nurses Association (ANA). (2016). *Position statement: Nurses' roles and responsibilities in providing care and support at the end of life.* https://www.nursingworld.org/~4af078/globalassets/docs/ana/ethics/endoflife-positionstatement.pdf

ANA Ethics Advisory Board. (2019, September 16). ANA position statement: The nurse's role when a patient requests medical aid in dying. *The Online Journal of Issues in Nursing, 24*(3). https://www.doi.org/10.3912/OJIN.Vol24No03PoSCol02

Bazarko, D. (2014). *Mindfulness and you: Being present in nursing practice.* American Nurses Association.

Beauchamp, T. (2019, February 11). *The principle of benevolence in applied ethics (Part 1, Para. 2).* https://plato.stanford.edu/entries/principle-beneficence/

Beauchamp, T. L., & Childress, J. F. (2019). *Principles of biomedical ethics* (8th ed.). Oxford University Press.

Benner, P., Hooper-Kyriakidis, P., & Stannard, D. (1999). Thinking-in-action and reasoning-in-transition: An overview. *Clinical wisdom and interventions in critical care: A thinking-in-action approach* (pp. 1–26). Saunders.

Bennett, W. J. (Ed.). (1993). Honesty. In W. J. Bennett (Ed.), *The book of virtues: A treasury of great moral stories* (pp. 597–662). Simon & Schuster.

Bickoff, L., Sinclair, P. M., & Levett-Jones, T. (2017). Moral courage in undergraduate nursing students: A literature review. *Collegian, 24,* 71–83.

Broadie, S. (2002). Philosophical introduction. In S. Broadie & C. Rowe (Eds.) & C. Rowe (Trans.), *Aristotle Nicomachean ethics* (pp. 1–91). Oxford University Press.

Bu, X., & Jezewski, M. A. (2006). Developing a mid-range theory of patient advocacy through concept analysis. *Journal of Advanced Nursing, 57*(1), 101–110.

Buppert, C. (2018, January 3). *Should I interact with patients on social media?* https://www.medscape.com /viewarticle/890658

Butts, J. B. (2011). *PRISMS—Acronym for key action verbs for strategies to promote patient advocacy.* Unpublished raw data.

Christie, W., & Jones, S. (2013). Lateral violence in nursing and the theory of the nurse as wounded healer. *Online Journal of Issues in Nursing, 19*(1). https://doi .org/10.3912/OJIN.Vol19No01PPT01

Churchman, J. J., & Doherty, C. (2010). Nurses' views on challenging doctors' practice in an acute hospital. *Nursing Standard, 24*(40), 42–47.

Conti-O'Hare, M. (2002). The wounded healer: Theoretical perspectives. *The nurse as wounded healer: From trauma to transcendence* (pp. 33–50). Jones and Bartlett Publishers.

Corley, M. C. (2002). Nurse moral distress: A proposed theory and research agenda. *Nursing Ethics, 9*(6), 636–650.

Corley, M. C., Minick, P., Elswick, R. K., & Jacobs, M. (2005). Nurse moral distress and ethical work environment. *Nursing Ethics, 12*(4), 381–390.

Croke, E. M. (2003). Nurses, negligence, and malpractice: Continuing education. *American Journal of Nursing, 103*(9), 54–63.

Davis, A. J., Fowler, M. D., & Aroskar, M. A. (2010). *Ethical dilemmas and nursing practice* (5th ed.). Pearson.

Edson, M. (1999). *Wit.* Faber & Faber.

Ehrenreich, B., & English, D. (1973). *Witches, midwives, and nurses: A history of women healers.* Feminist Press.

Erichsen, E., Danielsson, E. H., & Friedrichsen, M. (2010). A phenomenological study of nurses' understanding of honesty in palliative care. *Nursing Ethics, 17*(1), 39–50.

Esterhuizen, P. (2006). Is the professional code still the cornerstone of clinical nursing practice? *Journal of Advanced Nursing, 53*(1), 104–113. (Original work published 1996)

Burge, M. (2010, June 10). Five nurses fired for Facebook postings. *The San Diego Union-Tribune.* https://www .sandiegouniontribune.com/sdut-5-employees-fired -for-discussing-patients-cases-2010jun10-story.html

Fry, S., & Johnstone, M. J. (2002). *Ethics in nursing practice: A guide to ethical decision making* (2nd ed.). Blackwell Science.

Fry, S. T., Veatch, R. M., & Taylor, C. (2011). Introduction. In S. T. Fry, R. M. Veatch, & C. Taylor (Eds.), *Case studies in nursing ethics* (4th ed., pp. xv–xxix). Jones & Bartlett Learning.

Greater Good. (2010, May). *The stars of our own movie.* https://greatergood.berkeley.edu/video/item/the _stars_of_our_own_movie

Greater Good. (2014). *Mindfulness defined.* https:// greatergood.berkeley.edu/topic%20/mindfulness /definition#what_is

Groesbeck, C. J. (1975). The archetypal image of the wounded healer. *Journal of Analytical Psychology, 20*(2), 122–145.

Hakesley-Brown, R., & Malone, B. (2007). Patients and nurses: A powerful force. *Online Journal of Issues in Nursing, 12*(1). https://doi.org/10.3912/OJIN.Vol12 No01Man04

Hamric, A. B. (2000). What is happening to advocacy? *Nursing Outlook, 48*(3), 103–104.

Hanks, R. G. (2007). Barriers to nursing advocacy: A concept analysis. *Nursing Forum, 42*(4), 171–177.

Holm, S. (2006). What should other healthcare professions learn from nursing ethics? *Nursing Philosophy, 7,* 165–174.

Hwang, K.-K. (2001). The deep structure of Confucianism: A social psychological approach. *Asian Philosophy, 11*(3), 179–204. https://doi.org/10.1080/09552360120116928

International Council of Nurses. (2021). *The ICN code of ethics for nurses.* https://www.nzno.org.nz/Portals/0 /Files/Documents/Consultation/Sue%20Gasquoine %20Feedback%202020-08-11/2020-11-11%20CoE _Version%20for%20Consultation_October%202020 _EN.pdf?ver=IgEV1G-xTMg4UIaBMDf5Cw%3D%3D

Jameton, A. (1984). *Nursing practice: The ethical issues.* Prentice Hall.

Johnson, C. E. (2012). Ethical interpersonal information. *Organizational ethics: A practical approach* (2nd ed., pp. 115–143). Sage.

Johnstone, M. J. (2008). *Bioethics: A nursing perspective* (5th ed.). Saunders Elsevier.

Kabat-Zinn, J. (2009). *Wherever you go, there you are: Mindfulness meditation in everyday life.* Hyperion.

Kelly, C. (2000). *Nurses' moral practice: Investing and discounting self.* Sigma Theta Tau International Center Nursing Press.

Kidder, R. M. (1995). *How good people make tough choices.* William Morrow.

Laabs, C. (2011). Perceptions of moral integrity: Contradictions in need of explanation. *Nursing Ethics, 18*(3), 431–440.

Lachman, V. D. (2007). Moral courage: A virtue in need of development? *MedSurg Nursing, 16*(2), 131–133.

Lachman, V. (2010). Do-not-resuscitate orders: Nurse's role requires moral courage. *Journal of Medical Surgical Nursing, 19*(4), 249–252.

Lipson, J. G., & Dibble, S. L. (2005). Introduction: Providing culturally appropriate health care. In J. G. Lipson & S. L. Dibble (Eds.), *Cultural and clinical care* (pp. xi–xviii). University of California, Nursing Press.

Loprinzi, C. L., Schapira, L., Moynihan, T., Kalemkerian, G. P., von Gunten, C., & Steensma, D. (2010). Compassionate honesty. *Journal of Palliative Medicine, 13*(10), 1187–1191.

Lutzén, K., & Nordin, C. (1993). Benevolence, a central moral concept derived from a grounded theory study of nursing decision making in psychiatric settings. *Journal of Advanced Nursing, 18,* 1106–1111.

Maes, S. (2003). How do you know when professional boundaries have been crossed? *Oncology Nursing Society, 18*(8), 3–5.

Malloy, D. C., Hadjistavropoulos, T., McCarthy, E. F., Evans, R. J., Zakus, D. H., Park, I., Lee, Y., Williams, J. (2009). Culture and organizational climate: Nurses' insights into their relationship with physicians. *Nursing Ethics, 16*(6), 719–733.

McCue, C. (2011). Using the AACN framework to alleviate moral distress. *Online Journal of Nursing Issues, 16*(1). https://doi.org/10.3912/OJIN.Vol16No01PPT02

McKenna, B. G., Smith, N. A., Poole, S. J., & Coverdale, J. H. (2003). Horizontal violence: Experiences of registered nurses in their first year of practice. *Journal of Advanced Nursing, 42*(1), 90–96.

Miller, R., & Zois, L. (2021). Nursing malpractice statistics. Baltimore, MD: Medical Malpractice Attorney. https://www.millerandzois.com/nurse-malpractice-statistics.html

Milliken, A. (2018, January 31). Ethical awareness: What it is and why it matters. *The Online Journal of Issues in Nursing, 23*(1), Manuscript 1. https://doi.org/10.3912/OJIN.Vol23No01Man01

Morley, G., Grady, C., McCarthy, J., & Ulrich, C. M. (2020, May-June). Covid-19: Ethical challenges for nurses. *Hastings Center Report, 50*(3), 35–39. https://doi.org/10.1002/hast.1110

National Council of State Boards of Nursing (NCSBN). (2018a). *A nurse's guide to professional boundaries.* https://www.ncsbn.org/ProfessionalBoundaries_Complete.pdf

National Council of State Boards of Nursing (NCSBN). (2018b). *A nurse's guide to use of social media.* https://www.ncsbn.org/NCSBN_SocialMedia.pdf

National Council of State Boards of Nursing (NCSBN). (2018c). *State and territorial boards of nursing: What every nurse needs to know about.* https://www.ncsbn.org/What_Every_Nurse_Needs_to_Know.pdf

National Council of State Boards of Nursing (NCSBN). (2011). *White paper: A nurse's guide to the use of social media.* https://www.ncsbn.org/Social_Media.pdf

Pearce, E. C. (1975). The patient. *A general textbook of nursing* (19th ed., pp. 3–10). Faber & Faber.

Pellegrino, E. D., & Thomasma, D. C. (1993). Phronesis: Medicine's indispensable virtue. *The virtues in medical practice* (pp. 84–91). Oxford University Press.

Pendry, P. S. (2007). Moral distress: Recognizing it to retain nurses. *Nursing Economics, 25*(4), 217–221.

Pinch, W. J. E. (2009). Honoring American nurse ethicists. *Nursing Ethics, 16*(2), 238–246.

Plante, T. G. (2004). *Do the right thing: Living ethically in an unethical world.* New Harbinger.

Ponte, P. R., Glazer, G., Dann, E., McCollum, K., Gross, A., Tyrrell, R., Branowicki, P., Noga, P., Winfrey, M., Cooley, M., Saint-Eloi, S., Hayes, C., Nicolas, P. K., & Washington, D. (2007). The power of professional nursing practice—An essential element of patient and family centered care. *Online Journal of Issues in Nursing, 12*(1), 4.

Pullon, S. (2008). Competence, respect, and trust: Key features of successful interprofessional nurse-doctor relationships. *Journal of Interprofessional Care, 22*(2), 133–147.

Purnell, L. (2002). The Purnell model of cultural competence. *Journal of Transcultural Nursing, 13*(3), 193–196.

Purnell, L. (2017). Models and theories focused on culture. In J. B. Butts & K. L. Rich (Eds.), *Philosophies and theories for advanced nursing practice* (pp. 565–601). Jones & Bartlett Learning.

Redman, B. K., & Fry, S. T. (2000). Nurses' ethical conflicts: What is really known about them? *Nursing Ethics, 7,* 360–366.

Reinhart, R. J. (2020, January 6). Nurses continue to rate highest in honesty, ethics. *Gallup.* https://news.gallup.com/poll/274673/nurses-continue-rate-highest-honesty-ethics.aspx

Reising, D. L. (2007, February 11). Protecting yourself from malpractice claims. *American Nurse.* https://www.myamericannurse.com/protecting-yourself-from-malpractice-claims/

Robb, I. H. (1916). *Nursing ethics: For hospital and private use.* E. C. Koeckert. (Original work published 1900)

Rowe, C., & Broadie, S. (Eds.). (2002). *Aristotle Nichomachean ethics* (C. Rowe, Trans.). Oxford University Press.

Schluter, J., Winch, S., Holzhauser, K., & Henderson, A. (2008). Nurses' moral sensitivity and hospital ethical climate: A literature review. *Nursing Ethics, 15*(3), 304–321.

Spector, R. E. (2016). *Cultural diversity in health and illness* (9th ed.). Pearson.

Stein, L. I. (1967). The doctor-nurse game. *Archives of General Psychiatry, 16*(6), 699–703.

Stein, L. I., Watts, D. T., & Howell, T. (1990). The doctor-nurse game revisited. *Nursing Outlook, 38*(6), 264–268.

Stenburg, M. J. (1988). "The responsible powerless": Nurses and decision about resuscitation. *Journal of Cardiovascular Nursing, 3,* 47–56.

Sulmasy, D. P., He, M. K., McAuley, R., & Ury, W. A. (2008). Beliefs and attitudes of nurses and physicians about do not resuscitate orders and who should speak to patients and families about them. *Critical Care Medicine, 36*(6), 1817–1822.

Thomas, S. P. (2009). *Transforming nurses' stress and anger: Steps toward healing* (3rd ed.). Springer.

Tschudin, V. (2006). 30th anniversary commentary on Esterhuizen P. (1996) Is the professional code still the cornerstone of clinical nursing practice? *Journal of Advanced Nursing 23,* 25–31.

Turnbull, D. (2003). Genetics and disability: Exploring moral space. *Journal of Future Studies, 7*(4), 3–14.

U.S. Department of Health and Human Services (HHS). (1996). *Health Insurance Portability and Accountability Act of 1996.* https://www.cdc.gov/phlp/publications /topic/hipaa.html

U.S. Department of Health and Human Services (HHS). (2003). *Summary of the HIPAA privacy rule.* https:// www.hhs.gov/hipaa/for-professionals/privacy/laws -regulations/index.html

Vaartio, H., Leino-Kilpi, H., Salanterä, S., & Suominen, T. (2006). Nursing advocacy: How is it defined by patients and nurses, what does it involve and how is it experienced? *Scandinavian Journal of Caring Science, 20,* 282–292.

Volker, D. L. (2003). Is there a unique nursing ethic? *Nursing Science Quarterly, 16*(3), 207–211.

Wright, D., & Brajtman, S. (2011). Relational and embodied knowing: Nursing ethics within the interprofessional team. *Nursing Ethics, 18*(1), 20–30.

Zerubavel, N., & Wright, M. O. (2012). The dilemma of the wounded healer. *Journal of Psychotherapy, 49*(4), 482–491.

Zurik, L. (2012, May 22). *Lee Zurik investigation: Nurse witnesses patient mistreatment.*

© Seller 1234/Shutterstock

PART II

Nursing Ethics Across the Life Span

CHAPTER 4

Reproductive Issues and Nursing Ethics

Janie B. Butts

You and I are persons. More specifically, we are human persons—persons who are members of the species Homo sapiens. *But what does it mean to say that someone is a person? And what is the significance of being human?*

—**David DeGrazia**, *Human Identity and Bioethics* (2005)

OBJECTIVES

After reading this chapter, the reader should be able to do the following:

1. Describe the current global and U.S. landscape of reproductive rights and reproductive health.
2. Explore the rationale for the worldwide morbidity rate of reproductive women.
3. Discuss the theories for full moral standing.
4. Explore the maternal–fetal conflict as it relates to the legal and ethical issues of human and reproductive rights, autonomy, beneficence, nonmaleficence, and justice in health care and treatment.
5. Explore legal and ethical issues of abortion.
6. Compare the two sides of the debate on abortion: pro-choice groups and pro-life groups.
7. Distinguish between the ethical issues for each major type of assisted reproductive technology.
8. Discuss the rationale for couples to make informed choices about pregnancy and the type of assisted reproductive technology in terms of genetic screening, testing, and counseling.
9. Discuss the ethical considerations for maternal substance abuse.
10. Integrate Bergum's relational ethics into the essential interpretational aspects of the American Nurses Association *Code of Ethics for Nurses with Interpretive Statements* for the care of childbearing women.

▶ Introduction to Ethics in Reproductive Health

Most organizations and healthcare professionals support women's rights and the availability of safe, effective, and accessible reproductive health care and contraceptive counseling. The Centers for Disease Control and Prevention (CDC, 2019a) adopted an overall mission of promoting optimal and equitable health for women and infants through public health efforts. Efforts to accomplish the mission include "surveillance, research, leadership, and partnership to move science to practice" (CDC, 2019a, Mission). Many individual countries around the world share the same values as the United Nations' goals for the rights of reproductive women and children. The International Conference on Population and Development (ICPD) in Cairo in 1994 adopted a definition of reproductive health, which still stands today.

▶ Reproductive Health

Reproductive health is a state of complete physical, mental, and social well-being and not merely the absence of disease or infirmity, in all matters relating to the reproductive system and to its functions and processes. Reproductive health therefore implies people are able to have a satisfying and safe sex life and that they have the capability to reproduce and the freedom to decide if, when and how often to do so. Implicit in this last condition are the right of men and women to be informed and to have access to safe, effective, affordable and acceptable methods of family planning of their choice, as well as other methods of their choice for regulation of fertility which are not against the law. (United Nations Population Fund, 2014b, p. 59)

Since 1994, many policies and programs have grown from the ICPD reproductive rights and reproductive health goals, but some critical issues continue to persist in the areas of human rights, self-determination, exclusion, discrimination, and inequality (United Nations Population Fund, 2014a). Some of the major worldwide and U.S. organizations refer to these problems as being a complex social and human rights failure that needs immediate attention.

A turning point for decisive action by world organizations and the United States was in 2010 after the release of an alarming report of compiled data from major world organizations. Amnesty International's updated spring 2010 report and an updated report in 2011, titled *Deadly Delivery: The Maternal Health Care Crisis in the USA*, reflected perilous statistics for those who are giving birth. For instance, maternal death in the United States worsened and fell from a ranking of 41 to 50 in the world, which placed the U.S. maternal death rate higher than 49 other countries. In fact, the United States was the only developed country with a rising maternal mortality rate, from 6.6 deaths per 100,000 in 1987 to 12.7 deaths per 100,000 in 2010. A majority of other countries reduced their maternal mortality ratios to result in a total global decrease to 34%. Even with the reductions in other countries, the global percentage is still reflective of an unacceptable maternal mortality rate, and it is largely preventable.

The unresolved nature of general global reproductive issues causes millions of women, men, and young people to suffer to varying degrees. A large proportion of these statistics relate to inadequate maternal health care, but a significant percentage of the statistics relate to women who would have preferred to use contraceptives to prevent pregnancy and sexually transmitted infections but did not have a choice or did not have access to modern forms of contraceptives. Further, many of the pregnant women who did not have access to modern forms of contraceptives resorted to having abortions with inadequate, unsafe care, which results in life-threatening health conditions and even mortality. Selected worldwide statistics on reproductive health illustrate this impact.

RESEARCH NOTE: SELECTED WORLDWIDE STATISTICS ON REPRODUCTIVE RIGHTS AND REPRODUCTIVE HEALTH

Did you know that . . .

- More than 800 women die every single day with complications related to childbirth and pregnancies that could have been prevented?
- In 2015 alone, approximately 303,000 women worldwide died during or following childbirth?
- Ninety-nine percent of the worldwide maternal deaths occur in developing countries?
- Approximately 222 million women in developing countries wish to prevent pregnancy, and they are not using modern methods of contraception?
- The worldwide rate of use in modern methods of contraception is 57% as compared to 30% in developing countries?
- Sixteen million adolescents give birth each year, and maternal mortality is the leading cause of death for adolescents in poor and developing countries?
- Between 1990 and 2015, maternal deaths declined by 2.3% worldwide?

United Nations Population Fund. (2014a). ICPD beyond 2014 issue brief: Health: Sexual and reproductive health and rights (SRHR). https://www.unfpa.org/sites/default/files/resource-pdf /Sexual_and_Reproductive_Health_Rights.pdf; and World Health Organization (WHO). (2018a). Maternal mortality. http://www.who .int/news-room/fact-sheets/detail/maternal-mortalit

Reasons cited by Amnesty International (2011) for the issues causing the maternal health crisis include the following:

1. Discrimination and exclusion
2. Socioeconomic and bureaucratic barriers
3. No choice about pregnancy
4. Lack of information about and participation in maternal care and family planning
5. Inadequate postpartum care and staffing and inadequate quality protocols and accountability

These ongoing problems have perpetuated numerous legal and ethical issues associated with reproductive health, such as the challenge for providing basic beneficent-principled care for the mother or the mother and fetus dyad. Other legal and ethical issues, such as self-determination, human rights for choice and equality, and discrimination, are rooted in the bioethical principles of autonomy and justice.

This chapter on ethics in reproductive health illustrates only selected topics, which include theories of moral standing of humans; the maternal–fetal conflict in relation to abortion and pro-life and pro-choice positions, reproductive technology, and genetic screening as well as nursing care of childbearing women.

Moral Standing of Humans

When someone mentions the phrase "moral standing of humans," what comes to mind? Experts do not know exactly at what point full moral standing begins, but Veatch (2003) did note that people tend to view ethical issues of a late-term fetus and postnatal infant as more troublesome than ethical issues during the early phase of sperm and ova and then embryo. He pondered general questions: Are there specific physiological or neurological criteria signaling when full moral standing begins and ends? Could the criteria used for determining when death occurs be the same criteria to determine when life or full moral standing begins? To explore these questions requires more detailed discussion.

First, a general brief explanation is provided for readers who want to develop a moral position on any topic. For example, moral philosophers have argued in a highly complex structure for and against and to differing degrees about every single view of when full moral standing begins and who or what qualifies as having moral standing. Therefore, it is not plausible for nurses and other readers to attempt to come to a strong belief about when full moral standing begins without substantially more in-depth reading than what is presented here or without wide-ranging consideration of the historical arguments within the moral philosophy and bioethical literature. For application of ethical conduct in the majority of everyday nursing decisions in ethics, nurses should refer to the *Code of Ethics for Nurses with Interpretive Statements* (American Nurses Association [ANA], 2015) and nursing ethics books, such as this one and others, for guidance. However, developing a justified belief, such as a stance on full moral standing, requires a much deeper reflection. Nurses must defend their position by reading a broad range of literature that supports the position taken. Taking an ethical stance always requires justifying the position by backing it up with support from the moral experts and the premium and original literature on the ethical topic. This thought is threaded throughout this text.

There are many specific views about the exact point when full moral standing begins, how it fits with the concept of personhood, and whether moral standing denotes only human beings or includes other beings. For the purpose of this chapter, moral standing refers only to human beings. One commonly held belief is that **full moral standing** indicates human beings have or sentient fetuses have the potential for privileges and the capacity to reason and make autonomous decisions. They consider themselves the unique subjects of their own interests and experiences. "To have moral status is to bear direct or independent moral importance" (DeGrazia, 2008, p. 183). Moral importance entails human beings having certain properties possessed by all or most members of their group and the way in which human beings should conduct themselves toward other members of their group.

Like full moral standing, the concept of personhood is most complex, and philosophers frequently use the term **personhood** when deliberating about positions on moral standing. Numerous conflicting positions on personhood exist, some with a legal designation. Many, but not all, philosophers believe that personhood denotes a capacity for human beings to have complex forms of consciousness, in which case personhood would indicate already-born humans, and in fact, it occurs some time later when complex thinking actually develops. Most philosophers agree that sentience of the fetus is required for a determination of some degree of moral standing, but how is personhood related to moral standing? Personhood, defined in this paragraph as an already-born human being, would not enter into the picture during fetal development. From a more complete list, only a few of the common theories of full moral standing related to the embryo and fetus have been selected. The explanations are only brief summaries and do not include personhood as a moral standing view or the for-and-against arguments of each theory.

▶ Potentiality View

Potentiality includes two positions: the basic potentiality view and a broader position known as the future-like-ours argument. The **potentiality view** means a fetus, from the time of conception, possesses the potential to be a person with the same rights and protections that already-born persons appoint to themselves (Feinberg, 1984). According to this view, a fertilized egg does not have the attributes of a person yet, but if it is allowed to develop, it will become a sentient being with rationality. A **sentient being** is a person with awareness, perception, and a capacity for feelings. The overall view of potentiality generally encompasses two assumptions: each person originates as a single-cell zygote at the time of conception, and full moral standing begins at origination. This potentiality position is a basic view held by some moral philosophers.

A broader argument evolving from the basic potentiality view is the **future-like-ours argument** (Marquis, 1989). Pro-life groups have used the future-like-ours argument as a strong contention to suggest that, just like living human beings, a fetus has the potential to become a person with a future full-life experience and the possibility of successful self-actualization goals, a normal life span, rational decision-making abilities, and relationships. This argument indicates a potential for a fetus, once born, to have a future experience of life's full offerings.

Biological View

The biological position is a scientific-based approach for determination of moral status, but this view consists of several theories, each one guided by the biological stage of development of a fetus. DeGrazia (2006) endorsed one view of the biological theory of moral standing, which is presented here. As previously stated, many moral philosophers and bioethicists have believed that sentience of the fetus is essential to determination of moral standing and to have sentience requires the fetus to have awareness, perception, and a capacity for feelings.

Evidence indicates a single-cell zygote is derived from the sperm and ovum; the single-cell zygote is a nonsentient entity and has not yet come into existence. The inference of this **biological view** is that a single-cell zygote does not come into being until the cell has completed the division process, at which time the entity becomes a uniquely individuated human organism (DeGrazia, 2006). During the 2-week division process after the formation of the single-cell zygote, the embryo has the potential to split into two or more identical embryos, known as identical twinning (or multiembryos). Nonidentical fraternal twins are different because they are derived from two separate fertilized eggs, but each one of the embryos has the potential to split into twin embryos that would become identical twins. Based on the process, the single-cell zygote cannot be uniquely individuated until the division has been completed, and

> if not uniquely individuated, the zygote is not yet a unique member of our basic kind (according to the biological view): human organism. By the time all parts of the embryo are differentiated and twinning is precluded, one of us has come into existence. (DeGrazia, 2006, pp. 51–52)

After it has been uniquely individuated, the being becomes a member of the human organism with moral standing.

Interests View

The possession of interests is essential to having rights (Feinberg, 1984). Steinbock (1992, 2006) and DeGrazia (2006) extended the interests–rights requirement to the concepts of sentience and moral standing. In other words, sentience is central to having moral standing, rights, and interests. They believe the more important question to be answered is "Who really counts morally?" The **interests view** requires that a being must have rights and interests at stake, which implies sentience and some degree of moral standing; those interests must matter morally to the being, and the being must be sentient enough to know what could be done to it. The absence of interests means that rights cannot be assumed. In other words, only sentient beings can have a stake in something; nonsentient beings do not have any interests of their own, and moral standing would be difficult to determine. Steinbock (2006) explained her position:

> Embryos are not mere things. They are alive and have the potential to become beings with interests—indeed to become people, like you and me. But their potential to become persons does not give them the moral status or the rights of actual persons. Early embryos, indeed early-gestation fetuses, have no consciousness, no awareness,

no experiences of any kind, even the most rudimentary. . . . Within even the precursor of a nervous system . . . or without consciousness, they cannot have desires; without desires, they cannot have interests. (p. 29)

These different approaches to full moral standing, among the many others not mentioned here, illustrate some profound disagreements. Philosophers of moral standing theories attempt to answer the following questions: When do we come into existence, or sentience? Does life begin at conception? Do sentience and full moral standing occur simultaneously?

▶ Maternal–Fetal Conflict

Maternal–fetal conflict occurs "when a pregnant woman's interests, as she defines them, conflict with the interests of her fetus, as defined by the woman's physician" (Tran, 2004, p. 76). A maternal–fetal conflict can occur when a pregnant woman's treatment is hazardous to the fetus or when a pregnant woman does not comply with a physician's recommendations that are traditionally believed to nurture the fetus's growth and development. This ethical issue relates to each person's right to life versus the possibility of bringing harm to one person when treating the other of the two biologically connected persons. In years past, when physicians and nurses cared for a pregnant woman, they considered in detail the mother and fetus as one patient unit. Physicians contemplated all viewpoints of the care and treatment of the whole patient, both the mother and fetus together, by comparing the perceived benefits of the whole compared with perceived combined burdens. The dual-care concept gained prominence during the same era of the development of fetal medicine and treatment (Iris et al., 2009).

Historically, some of the reasons for maternal–child conflict included lifestyle choices and issues, such as abortion and use of substances, refusal of treatment by the mother, issues of maternal brain death, and issues surrounding occupational health (Coutts, 1990; Post, 1996). Authors commonly have cited abortion as their first example among the various reasons for maternal–fetal conflict, but a few experts believe abortion is not even a maternal–fetal conflict (Coutts, 1990).

Society, nurses, and physicians share an overall goal of optimal pregnancy outcomes. However, with the dual-care frame of mind, physicians and nurses should consider the best care and medical treatment possible for the mother and fetus separately and distinctly, yet they should realize the biological link. The basic dispute in the maternal–fetus conflict is human rights for each, resulting in ethical issues embedded in a dilemma between the principle of respect for autonomy and the moral standing of the woman and a principle of respect for autonomy of the fetus. Other issues surrounding the maternal–fetal conflict focus on a dilemma between the principle of respect for the autonomy of the woman person and the principle of nonmaleficence of the fetus. Ludwig (2008) posed these questions:

- What happens when medical therapy is indicated for one patient, yet it is contraindicated for the other?
- When does the fetus or newborn become a person?
- People have rights. Does a fetus have rights?
- What about obtaining court orders to force pregnant women to comply?

▶ Conflict of Rights Issues

Reproductive Rights

A woman's decision to have a baby, not to have a baby, or to have an abortion are among the most critical decisions she will make in her life. Although a woman may involve significant others, this type of decision is intensely personal, and it is one she will hope to make on her own without coercion or mandates from healthcare professionals or federal and state governments.

One of the ethical questions is "Does a woman have a right to have a child?" Infertility, for instance, is not a life-threatening disorder, but it does cause undue suffering and shame to millions of women and couples. A legal question is "If there is a right to reproduce, should it include the right to unlimited and scarce resources?" As technology advances, more questions begin to surface; for example, should fertility medicine be regulated? Healthcare professionals must attempt to resolve the question of how society should strike a balance among the various options of procreation, reproduction, testing, and maternal rights.

Many times, legal rights and moral rights overlap because lawmakers often legislate the policies into laws to enforce certain rights. **Moral rights** include liberty rights and claim rights (Mahoney, 2007). **Liberty rights**, sometimes called negative rights, are those rights a person can impose on others without a fear of someone or some group preventing those rights from being exercised. Liberty rights include freedom of speech, autonomy, privacy, and others as stated in the first 10 amendments of the U.S. Constitution. Health care in the United States is a liberty right.

Claim rights, sometimes called positive or welfare rights, are those rights owed to people through active and positive steps taken by others or groups to ensure the claim is met. There are two population exceptions in the United States to healthcare liberty rights— low-income people and elders—and they fall under claim rights. Social federal and state programs help ensure fulfillment and preservation of claim rights.

If there is a right to reproduction, is it a liberty right, a claim right, or both? In addition, does an unborn fetus or child have healthcare rights? Answers to these questions remain unclear, but most experts agree all healthcare rights are of critical importance to everyone. Reproductive rights are about human rights, quality health care, choice, liberation from enforced sexual pleasures and abuse, and population growth and distribution.

Civil Liberties and Legal Decisions

Historical records indicate that multiple and complex ethical, legal, and political issues have arisen, including criminalization of pregnant women. Courts have ordered physician-sanctioned cesarean deliveries for the sake of the fetus against the mother's wishes; pregnant women have been prosecuted for their abuse of alcohol and other drugs; and courts have ordered pregnant women to receive blood transfusions in life-threatening or other conditions, even when the women were refusing blood transfusions because of religious beliefs (American Civil Liberties Union [ACLU], 1997; Chandis & Williams, 2006). Issues of abortion and forced treatments tap into questions of whether the fetus is viewed as a person, has a right to life, or is viewed as having equal moral status as the mother versus a pregnant woman's right to bodily integrity and the right to privacy, dignity, and choice.

It is important for the reader to know the ACLU's opinion of government officials tampering with women's rights during pregnancy. In a 1997 article titled "Coercive and Punitive Governmental Responses to Women's Conduct During Pregnancy," the ACLU created strong statements, as highlighted in the quoted passages in the following Legal Perspective box.

Since the ACLU's position in 1997, various states have proceeded with laws or rulings criminalizing mothers for certain behaviors. In 2013, the State of Tennessee passed the Tennessee Fetal Assault Law (SB1391) as a 2-year trial providing for the prosecution of any woman illegally using a narcotic drug while pregnant if her child was born addicted to or

LEGAL PERSPECTIVE: WOMEN'S REPRODUCTIVE RIGHTS VIOLATED

A decade ago [in the 1980s], we saw a rash of cases in which government officials zealously embraced a misguided mission to protect fetuses by attempting to control the conduct of pregnant women. . . . Inevitably, such actions backfire: women who fear the government's "pregnancy police" will avoid prenatal care altogether, and both they and their fetuses will suffer as a result.

The ACLU . . . defended many of the women who were subject to coercive or punitive state actions. We won case after case, and attempts to bully and punish pregnant women eventually diminished.

Recently, however, we have seen this dangerous trend revive. (Arresting the Pregnancy Police)

Coercive and punitive treatment of pregnant women violates the civil liberties of individual women and fosters distrust of health care providers. . . . An influential 1988 Illinois Supreme Court decision, *Stallman v. Youngquist*, warned courts not to make "mother and child . . . legal adversaries from the moment of conception until birth." Rejecting a child's claim of damages from its mother, the court wrote:

> Holding a mother liable for the unintentional infliction of prenatal injuries subjects to state scrutiny all the decisions a woman must make in attempting to carry a pregnancy to term, and infringes on her right to privacy and bodily autonomy.

> Although we may not always approve of a woman's conduct during pregnancy, we must insist women be offered educational, social, and medical services that can persuade them to make the wisest and healthiest choices. Coercion is both a counterproductive and an illegal alternative. (The Implications for Reproductive Rights in General)

American Civil Liberties Union (ACLU). (1997). *Coercive and punitive governmental responses to women's conduct during pregnancy*. https://www.aclu .org/other/coercive-and-punitive-governmental-responses-womens-conduct-during-pregnancy

harmed by the narcotic drug. The first woman in Tennessee to be arrested for a misdemeanor used an illegal drug while pregnant (ACLU, 2014). The woman admitted to using methamphetamine after the baby tested positive for it. Castelli, the director of the ACLU, stated that the new law is unconstitutional and singles out mothers with substance abuse problems. The other side of the argument involves prosecutors and law enforcement officers who argued in support of the law because they believe it is the only way to help the mothers get into a drug treatment program and prevent harm to their babies (Kemp, 2014).

The ACLU (2014) in Tennessee and medical experts immediately began to challenge this criminal law. In January 2017 after the trial period had concluded, the State of Tennessee discontinued the Tennessee Fetal Assault Law (2018, SB1391) as no longer in effect. Republican Andrew Farmer of East Tennessee stated that he had heard too many stories of addicted women who were scared away from prenatal care because they feared they would have jail time (Farmer, 2016). Medical experts and some law officials believed that exercising the law had many unintended consequences.

Since the latter part of the 20th century, astounding advances have occurred in reproductive technologies, so much so that they have sparked public, ethical, and political scrutiny concerning a woman's private choice (autonomy) versus public regulation and law (Harris & Holm, 2000). Sometimes, nurses believe they are caught in the middle, and they do not know how to manage the care related to the maternal–fetal conflict. In Provisions 1 and 2 of the *Code of Ethics for Nurses with Interpretive Statements*, the ANA (2015) clarified nurses' roles in terms of appropriate ethical behavior and action toward patients. Included in these two code provisions are concepts to which nurses are ethically bound, such as the respect for human dignity, the patient's right to self-determination, a commitment to the patient's interest, the respect of privacy and confidentiality, and the protection of the patient's rights. Individual nurses need to make certain they follow these ethical guidelines in a nonjudgmental and caring way. Protecting the woman's rights and decisions and maintaining dialogue of the highest quality among the woman, her family, and other healthcare professionals are most critical because of the deeply sensitive issues women face in reproduction, procreation, or abortion. The manner in which nurses interact and intervene with these patients often will affect the patient's health and emotional outcomes.

▶ Abortion

The center of the pro-choice and pro-life debates is about human rights: the right to life of the fetus or the woman's right to control her own body by choosing whether to carry a pregnancy to term, have a baby, and parent it. Often, a woman is not sure of her plans for the future and must make a difficult decision about whether to have an abortion, carry the fetus and parent it, or give it up for adoption. She may struggle about making her choice and most likely will experience mild to severe discomfort in her decision.

The debaters of each group argue about the position they support by providing rationales and justifications about when they believe life begins and sentience and moral standing occur during fetal development. Because pro-choice and pro-life debaters justify their claims and arguments on each side, the dilemma is deadlocked with no hope for resolution. These diametrically opposed sides have ethical, political, legal, and religious implications. Opposition even occurs regarding the use of labels. The opposing groups have historically been labeled as pro-choice and pro-life, but as both sides tightened the reins on their beliefs and values, the pro-choice groups began labeling pro-life groups as anti-choice. The rationale behind this decision was that pro-life groups were making claims about pro-choice groups not valuing life. Some pro-life groups refer to themselves as pro-life while a few pro-choice groups refer to pro-life groups as anti-choice. This labeling controversy has somewhat diminished. The author of this chapter takes the stance that the argument about labels is largely irresolvable. Therefore, the terms *pro-choice* and *pro-life* are used because of their widespread use in the media.

On January 22, 1973, the U.S. Supreme Court ruled in the landmark decision of *Roe v. Wade* that the Constitution of the United States protects a pregnant woman's liberty to choose to have an abortion based on the right of privacy. Although abortion, especially in the first trimester, is legal in many countries, intense moral and political scrutiny and legal actions have continued to occur, particularly in the United States. Almost a half century after its initial ruling, the *Roe v. Wade* decision of 1973 was officially reversed by the U.S. Supreme Court on June 24, 2022, in the case of *Dobbs v. Jackson Women's Health Organization.* Supreme Court justices voted 6-3 that the Constitution does not support a woman's right to an abortion, which means that abortion no longer exists as a Constitutional right in the United States. In the 1973 *Roe v. Wade* court ruling, states could not make laws banning abortions in the first or second trimester, except for certain reasons. In the third trimester, states could make laws banning abortions; unless a third-trimester abortion was critical to a woman's survival, the woman was required to follow her state law. Since the decision was overturned on June 24, 2022, regulation of abortion was given to the states, which now are making their own laws on the various restrictions on abortion.

The support for the *Roe v. Wade* decision of 1973 included a landscape of political and moral positions from women, politicians, and other protesters from pro-life and pro-choice groups. A particular instance was in the form of an article written by a moral philosopher 2 years before the *Roe v. Wade* decision. Thomson (1971) wrote a classic and well-known article titled "A defense of abortion," which served as a foundation for the abortion debate by the court and the protesters. At the beginning of her article, Thomson agreed that every person has a right to life and this right is extended to fetuses. Then, to make her argument, she stated that she was pretending a fetus is a person because it, in fact, becomes a human person at some time before birth. Her conclusive premise was, even assuming the fetus has a right to life, the fetus morally could not infringe on the mother's own right to control her body or use her body to stay alive.

Abortion is a term that sometimes refers to **induced abortion**, which is the result of a woman's intentional termination of a pregnancy either artificially or therapeutically (MedicineNet.com, 2021). Induced abortion is the core of the pro-choice and pro-life debate. The debaters argue with political fervor and bitterness, sometimes resulting in violence, about the legality or rightness and wrongness of a woman's choosing to terminate her pregnancy. In the pro-choice view, abortion is almost always permissible and can be justified.

From 1973, after *Roe v. Wade*, to 2021, there have been more than 61 million registered abortions in the United States. Since 1980, there have been more than 1.6 billion abortions worldwide (Guttmacher Institute, 2021a). These statistics were almost all considered documented surgical abortions. However, the Pharmacists of Life organization estimated that as many as 250 million babies aborted chemically, such as with mifepristone, since 1973 just in the United States. In a 4-year span between 2010 and 2014, there were more than 54 million abortions each year worldwide, and 45% of those were unsafe and mostly in developing countries (WHO, 2021). Deaths from unsafe abortions in women in developing countries are disproportionately higher as compared to developed countries. Of the unsafe abortions, 30 women die per 100,000 in developed countries as compared to 520 deaths per 100,000 in sub-Saharan Africa.

Documented reasons for abortions include rape, incest, physical life of mother, physical health of mother, fetal health, mental health of mother, and personal choice. Personal choices included being too young, not ready for responsibility, too immature, and inadequate economic means. Additional reasons include rejecting a change of lifestyle, single motherhood, a poor relationship, or additional children.

Federal Abortion Ban Preventing Partial-Birth Abortion

The National Right to Life Committee (NRLC) and other pro-life groups for years have campaigned for equal rights and protections for the unborn fetus, based on the viewpoint of the fetus as a human life—one that, if not a person yet, has the potential to be a person. On November 5, 2003, President George W. Bush signed into law the Partial-Birth Abortion Ban Act of 2003 (Daliard, 2004).

The definitions of partial-birth abortion and late-term abortion can be misunderstood by healthcare professionals and providers. **Partial-birth abortion**, a nonmedical term, refers to late-term or third-trimester abortions by way of a procedure called intact dilation and extraction (abbreviated as intact D&E) (Shimabukuro, 2008). In other words, a **late-term abortion** consists of physicians delivering a live fetus vaginally, yet only partially, for the sole purpose of terminating a pregnancy by way of an intact D&E. The term *partially* means that for head presentation, the entire head must be outside the mother's vagina before the fetus can be terminated, and for breech presentation, any part of the fetus's trunk past its navel must be outside the mother's vagina before the fetus can be terminated.

An historical presentation of the last two decades will update the reader on some events that have led to the current state of the protections and restrictions of abortion. Since the federal ban of partial-birth abortion of 2003, many states agreed with the ACLU (2007) by striking down the ban, ruling it unconstitutional, whereas other states have been pushing for the abortion ban to apply as early as 12 or 13 weeks or earlier gestation, a push viewed by the ACLU as deceptive. The time line of 12 to 13 weeks trickles into the first trimester of pregnancy, meaning that the term *partial-birth abortion* could no longer be used; rather, the term *abortion* must be applied.

The U.S. Supreme Court reviewed the Federal Abortion Ban because of the strike downs by several states, even though some states are continuing to support the ban, which has resulted in unresolved issues, anger, and moral fanaticism on each side of the argument. The public anxiously awaited the final decision, and on April 18, 2007, under the direction of Chief Justice John Roberts, the U.S. Supreme Court announced a 5-4 decision to uphold the Federal Abortion Ban. According to the ACLU (2007), the U.S. Supreme Court's decision of upholding the ban undermined the core tenet of *Roe v. Wade*: a woman's health must remain unrivaled. No health exception for women was written in the law. In a written dissent, Justice Ruth Bader Ginsburg made a strong criticism by warning the majority justices they were placing women's health in danger and undermining women's battle for equality. Justice Ginsburg stated, "the Act, and the Court's defense of it, cannot be understood as anything other than an effort to chip away at a right declared again and again by the Court—and with increasing comprehension of its centrality to women's lives" (ACLU, 2007, para. 5). For a condensed historical time line of the Federal Abortion Ban, refer to ProCon.Org.'s discussion on the "History of Abortion" (2021).

Before and since the 2007 Supreme Court decision, each state continued to develop laws to limit the circumstances in which a woman may have an induced abortion (Guttmacher Institute, 2021b). All states have one or more codifications and regulations (ProCon.Org., 2021). In fact, since 1973, there were 1,193 restrictions by various states on *Roe v. Wade*. Since 2010, state abortion restrictions have soared for a variety of reasons, including the 20-week abortion bans, ultrasound laws, fetal heartbeat laws, or 6-week bans, etc. "Between 2011 and 2017, states enacted over 400 new abortion restrictions" (ProCon.Org., 2021, Section State Restrictions).

Funding of abortions has been largely determined by the ruling political party. For instances, President Barack Obama rescinded the amendment banning federal funding for abortions, President Donald Trump reinstated it, and President Joe Biden rescinded it (ProCon.Org, 2021).

By 2020, at least seven states had placed Covid-19 restrictions on abortions by listing them as a nonessential medical procedure, but federal judges blocked most of these restrictions (ProCon.Org.). Some states have already passed laws on various levels of restricted abortion access. Until the U.S. Supreme Court justices reversed the 1973 *Roe v. Wade* decision on June 24, 2022, Mississippi had been waiting since 2020 to write restrictions that would ban nearly all abortions after 15 weeks of pregnancy. In May 2021, Texas passed a law that does not allow pregnant women to obtain abortions after 6 weeks. The U.S. Supreme Court did not block the Texas law. Texas then banned all abortions to await the *Roe v. Wade* ruling. Many Texans continue to travel every month to other states for abortions. As this book went to publication, Texas had temporarily resumed abortions up to 6 weeks of pregnancy. Nearly all states have considered or adopted laws to protect or place various restrictions on abortion.

As of September 2021, other states were considering the adoption of similar abortion laws. States continue to write various levels of abortion restrictions. States are anticipating the U.S. Supreme Court to review and potentially vote on a landmark decision, which could leave states to create their own abortion laws, either partially or completely.

Pro-Choice Versus Pro-Life Views

Pro-Choice View

In the pro-choice view, a common argument is that abortion is legally permissible, regardless of the morality involved. A woman has a basic right to make up her own mind about choices of pregnancy or abortion, and her right always prevails over any other right, including any fetal rights. At the core of the pro-choice stance is the right of privacy based on the U.S. Constitution, U.S. Declaration of Independence, and the worldwide Universal Declaration of Human Rights. Sentience, moral status, and personhood are among the various arguments used in the pro-choice view.

To the pro-choice group, abortion is morally and legally permissible. Many people contend a fetus that cannot survive outside a woman's body is not considered viable; therefore, a fetus cannot override the woman's right to choose an abortion when the fetus is not viable outside the womb. In this pro-choice view, there are various opinions about the beginning of life. Two of those opinions are (1) the fetus does not have human life until the mother is in the 17th week of gestation, or (2) the fetus with sentience and moral status has human life at the seventh month of gestation, when its nervous system has fully developed.

The pro-choice group supports the use of emergency contraceptives. **Emergency contraception (EC)** is defined as postcoital birth control measures preventing pregnancy (Planned Parenthood, 2021). Two types of EC exist, which are both considered early abortion, after sexual intercourse methods for an unintended pregnancy. One option is known as the morning-after pill, which includes ulipristal acetate (Ella), levonorgestrel pill (Plan B). The morning after pill, ulipristal acetate, must be taken within 120 hours (or 5 days) after having unprotected sex, and the levonorgestrel pill must be taken within 72 hours (or 3 days).

The other option of EC is the use of a copper IUD, which is 99% effective. The copper IUD must be inserted within 120 hours (or 5 days) after having unprotected sex. A healthcare provider needs to insert the copper IUD, as either a postcoital procedure or a method to prevent pregnancy before anticipated sexual intercourse.

The arguments do not ever cease as to when a fetus becomes a person—at conception, when the heartbeat develops, when the nervous system develops, when it is considered viable outside the womb, or when the fetus begins the process of thinking. From trying to determine the personhood of the fetus, people

---

LEGAL PERSPECTIVE: SUMMARY OF STATE REGULATIONS FOR HAVING AN INDUCED ABORTION

- Licensed physician and/or performed in hospital: required by a majority of states
- Gestational limits: prohibited by 43 states except where necessary for mother's life
- Partial-birth abortion: prohibited by 21 states
- Healthcare providers and hospitals allowance of refusal to participate in abortion: allowed by a majority of states
- Waiting periods required before an abortion procedure: mandated by 25 states
- Parental involvement mandated: required by 37 states to have some type of parental involvement if a minor is asking for an abortion procedure, required by 27 states for one or both parents to consent to the procedure if a minor, and required by 10 states one or both parents should only be notified

Three other regulations delineated by states include public funding allocations, private insurance restrictions, and mandated counseling before an abortion.

Data from Guttmacher Institute. (2018, June). An overview of abortion laws. https://www.guttmacher.org/print/state-policy/explore/overview-abortion-laws

ETHICAL REFLECTION: PRO-CHOICE VIEWS ON EQUAL MORAL STANDING FOR MOTHER AND FETUS

Pro-choice groups believe if a woman and fetus are warranted as having equal moral standing, as believed by pro-life groups, a woman's rights are weakened, causing the woman and the fetus to be at odds with each other. Some pro-life groups argue that in special circumstances the woman may have an abortion, such as in cases of incest or rape or if the infant is severely deformed.

What are your thoughts? Are these circumstances viewed as a double standard, meaning abortion is accepted when the procedure is subjectively needed?

person living outside the womb. Historically, unless a mother's life was threatened, the embryo (or fetus) was protected because it is worthy of respect yet vulnerable to murder and harm. This protection begins at the time of conception, but it especially applies in the second and third trimesters.

Most pro-life groups believe that life begins at conception as a single-cell zygote and moral status is acquired at conception; the belief is taken based on faith values and cultural origins rather than scientific, biological evidence. Opinions vary among pro-life groups as to when personhood begins in lieu of conception (see Ethical Reflection: Pro-Life Views on When Personhood Begins for some of these times).

Pro-life groups sometimes quote several passages from the Bible, but the Roman Catholic Church's position about abortion is a little more complex (Harris & Holm, 2003). According to the Roman Catholic Church, the whole issue regarding the morality of abortion stems from the greater question of when the fetus receives a soul. Because many interpretations of the Bible exist, the Roman Catholic Church has taken a general stance on this moral issue, as Harris and Holm (2003) stated, "because killing is such a grave moral wrong, one should act cautiously and presume that there may be ensoulment from conception. . . . Abortion and the destruction of embryos should therefore be treated as the killing of an ensouled being" (p. 122).

should use rational thinking and employ the highest possible moral importance.

Pro-Life View

In the pro-life group, the personhood view stems from a fundamental understanding of the embryo or fetus as a person. Most pro-life groups argue that life and full moral status begin at conception and abortion is immoral and murderous and should be illegal. According to this view, the embryo, from the time of conception and throughout the development of the fetus, has the same right to life due each

ETHICAL REFLECTION: PRO-LIFE VIEWS ON WHEN PERSONHOOD BEGINS

- At conception
- After the fertilized egg splits into two cells a few days after conception
- Twelve days after conception, when the fertilized ovum has attached itself to the uterine lining
- Two weeks from conception, when the yellow streak develops, which is the neural tube that protects the backbone and prevents splitting into two embryos (before the yellow streak develops, the embryo may split into identical twins)

(continues)

ETHICAL REFLECTION: PRO-LIFE VIEWS ON WHEN PERSONHOOD BEGINS

(continued)

- Three weeks from conception as the fetus begins to develop body parts
- End of first month when the fetus is about ¼ inch long (size of grain of rice)
- Five weeks or sooner from conception, when the heartbeat begins
- Seven weeks from conception as the first brain waves are sensed
- Two months, and again at 3 months, from conception when the fetus begins to resemble a human being and is about 1 inch long
- Four months from conception, when the fetus has its own differentiating characteristics and is about 6 inches long and weighs 4 ounces
- Twenty-three to 24 weeks from conception, when the fetus is said to become viable and is about 12 inches long and weighs 2 pounds
- Twenty-seven weeks from conception, when the fetus's higher brain begins to function
- Seven months from conception, when the fetus is 14 inches long and weights 2 to 4 pounds, and is likely to survive
- Eight months from conception, when most internal organs have developed, the brain continues to develop rapidly, and the fetus is 18 inches long and weights up to 5 pounds
- At birth, only after delivery and breathing is separate from the woman's body, and the fetus is about 17 to 19 inches long and weighs from 5.5 pounds to 6.5 pounds.

What are your thoughts on personhood?
What is your opinion on when the fetus becomes a person?

Cleveland Clinic. (2020, April 16). Fetal development. Stages of growth. https://my.clevelandclinic.org/health/articles/7247-fetal-development-stages-of-growth

Speaking Out

Legal and moral arguments about abortion and women's reproductive rights continue. NARAL Pro-Choice America and the National Right to the Life Committee (NRLC, n.d.) speak out. NARAL Pro-Choice America (2021) publicizes its belief that the choice of abortion should be women's right based on the *Roe v. Wade* federal decision in 1973. The NRLC also publicizes its longstanding mission, which is the right to life. The following is the first sentence from the mission statement of the NRLC:

> The mission of National Right to Life is to protect and defend the most fundamental right of humankind, the right to life of every innocent human being from the beginning of life to natural death.

ETHICAL REFLECTION: WHAT IS YOUR VIEW ON THE MORALITY OF ABORTION?

After reading all the arguments on rights and human life in this section, **what do you believe about abortion?** Address your views to the following points, and use an ethical framework (theory, approach, or principle) to justify your answers:

- If most abortions during the first trimester are considered legally permissible, how should one view a woman taking an over-the-counter morning-after pill?
- What are your ethical views on abortion?
- When do you believe human life begins?
- When do you believe a human life becomes a person?

Please describe these points by clarifying your own beliefs and values regarding these issues. Remember, there is no one right answer. These views are your opinions based on your values, an ethical theory justification, and readings in this text and other sources.

A final ethical reflection:

■ If you are giving nursing care to a woman who just received a partial-birth abortion by way of an intact D&E, describe your own beliefs concerning partial-birth abortion.

ETHICAL REFLECTION: DISENFRANCHISED GRIEF—FORBIDDING THE GRIEF OF ABORTION

The Words of Tina

If you regret an abortion, nobody wants to hear about it. After all, there's nothing anyone can do to fix the problem. So you have to tell yourself what happened was good—and everyone around you tells you the same thing. After that, I knew I would never bring up the subject again.

The Words of Kathy

Dear Mom, I'm sorry I never told you the truth about my abortion for so long. I told you I was having minor surgery—female problems. Remember? . . . And what really kills me the most is that you and Daddy came to see me that night in the hospital . . . I was so scared—scared you'd find out what really happened that day. Man, I was hurting inside. And there you two were standing at the foot of my bed extending your love and concern. Mom, didn't you notice I couldn't even look you in the eyes? And over the years the times I turned from you whenever the abortion issue was raised? I can still see your face the moment I finally told you. Eight years later . . . you never looked up at me . . . [and] you sat quietly and gently spoke to me. Just as long as I kept my shameful secret, you were willing to keep it too. . . . Oh how I wish you had been able to talk about it . . . to cry with me, to help me get through that horrible time. You knew it all . . . but we never talked. I was so desperately alone.

Reproduced from Burke, T. (with Reardon, D.). (2002). *Forbidden grief: The unspoken pain of abortion*. Acorn.

America's first document as a new nation, The Declaration of Independence, states that we are all "created equal" and endowed by our Creator "with certain unalienable Rights, that among these are Life . . ." Our Founding Fathers emphasized the preeminence of the right to "Life" by citing it first among the unalienable rights this nation was established to secure.

National Right to Life carries out its lifesaving mission by promoting respect for the worth and dignity of every individual human being, born or unborn, including unborn children from their beginning; those newly born; persons with disabilities; older people; and other vulnerable people, especially those who cannot defend themselves. Our areas of concern include abortion, infanticide, euthanasia, assisted suicide, and the killing of unborn children for their stem cells. (n.d., para. 3)

Many times, women who are pro-choice and believe in women's reproductive rights receive abortions but do not necessarily want the procedure. They may find themselves in situations of unintended pregnancy where they must have an abortion for reasons already described in this section. Just because a woman believes in her right to choose in no way means her intentional decision to have an abortion and lose her fetus will not be emotionally traumatizing (Burke, 2002). Sometimes, women feel restricted from expressing their grief because they fear no one wants to hear about it. They may believe they cannot discuss the abortion or loss of their fetus with anyone because it needs to be kept a deep, dark secret. Some women may believe they do not have permission to grieve openly for the loss of their fetus, and therefore they experience extreme and extended sorrow, which is a type of grief called **disenfranchised grief**. When one is not allowed to grieve or must hide it, the grief process is prolonged and far worse. "Such 'impacted' [disenfranchised] grief can even become integrated into one's personality and touch every aspect of one's life" (Burke, 2002, p. 51).

▸ ## Reproductive Technology

On July 14, 1978, the first test-tube baby, Louise Joy Brown, was born in Great Britain (Louise Brown biography, 2014). The Browns had tried to conceive for 9 years. But Lesley Brown's fallopian tubes were blocked, so they tried in vitro fertilization.

Reproductive failure can be emotionally and financially devastating to couples. Because of infertility, more than 1% of all infants born in the United States are conceived with assisted reproductive technology (Centers for Disease Control and Prevention [CDC], 2014). Based on the CDC's preliminary data on successes in assisted reproductive technology, there were

> 330,773 ART cycles performed at 448 reporting clinics in the United States during 2019, resulting in 77,998 live births (deliveries of one or more living infants) and 83,946 live born infants. Of the 330,773 ART cycles performed in 2019, 121,086 were egg or embryo banking cycles in which all resulting eggs or embryos were frozen for future use. (CDC. 2019a, Preliminary Data)

From 2006 to 2010 in the United States, 12% of all women of reproductive age or their partners used infertility services, such as assisted reproductive technology. As women's ages increase, so too does their use of infertility services; in fact, 20% of women ages 35 to 44 have used infertility services (CDC, 2019a).

Infertility is generally defined as a woman not being able to become pregnant after the couple has tried for 1 year. The term **assisted reproductive technology (ART)** refers to the handling and management of sperm and eggs and every kind of fertility treatment or drug used for the purpose of retrieving eggs to be used in the treatment (CDC, 2019a). Treatments not included under the ART umbrella consist of those in which only sperm are managed, such as artificial insemination, surgical procedures on women or men, or drugs involving infertility when eggs will not be retrieved.

The CDC recognizes five types of ART (CDC, 2021):

1. In vitro fertilization (IVF): Extracting the woman's eggs, fertilizing them with sperm outside the body, and then transferring the embryo through the cervix into the uterus

2. Intracytoplasmic sperm injection (ICSI): Injecting a single sperm into a mature egg, a method often used for couples with male infertility

3. Conventional fertilization: Placing the egg with many sperm outside the body into a petri dish until one sperm fertilizes the egg, which is another method used for couples with male infertility

4. Gamete intrafallopian transfer (GIFT): Transferring unfertilized eggs and sperm into the fallopian tubes and then transferring the embryo into the uterus (rarely used in the United States)

5. Zygote intrafallopian transfer (ZIFT): Fertilizing eggs in the laboratory with sperm and then transferring the zygote into the fallopian tubes (rarely used in the United States)

Embryos resulting from IVF can be frozen until the time when the woman or couple will need one or more of them. The embryo is then unfrozen and implanted without significant risks to the fetus.

The concerns over the future of human life and family structure, human cloning, the less than optimal success rate of ART, and the cost of reproductive technology give society enough reasons to ask a most basic ethical question: Should reproductive technology be used at all (Munson, 2004)? The cost of reproductive technology is a global concern because of scarce medical and healthcare resources. In a Center for American Progress report on future choices of ART, Arons (2007) stated that assisted reproductive technologies has prompted Americans to ask questions about society and family.

ETHICAL REFLECTION: WHAT ARE THE REPRODUCTIVE HEALTH RIGHTS IN THE UNITED STATES?

- Reproductive health in the United States is currently a liberty right, one a couple may pursue without interference from any governmental agency, provided there are no laws against what is being pursued. Many reimbursement agencies do not pay for some of these expensive reproductive medical procedures.
- How should private insurance companies and other reimbursement agencies weigh the priorities of healthcare resource allocation and distribution for those who are dying and critically ill against those who believe they have an autonomous right to a child?
- What does the future hold for autonomy and rights to reproductive services?
- How will distributive justice be managed?

Ethical Issues of Reproductive Technology

There are specific ethical issues about reproductive technologies other than the broad ones already mentioned. These issues are divided into five groups: (1) the risks resulting from technology; (2) surrogacy (for donor eggs, embryo donation, or carrying fetuses); (3) the handling of surplus reproductive products, such as eggs or embryos that are not used; (4) the implications of sperm sorting or gender selection; and (5) genetic modification and enhancement (Frankel, 2003; Wachbroit & Wasserman, 2003).

The first group of ethical issues involves risks created as a result of technology. Examples include ART and freezing embryos. One risk is multiple-infant live births. Worldwide, millions of babies have been born from IVF. The ethical principles include beneficence, nonmaleficence, and justice—promoting human good for the woman or the couple who strongly desire a baby, doing no harm to the fetuses, and distribution and allocation of resources during the process and after the births.

The second group of ethical issues pertains to third-party involvement through donor eggs and embryos and carrying fetuses through surrogacy. **Surrogacy** is a particularly good example, such as when a man can fertilize the woman's egg but the woman cannot carry the fetus to term for some reason. In this case, the couple may ask a surrogate woman to carry the fetus to term, a process called **gestational surrogacy**. Other types of surrogacy include **traditional surrogacy**, in which the surrogate uses her own eggs and is artificially inseminated with semen from the prospective father and carries the fetus to birth; **egg donation**, in which a woman donates her eggs for IVF with specific semen; and **embryo donation**, when a couple with a history of past successful pregnancy and delivery donates embryos to prospective couples seeking parenthood by way of IVF and implantation.

The ethical issues regarding surrogacy are many. Who owns the infant after it is delivered by the surrogate? Who is the mother—the woman who produced the egg or the one who carried the fetus to term and delivered it? Is the meaning of family integrity or biological relationships at stake, or does it matter? Other concerns are legal issues: finding a legal way to pay the surrogate woman for her time and effort because the selling of children usually is illegal, avoiding treating babies as commodities, and avoiding exploitation of financially needy women (Munson, 2004; Wachbroit & Wasserman, 2003). As the population increases, so will surrogacy. The principles involved are autonomy and nonmaleficence. These principles involve the issues of a couple's feelings about the right to choose; the surrogate's right to choose to be a surrogate; and doing no harm to the outcome of the child, the family biological structure, and individual freedoms.

The third group of ethical issues consists of **surplus reproductive products** resulting from technology. For example, because the success rate is low for IVF, a woman may have stored many frozen eggs in an attempt for a successful pregnancy. After the woman is pregnant, what happens to the remaining eggs? Many of the eggs are fertilized, but only a few are implanted. What happens to these embryos? For people who believe life begins at conception, is it considered murderous to destroy the remainder of the fertilized eggs? Beliefs about the right to life, the point at which life and full moral standing begin, and the question of whether destroying embryos is murder are at the center of this debate, as are the principles of autonomy and nonmaleficence.

The fourth group of ethical issues is called **sperm sorting**, or **gender selection**, which is advanced technology that enables persons to create the kind of child they want to have, to balance the family, or to prevent X-linked or other genetic diseases (Harris & Holm, 2003). The medical procedure through which sperm sorting is accomplished is called **preimplantation genetic diagnosis (PGD)**. Family balancing, or evening out gender representation in children, is a concept used to help justify and promote the use of gender selection prior to implantation. The principles to be considered in sperm sorting, family balancing, and gender selection include autonomy, beneficence, nonmaleficence, and justice.

X-linked diseases occur in 1 of every 1,000 live births overall; more than 500 X-linked diseases have now been identified, including hemophilia, Duchenne muscular dystrophy, and X-linked mental retardation. Other genetic diseases identified through PGD include Fanconi anemia, thalassemia, sickle-cell disease, neurofibromatosis, and many others (University of Minnesota Masonic Cancer Center, n.d.). Sperm sorting dramatically increases a couple's chance of having an unaffected child.

The last ethical issue, the fifth group, is **inheritable genetic modification (IGM)**, which is a procedure used to modify genes along the germ lines that are transmitted to

ETHICAL REFLECTION: MOLLY AND ADAM NASH

Adam Nash was born in Colorado on August 29, 2000. He had been an embryo that was sorted, screened, and selected from at least 12 embryos from the Nash couple, Lisa and Jack, for the purpose of tissue matching for their critically ill daughter, Molly.

Molly Nash was born to the Nash parents on July 4, 1994, with Fanconi anemia, a fatal autosomal recessive bone marrow failure (aplastic anemia), which is treatable only with a bone marrow transplant from a sibling's umbilical cord blood. At the time, the success rate of a bone marrow transplant from an unrelated donor was only 42%, but from a sibling, the success rate increased to 85%.

The Nash parents, with support of physicians, made the decision to have preimplantation genetic testing on their embryos in the hopes of saving their only child. In the process, 12 of Lisa's eggs were fertilized by Jack's sperm via IVF; two of the embryos had Fanconi anemia and were discarded. Of the remaining 10 embryos, only 1 matched Molly's tissue. This one became Adam Nash.

Data from Grady, D. (2000, October 4). Son conceived to provide blood cells for daughter. *New York Times*, p. 24. https://www.nytimes.com/2000/10/04/us/son-conceived-to-provide-blood-cells-for-daughter.html

offspring (Frankel, 2003). Stem-cell research could help prevent genetic diseases from occurring in families through the generations by modifying the germ lines of the embryos. Genetic traits in the embryo can be enhanced with IGM. What if researchers could help a couple create the perfect baby? In 1932, Aldous Huxley suggested in his book *Brave New World* that genetics and reproductive technology would be society's worst nightmare because of the government's involvement in these activities (Frankel, 2003).

ETHICAL REFLECTION: ARE COUPLES JUSTIFIED IN USING ONE PERSON FOR THE PURPOSE OF CREATING ANOTHER PERSON?

What are your thoughts?

- Were the Nashs justified in creating Adam for the purpose of helping Molly get well? In other words, should humans be used as a means to an end? Explore the rationale for using Kant's deontology theory in the Nashs' situation. Then, explore the rationale for using utilitarianism in the Nashs' situation. Compare the two rationales.
- Once the two Fanconi anemia embryos were discarded, 10 embryos were left. One of the 10 embryos became Adam, but what could have potentially happened to the 9 remaining embryos?
- How was it justified to discard the two embryos with Fanconi anemia and keep the one that became Adam? Consider your beliefs regarding when life begins and the moral equality of each life.

What is the future of genetic modification? No one knows exactly, but Huxley's 1932 prediction for the future of genetic technology is strikingly different from Frankel's (2003) forecast:

But as we begin the twenty-first century, the greater danger, I believe, is a highly individualized marketplace fueled by an entrepreneurial spirit and the free choice of large numbers of parents that could lead us down a path, albeit incrementally, toward a society that abandons the lottery of evolution in favor of intentional genetic modification. The discoveries of genetics will not be imposed on us. Rather, they will be sold to us by the market as something we cannot live without. (p. 32)

When these genetic issues are mentioned, emotions flare between people with divided opinions. One side's view is how great society's future will be with the new developments. The other side's view is science should not be interfering with nature or God's work. Not only do these genetic issues spark extreme emotions; they are also the most complex of all the ethical issues people in society face today. The prospect of designing, altering, enhancing, or ending the life of fetuses or embryos is challenging.

The standard principles of autonomy, beneficence, nonmaleficence, and justice should be addressed in the ethics involved with all PGD and other genetic manipulations such as IGM. However, the issues seem much more complex than just principle-driven or even theory-driven justifications. Genetic manipulation is essentially an unexplored territory leaving nurses and other healthcare professionals in moral distress. Frankel's (2003) statement with regard to IGM, which could be applied to all genetic manipulation, is the question of "whether we will shape it or be shaped by it" (p. 36).

Issues of Other Reproductive Services

Prenatal care is critical to the future health of the child. There are numerous prenatal health issues, but only the critical ethical issues of genetic counseling and testing and maternal substance abuse are included in this section.

ETHICAL REFLECTION: FAMILY BALANCING

- Do you believe that destroying a fetus or embryo is the same as killing? Explain your thoughts.
- Ben and Lynn want to select the gender of their next baby. They currently have a girl, and this time they want a boy to balance the family. Do you think the destruction of their remaining embryos would be for an inconsequential reason— family balancing? Explain your thoughts based on an ethical framework: theory, approach, or principle.
- Do you think family balancing, sperm-sorting procedures, and the prevention of genetic diseases are reasons for consideration of moral standing when extra embryos will be destroyed? Explain your thoughts.
- Explore your own feelings regarding sperm sorting involving PGD and genetic modification involving IGM. Write down your feelings about these two procedures.
- What are ethical strategies nurses can use for caring for two couples using gender selection (sperm sorting), one seeking family balancing and one preventing an X-linked mental retardation? Be specific when listing these strategies.

Genetic Screening and Testing

Scientists have discovered thousands of genetic diseases, and the number increases every day. Genes causally linked to biochemical, cellular, and physiological defects are responsible for these genetic diseases (Munson, 2004). DNA testing can identify some of these diseases in the fetus, and many new technologies are available. For example, today Down syndrome can be detected at 10 to 14 weeks' gestation by performing a chorionic villus sampling (CVS) of the products of conception or by an older method of amniocentesis, which cannot be performed until 16 to 18 weeks' gestation.

Diseases such as sickle cell, phenylketonuria (PKU), and Tay-Sachs can be screened with high accuracy. As an example, let us look at sickle-cell disease, an autosomal recessive disease. If one parent has the disease and the other is not affected, all four children will be carriers. However, if both parents are carriers, there is a chance that one in four children will have the disease, which makes for a 25% chance overall.

Genetic screening involves professionals counseling individuals or couples about their risk for genetically linked diseases (Munson, 2004). Genetic screening can be useful for couples with a background of genetic disease, such as sickle-cell anemia, because of its inheritance pattern. As Munson pointed out, however, after couples have this information, they often have no idea what to do with it. Should couples decide not to have children at all based on this 25% chance? Should couples take their chances and get pregnant anyway with the 25% risk? If so, should the woman be allowed to have a prenatal genetic test with only a 25% risk involved? If it is found that the fetus has a recessive disease, would the mother need to consider an abortion? If an abortion is out of the question, what would be the next step? Last, should there perhaps have been no reason for the prenatal genetic test in the first place?

Couples need to consider these questions before wandering down the path of expensive prenatal testing. There is the possibility that a woman can have embryo selection, sometimes called sperm sorting, via IVF before implantation of the embryo. As previously discussed, however, embryo selection means the remaining embryos will be discarded, diseased or not, unless the couple donates them to other couples or for research purposes. Even when they are used for research, the embryos are destroyed after they are used.

A variety of prenatal tests allow for a close inspection of tissue and bone, including ultrasound, radiography, and fiber optics. **Prenatal genetic diagnosis** is accomplished through an examination of the fetal DNA. Prenatal genetic diagnosis is commonly performed through amniocentesis at 15 weeks of pregnancy or later, or by CVS, which is performed between 10 and 12 weeks of pregnancy (American Academy of Family Physicians, 2020). The CVS test carries a risk for fetal foot or toe deformities; with amniocentesis, a risk of miscarriage exists. The most common test used for prenatal genetic diagnosis is a blood test for alpha fetoprotein. It is performed several weeks after conception and predicts disorders such as spina bifida or anencephaly with high accuracy.

Knowing when and when not to test could pose an ethical conflict for healthcare professionals. Many women want to know prior to delivery that everything is all right, and often they believe genetic testing will provide a certain degree of personal control and comfort. Should women have prenatal tests performed for what would seem like trivial reasons to other people? Will the woman's insurance company pay for these tests? What if she has no insurance but still wants them? Does she have an autonomous right to testing just because the technology is available?

Many experts hold two basic views: prenatal testing should be done (1) if the woman strongly believes in her right to have the procedure and wants it performed and (2) when the cost of the prenatal testing is very small compared to the costs of raising a child with a genetic disease or debilitating disorder (Munson, 2004). These decisions reach to the very core of family values and biological structure.

Stem-cell research offers considerable hope for correction of genetic diseases, but until the time comes for its full use, couples must make their decisions based on the technology available to them. Testing is appropriate when a couple can depend on accurate information, make an informed choice and decision, and live with the outcome after the decision about prenatal testing is made.

Maternal Substance Abuse

Maternal substance abuse is detrimental to a fetus or newborn. However, according to research, some pregnant women who abuse drugs do not seem to understand the potential harm they are inflicting on their unborn children (Perry et al., 2003). As one would expect, the women who are unaware of the danger they are posing to their unborn children are those who are abusing drugs but do not seek help. This same group of women was found to be more likely to believe having a small baby is a positive occurrence. The results of this research underscore the need for wide-scale community education programs about maternal drug abuse. Nurses can be a valuable resource in this effort.

Maternal drug screening is not performed routinely, and testing a woman or an infant without informed consent is considered a violation of a patient's right to privacy (Keenan, 2006). If healthcare providers perform maternal or newborn testing without the mother's consent and the test results are positive, any decision to restrict or remove parental rights would be based on illegally obtained evidence.

The handling and treatment of maternal drug abuse varies from state to state, but it is important to remember violations of women's rights (liberty rights) have occurred in some states. Possible violations may include the following:

- Prosecution of a pregnant woman who abuses drugs
- Charging a pregnant woman with drug possession if she is arrested for drug abuse prior to fetal viability
- Charging a pregnant woman with distribution of drugs to a minor if she is arrested for drug abuse after the fetus is considered viable
- Reduction of parental rights

Nurses have an ethical responsibility to recognize maternal substance abuse. Although nurses might personally find a pregnant woman's substance abuse morally objectionable, compassion is warranted. A family, rather than an individual person, is wounded by the woman's abusive behavior. Action is sometimes taken based on state laws to protect a fetus or

ETHICAL REFLECTION: PREGNANCY AND PRENATALLY DIAGNOSED GENETIC DISEASES

- Do you think a couple has a right to have a child with a prenatally diagnosed disabling genetic disease? Explain your thoughts.
- Do you think physicians and nurses should inform couples who want a baby about all the genetic tests available to them? Why or why not? Explain your thoughts.
- Do you think a mother has a right to know the results of theher prenatal genetic tests, whether positive or negative? Explore both sides based on the literature, and justify your answer based on an ethical framework: theory, approach, or principle.
- What approaches would you take as a nurse caring for a pregnant mother carrying a fetus with Down syndrome? Consider all the options.

ETHICAL REFLECTION: PREGNANCY AND DRUG ABUSE

- If you were a maternal–child nurse, after considering the ACLU's 1997 statement regarding women's rights, what action would you take if you suspect a pregnant patient at the clinic where you work is abusing drugs? What information would you need to guide your actions?
- What would you do if you suspect the woman will avoid the clinic in the future if you address the abuse issue?

child who is at risk from maternal substance abuse, but nurses must consider that a woman's decision or desire to seek treatment might result in a violation of the woman's rights. A woman's decision to obtain help often involves limited trust toward healthcare providers.

▷ Nursing Care of Childbearing Women

Ethical and legal issues in reproductive health are incredibly complex and challenging, but at the same time they encourage us with the promise of correcting genetic diseases. Sometimes, the possibilities inherent in new genetic technologies, including human cloning, cause people to become apprehensive or fearful. First, nurses caring for childbearing women must be educated and remain current with reproductive ethics. Nurses need to understand and respect the beliefs and practices about pregnancy and childbearing of various cultures.

Certain aspects of Provisions 1.4, 2.2, and 5.3 in the *Code of Ethics for Nurses with Interpretive Statements* (2015) particularly relate to the care of childbearing women. Those aspects are presented in a summary of those Provisions:

1. Nurses must maintain respect for human dignity and autonomy.
2. Nurses must recognize and protect patients' rights for understanding information and potential implications with their decisions.
3. Nurses must acknowledge the struggles between their own personal values and professional values regarding their responsibility for respecting the interests of patient care and patients' decisions.
4. When asked, nurses may express a personal and informed opinion but also must observe the moral and professional boundaries regarding patient self-determination.
5. Nurses may potentially influence their patients during health care, whether intended or unintended. Therefore, they must avoid any behavior that may be manipulative or coercive.

Nursing management for childbearing women is focused on the ethical relationship between the nurse and the woman. Related to the *Code of Ethics for Nurses* (ANA, 2015) is a relational care approach. With this framework, the nurse will always ask, "What is the 'right thing to do' for oneself and others?" (Bergum, 2004, p. 485). The nurse–patient relationship, as Bergum has experienced it, is a moral entity. Relational ethics is an action ethic created within the moral space of a relationship (Bergum, 2004; Jopling, 2000). A moral space is where the relationship is created and nurses display responsibility and respond to others. Nurses must be morally responsible to the childbearing women for whom they care, whether they are caring for them clinically, educating them, or overseeing their care. In so doing, nurses need to remember the dual-care framework for pregnant women: woman and fetus.

Bergum (2004) identified four themes to define relational ethics: environment, embodiment, mutual respect, and engagement. No matter which ethical issue is of concern, nurses need to focus on the quality of the moral relationship between the nurse and patient. In relational ethics, the first theme, environment, is a living system. It is important to understand how the whole environment is affected by the actions of each person. The living environment is in every nurse, and every action taken by nurses affects the outcome of the healthcare system as a whole. For example, the goal of a healthcare agency for a woman who had a partial-birth abortion could be to discharge her after 1 day. The patient and agency depend on the responsible and competent actions of nurses and others to meet the goal of a 1-day discharge.

Embodiment is the second theme, which is defined as having scientific knowledge, compassion for human life, and experiencing feeling and emotion for another person. For example, if a pregnant woman at 16 weeks' gestation has just been told after a prenatal genetic test that her fetus has Down syndrome, the nurse would understand the science behind the test and know the aftercare procedure. The nurse would have a mindful reality of the woman's pain and suffering and therefore have compassion for her.

Mutual respect is the third theme in relational ethics. Mutual respect is a way for people to exist together and have equal worth and dignity; it often is difficult to attain, but it is the central theme of relational ethics. In the example of the woman and her fetus with Down syndrome, mutual respect could be initiated by the nurse's regard for the woman's feelings, values, beliefs, and attitudes. The word *mutual* means to have a reciprocal and interactive focus. Based on this concept, the woman would need to reciprocate respect toward the nurse.

The fourth theme, relational engagement, is when the nurse and patient can find a few minutes to interact about something important to them. The nurse needs to understand the patient's circumstances and vulnerability. An example of engagement for the woman and her fetus with Down syndrome can be accomplished by the nurse's engaging in a conversation with the woman about her feelings concerning the diagnosis and options for her and her fetus.

Dialogue is in the center of the moral space, at the focus of relational ethics, and is the venue for the four themes to emerge. Depersonalization and coldness often surround the healthcare systems that women use. Nurses must give personalization to childbearing women by practicing relational ethics. On relational ethics and the moral life, Bergum (2004) stated:

> With relational space as the location of enacting morality, we need to consider ethics in every situation, every encounter, and with every patient. If all relationships are the focus of understanding and examining moral life, then it is important to attend to the quality of relationships in all nursing practices, whether with patients and their families, with other nurses, with other health care professionals, or with administrators and politicians. (p. 485)

KEY POINTS

- Reproductive health rights imply that people have the capability to reproduce and the freedom to decide if and when to reproduce. The definition includes the right of men and women to be informed and have access to safe, effective, affordable, and acceptable methods of reproductive health and family planning of their choice.

- A turning point for improving worldwide and U.S. maternal health was in 2010 after the release of an alarming report that reflected perilous statistics for women giving birth. The U.S. maternal death rate is higher than in 49 other countries, and in those statistics, the United States was the only developed country with a rising maternal mortality rate.

- There are different variations of how organizations and people view the moral standing of a fetus. Generally, the degree to which moral standing is placed on the fetus influences maternal rights—the greater the degree of moral standing of the fetus, the more restraint of maternal rights. The central ethical dilemma regarding abortion is about rights—the right to life of the fetus or the woman's right to control own body. The U.S. Supreme Court upheld the Partial-Birth Abortion Ban Act of 2003, also known as the Federal Abortion Ban, on April 18, 2007 (ACLU, 2007). The *Roe v. Wade* decision of 1973 was officially reversed by the U.S. Supreme Court on June 24, 2022, almost half a century later, which means that the constitutional right for a pregnant women to have an abortion no longer exists.

- Most women who have abortions agree they could not have a baby, carry a fetus, or raise a family for personal or health reasons. Some women, though they may strongly believe in maternal rights, experience disenfranchised grief because they believe they do not have permission to grieve the loss of their fetus; thus, they experience extreme sorrow.

- ART has been a miracle and a relief for women or couples who experience infertility. There are five types of ART: in vitro fertilization (IVF), intracytoplasmic fertilization, conventional fertilization, zygote intrafallopian transfer (ZIFT), and gamete intrafallopian transfer (GIFT). Ethical issues regarding ART include the risks resulting from technology; surrogacy (donor eggs, embryo donation, or carrying fetuses); the handling of surplus embryos and fetuses; implications of sperm sorting, gender selection, and family balancing; and genetic modification and enhancement—the dream of creating a perfect child.

- Preimplantation genetic diagnosis (PGD) is a procedure that allows implantation of a selected gender or a perfect or near-perfect embryo. Many genetic diseases can be detected through gene technology, screening, and genetic diagnosis. Knowing when to test and when not to test could be an ethical difficulty for all people concerned with the issue. Maternal rights should be respected, but weighing maternal rights against burdens of costs may be a hard choice for couples and providers of care.

- Maternal substance abuse, including alcohol and other drugs, can be detrimental to the fetus or newborn infant. There tends to be lack of education from providers of care or a deficit of pregnant women in comprehending the adverse effects of substance abuse. Maternal and infant drug screening is not performed on a routine basis and may not be done without express informed consent. Nurses have a moral responsibility to educate their patients and recognize maternal substance abuse. However, a woman's decision to obtain help is her decision, and her decision is dependent on the degree of trust she has developed with her providers of care.

- Nurses should incorporate essential concepts from the ANA *Code of Ethics for Nurses with Interpretive Statements* (2015) with Bergum's (2004) relational ethics. Bergum's themes of relational ethics are environment, embodiment, mutual respect, and engagement. Dialogue is in the center of the moral space and serves as the venue in which Bergum's four themes can emerge.

References

American Academy of Family Physicians. (2020, April 1). *Prenatal diagnosis: Amniocentesis and CVS.* https://familydoctor.org/prenatal-diagnosis-amniocentesis-and-cvs/

American Civil Liberties Union. (1997). *Coercive and punitive governmental responses to women's conduct during pregnancy.* https://www.aclu.org/other/coercive-and-punitive-governmental-responses-womens-conduct-during-pregnancy

American Civil Liberties Union. (2007, May). *Case summaries: U.S. Supreme Court upholds federal ban on abortion methods: Ruling undermines women's health and equality.* https://www.aclu.org/other/case-summaries-us-supreme-court-upholds-federal-ban-abortion-methods

American Civil Liberties Union. (2014). *ACLU-TN seeks to challenge new law criminalizing addicted mothers.* https://www.aclu.org/press-releases/aclu-tn-seeks-challenge-new-law-criminalizing-addicted-mothers

American Nurses Association. (2015). *Code of ethics for nurses with interpretive statements.*

Amnesty International. (2010). *Deadly delivery: The maternal health care crisis in the USA.* https://www.amnestyusa.org/files/pdfs/deadlydelivery.pdf

Amnesty International. (2011). *Deadly delivery: The maternal health care crisis in the USA: One year update spring 2011.* https://www.amnestyusa.org/reports/deadly-delivery-the-maternal-health-care-crisis-in-the-usa/

Arons, J. (2007, December 17). *Future choices: Assisted reproductive technologies and the law.* Center for American Progress. https://www.americanprogress.org/issues/women/reports/2007/12/17/3728/future-choices-assisted-reproductive-technologies-and-the-law/

Arons, J., & Chen, E. (2013, March 25). *Future choices II. An update on legal, statutory, and policy landscape of assisted reproductive technologies.* Center for American Progress. https://www.americanprogress.org/issues/women/reports/2013/03/25/57951/future-choices-ii/

Bergum, V. (2004). Relational ethics in nursing. In J. L. Storch, P. Rodney, & R. Starzomski (Eds.), *Toward a moral horizon: Nursing ethics for leadership and practice* (pp. 485–502). Pearson.

Burke, T. (2002). *Forbidden grief: The unspoken pain of abortion.* Acorn.

Centers for Disease Control and Prevention. (2014). *National public health action plan for the detection, prevention, and management of infertility.* https://www.cdc.gov/reproductivehealth/infertility/pdf/drh_nap_final_508.pdf

Centers for Disease Control and Prevention. (2019a, January 16). *Strategic plan: Improving women's reproductive health, pregnancy health, and infant health.* https://www.cdc.gov/reproductivehealth/drh/about-us/DRH-strategic-plan.htm

Centers for Disease Control and Prevention. (2019b, October 8). *What is assisted reproductive technology?* https://www.cdc.gov/art/whatis.html

Centers for Disease Control and Prevention. (2021, April 13). *Infertility FAQs.* https://www.cdc.gov/reproductivehealth/infertility/index.htm

Chandis, V., & Williams, T. (2006). The patient, the doctor, the fetus, and the court-compelled cesarean: Why courts should address the question through a bioethical lens. *Medicine and Law, 25,* 729–746.

Cleveland Clinic. (2020, April 16). *Fetal development: Stages of growth.* https://my.clevelandclinic.org/health/articles/7247-fetal-development-stages-of-growth

Coutts, M. C. (1990). *Maternal-fetal conflict: Legal and ethical issues.* https://repository.library.georgetown.edu/bitstream/handle/10822/556868/sn14.pdf?sequence=1&isAllowed=y

Daliard, C. (2004, October). Courts strike 'partial-birth' abortion ban; Decisions presage future debates. *The Guttmacher Report, 7*(4), 1–4.

DeGrazia, D. (2005). *Human identity and bioethics.* Cambridge University Press.

DeGrazia, D. (2006). Moral status, human identity, and early embryos: A critique of the president's approach. *Journal of Law, Medicine, & Ethics, 34*(1), 49–57.

DeGrazia, D. (2008). Moral status as a matter of degree? *The Southern Journal of Philosophy, 46,* 181–198.

Farmer, B. (2016, March 23). *Tennessee lawmakers discontinue controversial fetal assault law.* https://www.npr.org/2016/03/23/471622159/tennessee-lawmakers-discontinue-controversial-fetal-assault-law

Feinberg, J. (1984). Potentiality, development, and right. In J. Feinberg (Ed.), *The problem of abortion* (2nd ed., pp. 145–150). Wadsworth.

Frankel, M. S. (2003). Inheritable genetic modification and a brave new world: Did Huxley have it wrong? *Hastings Center Report, 33*(2), 31–36.

Grady, D. (2000, October 4). Son conceived to provide blood cells for daughter. *New York Times,* Section A, p. 24. https://www.nytimes.com/2000/10/04/us/son-conceived-to-provide-blood-cells-for-daughter.html

Guttmacher Institute. (2021a). *Number of abortions: Abortion counters.* http://www.numberofabortions.com

Guttmacher Institute. (2021b). *An overview of abortion laws.* https://www.guttmacher.org/state-policy/explore/overview-abortion-laws

Guttmacher Institute. (2022, April 15). *2022 state legislative sessions: Abortion bans and restrictions on medication abortion dominate.* https://www.guttmacher.org/article/2022/03/2022-state-legislative-sessions-abortion-bans-and-restrictions-medication-abortion

Harris, J., & Holm, S. (2000). Introduction. In J. Harris & S. Holm (Eds.), *The future of human reproduction: Ethics, choice, & regulation* (pp. 1–37). Clarendon.

Harris, J., & Holm, S. (2003). Abortion. In H. LaFollette (Ed.), *The Oxford handbook of practical ethics* (pp. 112–135). Oxford University Press.

Iris, O., Amalia, L., Moshe, M., Arnon, W., & Eyal, S. (2009). Refusal of treatment in obstetrics—A maternal-fetal conflict. *Journal of Maternal-Fetal and Neonatal Medicine, 2*(7), 612–615.

Jopling, D. A. (2000). *Self-knowledge and the self.* Routledge.

Keenan, C. (2006). Maternal versus fetal rights: Part I. In S. W. Killion & K. Dempski (Eds.), *Quick look nursing: Legal and ethical issues* (pp. 144–145). Jones and Bartlett Publishers.

Kemp, J. (2014, July). *Tennessee mom arrested under new drug law after newborn tests positive for meth.* https://www.nydailynews.com/news/crime/tennessee-mom-busted-new-drug-law-baby-tests-positive-meth-article-1.1865979

Louise Brown biography. (2014). https://www.biography.com/personality/louise-brown

Ludwig, M. J. (2008). *Maternal-fetal conflict.* https://depts.washington.edu/bhdept/ethics-medicine/bioethics-topics/detail/69

Mahoney, J. (2007). *The challenge of human rights: Origin, development, and significance.* Blackwell.

Marquis, D. (1989). Why abortion is immoral. *Journal of Philosophy, 86,* 183–202.

MedicineNet.com. (2021, March 29). *Medical definition of induced abortion.* https://www.medicinenet.com/induced_abortion/definition.htm

Munson, R. (2004). *Intervention and reflection: Basic issues in medical ethics* (7th ed.). Wadsworth-Thomson.

NARAL: Pro-Choice America. (2021). *Abortion access.* https://www.prochoiceamerica.org/issue/abortion-access/

National Right to Life Committee. (n.d.). *National right to life mission statement.* https://www.nrlc.org/about/mission/

Perry, B. L., Jones, H., Tuten, M., & Svikas, D. S. (2003). Assessing maternal perceptions of harmful effects of drug use during pregnancy. *Journal of Addictive Diseases, 22,* 1–9.

Planned Parenthood. (2021). *Which kind of emergency contraception should I use?* https://www.plannedparenthood.org/learn/morning-after-pill-emergency-contraception/which-kind-emergency-contraception-should-i-use

Post, L. F. (1996). Bioethical considerations of maternal-fetal issues. *Fordham Urban Law Journal, 24*(4), 757–775.

ProCon.org. (2021, September 22). *History of abortion.* https://abortion.procon.org/history-of-abortion/

Shimabukuro, J. O. (2008, January 14). Partial-birth abortion: Recent developments in the law. *Congressional Research Report* (RL30415). https://www.everycrsreport.com/files/20080114_RL30415_633702d0760538f656ce04fba856876f61256cb4.pdf

Steinbock, B. (1992). *Life before birth: The moral and legal status of embryos and fetuses.* Oxford University Press.

Steinbock, B. (2006). The morality of killing human embryos. *Journal of Law, Medicine, & Ethics, 34*(1), 26–34.

Tennessee Fetal Assault Law, SB1391, 108th General Assembly. (2013-2014). https://legiscan.com/TN/bill/SB1391/2013

Tennessee Fetal Assault Law, SB1391. (2018, December 6). https://rewirenewsgroup.com/legislative-tracker/law/tennessee-pregnancy-criminalization-law-sb-1391/

Thomson, J. J. (1971). A defense of abortion. *Philosophy and Public Affairs, 1*(1), 47–66.

Tran, L. (2004). Legal rights and the maternal-fetal conflict. *BioTeach Journal, 2,* 76–80.

United Nations Population Fund. (2014a). *ICPD beyond 2014 issue brief: Health: Sexual and reproductive health and rights (SRHR).* https://www.unfpa.org/sites/default/files/pub-pdf/ICPD_UNGASS_REPORT_for_website.pdf

United Nations Population Fund. (2014b). Reproductive rights and reproductive health. *Program of Action: International Conference on Population and Development* (pp. 58–77). https://www.unfpa.org/sites/default/files/pub-pdf/programme_of_action_Web%20ENGLISH.pdf

University of Minnesota Masonic Cancer Center. (n.d.). *Umbilical cord blood transplantation.* https://cancer.umn.edu/umbilical-cord-blood-transplantation

Veatch, R. (2003). *The basics of bioethics* (2nd ed.). Prentice Hall.

Wachbroit, R., & Wasserman, D. (2003). Reproductive technology. In H. LaFollette (Ed.), *The Oxford handbook of practical ethics* (pp. 136–160). Oxford University Press.

World Health Organization (WHO). (2019, September 19). *Maternal mortality.* https://www.who.int/news-room/fact-sheets/detail/maternal-mortality

World Health Organization. (2021, November 25). *Preventing unsafe abortion.* https://www.who.int/news-room/fact-sheets/detail/preventing-unsafe-abortion

CHAPTER 5

Infant and Child Nursing Ethics

Karen L. Rich

Heaven lies about us in our infancy.

—**William Wordsworth**, "Intimations of Immortality," 1807

OBJECTIVES

After reading this chapter, the reader should be able to do the following:

1. Discuss issues of vulnerability as they relate to the care of infants and children.
2. Understand ethical issues regarding the vaccination of children and the nurse's role.
3. Understand ethical issues regarding global childhood poverty.
4. Identify justifiable, ethical decision-making processes in the care of children.
5. Evaluate factors regarding refusing treatment for infants and children.
6. Discuss landmark cases in the ethical and legal care of infants and children.
7. Understand the nurse's role as an advocate in the care of infants and children.

Mothering

In his book *Ethics for the New Millennium*, the Dalai Lama (1999) emphasized the importance of the ethic of compassion. Empathy, which is one's "ability to enter into and, to some extent, share others' suffering" (p. 123), represents compassion (*nying je*) at a basic level. The Dalai Lama stated compassion can be developed, going beyond empathy to the extent that it arises without effort and "is unconditional, undifferentiated, and universal in scope" (p. 123). Compassion is a desire to separate another being from suffering. Compassion is also a sense of intimacy toward all feeling and perceiving beings (Dalai Lama, 1999). Persons with this well-developed level of compassion include in the scope of their compassion even those beings who may harm them. According to the Dalai Lama, this profound form of intimacy and compassion can be likened "to the love a mother has for her only child" (p. 123).

All animals are born into an initial condition of vulnerability and dependence. Human infants and children "arrive in the world in a condition of needy helplessness more or less unparalleled in any other animal species" (Nussbaum, 2001, p. 181). Historically, Western ethics generally has ignored human vulnerability and its resultant consequence of creating a need for humans to depend on one another (MacIntyre, 1999). However, some feminist philosophers, such as Virginia Held (1993) and Sara Ruddick (1995), used the underlying premise of human dependence as the foundation for their philosophy of ethics. In fact, some feminist philosophers proposed that the caring that occurs between a mother and her vulnerable and dependent child can be used as a model for all moral relationships. This model is like the model of compassion discussed by the Dalai Lama.

In considering how a feminist approach to ethics is relevant to the care of infants and children, nurses can think in terms of what Tong (1997) called a care-focused feminist ethics approach; this type of approach to ethics supports feminine values, such as "compassion, empathy, sympathy, nurturance, and kindness" (p. 38), which often have been marginalized in male-dominated societies. These values and virtues are ones traditionally associated with good mothering.

There have been heated debates about the differences between the types of moral reasoning engaged in by males and females. However, Stimpson noted "crucially, both women and men can be feminists" (Stimpson, 1993, p. viii). In accepting and using the feminine model of social relationships existing between mothers and children, Stimpson stated "a moral agent, female or male, will be [what Held (1993) called] a 'mothering person'" (p. viii).

Held (1993) proposed the concept of **mothering person** as a gender-neutral term used to describe the type of mothering that would occur in a society without male domination. Held stated there are good reasons to believe mothering should be a practice performed by both women and men. Ruddick (1995) defined a mother as one who can do maternal work and

> a person who takes on responsibility for children's lives and for whom providing child care is a significant part of her or his working life. . . . I am suggesting that, whatever difference might exist between female and male mothers, there is no reason to believe that one sex rather than the other is more capable of doing maternal work. (pp. 40–41)

When providing ethical care to infants and children, nurses support mothers and mothering persons, both females and males, who share in the unconditional compassion toward their children as described by the Dalai Lama.

FOCUS FOR DEBATE

Engage in a debate with your colleagues using the following positions: (1) mothering is an inherently female trait versus (2) mothering is not an inherently female trait.

▶ Foundations of Trust

A boy bathing in a river was in danger of being drowned. He called out to a passing traveler for help, but instead of holding out a helping hand, the man stood by unconcernedly and scolded the boy for his imprudence. "Oh sir!" cried the youth, "pray help me now and scold me afterwards."

—Aesop, Aesop's Fables

"Children are vulnerable, often frightened small people" (Ruddick, 1995, p. 119). An infant's development of basic trust versus basic mistrust is the first of Erik Erikson's (1950/1985) eight stages of psychosocial development. According to Ruddick, it is the responsibility of mothers to establish the feeling of trust between themselves and their children because children's trust ideally is founded on the nurturance and protectiveness of their mothers. Unless there are unusual circumstances, guardians are entrusted with the autonomy to make decisions for their minor children. This autonomy is an endorsement of the trust societies place in parents and guardians' ability and desire to provide care in the best interest of their children. Although guardians generally have autonomy privileges in decision making for their children, children have their own basic dignity as human beings.

ETHICAL REFLECTION

With your colleagues, use the Socratic method to analyze the concept of nurse–family trust.

Because most children depend on their mothering persons to be trustworthy, mothering persons often are wary when they are judging healthcare policies and choosing the people they entrust to meet their children's healthcare needs. Trust becomes an even greater issue when mothering people are not able to choose their children's healthcare providers, as is usually the case with nurses. Justified maternal wariness includes a cautious trust of nurses and other healthcare professionals who interact with and treat one's children. However, it is natural, and often a source of comfort, for parents and guardians to believe that healthcare professionals have a more complete grasp of the medical facts and probabilities related to their child's health care than they themselves have in many instances. Consequently, mothering figures depend on and trust healthcare professionals to support or guide them in

making difficult healthcare decisions for their children. Sometimes, this trust is like unavoidable trust (see an earlier chapter 2).

Vaccinations

Because of the grave threat of nonpreventable infectious diseases, people living before and during the early 1900s would have been delighted to have had a wide array of available vaccines. However, because of successful public health advances in the 20th and 21st centuries, many people in the United States have not personally encountered some of the older diseases that are now preventable by vaccines, such as measles and polio. Therefore, some people take for granted the benefits of available vaccines. Rus and Groselj (2021) described this as vaccines being "victims of their own success" (p. 1).

Vaccines being victims of their own success has contributed to some guardians deciding not to vaccinate their children. When guardians do not see in the flesh historical infectious diseases like measles and polio, they assume their children will be safe from them, but these diseases have not been eradicated. Other reasons for guardians' vaccine hesitancy include distrust of the medical system and the safety of medical products; receipt of incorrect vaccine information; negative influences of media, family, and friends; and not realizing that some vaccine preventable diseases can be debilitating or deadly. During the Covid-19 pandemic issues of vaccine mistrust and misinformation exploded. With some diseases, such as Covid-19, herd immunity is not likely to be reached without widespread vaccinations. Herd immunity is one of the primary goals of vaccination programs. Herd immunity can be defined in various ways, but its basic meaning is that about 80% of people in a geographic area must be vaccinated against the target disease and those vaccinated must be evenly distributed within the population. Herd immunity was achieved with measles, but vaccine hesitancy began to break this immunity down and sporadic outbreaks of measles have occurred. Also, measles infections have been imported from other countries and infected children in the United States who are unvaccinated against it.

Ethics regarding the responsibility to be vaccinated is discussed in a later chapter 11. In the case of minor children, general ethical considerations apply to parental decisions with the added issue that minor children are dependent on their guardians' for maintaining their safety from vaccine preventable diseases.

Historically, some guardians opposed to a program of traditional universal vaccination have sought ways to achieve natural immunity for their children. A method that sometimes has been used is to have children attend "exposure parties." Groups of well and previously uninfected children are brought together with a child or children who are currently believed to be infectious with a specific vaccine-preventable disease, such as chicken pox, rubella, or measles, so that the uninfected children can become infected and thus naturally immunized. These parties are not without risks to children, including the most obvious result of having one's child endure unnecessary and sometimes dangerous illnesses. On its website about chickenpox transmission, the CDC (2021a) has a profile box covering exposure parties. The title of the box is "'Chickenpox Parties'—Don't Take the Chance."

States vary regarding mandatory childhood vaccination laws, and the CDC (2022) has a Public Health Law program that compiles data about school vaccination laws in each state, including eligible exemptions (see **FIGURE 5-1**). Most of the state laws cover both public and private schools and day-care centers. The following list includes eight characteristics of school vaccination exemptions covered by laws:

1. Permits medical exemptions only
2. Permits medical and religious exemptions
3. Permits medical, religious, and philosophical exemptions
4. Requires parental acknowledgment during the exemption application process that exempted students can be excluded from school during outbreaks
5. Establishes that exemptions might not be recognized in the event of an outbreak
6. Requires notarization of documents in the exemption application process
7. Requires parental education on vaccinations in the exemption application process
8. Addresses the duration of medical exemptions (e.g., temporary or permanent) (p. 3)

In 2012, the CDC (2012) published the following document as a guide for guardians: "If You Choose Not to Vaccinate Your Child, Understand the Risks and Responsibilities." Though it is aimed at guardians, this document is helpful for nurses working with guardians who choose to delay vaccinations or to not vaccinate their children. This information is located on the CDC's website. The CDC (2021b) also has a web page titled "Provider Resources for Vaccine Conversations with

ETHICAL REFLECTION

Research some of the reasons guardians refuse immunizations for their children. Imagine you are a public health nurse working at a county health department. A mother brings her newborn in for a well-baby checkup. The baby's mother tells you she has a "philosophical objection" to childhood vaccinations.

- How would you respond to the mother's comment?
- Would you discuss vaccine ethics with this mother? Why or why not? If so, what would you say? You may want to refer to a later chapter 11 to answer this question.

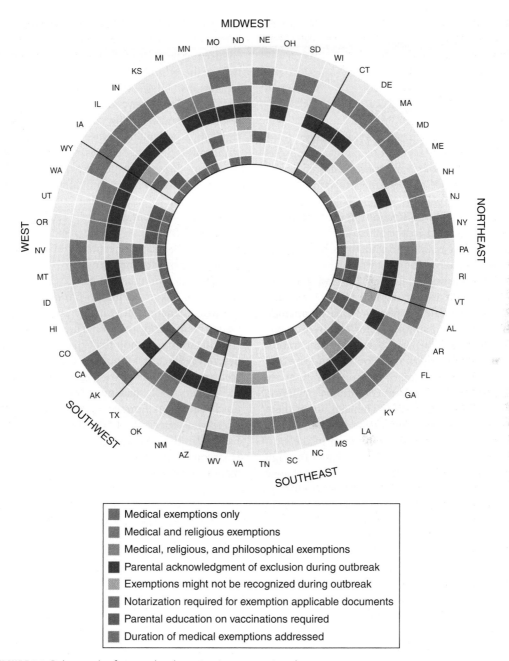

FIGURE 5-1 Polar graph of state school vaccination exemptions law.

Reproduced from Centers for Disease Control and Prevention (CDC). (2022). *Public health law: State school immunization requirements and vaccine exemption laws*. https://www.cdc.gov/phlp/docs/school
-vaccinations.pdf

Parents" that provides a plethora of resources for healthcare providers to use when discussing vaccines with guardians.

Undocumented Immigrant Children

The plight of immigrant children from Mexico and Central America came to the forefront of people's awareness in the Obama and Trump administrations and continued to be newsworthy in the Biden administration. The salient issues and situations have waxed and waned, but they continue to involve immigrant children at the U.S. and Mexican border who are accompanied by their family as well as children who are unaccompanied by family, i.e., simply minor children on the run. People have been outraged at separation of family members at the border and the care and treatment of unaccompanied children being housed in various conditions, including those that are cage-like. The facts about these issues are hard to understand because there are so many particulars involved in the situations, the facts have been presented through a political lens, and the facts seem to change continuously, which makes it difficult for the public to keep up with the changes. Consequently, it is difficult to discuss children as undocumented immigrants.

Regarding the position of America's primary nursing professional organization, in 2018, the American Nurses Association (ANA) released a statement saying the organization "adamantly opposes the Administration's policy and practices toward migrants and asylum seekers that result in the forcible separation of children from their families" (para. 2). This statement was issued during the Trump administration's Zero Tolerance Policy that called for criminal prosecution of any adult immigrating to the United States undocumented. As part of this policy, United States officials separated many children from their

guardians; and in some cases, adults were sent back to their country of origin without their children. Stange and Stark (2019) outlined two of the ethical issues involved with these separations. First, both guardians and children experience psychological trauma with resultant manifestations such as depression, children experiencing bedwetting, and social withdrawal. Second, there is a disruption of guardians' legal rights to provide informed consent for their children's treatment. To add to the problems, it seems that little to no records were maintained to help reunite these families. In May 2021, President Biden formed a task force to make concentrated efforts to reunite children with their families.

The care of unaccompanied immigrant children was moved to the Office of Refugee Resettlement (ORR) in March 2003 (U.S. Department of Health and Human Services (HHS), Administration for Children & Families, n.d.). Since this time, the ORR has overseen the treatment of over 409,550 children. In February 2021, the United Nations International Children's Emergency Fund (UNICEF) released a report titled "Building Bridges for Every Child: Care and Services to Support Unaccompanied Children." The report recommended 8 policy essentials:

1. Call for children to receive due process, protection in seeking asylum, and to be reunited with family members.
2. Ensure that processes are child sensitive.
3. Minimize detention and institutional-based care and maximize family and community-based care. Prioritize case management services.
4. Link HHS children's programs with immigrant care. Provide inclusiveness, non-discrimination, and equity in care.
5. Use the best interest standard (see best interest standard covered later

in this chapter). Appoint child advocates.

6. Based on children's age and maturity, allow them to participate in decisions about their care.

7. Provide continuity of care when children are released from ORR care. Provide free legal assistance for children.

8. Assure child-sensitive support and make sure the return is in a child's best interests when returning children to their home country.

The entire report is downloadable from UNICEF's website. Fortunately, as of May 2021, the number of unaccompanied immigrant children being housed in U.S. detention facilities has decreased after a 20-year high (British Broadcasting Corporation [BBC], 2021). Unfortunately, there were still approximately 13,730 children in ORR custody as of September, 2021 (USDHHS, 2021, November 15).

Stephen and Zoucha (2020) discussed ethical issues involved with undocumented immigrant children, and they called on nurse leaders to use the theory of bureaucratic caring when trying to improve the predicament of these children. Some of the foundational principles related to the children's care include the following: human dignity, right to health care, nurses' duty to care, and primacy of the family. These issues also are covered in the ANA's (2015) *Code of Ethics for Nurses with Interpretive Statements*. The theory of bureaucratic caring was developed by Ray (1989, 2001) for use in organizational settings. Ray proposed that healthcare bureaucracies' aims, such as economic and political stability, sometimes conflict with nurses' desire to practice from a humanistic perspective. Thus, bureaucratic caring is the antithesis of humanistic caring. According to the theory, organizations can be transformed when nurses introduce spiritual and ethical caring to the system (Turkel, 2007). In recommending use of the theory with immigrants, Stephen and Zoucha (2020) proposed that organizational nurse leaders assure their voices are heard in discussions that drive change regarding care of immigrants.

ETHICAL REFLECTION

1. Research the current situation regarding undocumented immigration in the United States.
2. Describe your ethical analysis of undocumented immigration and treatment of immigrants, especially children. Defend your position with ethics theories and approaches. Refer to earlier chapters 1 and 2, as needed.
3. How does the reason immigrants try to enter the United States undocumented affect your position? For example, guardians sending their unaccompanied children to the United States in an attempt to protect the children from dangers in their home country.
4. Is the United States morally obligated to help solve problems that prompt immigrants to seek asylum in the United States? Defend your answer.

Global Problems of Childhood Poverty and Infectious Diseases

Statistical data regarding the unmet needs of infants and children worldwide should concern all compassionate people, but especially nurses. According to UNICEF (n.d.), "children are more likely to live in poverty [than adults]. They're also more vulnerable to its effects" (para. 1). UNICEF listed the following global health facts:

- 1 billion children worldwide are multidimensionally poor—without access to education, health, housing, nutrition, sanitation or water
- 356 million children are living in extreme poverty, forced to survive on less than $1.90 a day

- Children are more than twice as likely to live in poverty than adults
- Children from the poorest households die at twice the rate of their better-off peers. (para. 8)

Childhood poverty does not exist only in low-income countries. In the United States almost 11 million children, or 1 in 7 children, are living in economically disadvantaged circumstances (Haider, 2021). Writing for the Center for American Progress, Haider recommended these, among other, ways to end childhood poverty in America:

- Policy enactment that provides for basic needs—food, housing, health care
  - Scale up food assistance programs, such as SNAP, provide more free meals at schools
  - Strengthen and expand the Section 8 housing program
  - Ensure there are strong programs for affordable health care for children, such as Medicaid and the Children's Health Insurance Program (CHIP)
- Reduce policy barriers

The burden of child poverty is closely correlated with poor health among the world's children. According to UNICEF (2020), "150 million additional children plunged into poverty due to COVID-19" (para. 1). Public health professionals have known for many years that many of the deaths reported in global child health data are the result of conditions for which there are low-cost prevention measures or treatments. Global child health data taken from the World Health Organization (WHO, 2020) website includes the following:

- In 2019 an estimated 5.2 million children under 5 years died mostly from preventable and treatable causes. Children aged 1 to 11 months accounted for 1.5 million of these deaths while children aged 1 to 4 years accounted for 1.3 million deaths. Newborns (under 28 days) accounted for the remaining 2.4 million deaths.

- An additional 500,000 older children (5 to 9 years) died in 2019.
- Leading causes of death in children under 5 years are preterm birth complications, birth asphyxia/trauma, pneumonia, congenital anomalies, diarrhoea, and malaria, all of which can be prevented or treated with access to simple, affordable interventions including immunization, adequate nutrition, safe water and food, and quality care by a trained health provider when needed.
- Older children (5 to 9 years) had one of the largest declines in mortality since 1990 (61%) due to a decline in infectious diseases.
- Injuries (including road traffic injuries and drowning) are the leading causes of death among older children (para. 1).

The UNICEF Office of Research-Innocenti published a working paper titled "Why Assist People Living in Poverty? The ethics of poverty reduction" (Barrientos et al., 2016). According to the document, the basis for associating poverty and ethics is because poverty is a matter of injustice. The basis of injustice being at the center of ethics and childhood poverty is echoed by Schweiger (2019). Other relevant ethical frames of reference include "egalitarian, utilitarian, priority, sufficiency and humanitarian perspectives" (Barrientos et al., 2016, p. 6).

The last three provisions of the American Nurses Association's (ANA, 2015) *Code of Ethics for Nurses with Interpretive Statements* focus on nursing "aspects of duties beyond individual patient encounters" (p. xiii). Provision 7.3 addresses nurses' responsibilities in developing health policy whether the nurse serves as a clinician, an educator, or an administrator. The scope of this responsibility is global. Student nurses often wonder why they need health policy content in their nursing curriculum; one important reason is that it is a matter of ethics. Compassion is a desire to separate beings from suffering. Being active in developing and changing health policies locally, statewide, regionally, nationally, or globally can be a compassionate nursing action to help vulnerable children who are subjected to and die from preventable diseases and conditions. Provision 8 of the *Code of Ethics* (ANA, 2015) also includes a focus on global health. Provision 8.2 directs nurses to "address the context of health, including social determinants of health such as poverty, access to clean water and clean air, sanitation, human rights violations, hunger, nutritionally sound food, education, safe medications and health disparities" (pp. 31–32).

ETHICAL REFLECTION

Consider the problems of global poverty and infectious diseases as they affect children and relate them to social justice.

- What can nurses do to improve social justice for the world's population of children?

Abused and Neglected Children

Child abuse and neglect, at a minimum, are defined at the Federal level by the Child Abuse Prevention and Treatment (CAPTA) Reauthorization Act of 2010 as

> any recent act or failure to act on the part of a parent or caretaker which results in death, serious physical or emotional harm, sexual abuse or exploitation; or an act or failure to act which presents an imminent risk of serious harm. (Child Welfare Information Gateway, 2019b, p. 1)

Civil and criminal state statutes also define these terms. Nurses should be familiar with both federal and their state information about child abuse and neglect. The major types of child abuse and neglect outlined by the U.S.

government's Child Information Gateway (2019c) include:

- Physical abuse
- Neglect
- Sexual abuse
- Emotional abuse
- Abandonment
- Parental substance use
- Human trafficking

LEGAL PERSPECTIVE: CAPTA

A federal law originally enacted in 1974 titled the Child Abuse Prevention and Treatment Act (CAPTA) was reauthorized in 2010 and last amended in 2019. It is "the key federal legislation addressing child abuse and neglect" (Child Welfare Information Gateway, 2019a, p. 1).

The U.S. Department of Health and Human Services (HHS) Administration for Children and Families, Administration on Children, Youth, and Families, Children's Bureau (2022, January 19) annual Child Maltreatment report from federal fiscal year 2020 contained the following data:

- The national rounded number of children who received a child protective services investigation response or alternative response decreased from 3,476,000 for federal fiscal year (FFY) 2019 to 3,145,000 for FFY 2020.
- Comparing the national rounded number of victims from FFY 2019 (656,000) to the national rounded number of victims in 2020 (618,000) also shows a decrease.
- The FFY 2020 data show three-quarters (76.1%) of victims are neglected, 16.5 percent are physically abused, 9.4 percent are sexually abused, and 0.2 percent are sex trafficked.
- The national estimate of victims who died from abuse and neglect decreased from

1,830 for FFY 2019 to 1,750 for FFY 2020. The rate of child fatalities also decreased from 2.48 per 100,000 children in the population to 2.38 per 100,000 children in the population. (p. ii)

The complete report can be found online at the government author's website.

Nurses must be aware of high-risk situations for child abuse and neglect and be able to recognize the signs and symptoms of maltreatment. Reporting suspected maltreatment can help children and families receive critically needed assistance. Healthcare professionals are not the only people who can report suspected child maltreatment; any concerned person can do this. Nurses need to remember and educate others that "reporting your concerns is not making an accusation; rather, it is a request for an investigation and assessment to determine if help is needed" (Child Welfare Information Gateway, 2019c, p. 4). Nurses also need to be aware that children may directly disclose that they have experienced maltreatment. Nurses and others can find help in handling abuse disclosures at the Childhelp National Child Abuse Hotline website (Childhelp, n.d.). Key recommendations include:

- Avoid denial
- Provide a safe environment
- Reassure [the] child
- Listen and don't make assumptions
- Do not interrogate
- Make no promises
- Document exact quotes
- Be supportive, not judgmental
- Have an understanding about abuse and neglect
- Report any suspicion of child abuse and neglect (pp. 2–3)
- The Child Welfare Information Gateway (2019c) provides a list of general maltreatment that can help determine when a child needs help. Specific signs and symptoms relating to physical abuse, neglect, sexual abuse, and emotional maltreatment can

be found on the Child Welfare Information Gateway website.
- The child shows sudden changes in behavior or school performance
- Has not received help for physical or medical problems brought to the guardians' attention
- Has learning problems (or difficulty concentrating) that cannot be attributed to specific physical or psychological causes
- Is always watchful, as though preparing for something bad to happen
- Lacks adult supervision
- Is overly compliant, passive, or withdrawn
- Comes to school or other activities early, stays late, and does not want to go home
- Is reluctant to be around a particular person
- Discloses maltreatment

Parent [guardian] may exhibit the following signs:

- Denies the existence of or blames the child for the child's problems in school or at home
- Asks teachers or other caregivers to use harsh physical discipline if the child misbehaves
- Sees the child as entirely bad, worthless, or burdensome
- Demands a level of physical or academic performance the child cannot achieve
- Looks primarily to the child for care, attention, and satisfaction of the parent's [guardian's] emotional needs
- Shows little concern for the child
- Parent [guardian] and child touch or look at each other rarely (p. 5)

The usual responsibility of handling a patient's treatment confidentially is waived in the instance of suspected child abuse, even when the person reporting the abuse is the patient (Ramsey, 2006). Abuse does not need to be confirmed as factual to be reportable. The identification of suspected abuse should be promptly reported to the agency designated by each state. There is legal protection in most states for professionals, including nurses, who are reporting suspected abuse in good faith, though healthcare professionals may be exposed to legal sanctions if they fail to report suspected abuse to the appropriate agencies.

Surrogate Decision Making

Children are legally incompetent individuals who, in most cases, must have surrogate decision makers for important life decisions, including healthcare decisions. Ethicists have established standards accepted as being ethically appropriate for guiding healthcare decisions made on behalf of infants and children. The most accepted ethical standard that underlies surrogate decision making for children is based on a standard of best interest. When using the **best interest standard**, surrogate decision makers base their decisions on what they believe will provide the most benefits and the least burdens for the child. The best interest standard is a quality-of-life assessment; when using it, a surrogate decision maker must "determine the highest probable net benefit among the available options, assigning different weights to interests the patient has in each option" and discounting or subtracting inherent risks or costs (Beauchamp & Childress, 2019, p. 141). "The best interest standard protects an incompetent person's welfare interests by requiring surrogates to assess the risks and probable benefits of various treatments and alternatives to treatment" (p. 141). Because of its basis and use, the best interest standard is a quality of life standard.

The standard of best interest is like the standard of substituted judgment, but the two standards are distinctly different. The aim of the **standard of substituted judgment** is for a surrogate to make decisions that abide by the previously known (either verbalized or inferred) treatment preferences persons had when they were able to express those preferences (i.e., when they were competent) at a time when persons are no longer able to express treatment preferences (i.e., when they are no longer competent). Thus, some ethicists argue that only a standard of best interest is appropriate when decisions are made for children or persons incompetent since childhood. When decisions are being made for persons who have never been legally competent, there is no history of known preferences based on the person's competent thinking.

In using the best interest standard, guardians must sacrifice their personal goals for their child in favor of the child's needs and interests. Guardians are put in a difficult situation when they must be uncompromising in trying to attend to one child's best interest when it may conflict with the best interest of another child or children within the same family (Ross, 1998).

Withholding Information from Children

Just as with adults, family members may want health information withheld from children when the children are seriously ill or have a terminal condition. This can present a dilemma for healthcare professionals caught between their patients and patients' parental surrogate decision makers. In evaluating the ethical acceptability of withholding information from children, nurses should consider the decreasing acceptability of using therapeutic privilege (see an earlier chapter 2). Harrison (2011) proposed that principles of fidelity and truthfulness are at the heart of the issue in these circumstances. Fidelity and truthfulness also can be viewed from the perspective of virtues. Healthcare professionals are charged with being faithful to their professional, ethical commitments to their patients and to interact with their patients truthfully. Truthfulness in practice can be clouded by feelings of paternalism and confusion about where to draw lines with therapeutic privilege.

Withholding information from children and adolescents, like allowances for minors refusing treatment, should be guided by the minor patients' maturity and developmental status. Consequently, there is no one correct answer to whether health information should be withheld from minors, but there are guidelines for making decisions (Harrison, 2011):

- It is difficult to keep secrets in a hospital. Sometimes, patients' fears arising from lack of information while observing and listening to what actually is happening in the environment is worse than fears resulting from truthful disclosure. Also, older children and adolescents are adept at gathering information via technological sources.
- Professionals and guardians must determine the risk of harm to the patient if information is withheld.
- A multidisciplinary team and an ethics consultation should be involved in decision making.
- If the team's determinations differ from those of the guardians, attempts should be made to negotiate. Negotiation in terms of when information is disclosed, how quickly it is disclosed, how it is disclosed, and by whom it is disclosed sometimes helps guardians accept the importance of adhering to the principles of fidelity and truthfulness in their child's care.

Refusal of Treatment

Parents and guardians sometimes refuse treatment for their children, and children themselves may, in some cases, be deemed to have decisional capacity to refuse treatment based on religious beliefs or other reasons. In general, religious and cultural beliefs are given respect in healthcare matters and protected through liberties granted by the U.S. Constitution (Jonsen et al., 2022). Serious consideration must be given to the wishes of maturing children who are judged to have good insight

about the benefits and burdens of their healthcare treatment. The following factors should be taken into consideration and carefully weighed when evaluating the extent of autonomy to be granted to minor children in refusing health care, keeping in mind, however, that efforts need to be made not to undermine the relationship between children and their mothering persons (Jonsen et al., 2006):

- The support for the child's request by the child's mothering person
- The severity of the child's condition, such as a child with a terminal and irreversible condition who refuses additional painful treatment versus a situation, such as meningitis, in which the child's condition is acute and reversible
- The consequence of direct harm to the child that potentially could result from the child's decision and the child's realistic understanding of the possible consequences
- Fear, distress, or parental pressure as a motivation for the child's decision

LEGAL PERSPECTIVE: PROTECTION OF VULNERABLE CHILDREN

Courts have consistently intervened to order blood transfusions for the minor children of Jehovah's Witnesses. Courts were once inclined to order transfusion for a guardian whose death would leave children orphaned but now rarely do so because alternative care for children is usually available.

Jonsen, A. R., Siegler, M., & Winslade, W. J. (2022). Clinical ethics: A practical approach to ethical decisions in clinical medicine (9th ed.). McGraw-Hill, p. 79.

Parental autonomy with regard to a child's healthcare treatment is usually given wide latitude (Jonsen et al., 2006, 2010; Ross, 1998); however, some parental refusals are considered to be abusive or neglectful. State laws protect children from parental healthcare decisions based on religious or other beliefs that can result in serious risk or harm to the child (Jonsen et al., 2006). Nevertheless, many states do not prosecute guardians for abuse or neglect if they try to refuse treatment based on religious beliefs. In general, the following principles are followed in overriding parental autonomy in the treatment of children:

- The guardian or guardians are not given the right of parental autonomy if they are deemed to be incapacitated or incompetent because of factors such as substance abuse, certain psychiatric disorders, minimal ability to comprehend the best interest of the child, or habitual physical abuse.
- As is done when considering respect for the autonomy of a child, the severity of the child's condition and the direct harm to the child that could result from nontreatment should be evaluated. The child should be treated even against the wishes of the guardians to prevent or cure serious disease or disability.
- Blood transfusions should be given to a child of a Jehovah's Witness when transfusions are needed to protect the child from the serious complications of disease or injury. Court authority need not be sought in an emergency situation because legal precedent protects the safety of the child.

When analyzing the ethical path to take regarding refusals of treatment for children, consultation may need to be sought from mental health practitioners or an ethics committee.

Impaired and Critically Ill Children

When neonatal intensive care units (NICUs) were developed in the 1960s, the goal was to increase the likelihood that premature babies would survive. Many medical and technological advances followed, and researchers are still making strides in neonatology today. NICUs are often complicated and scary

places for guardians who are grappling with the trauma of having a severely impaired or terminally ill neonate. Guardians frequently must make life-and-death decisions about their infants within a context that would be highly stressful even in the best of circumstances. NICUs are often emotionally charged places for nurses too as they watch the miracles of life play out before them while they also share in the experience of a family's deepest suffering.

Quality of Life

A term pregnancy is 40 weeks. In developed countries, the lower limit of viability for newborns is about 23 to 24 weeks. However, some people believe "the survival rate for babies born at 22 to 24 weeks is too low and the rate of disabilities among survivors is too high" to be justifiable in expending scarce resources on active interventions (Janvier & Lantos, 2011, loc. 3935). Whether one focuses on the justice of fairly distributing scarce healthcare resources, not violating the principle of nonmaleficence by inflicting harm on a newborn or child, or on matters of beneficence in trying to do good for both patients and families, quality-of-life determinations become a part of these important ethical analyses.

In regard to quality-of-life determinations for newborns and children, it is important to refer back to the ethical foundation of surrogate decision making for children, that is, the standard of best interest. There are at least two differences between how quality-of-life decisions are judged for infants and children as opposed to how they are judged for adults (Jonsen et al., 2010). Adults are either able to verbalize preferences reflecting their personal evaluations about the quality of their lives or other people have a general idea of those preferences when an adult becomes incapacitated. In contrast, "in pediatrics, the life whose quality is being assessed is almost entirely in the future, and no expression of preferences is available" (p. 158). Quality of life cannot be measured objectively like an Apgar score, though efforts have been made to measure it through quantitative tools (Wyatt, 2011).

Healthcare professionals must be aware of any tendencies they have to judge the quality of life of pediatric patients as lower than the children, to the best of their ability, or their mothering person would judge it. In reviewing research about health-related quality of life (HRQL) and children, Wyatt (2011) found studies showing the following:

- Children with cerebral palsy rated their HRQL higher than their guardians rated it.
- Healthcare professionals rated children's HRQL even lower than guardians' negative perceptions.
- Family dysfunction of various types in families with extremely low-birth-weight infants with neuroimpairment was no higher than in families with normal-birth-weight babies.
- Healthcare professionals' assumptions that infant impairment will lead to lower well-being in adolescence and adulthood was not borne out by data.

Healthcare professionals talk considerably about the importance of evidence-based practice. However, do nurses and other healthcare professionals take time to find evidence in forming perspectives about HRQL? Nurses are not in a position to make major, ethics-laden treatment decisions in the care of infants and children; even advanced practice nurses, such as nurse practitioners who work in obstetrics and NICUs, work in collaboration with other healthcare professionals. However, all nurses who work with children should be patient advocates and are potentially very influential in the healthcare decisions made by guardians and other healthcare providers. Practical wisdom, in the tradition of Socrates, Plato, and Aristotle, and the good character of nurses are essential elements in the compassionate care of children.

Withholding and Withdrawing Treatment

A comprehensive discussion of end-of-life issues generally can be used as a basis for considering decisions about withholding and withdrawing treatment for children; infants, however, fall into a special class of persons regarding withholding and withdrawing treatment.

Anyone who is seriously interested in the study of nursing and healthcare ethics realizes it is difficult to separate ethics from related laws, governmental regulations, and public policies. In evaluating the ethical care of infants in terms of withholding and withdrawing treatment, it is helpful to understand the history and circumstances involved with several landmark cases. Some of these cases help to summarize and clarify the usual expected actions with regard to the treatment of infants, although conclusions about the ethical directions provided by these cases are by no means without dispute. The following discussion is based on public information about these cases and a history provided by Pence (2004).

ETHICAL REFLECTION

Infant Charlie Gard was born in Great Britain on August 4, 2016, with a rare, inherited, and fatal condition called encephalomyopathic mitochondrial DNA depletion syndrome (MDDS). A legal battle ensued among Charlie's guardians, the Great Ormond Street Hospital in London, and the British court system when the Gards wanted to take their infant to the United States for a noninvasive experimental treatment. The fight was publicized worldwide, and a U.S. physician agreed to accept Charlie. Though Charlie's guardians raised money for the treatment, the case stalled so long in the court system that

Charlie's condition deteriorated to the point that his guardians gave up their fight. Charlie died on July 28, 2017, in hospice care.

1. With your peers, form at least two groups. In your group, thoroughly research the events in Charlie's case.
2. Use the Four Topics Method (see Table 2-1 in an earlier chapter 2) to analyze Charlie's case.
3. One group should approach the case from the perspective of an ethics committee at the Great Ormond Street Hospital, and the other group should approach the case from the perspective of an ethics committee at the U.S. hospital considering accepting Charlie for treatment.
4. Make a recommendation about Charlie's care based on your analysis of the case.
5. Present your group's analysis to your peers.

1971: Johns Hopkins Cases

In the 1970s, two infants with Down syndrome were "allowed to die" at Johns Hopkins Hospital, based on what some people believe were the selfish motives of the guardians (Pence, 2004, p. 217). A third infant with Down syndrome was referred to Johns Hopkins shortly thereafter because of the hospital's reputation for allowing the other two infants to die. However, at this point the hospital staff presented a more balanced view of the infant's prognosis that resulted in a different outcome: the third baby was treated and lived.

1984: Child Abuse Amendments (Baby Doe Rules)

The Child Abuse Amendments of 1984, also referred to as the Baby Doe rules, are based on the case of Infant Doe, who was born in Indiana in 1982. "Baby Doe cases arise when parents of impaired neonates or physicians charged with the care of these neonates question whether continued treatment is worthwhile and consider forgoing treatment in order to hasten death" (Pence, 2004, p. 216).

Many of the events in the short life of Infant Doe greatly influenced precedence and directions of the treatment for impaired newborns. Infant Doe was born on April 9, 1982, and died 6 days later (Pence, 2004). The controversy surrounding the care of Infant Doe was based on disagreements about whether treatment should be withheld because the infant had Down syndrome and a tracheoesophageal fistula. The obstetrician who delivered Infant Doe discouraged the parents from seeking surgical correction of the fistula and indicated the baby might become a "mere blob" (Pence, 2004, p. 220). Based on the obstetrician's recommendations and their own beliefs, the parents refused care for their infant. Hospital staff and administrators disagreed with this decision and appealed the decision to a county judge. No guardian ad litem was appointed for the baby, and an unrecorded, middle-of-the-night hearing was conducted by the judge at the hospital. The meeting resulted in the judge's support for the parents' decision. The hospital staff appealed the decision unsuccessfully all the way to the Indiana Supreme Court. They were in the process of taking the case to the U.S. Supreme Court when Infant Doe died.

The specific details of what followed these events are interesting but beyond the scope of this chapter. The ultimate outcome is that the media attention given to the Infant Doe case precipitated action by the Reagan administration, specifically the U.S. Department of Justice and the U.S. Department of Health and Human Services (Pence, 2004). **Baby Doe rules** were published by the federal government and became effective on February 12, 1984. The rules were based on Section 504 of the Rehabilitation Act of 1973, which forbids discrimination based entirely on a person's handicaps. The Baby Doe rules provide for a curtailment of federal funds to institutions that violate the regulations.

According to Pence (2004), "this interpretation by the Justice Department created a new conceptual synthesis: imperiled newborns were said to be handicapped citizens who could suffer discrimination against their civil rights" (p. 221). It is noteworthy that the federal Second Circuit Court of Appeals issued a ruling within 10 days of the Baby Doe rules that made the new rules essentially unenforceable. This ruling was based on the case of Baby Jane Doe.

LEGAL PERSPECTIVE: THE CASE OF INFANT DOE

The U.S. Civil Rights Commission reviewed the Infant Doe case in 1989, along with other Baby Doe cases, and "the commission concluded that [the obstetrician's] evaluation was 'strikingly out of touch with the contemporary evidence on the capabilities of people with Down syndrome.'"

Reproduced from U.S. Commission on Civil Rights, as cited by Pence, G. (2004). Classic cases in medical ethics. McGraw-Hill, p. 220.

Baby Jane Doe: Kerri-Lynn

Baby Jane Doe, Kerri-Lynn A., was born in 1983 at St. Charles Hospital in Long Island, New York. She was transferred to the NICU at the University Hospital of the State University of New York (SUNY) at Stony Brook because of her complicated condition at birth. Kerri-Lynn was born with spina bifida, hydrocephalus, an impaired kidney, and microcephaly (Pence, 2004). Her parents were lower middle-class people who had been married for only 4 months when Kerri-Lynn was conceived. After Kerri-Lynn was born, there was disagreement among the medical staff and other people about whether she should be treated or provided with comfort measures (food, hydration, and antibiotics) and allowed to die. The parents decided in favor of withholding aggressive treatment.

The controversy resulted in legal proceedings, eventually including the involvement of the U.S. Department of Justice and the U.S. Department of Health and Human Services. Leaders within these agencies wanted to send representatives to review Kerri-Lynn's medical records to ascertain whether the Baby Doe rules were being violated. However, the parents and the hospital objected to allowing the government representatives to review the records. Ultimately, a federal appeals court and then the U.S. Supreme Court ruled in favor of the parents and the hospital in the case of *Bowen v. American Hospital Association et al.* in 1986 (Pence, 2004).

This ruling essentially removed the enforcement potential from the Baby Doe rules. The rules cannot be enforced if the government has no authority to review the individual medical records of infants to determine if the rules are being violated. The Supreme Court explained that because the guardians do not receive federal funds for the provision of medical care, their decisions are not bound by Section 504 of the Rehabilitation Act (Pence, 2004). Baby Jane Doe's parents later allowed the recommended surgery to be performed (see **BOX 5-1**). The attorney who represented

BOX 5-1 The Case of Kerri-Lynn

In 1994, B. D. Colen was a lecturer in social medicine at Harvard University. He provided an update on Kerri-Lynn:

> Now a 10-year-old . . . Baby Jane Doe is not only a self-aware little girl, who experiences and returns the love of her parents; she also attends a school for developmentally disabled children—once again proving that medicine is an art, not a science, and clinical decision making is best left in the clinic, to those who will have to live with the decision being made.

Pence, G. (2004). Classic cases in medical ethics. McGraw-Hill, p. 226.

her parents reported in 1998 that Kerri-Lynn was 15 years old and living with her parents.

Although "in reality [the Baby Doe regulations] do not apply directly to physicians, nurses, or parents, it does get the attention of many" (Carter & Leuthner, 2003, p. 484). The Child Abuse Amendments of 1984 (Baby Doe rules) generally provide three reasons to withhold treatment from newborns; confusion remains, however, about whether the rules are an attempt to mandate nutrition, hydration, and medications for all neonates. This confusion, in addition to the compassion most people feel toward a dying or severely impaired child, is one reason healthcare professionals experience moral uncertainty in relation to decisions about withholding and withdrawing treatment from neonates. The 1984 amendments state the following:

> The term "withholding of medically indicated treatment" does not include the failure to provide treatment (other than appropriate nutrition, hydration, or medication) to an infant when, in the treating physician's . . . reasonable medical judgment:
>
> 1. the infant is chronically and irreversibly comatose,
> 2. the provision of such treatment would
>   a. merely prolong dying,
>   b. not be effective in ameliorating or correcting all of the infant's life-threatening conditions, or
>   c. otherwise be futile in terms of the survival of the infant, or
> 3. the provision of such treatment would be virtually futile in terms of the survival of the infant and the treatment itself under such circumstances would be inhumane. (U.S. Child Abuse Amendments of 1984, as cited in Carter & Leuthner, 2003, p. 484)

According to Carter and Leuthner (2003), the language in these rules addressing situations in which aggressive treatment of infants is not required can be interpreted to mean two things with regard to nutrition: "(1) every infant should always be provided with medical means of nutrition [or] (2) every infant should receive nutrition appropriate for his/her medical situation" (p. 484).

Carter and Leuthner (2003) proposed that the Baby Doe rules should not be interpreted to restrict or prevent the withdrawal of nutrition. However, interpretations of the rules with regard to withholding and withdrawing nutrition, hydration, and medications vary among healthcare providers and institutions, and as mentioned previously, healthcare providers experience moral uncertainty regarding these rules. When situations arise that precipitate discussions about withholding and withdrawing nutrition and hydration from newborns, the involvement of an ethics committee is recommended. It also may be helpful for healthcare professionals serving on an ethics committee to obtain consultation from ethicists who specialize in pediatric care.

In 2007, the American Academy of Pediatrics issued a policy statement covering the noninitiation or withdrawal of intensive care for high-risk newborns (Committee on Fetus and Newborn, 2007). The directive to make decisions in partnership with parents or guardians and in the best interest of the child is emphasized throughout the statement. The committee reaffirmed its previous position that treatment decisions should consider serious birth defects, prognosis, and future disability as predicted by the best data available. Because ethicists agree in regard to adult patients, the committee asserted that there is essentially no ethical difference between withholding and withdrawing care with high-risk neonates.

The difficulty in predicting long-term outcomes of extremely premature or terminally ill infants serves to intensify decision dilemmas. An ethical dilemma involves a situation in which one must choose between two choices and neither choice is good or the better choice is unclear. If intensive care is chosen, an infant may experience a prolonged dying process, suffering, or futile care (Committee on Fetus and Newborns, 2007). If intensive care is not chosen, increased morbidity and mortality occur.

Generally, healthcare professionals are not obligated to provide patients with futile care, though this practice was successfully challenged in the case of Baby K (as seen in the next section). Regardless, healthcare professionals must remember that the patient should be their primary focus of concern. If parents or guardians and healthcare professionals disagree about a child's treatment, discussion should occur to reach an agreement. If agreement is still not forthcoming, an ethics committee consultation should be sought. Offering to transfer the child to other healthcare providers may be necessary. Finally, getting help from the legal system should be the last option in the process of resolving disagreements.

1993: In the Matter of Baby K

Although the Baby Doe rules provide a basis for the right of guardians to refuse treatment for their severely disabled newborns, the ruling left the unanswered question of whether guardians also have the right to insist on treatment for their newborns when medical staff believe the treatment would be futile or useless. The landmark case that provides a precedent for this type of situation involved Baby K, born with anencephaly in 1992. Baby K's mother insisted that a hospital provide maximum treatment for her child, including ventilator support. Hospital physicians disagreed with the mother's wishes and proposed that warmth, nutrition, and hydration were all that should be provided in Baby K's care. The case was taken to the legal system for resolution. In reviewing this case, judges noted that medical assessments indicated Baby K was not being subjected to care requested by her mother that would cause the baby pain or suffering. Judges

serving on the U.S. Court of Appeals for the Fourth Circuit ruled in favor of the mother and ordered the hospital to provide the level of care Baby K's mother requested (*In the Matter of Baby K*, 1993).

▶ The Influence of Nurses: Character

Those who stand for nothing, fall for anything.

—Alexander Hamilton

The good character or virtuous behavior of nurses, other healthcare professionals, and parents or guardians is not the only character relevant to the well-being of children. A child's own character development is important too. School nurses are in a special position to help with this, and any nurse who works with children would do well to keep in mind the importance of influencing the development of a child's good character and educating others about this development. Ryan and Bohlin (1999) suggested that children need to be engaged in "heart, mind, and head" to know "who [they] are" and "what [they] stand for" (pp. xvi–xvii).

The search for the meaning of life overshadows almost all human endeavors in people young and old. In the fast-paced world of the 21st century, parents and guardians are busy trying to provide their families with necessities and physical comforts, and children are often busy playing video games and watching television—there is scarcely time to ponder the greater mysteries of life. Ryan and Bohlin (1999) proposed that "detached from a conception of the purpose of life, virtues become merely nice ideals, empty of meaning" (p. 39). They suggested adults should not fear stimulating children to ponder the age-old question about why they were born. Many children, but particularly children who are ill, think about the meaning of life even when they do not know how to articulate their feelings. Nurses can provide these children with a kind hand and a warm heart during frightening times.

Anytime is a good time to take the opportunity to educate children in the development of moral and intellectual virtues. Stenson (1999) proposed three ways to help children internalize virtuous habits and strengths of character when they are on their journey from infancy to adulthood. The three means of internalization, and the order in which they occur, are as follows:

1. By example: Children learn from what they witness in the lives of parents and other adults they respect (and thus, unconsciously imitate).

2. Through directed practice: Children learn from what they are repeatedly led to do or are made to do by parents and other respected adults.

3. From words: Children learn from what they hear from parents and other respected adults as explanations for what they witness and are led to do (p. 207).

Nurses are patient advocates, but they also are role models. Nurses may never know when the example they show to children and their mothering person may influence the future of a child or the future of nursing.

KEY POINTS

- The words *mother* and *mothering person* can be gender neutral.
- Children and other people may be harmed when children are not immunized. Nurses must understand the best ways to interact with guardians who refuse to have their children immunized.
- Globally, many children become sick and die every year from preventable diseases and conditions.
- Nurses are mandatory reporters of child abuse. There is legal protection in most states for nurses who report suspected child abuse in good faith.
- The best interest standard is generally the ethical approach used in making difficult decisions about the healthcare treatment of children.
- Children often perceive their own health-related quality of life to be higher than their guardians or healthcare professionals perceive it to be.
- The ethics of allowing children themselves or their guardians to refuse healthcare treatments is based on a number of factors. These factors include the severity of the potential harm to the child that may result from the refusal.
- The Child Abuse Amendments of 1984 are frequently referred to as the Baby Doe rules. Although these rules lack power in actual enforcement, they are influential in decisions regarding the withholding and withdrawing of supportive care for infants.

References

American Nurses Association. (2018). *American Nurses Association calls for an immediate end to immoral and cruel practice of separating children from their families.* https://www.nursingworld.org/news/news-releases/2018/separation-of-children-families/

American Nurses Association. (2015). *The code of ethics for nurses with interpretive statements.*

Barrientos, A., Abdulai, A-G., Demirag, D., de Groot, R., & Ragno, L.P. (2016). Why assist people living in poverty? The ethics of poverty reduction. *Innocenti Working Paper,* IWP_2016_27. https://www.unicef-irc.org/publications/871-why-assist-people-living-in-poverty-the-ethics-of-poverty-reduction.html

Beauchamp, T. L., & Childress, J. F. (2019). *Principles of biomedical ethics* (8th ed.). Oxford.

British Broadcasting Corporation (BBC). (2021). *Child migrants: Massive drop in children held by border officials.* https://www.bbc.com/news/world-us-canada-56405009

Carter, B. S., & Leuthner, S. R. (2003). The ethics of withholding/withdrawing nutrition in the newborn. *Seminars in Perinatology, 27*(6), 480–487.

Centers for Disease Control and Prevention (CDC). (2012). *If you choose not to vaccinate your child, understand the risks and responsibilities* [PDF file]. https://www.cdc.gov/vaccines/hcp/conversations/downloads/not-vacc-risks-bw-office.pdf

Centers for Disease Control and Prevention (CDC). (2021a). *Chickenpox (Varicella): Transmission.* https://www.cdc.gov/chickenpox/about/transmission.html

Centers for Disease Control and Prevention (CDC). (2021b). *Provider resources for vaccine conversations with parents.* https://www.cdc.gov/vaccines/hcp/conversations/index.html

Centers for Disease Control and Prevention (CDC). (2022). *Public health law: State school immunization requirements and vaccine exemption laws.* https://www.cdc.gov/phlp/docs/school-vaccinations.pdf

Child Welfare Information Gateway. (2019a). *About CAPTA: A legislative history.* https://www.childwelfare.gov/pubPDFs/about.pdf

Child Welfare Information Gateway. (2019b). *Definitions of child abuse and neglect.* https://www.childwelfare.gov/pubpdfs/define.pdf

Child Welfare Information Gateway. (2019c). *What is child abuse and neglect? Recognizing the signs and symptoms.* https://www.childwelfare.gov/pubpdfs/whatiscan.pdf

Childhelp. (n.d.). *Handling child abuse disclosures.* https://www.childhelp.org/wp-content/uploads/2021/11/Handling-Disclosures.pdf

Committee on Fetus and Newborn. (2007). Noninitiation of withdrawal of intensive care for high-risk newborns. *Pediatrics, 119*(2), 401–403.

Dalai Lama. (1999). *Ethics for the new millennium.* Riverhead Books.

Erikson, E. H. (1985). *Childhood and society* (35th ed.). W. W. Norton. (Original work published 1950)

Haider, A. (2021). *The basic facts about children in poverty.* https://www.americanprogress.org/issues/poverty/reports/2021/01/12/494506/basic-facts-children-poverty/

Harrison, C. (2011). Fidelity and truthfulness in the pediatric setting: Withholding information from children and adolescents. In D. S. Diekema, M. R. Mercurio, & M. B. Adam (Eds.), *Clinical ethics in pediatrics: A case-based textbook* [Kindle version] (loc. 1545–1773). Cambridge University Press.

Held, V. (1993). *Feminist morality: Transforming culture, society, and politics.* University of Chicago Press.

In the Matter of Baby K, 832 F. Supp. 1022 (E.D. Va. 1993).

Janvier, A., & Lantos, J. D. (2011). Variations of practice in the care of extremely preterm infants. In D. S. Diekema, M. R. Mercurio, & M. B. Adam (Eds.), *Clinical ethics in pediatrics: A case-based textbook* [Kindle version] (loc. 3935–4150). Cambridge University Press.

Jonsen, A. R., Siegler, M., & Winslade, W. J. (2006). *Clinical ethics: A practical approach to ethical decisions in clinical medicine* (6th ed.). New York, NY: McGraw-Hill.

Jonsen, A. R., Siegler, M., & Winslade, W. J. (2010). *Clinical ethics: A practical approach to ethical decisions in clinical medicine* (7th ed.). New York, NY: McGraw-Hill.

Jonsen, A. R., Siegler, M., & Winslade, W. J. (2022). *Clinical ethics: A practical approach to ethical decisions in clinical medicine* (9th ed.). [Kindle Edition]. McGraw-Hill.

MacIntyre, A. (1999). *Dependent rational animals: Why human beings need the virtues.* Chicago, IL: Open Court.

Nussbaum, M. C. (2001). *Upheavals of thought: The intelligence of emotions.* Cambridge University Press.

Pence, G. E. (2004). *Classic cases in medical ethics: Accounts of cases that have shaped medical ethics, with philosophical, legal, and historical backgrounds* (4th ed.). McGraw-Hill.

Ramsey, S. B. (2006). Abusive situations. In S. W. Killion & K. Dempski (Eds.), *Quick look nursing: Legal and ethical issues* (pp. 58–59). Jones and Bartlett Publishers.

Ray, M. (1989). The theory of bureaucratic caring for nursing practice in the organizational culture. *Nursing Administration Quarterly, 13*(2), 31–42.

Ray, M. (2001). The theory of bureaucratic caring. In M. Parker (Ed.), *Nursing theories and nursing practice* (pp. 421–444). F.A. Davis.

Ross, L. F. (1998). *Children, families, and health care decision-making.* Oxford University Press.

Ruddick, S. (1995). *Toward a politics of peace.* Beacon Press.

Rus, M., & Groselj, U. (2021). Ethics of vaccination in childhood—A framework based on the four principles of biomedical ethics. *Vaccines, 9*(2), 113.

Ryan, K., & Bohlin, K. E. (1999). *Building character in schools: Practical ways to bring moral instruction to life.* Jossey-Bass.

Schweiger, G. (2019). Ethics, poverty, and children's vulnerability. *Ethics and social Welfare, 13*(3) 288–301.

Stange, M., & Stark, B. (2019). The ethical and public health implications of family separation. *Public Health and the Law, 47*(S2), 91–94.

Stenson, J. B. (1999). Appendix C: An overview of the virtues. In K. Ryan & K. E. Bohlin (Eds.), *Building character in schools: Practical ways to bring moral instruction to life* (pp. 207–211). Jossey-Bass.

Stephen, J.M., & Zoucha, R. (2020). A call for nurse leader action: Ethical nursing care of Latinx unauthorized immigrant children and families. *Nurse Leader.* https://doi.org/10.1016/j.mnl.2020.08.002

Stimpson, C. R. (1993). Series editor's foreword. In V. Held (Ed.), *Feminist morality: Transforming culture, society, and politics* (pp. vii–ix). University of Chicago Press.

Tong, R. (1997). *Feminist approaches to bioethics: Theoretical reflections and practical applications.* Westview.

Turkel, M. C. (2007). Dr. Marilyn Ray's theory of bureaucratic caring. *International Journal for Human Caring, 11*(4), 57– 67.

United Nations International Children's Emergency Fund (UNICEF). (n.d.). *Child poverty.* https://www.unicef.org/social-policy/child-poverty

United Nations International Children's Emergency Fund (UNICEF). (2020). *East Asia and Pacific press release.* https://www.unicef.org/eap/press-releases/150-million-additional-children-plunged-poverty-due-covid-19-unicef-save-children

United Nations International Children's Emergency Fund (UNICEF). (2021). *New approach needed to ensure protection and care for unaccompanied migrant children in the United States.* https://www.unicef.org/press-releases/new-approach-needed-ensure-protection-and-care-unaccompanied-migrant-children-united

U.S. Department of Health and Human Services (HHS), Administration for Children and Families. (2021, November 15). *Latest UC data—FY2021.* https://www.hhs.gov/programs/social-services/unaccompanied-children/latest-uc-data-fy2021/index.html

U.S. Department of Health and Human Services (HHS), Administration for Children and Families, Administration on Children, Youth and Families, Children's Bureau. (2022, January 19). *Child Maltreatment 2020.* https://www.acf.hhs.gov/cb/report/child-maltreatment-2020

U.S. Department of Health and Human Services (HHS), Administration for Children & Families. (n.d.). *Unaccompanied children.* https://www.acf.hhs.gov/orr/programs/uc

World Health Organization (WHO). (2020). *Children: Improving survival and well-being.* https://www.who.int/news-room/fact-sheets/detail/children-reducing-mortality

Wyatt, J. (2011). The role of quality of life assessments in neonatal care. In D. S. Diekema, M. R. Mercurio, & M. B. Adam (Eds.), *Clinical ethics in pediatrics: A case-based textbook* [Kindle version] (loc. 3749–3920). Cambridge University Press.

CHAPTER 6

Adolescent Nursing Ethics

Janie B. Butts

OBJECTIVES

After reading this chapter, the reader should be able to do the following:

1. Explore the phases of adolescent development.
2. Compare trust, privacy, and confidentiality and their significance regarding healthcare information, nursing care of adolescents, and adolescent decision-making capacity.
3. Delineate the major at-risk behaviors in which adolescents engage.
4. Examine the major causes of adolescent deaths.
5. Evaluate the significance of appropriate and inappropriate communication by health educators who teach adolescents a prevention program with health risk messages.
6. Analyze the safety and effectiveness or the Covid-19 vaccine for adolescents in relation to monitoring systems, side effects, and the ethics of the vaccine.
7. Explore the HPV vaccination, benefits, and ethical issues related to HPV vaccines for adolescents.
8. Discuss other critical health issues triggering ethical concerns, pregnancy and abortion, HIV infection and STDs, alcohol and other drug use, eating disorders and Ana Book Camp and Mia websites, sexual assault, and suicide, depression and suicidal ideation.
9. Delineate the five stages of grief that adolescents and others experience during their own dying process.
10. Discuss essential competencies that nurses should demonstrate during the planning and care of adolescents, and include the major concepts from the American Nurses Association (ANA, 2015) *Code of Ethics for Nurses with Interpretive Statements.*

▶ The Age of Adolescence

Good and bad experiences shape the way adolescents make life decisions and move toward independence. Through these tempestuous times, adolescents somehow develop their identity and sense of sexuality. Experts describe adolescence as a period of transition that differs in length for each person and occurs during the second decade of life (DiClemente et al., 1996; Leffert & Petersen, 1999). It is a time of a remarkable succession of physical, cognitive, emotional, moral, and psychosocial development changes.

Three separate phases, spanning 11 years, characterize the **adolescent developmental process** (*Journal of Advanced Practice eJournal*, "Issues in Providing Health Maintenance to Adolescents," 2002). **Early adolescence** (ages 11 to 13) is a transitional period from childhood to middle adolescence and is usually marked by the onset of puberty, concrete thinking, testing the guardian value system, preferring peers to guardians, experimentation, and discovery. **Middle adolescence** (ages 14 to 18) is dominated by peer pressure; peer orientation; self-centeredness; concrete thinking with a developing ability to think abstractly; and stereotypical behaviors, such as following clothing trends and listening to music that is accepted by peers. **Late adolescence** (ages 18 to 21) usually indicates a transition from adolescence to adulthood and is characterized by abstract thinking, idealism, and individual relationships rather than a focus on peer groups. Late-stage adolescents generally begin to place more importance on their future and life plans as they advance through this stage.

Adolescents have a need to find out who they are and a desire to push limits and test unknown waters. Most adolescents, especially in the early and middle stages, make decisions based on their values from concrete thinking, the pressure of peer approval, and exposure to a quickly changing world around them. Mistakes and failures, but also successes, will occur along the way. Adolescents need to be encouraged to make autonomous decisions and express their values and preferences on a continuous basis so they will evolve to maturity with a defined sense of self.

Ethical Issues and Concerns Involving Adolescents

The age of adolescence brings with it overpowering family decision-making issues and health concerns, and as a result, complex ethical issues arise (**BOX 6-1**). Perplexing questions arise when relationships between guardian or others and adolescents begin to disintegrate swiftly into disharmony.

BOX 6-1 Ethical Issues and Concerns Involving Adolescents

- Adolescent relationships and communication
- Confidentiality, privacy, and trust
  - Trust–privacy–confidentiality dilemma
  - Limits of confidentiality
- Respect for autonomy and the consent process
- Covid-19 vaccines for adolescents, autonomy, nonmaleficence, and beneficence
  - Monitoring systems and side effects
  - The ethics of Covid-19 vaccines and adolescents
- Adolescent health risk behaviors, vaccines, nonmaleficence, and beneficence
  - Prevention education for adolescent health risk behaviors
    - Abstinence-only programs or comprehensive sex education programs
  - Pregnancy and abortion related to unprotected sex
  - Human papillomavirus (HPV), HPV Vaccines and Benefits, human immunodeficiency virus (HIV), and other sexually transmitted diseases (STIs) related to unprotected sex
    - HPV infection
    - HPV vaccines and benefits
    - HIV infection
    - Other STDs
  - Alcohol and other drug abuse related to adolescents
  - Eating disorders related to adolescents
  - Sexual abuse related to adolescents
  - Depression and suicidal ideation related to adolescents
  - Facing death
    - Losing a loved one
    - Adolescents facing their own death

The focus of adolescents' ethical issues is mostly on rights—the rights all people expect. Some of those rights include

- the right of freedom to consent to or refuse treatment—examples include receiving vaccines for HPV or Covid-19 or chemotherapy treatment for cancer
- the right to confidentiality and privacy—such as an adolescent's medical record
- the right not to be violated, exploited, or taken advantage of in terms of membership in a vulnerable age group—such as participating as a subject in research

Adolescent Relationships and Communication

Relationships are central to the adolescent's life. Because of the value adolescents place on relationships, nurses need to remember that positive and negative relationship skills learned within a family continue with children into the adolescent stage. As a result of these persistent skills, adolescents experience a complex set of feelings, ranging from excitement and happiness to sadness and loneliness.

When any changes in adolescent behavior go unnoticed by guardians or other people in authority, adolescents sometimes resort to silent suffering (San Francisco Bay Area Center for Cognitive Therapy, 2021). Additionally, if adolescents believe no one listens to their needs and desires at all, they may become silent sufferers. One of the most common assertions nurses hear from adolescents is "They don't listen to me!" Ironically, guardians often say, "My kid won't listen to me!" When it comes to other relationships involving adolescents, similar statements are sometimes made: "My teacher doesn't listen to my complaints," "That nurse didn't understand my problem," and so on. When guardians, teachers, and nurses do begin to notice behaviors that seem strange or extreme, they may have difficulty in discerning between an adolescent's everyday sense of angst, frustration, anger, or fear and

a serious mental health issues, such as anxiety or depression.

Adolescents want and need to be heard and understood; guardians want to give their opinions and be heard. Adolescents want relationships of their own with each other without interference from authority figures. On the other hand, healthcare and other professionals want to educate adolescents on illness management or prevention of harm, and media personnel want to grab adolescents' attention by whatever means necessary. Between adolescents' own notions about relationships and interactions with others and the incoming everyday opinions and prevention education messages from guardians, teachers, nurses, and media, a clear form communication and mutual respect become critical elements in adolescent relationships.

The question is *how do nurses help*? **Mindfulness** and **effective listening** are important strategies to implement and, when used, indicates the nurse is paying close attention to what is being said and will give a signal of awareness and understanding to the speaker. **Communication** is an ideal ethical nursing competency that encompasses mindfulness and effective listening (see an earlier chapter 3). Nurses have an ethical obligation to provide beneficent competent care, and one way is for them to create positive relationships to work toward better patient outcomes. By practicing mindfulness and effective listening, nurses will earn the respect of most young people, which is a critical factor in nurse–adolescent relationships.

Confidentiality, Privacy, and Trust

Confidentiality, privacy, and trust cannot be viewed as separate entities in a nurse–adolescent relationship. From an ethical standpoint, confidentiality, privacy, and trust are tightly woven with respect for autonomy, the adolescent's right to privacy, and the rights of

service. **Confidentiality** is linked with privacy and trust and usually means information given to the nurse or physician is to be kept secret and not shared with third parties without express consent. Nurses have an ethical and legal obligation to keep records confidential. **Privacy** allows the freedom from an intrusion into one's personal information and matters, such as any action for which a person has a reasonable expectation of privacy. **Trust** means that adolescents sometimes explore their vulnerabilities with healthcare providers while believing that providers will not take advantage of them. In other words, adolescents believe providers are reliable and dependable in managing their health and vulnerabilities. Any breach of confidentiality, privacy, or trust is viewed as a violation of autonomy.

Trust is important to a healthy and respectful relationship. If trust is broken and mistrust develops, it is very difficult for the informer (nurse) to regain trust. Adolescents will probably refuse to listen to anything nurses try to convey. Trust is a basic need that must be developed in the first stage of life, according to Erikson (1963). If trust is broken early in an individual's life, mistrust carries to all of the person's relationships.

If adolescents do not trust the nurse, they may not listen to explanations during an informed consent process. Nursing strategies to promote a trusting relationship with adolescents are highlighted in the Ethical Reflection:

ETHICAL REFLECTION: STRATEGIES FOR PROMOTING A TRUSTING RELATIONSHIP WITH ADOLESCENTS

The most important way for nurses to gain the trust of adolescents is by relentlessly proving themselves in the following ways:

- Be consistent.
- Give correct information.
- Keep commitments.
- Show concern and caring.

Strategies for Promoting a Trusting Relationship with Adolescents. These activities, when combined, help indicate the trustworthiness of nurses, meaning that nurses are dependable and commit to their obligations (Gullotta et al., 2000).

Trust–Privacy–Confidentiality Dilemma

A legal, ethical, political, and practical issue surfaces when a trusting relationship exists and the nurse is entrusted with an adolescent's confidential information. Sometimes, the nature of the information pertaining to a sensitive issue is potentially harmful to the adolescent if it is not reported to proper authorities or others (University of Chicago, 2013). Adolescents are concerned about their privacy and what others think of them, especially their guardians and peers. Nurses need to ensure that adolescents are examined privately and away from their guardians and peers. Often, the physical and emotional health outcomes of risky behaviors force adolescents to seek medical treatment. Because of the sensitive issues involved and a potential for these issues to cause embarrassment, adolescents want to keep the information private and especially do not want their guardians to know.

Well-established research findings in the United States reveal that the likelihood of adolescents seeking health services for sensitive issues depends on how well their sensitive issues remain confidential. Adolescents can seek family planning services at the state level, such as counseling and contraception through the *Planned Parenthood Federation of America*. Each state has a broad range of laws stemming from federal laws concerning confidentiality and consent of adolescents.

In the United States, one of several exceptions to adolescent autonomy over medical records sometimes involves the issue of abortion. Even with 38 states requiring some degree of guardian consent, 37 of these 38 states have sought ways to work completely around guardian involvement by exercising the judicial bypass, meaning adolescents may obtain approval from a court to bypass guardian involvement. See the Legal Perspective: Parental Involvement in Minors' Abortions by States 2021. If a minor below the age of 18 asks for an abortion procedure, some degree of guardian involvement for most states will be required or judicially bypassed, and 11 states require only guardian notification but no guardian consent (Guttmacher Institute. (2021a). Additionally, when the state does require guardian involvement, situations of medical emergency or extraordinary conditions will prompt exceptions to the guardian involvement law through the judicial process, such as when the pregnancy was the result of sexual assault or incest.

Limits of Confidentiality

From the beginning of their interaction, nurses need to assure adolescents of the importance they place on confidentiality in the nurse–patient relationship. However, confidentiality must never be guaranteed because it can be breached in instances that place the adolescent or others at harm or in danger—an exception called **limits of confidentiality** (University of Chicago, 2013).

Nurses should ensure they will not breach confidentiality *unless* harm or a potential threat to the patient or to known others is involved. In cases of potential harm, an adolescent must always be given a chance to disclose sensitive or controversial information to guardians or others involved, as appropriate. If the adolescent refuses to do so, nurses and other healthcare professionals are obligated to report certain information to state officials according to state laws. The reporting requirements vary from state to state, but reportable threats and harm are reasonably consistent from state to state.

Nurses must hold to these confidentiality and limits of confidentiality standards. Even if the situation is not considered a limit of

confidentiality, the nurse will find that holding to these confidentiality and limits of confidentiality standards with guardians may be difficult. However, the nurse should make an effort to involve the guardians for adolescents younger than age 14 because the guardianship lines of demarcation in these teens' younger years become even more blurry and questionable.

LEGAL PERSPECTIVE: GUARDIAN INVOLVEMENT IN MINORS' ABORTIONS BY STATES IN 2021

- 38 states require some degree of Guardian involvement in an adolescent's choice to have an abortion.
- 21 of the 38 states require guardian consent.
- 11 of the 38 states only require guardian notification, not consent.
- 6 of the 38 states require guardian consent and notification.
- 7 of the 38 states permit a minor to obtain an abortion if a grandparent or another adult relative is involved in the decision.
- 37 of the 38 states requiring guardian involvement have a judicial bypass procedure in place, which allows a minor to obtain approval from a court, and 7 of these require judges to use specific criteria to waive guardian involvement.
- 15 of these 37 states with judicial bypass the judge can use the clear and convincing evidence standard to determine if abortion is in the best interest when deciding whether or not to waive guardian involvement.
- 35 states permit a minor to obtain an abortion in a medical emergency without guardian consent.
- 16 states permit a minor to obtain an abortion without guardian consent in cases of abuse, assault, incest, or neglect.

Data from Guttmacher Institute. (2021b, September 1). *Parental involvement in minors' abortions.* https://www.guttmacher.org /state-policy/explore/parental-involvement-minors-abortions

Respect for Autonomy and Consent Process

Though adolescents should be age 18 or more to have full autonomy to give consent, those younger than age 18 years can give consent for their own care in a broad range of circumstances and services. Age 16 is usually the unofficial demarcation for many states (Drobac, 2017). The minors who can consent are those who act older by showing more maturity than a certain age or those who are legally emancipated, married, in the armed forces, living apart from their guardians, high school graduates, pregnant, or have already become guardians themselves (University of Chicago, 2013). They may also refuse treatment. The right for minor adolescents to consent to or refuse treatment is more frequently honored with certain types of services.

Deciding whether adolescents really have autonomous decision-making capacity is a consideration tightly linked to their personal self-directedness and characteristics, what Blustein and Moreno (1999) called **moral self-government**. The goal during adolescence is development of the moral self because most adolescents' moral selves are not yet fully formed. Blustein and Moreno stated that adolescents have an emerging capacity, which means the moral self is evolving but it is not doing so evenly or consistently. Traditionally, age and the stage of cognitive, emotional, and social development influence a person's ability to make mature decisions. The University of Chicago (2013) specified that an adolescent's capacity for decision making does not occur before age 15, but some experts delineate the cutoff for significant autonomous decision making as age 14.

For many years, adults in the United States and most of the world have valued the right to control their medical decisions. Adolescents are no different. In most states, these decisions are left up to healthcare professionals. If a valid consent between a nurse and an adolescent takes place, the initial phase should be more

LEGAL PERSPECTIVE: SERVICES RELATED TO AN ADOLESCENT'S RIGHT TO CONSENT

An adolescent's right to consent to or refuse treatment is honored more often with these services:

- Emergency care
- Family planning services, such as abortion, pregnancy care, and contraceptive services
- Diagnosis and treatment of STIs or any other reportable infection or communicable disease
- HIV or acquired immune deficiency syndrome (AIDS) testing and treatment
- Treatment and counseling for alcohol and other drugs
- Treatment for sexual assault and collection of medical evidence for sexual assault
- Inpatient mental health services
- Outpatient mental health services

FOCUS FOR DEBATE: ETHICAL ISSUES RELATED TO ADOLESCENT ABORTION

Kelly, age 16 years, has come to a clinic where you work as a nurse. She states that she is at least 12 weeks pregnant but has not told anyone, not even her guardians or boyfriend. She is fearful of losing her boyfriend if she tells him. She wants an abortion, has cash, and does not want anyone to know about the pregnancy or the abortion. The clinic is in a state that does not require direct guardian involvement but does require consent by someone of legal age, such as a grandmother or aunt.

- Explore the ethical issues and nursing strategies surrounding this situation with Kelly.
- Examine the trust–confidentiality–privacy issues, the consent process, autonomy, and communication.

of a dialogue and an educational exchange. During the consent process, the nurse's responsibility is to evaluate the adolescent's capacity for understanding and appreciating the process, especially with anticipated treatments or interventions. Examine the Legal Perspective: Services Related to an Adolescent's Right to Consent and consider the scenario in the Focus for Debate: Ethical Issues Related to Adolescent Abortion.

The consent process may not be just a one-time event, such as in a complex disease like cancer. Instead, when the required treatments and tests associated with the disease increase, so do the number of consents. During the initial treatment of the disease, one or both guardians may be highly involved in the consent process. Later in the treatment stages, adolescents may develop considerable maturity in decision making and therefore have the capacity to consent or not consent to subsequent treatments. The adolescent's level of understanding and appreciation of the content of the consent may have progressively increased. Over time, the adolescent can take on more, if not all, of the responsibility in the decision-making process, and dialogue and education continue throughout the treatment. During the treatment and consent phases, documentation of the adolescent's progress in development of the moral self is essential.

Covid-19 Vaccines for Adolescents, Autonomy, Nonmaleficence, and Beneficence

Just as all nonmandated or recommended vaccines for adolescents traditionally have been controversial between guardians, children, and recommendations from the Centers for Disease Control and Prevention (CDC), the controversy with the Covid19 vaccine is no different. On May 10, 2021, the Food and Drug Administration (FDA) authorized the PfizerBioNTech Covid-19 Vaccine for emergency use for adolescents, ages 12 to 15, so for now, the CDC recommends that everyone 12 years and older receive the Covid-19 vaccine (FDA, 2021). The Moderna Covid-19 Vaccine for adolescents will most likely be authorized for emergency use soon, if not already. The younger children, ages 5 to 11, will be authorized for use in the short future. By July 16, 2021, approximately 8.9 million adolescents, ages 12 to 17, had received the vaccine (Hause et al., *MMWR*, 2021). Although a specific number of adolescent vaccines by mid-August 2021 have not been clearly reported, four (4) in every 10 guardians reported their adolescents from ages 12 to 17 had already received at least one dose of the Covid-19 vaccine (Hamel et al., 2021).

Monitoring Systems and Side Effects

Indepth monitoring systems for the safety and efficacy of Covid-19 for all ages are at maximum priority by the FDA and CDC. The tracking and monitoring systems function on a continual ongoing basis and are classified in two ways: (1) passive surveillance, which can detect any safety issues and adverse effects quickly by way of reporting systems to the FDA and CDC; and (2) active surveillance, which has the ability to detect safety signals, severity, and complications of the vaccine very quickly in an extremely large data system that contains information for millions of people (FDA, 2021). For adolescents, ages 12 to 15, the majority of the Covid-19 vaccine reports have been positive and consistently effective.

Side effects do occur at varying degrees but the majority of the side effects have been consistently nonserious as reported by adolescents, ages 12 to 15 and ages 16 and older. Refer to the two Research Notes: first, Nonserious Side Effects from the Covid-19 Vaccine, Ages 12 and Older, and second, Nonserious and Serious Side Effects of Adolescents Ages 12 to 17 After Receiving the Covid-19 Vaccine.

RESEARCH NOTE: NONSERIOUS SIDE EFFECTS FROM THE COVID-19 VACCINE, AGES 12 AND OLDER

- Commonly Reported Side Effects
  - Arm pain at or surrounding the injection site
  - Tiredness and headache
  - Joint pain and muscle pain
  - Chills and fever
- Annotations and Explanations
  - Side effects tend to be more common after the second dose of the vaccine
  - People generally experience the side effects differently and uniquely
  - No side effects will be reported in some people

Data from Hause, A. M., Gee, J., Baggs, J., Abara, W. E., Marquez, P., Thompson, D., Ru, J. S., Licata, C., Rosenblum H. G., Myers, T. R., Dhimabukuro, T. T., & Shay, D. K. (2021). *COVID-19 vaccine safety in adolescents aged 12–17 years*—United States, December 14, 2020-July 16, 2021. Centers for Disease Control and Prevention. *Morbidity and Mortality Weekly Report, 70* (31), 1053–1058. https://www.cdc.gov/mmwr/volumes/70/wr/mm7031e1.htm

The Ethics of Covid-19 Vaccines and Adolescents

Historically, vaccines for all populations have been questioned by many regarding mandates, safety, and effectiveness. People in the communities and guardians of adolescents sometimes have religious and other political, philosophical, and conspiracy beliefs that provoke fear of the vaccines. Their beliefs potentially come into direct conflict with the recommendations of vaccines by the government. The ethical issues involved with vaccines could be endless. For the purpose of this section, the focus is narrowed to the principles of autonomy, beneficence, and nonmaleficence.

The government agencies, such as the CDC and the U.S. Department of Health and Human Services, have a beneficent obligation to contribute to the well-being of its people. In the Covid-19 pandemic, as with other crises,

RESEARCH NOTE: NONSERIOUS AND SERIOUS SIDE EFFECTS OF ADOLESCENTS AGES 12 TO 17 AFTER RECEIVING THE COVID-19 VACCINE

Shortly after the emergency use authorization, some cases of serious side effects, such as inflammation of the heart muscle (myocarditis) and the membrane enclosing the heart (pericarditis), among several other effects, began appearing in the reports at first by mostly males after the second dose of the vaccine.

- Between December 14, 2020 and July 16, 2021
  - 8.9 million adolescents vaccinated
  - 9,246 reported signs and symptoms, both nonserious and serious
- Of those 9,246 reporting, 8,383 (90.7%) categorized as nonserious side effects
  - Female 55.3%
  - Male 43.2%
- Of the 9,246 reporting, 863 (9.3%) categorized as serious side effects with heart-related events
  - Female 29.1%
  - Male 70.7%
- Of the 9,246 reporting, 14 deaths resulted
  - pulmonary embolism (2)
  - intracranial hemorrhage (2)
  - heart failure (1)
  - immune disorder and infection (1)
  - unknown (6)

Data from Hause, A. M., Gee, J., Baggs, J., Abara, W. E., Marquez, P., Thompson, D., Ru, J. S., Licata, C., Rosenblum H. G., Myers, T. R., Dhimabukuro, T. T., & Shay, D. K. (2021). COVID-19 vaccine safety in adolescents aged 12-17 years—United States, December 14, 2020-July 16, 2021. Centers for Disease Control and Prevention. *Morbidity and Mortality Weekly Report, 70* (31), 1053–1058. https://www.cdc.gov/mmwr/volumes/70/wr/mm7031e1.htm

this obligation is expressed in terms of applying a utilitarian approach to protect the citizens from illness and disease. The utilitarian approach allows the government, in this case, to distribute resources to the people with the intention of providing the greatest good for the greatest number of people with the least amount of harm. For the most part, utilitarianism encourages a beneficence principle of promoting good and a nonmaleficence principle of doing no harm (Beauchamp & Childress, 2019). Covid-19 vaccines are one way to accomplish providing the greatest good for the greatest number of people only if people consent to them. Individuals often view the government's efforts as meddling or interfering with their rights of autonomy and liberty, and refusing the vaccine is a way for people to exercise their autonomy rights. Based on their beliefs and opinions, they may determine there is not enough evidence to persuade them to take the vaccine.

Guardians and adolescents could be in disagreement about the Covid-19 vaccine. For instance, the teen may see the need to be vaccinated after researching safety, benefits, and risks, but the guardian(s) may disagree with the teen's wish. Just as with other legal matters of consent previously discussed in this chapter, adolescents may be allowed to consent to their own treatment under certain conditions, such as they should have the mental and emotional maturity and be informed of the risks and benefits of the vaccine to give an informed consent (Smith, 2021). Winning over the guardians or guardians winning over their teen would be a key factor for all people concerned in the decision, but everyone needs to understand the consent and the full range of safety, benefits, and risks involved. True, the Covid-19 vaccine has some serious side effects but statistics reveal that overall it is very safe and effective.

Adolescent Health Risk Behaviors, Nonmaleficence, and Beneficence

There are more than 1.8 billion young people living in the world, the largest number of adolescents in history, and of these 1.8 billion young people, 89% live in developing countries (United Nations Population Fund, 2016). More than 65 million young people between the ages of 10 and 24 live in the United States. Risk taking and believing "it's not going to happen to me," or feeling invincible are the hallmarks of adolescence, despite the high risks and intensified societal and technological pressures placed on them like no other time in history. The realities of massive global social, economic, political, and cultural changes affect adolescents' development process.

Research in health risk behaviors in adolescents has produced solid evidence. **Health risk behaviors** are described as having a negative effect on people's health (Lindberg et al., 2000). Adolescents are particularly prone to engaging in health risk behaviors—sometimes multiple risky behaviors. In fact, researchers indicate that engaging in one risky behavior leads to engaging in at least one or more other risky behaviors, especially paired behaviors such as smoking cigarettes and drinking alcohol or smoking marijuana and engaging in risky sexual activities (Lindberg et al., 2000; Lytle et al., 1995). In a literature review on adolescents' risky behaviors, McKay (2003) and Cook and colleagues (2003) found that most risky behaviors originate socially and can result in injury from accidents, violence, and sexual abuse. These health risks are still prevalent today.

In 2019, the Centers for Disease Control and Prevention (CDC) collected data by way of the Youth Risk Behavior Survey Surveillance System (YRBSS) on thousands of U.S. and national students in public-funded and private schools in at least one grade or more from grades 9 to 12 across the 44 states (CDC, *MMWR*, 2020). The four priority topics of research are: (1) sexual behavior, (2) high-risk substance abuse, (3) experiencing violence, and (4) mental health and suicide. Other new topics were introduced in the summarized in the summary of data and trends report, which included opioid misuse, sexually transmitted disease (STD) testing, and health behaviors of sexual minority youth. The CDC reported, "Some high school-aged youths experience disparate health risks that increase the possibility

RESEARCH NOTE: GENERAL HEALTH RISKS REPORTED IN 2019 ACROSS THE UNITED STATES IN ADOLESCENTS GRADES 9 TO 12

- **Driving or Riding**: 6.5% rarely ever wore a seatbelt when riding with a person driving; 39.0% texted or emailed while driving during the last 30 days prior to survey; 5.4% drove while drinking alcohol during the last 30 days prior to survey; 16.7% rode with a driver who had been drinking alcohol
- **Substance Use**: 36.8% ever used marijuana; 21.7% used marijuana during the last 3 days prior to survey; 3.9% ever used cocaine (powder, crack, or freebase); 7.0% ever hallucinogenic drugs (LSD, PCP, angel dust, mescaline, or mushrooms); 3.6% ever used ecstasy (MDMA); 1.8% ever used heroin (smack, junk, or China white); 1.6% ever used any illegal drug; 14.8% ever used any illicit drugs (cocaine, inhalants, heroin, methamphetamines, ecstasy, or hallucinogens).
- **Smoking or Vaping** : 24.1% ever tried cigarettes; 32.7% currently use any electronic vapor products 20 days of the 30 days prior to survey.
- **Sexual Experiences** : 38.4% of all students have ever engaged in sexual intercourse; 27.4% were sexually active 3 months before the survey; 8.6% ever had sexual intercourse with four or more people during their lives; and of the 27.4% currently sexually active, 54.3% used a condom during their last sexual intercourse; 11.9% did not use any method to prevent pregnancy.
- **Physical Activity** : 17.1% were physically active 1 or more days per week; 44.1% were physically active 5 or more days per week; 46.1% played video or computer games or used a computer 3 or more hours per day; 57.4% played on any school or community sports team 12 months prior to survey.

Data from Centers for Disease Control and Prevention (CDC). (2020, August 21). Youth risk behavior surveillance-United States, 2019. *Morbidity and Mortality Weekly Report, Supplement, 69*(1), 1–84. https://www.cdc.gov/mmwr/volumes/69/su/pdfs/su6901-H.pdf

of acquiring a sexually transmitted disease (STD), including human immunodeficiency virus (HIV) infection, and increase opportunities for substance use, mental health problems, and interpersonal violence or self-harm" (CDC, *MMWR*, 2020, p. 1).

According to that 2019 report, students were sampled on their risks often leading to unintentional injuries or death in adolescents. Four critical actions were connected to the leading causes of death and disability among adolescents in the United States: (1) motor vehicle crashes, (2) other unintentional injuries, (3) suicide, and (4) homicide (CDC, *MMWR*, 2020). Refer to the next two Research Notes: first, General Health Risks Reported Across the United States in Adolescents Grades 9 to 12 from the 2019 YRBSS, and second, (2) Most Risky Behaviors Leading to Major Causes of Death in 2019 Across the United States in Adolescents Grades 9 to 12.

RESEARCH NOTE: MOST RISKY BEHAVIORS LEADING TO MAJOR CAUSES OF DEATH IN 2019 ACROSS THE UNITED STATES IN ADOLESCENTS GRADES 9 TO 12

- Motor vehicle injuries
- Unintentional injuries
- Suicide (12 months before the survey, 8.9% had actually attempted suicide one or more times; 18.8% had seriously considered attempting suicide; 15.7% of students nationwide had made a plan about how they would attempt suicide.)
- Homicide

Data from Centers for Disease Control and Prevention (CDC). (2020, August 21). Youth risk behavior surveillance-United States, 2019. *Morbidity and Mortality Weekly Report, Supplement, 69*(1), 1–84. https://www.cdc.gov/mmwr/volumes/69/su/pdfs/su6901-H.pdf

Prevention Education for Adolescent Health Risk Behaviors

Mindfulness and effective listening are important strategies for communication, but being the **giver of communication**—how, where, and to what extent—is a critical ethical concern for adolescent relationships of all kinds, especially in professional nurse–adolescent relationships. See the Ethical Reflection: Check Yourself on Mindfulness and Effective Listening Skills. Beneficence and nonmaleficence are ethical principles of concern when planning and implementing prevention education and health risk message programs involving this age group. Health risk messages, or **fear appeals**, are persuasive messages that arouse adolescents by "outlining the negative consequences that occur if a certain action is not taken" (Witte et al., 2001, p. 2). Sensationalists, political campaign personnel, and religious leaders tend to use fear appeals, as do health educators, nurses, physicians, and professionals in other related disciplines if they suspect health issues are associated with a risky behavior. If fear appeals are effective, the target population will be more likely to make healthy choices and practice safe behaviors.

Fear appeals also can be used incorrectly and can do more harm than good. Giving health risk messages without the integration of a theory can be time consuming and fragmented. A **theory** provides "an explanation of how two or more variables work together to produce a certain outcome(s)" (Witte et al., 2001, p. 3). A theoretical framework guides the development of a health risk message, which eliminates the guesswork and shortens the duration of the developmental phase. Many current education programs for adolescents are theory-based prevention programs with an inclusion of health risk messages. When nurses provide prevention or intervention programs, they have an ethical obligation to focus not only on promoting good but also on doing no harm—a beneficent, nonmaleficent approach. Offering theory-based education programs with health risk messages requires nurses to incorporate a goal of teaching skills that are necessary to make healthy choices and practice healthy behaviors. This aim is consistent with a beneficent, nonmaleficent approach. See the Ethical Reflection: Planning a Prevention Educational Program.

An example of a prevention program of more intensity is the harm-reduction program. Most adolescents will never need the type of

ETHICAL REFLECTION: CHECK YOURSELF ON MINDFULNESS AND EFFECTIVE LISTENING SKILLS

- *Do I pay attention* by making eye contact and concentrating on the communication exchange?
- *Am I nonjudgmental* by showing a genuine interest in what the person is saying?
- *Do I provide nonverbal cues of understanding* by hearing the person's comments and acknowledging with nods, smiles, or other expressions?
- *Do I reflect* by summarizing the person's thoughts and clarifying the meaning of the message?

ETHICAL REFLECTION: PLANNING A PREVENTION EDUCATIONAL PROGRAM

Answer these basic questions:

1. How much information is too much information?
2. When and at what age will the information be presented?
3. What types of information are appropriate?
4. Where and how should the information be presented to be effective?

strategies used in a harm-reduction program (Patton et al., 2016). In this type of program, nurses teach the adolescents or adults, who engage in certain high-risk behaviors, to live safely. An extreme example of harm reduction is the needle exchange program for people of any age who are addicted to intravenous or other needle-requiring drugs. Adolescents have some or many complex, unmet needs because of inexperience and lack of knowledge with risky behaviors, how to access health care, and confidentiality issues. Examine the multifaceted needs in the Research Note: Approaches for Meeting the Educational Needs of Teens Engaging in Health Risk Behaviors.

RESEARCH NOTE: APPROACHES FOR MEETING THE EDUCATIONAL NEEDS OF TEENS ENGAGING IN HEALTH RISK BEHAVIORS

Current approaches in adolescent health include "intersectoral and multi-component" considerations (Patton et al., 2016, p. 4). Among these approaches include a mix of media, community, online, structured, and school-based programs to meet a complexity of issues experienced by adolescents.

Prominent differences in adolescent health between regions and countries and within different adolescent groups have resulted in global changes that require a range of multifaceted approaches when relating to and meeting the educational needs of teens. The complexity of providing intersectoral and multicomponent approaches derives from gender orientation: (1) LGBTQ+ teens (lesbian, gay, bisexual, transgender and queer, but the Q sometimes stands for questioning); (2) differentiated minority groups; and (3) other groups. Other issues that further complicate educational needs are teens

- living with disabilities,
- living homeless,
- living in poverty, and
- housed in juvenile detention centers.

Another example of an older, but still current structured prevention program, is a behavioral intervention program with theory-based health risk messages. An older effective prevention program was developed by St. Lawrence in 1994. She and her research team continued the development of this program (St. Lawrence et al., 1995). The prevention program is titled Becoming a Responsible Teen (BART) training manual, which is an eight-session curriculum based on two theoretical frameworks: (1) Bandura's (1977) social cognitive and self-efficacy theory and (2) Fisher and Fisher's (1992) information–motivation–behavioral (IMB) skills model. Later, Butts and Hartman (2002) conducted research using BART. For many years, and sometimes still today but with variations, the **BART behavioral intervention program** has been a popular evidence-based program among health educators.

Abstinence-Only Programs or Comprehensive Sex Education Programs

Other than through fundamental religious teachings, sexual education was rarely taught in formal institutions in the United States before the HIV and AIDS epidemic began in the 1980s. In the 1990s and early 2000s, examining how abstinence-only programs measure up to comprehensive sexual education programs was a popular issue. Many states sought and received federal funding for abstinence-only prevention education programs during that time, but by 2010, 25 states did not seek federal funding for abstinence-only programs (Wiley, 2012). Before 2010, there was a much stronger religious and political focus on, and plenty of funding for, teaching sexual abstinence in schools, homes, and churches than in previous years, especially since the sexual revolution movement of the 1960s. In the past decade, the political landscape has shifted from a focus on sexual abstinence to comprehensive sexual education programs.

Although **sexual abstinence** is defined as no participation in any genital contact, adolescents often do not have a clear meaning of sexual abstinence. Traditionally, adolescents have equated "having sex" with intercourse alone. Young people have sought more creative ways, other than coital sex, to express sexual intimacy (Remez, 2000). Meanwhile, guardians, educators, and others who teach sexual abstinence continue to say "just say no to sex," "don't have sex before marriage," or "delay the onset of sex." What do these statements mean exactly?

Could abstinence be defined today as a person being able to engage in any type of sexual activity as long as the couple or group is protected with latex and does not exchange bodily fluids? Without a clear definition, educators, guardians, and other adults have only vague communication between themselves and adolescents about the meaning of sexual abstinence. What adolescents perceive as the definition of sexual abstinence and what adults are trying to teach as sexual abstinence will likely differ. Ethically, vagueness itself can be harmful, not beneficial, because information may be misperceived. As a result, adolescents are left to their own interpretations, which leads to unprotected sex with consequences of unwanted pregnancy and HIV or STIs. Abstinence-only programs continue to decline as funding dwindles. Instead, funding is focused on comprehensive sexual education programs because research is beginning to support their effectiveness.

The issue of which type of program works best is of great concern for nurses who work with adolescents. Inconsistency exists across all the programs. Ethically, nurses need to think about the potential for harm to adolescents as a result of the type of sexual education program they choose. Nurses need to evaluate the program early in the planning process by using the guidelines already mentioned in this chapter. It is important for nurses to think about the ways in which adolescents may perceive, interpret, or put into practice the content being presented to them.

When nurses can focus effectively on the adolescents who are receiving the message, they need to clarify the message; try to focus on what they are really saying to adolescents; and, most of all, attempt to clarify and anticipate the message that adolescents are actually hearing. The overall ethical concern about sexual education is complex, but generally nurses must evaluate at what point along the sexual abstinence–comprehensive sex education continuum the information conveyed becomes unethical, nonbeneficial, or even harmful. Adolescents need sexual education more than ever today.

If a nurse takes the time to focus on the audience and the content of the message, adolescents will hopefully realize that nurses care for them and respect their values and beliefs. As the nurse provides well-defined content and becomes an effective listener, a reciprocal trusting and respectful relationship is more likely to develop.

Current prevention and intervention programs in the last decade for teens are highlighted by Healthy People 2020 ("Adolescent Health," 2021). These programs usually include a wide variety of programs for adolescents that narrowly target specific risks.

RESEARCH NOTE: EXAMPLES OF HEALTH RISKS INTERVENTION PROGRAMS FOR TEENS IN THE PAST 10 YEARS

- Violence prevention, 2018
- School bullying, 2017
- Six different adolescent health equity programs, 2013
- Skin cancer, 2012
- Testicular cancer, 2011

Data from Healhy People 2020. (2021, September 27). *Adolescent health*. U. S. Department of Health and Human Services. Office of Disease Prevention and Health Promotion. https://www.healthypeople.gov/2020/topics-objectives/topic/Adolescent-Health

This Healthy People 2020 goal for adolescent health is to "improve the healthy development, health, safety, and well-being of adolescents and young adults (AYAs)" (Healthy People, "Adolescent Health," 2021, p. 1). Consider the few examples listed in the Research Note: Examples of Health Risks Intervention Programs.

Nurses who are involved in any structured prevention or intervention program need to use a theory-based curriculum and evaluate the program early in the planning phase. Educators should consider answering the questions such as those in the Ethical Reflection: Ethical Questions for School Nurses to Answer in Planning a Prevention Education or an Intervention Program.

Nurses who give information to adolescents may potentially harm them if they choose a wrong or inappropriate prevention or intervention program. This situation poses a critical ethical dilemma for nurses when they must choose among the many standardized and accepted programs that are available for adolescents. For example on sexual education, nurses sometimes need to choose between teaching sexual abstinence and the use of safe sexual practices, or they could be asked to focus a program on religious beliefs. Choosing an age- or content-inappropriate program for a particular group or easily misinterpreted information could result in misled adolescents, or adolescents may perceive the health risk messages differently from the way the educator intended. Blunders could be critical to how adolescents will react to the information.

Many adolescent programs continue in the United States, but gaps still exist in prevention education and intervention programs. The gaps could be symptoms of problems related to managing and implementing prevention or intervention programs, such as controversial or inadequate content, complacency in creating and instituting programs, and not enough programs in place. For example, lack of teacher training, not enough material resources, inconsistent use of lesson plans, and failure to match lesson plans with the appropriate age

are factors with significant negative ramifications for adolescent prevention and intervention programs in the nation.

> ### ETHICAL REFLECTION: ETHICAL QUESTIONS FOR SCHOOL NURSES TO ANSWER IN PLANNING A PREVENTION EDUCATION OR AN INTERVENTION PROGRAM
>
> 1. If a school nurse is planning a prevention education or intervention program for rural or urban middle-school students, what are some considerations before or during the planning phase of the program?
> 2. What is the most effective prevention or intervention program that can be used for the specific topic?
> 3. What ethical considerations would be incorporated into program planning?
> 4. What message do adolescents need to hear?
> 5. What type of relationship should be established with the students who are receiving the education?

Sometimes, school nurses are the ones who plan and implement educational programs, so they need to know the objectives and content and anticipate the message intended to be heard by adolescents who participate in the program. Adolescents will usually assume the message they hear is correct because the information came from professional school nurses. When adolescents incorporate misinterpreted information into their viewpoints and behaviors, they place themselves at a higher incidence of health risk behaviors.

Pregnancy and Abortion Related to Unprotected Sex

Adolescents in the United States continue to have unprotected sex but at a lower rate. It is noticeable that the lower rates of unprotected sex has also resulted in lower teen pregnancy and abortions. Pregnancy rates for teens and abortion rates women, ages 15 to 44, continue to decline to all-time lows. In 2019, the United States teen birth rate declined to 16.7 per 1,000 females, ages 15 to 19. The teen birth rate in the United States has steadily declined in the past 3 decades and is at an all-time low in 2019 (CDC, "About teen pregnancy," 2021). "From 2009 to 2018, the number, rate, and ratio of reported abortions decreased 22%, 24%, and 16%, respectively" (CDC, *MMWR*, "Abortion surveillance—United States, 2018" 2020). Abortion rates among adolescents peaked in the 1970s and 1980s and then is thought to have historical lows by 2019. Overall for ages 15 to 44, the number, rate, and ratio of reported abortions decreased to all-time lows. Reasons cited for the these declines were because of more teens abstaining from sexual activity, more sexually active teens and adults using birth control methods because of great teen access to health services, and comprehensive sexual education programs.

HPV, HPV Vaccines and Benefits, HIV, and other STDs Related to Unprotected Sex

Even though pregnancy rates have slowly declined over the past decade for adolescents, STDs have remained high and of deep concern to public health officials. Half of all new STDs reported on the United States YRBSS of 2019 were among ages 15 to 24, which may be related to the statistic that 46% of sexually active students did not use a condom during their last sex episode (CDC, *MMWR*, 2020). Condom use among teens has declined in the past decade while STDs have increased among ages 15 to 44. By the 12th grade, at least 6 of 10 adolescents have had sexual intercourse one or more times, which is a decline from years past. Data from the YRBSS in 2019 on United States high school students, grades 9 to 12, indicated that 38% of students reported

having sexual intercourse in their teen history; of those 38%, 9% had 4 or more sexual partners, and 7 % were physically forced to have sexual intercourse when they did not want to have sex (CDC, *MMWR*, 2020). During the last 3 months prior to the YRBSS of 2019, 27% had sexual intercourse; of these 27%, 46% did not use condoms, 12% did not use any pregnancy prevention method, and 21% had drank alcohol or used drugs before the last sexual intercourse. The rate of reported STDs for both genders in the United States increased. The STDs include chlamydia, gonorrhea, and syphilis, which places teens at a high risk for acquiring HIV (human immunodeficiency virus) infection and HPV (human papillomavirus) infection.

HPV Infections

"Most new HPV infections occur in adolescents and young adults" (Meites, et al., *MMWR*, 2019, p. 698). No matter what age, a new sex partner places the person at a high risk for acquiring HPV infection. In fact, 85% of people will get an HPV infection in their lifetime. HPV is spread through sexual contact, and history reveals that HPV usually occurs soon after the person's first sexual activity. Many people with HPV are symptomless and do not know they are infected, but some have transient symptoms. With many, however, HPV can lead to the development of cancers in various locations: the cervix, anus, penis, vagina, vulvar, mouth, and throat. In addition to these various cancers, HPV causes genital warts. Worldwide, the majority (80%) of these HPV-associated cancers occur in the cervix (Bray et al., 2015).

HPV Vaccines and Benefits

The HPV-vaccinated rate worldwide for children and adults, ages 9 to 45, is less than 2%, but in the countries where cervical cancer has the highest rates, HPV vaccinations are minimal or absent (Harper & DeMars, 2017).

In the United States, 33,700 cancers each year are caused by HPV infection, and of those, 10,800 are cervical cancers in women (Meites et al., 20190. The HPV infection prevention programs in the United States could likely help to decrease the chance of adolescents' developing these cancers.

The HPV vaccination program in the United States has placed its greatest importance on the adolescent age group, especially ages 11 to 12 (Meites et al., *MMWR*, 2019). Vaccination against HPV infection before the first unprotected sexual encounter is recommended by experts, such as the CDC and advisory committees regarding vaccinations. In 2017-2018, 7.3 million adolescents eligible for HPV vaccinations remained unvaccinated (Sonawane, 2021). Recommendations differ among the age groups, and of the 7.3 million unvaccinated, more than 60% had guardians who maintained they would not initiate a series of HPV vaccinations. For minors, usually but not always, guardian consent is required for vaccines (Sonawane et al., 2021). The CDC recommended that all adolescents should get a 2-dose HPV vaccine series before they reach age 15 (CDC, "HPV vaccine schedule and dosing," 2019). For specific details, see the Research Note: The CDC's Evidence-Based Recommendations for HPV Vaccine Dosing.

The HPV vaccine has been approved by the U.S. Food and Drug Administration ([FDA], CDC, "HPV vaccination is safe and effective," 2021). Guardians and adolescents sometimes question the safety and efficacy of the HPV vaccine. Guardians have a concern that having the HPV vaccines would promote sexual promiscuity because their teens would not have to worry about acquiring an HPV infection, thus would take advantage of sexual opportunities.

Two of the most common questions both guardians and teens have about the HPV vaccines are (1) Do they cause infertility? and (2) Are the vaccines harmful in other ways? The HPV vaccines do not cause infertility. In fact, not having the HPV vaccine would place a sexually active teen at risk for acquiring HPV and, later, cervical cancer. The cancer treatments, such as hysterectomy, radiation, or chemotherapy, potentially could lead to infertility at which point the teen would probably never give birth to children. Based on the FDA approval and more than 15 years of tracking data through research and 135 million doses of HPV vaccines, the findings consistently illustrate safety in the vaccines and long-term effectiveness against HPV-related cancers. See the Research Note: Safety and Effectiveness of HPV vaccines.

RESEARCH NOTE: THE CDC'S EVIDENCE-BASED RECOMMENDATIONS FOR HPV VACCINE DOSING

- Ages 9 to 14 (routinely recommended most for ages 11 to 12)
  - Recommended initiation of a 2-dose HPV vaccine series
  - Second dose 6 to 12 months after the first dose (best protection provided)
  - Third dose within 12 weeks after second dose for those getting the second dose of HPV vaccine if a shorter interval between the first and second dose.
- Ages 15 to 26
  - Initiation of 3-dose HPV vaccine series if after age 15
  - Second dose 1 to 2 months after the first dose
  - Third dose 6 months after the first dose
  - Note: All three doses should be within 6-month period

Data from Centers for Disease Control and Prevention (CDC). (2019, August 15). *HPV vaccine schedule and dosing*. https://www.cdc.gov/hpv/hcp/schedules-recommendations.html

HIV Infection

HIV goes as far back as the 1800s when it jumped from chimpanzees to humans. HIV is still prevalent in the world. See the Research Note: Examples of Global Statistics

RESEARCH NOTE: SAFETY AND EFFECTIVENESS OF HPV VACCINES

- Safety of Vaccines
  - FDA-approval in 2006
  - 135 million doses administered since FDA-approval
  - Research consistently illustrates safety in HPV vaccines
- Effectiveness of Vaccines
  - Since the 2006 initiation of HPV vaccines in the United States, HPV-related cancers and genital warts have dropped 88% in teen women and 81% in adult women
  - Cervical precancers caused by HPV infection has dropped by 40%
  - Evidence suggests a long-lasting protection against HPV infections and HPV-related cancers

Data from Centers of Disease Control and Prevention. (2021, July 23). *HPV vaccination is safe and effective.* https://www.cdc.gov/hpv/parents/vaccinesafety.html

on the AIDS Epidemic for 2020. The human immunodeficiency virus (HIV) infection attacks and destroys the body's immune system and weakens it to the point of allowing infections and diseases an opportunity to invade the body, a scenario labeled acquired immunodeficiency syndrome (AIDS). The HIV-related infections and diseases that invade the body are called **opportunistic infections and diseases**. There is no treatment that effectively cures HIV, so once infected, the person has lifelong infection (CDC, "HIV basics," 2021). HIV infection is usually treated with antiretroviral therapy, and the opportunistic infections and diseases are treated individually as they arise. With proper treatment and care, a person can live a long life relatively healthy.

The recommendations for lowering the risk of partners contracting HIV and other STDs include not exchanging bodily fluids, not coming into contact with blood, and using

latex protection for sexual behaviors involving exchange of all bodily fluids, including blood, semen, pre-seminal fluid, rectal fluids, vaginal fluids, and breast milk (CDC, "HIV basics," 2021). Adolescents are at risk when they have unprotected sexual relations because of body fluid (and blood) exposures. Some ways to prevent HIV include making a choice not to have sex (abstinence), limiting sexual partners, using condoms the right way every time, and never sharing needles or any other incident causing blood exposures.

Many experts would like to see an implementation of more comprehensive sexual educational or intervention programs on healthy choices, abstinence, and strategies to be safe. In the 1990s the Joint United Nations Programme HIV/AIDS (UNAIDS) adopted a declaration to end AIDS. In many countries, HIV statistics are stabilizing or showing a slight decline because HIV prevention programs are improving. In all countries, particularly in

RESEARCH NOTE: EXAMPLES OF GLOBAL STATISTICS ON THE AIDS EPIDEMIC FOR 2020

- People living with HIV worldwide in 2020
  - 37.7 million people with HIV in 2020
  - 1.5 million new HIV infections in 2020
  - 1.3 million new HIV infections (ages 15 and up) in 2020
  - 150,000 new HIV infections for children (ages 0 to 14)
  - 79.3 million people worldwide infected with HIV since the beginning of the epidemic
- Deaths from AIDS-related illnesses worldwide in 2020
  - 680,000 deaths from AIDS-related illnesses in 2020
  - 36.3 million deaths from AIDS-related illnesses since beginning of epidemic

Data from Joint United Nations Programme on HIV/AIDS (UNAIDS). (2021). *Fact sheet 2021.* https://www.unaids.org/en/resources/documents/2021/UNAIDS_FactSheet

many developing countries, people acquiring HIV and other STIs remains a top concern.

Other STDs

The four prominent STDs reported in the 2019 YRBSS, not counting HPV or HIV, are chlamydia, gonorrhea, syphilis, and congenital syphilis (CDC, *MMWR*, 2020). All four STDs have alarming i1ncreases since 2015. See the Research Note: Other STDs Reported in the United States YRBSS in 2019. More than 2.5 million cases of STDs were reported on the YRBSS in 2019. The CDC ("Information for teens: Staying healthy and preventing STDs," 2021) provided rationale for adolescents' higher risks of acquiring an STD because they

- Are more susceptible because of their immature cervical tissue and vaginal mucosa
- Do not have STD testing as much for various reasons
- Are hesitant to discuss their sex lives in open and honest ways
- Often have more than one sex partner

Transmission of these STDs are similar to HPV and HIV infections: exchanging body fluids by having vaginal or oral sex with another person with an STD infection. Some STDs do not have symptoms yet can be

harmful and passed on, such as chlamydia. Adolescents can protect themselves by not having sex, being testing if the partners decide to have sex, agreeing to mutual monogamy once tested, not drinking alcohol or using drugs with sexual contact, and seek healthcare services for prevention of STD strategies and family planning (CDC, "Information for teens: Staying healthy and preventing STDs," 2021). Prevention is critical, but prevention must go beyond education. Adolescents need to be able to access healthcare services with a provision for family planning and STD treatment on a regular basis because many STDs are treatable and curable.

Alcohol and Other Drug Abuse Related to Adolescents

Adolescent alcohol and other drug prevention and intervention programs are available across the United States, and some of these programs have shown some effectiveness in past years. However, among adolescents between 2016 and 2020, drug use and alcohol abuse reports have revealed alarming escalation to public health officials and the public (National Center for Drug Abuse Statistics [NCDAS], 2021). "Alcohol abuse is by far the most commonly abused substance among teens and young adults" (NCDAS, 2021). For more detailed statistics, refer to the Research Note: Drug Use and Alcohol Abuse in Teens Between 2016 and 2020.

Teens continue to engage in too many health risk behaviors. The YRBSS of 2019 illustrated six categories of adolescent behavior that contribute to the leading causes of death and disability (CDC, *MMWR*, 2020). These include unintentional injuries and violence, sexual behaviors and unintended pregnancy, alcohol and other drug use, tobacco use, unhealthy dietary behaviors, inadequate physical therapy. Correlations exist among alcohol and other drug use and conduct disorder, depressions, and suicidal behavior.

RESEARCH NOTE: OTHER STDS REPORTED IN THE UNITED STATES YRBSS IN 2019

- Chlamydia 1.8 million cases—up 19% from 2015
- Gonorrhea 616,392 cases—up 56% from 2015
- Syphilis 129,813 cases—up 74% from 2015
- Congenital syphilis 1,870 cases—up 279% from 2015

Data from Centers for Disease Control and Prevention (CDC). (2020, August 21). Youth risk behavior surveillance-United States, 2019. *Morbidity and Mortality Weekly Report, Supplement, 69*(1), 1–84. https://www.cdc.gov/mmwr/volumes/69/su/pdfs/su6901-H.pdf

RESEARCH NOTE: DRUG USE AND ALCOHOL ABUSE IN TEENS, AGES 12 TO 17, BETWEEN 2016 AND 2020

General Statistics

- 86% of teens know others who smoke, drink, and/or use drugs during the school day hours.
- 33% of teens who have prescribed opioids are 33% more likely to misuse them after high school.

Alcohol Abuse

- 62% of 12th graders gave abused alcohol, and 17% of 12th graders consume 5+ drinks in a row
- 26% of 8th grades abused alcohol at least once.
- 1.19 million teens reported binge drinking in the last 30 days prior to the survey.

Drug Use

Marijuana

- 44% of teens have tried marijuana in their lifetime, and 63% of 12th grades used marijuana by way of vaping.
- Opioid overdose death have increased by 31% annually since the beginning of the 21st century
- 35% of teens reported using marijuana in the last year prior to the survey.

Stimulants (Cocaine and Amphetamines)

- 5% of teens reported using cocaine in the last year prior to survey.
- 9% of 8th grades have tried amphetamines in their lifetime.

Data from National Center for Drug Abuse Statistics. (2021). *Drug use among youth: Facts & statistics.* https://drugabusestatistics.org/teen-drug-use/

Adolescents with a family history of substance or physical abuse are at high risk for developing substance abuse problems and an **alcohol use disorder**, which indicates that the use of alcohol has become a person's normal function of living or has progressed to the point of causing physical, mental, social, or personal adverse effects. Such persons may also be prone to depression, low self-esteem, feeling like outcasts, or not fitting in with their peers. An ethical issue that is associated with the use and abuse of alcohol and other drugs is the dilemma of balancing adolescents' rights to **autonomy**, privacy, and **freedom** to determine their own actions against the harmful effects of irresponsible use of alcohol and other drugs. Dryfoos and Barkin (2006) and Jessor et al. (1995) delineated some early predictors of alcohol and other drug abuse and protectors. See the Ethical Reflection: Early Alcohol and Other Drug Abuse Predictors and Protectors.

Even though alcohol and other drugs are harmful when abused or misused, a small glass of red wine is reported to protect the heart against disease (Gullotta et al., 2000). Messages like this can be quite confusing to adolescents. Another message that could be misleading is the use of marijuana. in the United States have legalized or decriminalized medical use of marijuana. As of September 2021, forty-three (43) states have legalized marijuana for personal and recreational use (20 states), medicinal purposes only (37 states), or just CBD oil use (6 states) (DISA Global Solutions, 2021). Seven (7) states still have totally illegal status. Adolescents receive conflicting information on marijuana and alcohol use. For one example, advertisers often show groups of attractive young people socializing and drinking beer. Many companies intend to convey a subtle message that drinking beer makes one more attractive and popular.

Substance Abuse and Mental Health Services Administration (SAMHSA, 2017) published a federal government prevention campaign titled "Focus on Prevention: Strategies and Programs to Prevent Substance Use" as a starting point to decrease the use of substances by adolescents. This program provides a framework for any prevention program that addresses substance use and mental health issues.

Underground, or **secret drinking**, can lead to major unintended consequences. Another concern is the over-moralizing of the issue. Many professionals believe moralizing should not be part of the message. **Underage drinking**, which is drinking by anyone younger than age 21 years, is an illegal act because the legal drinking age in the United States is 21 years old. The other issue is parenting—knowing what to teach and what not to teach (Underage drinking debate: Zero tolerance vs. teaching responsibility, 2006). School nurses need to take part in educating teens and guardians about underage drinking. Striking a balance between a nurse's confidentiality regarding information learned and protecting the adolescent is a complex situation. The trust between a nurse and an adolescent should not be broken unless there is evidence of impending physical harm, which is a limit of confidentiality.

Eating Disorders Related to Adolescents

Physical appearance is one of the most important aspects of self-image for all adolescents, but this is especially true for girls. Girls dream and wish for beautiful, lean, and trim bodies, and many of them tend to not be satisfied with their own bodies. In the past few decades, adolescent boys have begun developing eating disorders; 20 million women and 10 million men currently have an eating disorder in the United States (Harris & Cumella, 2006; National Eating Disorders Association, 2021c).

For many adolescents, **obesity**, which means having too much body fat or weight, has become a disturbing problem. Adolescents who are obese tend to be very self-conscious of how they look to others, which may lead to a lifelong cycle of anxiety, depression, and overeating. Chronic overeating and obesity lead to severe health problems, such as heart disease, hypertension, type 2 diabetes, and respiratory problems.

As many as 50 to 75% of adolescent girls in the United States continually diet, although only 16% are actually overweight (Whitlock et al., 2005). Twice as many girls compared to boys experience an eating disorder in their lifetime, but most people never report their eating disorder. By age 6 years, girls begin to express their worries about their own weight or size, and by grade 3, almost half of girls (42%) view their weight as an enormous issue (National Eating Disorders Association, 2021b). More than half of adolescent girls and one-third of adolescent boys engage in unhealthy behaviors to lose weight, such as skipping meals, fasting, smoking cigarettes, vomiting, and taking laxatives. Common eating disorders, which lead to serious medical complications and even death if not treated correctly or at all, are illustrated in the Research Note: Types of Eating Disorders.

The tragedy is that most adolescents who experience these disorders are skilled at hiding them until medical problems become severe. Nurses who work closely with adolescents need to be highly skilled in assessing and monitoring adolescents who are at risk for these

RESEARCH NOTE: TYPES OF EATING DISORDERS

- **Anorexia nervosa**: An eating disorder that causes people to obsess about their weight and the food they eat; therefore, they lose large amounts of weight.
- **Bulimia nervosa**: An eating disorder that causes people either to excessively binge and purge by vomiting and taking laxatives or not to purge but to engage in other unsafe methods for losing weight, such as excessive exercise or fasting.
- **Binge eating disorder**: An eating disorder that causes people to binge eat large amounts of food, sometimes in secret.
- **Eating disorder not otherwise specified (EDNOS)**: An eating disorder that a care provider has not yet specified.

Data from National Eating Disorders Association. (NEDA, 2021a). *Statistics and research on eating disorders.* https://www .nationaleatingdisorders.org/statistics-research-eating-disorders

eating disorders. Other than weight loss, some signs that can alert nurses to these disorders include an obsessive need to be perfect or to be a high achiever; low self-esteem; open displays of intense guilt; signs of depression; or signs of fixation on food, calories, fat grams, or weight.

A critical message regarding child and adolescent eating disorders, such as anorexia nervosa or bulimia nervosa, is the fashion industry's blatant promotion of super-thin models, conveying a message that one must be thin to be beautiful. **Ana** is a popular abbreviation for anorexia nervosa, and **Mia** is a popular abbreviation for bulimia nervosa. Sometimes, adolescents personify Ana or Mia as a girl's name. Pro Ana and pro Mia websites support and encourage anorexic and bulimic behaviors, although some sites claim they do not. Websites such as Ana Boot Camp, Thin Intentions Forever, My Pro Ana Forum, and other sites send dangerous messages for teen girls and, sometimes, even for boys.

All these eating disorders serve as a warning of the presence of severe emotional hurting. In turn, if left undetected or untreated, the emotional distress may progress to more disturbing behavior, such as complete withdrawal, being friendless, expressions of anger and aggression, and self-harm. See the Research Note: Warning Signs of Eating Disorders—Anorexia Nervosa and Bulimia Nervosa. Psychotherapy is the treatment of choice, and nurses need to monitor for warning signs of all these disorders and talk with the adolescent and guardians so the nurse can make appropriate referrals to a primary care provider and a psychotherapist.

Sexual Abuse Related to Adolescents

According to Banks (1999), **sexual abuse** is unwanted sexual activity by one person on another, with perpetrators using force or making threats surrounded by apprehension and fear. Hundreds of thousands of minors are physically or sexually abused each year, most of the

> ## RESEARCH NOTE: WARNING SIGNS OF EATING DISORDERS— ANOREXIA NERVOSA AND BULIMIA NERVOSA
>
> - Sudden and dramatic weight loss
> - Relentless exercising
> - Ritual eating, such as tiny bites and rearranging food on the plate
> - Obsession with counting calories
> - High achiever or a need to be perfect
> - Frequent weighing on scales
> - Common use of laxatives, diuretics, and appetite suppressants
> - Binge eating or purging
> - Avoiding meals altogether or often eating alone
> - Self-image of being and looking fat even though weight loss continues
> - Interpersonal relationship problems
> - Sense of helplessness often curbed with controlling eating

Data from Harris, M., and Cumella, E. J. (2006). Eating disorders across the life span. *Journal of Psychosocial Nursing, 44*(4), 20–26.

time within the family. Sexual abuse, however, occurs outside the home as well. All states have clear laws, policies, and guidelines for child protection from abuse. Many adolescents will keep quiet about being sexually abused, mainly because of fear that no one will believe them or fear of the abuser (Reilly & Williams, 2015). Sexual abusers persuade their abused adolescents into believing they are at fault.

Dating violence has come to the forefront in the past couple of decades, though it has always been a problem. Just as adults have and must solve romantic conflicts, so do adolescents. Middle to late adolescents are more apt than younger adolescents to be in a relationship involving violence related to anger, jealousy, emotional hurting, one partner's behavior, and one person trying to gain control over the other one (Wolfe et al., 2006). People have reported jealousy as the main reason for aggression in a dating relationship. Other types of violence and abuse are evident within the adolescent population, such as gang violence, baiting violence, homophobic violence, bullying, harassment, and rape.

Nurses are responsible for critical event changes encountered during discussions with adolescents. Sexual abuse or other abuses fall under the limits of confidentiality. Nurses who work with adolescents must report any encountered cases to the proper officials or healthcare professionals. For example, a school nurse would report abuse or violence to the principal, or a nurse in an emergency department would report sexual abuse to a physician, mental health worker, or social worker; subsequently, they would report the incident to law enforcement. Before explaining the severity of the situation to the adolescent, nurses should make every effort to help adolescents express their own feelings and reactions about the situation. The most effective programs for prevention of health risk behaviors, including violence, are those in which the content is focused on the risk factors associated with the problem area. Prevention programs must be multifaceted to be successful. After nurses provide prevention education, the focus shifts to educating adolescents about strategies to provide protection in interpersonal relationships and about conflict resolution and decision-making skills. Interpersonal relationship skills are the focus of violence prevention programs.

Depression and Suicide Ideation Related to Adolescents

Depression, which is a persistent feeling of sadness or loss of interest, and **suicide**, which is an act of slaying oneself, are sometimes associated with the great emotions and drama during the age of adolescence. Depressive behavior may be hidden in daily displays of extremes. There are risk factors for adolescent suicidal ideation and attempts, many of which include family disturbances, familial tendencies, school bullying, cyber bullying, sexual orientation conflicts, and socioenvironmental problems.

Suicide is the 10th leading cause of death overall in the United States (Ivey-Stephenson et al., *MMWR*, 2021). Suicide in adolescents aged 14 to 18 years is the second leading cause of death after unintentional injuries. In that same age group (14 to 18), 2,039 suicides occurred, which accounted for 33.9% of all unintentional injuries.

Suicides among teens are of significant concern for decision makers because one of the *Healthy People 2020* objectives is to reduce suicide attempts resulting from injury, poisoning, or overdose. The focus is prevention and intervention programs. For adolescents, the top three methods for death by suicide are firearms, suffocation, and poisoning, respectively. Teen suicides are often linked to a history of mental health issues. Obtaining treatment for depression is essential for the prevention of suicide. Nurses may be fearful of making a mistake or missing signs of changes in adolescents. See the Ethical Reflection: Observable Signs and Subjective Comments of Adolescent Suicide.

Suicidal tendency is a person's having a propensity for suicidal ideation or to attempt suicide. **Suicidal ideation** is a person who has a preoccupation with suicide. In the 2019 YRBSS (Stephenson et al., *MMWR*, 2021), 18.8% of teens aged 14 to 18 seriously considered attempting suicide, 15.7% made a suicide plan, 8.9% attempted suicide, and 2.5% of the attempts required medical treatment, such as in injury, poisoning, or overdose.

What is alarming is the rise in adolescent suicide attempts during the Covid-19 pandemic (Yard et al., *MMWR*, 2021). During the 2020 study period as compared to 2019, a significant increase in mental health-related emergency department visits among teens aged 12 to 17. Yard et al. surmised, "Beginning in March 2020, the Covid-19 pandemic and response, which included physical distancing and stay-at-home orders, disrupted daily life in the United States".

ETHICAL REFLECTION: OBSERVABLE SIGNS AND SUBJECTIVE COMMENTS OF ADOLESCENT SUICIDE

Observable signs of adolescent suicide are as follows:

- Change in eating and sleeping habits
- Withdrawal from friends, family, and regular activities
- Violent actions, rebellious behavior, or running away
- Drug and alcohol use
- Unusual neglect of personal appearance
- Marked personality change
- Persistent boredom, difficulty concentrating, or a decline in the quality of schoolwork
- Frequent complaints about physical symptoms, often related to emotions, such as stomachaches, headaches, fatigue, and others
- Loss of interest in pleasurable activities
- Not tolerating praise or rewards
- Giving away favorite possessions or throwing away valuable belongings
- Becoming suddenly cheerful after a period of depression
- Showing signs of psychosis

Subjective comments of adolescent suicide are as follows:

- Complaints of being a bad person or feeling rotten inside
- Verbal hints with comments such as "I won't be a problem for you much longer"
- Comments such as "I want to kill myself" or "I'm going to commit suicide"

Modified from American Academy of Child and Adolescent Psychiatry. (2018). *Suicide in children and teens.* https://www.aacap.org/AACAP/Families_and_Youth/Facts_for_Families/FFF-Guide/Teen-Suicide-010.aspx.
Reprinted with the permission from the American Academy of Child and Adolescent Psychiatry ©2017. All Rights Reserved.

RESEARCH NOTE: ADOLESCENT SUICIDE ATTEMPTS BY GENDER ON THE RISE DURING THE COVID-19 PANDEMIC

- Research indicated that in 2020 as compared to 2019, an increase in emergency department visits for mental health-related issues among teens aged 12 to 17 increased by 31%, especially with girls.
- Suspected suicide attempts by girls aged 12 to 17 requiring emergency department visits during February and March 2020 were 50.6% higher among girls 12 to 17 and 3.7% higher among boys, both as compared to 2019.

Data from Yard, E., Radhakrishnan, L. Ballesteros, M. F., Sheppard, M., Gates, A., Stein, Z. , Hartnett, K., Kite-Powell, A., Rodgers, L., Adjemian, J., Ehlman, D. C., Holland, K., Idaikkadar, N., Ivey-Stephenson, A., Martinez, P., Law, R., & Stone, D. M. (2021, June 18). Emergency department visits for suspected suicide attempts among persons aged 12 to 25 years before and during the Covid-19 pandemic—United States, January 2019-May 2021. Centers for Disease Control and Prevention. *Morbidty and Mortality Weekly Report, 70* (24), 888–894. https://www.cdc.gov/mmwr/volumes/70/wr/pdfs/mm7024e1-H.pdf

(p. 888). Consider the gender statistics related to this same study in the Research Note: Adolescent Suicide Attempts by Gender on the Rise During the Covid-19 Pandemic.

If a nurse finds that an adolescent is exhibiting behaviors with signs of depression, suicidal ideation, or suicidal tendency, the nurse must quickly identify the problem, ascertain the intention of the adolescent, and clearly explain the process of notification while offering hope and the prospect of a treatment plan. Many state educational systems have initiated a program called **Gatekeepers** to spot suicidal youth. Gatekeepers trainers first educate school nurse coordinators to be trainers, and then those school nurse trainers provide training to other school nurses. Gatekeepers learn to recognize the risky behaviors of suicidal ideation. See the Ethical Reflection: Case Scenario—What Are Nurse Nan's Ethical Obligations in the Care of Eric?

ETHICAL REFLECTION: CASE SCENARIO—WHAT ARE NURSE NAN'S ETHICAL OBLIGATIONS IN THE CARE OF ERIC?

Nan, a school nurse, notices that Eric, a 15-year-old student, keeps to himself and never talks to anyone. Lately, his behavior has become extreme; he does not eat in the cafeteria with other students, keeps his head down at all times, and never makes eye contact with anyone. He has completely withdrawn from any social interaction at school. The other teens notice Eric's strange behavior and begin making fun of him, and then they begin bullying him. These actions just seem to make him go deeper into withdrawal, into silent suffering. Nan took note of his depressive signs and searched for current literature, which indicated that Eric is at risk for committing suicide. Then, Nan analyzed her ethical obligations as a school nurse as they pertain to Eric. What are Nan's ethical obligations to Eric?

Facing Death

Losing a Loved One

A catastrophic tragedy for all adolescents is losing a person they love. Healing strategies include simple activities for the nurse, such as being present, conducting effective listening, and allowing adolescents to express themselves as long as they need to. Some adolescents do not want to disclose information about their feelings of losing someone, and they need to be alone. Many adolescents turn to prayer, hope, and a belief in absoluteness or a higher being. Some adolescents heal through self-talk, memories, and dreams. It is a difficult thing for an adolescent to lose a guardian. For instance, one boy, age 16, expressed his thoughts about the memory of his mother 3 years after her death (Markowitz & McPhee, 2002). He was only 13 years old when his mother died.

Although people can expect death at some point in life, most of the time people are not prepared for it, especially adolescents. In 2000, more than 20,000 school-aged children or teens, ranging in age from 5 to 18 years, died in the United States (Lazenby, 2006). When a student dies, often the teacher and the school nurse will hold off on their grief and focus on the children left behind in the school. Lazenby (2006) conducted qualitative research to explore how teachers deal with the death of a student. When the researchers interviewed teachers about their perception of received support, one of the participants stated, "They never acknowledged to us [teachers] that maybe we needed to do something too and we were not allowed time to sit down and gather all our thoughts or listen to the counselors" (p. 56).

Adolescents are often encouraged to be strong, which sometimes leads to a lack of support for them (Wolfelt, 2016). However, if they have adequate support and are allowed to grieve appropriately, in most cases adolescents will heal without permanent scarring. When death is unexpected, such as in violence or an accident, screams and loud bursts of "Oh my God, why?" and "No!" from adolescents are often voiced. The death of a fellow student may shock others to a state of numbness and disbelief. When adolescents unexpectedly or expectedly lose someone they love, be it a friend or family member, how do they say goodbye, progress through the hurting and pain, and move on?

Adolescents realize how final and irreversible death is. When grieving has not progressed appropriately, however, dysfunctional grieving may occur. It is normal for adolescents to live in the present and often not think in terms of consequences. Grief is a complex process for anyone, but especially for adolescents (Wolfelt, 2016). During the grieving process, they may take more risks than usual and harm themselves. They may even seek potentially life-threatening thrills as a distraction.

Ethically, the nurse or school nurse must try to promote beneficence and nonmaleficence by helping adolescents through the stages of grief when they lose a loved one. If a long-term nurse–adolescent relationship exists, the nurse must try to help the adolescent overcome barriers to development tasks. Nurses and teachers need to be aware of dysfunctional grieving signs other than adolescents taking abnormal risks, such as the following: (1) symptoms of chronic depression, sleeping problems, and low self-esteem issues; (2) low academic performance or indifference to school-related activities; and (3) relationship problems with family members and old friends. School nurses are in an ideal situation to provide support to grieving adolescents and to educate teachers on how to cope with death and dying in school settings. Teachers have reported a deficit of knowledge and know-how when working with adolescents who are trying to cope with death and dying of their peers and family members (Lazenby, 2006).

Adolescents Facing Their Own Deaths

Adolescents who are facing their own deaths may have a terminal illness. In this case, they also may take life-threatening risks to impress their peers or others. Stillion and Papadatou (2002) poignantly stated: "Terminally-ill young people find themselves struggling with major issues of identity in the face of a foreclosed future" (p. 302). They ask questions such as "Who am I now?," "Who was I?," "Who would I like to become?," "Who will I be?," and "How will I be remembered by my friends?" (p. 303). The stages of grief experienced by adolescents when they know they are dying are different than when an adolescent is grieving for another person. When people know they are dying, the five stages of grief are (1) denial, (2) anger, (3) bargaining, (4) depression, and (5) acceptance (Kübler-Ross, 1970).

While struggling with whether to engage in intimate relationships and searching for purpose and meaning to their time-limited lives, adolescents with a terminal illness may live almost aimlessly from day to day. They

may fear they will hurt others if they die. "They [adolescents] must learn to live in two worlds—the medical world with the threat of painful treatment, relapse, and death; and the normal world of home, school, and community, with all the challenges that healthy children face" (Stillion & Papadatou, 2002, p. 303).

The central ethical principles involved in this type of nurse–adolescent relationship are beneficence, nonmaleficence, and autonomy. The five grief stages people experience when they know they are dying are at work here as well, and nurses who are involved with dying adolescents need to first explain the stages to the adolescent. Then, nurses and family members need to be alert to potential problems. Extreme behaviors and risk taking are signs alerting nurses and family members to take measures to prevent harm (nonmaleficence). Benefiting or doing good for terminally ill adolescents includes maintaining or improving their quality of life as much as possible. Ways to improve quality of life are to allow expressions of their fears and concerns, be sensitive to meeting cultural and spiritual needs, have compassion and show benevolence (kindness), and remember they experience most of the same challenges that healthy adolescents experience. Nurses must encourage sick adolescents to engage in autonomous decision making, as appropriate, as they progress through these developmental challenges.

Nursing Care of Adolescents

The discussion in this chapter illustrated ethical management of adolescents concerning consent, confidentiality, prevention, and illness. Consistently practicing ethical nursing competencies is important in nurse–adolescent relationships. These competencies include moral integrity (honesty, truthfulness and truthtelling, benevolence, wisdom, and moral courage), communication (mindfulness and effective listening), and concern (advocacy, power, and culturally sensitive care) (see an earlier chapter 3).

The ANA *Code of Ethics for Nurses with Interpretive Statements* (2015) contains essential aspects of moral integrity for nurses (Provisions 3.1 and 5.4), which include (1) duty to maintain confidentiality but sometimes with limits of confidentiality and (2) a right and duty to act in accordance with personal and professional values with compromise on a very limited basis. Nurses who base their practice on ethical competencies are more successful in developing respectful nurse–adolescent relationships. Adolescents need more of a nurturing relationship with nurses, which necessitates the use of qualities beyond the ethical competencies, including trustworthiness, genuineness, compassion, honesty (an identified ethical competency), and spirituality. This section illustrates those additional nurturing qualities.

Trustworthiness

Trustworthiness, as previously defined, means that nurses are dependable and authentic because they take responsibility for their own behavior and commit to their obligations (Gullotta et al., 2000). For example, a teen girl trusts a school nurse to follow through with an appointment to discuss a sensitive issue, such as the possibility of her being pregnant and the choices available to her.

Genuineness

Adolescents are more perceptive to how genuine a person is than any other population (Gullotta et al., 2000). **Genuineness** is how credible or real the nurse is. For example, if the nurse puts on a facade of genuineness with an adolescent but really does not desire a genuine relationship, the adolescent will perceive that disingenuousness. This pretense may be more damaging to the adolescent than if the nurse admitted the desire to *not* have a genuine relationship.

Compassion

Compassion means for the nurse to have an understanding of the adolescent's suffering and a desire to take action to alleviate the suffering. The display of compassion is uncommon but is a human quality that nurses should possess. In the ANA *Code of Ethics for Nurses with Interpretive Statements* (2015) and the International Council of Nurses *Code of Ethics for Nurses* (2021), compassion and alleviation of suffering are common themes.

An example of a compassionate action by a nurse is to intervene on behalf of an adolescent who has a hidden hurt. A **hidden hurt** in adolescents can lead to silent suffering (San Francisco Bay Area Center for Cognitive Therapy, 2021). Causes of silent suffering potentially can cause a great degree of mental stress, such as when family members or peers tease, make fun of, or bully a person because of a weight problem, poor grades in school, freckles, a big nose, other facial distortions, or other perceived shortcomings. The victimized person feels emotionally abused and belittled and, over time, a lowered sense of self-worth will occur, with a display of extremes in behaviors, such as aggression, violence, passiveness, or becoming withdrawn. An example of a compassionate school nurse is one who takes immediate measures to stop the aggressive behavior and compassionately acts by attempting to establish a trusting relationship with an adolescent who is continuously being bullied or teased. Notifying the school counselor or the principal and talking with the adolescent's guardians are important considerations.

Honesty

The old cliché "honesty is the best policy" has proved to be a good one for nurse relationships. **Honesty** means being forthright, truthful, and not deceptive. According to Gullotta et al. (2000), "without honesty there can be no relationship" (p. 281). Nurses should express their feelings and emotions in relationships. For example, expressing sadness, dissatisfaction, pleasure, or displeasure about an adolescent's behavior is better than trying to cover up feelings. Hiding one's feelings can cause a barrier—and irreparable damage—in the relationship.

If nurses practice the virtues of trustworthiness, genuineness, compassion, and honesty in adolescent care, a healthy and respectful relationship between the nurse and adolescent is more likely to develop. The adolescent must see evidence of the virtues in the nurse's practice if a relationship built on trust is to develop and evolve.

Spiritual Considerations

One of the most important things nurses can do to nurture the spiritual growth of youth is listen to their stories and, reciprocally, share stories with them. A spiritual emptiness exists in our society, even in the face of spirituality as an essential part of being human. If adolescents believe in a higher being, or what some may call absoluteness, they usually voice comfort in living with this belief. For adolescents, spirituality can provide a type of healthy, nonpunitive socialization and acceptance. Nurses can facilitate an adolescent's spiritual growth by remembering the little actions to aid in adolescents' spirituality, such as mindfulness and effective listening, being present, or keeping commitments to them. Spirituality transcends all religious beliefs; therefore, nurses could better help teens by being familiar with different religious beliefs.

Nurses can do several things to help adolescents with spiritual growth. There is one caution that can be a negative or positive experience, depending on the nurse's degree of spiritual commitment. When nurses help promote adolescents' spirituality, they may consciously or unconsciously begin developing their own spiritual growth. Small actions sometimes result in very positive effects, such as having benevolence and showing compassion.

Benevolence, an ethical nursing competency, is a feeling of and a proclivity for kindness that is experienced by many people. Being benevolent toward patients is necessary, but it requires a certain degree of willingness. Nurses need to remain mindful that their nurturing and kindness are not perceived as inappropriate, unethical, or illegal sexual advances.

Compassion is one of the virtues already mentioned in the Nursing Care of Adolescents section of this chapter. Nurses can promote spiritual growth by practicing compassion. See the Ethical Reflection: Virtues Related to Compassion.

Many Americans have taken a renewed interest in **spirituality** and prefer the term *spiritual* rather than *religious*. One reason for this interest is that most people believe spirituality is at the core of human life experience. If nurses talk with adolescents and truly listen to them, spiritual growth may occur for both adolescents and nurses.

ETHICAL REFLECTION: VIRTUES RELATED TO COMPASSION

- **Forgiveness** : Always being open to others' situations and reasons for the circumstances
- **Patience** and **tolerance** : Detaching from one's own agenda and outcomes and waiting on and being open to another's agenda
- **Equanimity** : A virtue that illustrates being balanced and calm. For example, with adolescents, being engaged in a situation with a patient and working toward a patient's well-being without an unhealthy attachment that potentially causes harm to the relationship
- **Sense of responsibility** : Knowing that people are interconnected and responsibility grows from that interconnectedness
- **Sense of harmony** : Remaining in contact with the reality of a situation and with others
- **Contentment** : An intermittent feeling of comfort that comes to a person as a result of practicing and following a spiritual direction

KEY POINTS

- An adolescent's three-phase developmental process includes early adolescence, middle adolescence, and late adolescence. Health risk behaviors are more prominent in middle adolescence.
- Nurses must gain trust by relentlessly proving themselves to adolescents by being consistent, giving correct information, keeping commitments, and showing concern and caring. These strategies are tried-and-true ways to gain trust with others, especially adolescents. A trust–privacy–confidentiality dilemma emerges when the nurse is entrusted with an adolescent's confidential health and social information. In fact, research has revealed that the likelihood of adolescents seeking health services for sensitive issues depends on how well their confidential issues will be maintained.
- There are limits to confidentiality when potential harm to others or self is at stake. Limits of confidentiality generally include suicidal ideation, homicidal ideation, physical abuse, sexual abuse, and other behaviors placing the adolescent at risk of physical harm.
- If adolescents ever really have autonomous decision-making capacity for consenting to or refusing treatments, it is closely linked to their moral self-development characteristics and how self-directed they are. Information collected in a nurse–adolescent relationship must be kept private and confidential by the nurse, with the exception of limits of confidentiality.
- When implementing any type of prevention education or intervention program with an emphasis on behavioral intervention for adolescents, nurses need to incorporate theory-based health risk messages along with behavioral interventions that are beneficial and not harmful.
- Nurses are faced with the dilemma of choosing a program that is appropriate and healthy for a particular group. There are a variety of standardized and evidence-based programs for adolescents. Misleading, age- or content-inappropriate information, or information that is not based in theory can cause more harm than good and may be a contributing factor to increased risks.
- An increasingly difficult challenge exists for nurses to provide ethical and acceptable sexual education to adolescents who are engaging in risky behaviors and to ensure that the information they teach is heard as intended. Nurses need to know where along the sexual abstinence–comprehensive sexual education continuum that information becomes unethical, nonbeneficial, or even harmful.
- Controversy between guardians, authorities, and adolescents has arisen during the Covid-19 pandemic relating to the Covid-19 vaccinations. The FDA authorized the emergency use of the PfizerBioNTech vaccine for teens, ages 12 to 15.
- Overall, the continual tracking and monitoring systems of the Covid-19 vaccine for adolescents have shown safety and effectiveness.
- The ethical issues involved with the administration of the Covid-19 vaccine for adolescents is based on the utilitarian theory of providing the greatest good for the greatest number of people with the least amount of harm with the competing principles of autonomy, beneficence, and nonmaleficence.
- Adolescent health risk behaviors and various vaccines and reported benefits lead to ethical issues and concerns, which include: unintended pregnancy and abortion related to unprotected sex, HPV infection, HPV Vaccines and Benefits, HIV infection, and other STDs related to unprotected sex, alcohol and other drugs, eating disorders, sexual abuse, depression and suicidal ideation, and issues in adolescents facing death of a loved one or peer or facing their own death.
- Alcohol and other drug use among adolescents continues to be a life-threatening problem. Predictors of drug and alcohol abuse include aggressiveness in early years, high-risk friends, unconventional behavior, conduct problems, alcoholic guardians, depression, peers who drink, and lack of guardian support and supervision.
- More than half of adolescent girls and one-third of adolescent boys engage in unhealthy behaviors to lose weight, such as skipping meals, fasting, smoking cigarettes, vomiting, and taking laxatives.

Eating disorders, such as anorexia nervosa, bulimia nervosa, binge eating disorders, or eating disorder can lead to serious medical complications and even death if not treated correctly or at all. Websites such as Ana Boot Camp, Thin Intentions Forever, My Pro Ana Forum, and other sites send dangerous messages for teen girls and boys.

- Because sexual abuse or other abuses fall under the limits of confidentiality, nurses must report any encountered cases to proper officials.
- Depression and suicide are sometimes related. Suicide is the second leading cause of death for adolescents who experienced unintentional injuries. The top three methods of suicide are firearms, suffocation, and poisoning. Observable signs of adolescent suicidal ideation and the tendency for suicide include the following: change in eating and sleeping habits, withdrawal, violent behaviors, personal neglect, drug and alcohol use, boredom, physical complaints, loss of pleasure, signs of psychosis, giving away personal items, and suddenly becoming cheerful after depression.
- Adolescents cope differently and sometimes worse than adults. When a peer at school dies suddenly, reactions are usually widespread throughout the community and school. Shock and disbelief will emotionally paralyze adolescents. Teachers and school nurses must hold off on their grief to focus on supporting and helping the grieving adolescents. The school nurse or community nurse must try to promote beneficence and nonmaleficence by helping adolescents through the stages of grief when they try to cope with the death of a loved one.
- Adolescents who know they will die experience the five stages of grief identified by Kübler-Ross (1970). It is likely that adolescents who are grieving for themselves or a classmate will intermittently engage in high-risk behaviors.
- Nurses need to base their practice with adolescents on a moral framework of virtues that include trustworthiness, genuineness, compassion, and honesty. The ANA *Code of Ethics for Nurses with Interpretive Statements* (2015) and the International Council of Nurses *Code of Ethics for Nurses* (2021) emphasize moral integrity in practice. Spiritual considerations are important to adolescents in all aspects of tribulations they experience. Nurses should practice the virtues of spirituality and teach them to adolescents.
  - Listen to adolescents' stories and problems.
  - Remember the little things nurses can do in times of stress and need.
  - Be compassionate.
  - Be forgiving and remain open to others.
  - Stay engaged in a situation with adolescents as needed.
  - Maintain a sense of responsibility.
  - Develop a sense of harmony.
  - Be content.

References

Advanced Practice Nursing eJournal. (2002). Issues in providing health maintenance to adolescents. *Advanced Practice Nursing eJournal, 2* (2). https://www.medscape.com/viewarticle/430530_2

American Academy of Child and Adolescent Psychiatry. (2018). *Suicide in children and teens*. https://www.aacap.org/AACAP/Families_and_Youth/Facts_for_Families/FFF-Guide/Teen-Suicide-010.aspx

American Nurses Association. (2015). *Code of ethics for nurses with interpretive statements*.

Bandura, A. (1977). *Social learning theory*. General Learning Press.

Banks, S. (1999). *Ethical issues in youth work*. Routledge.

Beauchamp, T. L., & Childress, J. F. (2019). Beneficence (Chap. 6, pp. 217–256). *Principles of biomedical ethics* (8th ed.). Oxford University Press.

Blustein, J., & Moreno, J. D. (1999). Valid consent to treatment and the unsupervised adolescent. In J. Blustein, C. Levine, & N. N. Dubler (Eds.), *The adolescent alone: Decision making in health care in the United States* (pp. 100–110). Cambridge University Press.

Bowman, D. H. (2004). Cover story: Abstinence-only debate heating up. *Education Week, 23*(22), 1–2.

Bray, F., Ferlay, J., Laversanne, M., Brewster, D. H., Mbalawa, C. G., Kohler, B., Piñeros, M., Steliarova-Foucher, E., Swaminathan, R., Antoni, S., Soerjomataram, I., & Forman, D. (2015, November 1). Cancer incidence in five continents: Inclusion criteria, highlights from Volume X and the global status of cancer registration. *International Journal of Cancer, 137*(9), 2060–2071. https://.org/10.1002/ljc.29670

Butts, J. B., & Hartman, S. (2002). Project BART: Effectiveness of a behavioral intervention to reduce HIV risk in adolescents. *Journal of Maternal Child Nursing, 27*(3), 163–169.

Centers for Disease Control and Prevention (CDC). (2019, August 15). *HPV vaccine schedule and dosing.* https://www.cdc.gov/hpv/hcp/schedules-recommendations.html

Centers for Disease Control and Prevention (CDC). (2020, August 21). Youth risk behavior surveillance–United States, 2019. *Morbidity and Mortality Weekly Report, Supplement, 69*(1), 1–84. https://www.cdc.gov/mmwr/volumes/69/su/pdfs/su6901-H.pdf

Centers for Disease Control and Prevention (CDC). (2020, November 20). Abortion surveillance–United States, 2018. *Morbidity and Mortality Report, 69* (7), 1–29. https://www.cdc.gov/mmwr/volumes/69/ss/ss6907a1.htm

Centers for Disease Control and Prevention. (2021). *Information for teens: Staying healthy and preventing STDs.* https://www.cdc.gov/std/life-stages-populations/stdfact-teens.htm

Centers for Disease Control and Prevention. (2021, April 7). *HIV basics.* https://www.cdc.gov/hiv/basics/index.html

Centers for Disease Control and Prevention. (2021, July 23). *HPV vaccination is safe and effective.* https://www.cdc.gov/hpv/parents/vaccinesafety.html.

Centers for Disease Control and Prevention. (2021, September 3). *About teen pregnancy.* Division of Reproductive Health. https://www.cdc.gov/teenpregnancy/about/

Cook, R. J., Dickens, B. M., & Fathalla, M. F. (2003). *Reproductive health and human rights: Integrating medicine, ethics, and law.* Oxford University Press/Clarendon.

DiClemente, R. J., Hansen, W. B., & Ponton, L. E. (1996). *Handbook of adolescent health risk behavior.* Plenum.

DISA Global Solutions Inc. (2021, September). *Map of marijuana legality by state.* https://disa.com/map-of-marijuana-legality-by-state

Drobac, J. A. (2017, November 2). *Age-of-consent laws don't reflect teenage psychology. Here's how to fix them.* Vox Media, LLC. https://www.vox.com/the-big-idea/2017/11/20/16677180/age-consent-teenage-psychology-law-roy-moore

Dryfoos, J. G., & Barkin, C. (2006). *Adolescence: Growing up in America today.* Oxford University Press.

Erikson, E. (1963). *Childhood and society* (2nd ed.). Norton.

Fisher, J. D., & Fisher, W. A. (1992). Changing AIDS risk behavior. *Psychological Bulletin, 111,* 455–474.

Gullotta, T. P., Adams, G. R., & Markstrom, C. A. (2000). *The adolescent experience* (4th ed.). Academic.

Guttmacher Institute. (2021a, September 1). *An overview of abortion laws.* https://www.guttmacher.org/state-policy/explore/overview-abortion-laws

Guttmacher Institute. (2021b, September 1). *Parental involvement in minors' abortions.* https://www.guttmacher.org/state-policy/explore/parental-involvement-minors-abortions#

Hamel, L., Lopes, L., Kearney, A., Kirzinger, A., Sparks, G., Stokes, M. & Brodie, M. (2021, August 11). *KFF COVID-19 vaccine monitor: Parents and the pandemic.* Kaiser Family Foundation. https://www.kff.org/coronavirus-covid-19/poll-finding/kff-covid-19-vaccine-monitor-parents-and-the-pandemic/

Harper, D., & DeMars, L. R. (2017). Review article: HPV vaccines – A review of the first decade. *Gynecologic, 146,* 196–204. https://www.sciencedirect.com/science/article/pii/S0090825817307746. https://doi.org/10.1016/j.ygyno.2017.04.004

Harris, M., & Cumella, E. J. (2006). Eating disorders across the life span. *Journal of Psychosocial Nursing, 44*(4), 20–26.

Hause, A. M., Gee, J., Baggs, J., Abara, W. E., Marquez, P., Thompson, D., Su, J. R., Licata, C., Rosenblum, H. G., Myers, R., Shimabukuro T. T., & Shay, D. K. (2021). COVID-19 vaccine safety in adolescents aged 12-17 years—United States, December 14, 2020-July 16, 2021. Centers for Disease Control and Prevention. *Morbidity and Mortality Weekly Report, 70*(31), 1053–1058. https://www.cdc.gov/mmwr/volumes/70/wr/mm7031e1.htm

Healthy People 2020. (2021, September 27). *Adolescent health.* U.S. Department of Health and Human Services. Office of Disease Prevention and Health Promotion. https://www.healthypeople.gov/2020/topics-objectives/topic/Adolescent-Health

International Council of Nurses (2021). *The ICN code of ethics for nurses.* https://www.icn.ch/system/files/2021-10/ICN_Code-of-Ethics_EN_Web_0.pdf

Ivey-Stephenson, A. Z., Demissie, Z., Crosby, A. E., Stone, M. S., Gaylor, E., Wilkins, N., Lowry, R. & Brown, M. (2021, August 21). Suicidal ideation and behaviors among high school students—Youth risk behavior survey, United States, 2019. Centers for Disease Control and Prevention. *Morbidity and Mortality Weekly Report, 69*(1), 47–55. https://www.cdc.gov/mmwr/volumes/69/su/pdfs/su6901a6-H.pdf

Jessor, R., Van Den Bos, J., Vanderryn, J., Costa, F., & Turbin, M. (1995). Protective factors in adolescent problem behavior: Moderator effects and developmental change. *Developmental Psychology, 31,* 923–933.

Joint United Nations Programme on HIV/AIDS (UNAIDS). (2021). *Fact sheet 2021*. https://www.unaids.org/en/resources/documents/2021/UNAIDS_FactSheet

Kübler-Ross, E. (1970). *On death and dying*. Macmillan.

Lazenby, R. B. (2006). CE education: Teachers dealing with the death of students: A qualitative analysis. *Journal of Hospice and Palliative Nursing, 8*(1), 50–56.

Leffert, N., & Petersen, A. C. (1999). Adolescent development: Implications for the adolescents alone. In J. Blustein, C. Levine, & N. N. Dubler (Eds.), *The adolescent alone: Decision making in health care in the United States* (pp. 31–49). Cambridge University Press.

Leman, K. (2019, January 7). How to respond when your teen is hurting. *Focus on the Family: Helping Families Thrive*. https://www.focusonthefamily.com/parenting/how-to-respond-when-your-teen-is-hurting/

Lindberg, L. D., Boggess, S., & Williams, S. (2000). *Multiple threats: The co-occurrence of teen health risk behaviors*. https://www.urban.org/sites/default/files/publication/62731/410248-Multiple-Threats-The-Co-Occurence-of-Teen-Health-Risk-Behaviors.PDF

Lytle, I. A., Kelder, S. H., Perry, C. L., & Klepp, K. I. (1995). Covariance of adolescent health behaviors: The class of 1989 study. *Health Education Research, 10,* 133–146.

Markowitz, A. J., & McPhee, S. J. (2002). Adolescent grief: "It never really hit me until it actually happened." *Journal of the American Medical Association, 288*(21), 2741.

McKay, S. (2003). Adolescent risk behaviors and communication research: Current directions. *Journal of Language and Social Psychology, 22*(1), 74–82.

Meites, E., Szilagyi, P. G., Chesson, H. W. Unger, E. R., Romero, J. R., & Markowitz, L. E. (2019). Human papillomavirus vaccination for adults: Updated recommendations of the advisory committee on immunization practice. Centers for Disease Control and Prevention. *Morbidity and Mortality Weekly Report, 68* (32), 698–702. https://www.cdc.gov/mmwr/volumes/68/wr/pdfs/mm6832a3-H.pdf

National Eating Disorders Association. (2021a). *Statistics and research on eating disorders*. https://www.nationaleatingdisorders.org/statistics%20research-eating-disorders

National Eating Disorders Association. (2021b). *Warning signs and symptoms*. https://www.nationaleatingdisorders.org/warning-signs-and-symptoms

National Eating Disorders Association. (2021c). *Body image and eating disorders*. https://www.nationaleatingdisorders.org/body-image-eating-disorders

National Center for Drug Abuse Statistics. (2021). *Drug use among youth: Facts & statistics*. https://drugabusestatistics.org/teen-drug-use/

Patton, G. C., Sawyer, S. M., Santelli, J. S., Ross, D. A., Afifi R., Allen, N. B., . . . Viner, R. M. (2016, June 11). *Our future: A* Lancet *commission on adolescent health and wellbeing*. Lancet, 387 (10036). https://doi.org/10.1016/S0140-6736(16)00579-1

Reilly, M., & Williams, B. H. (2015, September 15). Teens and sexual abuse. *Journal of the American Medical Association, 314*(11), 1192. https://jamanetwork.com/journals/jama/fullarticle/2441263

Remez, L. (2000). Oral sex among adolescents: Is it sex or is it abstinence? *Family Planning Perspectives, 32*(6), 298–304.

San Francisco Bay Area Center for Cognitive Therapy. (2021). *Silent suffering: Anxiety and depression in teenagers*. https://www.sfbacct.com/teen-topics/silent-suffering-anxiety-and-depression-in-teenagers/

Sonawane, K., Zhu, Y., Lin, Y.-Y., Damgacioglu H., Lin, Y., Montealegre, J. R., & Deshmukh, A. A. (2021, March). HPV vaccine recommendations and parental intent. *Pediatrics: Official Journal of the American Academy of Pediatrics, 147*(3). https://pediatrics.aappublications.org/content/147/3/e2020026286. https://doi.org/10.1542/peds.2020-02628

Smith, T. M. (2021, August 25). COVID-19 vaccination: Ethics—What to do when teens, parents disagree. *American Medical Association*. https://www.ama-assn.org/delivering-care/ethics/covid-19-vaccination-what-do-when-teens-parents-disagree

Stillion, J. M., & Papadatou, D. (2002). Suffer the children: An examination of psychosocial issues in children and adolescents with terminal illness. *American Behavioral Scientist, 46*(2), 299–315.

St. Lawrence, J. S. (1994). *Becoming a responsible teen [BART]: An HIV risk program for adolescents*. Jackson State University.

St. Lawrence, J. S., Brasfield, T., Jefferson, K. W., Alleyne, E., O'Bannon, R. E., & Shirley, A. (1995). Cognitive-behavioral intervention to reduce African-American adolescents' risk for HIV infection. *Journal of Consulting and Clinical Psychology, 63*(2), 221–237.

Substances Abuse and Mental Health Services Administration (SAMHSA). (2017, March). *Focus on prevention: Strategies and programs to prevent substance use*. U.S. Department of Health and Human Services (HHS), Pub. No. [SMA], 10-4120. https://store.samhsa.gov/sites/default/files/d7/priv/sma10-4120.pdf

Underage drinking debate: Zero tolerance vs. teaching responsibility. (2006). *The Brown University Child and Adolescent Behavior Letter, 22*(3), 1, 6–7.

United Nations Population Fund. (2016). *Ending the AIDS epidemic for adolescents, with adolescents: A practical guide to meaningfully engage adolescents in the AIDS response*. https://www.unaids.org/sites/default/files/media_asset/ending-AIDS-epidemic-adolescents_en.pdf

University of Chicago. (2013). *Approach to assessing adolescents on serious or sensitive issues and confidentiality*. https://pedclerk.uchicago.edu/page/adolescent-confidentiality

Whitlock, E. P., Williams, S. B., Gold, R., Smith, P. R., & Shipman, S. A. (2005). Screening and interventions for childhood overweight: A summary of evidence for the U.S. Preventive Services Task Force. *Pediatrics, 116,* e125–e144.

Wiley, D. C. (2012). Using science to improve the sexual health of America's youth. *American Journal of Preventive Medicine, 42*(3), 308–310.

Witte, K., Meyer, G., & Martell, D. (2001). *Effective health risk messages: A step-by-step guide.* Sage.

Wolfe, D. A., Jaffe, P. G., & Crooks, C. V. (2006). *Adolescent risk behaviors: Why teens experiment and strategies to keep them safe.* Yale University Press.

Wolfelt, A. D. (2016, December 16). Helping teenagers cope with grief. *Center for Loss and Life Translation.* https://www.centerforloss.com/2016/12/helping -teenagers-cope-grief/

Yard, E., Radhakrishnan, L. Ballesteros, M. F., Sheppard, M., Gates, A., Stein, Z., Hartnett, K., Kite-Powell, A., Rodgers, L., Adjemian, J., Ehlman, D, C., Holland, K., Idaikkadar, N., Ivey-Stephenson, A., Martinez, P., Law, R., & Stone, D. M. (2021, June 18). Emergency department visits for suspected suicide attempts among persons aged 12 to 25 years before and during the COVID-19 pandemic–United States, January 2019-May 2021. Centers for Disease Control and Prevention. *Morbidty and Mortality Weekly Report, 70*(24), 888–894. https://www.cdc.gov /mmwr/volumes/70/wr/pdfs/mm7024e1-H.pdf

CHAPTER 7

Adult Health Nursing Ethics

Janie B. Butts

OBJECTIVES

After reading this chapter, the reader should be able to do the following:

1. Explore the concept of medicalization as it relates to the societal shift away from physician predominance of the 1970s.
2. Differentiate among the following terms: compliance, noncompliance, adherence, nonadherence, and concordance.
3. Examine cultural views with regard to self-determination, decision making, and American healthcare professionals' values of medicalization and treatment regimens.
4. Identify ways nurses can create an ethical environment when they care for patients with chronic disease and illness.
5. Explore a utilitarian or deontology framework to justify the use of various organ procurement methods.
6. Analyze the Organ Procurement and Transplantation Network's guiding factors for allocation of organs across the United States.
7. Define death in relation to the Uniform Determination of Death Act of 1981.
8. Explore the rationale for the two guiding moral principles of the dead donor rule.
9. Delineate the nurse's role in terms of essential aspects of the American Nurses Association's *Code of Ethics for Nurses with Interpretive Statements* in the care of adult patients undergoing organ donation and transplantation.

▶ Medicalization

Medicalization developed from a process whereby medical professionals diagnose human social problems, disorders, and syndromes as medical conditions. Medicalization is an occurrence that is "defined in medical terms, described using medical language, understood through the adoption of a medical framework, or 'treated' with a medical intervention" (Conrad, 2007, p. 5). Cure over care is an emphasis in the medical model. Specifically, **medicalization** is an illness, disorder, or disease that "is not ipso facto a medical problem, rather, it needs to become defined as one" for the problem to become medicalized (Conrad, 2007, p. 6).

After considerable scrutiny by society in the media and literature, the concept of medicalization evolved over a number of years, mainly because of changes in the medical process and the healthcare system (Conrad, 2007). Some critics have expressed that medicalization has transformed nonmedical, social, or personal problems into medical conditions and therefore has narrowed the range of problems of what is considered acceptable for everyday living (Illich, 1975/2010). Medical professionals classify and label the symptoms and decide who is sick. What some individuals or groups perceive as advantages to medicalization may be perceived as disadvantages by others and vice versa. By labeling social conditions as medical problems, medicalization has allowed for the extension of the sick role, reduced individual blame for the problem, and led to a focus on the individual rather than the social context. On the other hand, many people have been helped by medications and treatment for their problems, such as alcoholism, erectile dysfunction, baldness, and many more human conditions.

Even though physicians remain the gatekeepers for medical treatment and continue to treat most disorders, three market-driven interests continue to expand the medicalization of society: (1) managed care; (2) biotechnology, such as genetic possibilities and pharmaceutical treatments; and (3) consumers. The trend for labeling human social conditions as medical problems continues to increase, with no signs of waning (Conrad, 2007).

As the shift to managed care emerged, patients began to think like consumers when it comes to the medical care they receive, the providers they want, and the types of health insurance policies they can purchase. Patients as consumers became more vocal and active in their own care and demanded more services. During the same era, pharmaceutical companies made enormous profits, and continue to do so, on new drug treatments; by the 1990s, the Human Genome Project shifted society's focus to new possibilities in diagnoses and treatments. As the 1990s ended, medical professionals' dominance in health care and treatments diminished somewhat, although physicians continue to practice with a significant degree of control. As the market has shifted some of the traditional power away from physicians, many consumers still experience a few hegemonic practices by the medical profession in regard to their health care, and medicalization will continue to be somewhat of a dominant force for a wide range of human problems.

Compliance, Adherence, and Concordance

The terms *compliance*, *adherence*, and *concordance* fall under the umbrella of medicalization. In the healthcare context, **compliance** refers to a patient's written or unwritten approval of a provider's medical treatment or a nurse's healthcare regimen, which represents the patient's intentions of following the wishes of the provider and the suggested course of treatment. Compliance borders on coerciveness and could indicate a paternalistic approach that persuades patients to behave in a submissive manner to a prescribed regimen.

In the past decades, society realized a decline in the use of the term *compliance* because of certain negative connotations that healthcare providers might interpret as **noncompliance** if they perceive a certain degree of incompetence and deviance when observing nonconforming patient behaviors. Patient noncompliance remains a persistent concern, but by nurses broadening their approach to compliance, more effective inventions will result (Berg et al., 2002). In 1978, Barofsky discussed three types of patient responses to healthcare provider treatments: (1) compliance; (2) adherence; and (3) concordance, which Barofsky characterized as therapeutic alliance. These responses are still relevant today. In Barofsky's continuum, compliance means coercion, adherence means conformity, and concordance is a therapeutic alliance between the providers of care and the patient.

Conformity is not the only way to define adherence. It became a substitute for compliance in an attempt to deemphasize provider control and emphasize patient choice in treatments and whether the patient chooses to adhere to a prescribed medical regimen. A more specific definition of **adherence** is the extent to which patients' behaviors match the recommendations agreed upon by the provider or nurse and the patient (Horne et al., 2005).

Providers often use the term **nonadherence** to indicate an all-or-nothing patient approach, meaning that patients follow either the entire treatment regimen or none of it. The extent to which a desired treatment plan or therapeutic result is unlikely to be realized seems to more comprehensively capture the meaning of *nonadherence*. Patients cite unintentional and intentional reasons for not adhering to a treatment plan. Unintentional reasons for nonadherence include financial or other constraints or limitations of memory or dexterity; intentional reasons occur when the patients' beliefs, attitudes, and expectations from their family's value system differ from the treatment plan. Patient adherence or nonadherence should not be characterized as good or bad; instead, it should be considered high or low adherence. Nurses and physicians often find it difficult to determine the level of adherence because, during a clinical encounter, patients do not necessarily mention or clearly verbalize how well they adhere to the treatment plan.

Concordance is similar to Barofsky's (1978) term *therapeutic alliance*. Concordance indicates a more shared approach, or partnership, to the treatment plan between the provider and the patient. Important to a concordant agreement is a negotiation between the patient and the provider regarding the beliefs and wishes of the patient and whether, when, and how treatments will be administered and medicines will be taken (Horne et al., 2005). Providers have engaged in concordance more in the United Kingdom than in any other country. The practice of concordance has many advantages, but the term needs more conceptualization and understanding for its increased use in medical and nursing practice. Providers who practice concordance have encountered frequent issues when it comes to discriminating concordance from compliance and adherence.

Valuing Self-Determination in a Medicalized Environment

Within the healthcare system today, doing more work with fewer resources is a concern when providers plan strategies to improve a person's health. Promoting healthy behaviors and prescribing treatment regimens yet trying to respect one's rights to self-determination is a complex situation. One ethical question that needs to be answered is how far providers of care should go in terms of respecting the autonomy of patients when some of the patients' behaviors burden society with enormous costs, both in terms of money and other resources. If providers and nurses are to practice ethically, they need to avoid paternalistic and coercive behaviors when educating patients on strategies to promote healthy behaviors (Berg et al., 2002). Self-determination and decision making are critical elements in the principle of respect for autonomy. Married couples and cohabiting partners often make healthcare decisions together (Osamor & Grady, 2018). Whether decisions are made jointly or individually, a careful balance between a person's freedom from controlling influences and capacity for intentional action is necessary. The principle of respect for autonomy means that healthcare professionals respect patients' choices and their right to their opinions. While respecting the principle for autonomy, providers should offer information on efficient, cost-containing treatments with a balance between risks and benefits of the proposed treatments, the costs to society for patients to maintain unhealthy behaviors, and patients' responsibility for self-care.

Cultural Views on Medicalization and Treatment Regimens

In a complex mix of treatment regimens and medicalization, effective care involves respecting the cultural values with regard to autonomy, independence, self-care, and authoritative figures of the family. In the United States, healthcare professionals value and depend on their ability to teach self-care strategies to patients in an effort to reduce illness and disease (Galanti, 2004). The patient's values often conflict with the Western values acquired by providers of care. Some patients and families of diverse cultures may not necessarily value a provider's or nurse's demonstrated eagerness to provide education. Instead, they may view the up-front eagerness as more of a coercive warning tactic with negative consequences rather than as a care strategy.

Another cultural consideration is the manner in which the decision is made. Generally speaking, people want to know how to care for themselves, but sometimes patients value input from their families and will not make decisions without direction from them. In this case, a decision will come from a family think-and-do approach rather than a unilateral patient decision. Some cultures from Eastern traditions, such as Asian cultures, believe the head of the family should make the decisions, whereas Native Americans prefer grandparents to make all the healthcare decisions. Beliefs such as these can be in conflict with the Western tradition in the United States, where there is an emphasis on self-control, self-care, autonomy, money, and cure over care. Practices such as the extensive use of life-sustaining methods and complex treatments demonstrate the focus on curing over caring, no matter how much the cure costs.

The application of an **adaptation theory** has the potential to reduce cultural conflicts. The question is, to what extent, if at all, will a person choose to adapt in the physical and social environment where they live? Some, but not all, people choose to adapt their cultural traditions to the broader environment. "When cultural conflicts occur, it is often because what is successful under one set of environmental circumstances may be less so under others" (Galanti, 2004, p. 17). Nurses have a role in adaptation; specifically, they can promote adaptation to a point of individual comfort to reduce the chance of social isolation and anonymity. In their codes of ethics, the American Nurses Association (ANA, 2015) and the International Council of Nurses (ICN, 2021) emphasized that nurses should care for patients in a respectful and unbiased way (see Appendix B for the ICN code

ETHICAL REFLECTION: CRITICAL ELEMENTS IN THE PRINCIPLE OF RESPECT FOR AUTONOMY

Respect for autonomy is one of the four biomedical principles (respect for autonomy, beneficence, nonmaleficence, and justice). Beauchamp and Childress (2019) recognized three conditions for a person's choice to be considered autonomous.

Intentionality: the patient's intention to act
Understanding: the patient's understanding of the action
No external control: the patient is not controlled by another person

- Describe a clinical situation you have seen in which all three factors of autonomy were evident before or when the patient made a choice.
- Describe a clinical situation you have seen in which one or more of the factors of autonomy were not present before or when the patient made a choice.

of ethics). The ICN *Code of Ethics for Nurses* (2021) states the following:

> Inherent in nursing is a respect for human rights, including cultural rights, the right to life and choice, to dignity and to be treated with respect. Nursing care is respectful of and unrestricted by considerations of age, colour, creed, culture, disability or illness, gender, sexual orientation, nationality, politics, race, religious or spiritual beliefs, legal, economic, or social status. (Preamble, para. 2)

ETHICAL REFLECTION: EXPLORE YOUR EXPERIENCE WITH MEDICALIZATION

Discuss one situation in which you have experienced the effects of medicalization and a treatment regimen for a patient. This scenario can come from a personal family experience or your own nursing practice, either as a nurse or a student.

- Explore the dynamics you observed among nurses and other providers of care, the healthcare system, and the family that influenced the patient's choice of treatment and outcomes.
- Describe the provider and nurse practice approaches in terms of their use of concordance, compliance, and adherence.
- Discuss if and to what extent you observed a balance, if any, between patient choice and provider-prescribed treatment. Consider your perceptions of the degree to which providers and nurses exercised paternalism and respected human dignity, cultural values, and autonomy.
- What ethical framework would guide your practice to facilitate meeting moral obligations described by the ANA and ICN codes of ethics? Consider a framework of utilitarianism, deontology, or virtue ethics. Please explain your rationale.

Chronic Disease and Illness

The leading cause of death and disability in the United States is chronic disease, which is generally characterized by long-lasting multiple etiologies and no cure. Often, though, chronic disease is manageable with ongoing medical attention to the disease (Martin, 2007). **Chronic disease** is any condition with a duration of one or more years that requires ongoing medical responsiveness or treatment and/or limits activities of daily living (Centers for Disease Control and Prevention [CDC], 2021, April 28, para. 1). Even with exponential advances in medical technology and treatments, the number of people with chronic disease has continued to increase very rapidly in the past few decades. Chronic diseases account for a

RESEARCH NOTE: STATISTICS ON CHRONIC DISEASES LEADING TO DEATH OR DISABILITY IN THE UNITED STATES IN 2020

- Most common and costly, but most preventable, chronic diseases include heart disease, stroke, cancer, diabetes, obesity, and arthritis.
- The highest risk factors that attributed to chronic diseases are alcohol use, overweight and obesity, decreased participation in physical activities or exercise, decreased sleep of less than 7 hours per 24-hour period, and smoking.
- Four in 10 adults in the United States had two or more chronic health conditions in 2021.
- Seven of 10 causes of death in 2020 were due to chronic disease, and of those, heart disease, cancer, and stroke account for more than 50% of all deaths each year.

Centers for Disease Control and Prevention (CDC). (2021, April 28). *About chronic diseases*. https://www.cdc.gov/chronicdisease/about/index.htm

large majority of the $3.8 trillion healthcare costs in the United States.

A few experts from different areas of the world label some diseases as lifestyle diseases because of their connection to lifestyle choices, such as smoking, the harmful use of alcohol and other drugs, an unhealthy diet, and physical inactivity. Some people have even questioned whether restricted and rationed access and resources to treatments for some lifestyle-related chronic diseases could be a justified ethical decision. Noncommunicable diseases account for more than 70% of deaths worldwide (World Health Organization [WHO], *Progress Monitor*, 2020). Among some of the leading causes of noncommunicable deaths worldwide are cardiovascular diseases, cancer, diabetes, and chronic respiratory diseases. A majority of the global burden of disease is a consequence of lifestyle choices and behaviors, and this statistic is rapidly rising.

Chronic illness refers to people's perception of their quality of life and the difficulty of living with and experiencing a chronic disease (Martin, 2007). People with chronic disease experience a collection of symptoms they describe as long-term affliction and suffering. The odds for a longer life span increase due to technology advances and better treatments, but considering this statistic, whether viewed as good or bad, people with chronic disease and illness experience a longer life of pain and suffering. Walker and Markos (2002) attempted to define chronic illness qualitatively and more comprehensively through research interviews with participants and an extrapolation of themes, but after analyzing the findings, the Chronic Illness Alliance never agreed on a universal definition of chronic illness. What is interesting in this research are the comments made by the participants about their experiences with chronic illnesses and how those illnesses have affected their lives. Most participants saw chronic illness as a negative state that robs them of any hope for recovery.

RESEARCH NOTE: SHARED MEANING OF CHRONIC ILLNESS—PARTICIPANTS' VIEWS

Participants in this Australian study reported their lived experiences with various chronic illnesses. Arthritis or musculoskeletal diseases topped the list of the 27 diseases and illnesses, followed by mental depression, multiple sclerosis, breast cancer, chronic pain, asthma, epilepsy, stroke, thyroid problems, and hypertension. Other diseases were less frequent. The researchers extrapolated nine major themes from the narratives of the 43 participants' lived experiences. The themes are as follows:

- Social impact of living with a chronic illness: This theme includes the following: (1) not being able to work; (2) living with an illness that will lead to dependency or even death, poverty, isolation, and loneliness; and (3) requiring many types of support in the home.
- Relationship between the patient with a chronic illness and medical providers: Patients felt that healthcare providers were frustrated by their chronicity, the healthcare staff were not properly trained to care for them, the medical model was dominant in terms of the many treatments and medications that did not seem to help, there was poor medical management, and the treatments were inconsistent.
- Stigma associated with chronic illness: Patients had feelings of discrimination and stigmatization, friends and family told the loved one to try harder, patients were labeled as noncompliant by medical and nursing providers if they did not or could not follow the regimen, and patients were labeled as difficult if they verbalized that the regimen was not working well.
- Labeling and classification: Patients felt that being labeled or classified in certain medical language brought about negativity from the wider global perception, and terms such as *chronic, long standing*, and *long term* were labels that brought about discrimination.

- ■ Need for a new definition of chronic illness: Patients desired a new definition with a broader perspective on chronic illness that includes the complexity of their experiences with the chronic illness.
- ■ Essential features of chronic illness: Patients believed their chronic illness had the following features:
  - Ongoing and problematic
  - Quality of work compromised
  - Relationships compromised
  - Lifelong and substantial commitment by caregiver
  - Elements of uncertainty
  - Expensive treatments and visits to providers
  - Incurable
  - Untreatable
  - Requires complex and ongoing management
  - Life threatening
  - Unresolved
  - Complex
  - Permeates the whole of life
  - Fatigue
- ■ Need for a health-promoting definition of chronic illness: Patients desired a new health-promoting definition to help others understand their difficulties and needs.
- ■ Consumers' views that policies should account for chronic illness: Patients feared that society and the government would punish them for their chronic illness.
- ■ Chronic illness and activism: Patients desired a commitment to fight for their rights.

Data from Walker, C., & Markos, S. (2002). *Developing a shared definition of chronic illness: The implications and benefits for general practice (GPEP 843: Final report).* Chronic Illness Alliance, Inc. Victoria: Health Issues Center

Ethical Concerns and Suffering

Carter et al.'s (2002) study uncovered significant global implications for those who care for patients with chronic disease and illness. Some fundamental ethical concerns are a patient's feeling of a lack of control, patient suffering, and difficulty in accessing services. These three concerns likely relate to the medicalization issues discussed in the previous section.

Patients with chronic disease and illness frequently feel as if their illnesses are controlling them rather than feeling they are in control of their own lives. As indicated in Carter et al.'s (2002) findings, the reality of power imbalances between vulnerable-feeling patients and the persuasion of healthcare providers magnifies negative feelings of lack of control. Unless patients are inclined to cause harm to themselves or others, healthcare professionals need to honor patients' desires to control their own lives.

Catherine Garrett (2004) based her work on chronic illness and suffering on her own chronic illness experience with irritable bowel syndrome, a cluster of symptoms of gastric pain, intestinal pain and spasms, and malfunctioning digestion. Garrett has lived with this pain and suffering for more than 50 years, and her desire in writing her book was to recount and share her story and scholarly research on sickness, disability, violence, grief, loss, confusion, and despair. These symptoms make up what she calls her suffering. Garrett explained suffering in chronic illness as just one of many types of suffering that has characteristics similar to how dying patients and families often describe their torment. Her work was a quest for the physical, emotional, intellectual, and spiritual components that link chronic illness and suffering.

Chronic illness results in a persistent, ongoing, and unhealing suffering, and if any inseparable part suffers, the whole person suffers.

Chronic conditions produce enormous demands and conflicts, to which the person must respond. Patient suffering related to chronic disease and illness results from a combination of unrelieved pain, the stigma of chronic illness, and disparities of living with the potential consequences of a perceived reduced quality of life. Patients with chronic disease and illness often feel alone and miserable, and signs of suffering become evident. Many chronically ill patients struggle with trying to attach meaning to their suffering through soul searching and spirituality to find out why they have to suffer so much. They sometimes conclude that they cause their own suffering.

Providing Ethical Care

How do nurses provide care for patients with chronic disease and illness? Two strong themes came from Carter et al.'s (2002) research. The first theme is that people with chronic disease and illness require special attention and understanding at a level that is not required by other patients, which means that nurses must first respect the patients' human dignity and worth. Respect includes acquiring a greater understanding of the experiences of patients who live with long-lasting disease and illness. The second predominant theme is the need for a clear and comprehensive health-promoting definition of chronic illness, ultimately to avoid labeling and stereotyping.

Nurses need to plan quality interventions to address these themes. Providing care requires that nurses exhibit ideal ethical competencies; people with chronic disease and illness require the same level of nursing competency or more. The competencies include the following: (1) moral integrity—honesty, truthfulness and truthtelling, benevolence, wisdom, and moral courage; (2) communication—mindfulness and effective listening; and (3) concern—advocacy, power, and culturally sensitive care.

Although all these ethical competencies are important, advocacy seems especially important for building a trustworthy, therapeutic relationship with patients who experience chronic disease and illness. One part of advocacy involves overseeing medical management, but a larger advocacy role requires emotional support with gentle nudging or teaching and a sense of security. To serve as an advocate, nurses will take certain risks, such as speaking out for their patients, possibly being caught in the middle of a conflict between the patient and others, and realizing the possibilities of what could be in the nurse–patient relationship.

Another ethical competency of particular importance for advocacy is communication, including two associated competencies: mindfulness and effective listening. Practicing good communication facilitates advocacy, which occurs at the point of care and thereafter for the patient and family and on broader state and national levels. At the broader range of advocacy,

ETHICAL REFLECTION: A MIDDLE-AGED PATIENT WITH CRIPPLING RHEUMATOID ARTHRITIS

A middle-aged female patient, Ms. S., has a 23-year history of crippling rheumatoid arthritis. One day Ms. S. presented to the emergency department with a possible injury after bumping her head in a fall. She had no complaints of head pain regarding her fall, and the X-ray showed no injury to her head; rather, while in the emergency department, Ms. S. complained of extreme arthritic pain. Her history revealed long-standing crippling from years of inflammation in her joints and bones, erosion to her joints and bones, severe fatigue, intermittent fever, bilateral swelling of her hands and feet, general aching and pain, several prescription medications for arthritis, and a complete dependence on others for care and support. As her nurse, you see that Ms. S. is exhibiting signs of suffering to the point that she seems weakened and compromised. According to her family, her suffering experience has robbed her of joy, contentment, and enthusiasm. In your conversations with Ms. S., she said her passion for living is gone and she wants to be free from the burden of pain and suffering.

- What is chronic disease and illness?
- How does Ms. S.'s chronic disease sequelae fit into the concept of medicalization?
- How do Ms. S.'s and her family's expressions of her chronic pain and mental outlook compare to Carter et al.'s (2002) findings about chronic illness?
- What ethical issues arise when caring for patients with chronic disease and illness?
- Integrate an ethical theory or approach in your plan of care, and then discuss nursing strategies.

When answering, explore ways you serve as an advocate for Ms. S. in terms of nursing practice and a multidisciplinary approach.

ETHICAL REFLECTION: NURSES AND SELF-CARE

Self-care practices are vital for nurses to replenish their physical and emotional energy.

- Self-care behaviors to promote mindfulness and self-healing include yoga, spiritual meditations, stress-relieving activities, Reiki, storytelling, writing, and other healing experiences. Nurses can choose their self-care practices, but it is equally important for nurses to encourage patients with chronic disease and illness to engage in some type of self-care behavior for their ongoing health.
- Another aspect of self-care is professional development and education. Nurses and nursing students can increase their knowledge and understanding of ethics and bioethics by attending ethics conferences, doing in-depth reading, participating in ethics dialogues in face-to-face groups of nurses or in online blogs and open forums, completing live or online courses on ethics, and identifying and consulting a mentor who has expertise in ethics.

nurses can serve on ethics committees and in political action groups and professional organizations. They can also address issues by writing for publication and engaging in media events to speak on behalf of patients with chronic disease and illness. One such media example is publicly supporting measures to improve access to healthcare services and individualized care instead of the Band-Aid type of care that many patients experience. However, serving in the role of advocate at any level of care can be emotionally and physically draining.

▶ Organ Transplantation

People appraised the organ transplantation success story as "an extraordinary leap in medicine and surgery" and "one of the miracles of modern medicine" (Jonsen, 2012, para. 1). Only after many years of experimental transplants, mostly on animals and occasionally on humans, did surgeons and researchers realize success. As of 2021 in the United States, more than 106,000 people were waiting on organs for transplants. Every day in the United States, more than 33,000 organs were obtained from deceased donors (Organ Procurement and Transplantation Network [OPTN], 2021a).

In 1954, a surgeon named Joseph Murray, with the help of a physician named John Merrill, performed the first successful kidney transplant from one monozygotic twin to another in Boston at Peter Bent Brigham Hospital, which is now known as Brigham and Women's Hospital (Jonsen, 2012; President's Council on Bioethics, 2003). The recipient lived for 8 years because the genetic materials of the twins were identical or similar. In 1990, Murray received a

Nobel Prize in Medicine for his contributions. In 1967, a surgeon named Christiaan Barnard, from Cape Town, South Africa, performed the first human heart transplant.

Organ Transplant Ethical Issues During the Early Years

Organ transplantation is more accepted in the 21st century than it was in the 1950s. Then, the ethical questions regarding removing organs from dead or living donors were just as intense and angst provoking as the ethical questions we face today regarding human cloning. Almost instantly, after that first heart transplant, some reasonable ethical issues arose:

1. Should surgeons invade a healthy living donor's body to retrieve an organ to benefit another person?
2. What method of selection can be used to maintain fairness?
3. Where will kidneys be obtained beyond the living donors?
4. If the donor is dead, what are the criteria for death? (Jonson, 2012)

Murray, the first kidney transplant surgeon, posed the first question as he was trying to decide whether to obtain an organ from a healthy living person, especially in light of his oath to help sick people get well and not to cause harm to others. Question 2 was an issue because, for the first time in history, surgeons were forced to decide on criteria for organ recipients because of a shortage of available organs; in other words, for the first time ever, surgeons were literally choosing who would live and who would die. Questions 3 and 4 related to unclear information in terms of whether surgeons could retrieve an organ from a dead donor and, if so, at what point they should retrieve an organ. The definition of death in the Uniform Determination of Death Act (UDDA) did not become law until 1981; therefore, clinical evidence to determine the death of a donor was uncertain. Another major issue was that many people were dying from organ rejection

because of inadequate and harmful antirejection medications. It was not until 1978 that the effective immunosuppressive medication cyclosporine was available for use.

Sixty years after the first kidney transplant, people are still debating ethical issues regarding organ donation and transplantation, but the issues in the 21st century have shifted to a more diverse set of problems. One current, major issue is societal pressure for organ harvesting, which results from a global demand for organs that far outweighs the supply. Another major issue involves individuals questioning their own moral beliefs about death, organ donation, and the legal definition of death.

Organ Procurement

Organ procurement is the obtaining, transferring, and processing of organs for transplantation through systems, organizations, or programs. There is evidence that people continue to choose not to donate their organs, which is one of the reasons for the severe imbalance in supply and demand (Kerridge et al., 2002; Rock, 2014). In the United States, 45% of adults are registered organ donors, compared to only 33% of people in the United Kingdom. Even though the number of registered organ donors is low in the United Kingdom, findings in U.K. polls have indicated that the majority of the population (90%) supports organ donation (Rock, 2014).

Some reasons for not having a higher number of registered organ donors stem from misconceptions about the definition of brain death, mistrust of the medical profession, and religious views. Organ donation is a delicate subject, and for many people, organ donation conjures up uncomfortable feelings with death in general. The very thought of donating an organ could lead to individuals having disturbing thoughts about their own death or loss of a body part.

The demand for organs far exceeds the supply. To counterbalance the supply–demand crisis, the U.S. Department of Health and Human Services continues to offer campaigns to increase the organ supply. For the reasons previously outlined, societal ethical conflicts exist between the national organ donor campaigns and the values of potential donors. Utilitarianism is a common ethical framework for planning and implementing goals to increase the organ supply. Conversely, at the core of many people's beliefs is the value of respect for autonomy and human dignity, which is a deontological ethical framework.

Because the public continues to place a high value on self-determination, utilitarian-based programs face challenges to increase the number of organ donors. From a utilitarian perspective, one organ donor can potentially save eight lives with his or her organs; however, people in the United States continue to die while waiting for an organ (OPTN, 2021a). Some countries apply a broader scope of utilitarianism by promoting either **presumed consent**, meaning that people automatically consent to donating their organs unless they specifically indicate otherwise, or **mandated choice**, meaning that competent people are required to indicate yes or no regarding their organ donation choice on license applications, tax returns, and other official state identification records. People are bound by this mandated choice, but an advance directive or a written change of mind can reverse the decision.

In the United States, donor cards are legal documents that are used along with other documentation in the organ donation process. A **donor card** gives permission for the use of a person's bodily organs in the event of death. Advance directives are also legal documents that are used to express one's desires about organ donation. Adults in the United States express their wishes regarding organ donation through a **required response**. People can decline or willingly agree to donate their organs, and they can allow a relative to be their designated surrogate.

Fair Allocation of Organs

The National Organ Transplant Act of 1984 led the way for the creation of a national list of candidates; it is currently maintained by the United Network for Organ Sharing (UNOS; https://unos.org). This organization assures the allocation of organs to the best-matched candidates. This act also designated the establishment of the OPTN, a national sharing organization that primarily safeguards fairness across the United States for all organ allocation. The scarcity of available organs prompted the OPTN to apply two factors to assure a balanced decision: justice and medical utility. Justice is the "fair consideration of candidates and medical needs," and medical utility is an effort to "increase the number of transplants performed and the length of time patients and organs survive" (OPTN, 2021b).

All the names of people in the United States who need an organ go on a national list only after a physician from one of the transplant centers evaluates each person for documented need. Although the criteria for organ donation varies by organ, the general guidelines include medical emergency, blood/tissue type and size match with the donor, time on the waiting list, and proximity between the donor and the recipient (Gift of Life Donor Program, 2021a).

The Gift of Life Donor Program began in 1974 as a small organization in Delaware for the purpose of managing a few kidney transplants. Today, it is a large national organization with an impeccable reputation that manages a variety of organs. The primary goal of the program is to "improve the quality of life of patients awaiting transplantation by maximizing the availability of donor organs and tissues while upholding the highest medical, legal, ethical, and fiscal standards" (Gift of Life Donor Program, 2021b). Additionally, the organization coordinates training for transplantation and donation professionals.

Ethical Issues of Death and the Dead Donor Rule

The 1981 **Uniform Determination of Death Act (UDDA)** defined **death** as an irreversible cessation of circulatory and respiratory functions or irreversible cessation of all functions of the brain (President's Commission for the Study of Ethical Problems in Medicine and Biomedical and Behavioral Research, 1981). Rubenstein et al. (2006) posed the following questions regarding this legal definition of death:

1. Why does having a sound definition of death matter at all?
2. What are the human goods at stake in getting this question right?
3. What are the moral hazards in getting it wrong? (Introduction, para. 5)

The medical community adopted two guiding moral principles, known collectively as the **dead donor rule**. This rule functions as the norm for managing potential organ donations. The principles of the dead donor rule are that the donor must first be dead before the retrieval of organs and a person's life and care "must never be compromised in favor of potential organ recipients" (DeGrazia & Mappes, 2001, p. 325).

There are three unresolved ethical issues regarding the retrieval of a person's organs in accordance with the legal definition of death: (1) properly caring for the dying person until death is pronounced, (2) the well-being of family members who must say goodbye to their dying loved one, and (3) the perceived good of the organ donation itself (Rubenstein et al., 2006).

The first ethical issue is assurance of uncompromised and competent care until the person is dead. The dead donor rule, if followed, applies here. Nurses and providers must first tend to the care of a dying patient, which could mean administering aggressive treatment or corroborating that the person's treatment is medically futile.

The second ethical issue is the well-being of families and healthcare professionals. Specifically, this ethical issue involves the risk of causing harm to the families when there has not been sufficient time for them to grieve and

process the information versus the risk of not having viable organs if the families wait too long to come to terms with the death. A point made by Rubenstein et al. (2006) is that "these final moments of life and first moments of death *belong* to the grieving at least as much as to the departed person" (Introduction, para. 7), yet this same window of time also belongs to the procurement team and surgeons. Quick actions to remove the organs and deliver them to the unknown beneficiary are necessary.

Following the pronouncement of death, providers of care maintain the physical body by way of ventilation and circulatory support until the organ procurement team can harvest the organs. The procurement teams, who are well trained, tread on morally shaky ground with the deceased's family. Approaching the grieving family is difficult, even when the team just needs to confirm the patient's or family's wish of wanting to donate organs. Sometimes, the person's death will have occurred suddenly, such as in a car accident or another injury, and families must have some time to come to terms with the death of their loved one.

When the potential donor is pronounced dead, the person continues to remain on a mechanical ventilator as if still living, with warm skin and up-and-down chest movements, and the person continues to receive intravenous fluids. The family sees their loved one's chest moving up and down, and even though the person has been pronounced dead, the family sees their loved one as still living. This leaves healthcare professionals and families with feelings of ambiguity. Nurses experience moral distress when a person is declared dead and will not be an organ donor, and the provider suspends medical treatment and ventilation support.

The third ethical issue involves the perceived good of organ donation itself. From one perspective, organ donation can give death a certain degree of meaning, allowing a last act of benevolence and selflessness. For example, when no hope exists for continuance of life, guardians might donate their child's organs as an imagined way to carry on that child's life.

From another perspective, patients are guaranteed some autonomy and self-determination when they preregister to donate their organs. The procurement team often views itself as an advocate for carrying out the patient's wish after death. This act of advocacy goes beyond the principle of autonomy in health care, but carrying out the recipient's wishes or releasing a dead person's organs for the good of another is a widely accepted utilitarianism paradigm in society.

An intensely debated ethical question involves the dead donor rule and its legitimacy. Is the dead donor rule outdated? Alan Shewmon (2004) clarified his thoughts on death as an unreal and unknowing ontological (study of being or existence) event without significant meaning, especially when society defines a person as dead by the legal standard created by people in the past 26 years.

As a consequence of questioning the soundness of the dead donor rule, a few bioethicists have attempted to define death as an event, instead of a process, as they grapple with the idea of expanding the scope of utilitarianism to overturn the dead donor rule; ultimately, organs could be retrieved from patients without higher brain function (Miller & Truog, 2008). Patients without higher brain function have no cognitive functioning, but they have an intact brain stem and usually breathe without the assistance of mechanical ventilation. An example is patients who have only lower brain function (and no higher brain), such as those in a persistent vegetative state, like Terri Schiavo.

This notion raises the question of whether this practice would be ethical or legally acceptable. Pronouncing patients' dead who have a functioning brain stem but no higher brain functioning would be a complete ontological shift in how society views death. Overturning the dead donor rule and retrieving organs from patients who are still alive by the UDDA definition of death would be a utilitarian ethical framework when viewed from the perspective of longer-term quality of life and the number of people who could be saved; for example, one person's organs may save eight lives. Society must answer these questions:

1. If the dead donor rule changes so organ teams can harvest organs from patients with only lower brain function, how will the definition of death change to include these patients?
2. Do patients without higher brain function, but who are not dead by the current legal definition of death, have full moral standing?

Society needs to search for what death really means in terms of the moral imperative of doing good for others versus acting within moral limits and respecting primum non nocere (first do no harm).

RESEARCH NOTE: ATTITUDES OF CARING FOR BRAIN DEAD ORGAN DONORS

Pearson et al. (2001) conducted a qualitative study of intensive care nurses' attitudes and experiences toward brain dead organ donors. The researchers discovered two major themes of caring: the family and the nurse.

The Family
Of central importance to the nurses in the study was meeting the needs of the patients' families. Some important considerations for nursing care of donor family members are as follows:

- Prioritizing the family's needs
- Empathizing with the family's tragedy

(continues)

RESEARCH NOTE: ATTITUDES OF CARING FOR BRAIN DEAD ORGAN DONORS
(continued)

- Supporting the family's decisions
- Realizing that caring for the patient shows care for the family
- Encouraging space and privacy for the family to grieve; say their goodbyes; and hopefully, accept the situation
- Not intruding on the family's grief (p. 135)

The Nurse

Another challenge for intensive care nurses is finding meaning in the case of each brain dead patient and the potential donors. In this study, nurses stated that brain dead patients should be treated as if they were alive because this action shows respect for the patients and their families and they were adamant that family members be shown respect and kindness. A compassionate way to show ultimate kindness is to give excellent care to the families' loved ones.

In the midst of giving competent care, tending to family's needs, and providing much-needed emotional support, nurses tend to become emotionally drained from feeling a need to clarify the definitions of brain death and other medical terms to families. Nurses also feel emotional strain in regard to their own ambiguities about the legal definition of brain death. With the expanding organ procurement system, nurses experience moral suffering associated with internal moral conflicts with regard to uncertainties of life and death. If nurses take advantage of extra education on organ transplantation nursing care and grieving families, they may be better prepared to manage their own personal emotions and those of families in crisis.

Nurses and Organ Donors

In intensive care units and on transplant teams, nurses manage care for potential organ donors, recipients, and their families on a daily basis. Organ procurement teams consist of nurses, surgeons, and other trained healthcare professionals. The psychosocial impact and outcome of the organ transplantation process for donors, donor families, and recipients are unique. According to the ANA *Code of Ethics for Nurses with Interpretative Statements* (2015), nurses work within a moral framework of good personal character to promote the principles of autonomy, beneficence, nonmaleficence, and justice. To review how those principles are evident in the essential aspects of the code, refer to the box Research Note: Attitudes of Caring for Brain Dead Organ Donors. Most nurses want to have a sense of satisfaction based on their belief that they are promoting human good, preserving their patients' dignity as much as possible, and maintaining a caring environment.

The ANA *Code of Ethics for Nurses with Interpretive Statements* (2015) includes some essential aspects for the care of adult patients in Provisions 1.2, 1.3, 1.4, 2.1, 5.1, 6.1, 6.2, and 8.3. These provisions consist of the importance of consideration of the following items:

- Culture, values systems, belief systems, social support, gender orientation, and primary language
- Interventions that optimize health and well-being of patients in nurses' care
- Patient autonomy in terms of decision making, cultural beliefs, and understanding of health, autonomy concerns, and relationships
- A commitment of nurses to respect the uniqueness, worth, and dignity of patients
- Respect for moral worth and dignity of all persons

- Practice the "good nurse" virtues of knowledge, skill, wisdom, patience, compassion, honesty, altruism, and courage
- Practice the promotion of human virtues and values of dignity, well-being, respect, health, and independence, among others
- Create and maintain excellence in practice environments that support nurses to fulfill their ethical obligations
- Respect and be sensitive to the culturally diverse populations' unique healthcare needs worldwide

KEY POINTS

- The traditional concept of medicalization from the 1970s, in what was known as the golden age of doctoring, and three market-driven forces have caused the provider's role to shift from one of dominance (in the 1970s) to one of more deference.
- The three market-driven forces contributing to this medical paradigm shift are managed care, biotechnology, and consumers. With the shift, patients now think like consumers as they choose types of medical services, providers, and insurance policies they want.
- The ethical issue of promoting healthy behaviors yet trying to respect a person's rights to self-determination is a complex situation. An ethical question to consider is "How far should providers of care go in terms of respecting the self-determination of patients when some noncompliant behaviors can cost society a great deal of money and other resources?"
- Under the umbrella of medicalization are the concepts of compliance, adherence, and concordance. Patients with chronic disease and illness generally fit within the notion of being medicalized.
- Chronic disease and illness include concepts such as suffering, labeling, isolation, and loneliness associated with long-standing disease.
- There is a supply–demand crisis for organ donation. Utilitarian-based programs to increase the number of organs remain challenged.
- Providing care to people with chronic disease and illness involves certain ideal nursing ethical competencies, which include the following: (1) moral integrity—honesty, truthfulness and truthtelling, benevolence, wisdom, and moral courage; (2) communication mindfulness and effective listening; and (3) concern—advocacy, power, and culturally sensitive care.
- Although all the ethical competencies are important for nursing practice, advocacy and communication are especially relevant for providing care to patients with chronic disease and illness.
- Primary nursing obligations to brain dead organ donors involve the care of the donor family and the high engagement of nurses in the care of the organ donor.

References

American Nurses Association (ANA). (2015). *Code of ethics for nurses with interpretive statements*.

Barofsky, L. (1978). Compliance, adherence, and the therapeutic alliance: Steps in the development of self-care. *Social Science and Medicine, 12*, 369–376.

Beauchamp, T. L., & Childress, J. F. (2019). *Principles of biomedical ethics* (8th ed.). Oxford University Press.

Berg, J., Evangelista, L. S., & Dunbar-Jacob, J. M. (2002). Compliance. In I. M. Lubkin & P. D. Larsen (Eds.), *Chronic illness: Impact and interventions* (5th ed., pp. 203–232). Jones and Bartlett Publishers.

Centers for Disease Control and Prevention (CDC). (2021, April 28). *About chronic diseases*. https://www.cdc.gov/chronicdisease/about/index.htm

Conrad, P. (2007). *The medicalization of society: On the transformation of human conditions into treatable disorders*. Johns Hopkins University Press.

DeGrazia, D., & Mappes, T. A. (2001). *Biomedical ethics* (5th ed.). McGraw-Hill.

Galanti, G. A. (2004). *Caring for patients from different cultures* (3rd ed.). University of Pennsylvania Press.

Garrett, C. (2004). *Gut feelings: Chronic illness and the search for healing.* Rodopi.

Gift of Life Donor Program. (2021a). *How does organ and tissue donation work?* https://www.donors1.org/learn-about-organ-donation/how-does-organ-and-tissue-donation-work/

Gift of Life Donor Program. (2021b). *Mission and core values.* https://www.donors1.org/about-gift-of-life/overview/mission-and-core-values/

Horne, R., Weinman, J., Barber, N., Elliott, R., & Morgan, M. (2005). *Concordance, adherence and compliance in medicine taking.* https://www.researchgate.net/publication/271443859_Concordance_Adherence_and_Compliance_in_Medicine_Taking

Illich, I. (2010). The medicalization of life. In I. Illich (Ed.), *Limits to medicine—medical nemesis: The exploration of health* (pp. 39–125). Marion Boyars. (Original work published 1975)

International Council of Nurses (ICN). (2021). *Code of ethics for nurses.*

Jonsen, A. R. (2012). *The ethics of organ transplantation: A brief history.* https://journalofethics.ama-assn.org/article/ethics-organ-transplantation-brief-history/2012-03

Kerridge, I. H., Saul, P., Lowe, M., McPhee, J., & Williams, D. (2002). Death, dying and donation: Organ transplantation and the diagnosis of death. *Journal of Medical Ethics, 28,* 89–94.

Martin, C. M. (2007). Commentary: Chronic disease and illness care. *Canadian Family Physician, 53,* 2086–2091.

Miller, F. G., & Truog, R. D. (2008). Rethinking the ethics of vital organ donations. *Hastings Center Report, 38*(6), 38–46. https://doi.org/10.1353/hcr.0.0085

Organ Procurement and Transplantation Network (OPTN). (2021a). *Annual record trend continues for deceased organ donation, deceased donor transplants.* https://optn.transplant.hrsa.gov/news/annual-record-trend-continues-for-deceased-organ-donation-deceased-donor-transplants/

Organ Procurement and Transplantation Network (OPTN). (2021b). *How organ allocation works.* https://optn.transplant.hrsa.gov/learn/about-transplantation/how-organ-allocation-works/

Osamor, P. E., & Grady, C. (2018). *Debate: Autonomy and couples' joint decision-making in healthcare.* https://www.researchgate.net/publication/322415844_Autonomy_and_couples%27_joint_decision-making_in_healthcare

Pearson, A., Robertson-Malt, S., Walsh, K., & Fitzgerald, M. (2001). Intensive care nurses' experiences of caring for brain dead organ donor patients. *Journal of Clinical Nursing, 10,* 132–139.

President's Commission for the Study of Ethical Problems in Medicine and Biomedical and Behavioral Research. (1981). *Defining death.* https://repository.library.georgetown.edu/bitstream/handle/10822/559345/defining_death.pdf

President's Council on Bioethics. (2003). *Organ transplantation: Ethical dilemmas and policy choices.* https://bioethicsarchive.georgetown.edu/pcbe/background/org_transplant.html

Rock, A. (2014). *Why don't more people want to donate their organs?* http://globalbioethics.org/gbi_old/2014/11/why-do-so-few-people-donate-organs/

Rubenstein, A., Cohen, E., & Jackson, E. (2006). PCBE: *The definition of death and the ethics of organ procurement from the deceased.* https://bioethicsarchive.georgetown.edu/pcbe/background/rubenstein.html

Shewmon, D. A. (2004). The dead donor rule: Lessons from linguistics. *Kennedy Institute of Ethics Journal, 14*(3), 277–300.

Walker, C., & Markos, S. (2002). *Developing a shared definition of chronic illness: The implications and benefits for general practice (GPEP 843: Final report).* Chronic Illness Alliance, Inc. Victoria: Health Issues Center.

World Health Organization (WHO). (2020). *Noncommunicable diseases progress monitor 2020.* https://www.who.int/publications/i/item/ncd-progress-monitor-2020

CHAPTER 8

Ethics and the Nursing Care of Elders

Karen L. Rich

OBJECTIVES

After reading this chapter, the reader should be able to do the following:

1. Define ageism.
2. Identify factors that influence elders' experiences of living meaningful lives.
3. Discuss the principle of autonomy as it relates to the ethical care of elders.
4. Assess the range of paternalism as it relates to ethical nursing practice.
5. Discriminate among different levels of moral agency.
6. Discuss different perspectives about quality-of-life assessments.
7. Identify the signs of elder abuse and appropriate nursing interventions.

▷ Aging in America

The President's Council on Bioethics (2005) proposed "we are on the threshold of a 'mass geriatric society,' a society of more long-lived individuals than ever before in human history" (p. xvii). People are living longer and healthier lives during the past century due to technological advances in medicine and public health. According to the *2020 Profile of Older Americans* report (U.S. Department of Health and Human Services [HHS], Administration on Aging, 2021):

In the U.S. the population age 65 and older numbered 54.1 million in 2019 (the most recent year for which data are available). They represented 16% of the population, more than one in every seven Americans. The number of older Americans has increased by 14.4 million (or 36%) since 2009, compared to an increase of 3% for the under-65 population. (p. 4)

Although the number of human life years has been extended, questions remain about how the quality of those years is threatened by chronic debilitating conditions, ageism, and limited support and resources for elders and their caregivers.

Often, chronic conditions such as cerebrovascular disease and Alzheimer's disease cause elders to lose their most crucial link with others: their voice within society. A loss of voice to express individual feelings, desires, and needs is arguably one of the most profound causes of isolation for elders (Smith et al., 2002). Considerations about the loss of elders' voices and society's diminished recognition of the meaningfulness of their lives underlie many of the ethical issues discussed in this chapter. A large portion of elder-focused ethics is based on relationships elders have with other people in society, including their families and healthcare professionals. Often, the lives of elders are set aside from the lives of other adults in communities. It is this overall view of generational separateness that makes it necessary to study elder-focused ethics.

Ageism, a way of thinking that was originally described by Butler (1975), has influenced some people within society to view elders as fundamentally different from others; consequently, some people cease to identify elders as normal human beings (Agich, 2003). Just as racism and sexism describe the stereotyping of and discrimination against people because of their skin color or gender, **ageism** involves the same type of negative perceptions toward older adults based on age. Ageism perpetuates the idea that elders as a population are cognitively impaired, set in their ways, and old-fashioned regarding their morals and abilities (Agich, 2003; Butler, 1975).

It can be disquieting to elders when they realize how youth oriented Western society is today. One can see that the media's target audience is most often young adults and the financially affluent middle-aged population. The target audience for television advertising is ages 24 to 54. Media emphasis is placed on having a beautiful body, even if expensive elective surgery is needed to do so. Pictures of beautiful and famous young people and couples are prominently displayed on magazine covers, and young athletes are revered in Western society. Older actors, and particularly actresses, lament the lack of good roles for them in the movie industry. It is not surprising that as people age they often become despondent about the losses they experience in regard to their appearance and physical abilities. The seemingly vital, active, and glamorous lives of young people portrayed in the media serve as a stark contrast to what many elderly persons may be experiencing. Agich (2003) proposed "a society that values productivity and material wealth above other values is understandably youth oriented; a natural consequence is that the old come to be seen, and to see themselves, as obsolete and redundant" (p. 54).

So who are the elders in today's society? Savishinsky (1991) stated:

> The class of the elderly includes both the rich and poor, sick and well, sane and insane; it also embraces the relatively healthy so-called young old between 60 and 75 and the more vulnerable old old who are living beyond their eighth decade. Some are intimately connected with family and community, whereas others are cut off from their kin. Some are active and ardent; others are disengaged and hopeless. (p. 2)

In the late 1700s and early 1800s, old people were encouraged to view their lives as a pilgrimage and to prepare for death while still participating in service to family and community. However, starting around the 1850s, societies began to instill the belief that thoughts about death should be avoided. The emphasis changed to a focus on valuing "the virtues of youth rather than age, the new rather than the old, self-reliance and autonomy rather than community" (Callahan, 1995, p. 39).

These views formed the foundation of the beginning of ageism in the 20th century. The realities of old age were not consistent with the new worldview of the morality of self-control and autonomy; rather, the decay inherent in aging was associated with dependence and failure. Though ageism began to be a general social theme after World War II, today it may be focused more on elderly persons who are disabled (Cohen, 1988).

The lives of people of all ages are overshadowed by an awareness of their eventual aging and death, and it is during one's later years that these issues can no longer be ignored. When one actually does confront the facts of unavoidable aging and death, the mysteries involved can be startling. The feminist philosopher Simone de Beauvoir (1972) proposed "the old are invisible because we see death with a clearer eye than old age itself" (p. 4). Agich (2003) interpreted this statement to mean that old people are set apart from the rest of society because people tend to look beyond the elderly persons themselves, who they perceive as close to death, and instead see the prospects of their own death.

Moody (1992) proposed that the modern advances in biomedical technology that have facilitated longer lives for many elderly persons have made it necessary to confront critical ethical questions that society may want to ignore. These questions involve dilemmas about death and dying, the perception of what is meant by quality of life, and judgments about the mental and physical functional capacity of old adults. Moody questioned whether typical models and approaches to bioethics based on rights and duties fit well with considerations of ethics and aging. He asked, "What ethical ideals are appropriate for an aging society?" (p. 243). According to Moody, focusing on individual autonomy and justice among generations will not provide people with the desired ethical model for engaging in relationships with elders. Elder-focused ethics includes negotiation and a foundation in the virtues. Principles and rules also must be included, but principles and rules can thwart desired ends

if the practical wisdom and good character of caregivers are not emphasized as part of the overall scheme of ethics.

ETHICAL REFLECTION

How can nurses combat ageism in their local, state, and national communities?

Life Meaning and Significance

Once, while Mahatma Gandhi's train was pulling slowly out of the station, a European reporter ran up to his compartment window. "Do you have a message I can take back to my people?" he asked. It was Gandhi's day of silence, a vital respite from his demanding speaking schedule, so he didn't reply. Instead, he scrawled a few words on a scrap of paper and passed it to the reporter: "My life is my message."

—**E. Easwaran,** *Your Life Is Your Message*, (1992), p. 1, Hyperion. Reprinted by permission.

The issues of autonomy, vulnerability, dependency, and good relationships are important when considering ethics and elders. However, there is another issue that is important to the moral world of elders and those with whom they relate: elderly persons' own feelings about the significance and meaning of their lives. According to Callahan (1995), underlying the strong desire by society and scientists to abolish the biology of aging is "a profound failure of meaning" (p. 39).

As people age, they often begin to realize the truth of Gandhi's words—their life is their message—but does Western society support elders reflecting on the meaning and significance of their lives? In earlier times, tradition was highly valued by society, and the meaning and significance of elderly persons' lives were viewed differently than they are today in our culturally and morally diverse society

(Callahan, 1995). In the past, elders had an elevated status in communities because their wisdom was prized for its own sake and their wisdom placed them in a special position of being called on to perpetuate and interpret societal moral traditions.

The diverse views in current Western culture sometimes undermine the community-wide role of elderly persons in passing on moral traditions; therefore, one of the traditional societal purposes for elders has diminished. Today, elderly persons are important to businesses if they are financially well off, to families if they are willing and able to provide financial support and care for grandchildren, to politicians as a voting block, and to nonprofit agencies as volunteers (Callahan, 1995). Some people believe these roles for elders make older persons valuable within society. However, upon closer inspection, one can determine that it is not age that is held in high regard, but the accidental features of old age such as disposable income and free time.

According to Cole (1986), meaning is "an intuitive expression of one's overall appraisal of living. Existentially, meaning refers to lived perceptions of coherence, sense, or significance, in experiences" (p. 4). Callahan (1995) described meaning as an inner feeling supported by "some specifiable traditions, beliefs, concepts or ideas, that one's life" has purpose and is well structured in "relating the inner self and the outer world—and that even in the face of aging and death, it is a life which makes sense to oneself; that is, one can give a plausible, relatively satisfying account" (p. 33). Callahan described significance as "the social attribution of value to old age, that it has a sturdy and cherished place in the structure of society and politics, and provides a coherence among the generations that is understood to be important if not indispensable" (p. 33).

Nurses may question why it is relevant to nursing ethics for them to consider elderly persons' pursuit of life meaning and significance. The answer is that nursing ethics is first and foremost about relationships, alleviating patients' suffering, and facilitating patients' well-being. In relation to elders, nursing ethics also is focused on helping elderly persons find and keep their voice or means of expressing their values and feelings. Finding meaning and significance alleviates suffering and promotes well-being for many elderly persons (see **BOX 8-1**).

The Search for Meaning

Viennese neurologist and psychiatrist Viktor Frankl (1905–1997) wrote the influential book *Man's Search for Meaning*, which was originally published in 1959. More than 10 million copies of this book have been sold, and it was rated as one of the 10 most influential books by respondents in a survey conducted by the Library of Congress (Greening, 1998). The book is about how Frankl found meaning in his experiences in Auschwitz and other

---

BOX 8-1 Discovering Meaning

In the story *The Fall of Freddie the Leaf,* a leaf named Freddie questioned a wise older leaf, Daniel, about life and its meaning. When Daniel told Freddie that all the leaves on their tree and even the tree itself would eventually die, Freddie asked, "Then what has been the reason for all of this? Why were we here at all if we only have to fall and die?"

Daniel answered, "It's been about the sun and the moon. It's been about happy times together. It's been about the shade and the old people and the children [that sat and played beneath the tree]. It's been about colors in Fall. It's been about seasons. Isn't that enough?"

Buscaglia, L. (1982). *The fall of Freddie the leaf: A story of life for all ages.* Charles B. Slack, pp. 19–20.

concentration camps during World War II. In the preface to the third edition of the book, Allport (1984) relayed Frankl's belief that "to live is to suffer, to survive is to find meaning in the suffering. If there is a purpose in life at all, there must be a purpose in suffering and in dying" (p. 9).

Frankl (1959/1984) suggested that meaning is the primary motivation in the lives of humans. He determined the last of his human freedoms in the concentration camp was to choose his attitude toward his suffering. Being in a concentration camp was an unchangeable situation for Frankl, as are the facts that aging will happen to all people who do not die young, and all people will eventually die. It is in continuing to choose to find meaning in the circumstances people encounter as their life stories are created and unfold that will eventually form the fabric of a meaningful life when people are old.

Frankl (1959/1984) believed the transitoriness, or fleeting nature, of life, similar to what Buddhists call impermanence, must not be denied by persons who are interested in putting the search for meaning at the center of their lives. Rather, even suffering and dying can be actualizing experiences. Though no one can supply another person's life meaning, nurses can help elderly people on their journey through life by aiding them to discover meaning in their lives and believe they are significant members of communities.

Updating the Eriksonian Life Cycle

In exploring the moral treatment of elderly persons, Callahan (1995) proposed that the search for common meaning in aging requires a consideration of the updated theory of the life cycle as described by Erik Erikson. Erikson's book *The Life Cycle Completed*, first published in 1982, emphasized that all eight stages of the Eriksonian life cycle cannot be distinctly separated but rather are interrelated. After Erikson's death at age 91, his wife, Joan, used

her own ideas and notes written by her husband to update the book. She proposed a ninth stage of development and addressed other issues related to old-old people. Joan Erikson was in her 90s when she wrote this updated book, and she used her voice to speak for many old-old people about their experiences.

The ninth stage of the life cycle is an extension of the eighth stage, which is a time when elders develop to some degree either despair and disgust or integrity. Wisdom is the strength or virtue some elders depend on to successfully navigate both the eighth and ninth stages of development. The ninth stage is the stage of the lived experiences of persons in their eighth or ninth decade of life. The following are some of the difficulties occurring in the ninth stage that make wisdom and integrity hard for elders to achieve (Erikson & Erikson, 1997):

- Wisdom requires the senses of sight and hearing to see, hear, and remember. Integrity is compared with tact (as in the word *intact*), which is related to touch. In their 90s, elderly persons often lose or have impaired senses of sight, hearing, and touch.
- When persons reach the age of late 80s or enter the decade of their 90s, despair may occur because people realize life is too short now to try to make up for missed opportunities.
- Despair may occur because old-old persons are just trying to get through the day because of their physical limitations, even without the added burden of regrets about their earlier life. When persons believe their lives are not what they wished them to be, the despair deepens.
- Persons in their 80s and 90s are likely to have experienced losses of relationships to a greater degree than at any other age. In addition to the suffering directly related to these losses, suffering is generated when the person realizes "death's door is open and not so far away" (Erikson & Erikson, 1997, p. 113).

Like virtue ethicists who have drawn connections between the good life and being a vital member of a community (Blum, 1994; MacIntyre, 1984), Joan Erikson (Erikson & Erikson, 1997) said her husband, Erik, often proposed that the life cycle cannot be appropriately understood if it is not viewed within a social context or in terms of the community in which it is actually lived. The Eriksons' belief that individuals and society are interrelated and people are constantly involved with the give and take of a dynamic community is a key position of communitarian ethicists today. When society lacks a sound ideal of old age, a holistic view of life is not well integrated into communities. If elders are excluded from the valued members of a community, they often are viewed as the embodiment of shame instead of the embodiment of wisdom.

Joan Erikson was convinced that if persons in their 80s and 90s had developed hope and trust in earlier life stages, they would be able to move further down the path to gerotranscendence, a concept she borrowed from the work of Lars Tornstam. Transcendence means "to rise above or go beyond a limit, [to] exceed, [to] excel" (Erikson & Erikson, 1997, p. 124). Erikson described the experiences of gerotranscendent individuals as follows:

- Feeling a cosmic union with the universal spirit
- Perceiving time as being limited to now or maybe only next week; otherwise, the future is misty
- Feeling that the dimensions of space have been decreased to the perimeter of what the person's physical capabilities allow
- Feeling that death is a sustaining presence for the person and viewing death as being "the way of all living things" (p. 124)
- Having an expanded sense of self that includes "a wider range of interrelated others" (p. 124)

Erikson then activated the word *transcendence* into the word *transcendance* to associate its meaning with the arts and specifically "the

dance of life [that] can transport us into all realms of making and doing with every item of body, mind, and spirit involved" (p. 127).

Moral Agency

It is generally believed that elders are a vulnerable population because of the natural progression toward frailty that occurs with aging. Because of this vulnerability, moral agency is a key consideration in relationships with elders. The ability to make deliberate choices and act deliberately in regard to important life experiences affecting the suffering and well-being of sentient beings, including oneself, refers to a person's moral agency. **Moral agency** implies that people are responsible for and have the capacity to direct their beliefs and actions. Arguments about moral agency generally result from debates about a person's mental capacity in regard to decision making. Referring to whether the person is or is not autonomous usually is at the heart of the debate.

Decisional Capacity

Decisional capacity or incapacity is the ability or inability to come to what most adults would consider to be reasonable conclusions or resolutions. Decisional capacity can generally be equated with the concept of competence, though competence has more of a legal connotation because it is closely tied to formal situations legally requiring informed consent. Questions of decisional capacity and competence are associated most often with the three populations of "(a) mentally disabled persons, (b) cognitively impaired elderly persons, and (c) children" (Stanley et al., 2003, p. 398).

There is no one set of published criteria to be used in all assessments of decisional capacity and competence. A method cited by Beauchamp and Childress (2019) is unique because it includes a range of the inabilities that someone who is incompetent exhibits as opposed to being based on the person's actual abilities. The standards begin by describing the behaviors persons with the least competence exhibit and moves toward standards requiring higher ability. The standards Beauchamp and Childress (2019) drew from literature are as follows:

- Inability to express or communicate a preference or choice
- Inability to understand one's situation and its consequences
- Inability to understand relevant information
- Inability to give a reason
- Inability to give a rational reason
- Inability to give risk- or benefit-related reasons
- Inability to reach a reasonable decision (as judged, for example, by a reasonable person's standard). (pp. 115–116)

Nurses must be sensitive to the fact that vulnerable and dependent elderly patients often are assumed to be mentally incapacitated or incompetent based on faulty impressions and ageism. When ungrounded assumptions are made based on a person's frail appearance, for example, elderly patients can be left out of the process of decision making that is important to their well-being. Elders who are physically frail may not be included in making decisions ranging from deciding when they want to take their bath in a long-term care facility to healthcare professionals aiding family members in legally taking away the older person's decisional capacity for treatment options and the management of their financial affairs.

Though in most cases family members have ethical motives when caring for elderly family members, this is not always the case. Occasionally, family members and caregivers are more interested in their own self-serving desires than the well-being of an elder when the family or caregivers want to deem the elder incompetent. Biased decisions, which can be intentional or unintentional, may be based on a desire to gain or maintain access to an elder's money or on feelings of disgust or exasperation. Nurses must be cautiously and wisely alert when assessing patients and situations that affect determinations of elders' decisional capacity. As directed in the *Code of Ethics for Nurses with Interpretive Statements* (American Nurses Association [ANA], 2015), a nurse's primary commitment is to the patient.

Autonomy and Paternalism

Autonomy in bioethics means that persons are rational and allowed to direct their own health-related and life decisions. **Paternalism** occurs when a healthcare professional makes choices for a patient based on the healthcare professional's beliefs about what is in the best interest of the patient or is best for the patient's own good. Physicians and nurses sometimes believe patients are unable to understand the full extent of their care needs; a less justifiable reason for paternalistic behavior is based on healthcare professionals' belief that their profession accords them a warranted place of power over patients.

Although the practice of paternalism was once an expected behavior among healthcare professionals, it is not as readily accepted today by professionals or recipients of care. However, elders are still at a high risk for having their autonomy violated by healthcare professionals. This often results from incorrect assumptions about elders' decisional capacities because of their frail appearance and the influences of societal ageism. Even when elders are confused regarding the minor details of a situation, they may retain decisional capacity. In fact, elderly persons may be disoriented regarding time and the names and roles of persons while still retaining the capacity to make reasonable decisions regarding their lives and treatment. For example, if an elderly patient does not remember the name of an emergency department physician when the physician comes and goes in and out of the room, this does not necessarily mean the patient is not competent to make treatment decisions. A more important assessment would be whether the patient knows she is in a hospital emergency department. Even this determination may not be sufficient to determine decisional capacity about treatment decisions.

When elders are confused about some of the details regarding their current situation, healthcare professionals may be tempted to act paternalistically. Even if an elder does not know she is in a hospital emergency department, healthcare professionals should not automatically overrule the patient's refusal of treatment. Instead, the whole context of the elder's life must be evaluated in terms of the ability to understand the benefits, risks, and consequences of decisions and the overall consistency of the elder's conversations and expressions of wishes over time. Healthcare professionals need to assess whether the elder's current wishes are consistent with previously expressed desires and ways of being. People sometimes want to quickly overrule elders' decisions and requests when their autonomy should rightfully be honored.

Some ethicists believe the excessive paternalistic behavior exhibited by physicians and nurses in the past has caused a backlash, currently resulting in an elevated and imbalanced interest in respecting a patient's autonomy. According to these ethicists, the pendulum has now swung too far in the direction of an overinflated interest in preserving autonomy, and this stance minimizes the importance of the give and take needed for good human relationships, a desire to cultivate a strong sense of community, and the usefulness of virtues (Agich, 2003; Callahan, 1995; Hester, 2001; MacIntyre, 1984, 1999; Moody, 1992). Therefore, behavior exhibited toward elderly patients may fall somewhere along a wide continuum from a point of unjustified paternalism to a point of rigid adherence to respecting

autonomy. Hester (2001), a communitarian ethicist, argued that healing requires communal involvement, not an overdeveloped interest in autonomy; when autonomy becomes the consuming focus in health care, the involvement of communities and personal relationships may be sidelined.

Elderly patients often need the care of nurses not because they need someone to respect their capacity for autonomy but because they have lost mental abilities, physical abilities, or both. Rather than focusing on the use of rules and principles such as autonomy, a humanistic focus on facilitating the well-being and alleviating the suffering of elders may be the more important focal point of care. Respect for autonomy remains extremely important in bioethics and nursing ethics, but a humanistic approach that puts the patient's humanity and well-being at the center of care is needed rather than an unquestioned allegiance to rule-oriented behavior.

Also, nurses may believe they should minimize family involvement to support an elderly patient's autonomy. Although healthcare providers need to support elders in maintaining self-direction, family caregivers usually should not be excluded from decision making regarding elders' care. Autonomous elderly patients are not necessarily bound by their family's decisions or recommendations, but often, elders appreciate the caring concern of their family and even the appropriate decisional support provided by trusted nurses. Caregivers, including nurses who are well-known by elderly patients through repeated contact over time, are intimates, not strangers, to the patient. It is unreasonable to believe that nurses who care about the well-being of their patients would be objectively detached from actively interacting with patients regarding their healthcare decisions. When providing decisional support to elders, nurses need to use practical wisdom in evaluating whether capricious assumptions, ageism, and prejudices are influencing the support and direction they are providing to patients. Ultimately, wise and compassionate decisional support is a critically important part of nursing care and patient advocacy.

Vulnerability and Dependence

In addition to autonomy, vulnerability and dependence are integrally related to moral agency. To facilitate communities working toward the common good of their members, MacIntyre (1999) emphasized that people need to acknowledge their animal nature. When realizing that human nature is also animal nature, vulnerability and dependence are accepted as natural human conditions. Vulnerability and dependence are inherent human conditions as people move from childhood to adulthood; barring complicating circumstances, people progress from vulnerability and dependence in childhood to being capable of independent practical reasoning as adults.

As adults, however, humans may reexperience vulnerability and dependence because of physical and cognitive changes during aging. According to MacIntyre (1999), ethicists frequently talk in terms of stronger, independent persons benevolently bestowing their virtues on people who are vulnerable and dependent. Nurses would do well to keep in mind that all people are subject to vulnerabilities and dependence, even nurses themselves. There is a vast amount of knowledge to learn from vulnerable and dependent elders if nurses are open to hearing and relating to their patients' life stories (Butts & Rich, 2004).

Dementia

Nurses, particularly those working in home care and long-term care settings, often provide care to patients with dementia. Kitwood (1997) suggested our evolving culture has supported society and healthcare communities treating persons with dementia as the "new outcasts of society" (p. 44). According to Jenkins and Price (1996), the loss experienced by persons with dementia can be likened to a loss of personhood. Examples of personal tendencies that depersonalize other people are listed in **BOX 8-2**.

BOX 8-2 Depersonalizing Tendencies to Avoid

1. Treachery: Using deception to distract or manipulate
2. Disempowerment: Not allowing persons to use their abilities
3. Infantilization: Patronizing; acting as an insensitive guardian would act toward a child
4. Intimidation: Inducing fear through physical power or threats
5. Labeling: Using a category, such as dementia, as the basis for interactions and explanations
6. Stigmatization: Treating someone as an outcast or a diseased object
7. Outpacing: Pressuring others to act faster than they are able; presenting information too rapidly
8. Invalidation: Failing to acknowledge others' subjective experiences and feelings
9. Banishment: Physical or psychological exclusion
10. Objectification: Treating others as a "lump of matter" rather than as sentient beings
11. Ignoring: Talking or interacting with others in the presence of a person as if he or she is not there
12. Imposition: Forcing a person to do something; overriding or denying the possibility of choice
13. Withholding: Refusing to provide asked-for attention or to meet evident needs
14. Accusation: Blaming for actions or failures that arise from lack of ability or misunderstanding
15. Disruption: Crudely intruding into a person's actions or reflections
16. Mockery: Humiliating; making jokes at another's expense
17. Disparagement: Damaging another person's self-esteem; conveying messages that someone is useless, worthless, [or] incompetent

Data from Kitwood, T. (1997). *Dementia reconsidered*. Open University Press, pp. 46–47.

When people become adjusted to the dwindling capacities of persons with dementia, they often begin reacting to these people as if they are less than persons (Moody, 1992). People with dementia can still be aware of their feelings even when the person they once seemed to be appears to be withering away. It is reasonable to assume that an extreme sense of vulnerability can occur as a person enters the early and middle stages of progressive dementia. This occurs when a remainder of cognitive ability may still exist in the awareness of personhood and connectedness to the environment and to others.

Kitwood's (1997) reference to persons with dementia becoming the outcasts of society is relevant when these people lose their dignity in terms of how other people perceive them. Dignity is acknowledged or denied in the relatedness of daily interactions between people with dementia and their significant others and healthcare professionals. Though families and nurses may not recognize the subtle risks involved, dignity may be jeopardized when caregivers are so focused on making ethical decisions regarding the care of persons with dementia that they forget to actually relate to the persons themselves (Moody, 1992).

Family and paid caregivers of people with dementia often become frustrated and anxious. Nurses can serve as mentors to other caregivers by exhibiting the virtues of compassion and equanimity when interacting with patients with dementia and their families. Gentle communication used by nurses helps to support the overall sense of dignity surrounding the care of patients with dementia. Environmental calm is created with gentle words as opposed to an environment of fear and anxiousness that can be created when loud and harsh words are used. Inexperienced caregivers learn by observing nurses. Nurses always must be aware of their potential to ultimately help or harm patients by the example they set for others.

Virtues Needed by Elders

May (1986) asserted that aging is a mystery rather than a problem and, as a society, people must focus on how they behave toward aging rather than on how to fix it. Doctors' and nurses' positions of power as compared to the seemingly passive beneficiary position of vulnerable patients is an important topic in bioethics. The behavior of healthcare professionals directed toward aged individuals is significant because elderly persons sometimes perceive the treatment they receive from healthcare professionals as symbolic of what they can expect from the larger community.

May (1986) proposed that even when they are seemingly powerless, elderly persons remain moral agents who are personally responsible for the quality of their lives. An ethic of caregiving that is one sided on the part of nurses and physicians is not the answer to power imbalances between healthcare professionals and patients. Elders may experience more meaning in their lives if they remain dynamically involved in creating their own sense of well-being. Life is not static; it can be vital into old age.

The following are virtues May (1986) proposed that elders need to cultivate to enhance the quality of their moral lives. These virtues were considered valuable enough to be included by the President's Council on Bioethics (2005) in their report *Taking Care: Ethical Caregiving in Our Aging Society*. Nurses who are aware of the continued moral development that occurs in old age can support elderly patients in cultivating these virtues as elders continue their journey of moral progress.

Courage

St. Thomas Aquinas's definition of courage as "a firmness of soul in the face of adversity" (May, 1986, p. 51) is applicable to elderly persons. Elderly persons need courage when facing the certainty of death and loss in their lives.

Humility

Elderly people need humility when their dignity is assaulted through seeing and feeling their bodily decay, they interpret the looks they receive from young people as a sign that their frailty is noticeable and possibly repugnant to others, and they progressively lose more people and things of value in their lives. Humility is a virtue also needed by caregivers to counteract the arrogance that may arise because of their position of power in their relationships with elders. Nurses need to be receivers as well as givers in patient–professional relationships; nurses can receive the gifts of insight and practical wisdom when they actively listen to the narratives of their elderly patients who have lived many years and experienced much joy and suffering.

Patience

Although old age sometimes stimulates the emotions of bitterness and anger, a positive conception of the virtue of patience can help combat these reactive emotions. "Patience is purposive waiting, receiving, willing . . . it requires taking control of one's spirit precisely when all else goes out of control" (May, 1986, p. 52). Patience is the virtue that can help elders bear the frustrations of their frail bodies rather than cursing their fate and becoming frustrated with issues such as being short of breath when trying to walk short distances.

Simplicity

Simplicity is a virtue referred to by Benedictine monks as a moral mark of old age. Simplicity becomes the virtue of a pilgrim who "has at long last learned how to travel light" (May, 1986, p. 53). Simplicity is exhibited

when elderly persons experience great joy in the small pleasures of life, such as a meal with friends, rather than in accumulating material possessions.

Benignity

Benignity is another moral mark of old age, according to the Benedictines. Benignity is defined "as a kind of purified benevolence" (May, 1986, p. 53). It is opposed to the vice of grasping and avarice (greed) associated with some elders' attempts to hold onto life in the face of death. Benevolence provides an answer to the tightfistedness of avarice, "not with the empty-handedness of death, but the open-handedness of love" (p. 53). Elders who exhibit the virtue of benignity usually have realized the meaning of their lives and the meaning that can be found in their deaths. They have learned to find joy in serving others.

Integrity

The virtue of integrity represents "an inclusive unity of character" (May, 1986, p. 53) summarizing all the other virtues of character in old age. Character is a moral structure and requires an overriding virtue when character is "at one with itself" (p. 53). Integrity, or an intactness of character, is the foundation that helps elders remain kind and optimistic in terms of their transcendent connection with the universe, even when loss and impermanence could easily pull them in a more negative direction.

Wisdom

Wisdom, or prudence, makes integrity possible through the lessons learned from the experiences of one's past. Prudence was defined by medieval moralists as consisting of three parts: *memoria*, *docilitus*, and *solertia*. *Memoria* "characterizes the person who remains open to his or her past, without retouching, falsifying, or glorifying it" (May, 1986, p. 57). *Docilitus*

BOX 8-3 Flexibility and Life

When a man is living, he is soft and supple; when he is dead he becomes hard and rigid. When a plant is living, it is soft and tender; when it is dead, it becomes withered and dry. Hence, the hard and rigid belongs to the company of the dead. The soft and supple belongs to the company of the living.

Reproduced from Tzu, L. (1989). *Tao teh ching* (J.C.H. Wu, Trans.). Shambhala, p. 155. (Original work published 1961). Reprinted by permission.

---

does not represent the passiveness of one who is merely docile but rather is "a capacity to take in the present—an alertness, an attentiveness in the moment" (p. 58). It implies a contrasting state from the need to talk excessively that sometimes serves to separate elders from others. *Solertia* is "a readiness for the unexpected" (p. 58). It provides a contrast to being inflexible with routines; however, some amount of ritual helps elders develop strength of character (see **BOX 8-3**).

Detachment and Nonchalance

Detachment and nonchalance are similar virtues. May (1986) proposed that detachment is a virtue linked with wisdom and is consistent with what Erikson defined as "an attitude that depends in part upon a store of experience" (p. 58). People who are experienced weigh and react to situations wisely, calmly, and with love; people who are inexperienced overreact and become engulfed by catastrophe. May based nonchalance on a biblical virtue that allows one the "capacity to take in one's stride life's gifts and blows" (p. 59). For example, the virtue of detachment or nonchalance might allow elderly persons who have serious medical problems to enjoy the gifts in their lives, such as being with their great-grandchildren, while calmly accepting the realistic assessment that they

---

BOX 8-4 Last Acts of Courtesy

Ida was a 79-year-old Alzheimer's patient seen by Dr. Muller, a psychiatrist, in the emergency room (ER) because she became agitated at her foster home. Ida looked younger than her years and "still had some of the light that usually leaves the face of the demented." Her score was 7 out of 30 on the Mini Mental Status Exam. "Ida gave little information during the interview, though she showed every sign of wanting to cooperate." Plans were made for Ida to be discharged back to the foster home with a prescription for haloperidol. When Dr. Muller went to say good-bye to Ida he found her "straightening the sheet and flattening out the pillow on the gurney where she had been placed prior to the interview. She was trying to put [Styrofoam cups and food wrappers] into a trash container" but was having difficulty in doing so. Dr. Muller stated, "I was struck by what was still left of this sweet lady's demented brain and mind—which did not know the year, season, month, or day—that made her want to attempt these last acts of courtesy before leaving the ER." Muller quoted neurologist Oliver Sacks, who stated "style, neurologically, is the deepest part of one's being, and may be preserved, almost to the last, in a dementia."

Data from Muller, R. (2003). *Psych ER*. The Analytic Press, pp. 63–65.

---

may not live to see their great-grandchildren graduate from college.

Courtesy

Courtesy too is based on a biblical link to wisdom. Courtesy is the "capacity to deal honorably with all that is urgent, jarring, and rancorous on the social scene" (May, 1986, p. 59) (see **BOX 8-4**).

Hilarity

A final virtue outlined by May (1986) is another virtue of old age identified by Benedictine monks. Though the risk for depression is more common in elders than at other ages because of conditions such as naturally lowered serotonin levels; anxiety over fixed incomes; physical, personal, and material losses; and disturbed sleep patterns, the monks wisely believed hilarity is a realistic virtue of old age. *Hilaritas* is "a kind of celestial gaiety in those who have seen a lot, done a lot, grieved a lot, but now acquire that humored detachment of the fly on the ceiling looking down on the human scene" (p. 60). It involves not taking oneself too seriously.

▶ Quality of Life

What do people mean when they discuss the issue of quality of life? Often, people, including healthcare professionals, talk about quality of life as if it were a self-evident concept. But is it? According to Jonsen and colleagues (2022), determinations of quality of life are value judgments. Value judgments imply variations among the people who are determining value. If it is determined that a patient's quality of life is seriously diminished, justifications often are proposed to refrain from life-prolonging medical treatments. Some people find this position problematic because of their views about the sanctity of life—these people believe because all human life is sacred, life must be preserved no matter what the quality of that life might be.

ETHICAL REFLECTION

Discuss your experiences with elders. Provide examples of situations in which you have observed elders displaying May's (1986) virtues. How can nurses help elderly persons cultivate the virtues identified by May?

Many people believe treatment can be withheld or withdrawn based on quality-of-life determinations while still preserving a reverence for the sanctity of life. Scales have been developed and measures of physical and psychological functions have been suggested to objectify quality-of-life determinations. However, people differ significantly in how they respond to scales and measurements to quantify the quality of their own or others' lives. Studies have shown at least one group of healthcare professionals—physicians—frequently rate the quality of a patient's life lower than the patient rates it (Jonsen et al., 2022).

The determination of the quality of a life can be divided into categories of personal evaluations and observer evaluations. According to Jonsen et al. (2022), a **personal evaluation** is "the personal satisfaction expressed or experienced by individuals in their own physical, mental, and social situation" (p. 119). **Observer evaluation** refers to quality-of-life judgments made by someone other than the person living the life. Observers tend to base their evaluations on some standard below which they believe life is not desirable. It is observer evaluations that generate most ethical problems about quality-of-life determinations because observer evaluations can reflect incorrect assumptions, biases, prejudices, or beliefs about conditions that are not necessarily permanent, such as homelessness or family conditions.

Problems with quality-of-life determinations specifically related to elderly patients can arise due to discrimination against patients by healthcare professionals based on the patient's chronological age, a perception of a patient's social worth, a patient's dementia, or differences between the professional's and the patient's life goals and values (Faden & German, 1994; Jonsen et al., 2022). Decisions regarding treatment always should be made based on honest determinations of medical need and patients' current or previously communicated preferences. If a patient's wishes were not previously communicated, decisions should be based on projections of what loved ones believe the patient would want done. Problems can easily arise when professionals try to project what they believe a reasonable person would want in a particular situation. It is at this point that prejudices and biased discriminations based on ageism can enter into observer evaluations.

When acting in regard to elderly patients, special attention needs to be focused on an assumption that values and goals are different among people of different age groups (Faden & German, 1994; Jonsen et al., 2022). The values that might be consistent among young healthcare professionals could be expected to be different from the values held by old-old adults. Automatic projections of values by nurses and other healthcare professionals are not consistent with the moral care of elderly persons. Elders may view their lives as having quality when younger persons, still in the prime of their lives, do not readily see the same quality. In addition to nurses using moral imagination in simply stopping to reflect about the dangers of forming automatic assumptions, conducting a values history with elderly patients when they enter a new healthcare system can be invaluable in trying to ensure the ethical treatment of elders. This history must be reevaluated as appropriate (see **BOX 8-5**).

As previously discussed, Frankl (1959/1984) maintained that "man's search for meaning is the primary motivation in his life" (p. 105). Humans embark on the search for meaning to alleviate and understand suffering and to move toward well-being. Frankl proposed inner tension, rather than inner equilibrium, may result from the search for meaning, and he believed that inner tension is a prerequisite for mental health. Valuing the need to strive toward equilibrium and homeostasis (a tensionless state) is a dangerous misconception, according to Frankl. This way of thinking can be especially true when interacting with elderly persons whose whole being does not generally remain in a state of equilibrium.

An acceptance of the belief that equilibrium is not necessarily the healthiest state supports the belief that suffering should not be attacked as if it were something to eliminate at all costs. Rather, well-being often involves the relief of suffering through the acceptance of suffering. In discussing the often-misguided goals of a modernist society, Callahan (1995) proposed that novelist George Eliot had captured this philosophy with the word *meliorism*.

BOX 8-5 Conducting a Values History

The following are sample questions for conducting a values history with elders:

1. What would you like to say to someone who is reading a document about your overall attitude toward life?
2. What, for you, makes life worth living?
3. How do you feel about your health problems or disabilities? What would you like others (family, friends, doctors, nurses) to know about these feelings?
4. How do you expect friends, family, and others to support your decisions regarding medical treatment you may need now or in the future?
5. If your current physical or mental health gets worse, how would you feel?
6. How does independence or dependence affect your life?
7. What will be important to you when you are dying (e.g., physical comfort, no pain, family members present)?
8. Where would you prefer to die?
9. What general comments would you like to make about medical treatment?
10. How do your religious background or religious beliefs affect your feelings toward serious, chronic, or terminal illness?

Modified from the Institute of Public Law, University of New Mexico School of Law. (n.d.). *Values history form*, (pp. 1–5). https://cdn.ymaws.com/www .hospicefed.org/resource/resmgr/hpcfm_pdf_doc/valueshistoryform.pdf

The concept of meliorism describes "an ethic of action oriented toward the relief, not the acceptance, of pain and suffering" (p. 30).

ETHICAL REFLECTION

How might ageism affect end-of-life decisions and the elderly? What can nurses do to combat end-of-life care and decisions based on ageism?

An emphasis on holistic care has helped to eliminate some of the beliefs from the Enlightenment period that the human body can be compared with a machine (sometimes referred to as reductionism). Mechanics fix machines, but the healthcare professional–patient relationship should not be viewed in a similar way. The healthcare system and healthcare professionals today often still perpetuate the meliorism described by Eliot. Meliorism causes doctors and nurses to work toward curing disease and relieving suffering at all costs. In working with patients of all ages, but especially in patients' later years, attempts must be made to alleviate suffering while realizing that completely relieving suffering and curing diseases is not always possible. In these instances, the nurse's goal is to help patients accept the pain and suffering that cannot be changed and find meaning in their suffering. Amid the chaos and pain of patients' suffering, nurses can be compared to the calm person described by the Buddhist monk Thich Nhat Hanh (see **BOX 8-6**). Patients' suffering can lead to a profound, transforming life experience for both patients and nurses.

▶ Assessing the Capacity to Remain at Home

Assessing elders' capacity to safely continue to live alone in their own homes is a problem often faced by nurses working in the community

BOX 8-6 Calm Within the Storm

In Vietnam there are many people, called boat people, who leave the country in small boats. Often the boats are caught in rough seas or storms, the people may panic, and boats can sink. But if even one person aboard can remain calm, lucid, knowing what to do and what not to do, he or she can help the boat survive. His or her expression—face, voice—communicates clarity and calmness, and people have trust in that person. They will listen to what he or she says. One such person can save the lives of many.

Data from Thich Nhat Hanh. (2001). *Thich Nhat Hanh: Essential writings* (R. Ellsberg, Ed.). Orbis Books, p. 162.

and helping to plan discharges of patients from acute care to home care. These determinations become particularly difficult when frail elders adamantly want to remain in or return to their homes and caregivers disagree with an elder's decision. Caregivers must consider the real and perceived capacities and incapacities of elders and question the safety of their living situation. Ways to assess cognitive capacity have been covered earlier in this chapter. If it is believed an elder is incapacitated, a consideration of respecting elders' autonomy versus supporting caregivers' beneficence may be needed. The ethical issue becomes a matter of deciding whether to act in a way Beauchamp and Childress (2019) called **soft (or weak) paternalism**.

ETHICAL REFLECTION

Healthcare professionals' beliefs about the proper treatment of elders falls along a continuum from discounting elders' personal quality-of-life judgments to believing only curing disease and being successful in eliminating physical suffering are worthwhile goals. Provide examples of nurses' opportunities to act as patient advocates in relation to this continuum.

"In soft paternalism, an agent intervenes in the life of another person on grounds of beneficence or nonmaleficence with the goal of preventing substantially nonvoluntary conduct" (Beauchamp & Childress, 2019, p. 233). Nonvoluntary, or nonautonomous, actions are actions not based on rational decision making. Persons who are the receivers of soft paternalistic actions must have some form of compromised ability for this form of weak paternalism to be justified. It is debatable as to whether soft paternalism qualifies as paternalism because acting in a person's best interest is not usually disputed when people must be protected from harm resulting from circumstances beyond their control, including a personal desire based on faulty information when a person is incapacitated. However, issues of self-harm often constitute dilemmas when elders with intact decisional capacity want to remain at home when it is not safe to do so because of the elder's physical limitations. Family caregivers and healthcare providers must carefully weigh when and the degree to which weak paternalism is justified in preventing self-harm.

Long-Term Care

Issues regarding moral relationships between nurses and patients in long-term care facilities are similar to other issues discussed in this chapter; that is, the relationships often are focused on issues of autonomy. As previously proposed, focusing too narrowly on respecting autonomy can cause nurses to miss the real day-to-day complexities that make up moral relationships with elders. In many instances, elders are in long-term care facilities because they are no longer able to exercise self-direction in safely caring for themselves. This fact sometimes makes attempts to respect and preserve autonomy a futile undertaking. When unrealistic goals are not acknowledged in long-term care, it often frustrates nurses and aides who work in long-term care facilities; unfortunately, these frustrations can ultimately be directed against long-term care residents.

Pullman (1998) proposed that an ethic of dignity be used, as opposed to an ethic of autonomy, in long-term care. With an ethic of dignity, the moral character of caregivers is the focus rather than the autonomy of the recipients of care. Of course, autonomy must be respected when it is realistic to do so, but when working with long-term care residents who are no longer able to exercise their full autonomy, a communal ethic of dignity can provide a compassionate means of care. Even when elders can fully exercise their autonomous choices, an ethic of dignity provides an appropriate grounding framework from which to work.

ETHICAL REFLECTION

Cohen (1988) said elders often focus all their energy toward avoiding "the ultimate defeat, which is not death but institutionalization and which is regarded as a living death" (p. 25) (see **BOX 8-7**). How can nurses help to change the experience of residence in a long-term care facility being like a living death?

Pullman (1998) divided dignity into **basic dignity**, which is the dignity inherent in all humans, and **personal dignity**, which is an evaluative type of dignity decided upon by communities that does not have to be solely tied to a person's autonomy. Personal dignity can be viewed as a community's valuing of the interrelationship of members of the community. Acknowledging elders' basic and personal dignity, through the adoption of an ethic of dignity, includes the "confidence that caregivers will strive to serve the on-going interests of their patients to the best of their abilities" (p. 37). If there is a belief that elderly residents of long-term care facilities need to be independent because being dependent is bad and the goal is to minimize the elders' need for care rather than to provide more care, then the

BOX 8-7 Look Closer, See Me

The author of the following poem is unknown, but it is said to have been written by an elderly woman living in a geriatric facility in Scotland. It was found among the elderly woman's belongings after she died and has been widely distributed since that time.

What do you see, nurse, what do you see, what are you thinking when you're looking at me? A crabbit [crabby] old woman, not very wise, uncertain of habit, with faraway eyes. Who dribbles her food and makes no reply when you say in a loud voice, "I do wish you'd try?" Who seems not to notice the things that you do, and forever is losing a stocking or shoe. Who, resisting or not, lets you do as you will with bathing and feeding, the long day to fill. Is that what you're thinking? Is that what you see? Then open your eyes, nurse; you're not looking at me.

I'll tell you who I am as I sit here so still, as I use [do] at your bidding, as I eat at your will. I'm a small child of ten with a father and mother, brothers and sisters, who love one another.

A young girl of sixteen, with wings on her feet, dreaming that soon now a lover she'll meet. A bride soon at twenty—my heart gives a leap, remembering the vows that I promised to keep. At twenty-five now, I have young of my own who need me to guide and a secure happy home. A woman of thirty, my young now grown fast, bound to each other with ties that should last.

At forty my young sons have grown and are gone, but my man's beside me to see I don't mourn. At fifty once more babies play round my knee, again we know children, my loved one and me.

Dark days are upon me, my husband is dead; I look at the future, I shudder with dread . . . For my young are all rearing young of their own, and I think of the years and the love that I've known.

I'm now an old woman and nature is cruel; 'tis jest to make old age look like a fool. The body, it crumbles, grace and vigour depart, there is now a stone where I once had a heart.

But inside this old carcass a young girl still dwells, and now and again my battered heart swells. I remember the joys, I remember the pain, and I'm loving and living life over again.

I think of the years; all too few, gone too fast, and accept the stark fact that nothing can last. So open your eyes, nurse, open and see, not a crabbit old woman; look closer—see ME!!

relationships between nurses and elderly residents of long-term care facilities are in trouble from their outset.

Pullman (1998) suggested that long-term care often requires paternalistic interventions from the beginning of patient–healthcare provider relationships. He defined a rule of **justified paternalism** as a guide for these paternalistic interventions: "the degree of paternalistic intervention justified or required is inversely proportional to the degree of autonomy present" (p. 37). Nurses must be extremely sensitive and aware in ensuring that they cultivate the intellectual virtue of practical wisdom so errors in judgment are not made about

respecting patients' autonomy versus practicing justified or weak paternalism in patient care.

When elders have the capacity to make choices regarding treatments and daily living activities, they should have the freedom to make personal decisions. Those options include such things as choosing to refuse medications and refusing physical therapy treatments. However, respecting elders' autonomy does not mean compassionate nurses should not take considerable time, if needed, to calmly discuss the potential consequences of controversial choices made by elderly persons. Nurses who work from an ethic of dignity are not emotionally detached from their patients but, instead, are willing to risk feeling a personal sense of failure or loss when their elderly patients make choices they believe are not in the elder's best interest.

▶ Elder Abuse

All people regardless of age or ability deserve justice.

—U.S. Department of Health and Human Services, Administration for Community Living, Elder Justice

Nurses are frequently the first people to recognize that patients are the victims of violence or abuse; this is especially true about emergency department and home care nurses. The moral care of elders requires nurses to be interested in recognizing the signs of abuse and in taking appropriate actions. "Elder abuse is a term referring to any knowing, intentional, or negligent act by a caregiver or any other person that causes harm or a serious risk of harm to an older adult" (National Center on Elder Abuse [NCEA], n.d. FAQ 1). It includes physical abuse, sexual abuse, neglect by caregivers, financial abuse, emotional abuse, and self-neglect . Self-neglect includes behaviors by elders that endanger their health or well-being.

Problems that may indicate elder abuse include the following:

- Physical Abuse: Bruises, pressure marks, broken bones, abrasions, and burns.
- Sexual Abuse: Bruises or injury to the genital area which may present as difficulty moving or sitting .
- Emotional Abuse: Withdrawal from normal activities, anxiety, depression, unusual behavior, or unease
- Neglect: Bedsores, unattended medical needs, poor hygiene, and unusual weight loss
- Financial Abuse: Uncharacteristic purchases by the individual or caregiver; failure to pay bills or keep appointments; questionable behavior (NCEA, n.d., FAQ 2)

Signs of abuse occurring within a healthcare facility include the following:

- Restraints: physician's orders for restraints (should be time-limited), the number of patients who are physically restrained, the type of restraints used, the correct application of restraints, and how often staff check restrained patients
- Signs of overmedication
- Signs of harassment, humiliation, or threats from staff or other patients
- Patients being uncomfortable around staff
- Signs of bruises or other injuries
- Evidence of patient neglect, such as patients left in urine or feces without cleaning. (Pozgar, 2013, p. 431)

LEGAL PERSPECTIVE

Because nurses are both ethically and legally considered to be mandatory reporters of abuse, they need to do the following:

- Report abuse to:
  - Child Protective Services
  - Adult Protective Services
  - Long-term care ombudsman (usually when an agency or healthcare provider is involved)
  - State licensing board (when healthcare provider is involved)
  - Law enforcement (if required under statute)
- When:
  - Written or verbal report within 24 hours of incident

Data from Westrick, S. J. (2014). *Essentials of nursing law and ethics* (2nd ed.). Jones & Bartlett, p. 133.

Many elders do not have the physical or cognitive capability to seek help. Thus, it is critical that healthcare professionals be on the lookout for signs of abuse. At a minimum, nurses should know the signs of elder abuse and report suspected abuse. A good resource for nurses is the Eagle Elder Abuse Guide for Law Enforcement website that provides specific reporting laws for each state and other useful information (University of Southern California [USC], n.d.). The website is sanctioned by NCEA. Nurses also can become active as volunteers in organizations and events to prevent elder abuse, such as becoming state long-term care ombudsmen or getting involved annually with World Elder Abuse Awareness Day.

ETHICAL REFLECTION

Discuss ways nurses can get involved with elder justice. Visit the HHS Elder Justice website and click on "Get Involved."

Humanistic Nursing Care of Elders

Travelbee (1971) described the human-to-human relationship between a nurse and the recipient of care as a "mutually significant experience" (p. 123). According to Travelbee, "each participant in the relationship perceives and responds to the human-ness of the other; that is, the 'patient' is perceived and responded to as a unique human being—not as 'an illness,' 'a room number,' or as a 'task to be performed'" (p. 124). Unfortunately, elders often feel dehumanized when interacting with healthcare professionals, which further compounds the dehumanization they encounter in society. Travelbee made a profound statement: "If an individual is related to as a 'human being' by at least one health worker he may be able to draw enough strength from the relationship to cope with ten other workers perceiving him as 'patient'" (p. 37).

Nurses who are compassionate dedicate themselves to helping patients transcend or accept unavoidable suffering. It is a challenge to relate to others compassionately, to really communicate to the heart, according to Chödrön (1997). "Compassion is not

a relationship between the healer and the wounded. It is a relationship between equals" (Chödrön, 2001, p. 50).

For many elders, the world is a lonely place. Nurses who have a sincere desire to alleviate or facilitate acceptance of the suffering of this vulnerable group are widening the circle of compassion in the world.

Compassion and healing can be thought of as paired needs of elders. Capra (1982) described healing as a "complex interplay among the physical, psychological, social, and environmental aspects of the human condition" (p. 124). Capra postulated that healing has been excluded from medical science because it cannot be understood in terms of reductionism. Healing suggests moving toward a wholeness that goes beyond a single human being; it is consistent with a belief in the interconnection of all beings and the universe. Healing does not imply curing; it is a realization that not all things can be fixed. This idea of healing encompasses the recognition of the nature of impermanence and accepts unpredictability and the inability to strictly control events.

Nurses must establish human-to-human relationships with elderly patients and recognize the interplay of many factors that may affect the older person's state of well-being. Many factors affecting elders cannot be changed; they must be peacefully accepted and used in achieving integrity. Caring for elders requires dynamic interventions blending art and science. Suffering and loss are inherent in the daily lives of elders, and the reality of impermanence forms a glaring presence that is difficult for the aged to ignore. Although there are many approaches in the ethical care of elderly patients, nurses might adopt an approach to care similar to a way of being suggested by Thich Nhat Hanh (1998), based on the Buddhist Lotus Sutra. Thich Nhat Hanh stated the sutra advises one "to look and listen with the eyes of compassion." He further stated that "compassionate listening brings about healing" (p. 86). Compassionate listening by nurses gives individual elders their voice in an often uncompassionate world.

KEY POINTS

- Ageism, or discrimination based on chronological age, underlies many ethical issues related to elders.
- Society often neglects to notice the meaning of elders' lives as scientists work to abolish the biology of aging.
- Determinations of decisional capacity in regard to elders are sometimes made based on prejudiced assumptions rather than facts.
- Elders may perceive the quality of their lives to be higher than healthcare professionals perceive it based on observational judgments.
- Soft paternalism is sometimes a compassionate approach to caring for elderly persons.
- Focusing on an ethic of dignity rather than a strict ethic of autonomy may be more realistic in caring for some elders, especially in long-term care facilities, when elderly persons are not completely able to exercise their autonomy.
  - Nurses should be aware of signs of elder abuse and neglect, and nurses actively can get involved in justice for elders.

References

Agich, G. J. (2003). *Dependence and autonomy in old age: An ethical framework for long-term care* (2nd ed.). Cambridge University Press.

Allport, G. W. (1984). Preface. In V. E. Frankl (Ed.), *Man's search for meaning: An introduction to logotherapy* (3rd ed., pp. 7–10). Simon & Schuster.

American Nurses Association. (2015). *Code of ethics for nurses with interpretive statements.*

Beauchamp, T. L., & Childress, J. F. (2019). *Principles of biomedical ethics* (8th ed.). Oxford University Press.

Blum, L. A. (1994). *Moral perception and particularity.* Cambridge University Press.

Buscaglia, L. (1982). *The fall of Freddie the leaf: A story of life for all ages.* Charles B. Slack.

Butler, R. (1975). *Why survive? Being old in America.* Harper & Row.

Butts, J. B., & Rich, K. L. (2004). Acknowledging dependence: A MacIntyrean perspective on relationships involving Alzheimer's disease. *Nursing Ethics, 11*(4), 400–410.

Callahan, D. (1995). *Setting limits: Medical goals in an aging society with "a response to my critics."* Georgetown University Press.

Capra, F. (1982). *The turning point: Science, society, and the rising culture.* Bantam Books.

Chödrön, P. (1997). *When things fall apart: Heart advice for difficult times.* Shambhala.

Chödrön, P. (2001). *The places that scare you: A guide to fearlessness in difficult times.* Shambhala.

Cohen, E. S. (1988). The elderly mystique: Constraints on the autonomy of the elderly with disabilities. *Gerontologist, 28*(Suppl.), 24–31.

Cole, T. R. (1986). The tattered web of cultural meanings. In T. R. Cole & S. Gadow (Eds.), *What does it mean to grow old? Reflections from the humanities* (pp. 3–7). Duke University Press.

de Beauvoir, S. (1972). *The coming of age* (P. O'Brien, Trans.). Putnam.

Easwaran, E. (1992). *Your life is your message: Finding harmony with yourself, others, and the earth.* Hyperion.

Erikson, E. H., & Erikson, J. M. (1997). *The life cycle completed* (extended version). W. W. Norton.

Faden, R., & German, P. S. (1994). Quality of life: Considerations in geriatrics. *Clinics in Geriatric Medicine, 19*(3), 541–551.

Frankl, V. E. (1984). *Man's search for meaning: An introduction to logotherapy* (3rd ed.). Simon & Schuster. (Original work published 1959)

Greening, T. (1998). Viktor Frankl, 1905–1997. *Journal of Humanistic Psychology, 38*(1), 10–11.

Hester, D. M. (2001). *Community as healing: Pragmatist ethics in medical encounters.* Rowman & Littlefield.

Institute of Public Law, University of New Mexico School of Law. (n.d.). *Values history form,* (pp. 1–5). https://cdn.ymaws.com/www.hospicefed.org/resource/resmgr/hpcfm_pdf_doc/valueshistoryform.pdf

Jenkins, D., & Price, B. (1996). Dementia and personhood: A focus for care? *Journal of Advanced Nursing, 24*(1), 84–90.

Jonsen, A. R., Siegler, M., & Winslade, W. J. (2022). *Clinical ethics: A practical approach to ethical decisions in clinical medicine* (9th ed.). [Kindle Edition]. McGraw-Hill.

Kitwood, T. (1997). *Dementia reconsidered: The person comes first.* Open University Press.

MacIntyre, A. (1984). *After virtue.* University of Notre Dame Press.

MacIntyre, A. (1999). *Dependent rational animals: Why human beings need the virtues.* Open Court.

May, W. F. (1986). The virtues and vices of the elderly. In T. R. Cole & S. Gadow (Eds.), *What does it mean to grow old? Reflections from the humanities* (pp. 43–61). Duke University Press.

Moody, H. R. (1992). *Ethics in an aging society.* Johns Hopkins University Press.

Muller, R. J. (2003). *Psych ER.* Analytic Press.

National Center on Elder Abuse (NCEA). (n.d.). *Frequently asked questions.* https://ncea.acl.gov/FAQ.aspx

Pozgar, G. D. (2013). *Legal and ethical issues for health professionals* (3rd ed.). Jones & Bartlett Learning.

President's Council on Bioethics. (2005). *Taking care: Ethical caregiving in our aging society.* https://repository.library.georgetown.edu/bitstream/handle/10822/559378/taking_care.pdf?sequence=1&isAllowed=y

Pullman, D. (1998). The ethics of autonomy and dignity in long-term care. *Canadian Journal on Aging, 18*(1), 26–46.

Savishinsky, J. S. (1991). *The ends of time: Life and work in a nursing home.* Bergin & Garvey.

Smith, N. L., Kotthoff-Burrell, E., & Post, L. F. (2002). Protecting the patient's voice on the team. In M. D. Mezey, C. K. Cassel, M. M. Bottrell, K. Hyer, J. L. Howe, & T. T. Fulmer (Eds.), *Ethical patient care: A casebook for geriatric health care teams* (pp. 83–101). Johns Hopkins University Press.

Stanley, B., Sieber, J. E., & Melton, G. B. (2003). Empirical studies of ethical issues in research: A research agenda. In D. N. Bersoff (Ed.), *Ethical conflicts in psychology* (3rd ed., pp. 398–402). American Psychological Association.

Thich Nhat Hanh. (1998). *The heart of the Buddha's teaching: Transforming suffering into peace, joy and liberation.* Broadway.

Thich Nhat Hanh. (2001). *Thich Nhat Hanh: Essential writings* (R. Ellsberg, Ed.). Orbis.

Travelbee, J. (1971). *Interpersonal aspects of nursing* (2nd ed.). F. A. Davis.

Tzu, L. (1989). *Tao te ching* (J. C. H. Wu, Trans.). Shambhala. (Original work published 1961)

University of New Mexico. (n.d.). *Values history.* https://hscethics.unm.edu/common/pdf/values-history.pdf

University of Southern California. (n.d.). *EAGLE Elder abuse guide for law enforcement.* https://eagle.usc.edu/law-enforcement-resources/state-mandated-reporting/

U.S. Department of Health and Human Services [HHS], Administration for Community Living. (2021). 2020 *Profile of older Americans.* https://acl.gov/sites/default/files/Aging%20and%20Disability%20in%20America/2020ProfileOlderAmericans.Final_.pdf

Westrick, S. J. (2014). *Essentials of nursing law and ethics* (2nd ed.). Jones & Bartlett Learning.

CHAPTER 9

Ethical Issues in End-of-Life Nursing Care

Janie B. Butts

A place to stay untouched by death does not exist. It does not exist in space, it does not exist in the ocean, nor if you stay in the middle of a mountain.

—**The Buddha**

OBJECTIVES

After reading this chapter, the reader should be able to do the following:

1. Discuss the issues and forces surrounding death anxiety and the ideal death.
2. Describe a scenario of an imaginative dramatic rehearsal of one's own death.
3. Explore the meaning of suffering.
4. Compare and contrast the different types of euthanasia: active, passive, voluntary, nonvoluntary, and involuntary.
5. Identify the historical death practices and issues that led to the president's commission on defining death and the Uniform Determination of Death Act of 1981.
6. Define death as it is expressed in the Uniform Determination of Death Act of 1981.
7. Discuss the three standards of death that materialized since the president's commission report in 1981.
8. Contrast the definitions and clinical procedures between whole-brain death and higher-brain death.
9. Delineate the strengths and weaknesses of the two types of advance directives and the nurse's role in communicating information about the types of advance directives to dying patients and their families, patients who are not necessarily dying, and the public.

(continues)

OBJECTIVES   *(continued)*

10. Analyze the different types of surrogate decision-making standards and the circumstances in which each of these standards would be needed.
11. Discuss the seven principles of surrogate decision making for incompetent patients.
12. Discuss the rationale for the decision-making standard used by the surrogate in the Terri Schiavo case.
13. Analyze the physician's requirements by the American Medical Association for a patient whose treatment has been evaluated as medically futile.
14. Describe nursing care and support for a patient in palliative care.
15. Compare the three highlighted legal cases of Quinlan, Cruzan, and Schiavo in terms of withholding life-sustaining treatment versus withdrawing life-sustaining treatment; withholding artificial nutrition and hydration versus withdrawing artificial nutrition and hydration; and letting go versus an intentional inducement of death.
16. Discuss the three conditions of the rule of double effect and the relationship of these conditions to the nurse's role according to the explanatory statements in Provision 1 of the American Nurses Association *Code of Ethics for Nurses with Interpretative Statements*.
17. Contrast two end-of-life circumstances: terminal sedation and physician-assisted suicide.
18. Define palliative care.
19. Delineate the World Health Organization's pain ladder for patients receiving palliative care.
20. Discuss nurses' moral distress associated with caring for dying patients and their families.
21. Explore ways in which nurses could manage the spiritual care of dying patients and their families.

▶ What Is Death?

Contemporary ethical discussions about death and dying relate to philosophers attempting to answer captivating questions such as "What is a good death?" and "How will we all die?" In recent years, the focus has been on the challenging issues of readiness to die, acceptance of death, and knowing the right time to die (Battin, 1994; Connelly, 2003; Hester, 2003). Many questions about death are unanswerable, but individuals can develop a subjective notion about the meaning of death. For people to face death more peacefully, they need to come to their own understanding of death and beyond, if a beyond exists, and develop a personal knowing of death's connection. Nietzsche, a German philosopher, proposed that everyone needs a philosophy of life in relation to death. Victor Frankl credited Nietzsche with saying, "He who has a *why* to live can bear almost any *how*" (Wackernagel & Rieger, 1878, as cited in Frank & Anselmi, 2011, p. 15).

A long, variable history of physicians trying to determine if and at what point a person could be pronounced dead with neurological criteria generated the legal definition of death in 1981. This definition specified that one of two criteria, or both, must be met for a physician to pronounce a person dead, either whole-brain death or cessation of circulatory and respiratory functions (President's Commission for the Study of Ethical Problems in Medicine and Biomedical and Behavioral Research, 1981). Advancements in technology enabled physicians to pronounce death with a stand-alone criterion of whole-brain death, which is one of the two criteria of death. The other stand-alone criterion was cessation of circulatory and respiratory functions. Since then, with continued advancements in technology and an increased demand for organs and organ harvesting, ethicists began challenging the legal definition of death, particularly death by neurological criteria (DNC) (Arbour, 2013). In this chapter, I will present the definition of death and its scope as well as ethical and legal issues and decisions related to death.

The Ideal Death

Philosopher Andrew Lustig (2003) expressed his amazement at how bioethicists are engaging in passionate conversations about the meaning of death, yet personalizing the truth of our own mortality is difficult. As the title character in the nonfiction best seller *Tuesdays with Morrie* puts it, "Everyone knows they're going to die, but nobody believes it" (Albom, 1997, p. 81). People "talk death" and romanticize death as if it were something ideal rather than a confrontation with mortality.

People use phrases such as "he passed away" to keep from saying the words "he died" or to avoid facing the apprehension associated with the reality of death (Spiegel, 1993). Yalom (1980) defined **death anxiety** as a "dread of death that resides in the unconscious, a dread that is formed early in life at a time prior to the development of precise conceptual formation, a dread that is terrible and inchoate and exists outside of language and image" (p. 189). Existential philosophers such as Kierkegaard, Heidegger, and Sartre emphasized that it is in facing death and the possibility of nonbeing that persons come to know themselves best; in other words, a person first has to put death in perspective to understand any portion of life.

Yalom (1980) stated individuals avoid facing their own mortality in two ways, or defenses. The first defense against death is through immortality projects, where people throw themselves into commendable projects, their work, or raising children. People thoroughly and completely engage in these activities and, by doing so, attempt to insulate themselves from death. The second defense is through dependence on a rescuer, believing another person can provide a sense of safety or protection from the fear of death.

Almost all people want to feel some sense of insulation from the fear of dying. Many times, patients look to nurses, physicians, and other healthcare professionals to fulfill a rescuer role. In Spiegel's (1993) large study about death and dying, several hundred participants discussed their greatest fears about death.

Death signifies the end of a person's living embodiment. Although death often remains a dark secret when people are still alive, one day when the time comes, they will wish for a good death. What exactly does that mean? When death is a known prognosis in a long-term illness, a **good death** generally means that people do not allow medical care and treatment to control all their thoughts about their death; rather, they focus on the illness trajectory and the best palliative care they can receive.

Nurses and other healthcare professionals need to be advocates for those who are dying and think of dying as a process everyone faces. Brogan (2006) related a story of how the concept of the modern hospice movement was started in 1967 in London by a nurse, Dame Cicely Saunders, who many regard as the Florence Nightingale of the hospice movement. In Saunders's own words about death and dying, she stated the following:

> I once asked a man who knew he was dying what he needed above all in those who were caring for him. He said, "For someone to look as if they are trying to understand me." I know it is impossible to understand fully another person, but I never forgot that he did not ask for success but only that someone should care enough to try.... The suffering of the dying is "total pain" with physical, emotional, spiritual, and social elements. (2006, p. 14)

Many people never get an opportunity to engage in death in an ideal manner. Instead, many people's experience with death resembles Saunders's suffering man. Nancy Dubler and David Nimmons presented what they called a cinematic myth of the good American death (see Ethical Reflection: Is This a Good Death or a Cinematic Myth?).

Lehto and Stein (2009) emphasized the significance of death anxiety and the role of nurses in everyday practice. Nurses need to take into account the possibility that some patients manifest ill effects or behaviors as a result of experiencing death anxiety. For most people, death is a mysterious event to be discovered rather than a comforting scene with the presence of family members and others hovering over them (Hester, 2003). Patients often find themselves, if at all conscious, connected to ventilators and other machines and intravenous lines and meters and receiving many medications. Technology and medicalization have exacerbated the problem of depersonalization. Family members or significant others experience difficulty communicating with their loved one because of physical, technological, and environmental barriers. During this perplexing time, the nursing staff could be a patient's most reliable and consistent contact.

ETHICAL REFLECTION: IS THIS A GOOD DEATH OR A CINEMATIC MYTH?

[The good death scene] includes the patient: lucid, composed, hungering for blissful release—and the family gathers in grief to mourn the passing of a beloved life. The murmurs of sad good-byes, the cadence of quiet tears shroud the scene in dignity. Unfortunately for many of us, our deaths will not be the spiritual, peaceful "passing" that we might envision or desire.

N. Dubler, & Nimmons, D. (1992). Ethics on call: A medical ethicist shows how to take charge of life-and-death choices (p. 146). Harmony Books//Crown/Penguin Random House.

When decisions about end of life need to be made, family members face uncertainty about the kind of treatment their loved one would want in particular circumstances. Even if patients have adequate decision-making capacity, they often want input from family members or significant others in treatment decisions. Sometimes, family members will find it difficult to discuss the uncertainties of treatments with their loved one. The difficulty could derive from something as simple as families having less time to discuss these uncertainties when hospital policies restrict family visitations. Another reason is families do not feel they have the ability to influence decisions and do not want their loved one to know how inadequate they feel.

Whatever death a person is to experience—a good death; an anticipated death; a sudden, unexpected death; or a painful, lingering death—most of the time, people do not have a choice in how they will die. Individuals, meanwhile, need to shift the focus from thoughts of "that we die" toward "how we die" so people can place substantial thought on future decisions about end-of-life care and what might be best for them (Hester, 2010, p. 3).

The benefit of persons envisioning an ideal death and reflecting on it from time to time is to help them develop a sense of readiness for a peaceful death. The American philosopher John Dewey (as cited in Fesmire, 2003) described a similar moral framework based on a person's development of intelligent habits through an imaginative dramatic rehearsal. Dewey discussed dramatic rehearsal as creative dialogue between two or more people in a particular scenario. In applying the **imaginative dramatic rehearsal**, a person can imagine one's own death by reconstructing the ideal death scenario; on continued reflection, they may later discover a rich, meaningful experience through this imagination (Fesmire, 2003; Hester, 2003). Persons who imagine an ideal death have a greater possibility of finding significance at the end of their lives and then, to some extent, shape their dying process.

The Concept of Human Suffering of Dying Patients

Philosophers, professionals, researchers, and religious leaders agree that suffering is difficult to condense into one succinct definition.

Human suffering can be connected to many episodes, contexts, and events, but a large part of the literature on suffering is associated with chronic disease and illness or dying patients and their families.

Hester (2010) emphasized that healthcare professionals should not reduce the concept of suffering to pain, explaining, "When we speak of suffering we mean far more than pain" (p. 18). Kahn and Steeves (1986) stated that an individual could experience suffering following a sense of threat to the being, the self, and existence. Similarly, Eric Cassell (2004) emphasized that suffering involves the whole person and body but pain and suffering are separate phenomena. After several years of studying suffering, Eriksson (1997) defined **suffering** as a perceived undesirable inner experience that could threaten the whole existence of being, yet it is a necessary element of life, as are joy and happiness. If others show compassion toward a suffering person, one could develop a more meaningful suffering existence.

Stan van Hooft (2000, 2006) was at the forefront of studying the Aristotelian framework of the human soul as a way to explain human suffering. Aristotle contended that a soul consists of a being with inseparable physical and spiritual interconnections. All parts of the whole being have one purpose, which Aristotle labeled as achieving *eudaimonia* (happiness, human fulfillment, and flourishing). If one part cannot reach this would-be goal, the whole being suffers because the mind and body are inseparable. As such, van Hooft (2000) concluded that suffering is the opposite of flourishing.

To differentiate pain from suffering, van Hooft (2000) stated that because pain is a hurtful and unpleasant sensation with varying intensities and degrees, it can interfere with individuals' achievement of a flourishing life and therefore will lead to suffering. Pain is a result of a malady or an illness of the vegetative or bodily state; pain can steal joy, contentment, and happiness and can cause individuals to suffer and lose a passion for life. Suffering saturates the whole body in all its four parts.

Catherine Garrett's (2004) life work on the differentiation of pain from suffering contributes to the meaning of suffering and describes the **suffering person** as a tormented being. Suffering is an inevitable but unwelcome component of experiencing life. Suffering is not only subjective; it is also objective in the sense that a suffering person's symptoms can become recognizable signs to others. Examples include a person who is experiencing death and dying, a chronic illness, or chronic violence.

Responsibility of Nurses Toward Suffering Patients

How an individual chooses to understand human suffering is personal. Nurses need to interpret the suffering of their patients in an attempt to alleviate or minimize pain or distress. Examples from official nursing documents in the box Ethical Reflection: Nurses' Moral Obligation Toward Human Suffering include statements about the need for nurses to reduce and alleviate suffering in patients.

Cassell (2004) made a connection between human suffering on the individual level and a person's need for compassion. Nurses' mindfulness of this connection can enrich their comprehension of patients' suffering. Nurses receive information on patients from nursing assessments, interviews, and interpersonal interactions, but one way for nurses to begin the journey of comprehending others' suffering is through the context of having compassion. Nurses generally use strategies such as empathy, compassion, and attentive listening to console suffering patients.

Euthanasia

The thought of extended agony and suffering prior to death provokes a sense of dread in most people, but keeping emotional, financial, and social burdens to a minimum and avoiding suffering are not always possible (Munson, 2004). Many people go to extremes to avoid suffering, as O'Rourke (2002) emphasized: "Suffering in all its forms is an evil, and every reasonable effort should be made to relieve it" (p. 221). However, an untold number of people die every day with tremendous suffering and pain. For many years, people have debated whether to legalize euthanasia, a process often referred to as mercy killing. Dr. Jack Kevorkian was one to argue strongly for euthanasia when patients were in a terminal state of dying (see the box Legal Perspective: Prison for Dr. Jack Kevorkian).

ETHICAL REFLECTION: NURSES' MORAL OBLIGATION TOWARD HUMAN SUFFERING

Nursing obligations and responsibilities are published in several official nursing documents. The following comments represent only two of these documents:

- ANA *Code of Ethics for Nurses with Interpretive Statements* (2015): "Nursing encompasses the protection, promotion, and restoration of health and well-being; the prevention of illness and injury; and the alleviation of suffering in the care of individuals, families, groups, communities, and populations" (p. vii).
- *The ICN Code of Ethics for Nurses* (2021): Four elements comprise the framework for the ethical conduct of nurses, which include "nurses and patients or other people requiring care or services, nurses and practice, nurses and the profession, and nurses and global health" (p. 3). See also Appendix B.

Data from International Council of Nurses (2012); American Nurses Association (2015).

Euthanasia, which has come to mean a good or painless death, has developed a strong appeal in recent years, partly because of the political muddle on the right-to-die issues and the association of these issues with the misery and suffering of dying patients. There are two major types of euthanasia (Munson, 2004). **Active euthanasia** is the intentional and purposeful act of causing the immediate death of another person, whether or not the dying person requested it; examples include a person with a terminal illness or a painful disease or a person who cannot be cured. Kevorkian did carry out the physician-assisted suicide procedure appropriately for many of his patients, but he carried out these actions in states without physician-assisted suicide sanctions. The action that sent him to prison was the active euthanasia of Thomas Youk on national television; this action was consistent with the definition of active euthanasia, not physician-assisted suicide. **Passive euthanasia**, or letting go, is the intentional withholding or withdrawing of medical or life-sustaining treatments. A debate continues in the United States whether there is a real moral difference between active and passive euthanasia, and although withdrawing or withholding medical or life-sustaining treatment has become widely accepted today, active euthanasia has not (Brannigan & Boss, 2001; Jonsen et al., 1998).

Other ways euthanasia has been described are voluntary, nonvoluntary, and involuntary. **Voluntary euthanasia** occurs when patients with decision-making capacity authorize physicians to take their lives. Voluntary euthanasia has become associated most with the term **physician-assisted dying** (formerly and also known as **physician-assisted suicide**), which is defined as the taking of one's own life with a lethal dose of physician-ordered medication. Eleven jurisdictions—California, Colorado, District of Columbia, Hawaii, Montana, Maine, New Jersey, New Mexico, Oregon, Vermont, and Washington—have laws approving the practice of physician-assisted death or medical aid in dying. Other states have bills up for vote or in dispute. **Nonvoluntary euthanasia** occurs when persons are not able to give express consent to end their lives and are unaware they are going to be euthanized. For example, a physician could euthanize a patient when a family member who serves as a decision maker gives consent. **Involuntary euthanasia** means a person's consent may be possible but is not sought and a physician could euthanize someone without express consent. An example of involuntary euthanasia is the euthanizing of a death-row inmate.

LEGAL PERSPECTIVE: PRISON FOR DR. JACK KEVORKIAN

Until his conviction on a second-degree murder charge for which he served 8 years in prison, from 1999 to 2007, Dr. Jack Kevorkian assisted with more than 100 suicides or mercy killings (Frontline, 2014). From 1990 to 1998, at the request of suffering patients from various parts of the United States, he helped them end their lives; he was nicknamed Doctor Death because of his euthanasia practices. Kevorkian was charged on several occasions but was later acquitted, prior to his conviction for euthanizing Thomas Youk. On November 22, 1998, 15 million viewers of the CBS program *60 Minutes* watched Dr. Kevorkian give a lethal injection to Youk, aged 52 years, who was dying with Lou Gehrig's disease. After this program aired, strong debates surfaced in the media and in healthcare, political, and legal systems worldwide. Dr. Kevorkian died in June 2011 with his long-held belief that people have a right to die and to request death (Schneider, 2011). His actions on that day went far beyond that of physician-assisted suicide to one of active euthanasia.

Data from Frontline. (1998). The Kevorkian verdict: The chronology of Dr. Jack Kevorkian's life and assisted suicide campaign. http://www.pbs.org/wgbh/pages/frontline/kevorkian/chronology.html

Salvageability and Unsalvageability Principle

In her book *The Least Worst Death*, Battin (1994) argued that euthanasia is a morally right and humane act on the grounds of mercy,

autonomy, and justice. The principle of mercy (mercy killing) includes two obligations: the duty not to cause further pain and suffering and the duty to act to end existing pain or suffering. The principle of autonomy involves the idea that health professionals ought to respect a person's right to choose a suitable course of medical treatment. The principle of justice is based on how unsalvageable the providers of care believe a permanently unconscious person to be.

Based on this salvageability/unsalvageability principle, however, a healthcare provider could justify performing euthanasia on still-competent but dying patients if they were regarded as unsalvageable (Battin, 1994). It is in knowing where to draw the legal and moral line with this principle that providers and families may face difficult decisions. Any decisions must be carefully examined, especially when the acts may go beyond the meaning of the principle of unsalvageability. There are many opponents who say this euthanasia argument is a slippery slope. Battin (1994), who is a supporter of euthanasia for the unsalvageable suffering person, opposes the notion of a slippery slope euthanasia argument.

Historical Influences on the Definition of Death

In Europe in the 18th and 19th centuries, there was widespread fear of being buried alive because of inadequate methods for detecting when a person was dead; sometimes, when a body was exhumed, claw marks were found on the inside of the coffin lid. There are documented accounts of people being buried alive, but some stories became embellished over time. As a result, many people came to believe exaggerated accounts of premature burial.

Whether or not stories were embellished, great fear persisted during that era, possibly for good reason. Out of fear of being buried alive, the great composer Frédéric Chopin left a request in his will to be dissected after his death and before being buried to make certain he was dead (Bondeson, 2001).

When laws preventing premature burials were enacted, the owners of funeral homes went to the extreme of having their staff monitor dead bodies during the wait time. Before the law had taken effect, special signaling devices were installed from inside the coffin to the outside world to help those buried alive to communicate with others above the ground.

For hundreds of years, when a person became unconscious, physicians or others would palpate for a pulse, listen for breath sounds with their ears, look for condensation on an object when it was held close to the body's nose, and check for fixed and dilated pupils (Mappes & DeGrazia, 2001). The invention of the stethoscope in 1819 led to reduced fear because physicians could listen with greater certainty for a heartbeat through a magnified listening device placed on the chest of the body.

A breakthrough in technology occurred at the beginning of the 20th century when Willem Einthoven, a Dutch physician, discovered the existence of electrical properties of the heart with his invention of the first electrocardiograph (EKG) in 1903 (Benjamin, 2003). The EKG provided sensitive information about whether the heart was functioning. From the middle of the 19th century to the middle of the 20th century, a consensus existed about determination of death; that is, when the heart stopped beating and the person stopped breathing, the person had ceased to live.

Society began to change its perceptions of death as technology became integrated into medicine. The 1950s and 1960s brought more uncertainty involving death as physicians kept patients alive in the absence of a natural heartbeat. When transplants were being performed in the 1960s and 1970s, it became apparent that a diagnosis of death would not necessarily depend on the absence of a heartbeat and respirations. Rather, in the future, the definition of death would need to include brain death criteria.

In 1968, an ad hoc committee at Harvard Medical School attempted to redefine death not only in terms of heart–lung cessation; it added reliable brain death criteria for ventilator-dependent patients with no brain function (described by committee members as patients in an irreversible coma) (Benjamin, 2003). Back then, this definition led to confusion about the term **brain death** and to a widespread misconception about whether the human organism—the person—was actually dead. Somehow, brain death, which technically means death of the brain, came to mean death of a human organism or person. Because of the way some individuals perceived the meaning of the term *brain death*, they translated the 1968 definition to mean that two kinds of death existed for human organisms: the traditional heart–lung death and now a new kind of death called brain death. Benjamin emphasized that ethicists and physicians had not given sufficient attention to clarifying this term before the article was published in 1968.

The Definition of Death

Ethicists, physicians, and others continued intense debates about death. It was not until 1981 that members of the President's Commission for the Study of Ethical Problems in Medicine and Biomedical and Behavioral Research wrote in the document *Defining Death* that a body was an organism as a whole:

> Three organs—the heart, lungs, and brain—assume special significance—because their interrelationship is very close and the irreversible cessation of any one very quickly stops the other two and consequently halts the integrated functioning of the organism as a whole. Because they were easily measured, circulation and respiration were traditionally the basic "vital signs." But breathing and heartbeat are not life itself. They are simply used as signs—as one window for viewing a deeper and more complex

reality: a triangle of interrelated systems with the brain at its apex. (p. 33)

The commission members sanctioned a definition of death in 1981 and recommended its adoption. Detailed and complex arguments continue concerning which criteria belong in the definition of death and, more specifically, death of the brain. Since this 1981 definition was adopted, criteria for death of the brain have been adopted by every state.

LEGAL PERSPECTIVE: DEATH LEGALLY DEFINED IN 1981

The members of the President's Commission for the Study of Ethical Problems in Medicine and Biomedical and Behavioral Research defined death in accordance with accepted medical standards. This definition was enacted as the Uniform Determination of Death Act (UDDA) of 1981. A person who is dead is one who has sustained either of the following:

- Irreversible cessation of circulatory and respiratory functions
- Irreversible cessation of all functions of the entire brain, including the brain stem

Data from President's Commission for the Study of Ethical Problems in Medicine and Biomedical and Behavioral Research. (1981). *Defining death: Medical, legal, & ethical issues in the determination of death*. Government Printing Office, p. 73. https://repository.library .georgetown.edu/bitstream/handle/10822/559345/defining _death.pdf?sequence=1&isAllowed=y

Veatch (2003) extended the debate on the definition of death by posing an intriguing question regarding the loss of full moral standing for human beings. This statement triggers the question as to when humans should be treated as full members of the human community. Almost every person has reconciled the notion that some persons have full moral standing and others do not, but there is continued controversy about when full moral standing ceases to exist and what characteristics

qualify for the cessation of full moral standing. Losing full moral standing is equivalent to ceasing to exist.

The Uniform Definition of Death Act (UDDA) of 1981 continues to stand as the legal definition of death. As the 20th century brought on rapid and advanced technologies, such as organ transplantations, mechanical ventilators, and defibrillators, physicians and philosophers began to address the practical concerns of what constitutes death, how to save more lives, and what is considered in tentional killing. These concerns prompted a discussion of three main approaches for the definition of death: (1) the older traditional cardiopulmonary only approach, (2) the current mainstream view—whole-brain approach, and (3) the higher-brain approach (DeGrazia, 2021).

ETHICAL REFLECTION: THREE APPROACHES FOR DEFINING DEATH

- **Cardiopulmonary death**: A person is dead by cardiopulmonary criteria when the cessation of breathing and heartbeat is irreversible.
- **Whole-brain death or permanent brain failure**: Death is regarded as the irreversible cessation of all brain functions, with no electrical activity in the brain, including the brain stem.
- **Higher-brain death**: Human death is considered the irreversible cessation of the capacity for consciousness, which implies that the person is dead even though the continual function of the brain stem regulates breathing and heartbeat (such as in a persistent vegetative state).

Reproduced from Degrazia, D. (2007; updated, substantive revision 2021, May 17). *The definition of death. Stanford encyclopedia of philosophy*. https://plato.stanford.edu/archives/sum2021/entries /death-definition/

With whole-brain death, the patient may survive physically for an indeterminate duration with a mechanical ventilator. This event is peculiar, as specified by Veatch (2003): "A brain-dead patient on a ventilator does, of course, make for an unusual corpse. On the ventilator, he is respiring and his heart is beating. But if his whole brain is dead, the law in most jurisdictions says that the patient is deceased" (p. 38). Philosophers and bioethicists have continued to explore the definition of death with several radical ideas.

At the point when the person has met brain death defined by 1981 UDDA criteria and is pronounced dead, mechanical ventilation and medical treatment can be discontinued (Benjamin, 2003). Because of the variation in the clinical evaluation for brain death from institution to institution, the American Academy of Neurology offered uniform clinical evaluation guidelines for determining brain death (Wijdicks et al., 2010).

An electroencephalogram (EEG) is a meter used to measure the electrical activity of the brain (Munson, 2004). If a person is on life-sustaining support while in the process of being pronounced dead, such as in whole-brain death, an EEG is needed in addition to the guidelines listed in the clinical evaluation guidelines. One EEG is usually sufficient for a physician to pronounce someone brain dead in the United States (Wijdicks et al., 2010), but some jurisdictions require that two EEGs, performed 24 hours apart, show no brain activity before physicians can disconnect a person from life-sustaining support. Physicians and nurses must also make certain that loss of brain function is not caused by mind-altering medications, hypoglycemia, hyponatremia, or any other cause.

With higher-brain death, or loss of higher-brain function, the patient lives in a persistent vegetative state indefinitely but without the need for mechanical ventilation. A person with higher-brain death may have permanently lost some, but not all, functions, which has been the cause of enormous dispute. Even very minimal brain functioning, such as limited reflexes in the brain stem, is cause for a patient to be diagnosed with higher-brain

death (Veatch, 2003). Questions persist as to when a person should or should not be treated as one who has full moral standing in society.

Some patients may seemingly have complete loss of brain function only to have the electrical activity of the brain reappear later, even if it is minimal, which makes the 1981 UDDA whole-brain death criteria difficult to use for pronouncing a person dead (Munson, 2004). Society, physicians, and nurses often have difficulty defining death by the 1981 UDDA definition, especially when they try to incorporate the standards of cardiopulmonary death, whole-brain death, or higher-brain death. Benjamin (2003) posed this question for people to consider: "Exactly what is it that ceases to exist when we say someone like you or me is dead?" (p. 197). No definite criteria exist on higher-brain death, but in 1994 a task force published general guidelines for a persistent vegetative state (Multi-Society Task Force on Persistent Vegetative State, 1994). Benjamin (2003) and Veatch (2003) affirmed there will be no answers to many questions until ethicists and others can come to a general consensus about what life is, when life begins, when life ends, and who does and does not have full moral standing.

Decisions About Death and Dying

Advance Directives

An **advance directive** is "a written expression of a person's wishes about medical care, especially care during a terminal or critical illness" (Veatch, 2003, p. 119). When individuals lose control over their lives, they may also lose their decision-making capacity, and advance directives become instructions about their future health care for others to follow. Advance directives can be self-written instructions or prepared by someone else as instructed by the patient. Under the federal Patient

Self-Determination Act of 1990, states, under mandated authority, have developed laws to protect the rights of individuals making decisions about end-of-life and medical care. (See Appendix C for an example of a complete legal packet for a healthcare advance directive.) Critical issues that need to be addressed in any advance directive include specific treatments to be refused or administered; the time the directive needs to take effect; specific hospitals and physicians to be used; which lawyer, if any, should be consulted; and specific other consultations, such as an ethics team, a chaplain, or a neighbor. There are two types of advance directives: living will and durable power of attorney.

A **living will** is a formal legal document that provides written directions concerning what medical care is to be provided in specific circumstances (Beauchamp & Childress, 2019; Devettere, 2000). The living will gained recognition in the 1960s, but the Karen Ann Quinlan case in the 1970s brought public attention to the living will and subsequently prompted legalization of the document. Although living wills were a good beginning, today they are not completely adequate. Problems can arise when living wills consist of vague language, contain only instructions for unwanted treatments, lack a description of legal penalties for those people who choose to ignore the directives of living wills, and are legally questionable as to their authenticity.

The **durable power of attorney** is a legal written directive in which a designated person can make either general or specific healthcare and medical decisions for a patient. The durable power of attorney has the most strength for facilitating healthcare decisions; however, even with a power of attorney, families and healthcare professionals may experience fear about making the wrong decisions regarding an incapacitated patient (Beauchamp & Childress, 2019).

In addition to the weaknesses previously discussed about advance directives, other weaknesses may arise; for example, very few people ever complete an advance directive, a surrogate decision maker may be unavailable for decision making, and healthcare professionals cannot overturn advance directives if a decision needs to be made in the best interest of a patient. The existence of advance directives can be a source of comfort for patients and families as long as they realize their limitations and scope. Ensuring the validity of the advance directive, realizing the importance of preserving patients from unwanted intrusive interventions, and respecting the possibility that patients may change their minds about their expressed written wishes are several ways that nurses must demonstrate benevolence toward patients and their families.

Surrogate Decision Makers

When patients can no longer make competent decisions, families may experience difficulty in trying to determine a progressive right course of action. The ideal situation is for patients to be autonomous decision makers, but when autonomy is no longer possible, decision making falls to a surrogate (Beauchamp & Childress, 2019). The **surrogate decision maker**, often known as a proxy, is an individual who acts on behalf of a patient and either is chosen by the patient, such as a family member; is court appointed; or has other authority to make decisions. Family members serving as proxies are generally referred to as surrogates.

Advances in healthcare technology and life-sustaining treatments precipitated the development of the surrogate decision-maker role, as it is known today. Decisions about treatment options and the motives behind these decisions may be complex and destructive. Before the surrogate makes a decision, there needs to be appropriate dialogue among the physicians, the nurses, and the surrogate (Emanuel et al., 1995). On behalf of the patient, surrogates endure an uncomfortable multistage decision-making process for gathering information and engaging the patient (when possible), extended family members, physicians, nurses, and other healthcare professionals. During this process, the surrogate decision makers consider their own subjective views, the perceptions of others on the status of the patient, the medical evidence, and patient preferences (Buckley & Abell, 2009).

Surrogate decision makers sometimes have difficulty distinguishing between their own emotions and the feelings of others, or they may have monetary motives for making certain decisions. It is the responsibility of nurses and physicians to be alert to these kinds of motives or concerns and look for therapeutic ways to deliberate with the surrogate. As Olick (2001) stated, "In many respects, [surrogate decision making principles] may be said to be a part of the legacy of Karen Ann Quinlan and her family" (p. 30). Of interest too is the influence these principles had on the Terri Schiavo case and her family, which is discussed later in this chapter.

There are three types of surrogate decision-making standards. The **substituted judgment standard** is used to guide medical decisions for formerly competent patients who no longer have any decision-making capacity (Beauchamp & Childress, 2019). This standard is based on the assumption that incompetent patients have the exact same rights as competent patients to make judgments about their health care (Buchanan & Brock, 1990). Surrogates make medical treatment decisions based on what they believe patients would have decided if they were still competent and able to express their wishes. In making decisions, surrogates use their understanding of the patients' previous overt or implied expressions of their beliefs and values (Veatch, 2003). Before losing competency, the patient could have either explicitly informed the surrogate of treatment wishes by oral or written instruction or implicitly made treatment wishes clear through informal conversations.

Many times, when more than one sibling is involved in the decisions regarding the care of a dying parent, misunderstandings occur and angry feelings over practical, legal, and financial matters become apparent. Siblings will be affected uniquely by their parent's death, depending on several factors: the type of relationship that exists between each sibling and the parent; if and how each sibling has experienced death in the past; each sibling's present life situation and stressors; any past grudges toward siblings by other siblings or other people; and current sibling relationships. One sibling usually takes charge, or the siblings designate one sibling to be the speaker for the group. Even when one sibling is empowered, however, the others usually desire an equal voice in the decision-making process. This may be a frustrating process for everyone if the siblings cannot agree. Dialogue is critically important so that people involved can come to an understanding and avoid further misunderstandings and pain.

The **pure autonomy standard** is based on a decision that was made by an autonomous patient while competent but who has later become incompetent. In this case, the decision is usually upheld based on the principle of autonomy extended (Beauchamp & Childress, 2019; Veatch, 2003). The **best interest standard** is an evaluation of what is good for an incompetent patient in particular healthcare situations when the patient has never been competent, such as in the case of an infant or mentally retarded adult (Beauchamp & Childress, 2019). The surrogate attempts to decide what is best for the incompetent patient based on the patient's dignity and worth as a human being without taking into consideration the patient's concept of what is good or bad. The surrogate will have no evidence or basis for determining the incompetent patient's desires or what is best for that patient, but the surrogate evaluates the benefits and burdens for available treatment options. Because the best interest standard is patient centered, the surrogate must make decisions based on current and future interests (Buchanan & Brock, 1990). These decisions inevitably involve muddy, subjective quality-of-life judgments, such as appraising the incompetent patient's simple life pleasures and contentment, sense of social worth, degree of pain and suffering experienced, and the benefits and costs of treatment.

ETHICAL REFLECTION: PATIENT SELF-DETERMINATION

According to the ANA *Code of Ethics for Nurses with Interpretive Statements* (2015) Provision 1.4, nurses have a moral obligation to respect human dignity and certain patient rights, especially patient self-determination. What are some strategies the nurse can implement to ensure the respect of human dignity and self-determination for an incompetent patient?

FIGURE 9-1 Humpty Dumpty cartoon.
Andy Marlette Cartoons

Medical Futility

Humpty Dumpty sat on a wall, Humpty Dumpty had a great fall; All the King's horses, And all the King's men, Could not put Humpty Dumpty together again.

—Lewis Carroll, *Adventures of Alice in Wonderland* and *Through the Looking Glass*

I propose an analogy between the meaning of medical futility and the life of Humpty Dumpty and his broken body after the fall (**FIGURE 9-1**).

The term **futile** means pointless or meaningless events or objects (O'Rourke, 2002). **Medical futility** is defined as "the unacceptably low chance of achieving a therapeutic benefit for the patient" (Schneiderman, 1994, para. 10). Questions to ask regarding futility as related to bioethics are as follows:

- What is at stake?
- What weight does the term *futility* carry?
- Is the meaning and weight of the term *futility* appreciated from the broader dominion of bioethics?
- What are healthcare professionals' ethical obligations insofar as thinking that a medical intervention is clearly futile?
- Who makes the final decision? Who has the power?

- How can hospitals and other healthcare agencies incorporate a reasonable, fair, objective, and clear policy on futility?

Schneiderman (1994) linked his definition of medical futility to the whole person, the wholeness similar to the way Aristotle spoke of a human being with four inseparable parts. In other words, a suffering person will seek a cure, healing, or care from a provider to become as whole as possible again. In weighing the concept of futility, the nurse must understand how integral the suffering–healing–provider relationship is to the health process and the goals of medicine and nursing. The provider of care is responsible for administering medical treatments and interventions to benefit the patient as a whole and not have just a small effect on some part of the body or an organ. Integrated throughout this process is the necessity of the patient to comprehend and appreciate the benefits of medical treatment. To comprehend these benefits, the person must at least be partially conscious; patients who are in a persistent vegetative state cannot possibly appreciate the beneficial effects of the treatment. The mere effect is of no benefit if the effect does not help a patient achieve some degree of life goals or human fulfillment, or the type of telos emphasized by Aristotle.

Medical futility goes back in history as long as can be remembered. In ancient Greece, there was an acceptance of physicians refusing to treat people who were overwrought with disease. The futility movement became more important in the 1970s, when medical technology brought about extraordinary life support and life-extending measures. As physicians began asking "What is a good death?" and "When do we let go?" medical futility emerged as an important concept. Throughout the 1970s and 1980s, philosophers and physicians strongly debated the concept of futility in an effort to define the term and create guidelines for putting it into practice. In the 1990s, definitions began to shift from the theme of blaming providers of care for failures to a focus on more quantitative and qualitative values of treatments with low probabilities of benefits in the past. Historical landmark legal cases on medical futility include the cases of Helga Wanglie, *In the Matter of Baby K*, and *Gilgunn v. Massachusetts General Hospital*.

Healthcare professionals and most other people have accepted and ethically justified withholding and withdrawing treatments deemed futile or extraordinary, but this acceptance does not mean that withholding or withdrawing treatment is universally accepted.

The case of Terri Schiavo (*Schiavo and Schindler v. Schiavo*) was not primarily about medical futility; rather, it was about Michael Schiavo's legal, not ethical, responsibility for carrying out Terri's express and previous verbal wishes of not wanting to stay alive in her current circumstances. Terri Schiavo, with all evidential information set forth by the physician who performed the autopsy, met the legal definition of a persistent vegetative state and therefore was a medically futile case regarding treatment.

When a healthcare provider cannot have reasonable hope that a treatment will benefit a terminally ill person, the medical treatment is considered futile. Treatments often considered medically futile include cardiopulmonary resuscitation (CPR), medications, mechanical ventilation, artificial feeding and fluids, hemodialysis, chemotherapy, and other life-sustaining technologies. When surrogates are the spokespersons for patients, one of the nurse's responsibilities is to make sure communication remains open between the healthcare team and the decision maker for the family. Everyone needs to have a chance to express feelings and concerns about treatment options that are viewed as medically futile (Ladd et al., 2002).

LEGAL PERSPECTIVE: LANDMARK LEGAL CASES INVOLVING MEDICAL FUTILITY DECISIONS

1988: The Case of Helga Wanglie

An elderly woman was aged 85 years when she fractured her hip after slipping on a rug, after which she developed severe ventilator-dependent pneumonia. She was later diagnosed with persistent vegetative state (PVS; higher-brain death) secondary to hypoxic-ischemic neuropathy and was ventilator dependent secondary to chronic lung disease. (Patients with PVS generally do not require mechanical ventilation because the brain stem is intact. Her dependency on the ventilator related strictly to her chronic lung disease.) Physicians at two facilities agreed that treatment would be futile, but the family members wanted her to be treated and kept alive as long as possible. They believed the physicians were playing God, but they did agree to a do-not-resuscitate physician order with much trepidation. After an intense legal battle, on July 1, 1991, the court authorized Mr. Wanglie, the patient's husband, to be the surrogate decision maker for Mrs. Wanglie. However, on July 4, 1991, only 3 days after the final court decision, Mrs. Wanglie died.

1993: *In the Matter of Baby K*

In 1992, Baby K was born with anencephaly, that is, with a brain stem but no capacity for a conscious life. Statistically, the baby was predicted not to be able to survive more than a few days to months. Physicians and ethics committee members argued not to keep Baby K alive on ventilator support because of medical futility, but the mother insisted that Baby K be kept alive because she believed all human life is precious and to be preserved. The federal court supported the mother's claim only if someone would assume the amount of the mother's bills for care of Baby K. The mother found monetary support, and Baby K lived for 2 years in a nursing home on ventilator support.

1995: *Gilgunn v. Massachusetts General Hospital*

In a rare early case of a court supporting a physician's claim of medical futility, a jury, after the fact, found that cardiopulmonary resuscitation need not be provided to a patient dying with multiple organ-system failure, as in the case of Ms. Gilgunn, aged 71 years, who was comatose. The family had sought treatment, but the physician objected. The jury's decision was the result of a retrospective evaluation of the medical decision. The jury's decision for stopping futile treatment was unique at the time.

ETHICAL REFLECTION: DEVELOPING YOUR BELIEFS AND OPINIONS ABOUT MEDICAL FUTILITY

Following are questions to ponder as you develop your beliefs and opinions about the medical futility of a patient, such as one in the last stages of metastasized cancer:

- What ethical theory, approach, or principle provides the rationale for your beliefs on autonomy and medical futility? Explain.
- How far does one go with patient autonomy?
- Do you believe patient autonomy should have limits?
- Should patient autonomy (and surrogate autonomy) be unlimited, no matter what the physician believes should and should not be done?
- Would the healthcare system's financial burden be a factor for setting limits on patient autonomy (and surrogate autonomy) in your personal opinion or as a societal stance?
- Do patients or families have a moral right to insist on medical treatment when two or more physicians and hospitals deem it futile? Give your rationale based on your ethical theory, approach, or principle.
- Do providers of care have a moral duty to provide medically futile treatment at the family's request, just because the family wants it?

Medical futility cannot be circumscribed within clear boundaries. There are usually questionable gray areas when debating issues of futility; even Humpty Dumpty's case was questionable. Remember, it was all the King's horses and all the King's men who could not put Humpty Dumpty together again. However, no men or horses from another King's court tried to put Humpty Dumpty together again, contrary to what occurs in real medical futility cases, because a second opinion is an essential component in declaring medical futility.

Grayness will always exist because healthcare providers and other professionals attempt to embrace the patient's hope and consider a patient's values and feelings, even when the patient is cognitively impaired and will not have feelings. However, nurses acknowledge that all human beings have limits. The human component exists on both sides of the futility–value issue, but gray areas that blur the boundaries will always exist. Patients, families, judges, patient advocacy groups, the media, those involved with sociopolitical issues, and the public will challenge these gray boundaries time after time.

▶ Palliative Care

Palliative care consists of comfort care measures that patients may request instead of aggressive medical treatments when their condition is terminal. Nurses are probably the most active of all healthcare professionals in meeting the palliative needs of dying patients. Palliative care has become an organized movement through official associations and organizations since the 1990s. **Palliative care** is defined as:

> An approach that improves the quality of life of patients (adults and children) and their families who are facing problems associated with life-threatening illness. It prevents and relieves suffering through the early identification, correct assessment and treatment of pain and other problems, whether physical, psychosocial of spiritual.

(World Health Organization [WHO], 2020, August 5, para. 1)

Understanding what quality of life means to the dying patient is an important part of end-of-life care for nurses, and no matter what stage of dying the patient is experiencing, the main goals of palliative care are to prevent and relieve suffering and allow for the best care possible for patients and families.

When nurses provide palliative care, they do not hasten or prolong death for these patients; rather, they try to provide patients with relief from pain and suffering and help them maintain dignity in the dying experience. Palliative treatment may include a patient's and family's choices to forgo, withhold, or withdraw treatment. Some patients will have a **do not resuscitate (DNR) order**, which is a written physician's order placed in a patient's chart that says hospital personnel are not to carry out any type of CPR or other resuscitation measures. Each hospital and agency has specific policies and procedures for how a DNR order is to be written and followed. A critical ethical violation to informed consent may occur if a physician writes a DNR order on a patient's record without discussing the order and decision with the patient, family members, or surrogate (O'Rourke, 2002). A DNR physician order needs to be justified by one of three reasons: no medical benefit can come from CPR, a person has a very poor quality of life before CPR, and a person's quality of life after CPR is anticipated to be very poor (Mappes & DeGrazia, 2001).

Unofficial—and unauthorized—slow codes have been practiced in the past and can be described as going through the motions or as giving half-hearted CPR to a patient whose condition has been deemed futile. At one time, nurses initiated slow codes when a physician had not yet written the DNR order of a terminally ill patient. However, a slow code is an unethical and illegal practice, and physicians and nurses should never initiate them. Slow codes are not recognized as a legal procedure.

The Right to Die and the Right to Refuse Treatment

The right to die is a patient's choice, based on the principle of autonomy. Well-informed patients with decision-making capacity have a right to refuse or forgo recommended treatments in an attempt to avoid a long period of suffering during the dying process. **Right to die** means a person has an autonomous right to refuse life-sustaining or life-extending treatment measures. Most of the time there are no ethical or legal ramifications if a person decides to forgo treatments; the courts generally uphold the right of competent patients to refuse treatment (Jonsen et al., 2006; Mappes & DeGrazia, 2001). Nevertheless, healthcare professionals need to make certain the patient's decision is truly autonomous and not coerced. Healthcare professionals may find it difficult to accept a competent patient's decision to forgo treatment.

Sometimes, in a patient's mind, the burdens of medical treatments outweigh the benefits (O'Rourke, 2002). Perceived burden is a concern for nurses, physicians, and patients because physical pain and emotional suffering from treatments or the prolongation and dread of carrying out treatments may be too much to bear. Other views of burden consist of the economic, social, and spiritual burdens on a patient and family. Whether or not at the end of life, adult autonomous patients with competent decision-making capacity may refuse medical treatments at any time in life and may base their refusal on religious or cultural beliefs.

Withholding and Withdrawing Life-Sustaining Treatment

Withholding and withdrawing treatment is the forgoing of life-sustaining treatment that the patient does not desire because of either a perceived disproportionate burden on the patient or family members or other reasons. Notable legal decisions led to many questions regarding the right to die and the right to withhold and withdraw life-sustaining treatments. Three landmark legal cases about withholding and withdrawing treatments, particularly for people in a persistent vegetative state, are presented in this section (Brannigan & Boss, 2001; Jonsen et al., 1998; U.S. Court of Appeals, Eleventh Circuit, Decided: 2005, March 25).

A somewhat more recent case was that of Terri Schiavo, who died on March 31, 2005. There were a total of 21 legal suits, but the last few cases involved her husband Michael's request to have her feeding tube discontinued, which would stop the artificial nutrition and hydration. Terri's parents fought this request. By Florida law, Michael Schiavo as a spouse and guardian had a legal right to serve as a surrogate decision maker for Terri.

Substituted judgment became the ethical and legal standard, with guardianship as the focal point, and it was a critical factor in decision making regarding Terri Schiavo's care and outcome in light of no advance directive. Surrogates must make unbiased, substituted judgments based on an understanding of what patients would decide for themselves, not the values of the surrogate. The court obtained documented evidence from Michael Schiavo and other people that Terri had stated she did not want to live in a condition in which she would be a burden to anyone else. This evidence served as the basis for many of the court denials to the Schindlers, the parents.

Nurses need to give compassionate and excellent care to patients. No matter what the decision will be, family members and patients need to feel a sense of confidence that nurses will maintain moral sensitivity with a course of right action. Nurses ethically support the provision of compassionate and dignified end-of-life care as long as they do not have the sole intention of ending a person's life (ANA, 2015).

A special statement concerning the Terri Schiavo case was released after the court ruling, which upheld the decision for the right of the patient or surrogate to choose forgoing artificial nutrition and hydration. Even if incapacitated, the patient has a right to have designated a surrogate or specified whether to continue medical treatment. Nurses are obligated to assist their patients and maintain their dignity. One such case regarding rights was in the Terri Schiavo case. Terri Schiavo had a right to self-determination or surrogate determination. She was in a persistent vegetative state for years, and evidence existed that she had expressed she did not want her life sustained by artificial means.

ETHICAL REFLECTION: GUIDELINES FOR A CLINICAL DIAGNOSIS OF PERSISTENT VEGETATIVE STATE

- No awareness of self or environment and an inability to interact with others
- No sustained, reproducible, purposeful, or voluntary responses to visual, auditory, tactile, or noxious stimuli
- No language comprehension or expression
- Intermittent wakefulness exhibited by the presence of sleep–wake cycles
- Preserved autonomic functions to permit survival with medical and nursing care
- Incontinence—bladder and bowel
- Variable degrees of spinal reflexes and cranial-nerve reflexes, such as pupillary, oculocephalic, corneal, vestibulo-ocular, and gag

Data from Multi-Society Task Force on Persistent Vegetative State. (1994). Medical aspects of the persistent vegetative state (p. 1500). *New England Journal of Medicine, 330*, 1499–1508.

LEGAL PERSPECTIVE: TWO LANDMARK LEGAL CASES ABOUT WITHHOLDING AND WITHDRAWING TREATMENTS AND PERSISTENT VEGETATIVE STATE

1975: Karen Ann Quinlan

The case of Karen Ann Quinlan in 1975 led to her parents receiving the right to have Karen Ann's mechanical ventilator discontinued (Jonsen et al., 1998; LEXIS-NEXIS, 1999). Karen Ann, who was aged 21 years, attended a party and ingested diazepam, dextropropoxyphene, and alcohol and then lapsed into a coma. She was placed on a ventilator, and consequently, her parents were involved in legal battles for several years to have Karen Ann removed from the ventilator. Physicians would not remove her from the ventilator because they could not establish Harvard Criteria for brain death. Finally, the New Jersey State Supreme Court ordered the physicians to unplug the ventilator. After it was unplugged, Karen Ann breathed without the help of the ventilator and continued living for 10 years; her death was a result of pneumonia and its complications. The legacy of Quinlan's case included the following: (1) contributing to the definition of the term **persistent vegetative state**; (2) setting precedence for parents (or legal guardians) to have a right to choose; (3) the formation of ethics committees in most healthcare settings; and (4) the creation and implementation of the advance directive.

1983: Nancy Cruzan

Nancy Cruzan, aged 25 years, was in a motor vehicle accident in 1983. She sustained severe injuries that led to a complete loss of consciousness and, later, a persistent vegetative state with continuous artificial nutrition and hydration. Nancy's parents and co-guardians made several pleas during the next few years to the Director of the Missouri Department of Health to have her feeding tube removed on the basis that there was no chance for a return of cognitive capacity. The Director declined to accommodate the Cruzans' request. The case then progressed to the next level where the Supreme Court of Missouri upheld the State of Missouri's decision to decline the Cruzans' wishes on the basis that they needed clear and convincing evidence of the patient's wishes to have the life support removed. The U. S. Supreme Court later upheld the Supreme Court of Missouri's ruling. In September 1990, the State of Missouri withdrew its case. With no opposition, a county judge ruled that the life support on Nancy Cruzan could be removed. The county judge issued the order to remove life support on December 14, 1990. Nancy was age 33 when she died on December 26, 1990, only a few days after the court's final decision. The judge based the decision on a previous comment by Nancy, who had stated to the housekeeper that she would not want to live in this type of condition. Of particular interest is Nancy Cruzan's grave marker. The family members, adapting their idea from a political cartoon about the case, had three dates etched on the grave marker: one date reflects her birth, one reflects her death at the time of the accident, and one reflects her actual physical death (Fine, 2005). The grave marker is slightly confusing based on the meanings of the terms *persistent vegetative state* and *brain death*. Nancy's persistent vegetative state never equated to the definition of brain death, as the grave marker implies. The etching on the grave marker shows the following:

Born July 20, 1957
Departed January 11, 1983
At Peace December 26, 1990

Significant to this case was the decisions. At the ruling of the Nancy Cruzan case, the judges of the Supreme Court of Missouri established three conditions for withdrawing treatments, including artificial nutrition and hydration: (1) the patient has a right to refuse medical treatment; (2) artificial feeding constitutes medical treatment; and (3) when the patient is mentally incompetent, each state must document clear and convincing evidence that the patient's desires had been for discontinuance of medical treatment. Another important component that came from this case was the use of advance directives.

Cornell Law School, Legal Information Institute. (n.d.). Cruzan by Cruzan v. Director, Missouri Department of Health [497 U.S. 261; No. 88-1503]. http://www.law.cornell.edu/supremecourt/text/497/261; and Jonsen, A. R., Veatch, R. M., & Walters, L. (1998). Source book in bioethics. Georgetown University Press.

In 2017, the ANA published an updated version of its position statement on forgoing nutrition and hydration. Previous ANA position statements on forgoing nutrition and hydration were in 1992 and 2011. The following statement is in the newly revised ANA (2017) position statement: "When a patient at the end of life or the patient's surrogate has made the decision to forgo nutrition and/or hydration, the nurse continues to ensure the provision of high quality care, minimizing discomfort and promoting dignity." The ANA emphasized that physiological nurses are responsible for understanding the physiologic aspects surrounding the clinical options.

LEGAL PERSPECTIVE: LEGAL FACTS IN THE THERESA "TERRI" MARIE SCHIAVO CASE

Major Final Court Rulings

- March 21, 2005: A federal court order denied the injunction relief sought by the Schindlers, and the court refused to compel Theresa Schiavo to undergo surgery for reinsertion of the feeding tube.
- March 24, 2005: The second federal court denied a motion by the Schindlers for a temporary restraining order against Michael Schiavo and the hospice regarding an alleged violation of Terri's right to artificial nutrition and hydration based on the Americans with Disabilities Act (ADA). The courts ruled that Terri's rights based on the ADA were not violated.
- March 24, 2005: The U.S. Supreme Court denied the application by the Schindlers for a stay of enforcement of the Florida judgment.
- March 25, 2005: The U.S. Court of Appeals Eleventh Court District denied an appeal by the Schindlers for a rehearing.

(continues)

LEGAL PERSPECTIVE: LEGAL FACTS IN THE THERESA "TERRI" MARIE SCHIAVO CASE

History and Facts of the Case

In 1990, Terri Schiavo's husband, Michael, found Terri unresponsive in the couple's home. Florida physicians affirmed that Terri, at age 26, had experienced prolonged cerebral hypoxia after an acute cardiac arrest. Physicians determined that a severely low potassium level, which was secondary to an eating disorder, brought on her cardiac arrest. Her condition was determined consistent with the diagnosis of persistent vegetative state because of the brain insult. In a 1992 medical malpractice suit against her fertility obstetrician, Terri Schiavo was awarded $750,000, which was placed in a trust fund for her future medical care. Michael Schiavo was awarded $300,000 (Cerminara, 2005). In 1992, the Schindlers (Terri's parents) and Michael became alienated over the management of Terri's therapy and the money awarded to the Schiavos. In February 1993, the Schindlers unsuccessfully demanded a share of Michael's money from the malpractice settlement.

The first lawsuit filed against a family member was initiated in 1993 by the Schindlers in an attempt to have Michael removed as Terri's guardian, but the judge dismissed the case. Rehabilitation efforts continued for several years without success. Michael first petitioned the court in 1998 to have Terri's feeding tube removed and artificial nutrition and hydration discontinued, which was vehemently opposed by the Schindlers. Before her 1990 event, Michael testified that Terri had told him that "If I ever have to be a burden to anybody, I don't want to live like that" (Lynne, 2005). Terri made similar statements about her wishes to other people, as evidenced by court-documented material. Judge Greer at the 6th Judicial Circuit Court in Clearwater, Florida, avowed there was clear and convincing evidence of Terri's wishes.

From 1993 to 2005, there were 21 lawsuits and appeals. The majority of the lawsuits were filed after 1998, and most of them upheld Michael's initial contention that he was attempting to carry out Terri's wishes. During the appeals, Terri's feeding tube was removed on three occasions; on the first two occasions, the feeding tube was reinserted and artificial nutrition and hydration were resumed.

Thirteen days after the third and final removal of her feeding tube, Terri died on March 31, 2005, at the age of 41 years. The ethics and legality of removing the feeding tube were scrutinized until her death through lawsuits; political and media statements; actions of the U.S. Congress; and pleas from high-ranking public figures, such as Pope John Paul II.

Reproduced from U.S. Court of Appeals, Eleventh District. (2005, March 21/Decided March 25). Theresa Marie Schindler Schiavo and ex relations Robert Schlindler and Mary Schindler (plaintiffs) v. Michael Schiavo, Judge George W. Greer, and The Hospice of the Florida Suncoast, Inc. (defendants). (Civ. Act. No. 8:05-CV-530-T-27TBM). https://caselaw.findlaw.com/us-11th-circuit/1360200.html; Cerminara, K. L. (2006). Theresa Marie Schiavo's Long Road to Peace, *Death Studies*, 30(2), 101–112. https://doi.org/10.1080/07481180500455574; and Lynne, D. (2005, September 1). Terri's story. Cumberland House Publishing.

Alleviation of Pain and Suffering in the Dying Patient

The degree of quality of life contributes to the choices patients make during the end-of-life process. Attempting to relieve pain and suffering is a primary responsibility for nurses and providers of care, which makes the whole arena of palliative care an ethical concern. Patients fear the consequences of disease—pain, suffering, and the process of dying. Most of the time it is the nurse who administers the pain medication and evaluates a patient's condition between and during pain medication injections. In an updated position statement on nurses' roles and responsibilities in providing care and support at the end of life, the ANA (2016) emphasized that nurses "are responsible for recognizing patients' symptoms, taking measures within their scope of practice to administer medications, providing other measures for symptom alleviation, and collaborating with other professionals to optimize patients' comfort and families' understanding and adaptation" (para. 1).

Rule of Double Effect

According to Cavanaugh (2006), the **rule of double effect** is based on an individual's reasoning that an act causing good and evil is permitted when the act meets the following conditions:

1. The act, considered independently of its evil effect, is not in itself wrong.
2. The agent intends the good and does not intend the evil either as an end or as a means.
3. The agent has proportionately grave reasons for acting, addressing his relevant obligations, comparing the consequences, and, considering the necessity of the evil, exercising due care to eliminate or mitigate it. (p. 36)

Some historians of ethics have attributed the double-effect reasoning to Saint Thomas Aquinas's writing about a person's self-defense in a homicide, and other historians have not. Today's double-effect reasoning is inclusive of actions that could cause harm, which is a foreseen but inevitable outcome. The use of the double-effect reasoning is an area of substantial concern when the healthcare professional sees some good in the action yet foresees with certainty that there will be bad in the action.

When the rule of double effect is applied, nurses need to be aware that the hastening of death must be a possible foreseen and inevitable but unintended effect. In the *Code of Ethics for Nurses with Interpretive Statements*, the ANA (2015) states, "The nurse should provide interventions to relieve pain and other symptoms in the dying patient consistent with palliative care practice standards and may not act with the sole intent to end life" (Provision 1.4, p. 3).

Nurses may have conflicting moral values concerning the use of high doses of opiate-containing drugs, such as morphine sulfate, or even opiate-synthetic medications. In times when nurses feel uncomfortable, they need to explore their attitudes and opinions with their supervisor and, when appropriate, in clinical team meetings. Individually evaluating each patient and circumstance is essential.

Terminal Sedation

Terminal sedation is an accepted practice in the United States and many other countries. Quill (2001) defined **terminal sedation** as a last resort "when a suffering patient is sedated to unconsciousness, usually through the ongoing administration of barbiturates or benzodiazepines. The patient then dies of dehydration, starvation, or some other intervening complication, as all other life-sustaining interventions are withheld" (p. 181). Terminal sedation is different than usual palliative sedation; in terminal sedation the healthcare team discontinues medications and feeding tubes. Some people think terminal sedation hastens death, but Ira Byock stated that terminal sedation is used only in the last stages of life when medications and nutrition and hydration do not prolong life (as cited in Kingsbury, 2008).

When the word *terminal* is used, there is an understanding among the healthcare team and family members that the outcome, and possibly a desired outcome, is death (Sugarman, 2000). The ANA (2015) does not directly address terminal sedation in the *Code of Ethics for Nurses with Interpretive Statements*, but it does address nurses' obligations to give compassionate care at the end of life and not have a sole intent of ending a person's life. Understanding the moral and ethical implications will guide nurses in their individualized direction.

ETHICAL REFLECTION: EXAMPLES OF DOUBLE-EFFECT REASONING CONDITIONS

Condition 1

An example of the first condition of the rule of double effect is applied when a nurse administers a medication that is neither good nor bad.

Condition 2

The second condition involves the intention of a nurse or physician. An example is a nurse's intent to relieve pain by administering a medication and not for the patient to be compromised in any way.

Condition 3

The third condition is that the bad effect cannot be the means to the intended good effect; for instance, a nurse cannot administer an opiate-containing or other type of medication to produce the harmful bad effect, such as respiration cessation, to achieve the intended good effect, which in this case is pain relief.

Physician-Assisted Suicide

Society has reacted with everything from moral outrage to social acceptance with regard to physician-assisted suicide. Four states in the United States have made physician-assisted suicide legal: Oregon in 1994, Washington in 2008, Montana in 2009, and Vermont in 2013. State congressional members have introduced physician-assisted suicide bills in a number of other states, two of them being Connecticut and Hawaii (Death with Dignity, 2018). With certain restrictions, patients who are near death may obtain prescriptions to end their lives in a dignified way. Sugarman (2000) defined physician-assisted suicide as "the act of providing a lethal dose of medication for the patient to self-administer" (p. 213). According to Kopala

and Kennedy (1998), physician-assisted suicide must meet three conditions in accordance with the ANA:

1. You [the nurse] must know the person intends to end his or her life.
2. You [the nurse] must make the means to commit suicide available to the person.
3. The person must then end his or her own life. (p. 19)

During a 20-year dispute over euthanasia practices, under certain guidelines, physicians could practice euthanasia in the Netherlands. In February 2002, the Dutch passed a law that permitted voluntary euthanasia and physician-assisted suicide. In the discussions of euthanasia in the United States, the scope has been limited to only physician-assisted suicide, whereas in the Netherlands, the discussion has a much wider perspective.

Special guidelines relating to the Death with Dignity Act in Oregon were written by the Oregon Nurses Association for nurses who care for patients choosing physician-assisted suicide (as cited in Kopala & Kennedy, 1998, and Ladd et al., 2002). The guidelines include maintaining support, comfort, and confidentiality; discussing end-of-life options with the patient and family; and being present for the patient's self-administration of medications and death. Nurses may not inject the medications themselves, breach confidentiality, subject others to any type of judgmental comments or statements about the patient, or refuse to provide care to the patient.

▶ Rational Suicide

The idea of saving people versus allowing people to die or commit suicide is at the very essence of one of the most debated and controversial dilemmas today. As long as there is difficulty in determining rationality in suicide, this controversy will remain. Moral progress in nursing necessitates that nurses ponder these ethical uncertainties . . .

with patients who are contemplating rational suicide. Meanwhile, nurses should never be caught off-guard in relation to the ethical and political changes in health care for fear of losing their power and voice.

—Reproduced from K. L. Rich and **J. B. Butts**, *Rational Suicide: Uncertain Moral Ground* (2004), p. 277

Rational suicide is a self-slaying based on reasoned choice and is categorized as voluntary, active euthanasia. Siegel (1986) stated that the person who is contemplating rational suicide has a realistic assessment of life circumstances, is free from severe emotional distress, and has a motivation that would seem understandable to most uninvolved people in the person's community.

Morally accepting a person's act of committing rational suicide seems outrageous to most people, and the very thought of it weighs heavily on their hearts. Should people criticize others for making a choice of rational suicide? More and more people view rational suicide as an acceptable alternative to life, especially when faced with unbearable pain, suffering, or loneliness (O'Rourke, 2002). However, the terms *rational* and *suicide* seem to contradict each other (Engelhardt, 1986; Finnerty, 1987).

David Peretz (as cited in O'Rourke, 2002), a noted psychiatrist and suicidologist, offered his interpretation of why rational suicides seem more accepted in society today. He believes that, increasingly, people are so overwhelmed with stress related to fears associated with life and dying that they begin searching for new ways to cope. Through searching, they often develop an interest in ways to die better, such as dying a good death, dying with dignity, and exercising their right to die.

Peretz stated that this motivation is unethical, dangerous, and harmful because it leads a person to a false sense of omnipotence. Two other elements may contribute to rational suicide but are also unrealistic and

unethical, according to Peretz. One element is that people who are advocates of rational suicide believe strongly in personal autonomy as the goal of human life; therefore, if a person cannot have complete personal autonomy, life is not worth living. The other element is an act of self-destruction, which has the potential to mythologize rational suicide. Peretz stated that by mythologizing an object, it is given false power. Advocates of rational suicide promote self-destruction as a way to realize a false sense of freedom from serious human problems, such as physical suffering, loneliness, or frailty.

For nurses to endorse any suicide seems contradictory to good practice because, traditionally, nurses and mental health professionals have intervened to prevent suicide. Many times, cultural, religious, and personal beliefs guide nurses in how they respond to patients who are thinking about suicide. Does a nurse have the right to try to stop a person from committing rational suicide, in other words, to act in the best interest of a patient? Or is a nurse supposed to support a person's autonomous decision to commit rational suicide, even when a decision is morally and religiously incompatible with the nurse's perspective? If the nurse knows of the plan for rational suicide, would care toward that patient be obligatory? Would nurses be obligated to render care despite their own value conflicts? What actions could the nurse take at this point?

According to Rich and Butts (2004), no clear answers exist to this ethical dilemma, but interventions become unique to each situation. Interventions may include everything from providing information regarding Compassion & Choices (a right-to-die organization) to answering questions about lethal injections. Nurses need to consider autonomy and beneficence when deciding on interventions for persons who are planning rational suicide. Nurses are closely involved with more end-of-life ethics as the issue of voluntary, active euthanasia is becoming increasingly prevalent.

Care for Dying Patients

Nurses must first sort out their own feelings about euthanasia and dying before they provide appropriate moral guidance and direction to patients and families. The sights, sounds, and smells of death can be an emotionally draining experience for nurses, but nurses must meet the needs of patients and families. Every day, nurses face disturbing moral conflicts and distress, such as whether they should keep giving a continuous morphine sulfate infusion to a dying patient for comfort in light of the risk of depressed respirations or whether they should assist in withdrawing and withholding artificial nutrition and fluids or other life-sustaining interventions. When nurses experience personal value and professional moral distress in decision making, they may find themselves on uncertain moral ground. The substance of decision making regarding ethical issues and the experience of moral distress needs documenting so as not to lose the richness of the narratives and the degree to which these diagnoses are used.

Barbara Couden (2002), a registered nurse, wrote a beautiful and poignant description of her emotional experiences with loss and death in intensive care, stating that, at times, she just wanted to run away. She portrayed her experiences of physical and emotional exhaustion; periods of fatigue, guilt, and sometimes relief when death finally came; the smell of death on her clothes and wetness on her face from crying families pressing against her face; tearfulness and sadness; and her own intense feelings of grief and loss. Couden experienced immeasurable unexpressed grief and unresolved personal losses, along with the losses of her patients, until she had no emotions left to express toward her patients and no energy left to spend on them.

After Couden (2002) sought ways to deal with her crisis, she discovered three important aspects of her emotional work. First, she had to face her own grief and loss, which includes continuous expressions of loss through tears and discussions. Second, she had to find ways to deal with her own intense feelings of grief and loss before she "could dare to give them [her feelings] utterance" (p. 42). She cries and expresses her own grief with patients, and as she does, the environment becomes a unique place for her and her patients as they exchange

ETHICAL REFLECTION: SOMETIMES I WANT TO RUN

Barbara A. Couden wrote the following:

Sometimes I want to run. It's work not to recoil from the rawness of life in those rooms. It is probably easier to behave as a starchy, mechanical nurse who staves off discomfort with a cheerful cliché. However, people deserve to experience hospitalization, grief, or even dying at its very best. To provide less isn't care at all. So I give my open heart and plunge into their circumstances, even though really I'm no one special to them—just there by default. In return, they honor me with the privilege of sharing their pain, struggle, and the richness of life, death, and love. In some way, we each live on in the other's memory: endeared by shared suffering, strivings to nurture hope, and our individual attempts to love. So there are nights that I reflect on my heartfelt efforts, smell death on my clothes, and feel dampness where the tears of grieving loved ones have pressed against my face. Sometimes it seems that my role as a nurse is to absorb the feelings of others: pain, sadness, and loss. I'm sitting up in bed tonight, waiting for mine to dissipate.

Reproduced from Couden, B. A. (2002). "Sometimes I want to run": A nurse reflects on loss in the intensive care unit. *Journal of Loss and Trauma*, 7(1), pp. 41–42. Reprinted by permission of the publisher Taylor and Francis Ltd., http://www.tandfonline.com

their emotions. She finds ways to pamper herself. Her third aspect of emotional work involves her mannerisms toward patients and feeling good about the way she responds to her patients. Couden confirmed her feelings about the way she responds to her patients when she saw her therapist emotionally moved by her own stories.

Relationships with patients are at the heart of nursing ethics. Nursing at its best is good for the souls of the patient and nurse; Wright (2006) stated, "For the heart is the seat of the soul, and when we nurse another, we nurse a soul too. Soulful work requires soulful individuals and communities" (p. 23). Without this soulful work, patients will feel disconnected. Relationships can become quite complex because of the accompanied interrelational experiences and emotions (Maeve, 1998).

Most nurses share in patients' emotional experiences of pain, suffering, and joy and do not just give superficial care and then forget about it. Providing care to their dying patients becomes an essential component of nurses' own lives, and the stories they remember about their patients become interwoven into their own life stories. Maeve (1998) studied nine nurses who worked with suffering and dying patients. As she listened to the nurses' stories, she realized that moral issues about practice and relationships were dominant where suffering and dying patients were concerned.

Three major themes were identified from the study (Maeve, 1998). One was "tempering involvement" (p. 1138), which means that nurses had a dilemma or conflict about becoming involved—how much involvement; setting limits; setting boundaries to distinguish their lives from their patients' lives; and becoming embodied, such as when nurses may actually live in the experience with their patients. The second theme, "doing the right thing/the good thing" (p. 1139), involved education, experience, courage, moral dilemmas, and past regrets for a few of their performances or decisions with patients. The third theme, "cleaning up" (p. 1140), marked the end of the involvement with the patient. During this time, the nurse needs to reflect on experiences and clean up grief.

In one Japanese study of 160 nurses, Konishi et al. (2002) studied withdrawal of artificial food and fluid from terminally ill patients. The majority of the nurses supported this act only under two conditions: if the patient requested withdrawal of artificial food and fluids and if the act relieved the patient's suffering. Comfort for the patient was of great concern by nurses. One nurse in the study stated, "[Artificial food and fluid] only prolongs the patient's suffering. When withdrawn, the patient showed peace on the face. I have seen such patients so many times" (p. 14). In the same study, another nurse who was experiencing moral conflict with a decision to withdraw artificial food and fluid stated, "Withdrawal is killing and cruel. I feel guilty" (p. 14).

Other end-of-life issues may be reasons for moral conflicts as well. Researchers conducted a literature review on the topic of ethical issues in terms of how nurses perceive their care of dying patients (Georges & Grypdonck, 2002). A dearth of systematic research exists on the topic of nurses' moral conflicts and distress. Some of the moral dilemmas particularly critical to end-of-life care found by Georges and Grypdonck were as follows:

- Communicating truthfully with patients about death because they were fearful of destroying all hope in the patient and family
- Managing pain symptoms because of fear of hastening death
- Feeling forced to collaborate with other health team members about medical treatments that, in the nurses' opinion, are futile or too burdensome
- Feeling insecure and not adequately informed about reasons for treatment
- Trying to maintain their own moral integrity throughout relationships with patients, families, and coworkers because of the feeling that they are forced to betray their own moral values

Although a nurse has an obligation to provide compassionate and palliative care, the nurse has a right to withdraw from treating and caring for a dying patient as long as another nurse has assumed the care. When care is such that the nurse perceives it to be violating his or her personal and professional morality and values, the professional nurse must pursue alternative approaches to care.

Nursing care for dying patients needs to be enriched over time because new nurses and nurses who do not routinely care for dying patients are not automatically skilled in this type of care. Nurses must acquire expertise and skills in end-of-life care, as in any other area of practice. As we will see, compassionate care is an essential component of nursing care for dying patients.

Compassionate Nurses and Dying Patients

Nurses find themselves on uncertain moral ground when they attempt to sustain dying patients, but they must be honest with patients and give sufficient information concerning advance directives and medical treatment options. However, the most important aspect is to offer support to dying patients by relating to their fear of death and alleviating pain and suffering. Family members need to support their loved one, and they can often learn support strategies from talking with nurses and observing how nurses interact with the patient. When dying patients experience the compassionate acts of nurses and family members, death can be a positive experience for them. Nurses must remember that little things make a big difference in the care of dying patients. Medical treatments aimed at relieving pain and suffering can coexist with palliative care, and nurses' compassionate acts are essential to this cohesive coexistence (Ciccarello, 2003). One particular compassionate act is for nurses to teach individuals and patients in community and hospital settings about treatment decisions at the end of life, such as life-sustaining treatments and palliative care with symptom management. Nurses can teach patients about advance directives and surrogate decision making. The case of Terri Schiavo could possibly have a positive influence on the need for understanding and having advance directives.

Physical and Emotional Pain Management

Understanding and upholding aggressive pain management precepts may be the most challenging moral dilemma that nurses face when caring for dying patients. The lack of understanding regarding the issues and fears of patient addiction or death causes nurses and physicians to undertreat pain and suffering in many cases. Miller et al. (2001) emphasized the importance of nurses applying three basic precepts when controlling pain. Nurses and physicians need to (1) follow the WHO's (2018) "cancer pain ladder" protocol for palliative pain management (see the following section); (2) treat pain early because, when pain is out of control, it is more difficult to treat; and (3) explain to terminally ill patients that addiction should not be feared and that dying patients rarely develop an addiction to properly administered pain medications. The goal of cancer pain management is to relieve pain to a level that allows for an acceptable quality of life (WHO, 2018, p. 9).

▶ Types of Pain

Miller et al. (2001) described two major types of pain: nociceptive and neuropathic. Nociceptive pain involving tissue damage occurs with two types of pain: somatic (musculoskeletal pain) and visceral (organ pain—the most common type of pain). After nurses have performed a thorough pain assessment, the

WHO's (2018) pain ladder is an excellent approach for providers of care. It is a step-by-step approach to managing pain with palliative care. At the first sign of a patient's pain, nurses should administer oral non-opioid medications or adjuvant therapy, as ordered by the primary care provider. The next progressive step involves use of opioids, such as codeine, for mild to moderate pain, in addition to interventions in the first step. The last step involves use of strong opioids, such as morphine sulfate, for moderate to severe pain, in addition to interventions in the previous steps of the ladder.

Moral conflicts among patients and family members can arise about pain relief and suffering. Sharing in each patient's experience of pain and emotional suffering will provide a better experience for nurses and their patients during the death process.

Spiritual Considerations

Spirituality is one of the most important aspects of end-of-life nursing care, but often, nurses feel helpless when it comes to providing the right type of spiritual care for their patients. Meaningful experiences, especially at the end of life, are important for nurses in their care of patients because nurses feel that they touch patients' lives in some way through generous or compassionate acts. One such way may be the facilitation of spirituality. Spirituality has become more essential to nursing care since it has been included in the definition of palliative care. Most Americans believe end-of-life spiritual care is an important part of the dying process, and at the same time, they believe nurses and others do not effectively provide spiritual care.

Spirituality is a deeply personal and integral part of a person's life (Taylor, 2002). Several definitions of spirituality exist in nursing (Dossey & Guzzetta, 2000; Narayanasamy, 1999; Taylor, 2002). Spirituality, as defined by Dossey and Guzzetta (2000), is "a unifying force of a person; the essence of being that permeates all of life and is manifested in one's being, knowing, and doing; the interconnectedness with self, others, nature, and God/Life Force/Absolute/Transcendent" (p. 7).

Taylor (2003) studied the expectations of patients and family members regarding spiritual needs and care from nurses. In-depth, tape-recorded interviews were conducted with 28 adult patients who had cancer and their family caregivers. Six categories, and consequently specific nursing interventions, are listed in the priority of responses; they are "kindness and respect," "talking and listening," "prayer," "connecting," "quality temporal nursing care," and "mobilizing religious or spiritual resources" (p. 588).

The category with the most responses was kindness and respect, and a few responses regarding this theme included "just be nice," "giving loving care," and "a smile does a lot" (Taylor, 2003, pp. 587–588). For the next category, talking and listening, the responses varied widely because some patients enjoyed the superficial chatter, whereas others were pleased about nurses sharing their own deep religious experiences as comforting measures. Another category, prayer and the nurse's offering to pray with patients, varied widely in responses according to individualized beliefs. The category of connecting relates to certain characteristics, such as nurses being authentic and genuine, having physical presence, and having symmetry with patients. (Symmetry with patients means patients want to have a sense of working with nurses in a notion of friendship.) Giving quality temporal nursing care, another category, relates to the mechanisms that support the spirit of the person, such as keeping the room clean and not allowing the patient to suffer. The last category is mobilizing religious or spiritual resources. Nurses can facilitate mobilization by consulting chaplains and having Bibles or other religious materials in the room available as needed.

There are no completely right ways to help a person die because dying processes are individual experiences (Benner et al., 2003). Nursing care depends on each situation. Stories told by family members and dying patients are particularly significant to the understanding of death and are central to paying proper tribute to human passage. As Benner et al. (2003) pointed out, "death forever changes the world of those who experience the loss of the person dying" (p. 558). The involvement of nurses in decisions about death becomes more complex every day as more technology emerges in the dying process. Family members and patients must be involved with all ethical decisions.

KEY POINTS

- Most of the time, whatever death a person is to experience—a good death; an anticipated death; a sudden, unexpected death; or a painful, lingering death—people do not have a choice of how they will die.
- Suffering is something that all human beings and every living thing experiences, and because of the multidimensional aspects of humans, suffering affects every part of people's lives—physical, mental, emotional, social, and spiritual.
- Types of euthanasia include active, passive, voluntary, nonvoluntary, and involuntary. Physician-assisted suicide is a type of voluntary euthanasia.
- Death was legally defined in 1981 in the Uniform Determination of Death Act.
- Three standards for death—cardiopulmonary, whole brain, and higher brain—emerged as a result of the landmark legal decisions associated with these terms.
- Nurses need to develop awareness and knowledge of the types of advance directives to provide education to patients.
- The surrogate decision maker, often known as a proxy, is an individual who acts on behalf of a patient and is chosen by the patient, such as a family member; is court appointed; or has another type of authority to make decisions.
- The surrogate decision-making standards include the substituted judgment standard, pure autonomy standard, principle of autonomy extended standard, and best interest standard.
- Before physicians consider a patient's treatment as medically futile, they must first consider the American Medical Association's guidelines for designating a patient as medically futile and then attempt to answer questions such as "How far does one go with patient autonomy?" and "What is the potential outcome of treatments for the patient?"
- Palliative care and terminal sedation are accepted practices in most countries, including the United States.
- The landmark legal cases of Karen Ann Quinlan, Nancy Cruzan, and Terri Schiavo brought recognition to the concepts of patient (or surrogate) self-determination as related to the right to die or refuse treatment; withholding and withdrawing life-sustaining treatment, such as artificial nutrition and hydration and mechanical ventilation; and persistent vegetative state and whole-brain death.
- Oregon, Washington, Montana, and Vermont have legally approved physician-assisted suicide.
- Death and dying can be a more positive experience if nurses give compassionate care to patients and families during the dying process.
- The ANA *Code of Ethics for Nurses with Interpretative Statements* emphasizes aggressive pain control for suffering patients at the end of life, but nurses should never have the sole intention of ending a patient's life.
- The ANA supports nurses in their attempts to relieve patients' pain, even when the interventions lead to risks of hastening death.

References

Albom, M. (1997). *Tuesdays with Morrie: An old man, a young man, and life's greatest lesson.* Broadway Books.

American Nurses Association. (2015). *Code of ethics for nurses with interpretive statements.* Author.

American Nurses Association. (2016). *Nurses' roles and responsibilities in providing care and support at the end of life.* https://www.nursingworld.org/~4af078/globalassets/docs/ana/ethics/endoflife-positionstatement.pdf

American Nurses Association. (2017). *Nutrition and hydration at the end of life.* https://www.nursingworld.org/~4af0ed/globalassets/docs/ana/ethics/ps_nutrition-and-hydration-at-the-end-of-life_2017june7.pdf

Arbour, R. B. (2013). Brain death: Assessment, controversy, and confounding factors. *Critical Care Nurse, 33*(6), 27–46. https://doi.org/10.4037/ccn2013215

Battin, M. P. (1994). *The least worst death: Essays in bioethics on the end of life.* Oxford University Press.

Beauchamp, T. L., & Childress, J. F. (2019). *Principles of biomedical ethics* (8th ed.). Oxford University Press.

Benjamin, M. (2003). Pragmatism and the determination of death. In G. McGee (Ed.), *Pragmatic bioethics* (2nd ed., pp. 193–206). MIT Press.

Benner, P., Kerchner, S., Corless, I. B., & Davies, B. (2003). Attending death as a human passage: Core nursing principles for end-of-life care. *American Journal of Critical Care, 12*(6), 558–561.

Bondeson, J. (2001). *Buried alive: The terrifying history of our most primal fear.* W. W. Norton.

Brannigan, M. C., & Boss, J. A. (2001). *Healthcare ethics in a diverse society.* Mayfield.

Brogan, G. (2006). Inventing the good death. *Registered Nurse: Journal of Patient Advocacy, 102*(7), 10–14.

Buchanan, A. E., & Brock, D. W. (1990). *Deciding for others: The ethics of surrogate decision making.* Cambridge University Press.

Buckley, J. W., & Abell, N. (2009). Factors affecting life-sustaining treatment decisions by health care surrogates and proxies: Assessing benefits and barriers. *Social Work in Health Care, 48,* 386–401.

Cassell, E. J. (2004). *The nature of suffering and the goals of medicine* (2nd ed.). Oxford University Press.

Cavanaugh, T. A. (2006). *Double-effect reasoning: Doing good and avoiding evil.* Clarendon Press.

Cerminara, K. L. (2005). Theresa Marie Schiavo's long road to peace. *Death Studies, 30*(2), 101–112.

Ciccarello, G. P. (2003). Strategies to improve end-of-life care in the intensive care unit. *Dimensions of Critical Care Nursing, 22*(5), 216–222.

Connelly, R. (2003). Living with death: The meaning of acceptance. *Journal of Humanistic Psychology, 43*(1), 45–63.

Cornell Law School, Legal Information Institute. (n.d.). *Cruzan by Cruzan v. Director, Missouri Department of Health* [497 U.S. 261]. https://www.law.cornell.edu/supremecourt/text/497/261

Couden, B. A. (2002). "Sometimes I want to run": A nurse reflects on loss in the intensive care unit. *Journal of Loss and Trauma, 7*(1), 35–45.

Death with Dignity. (2018). *Death with dignity around the U.S.* https://www.deathwithdignity.org/take-action/

DeGrazia, D. (2021, May 17). *The definition of death.* https://plato.stanford.edu/archives/sum2021/entries/death-definition/

Devettere, R. J. (2000). *Practical decision making in health care ethics: Cases and concepts* (2nd ed.). Georgetown University Press.

Dossey, B. M., & Guzzetta, C. E. (2000). Holistic nursing practice. In B. M. Dossey, L. Keegan, & C. E. Guzzetta (Eds.), *Holistic nursing: A handbook for practice* (3rd ed., pp. 5–26). Aspen.

Dubler, N. & Nimmons, D. (1992). *Ethics on call: A medical ethicist dhows how to takecharge of life-and-death choices* (p. 146). Harmony Books//Crown/Penguin Random House.

Emanuel, L. A., Danis, M., Pearlman, R. A., & Singer, P. A. (1995). Advance care planning as a process: Structuring the discussions in practice. *American Geriatrics Society, 43,* 440–446.

Engelhardt, H. T. (1986). Suicide in the cancer patient. *Cancer, 36*(2), 105–109.

Eriksson, K. (1997). Understanding the world of the patient, the suffering human being: The new clinical paradigm from nursing to caring. *Advanced Practice Nursing Quarterly, 3*(1), 8–13.

Fesmire, S. (2003). *John Dewey and moral imagination.* Indiana University Press.

Fine, R. L. (2005). From Cruzan to Schiavo: Medical, ethical, and legal issues in severe brain injury. *Baylor University Medical Center Proceedings, 18*(4), 303–310.

Finnerty, J. L. (1987). Ethics in rational suicide. *Critical Care Nursing Quarterly, 10*(2), 86–90.

Frank, R., & Anselmi, K. K. (2011). Washington v. Glucksberg: Patient autonomy v. cultural mores in physician-assisted suicide. *Journal of Nursing Law, 14*(1), 11–16.

Frontline. (2014). *Chronology of Dr. Jack Kevorkian's life and assisted suicide campaign.* https://www.pbs.org/wgbh/pages/frontline/kevorkian/chronology.html

Garrett, C. (2004). *Gut feelings: Chronic illness and the search for healing.* Rodopi.

Georges, J. J., & Grypdonck, M. (2002). Moral problems experienced by nurses when caring for terminally ill people: A literature review. *Nursing Ethics, 9*(2), 155–178.

Hester, D. M. (2003). Significance at the end of life. In G. McGee (Ed.), *Pragmatic bioethics* (2nd ed., pp. 121–136). MIT Press.

Hester, D. M. (2010). *End of life care and pragmatic decision making: A bioethical perspective.* Cambridge University Press.

International Council of Nurses. (2012). *The ICN code of ethics for nurses.* Author.

Jonsen, A. R., Siegler, M., & Winslade, W. J. (2006). *Clinical ethics* (6th ed.). McGraw-Hill.

Jonsen, A. R., Veatch, R. M., & Walters, L. (1998). *Source book in bioethics.* Georgetown University Press.

Kahn, D. L., & Steeves, R. H. (1986). The experience of suffering: Conceptual clarification and theoretical definition. *Journal of Advanced Nursing, 11,* 623–631.

Kingsbury, K. (2008, March 21). *When is sedation really euthanasia?* http://content.time.com/time/health/article /0,8599,1724911,00.html

Konishi, E., Davis, A. J., & Aiba, T. (2002). The ethics of withdrawing artificial food and fluid from terminally ill patients: An end-of-life dilemma for Japanese nurses and families. *Nursing Ethics, 9*(1), 7–19.

Kopala, B., & Kennedy, S. L. (1998). Requests for assisted suicide: A nursing issue. *Nursing Ethics, 5*(1), 16–26.

Ladd, R. E., Pasquerella, L., & Smith, S. (2002). *Ethical issues in home health care.* Charles C Thomas.

Lehto, R. H., & Stein, K. F. (2009). Death anxiety: An analysis of an evolving concept. *Research and Theory for Nursing Practice: An International Journal, 23*(1), 23–41.

LEXIS-NEXIS. (1999). *In the matter of Karen Ann Quinlan, an alleged incompetent* [70 N.J. 10; 355 A.2d 647; 1976 N.J. LEXIS 181; 79 A.L.R.3d205]. https:// euthanasia.procon.org/wp-content/uploads/sites/43 /in_re_quinlan.pdf

Lustig, A. (2003). End-of-life decisions: Does faith make a difference? *Commonweal, 130*(10), 7.

Lynne, D. (2005, September 1). *Terri's story.* Cumberland House Publishing.

Maeve, M. K. (1998). Weaving a fabric or moral meaning: How nurses live with suffering and death. *Journal of Advanced Nursing, 27,* 1136–1142.

Mappes, T. A., & DeGrazia, D. (2001). *Biomedical ethics* (5th ed.). McGraw-Hill.

Miller, K. E., Miller, M. M., & Jolley, M. R. (2001). Challenges in pain management at the end of life. *American Family Physician, 64*(7), 1227–1234.

Multi-Society Task Force on Persistent Vegetative State. (1994). Medical aspects of the persistent vegetative state. *New England Journal of Medicine, 330*(21), 1499–1508.

Munson, R. (2004). *Intervention and reflection: Basic issues in medical ethics* (7th ed.). Wadsworth-Thomson.

Narayanasamy, A. (1999). ASSET: A model for actioning spirituality and spiritual care education and training in nursing. *Nurse Education Today, 19,* 274–285.

Olick, R. S. (2001). *Taking advance directives seriously: Prospective autonomy and decisions near the end of life.* Georgetown University Press.

O'Rourke, K. (2002). *A primer for health care ethics: Essays for a pluralistic society* (2nd ed.). Georgetown University Press.

President's Commission for the Study of Ethical Problems in Medicine and Biomedical and Behavioral Research. (1981, July). *Defining death: Medical, legal, and ethical issues in the determination of death.* Government Printing Office. https://repository.library.georgetown .edu/bitstream/handle/10822/559345/defining_death .pdf?sequence=1&isAllowed=y

Quill, T. E. (2001). *Caring for patients at the end of life: Facing an uncertain future together.* Oxford University Press.

Rich, K. L., & Butts, J. B. (2004). Rational suicide: Uncertain moral ground. *Journal of Advanced Nursing, 46*(3), 270–283.

Schneider, K. (2011). *Jack Kevorkian dies at 83: A doctor who helped end lives.* https://www.nytimes.com/2011 /06/04/us/04kevorkian.html

Schneiderman, L. J. (1994). Medical futility and aging: Ethical implications. *Generations, 18*(4), 61–64.

Siegel, K. (1986). Psychosocial aspects of rational suicide. *American Journal of Psychotherapy, 40*(3), 405–418.

Spiegel, D. (1993). *Living beyond limits: New hope and help for facing life-threatening illness.* Times Books.

Sugarman, J. (2000). *20 common problems: Ethics in primary care.* McGraw-Hill.

Taylor, E. J. (2002). *Spiritual care: Nursing theory, research, and practice.* Prentice Hall.

Taylor, E. J. (2003). Nurses caring for the spirit: Patients with cancer and family caregiver expectations. *Oncology Nursing Forum, 30*(4), 585–590.

U.S. Court of Appeals, Eleventh District. (2005, March 21 /Decided March 25). Theresa Marie Schindler Schiavo and ex relations Robert Schlindler and Mary Schindler (plaintiffs) v. Michael Schiavo, Judge George W. Greer, and The Hospice of the Florida Suncoast, Inc. (defendants). (Civ. Act. No. 8:05-CV-530-T-27TBM). https://caselaw.findlaw. com/us-11th-circuit/1360200.html; Cerminara, K. L. (2006). Theresa Marie Schiavo's Long Road to Peace, *Death Studies, 30*(2), 101–112. https://doi .org/10.1080/07481180500455574; and Lynne, D. (2005, September 1). Terri's story. Cumberland House Publishing.

van Hooft, S. (2000). The suffering body. *Health, 4*(2), 179–195.

van Hooft, S. (2006). *Caring about health.* Ashgate.

Veatch, R. M. (2003). *The basics of bioethics* (2nd ed.). Prentice Hall.

Wijdicks, E. F. M., Varelas, P. N., Gronseth, G. S., & Greer, D. M. (2010). Evidence-based guideline update: Determining brain death in adults: Report of the Quality Standards Subcommittee of the American Academy of Neurology. *Neurology, 74*(23), 1911–1918.

World Health Organization (WHO). (2018). *WHO guidelines for the pharmacological and radiotherapeutic management of cancer pain in adults and adolescents.* Geneva: World Health Organization. License: CC BY-NC-SA 3.0 IGO. https://apps.who.int/iris/bitstream/handle/10665/279700/9789241550390-eng.pdf

World Health Organization (WHO). (2020, August 5). *Palliative care.* https://www.who.int/news-room/fact-sheets/detail/palliative-care

Wright, S. (2006). The heart of nursing. *Nursing Standard, 20*(47), 20–23.

Yalom, I. D. (1980). *Existential psychotherapy.* Basic Books.

PART III

Special Issues

© Seller 1234/Shutterstock

CHAPTER 10

Psychiatric/Mental Health Nursing Ethics

Karen L. Rich

OBJECTIVES

After reading this chapter, the reader should be able to do the following:

1. Identify how personal and professional values affect psychiatric/mental health nursing.
2. Discuss the ethical implications of diagnostic labeling.
3. Examine ways psychiatric patients are stigmatized by both healthcare professionals and the general public.
4. Adhere to appropriate boundaries in nurse–patient relationships.
5. Discuss differences among privacy, confidentiality, and privileged communication as they apply to psychiatric/mental health nursing.
6. Describe psychiatric patients' rights in directing their care.
7. Use humanistic theories in psychiatric/mental health nursing practice.

▶ Characteristics of Psychiatric Nursing

Although psychiatric/mental health nursing does not have what some nurses perceive to be the excitement of other nursing specialties, such as intensive care and emergency department nursing, mental health care is extremely important. As Schneider (2016) stated, "psychiatry is a critical yet often neglected area of medicine" (p. 567). Most nurses are inspired

when they realize psychiatric/mental health nursing care is focused on the very nucleus of personal identity. However, this realization brings with it an awesome moral responsibility. Issues concerning patient autonomy are inherent to the actual nature of psychiatry (Schneider, 2016).

According to Radden (2002a), there are three areas distinguishing psychiatry from other medical specialties: the characteristics of the therapeutic relationship, the characteristics of psychiatric patients, and what Radden called the *therapeutic project*. Keltner and Steele (2019) proposed that psychiatric nursing interventions can be divided into three components: the psychotherapeutic nurse–patient relationship (words), psychopharmacology (drugs), and milieu management (environment), all of which must be supported by a "sound understanding of psychopathology" (p. 2). Ethical implications involved with these different aspects of psychiatric care and special issues in mental health are addressed in this chapter.

In general, professional healthcare practices are made credible because of formal expert knowledge used in professional–patient relationships, but the nature of professional–patient relationships, the first distinguishing area of psychiatry, may be even more important in mental health care than in other healthcare specialties (Radden, 2002a; Sokolowski, 1991). One reason is because facilitative relationships are often the key to therapeutic effectiveness with psychiatric patients. For many years the nurse–patient relationship in psychiatry has been characterized from the perspective of the nurse's "therapeutic use of self," which has been defined as "the ability to use one's personality consciously and in full awareness in an attempt to establish relatedness and to structure nursing intervention" (Travelbee, 1971, p. 19). Radden (2002a) compared the therapeutic relationship to a "treatment tool analogous to the surgeon's scalpel" (p. 53). When nurses are using their personalities to effect changes in patients, it becomes very important that the nurses' behaviors reflect moral character.

The second distinguishing feature of psychiatry involves the characteristics of psychiatric patients. Psychiatric patients may be more vulnerable than other patients to exploitation, dependence, and inequality in relationships (Radden, 2002a). A presumed decrease in psychiatric patients' ability to exercise judgment and the stigma associated with mental illness lead to this special vulnerability. A central issue in psychiatric ethics is vulnerability regarding "treatment refusal, involuntary hospitalization

for care and protection, responsibility in the criminal setting, and the set of issues surrounding the criterion of competence (competence to stand trial, competence to refuse and consent to treatment, competence to undertake legal contracts, for example)" (Radden, 2002b, p. 400).

The third distinguishing feature of psychiatric care proposed by Radden (2002a), the therapeutic project, is an important part of the overall relationship between ethics and mental health. The therapeutic project is a major undertaking that involves "reforming the patient's whole self or character, when these terms are understood in holistic terms as the set of a person's long-term dispositions, capabilities and social and relational attributes" (p. 54). As with the nurses' use of self, nurses have an important moral responsibility in working with psychiatric patients in regard to the therapeutic project. Radden (2002a) stated there are only a few other societal projects that compare with the impact of the therapeutic project—one is the raising of children, which also places great responsibility on the person who is in a position of power with vulnerable others.

▶ A Value-Laden Specialty

We do not know our own souls, let alone the souls of others.

—**Virginia Woolf**, "On Being Ill," 1926

The Greek philosopher Socrates is credited with saying the unexamined life is not worth living. This thought underlies the aim of much of the care patients receive from psychiatric/mental health nurses. One might add two supplementary statements to the famous statement made by Socrates:

1. Many people are unable to adequately examine their lives, but these lives are still worth living.

2. Even for people who try to examine the content and context of their lives, understanding often is elusive.

Although personal values pervade all discussions of nursing ethics, an emphasis on values is even more relevant to psychiatric/mental health nursing because it is largely involved with subjective experiences rather than objective diseases. According to Dickenson and Fulford (2000), psychiatry is sometimes referred to as a moral discipline rather than a medical discipline. Human values are generally shared values regarding the experiences and behaviors addressed by physical medicine. However, in psychiatry, values relating to experiences and behaviors are usually diverse. These diverse values among mental health professionals and patients focus on motivation, desire, and belief as opposed to an overall agreement about objective findings, such as an agreement that cancer and heart disease are bad conditions. Problems arise in psychiatric/mental health care when nurses do not know how to use practical wisdom in navigating through value disparities and disagreements with patients and other healthcare providers.

Seedhouse (2000) proposed that there often is a fundamental values difference between what nurses are traditionally taught about the goals of nursing care and the priorities of the medical model in psychiatry (see **BOX 10-1**). According to Seedhouse, the psychiatric system often relegates nursing priorities to the rank of secondary importance.

In mental health organizations, professionals other than nurses may view it as an irritation when nurses try to reinforce the personal worth of patients by trying to find meaning in patients' behaviors and experiences rather than just providing medicalized treatment. The acknowledgment of this problem is not intended to mean nurses should make negative generalizations about the psychiatric healthcare system as a whole; instead, nurses' knowledge of the views of other healthcare professionals should encourage them to be

---

BOX 10-1 Possible Priority Disparities

Nursing Priorities

[Nurses are] supposed to be respectful of all other people's beliefs, treat people as equals, care personally to the extent that [they enter] patients' subjective worlds, uphold their dignity, ensure their privacy, be ethical at all times, nurture all patients and—of course—work for their health (in this case work for their mental health).

Psychiatric [System] Priorities

The psychiatrist is trained to diagnose and treat mental illnesses supposedly as real and independent of the psychiatrist as [if treating] cold sores and bronchitis.

Data from Seedhouse, D. (2000). *Practical nursing philosophy: The universal ethical code.* John Wiley & Sons, p. 138.

---

aware of the values influencing the systems in which they function.

It is important for psychiatric/mental health nurses to remember that truly knowing oneself is hard and understanding what underlies the emotions, words, and behaviors of other people often is even more difficult. Ethical practice in psychiatry generally is consistent with a foundationally nonjudgmental attitude. This does not mean nurses should not have thoughts, values, and considered judgments or opinions. It is unrealistic to believe nurses' values do not affect their work—that is, the work of nurses can be completely value neutral. The key to moral nursing care is for the nurse to have moral values. Nurses are responsible for using practical wisdom in their judgments, being truthful with themselves about their own values, and being compassionately truthful in their work with patients. Nurses need to take care that their attitude does not degenerate into one of condescension or pity. Keeping a "there but for the grace of God go I" attitude when working in a psychiatric/mental health setting may contribute to compassionate care.

The Practice Area of Mental Health: Unique Characteristics

Some people believe psychiatry is the one healthcare specialty in which 19th-century philosophies continue to exert a strong influence on today's approach to practice (Beresford, 2002). Even in the 21st century, *bad* is often equated with *mad*, and there is a tension between efforts to reduce the stigma of mental illness and forensic psychiatry (Pouncey & Lukens, 2013). Until the discovery of new drug therapies revolutionized the field of psychiatry, mentally ill patients were frequently warehoused in asylums, often for very long periods of time or even for life (Hobson & Leonard, 2001; Keltner & Steele, 2019). Research in the 1950s and 1960s produced new psychotropic medications that ushered in a metamorphosis in psychiatry. The new medications provided a way to manage psychiatric symptoms that had been difficult or impossible to manage before, but these drugs still caused many serious side effects related to their use.

ETHICAL REFLECTION

How has mental health care been shaped by the values of Western societies?

Because of the discovery of new drugs, there was a wide-scale release of patients from mental institutions in the 1960s and 1970s, and many of these people eventually became homeless or were jailed (Hobson & Leonard, 2001; Keltner & Steele, 2019). When patients were released from hospitals, the doors were almost literally locked and barred behind them. Patients were assured they would receive adequate treatment for their mental illnesses in the community, but society and the medical community did not keep their promises to these patients. Satisfactory community treatment never materialized, and access to care is still a problem in mental health today. Although healthcare professionals often use the term *mental health* when speaking about the specialty of psychiatry, the system of psychiatric care continues to be based on mental illness.

After the 1970s, patients still were not well managed with the new psychotropic drugs, and psychoanalysis started to lose favor. When in the 1980s and 1990s health maintenance organizations further constrained the care and treatment of psychiatric patients, holistic care almost fell apart (Hobson & Leonard, 2001). The payment psychiatrists received to conduct therapy sessions with their patients was no longer an incentive to provide these services; psychiatrists have been pushed in the direction of focusing on biomedical treatment, while nonphysician therapists provide counseling but no prescriptions for medications. Primary care and other nonpsychiatrist physicians now prescribe an abundance of psychotropic drugs to patients. This trend in treatment began a severe fragmentation in the environment of psychiatric care. Physicians and therapists traditionally have not communicated well among themselves and sometimes fight turf battles, further impeding the quality of patient care.

Although there have continued to be many more improvements in psychiatric medications, they still provide, at best, a symptom-only treatment, not a cure, and medications are often prescribed inappropriately (Frances, 2013b). Generally, there continues to be a fragmentary divide between professionals who treat mental illnesses biomedically and professionals who provide psychological therapy and counseling. This fragmentation, or treatment gap, has ethical implications for the quality of care patients receive. It is in filling this treatment gap that nurses can move forward from a moral perspective.

Nurses are in a crucial bridge, or in-between, position to advance the holistic care of psychiatric patients by assessing their behavior and responses to medications and by providing education and valuable psychological and spiritual care, counseling, and support. Advanced-practice psychiatric/mental health nurse practitioners can prescribe medications and provide therapeutic and supportive counseling.

Ethical Implications of Diagnosis

Although it is not always a case of such serious proportions, through the use of mental illness diagnostic categories "people may be locked up, subjected to compulsory (and health damaging) 'treatment' and have their rights restricted" (Beresford, 2002, p. 582). This issue is closely tied to considerations of the stigma psychiatric patients face. Pipher (2003), a psychologist, acknowledged that ethical guidelines in clinical mental health practice do not address some of the important moral issues. Disagreement about the application of psychiatric diagnoses is one of these issues. In a qualitative study conducted by Watts and Priebe (2002), psychiatric patient participants expressed that they perceived the psychiatric system and the labeling involved with psychiatric diagnoses as "an attack on their identity" (p. 446). Corey (2005) cautioned counselors that cultural differences must be considered when patients are diagnosed with mental disorders:

> Certain behaviors and personality styles may be labeled neurotic or deviant simply because they are not characteristic of the dominant culture. Thus, counselors who work with African Americans, Asian Americans, Latinos, and Native Americans may erroneously conclude that a client is repressed, inhibited, passive, and unmotivated, all of which are seen as undesirable by Western standards. (p. 45)

Because psychiatric diagnoses often represent the boundaries of what is categorized as normal versus abnormal in society, psychiatric diagnoses, along with cultural, gender, and class biases, can perpetuate oppressive power relationships (Crowe, 2000). Consequently, the psychiatric diagnosing of patients is a morally charged issue. Psychiatric/mental health advanced practice nurses are in a position to assign a psychiatric diagnosis to patients, but the assigning of diagnoses is an ethical issue about which generalist nurses also must be aware. Crowe (2000) proposed that even when nurses are not responsible for assigning a diagnosis to a patient, they are collaborators in the diagnostic process when they do the following:

- Provide data and descriptions of observations to enable a diagnosis
- Integrate the nomenclature of diagnosis into the language of mental health nursing practice
- Administer medications that have been determined by psychiatric diagnosis
- Engage in service user and family education based on psychiatric diagnosis and treatment (p. 585)

In psychiatry, there generally are few, if any, definitive tests that can be used to diagnose illness, which has led to arguments over the years about the subjectivity of diagnosing mental illness and deciding what is normal and abnormal (Frances, 2013b; Schneider, 2016). The third edition of the *Diagnostic and Statistical Manual of Mental Disorders* (*DSM-III*), published in 1980, radically changed how psychiatric diagnoses were categorized, which began to satisfy some of the critics. The *DSM-III* was the first in a series of *DSM* manuals to use research as a basis for categorizing diagnoses.

The developers of the *DSM-IV* went even further in using biological data for diagnostic categories. Diagnosing with the *DSM-IV-TR* (4th edition, text revision) was intended to be based on observed data rather than on what is subjective or merely based on theory. Seedhouse (2000) suggested that people who take an antipsychiatric view (see **BOX 10-2**) considered the *DSM-IV* to be a "house of cards" (p. 126) based on speculative assumptions. It is interesting that Frances (2013b), who worked

BOX 10-2 Antipsychiatry

Practitioners who have an antipsychiatry view want to focus more on the beliefs and values of their patients and to include the spiritual, political, and socio-cultural dimensions of experience in their practice. This approach indicates that the concept of illness is far too restrictive to assist us in understanding insanity and reminds us that in order to understand mental illness some deconstruction of what constitutes mental illness is necessary.

Data from O'Brien, O., Woods, M., & Palmer, C. (2001). The emancipation of nursing practice: Applying anti-psychiatry to the therapeutic community. *Australian and New Zealand Journal of Mental Health Nursing, 10,* 4.

on the task force for the *DSM-III* and chaired the task force that produced the *DSM-IV*, in his book, *Saving Normal*, seems to agree with Seedhouse. When Frances (2013b) and colleagues worked on the new *DSM* edition, he already believed the "DSM had become too powerful for its own good and for society's" (loc. 83). Though he tried to be conservative in leading changes, he later sadly contended that the *DSM-IV* was "misused to blow up the diagnostic bubble" (loc. 83), meaning it was used to support diagnostic inflation. Based on the use of the *DSM-IV*, Frances (2013a) cited diagnostic consequences in his book *Essentials of Psychiatric Diagnosis: Responding to the Challenge of the DSM-5*. Statistics cited by Frances (2013a) are as follows:

- Retrospective epidemiological studies report that 20% of the general population qualifies for a current psychiatric diagnosis and 50% for a lifetime one.
- Prospective epidemiological studies double these rates and suggest that mental disorder is becoming virtually ubiquitous.
- During the past 20 years, we have experienced three unanticipated fads partly precipitated by DSM-IV:
  - A 20-fold increase in Autism Spectrum Disorder;

  - A tripling of Attention-Deficit/Hyperactivity Disorder (ADHD), and a doubling of Bipolar Disorders;
  - And the most dangerous fad, which is a 40-fold increase in childhood Bipolar Disorders, stimulated not by DSM-IV but instead by reckless and misleading drug company marketing.
- Twenty percent of the U.S. population is taking a psychotropic drug; 7% of the population is addicted to one (pp. 4–5).

The current *DSM*, *DSM-5*, is based on a medical model of diagnosing illness (Morrison, 2014). Frances (2013a) stated that the new *DSM* was supposed to provide an advanced paradigm shift in psychiatry but instead, it is unsafe to use and is based on unsound scientific evidence. New disorders have been introduced that have blurred boundaries with normal behavior, requirements have been lowered for diagnosing some disorders, and some disorders have been collapsed into broad categories (Frances, 2013b). A petition of considerations from the Division 32 Committee on *DSM-5* within the American Psychological Association (APA) and 51 mental health associations was sent to the *DSM-5* task force and the APA before the final *DSM-5* manual was published (Frances, 2013a; Robbins, 2012). The petition was rejected by the *DSM-5* task force. Areas of particular concern presented in the petition are as follows:

- Lowering of diagnostic thresholds, which may expand the number of people who meet criteria for certain disorders and lead to an increase in false-positive diagnoses.
- Vulnerable populations: Certain proposed revisions may lead to misuse in vulnerable populations, such as children and the elderly. This is particularly concerning if some of the newly proposed disorders are to be treated with neuroleptics, which are known to have dangerous side effects.
- Sociocultural variation: The proposed wording of the new definition of mental

disorder is ambiguous and if read literally, may risk resulting in the labeling of sociopolitical deviance as mental disorder.

- Personality disorders: The personality disorders section is perplexing. A member of the Personality Disorders Workgroup publicly described the proposals as confused and incoherent (Livesley, 2010).
- Conditions proposed by outside sources include questionable suggestions such as Apathy Syndrome, Internet Addiction Disorder, and Parental Alienation Syndrome.
- Various changes throughout the manual place subtle emphasis on medico-physiological theory. *DSM-III* and *DSM-IV* were said to be "atheoretical" (i.e., useable by practitioners from any theoretical background). When viewed together, some of the proposed changes seem to depart from *DSM*'s former "'atheoretical' stance in favor of a pathophysiological model" (Robbins, 2012, para. 22). This move is problematic because growing evidence suggests that psychopathology cannot be reduced to purely biological explanations and psychotropic medications pose substantial iatrogenic hazards.

A summary of the conclusions from this position are as follows:

- People are harmed by the medicalization of natural or normal responses to their experiences.
- Value-free criteria were not used.
- The social causation of problems is not emphasized.
- Mental distress should be considered along a continuum, including normal experiences and social causes.
- As an empirical system, the classification should not be based on past theory; rather a bottom up approach should be used to create it.

The changes in the *DSM-5* were touted as being paradigm shifting, but they have ended up being just more of the same in the minds of mental health professionals interested in setting the scene for more holistic mental health practice. More than ever, *people* are at risk of becoming mental health *patients* based on loose diagnosing within the healthcare system. People who need mental health care often cannot get it, whereas people with normal fluctuations in emotions and behavior are considered abnormal.

Also, when mental health professionals feel forced by insurance companies to assign a diagnosis to patients, ethical dilemmas may arise (Corey, 2005). In suggesting there are ethical implications and problems with subjectivity in identifying the psychiatric diagnoses of patients, Pipher (2003) presented a story about a young boy with an apparent obsessive-compulsive disorder. The boy's hands were chafed from frequent hand washing, and he insisted that all of his possessions be rigidly organized. The young man might even have qualified for special services at school based on his having a specific diagnosis, but there was a question about whether the diagnosis would ultimately help or hurt the boy. How would a label affect the child's self-perception and the perception of other people who might learn about the diagnosis? In the end, Pipher decided a diagnosis was not necessary in this boy's case. Distraction was used as a treatment, and the child's family physician was available to prescribe appropriate medications as needed.

The point of Pipher's story is that clinicians must be very careful in labeling patients because healthcare professionals often are unable to project the additional problems that might be triggered by a psychiatric label. According to Pipher (2003), clinicians would do well to ask the following questions before diagnosing psychiatric patients: "Why are we doing this? Will a diagnosis allow clients to get the help they need? Can the diagnosis hurt the client?" (p. 143).

Diagnoses often are generated or changed based on information gathered and reported by nurses. Staff nurses must remember that loosely applied diagnoses the nurse might off-handedly repeat to other people, whether these people are coworkers, the patient, families, or healthcare insurers, can be harmful to the best interests of patients—in other words, a psychiatric diagnosis is not something to be applied without skillful and reflective consideration by professionals who are specially educated to do so. Even then, nurses should be aware that often the determination of psychiatric diagnoses is a subjective and inexact science and sometimes can be detrimental to a patient's well-being.

ETHICAL REFLECTION

What factors make an objective diagnosis difficult in the field of psychiatry? What are some of the moral implications related to this difficulty? How might this issue affect nursing care?

Anosognosia

In 2012, Amador published a booklet titled "I am not sick, I don't need help." Dr. Amador's brother has schizophrenia, and he had trouble trying to convince his brother and his psychiatric patients that they have a mental illness. Through his practice and research, he discovered that people with mental illnesses who refuse to admit they are ill are not being stubborn or in denial. He realized the problem is what might be called "a broken brain" (p. 37). The brain circuitry problem causing their mental illness is the same problem causing their lack of insight into their illness. This lack of insight is termed **anosognosia**. The National Alliance on Mental Illness (NAMI, 2021) also recognizes the concept of anosognosia. Amador (2012) suggested that caregivers, when faced with frustrating patient refusals, remember "*the enemy is brain dysfunction*, not the person[s]" who deny their mental illness (pp. 49–50).

Amador (2012) advised that the wrong thing to do when working with patients with anosognosia is to approach the problem with the medical model. Affected patients do not view themselves as *patients* or needing help. Amador developed a positive prescription for working with people with anosognosia. He recommended the correct way to help is to L.E.A.P.

L—Listen reflectively; do not argue with the patient

E—Empathize, which helps build trust

A—Agree with what you can find that is common ground; do not focus on your own agenda

P—Partner to achieve shared goals with the patient; this involves a joint decision to work together

Stigma

There is a long history of people with psychiatric illnesses and conditions being stigmatized by a broad spectrum of society (Bolton, 2003; Green et al., 2003; Knight et al., 2003; Mayo Clinic Staff, 2017; Rosen et al., 2000; Wahl, 2003). In fact, some people believe this stigma extends to even professionals, such as nurses and physicians, who care for psychiatric patients (Bolton, 2003; Halter, 2002; Verhaege & Bracke, 2012) with mental health professionals themselves being viewed as being crazy or lazy (Keltner & Steele, 2019). Rosen and colleagues (2000) defined psychiatric **stigma** as "the false and unjustified association of individuals who have a mental illness, their families, friends and service providers with something shameful" (p. 19). This negative perception is perpetuated by the media and frequently results in hostility in communities and discrimination by service providers and employers. Fears are exacerbated and illnesses are left untreated.

When referring to people with mental illnesses, the U.S. surgeon general stated, "stigma tragically deprives people of their dignity and interferes with their full participation in society" (U.S. Department of Health and Human Services, 1999, p. viii). Concern about stigma prevents some people from seeking and receiving psychiatric care (Mayo Clinic Staff, 2017), and healthcare professionals and patients from some cultures, especially Asian cultures, may be reluctant to give or accept a psychiatric diagnosis.

Unfortunately, even healthcare professionals perpetuate the stigma of mental illness. Bolton (2003), a hospital liaison psychiatrist, voiced his distress regarding healthcare professionals' negative perceptions of patients with mental illnesses. He stated that professionals who refer patients to him often say things such as "we've got another nutter for you" (pp. 104–105). Bolton followed up this concern by saying he no longer accepts this sort of language and stigmatization without tactfully educating the user of such language about its inappropriateness. Bolton outlined common stigmatizing beliefs about mental illness:

- People with mental illnesses are dangerous to others.
- Mental illness is feigned or imaginary.
- Mental illness reflects a weakness of character.
- Disorders are self-inflicted.
- The outcome is poor.
- Disorders are incurable.
- It is difficult to communicate with people who have mental illness.

Goffman (1963), a sociologist, did landmark work regarding stigma, contrasting the normal people of society with stigmatized people, or people who may be called the discreditables. He proposed that people with a particular stigma, such as mental illness, have common experiences in terms of how they learn to view their stigma and their very conception of self. Goffman described this phenomenon as a common moral career. These common experiences, or moral careers, involve four phases ranging from having an inborn stigma to developing a stigma later in life.

However, regardless of the progression of the moral careers of stigmatized persons, it is a significant point in time when these persons realize they possess the stigma and are exposed to new relationships with others who also have the same stigma. Goffman proposed that on first meeting other people who the stigmatized person must accept as his own, there often is a feeling of ambivalence but eventually a sense of identity develops.

It is important for nurses who practice in mental health settings to understand the meaning of relationships among psychiatric patients. If nurses become sensitive to the lived experiences of psychiatric patients and the therapeutic value of these patients' relationships with other people who are mentally ill, it ultimately may help to create a more supportive environment for these patients. Psychiatric patients who are marked with a stigma by society, their own families, and even healthcare professionals may feel a sense of camaraderie with other people who have experienced similar moral careers.

Frequently, nurses find patient-to-patient camaraderie disconcerting and sometimes attempt to minimize the support psychiatric patients develop among themselves. However, psychiatric patients often find encouragement in these relationships, as illustrated by the comments of a former psychiatric patient, Irit Shimrat (see **BOX 10-3**). Although sound judgment on the part of nurses is essential when assessing safety factors and the therapeutic value of relationships among psychiatric patients, compassionate nursing care involves being sensitive to the stigma experienced by psychiatric patients and how this stigma affects patients' perceptions of other people who have lived through similar experiences.

▶ Advocacy

There often is a fragmentation in mental health care when patient treatment is based on the medical model. Nurses are in a unique

BOX 10-3   A Common Moral Career

Former psychiatric patient Irit Shimrat stated the following:

> What saved me was the help I got from other patients, and the fact that I was able to help them. By showing each other compassion, by listening to each other, against all odds, we were able to remember that we were still alive. . . . When I'm feeling terrified of the world, I can talk to someone else who's been terrified of the world, but who isn't right now, and they can free me from that terror. The stories we tell ourselves about the world and our place in it have a huge influence on how we feel and what we're capable of. When people who have been labeled mentally ill can talk to each other about these stories, without fear of being judged, the feedback we get, and give, can be enormously liberating.

Shimrat, I. (2003, July/August). Freedom. *Off Our Backs*, 55, 18.

ETHICAL REFLECTION

After returning from the Iraq–Afghanistan Wars, soldiers stated they were uncomfortable seeking psychiatric treatment for posttraumatic stress disorder. One soldier interviewed on National Public Radio stated that his officers pressured him to cancel his mental health counseling appointments to participate in scheduled military maneuvers.

Research and discuss sources of discrimination and stigma associated with soldiers' postwar psychiatric treatment.

position to act as patient advocates in bridging the fragmentary divide between medicalized and holistic care. Advocacy in nursing involves nurses championing the needs and well-being of individual patients, families, groups, communities, or populations. According to Seedhouse (2000), "more than any other branch of nursing, mental health nursing exposes the rift between nursing's nurturing instincts and medicine's/society's insistence that aberrant behaviors are contained" (p. 153).

Nurses must try to bring to the forefront the idea that there need not be a sharp distinction between physical or biomedical health promotion and prevention and mental health promotion and prevention. This integration can be accomplished by nurse-led dialogue among the whole team of healthcare providers caring for psychiatric patients. Nurses must be open to listening and sensing the feelings, emotions, and goals of all members of the team while

practicing existential advocacy as described by Sally Gadow. According to Gadow (as cited in Bishop & Scudder, 2001), "the nurse as existential advocate does not merely help patients choose what they want—for example, the drug user who wants to be as 'high' as possible while in the hospital. The existential advocate is there to help patients recognize and realize their best selves, given their situation" (pp. 76–77).

With regard to stigma, Goffman (1963) proposed that people who are stigmatized often have a turning point in their lives. Sometimes, this turning point is recognized when it occurs, but sometimes it is recognized only in retrospect. Goffman stated that the turning point is an

> isolating, incapacitating experience, often a period of hospitalization, which comes later to be seen as the time when the individual was able to think through his problem, learn about himself, sort out his situation, and arrive at a new understanding of what is important and worth seeking in life. (p. 40)

Because nurses are unaware of when patients are ready to undergo such a significant or potentially life-changing event, nurses must constantly cultivate a humanistic environment or milieu that facilitates the personal growth of patients. Smart (2003) stated that he realized it is best to think of sanity as occurring along a continuum rather than as a them versus me event.

▸ Boundaries

A discussion of boundaries is particularly relevant to psychiatric/mental health nursing because of the vulnerability of mentally ill patients and the importance of trust in supporting therapeutic nurse–patient relationships. Boundary violations occur when a nurse or patient exceeds the therapeutic limits of the nurse–patient relationship. Professional boundaries are specifically covered in provision 2.4 of the American Nurses Association *Code of Ethics for Nurses with Interpretive Statements* (ANA, 2015). By keeping in mind that "nurse-patient and nurse-colleague relationships have as their foundation the promotion, protection, and restoration of health and the alleviation of pain and suffering" (ANA, 2015, p. 7), nurses can find guidance in maintaining professional boundaries. Nurses must ask themselves if the actions they take, the words they say, and the behaviors they model are in the best interest of patients; in other words, nurses must be very conscious of how their behavior might affect and be interpreted by patients. It cannot be assumed that psychiatric patients will react the same way other patients might react to the behaviors of the nurse.

ETHICAL REFLECTION

In what ways do you believe the media has contributed to the stigma of mental illness? In what ways might this media influence also affect the way the public views mental health nurses?

Concepts underlying nurse–patient boundaries include power, choice, and trust (Maes, 2003). The asymmetry of power in favor of the nurse can place nurses in a position of influencing the decisions of patients. Patients need complete information to make choices, and nurses must help patients receive the information they need. Though psychiatric patients may try to test nurses' good judgment by pushing nurse–patient boundaries to inappropriate limits, overall, patients trust nurses to have the knowledge, prudence, and skill necessary to provide them with ethical and competent care. Nurses must be faithful to that trust.

Potential violations of nurse–patient boundaries can involve gifts, intimacy, inappropriate limits, neglect, abuse, and restraints (Maes, 2003). Gifts often are nontherapeutic in psychiatric/mental health nurse–patient relationships, and gifts given to nurses by patients need to be considered in terms of why the gift was given and its value and whether the gift might provide therapeutic value for the patient. Gifts should not influence the type of care provided by the nurse or the quality of the nurse–patient relationship. General guidelines for the inappropriate acceptance of gifts from patients include situations in which the gift is expensive; the patient is seeking approval by giving the gift; the gift is given early in the relationship, which may set the stage for lax boundaries; the nurse does not feel comfortable accepting the gift but does so because of not wanting to hurt the patient's feelings; or the nurse is having difficulty setting boundaries (Corey et al., 2003). Nurses should never accept money as tips or gifts.

The cultural implications of gift giving also need to be considered. For example, patients from Asian cultures may view giving an inexpensive gift as a sign of gratitude and respect, whereas nurses responding from a Western perspective may view the taking of a gift from a patient as a boundary violation. If a nurse refused an inexpensive gift from an Asian patient, the patient may be insulted (Corey et al., 2003). It is important for nurses to keep ethical boundaries in mind, but sometimes, inflexibility is damaging to therapeutic relationships. Each situation must be evaluated individually and in accordance with the policies of the employing healthcare facility. Guidelines about accepting gifts is summed up as follows in Provision 2.4 of the ANA's (2015) *Code of Ethics for Nurses with Interpretive Statements:*

> Accepting gifts from patients is generally not appropriate; factors to consider include the intent, the value, the nature, and the timing of the gift, as well as the patient's own cultural norms. When a gift is offered, facility policy should be followed. Dating and sexually intimate relationships with patients are always prohibited. (p. 7)

Also, a violation of intimacy might occur if a nurse inappropriately shares information with other people in ways that violate a patient's privacy. The nature of nurses' work with both patients and colleagues has a personal element, but nurse–patient relationships are not to be confused with the common definition of friendship (ANA, 2001, 2015). Nurses are not discouraged from having a caring relationship with patients, patients' families, or colleagues; however, caring and jeopardizing professional boundaries are two very distinct issues. Although carefully chosen self-disclosure is sometimes therapeutic, revealing personal information to psychiatric patients often is detrimental to patient care. Nurses are cautioned to observe limits that prevent either the nurse or the patient from becoming uncomfortable in their relationship (ANA, 2001). Psychiatric patients are best helped when they remain the focus of nursing care rather than when attention is diverted to the personal experiences of nurses.

Physically, chemically, and environmentally restraining patients, which is discussed in most psychiatric/mental health nursing textbooks, can provide a major pitfall for nurses in terms of boundary violations. Nurses are responsible for providing safe, reasonable, and compassionate care to all patients according to appropriate ethical codes, professional standards, state nurse practice acts, and organizational policies. Nurses must do everything possible to prevent or stop patient abuse in whatever form it occurs, whether the abuse is perpetrated by a patient's family or a member of the healthcare team. The safe and appropriate use of physical, chemical, and environmental restraints is a particularly important issue that nurses must be continually aware of during patient care. It is essential that nurses know the policies of their employer and the standards set by professional organizations and accrediting agencies to safeguard patients. A few of the guiding principles of using seclusion and restraint published by the American Psychiatric Nurses Association (2018) include:

- Being treated with respect and dignity is a person's right.
- Staff convenience is never a valid reason to use seclusion or restraint.
- Minimal time of use and least restrictive measures are necessary.
- Physical safety must be assured while affording patients maximum freedom of movement.
- The patient must be continuously observed.

Whose Needs Are Being Served?

An issue closely tied to relationship boundaries and the restraint of patients is the ethical obligation of determining whose needs are being served in professional–patient relationships. When discussing counselor–client relationships, Corey (2005) proposed counselors need to be aware of when they may be placing their own needs before those of their client. This type of assessment and awareness of needs is equally applicable in nurse–patient relationships. It is easy for nurses to unintentionally become absorbed in their own self-interests during day-to-day patient care. Personal needs of the nurse that may be placed before the patient's needs include the following:

- The need for control and power
- The need to be nurturing and helpful

- The need to change others in the direction of our own values
- The need to persuade
- The need for feeling adequate, particularly when it becomes overly important that the client confirm our competence
- The need to be respected and appreciated (Corey, 2005, p. 38)

ETHICAL REFLECTION

What would you say to a patient who offered you his dead mother's pearl necklace? What would you do if a coworker told you that she accepted jewelry from a patient?

Nurses may have to take special care to keep in mind that patients' needs are to be placed first. As is stated in the second provision of the ANA's (2015) *Code of Ethics for Nurses with Interpretive Statements*, "the nurse's primary commitment is to the recipients of nursing and healthcare services—patient or client—whether individuals, families, groups, communities or populations" (p. 5). Because of the psychological nature of their conditions, psychiatric/mental health patients may be particularly vulnerable to nurses placing them in dependent positions.

Psychotropic drugs sometimes make patients more manageable for nurses, which raises the question of whose needs are being served: the nurse's or the patient's? Similar to the earlier point regarding nurses' complicity in the diagnostic labeling of patients, nurses have an important role in determining the type, frequency, and dose of medications ordered for and administered to psychiatric patients, particularly in hospital settings. Nurses are the professionals who spend the most time with hospitalized psychiatric patients, and physicians often base treatment decisions on nurses' formal or informal comments, reports, and documentation. Nurses must be aware of whose needs are being served, and they must

use careful reflection in determining how they choose to represent patients' behaviors and conditions to other people.

ETHICAL REFLECTION

What questions might nurses ask to evaluate their motives before giving PRN medications to psychiatric patients? What could a nurse do to positively influence a coworker who tends to oversedate patients because she likes patients to be easy to handle?

Privacy, Confidentiality, and Privileged Communication

Although privacy, confidentiality, and privileged communication are similar concepts, there are important differences to be considered. Confidentiality and privileged communication are both issues of a patient's right to privacy; confidentiality usually is more associated with ethics, whereas privileged communication pertains more to the legal nature of provider–patient relationships (Corey et al., 2003).

Privacy

The concept of privacy began receiving attention in the 1920s, when the U.S. Supreme Court addressed the liberty interest of families with regard to decision making about their children (Beauchamp & Childress, 2019). The court's rulings were designed to protect part of a person's private life from state intrusion, which incidentally is also the foundation for overturning restrictive abortion laws in 1973. However, the right to privacy cannot be reduced to a narrow context of having a right to act autonomously. In addition to autonomy, the rights that fall within the boundaries of

privacy include a person's right to be protected from no more than limited physical and informational access by others. One function of the Health Information Portability and Accountability Act of 1996 (HIPAA) is to protect patient's privacy (see **BOX 10-4**).

Allen (as cited in Beauchamp & Childress, 2019) described four types of privacy that address limited personal access:

1. Informational privacy: Communication of information
2. Physical privacy: With regard to personal spaces
3. Decisional privacy: With regard to personal choices

4. Proprietary privacy: Property interests, including interests with regard to bodily tissues, one's name, and so forth

Beauchamp and Childress added a fifth type of privacy to Allen's list: *relational* or *associational* privacy. This type of privacy represents the context of family and intimate relationships in which people collaborate to make decisions.

The value placed on privacy varies among situations and people. Sometimes, for example, persons may feel comfortable with other people knowing they have a psychiatric condition, but they are not comfortable with sharing the

---

BOX 10-4 How Well Do You Know HIPAA?

1. May mental health practitioners or other specialists provide therapy to patients in a group setting where other patients and family members are present?
2. Does HIPAA allow a healthcare provider to communicate with a patient's family, friends, or other persons who are involved in the patient's care?
3. When does mental illness or another mental condition constitute incapacity under the Privacy Rule? For example, what if a patient who is experiencing temporary psychosis or is intoxicated does not have the capacity to agree or object to a healthcare provider sharing information with a family member, but the provider believes the disclosure is in the patient's best interests?
4. If a healthcare provider knows that a patient with a serious mental illness has stopped taking a prescribed medication, can the provider tell the patient's family members?
5. When does HIPAA allow a doctor to notify an individual's family, friends, or caregivers that a patient has overdosed?
6. If an adult patient who may pose a danger to self stops coming to psychotherapy sessions and does not respond to attempts to make contact, does HIPAA permit the therapist to contact a family member to check on the patient's well-being even if the patient has told the therapist that they do not want information shared with that person?
7. When does HIPAA allow a hospital to notify an individual's family, friends, or caregivers that a patient who has been hospitalized for a psychiatric hold has been admitted or discharged?
8. Does HIPAA permit a doctor to contact a patient's family or law enforcement if the doctor believes that the patient might hurt herself or someone else?
9. What constitutes a "serious and imminent" threat that would permit a healthcare provider to disclose PHI [protected health information] to prevent harm to the patient, another person, or the public without the patient's authorization or permission?
10. What options do family members of an adult patient with mental illness have if they are concerned about the patient's mental health and the patient refuses to agree to let a healthcare provider share information with the family?

Find complete answers at U.S. Department of Health and Human Services. (2017). *HIPAA FAQs for professionals*. https://www.hhs.gov/hipaa/for -professionals/faq/index.html

exact nature of the condition. Clinton and colleagues (2013) called one means of violating mental health patients' privacy *patient-targeted Googling (PTG)*. These authors informally surveyed some of their psychiatrist colleagues and found most of them Googled their patients. The wide availability of information on the internet and the generally anonymous ability to access it has made it easier than in the past to delve into patients' private lives. One might consider PTG as analogous to purposely driving by a patient's home, which most healthcare professionals would agree is unethical. Currently, there are no professional guidelines about this emerging practice. Nurses need to err on the side of strictly maintaining a patient's privacy unless there is a justifiable reason for privacy to be violated, such as a duty to warn (see the following "Privileged Communication" section).

Confidentiality

In healthcare ethics, confidentiality is one of the oldest moral commitments, dating back to the Hippocratic Oath (Gillon, 2001). **Confidentiality**, or nondisclosure of information, involves limits on the communication of "any information a nurse obtains about a patient in the context of the nurse–patient relationship" (Westrick, 2014, p. 77). It includes limits on the communication of information related to any of the five types of privacy previously listed. Confidentiality is one of the most important ethical precepts in psychiatric/mental health nursing because the therapeutic nurse–patient relationship is grounded in trust.

Privileged Communication

Whereas confidentiality involves a professional duty not to disclose certain information, **privilege** provides relief from having to disclose information in court proceedings (Smith-Bell & Winslade, 2003). Patients have a legal right to believe their communication

with nurses will be kept confidential, but there are limits to confidentiality in psychiatric/mental health practice. Limits to both confidentiality and privilege permit disclosure of information by the nurse when the following circumstances arise:

- Patients are a threat to themselves (suicide, for example) or to identifiable others (duty to warn).
- Statutes require the disclosure of certain happenings, such as abuse, rape, incest, or other crimes.
- The patient consents to release of the information.
- A court mandates the release.
- The information is needed for other caregivers to provide care to the patient, that is, when certain people have a need to know information (Corey, 2005; Westrick, 2014).

Nurses cannot disclose patient information to unidentified or unauthorized telephone callers or to relatives, significant others, or friends of the patient without the patient's consent (Westrick, 2014). Nurses should not disclose information via "social media or electronic messaging" (p. 77).

In some cases, nurses may have a **duty to warn** that involves "a professional duty to disclose confidential information to protect an identifiable victim" (Westrick, 2014, p. 81). Documentation by nurses of patient threats is necessary, but this may not be enough in some cases. Nurses also may have a duty to warn appropriate authorities about threats made by patients or even to warn the specific person or persons targeted by the threats. The threatened person must be identifiable and state laws vary (Keltner & Steele, 2019). This duty is weighed by viewing it as a dilemma between respecting a patient's privacy and respecting society's need to be informed about acts that are dangerous to citizens (Everstine et al., 2003). The duty is based on the case of *Tarasoff v. Board of Regents of the University of California.*

LEGAL PERSPECTIVE: TARASOFF V. BOARD OF REGENTS OF THE UNIVERSITY OF CALIFORNIA

In August 1969, a voluntary outpatient, Prosenjit Poddar, was being counseled at the student health center at the University of California, Berkeley, campus. The patient threatened to kill a woman (Tatiana Tarasoff) who was unnamed but who was identifiable to the therapist. The therapist warned the campus police about the threat. The police spoke with Poddar and deemed him to be "rational" and therefore, did not take action to warn Ms. Tarasoff. The therapist continued to pursue the issue, but Ms. Tarasoff was not warned of the threat and was later killed by Poddar. Her family sued the Board of Regents and the university staff for failing to warn the victim. In 1976, the California Supreme Court ruled in favor of the parents. The court proclaimed: "The protective privilege ends where the public peril begins" (cited in Corey et al., 2003, p. 347).

■ Check the duty to warn law in your state.

Data from Corey, G., Corey, M. S., & Callanan, P. (2003). *Issues and ethics in the helping professions*. Wadsworth Group-Brooks/Cole.

▶ Decisional Capacity

According to Beauchamp and Childress (2019), some people distinguish competence and capacity based on who is making the determination; that is, capacity is assessed by healthcare professionals, and competence is determined within the court system. Singer (2003) defined competence as "a group of capacities" (p. 152). Some people propose that for all practical purposes, the consequences of the determination of capacity versus competence are basically the same (Grisso & Appelbaum, 1998). In psychiatric care, both capacity and competence are related to questions of whether patients have

a right to consent to and refuse treatment, and they are closely associated with the principle of autonomy.

Statutory Authority to Treat

Involuntary commitment poses ethical and legal problems for psychiatric healthcare professionals. Based on a general social policy of deinstitutionalization, involuntary hospitalization decisions can be made only after less restrictive options have failed or carefully been determined not to be a viable option (Corey et al., 2003). The decision usually is made based on a person being a danger to self; a danger to others; and in some states, being gravely disabled. Each state jurisdiction has statutes that allow psychiatrists to hold persons involuntarily for psychiatric treatment, and healthcare professionals are responsible for following their state's particular laws and regulations (Corey et al., 2003; Jonsen et al., 2022; Keltner & Steele, 2019). If a patient is determined by a psychiatrist to be incompetent, state statutes can be followed for a temporary involuntary commitment, which is legal in all states. Court proceedings are then initiated to extend the involuntary treatment or commitment. This legal process is expedited while the person is being temporarily held involuntarily.

This process begins with a presumption of competency (Dempski, 2009). When it is determined by a psychiatrist that the person exhibits a lack of decision-making capacity, a petition is filed with the court to determine competency. The person receives a court-appointed guardian or legal counsel and undergoes psychological testing procedures. A hearing is scheduled, and evidence is presented about the person's ability to handle personal affairs and understand the consequences of personal decisions. Negotiations are conducted with the aim of determining the least restrictive alternative for the person's care and treatment. Outcomes of the hearing can result in a dismissal of the petition, the appointment of limited guardianship, or the appointment of complete guardianship.

These outcomes may be appealed, and a restoration hearing can be held later if the person's circumstances change and warrant a removal of guardianship. This process is often inappropriately called a "medical hold" (Jonsen et al., 2022, p. 104). The psychiatric commitment process does not automatically include an authorization to treat a patient involuntarily for medical, in addition to psychiatric, conditions. A legally authorized appointee must also be specially assigned to make medical decisions other than those that are determined to be for a life-saving emergency, in which an implied consent is sufficient.

Competence and Informed Consent

Competence and informed consent are intricately connected. Informed consent, as required by legal authorities, is impossible in situations involving incompetent patients (Singer, 2003). A patient, even when involuntarily committed, has a right to refuse treatment, such as psychotropic medications, until or unless the patient has been deemed incompetent by formal legal proceedings or in an emergency situation if the patient is violent. This right to refuse medications and treatment is based on the Constitutional right to privacy. In the case of *Rivers v. Katz*, the New York State Court of Appeals established there are limited circumstances in which a patient's right to refuse unwanted treatment can be overridden—only on the determination that a patient is a danger to self or other people. Patients may not be prevented from refusing medications based on healthcare professionals' desire to create a therapeutic environment, for the convenience of hospital staff, or to facilitate the process of deinstitutionalization.

There are no uniform standards that can be used to determine competence, although it is accepted that incompetence is founded on cognitive impairment (Berg et al., as cited in Singer, 2003). Brody (1988) outlined general criteria of competency that also are applicable with regard to psychiatric patients. These criteria include the following:

- The ability to receive information from surroundings
- The capacity to remember the information received
- The ability to make a decision and give a reason for it
- The ability to use the relevant information in making the decision
- The ability to appropriately assess the relevant information (pp. 101–102)

To this list, Singer (2003) added the capacity to participate constructively in discussions with the caregiver regarding treatment, including the "ability to engage in mutual questioning and answering" (p. 153). Singer called this supplementary capacity of communicative interchange "dialogic reciprocity."

LEGAL PERSPECTIVE: MENTAL ILLNESS AND THE U.S. PRISON SYSTEM

The largest jail system in the U.S. is the Los Angeles County jail. This jail also has the distinction of being described as the largest mental health system in the world (Keltner & Steele, 2019; Kiefer, 2021).

Psychiatric Advance Directives

The Patient Self-Determination Act (PSDA) enacted by the federal government in 1990 has drawn focused attention to patients' right to autonomy in making healthcare decisions. The **psychiatric advance directive (PAD)** developed as an outcome of the PSDA. States' recognition of the right of patients to make advance directives for health care allows for some form of direction for psychiatric care. The National Resource Center on Psychiatric Advance Directives (2021) provides comprehensive information about PADs and statutes by state. Competent psychiatric patients who want to direct their psychiatric care, when and if they later lose their capacity to voice their treatment choices, may complete a PAD. A PAD also can be used by a person to choose a healthcare proxy.

LEGAL PERSPECTIVE: PADS

Visit the National Resource Center on Psychiatric Advance Directives website and answer the following questions based on information on this site.

- What is contained in your state's statute regarding PADs?
- How does a person create a PAD?
- When is a patient considered to be "incapable"?
- Will the PAD be followed if someone is involuntarily committed to a facility?
- How does a PAD differ from generic advance directives for health?

Person-Centered Approach

The concepts of humanistic psychology and existentialism form the basis of psychologist Carl Rogers's person-centered approach (Corey, 2005). According to Rogers (1980), the development of person is the central goal of any person-centered relationship. For a growth-promoting environment to exist in the relationship, three conditions are necessary: (1) genuineness or realness; (2) acceptance, caring, or prizing; and (3) empathic understanding. The nurse who employs the element of genuineness or realness does not maintain a distant professional facade with the patient— the nurse truly experiences the feelings that are occurring in the relationship. The nurse who is exhibiting Rogers's second condition

of a therapeutic relationship maintains an attitude of unconditional positive regard for a patient. The patient is prized in a total way, and whatever feelings are occurring are accepted. Acceptance of the patient is not conditional. The last of Rogers's facilitative factors, empathic understanding, is a deep sensitivity to the patient's feelings, both those feelings on the level of awareness and those below. The professional nurse is able to sense the personal meanings of the patient's experience and communicates this understanding to the patient.

Humanistic Nursing Practice Theory

Paterson and Zderad first published their humanistic nursing practice theory in 1976, when nurses were in the midst of assertiveness training as a result of the women's movement in the United States (Moccia, 1988). Moccia proposed the power of Paterson and Zderad's theory involves authentic dialogue with patients, students, and other healthcare professionals. According to Paterson and Zderad (1988), humanistic nursing emphasizes both the art and science of nursing. "Humanistic nursing embraces more than a benevolent technically competent subject–object one-way relationship guided by a nurse on behalf of another" (p. 3). Nursing, rather, involves a responsible searching for nurse–patient two-way interactions that receive their meaning from and are grounded in the nurse's and patient's existential experiences, or the experiences of living. A brief overview of Paterson and Zderad's perspectives about the domain of nursing—person, nurse (nursing), health, environment—provides some clarification of their theory, which can be used imaginatively by nurses in moral psychiatric/mental health practice.

Persons (including patients and nurses) have the freedom to make choices. Persons have individual, unique views of the world; are adequate, having the capacity to hope and envision alternatives to what is immediately apparent; have the capacity for authentic presence and intersubjective relatedness; and have meaningful personal histories, although their histories do not control them.

Nursing is an art–science, meaning that nursing is derived from subjective, objective, and intersubjective experiences. Nursing is a form of unique knowledge that is developed through dialogical human processes. Finally, nursing is both being and doing, with a focus on being present with another and engaging in two-way dialogue.

Health does not always mean the absence of disease. The nurse's aim is to provide comfort to patients, with comfort conceptualized as being all that one can be at a particular point in time. Nurses try to promote well-being and more-being of others, emphasizing that persons are adequate as they are (well-being) but are free to become more than they are (more-being).

Environment, the final part of the domain, focuses on time and space, the here and now, or the connectedness of past, present, and future. It also focuses on the nursing situation, which includes the whole world of people and things, a world that is more than just the patient and the nurse—the all-at-once or an awareness of all of the emotions, values, and experiences that work together to increase wisdom, a community of persons striving toward a common center, and a complementary synthesis or living out the tension between the objective scientific world and the subjective and intersubjective domains of nursing (O'Connor, 1993; Paterson & Zderad, 1988).

Human-to-Human Relationship Model

The human-to-human relationship model, developed by Joyce Travelbee, is based on her experiences in psychiatric nursing and grounded in the philosophy of existentialism. Travelbee (1971) proposed that nurses must possess a body of knowledge and know how to use it and must learn to use themselves therapeutically

if helping relationships are to be established. The phases leading to the establishment of human-to-human relationships, as described by Travelbee, can be used for ethical practice in psychiatric/mental health nursing. These phases are as follows:

1. The phase of the original encounter: First impressions of both the patient and nurse are perceived. The nurse must be aware of value judgments and feelings.
2. The phase of emerging identities: A bond is established between the nurse and the patient. There is again an emphasis on awareness by the nurse of how the patient is being perceived. Nurses must develop an awareness and a valuing of the uniqueness of others.
3. The phase of empathy: This is a conscious process of sharing in another person's experiences.
4. The phase of sympathy: In this phase, the nurse progresses further than empathy and wants to alleviate a patient's distress.
5. The phase of rapport: Rapport is the end goal of all nursing endeavors; it is a process, an experience, or a happening; it is the human-to-human relationship. (Rangel et al., 1998; Travelbee, 1971)

Recognizing Inherent Human Possibilities

Rogers (1980) believed there is an underlying movement toward inherent possibilities that all human beings exhibit. He proposed that it is a self-actualizing tendency for complete development and life is an active process that moves toward maintaining, enhancing, and reproducing, even when conditions are not favorable. Rogers compared this view of human flourishing to a story about sprouting potatoes he observed in his youth. He noticed that even when potatoes were stored in the basement during winter, they would produce pale (as opposed to healthy green) sprouts that twisted toward what little light they might have. Life was still trying to flourish, although conditions were not favorable. Rogers's words very eloquently compare how these potatoes can be likened to psychiatric patients, or any patients, whose lives nurses touch. Rogers (1980) said:

> In dealing with clients whose lives have been terribly warped, in working with men and women on the back wards of state hospitals, I often think of those potato sprouts. So unfavorable have been the conditions in which these people have developed that their lives often seem abnormal, twisted, scarcely human. Yet, the directional tendency in them can be trusted. The clue to understanding their behavior is that they are striving, in the only ways that they perceive as available to them, to move toward growth, toward becoming. To healthy persons, the results may seem bizarre and futile, but they are life's desperate attempt to become itself. (p. 119)

KEY POINTS

- Psychiatry may be thought of as a moral discipline rather than a medical discipline because it is often involved with subjective experiences and relationships rather than objective tests and diseases.
- Nurses must be sensitive to the moral implications of using diagnostic labels when referring to patients because diagnostic labels can be a source of harm and distress for patients.
- People in society often stigmatize mentally ill persons, and healthcare professionals sometimes perpetuate this stigma. Even people who care for mentally ill persons are often stigmatized.
- Confidentiality and privileged communication are issues of a patient's right to privacy. Confidentiality is usually thought of in ethical terms, whereas privileged communication pertains more to legal protection.
- In some situations, there are limits to a patient's right to confidentiality and privileged communication, such as when healthcare professionals have a duty to warn identifiable others of threats made by patients.
- The decision to involuntarily hospitalize a person is usually based on the person being a danger to self or to others and, in some states, being gravely disabled.
- Humanistic nursing care is grounded in the belief that through genuine, intersubjective experiences and relationships, nurses can help patients to be free to become all that they can be.

References

Amador, X. (2012). *I AM NOT SICK I don't need help.* (10th anniversary edition). Vida Press.

American Nurses Association. (2001). *Code of ethics for nurses with interpretive statements.*

American Nurses Association. (2015). *Code of ethics for nurses with interpretive statements.*

American Psychiatric Nurses Association. (2018). *APNA position statement on the use of seclusion and restraint.* https://www.apna.org/resources/apna-seclusion-restraint-position-paper/

Beauchamp, T. L., & Childress, J. F. (2019). *Principles of biomedical ethics* (8th ed.). Oxford University Press.

Beresford, P. (2002). Thinking about "mental health": Towards a social model. *Journal of Mental Health, 11*(6), 581–584.

Bishop, A., & Scudder, J. (2001). *Nursing ethics: Holistic caring practice* (2nd ed.). Jones and Bartlett Publishers.

Bolton, J. (2003). Reducing the stigma of mental illness. *Student British Medical Journal, 11,* 104–105.

Brody, B. A. (1988). *Life and death decision making.* Oxford University Press.

Clinton, B. K., Silverman, B. C., & Brendel, D. H. (2013). Patient-targeted Googling: The ethics of searching online for patient information. In D. A. Sisti, A. L.

Caplan, & H. Rimon-Greenspan (Eds.), *Applied ethics in mental health care: An interdisciplinary reader* (loc. 7456–7863). MIT Press.

Corey, G. (2005). *Theory and practice of counseling and psychotherapy* (7th ed.). Brooks/Cole-Thomson Learning.

Corey, G., Corey, M. S., & Callanan, P. (2003). *Issues and ethics in the helping professions*. Wadsworth Group-Brooks/Cole.

Crowe, M. (2000). Psychiatric diagnosis: Some implications for mental health nurse care. *Journal of Advanced Nursing, 31*(3), 583–589.

Dempski, K. (2009). Emergency psychiatric admissions. In S. J. Westrick & K. Dempski (Eds.), *Essentials of nursing law and ethics* (pp. 126–129). Jones and Bartlett Publishers.

Dickenson, D., & Fulford, K. W. M. (2000). *In two minds: A casebook of psychiatric ethics*. Oxford University Press.

Everstine, L., Everstine, D. S., Heymann, G. M., True, R. H., Frey, D. H., Johnson, H. G., & Richard, H. (2003). Privacy and confidentiality in psychotherapy. In D. N. Bersoff (Ed.), *Ethical conflicts in psychology* (3rd ed., pp. 162–164). American Psychological Association.

Frances, A. (2013a). *Essentials of psychiatric diagnosis: Responding to the challenge of* DSM-5 (Rev. ed.) [Kindle version]. Guilford Press.

Frances, A. (2013b). *Saving normal* [Kindle version]. HarperCollins.

Gillon, R. (2001). Confidentiality. In H. Kuhse & P. Singer (Eds.), *A companion to bioethics* (pp. 425–431). Blackwell.

Goffman, E. (1963). *Stigma: Notes on the management of spoiled identity*. Simon & Schuster.

Green, G., Hayes, C., Dickinson, D., Whittaker, A., & Gilheany, B. (2003). A mental health service users' perspective to stigmatization. *Journal of Mental Health, 12*(3), 223–234.

Grisso, T., & Appelbaum, P. S. (1998). *Assessing competence to consent to treatment: A guide for physicians and other health care professionals*. Oxford University Press.

Halter, M. J. (2002). Stigma in psychiatric nursing. *Perspectives in Psychiatric Care, 38*(1), 23–28.

Hobson, J. A., & Leonard, J. A. (2001). *Out of its mind: Psychiatry in crisis—A call to reform*. Perseus.

Jonsen, A. R., Siegler, M., & Winslade, W. J. (2022). *Clinical ethics* (9th ed.) [Kindle edition]. McGraw-Hill.

Keltner, N. L., & Steele, D. (2019). *Psychiatric nursing* (8th ed.). Elsevier.

Kiefer, F. (2021). *From LA jail, two inmates pioneer care for mentally ill peers*. https://www.csmonitor.com /USA/Justice/2021/0518/From-LA-jail-two-inmates -pioneer-care-for-mentally-ill-peers

Knight, M. T. D., Wykes, T., & Hayward, P. (2003). "People don't understand": An investigation of stigma in schizophrenia using interpretative phenomenological analysis (IPA). *Journal of Mental Health, 12*(3), 209–222.

Livesley, W. J. (2010). Confusion and incoherence in the classification of personality disorder: Commentary on the preliminary proposals for *DSM-5*. *Psychological Injury and Law, 3,* 304–313.

Maes, S. (2003). How do you know when professional boundaries have been crossed? *Oncology Nursing Society News, 18*(8), 3–5.

Mayo Clinic Staff. (2017). *Mental health: Overcoming the stigma of mental illness*. https://www.mayoclinic.org /diseases-conditions/mental-illness/in-depth/mental -health/art-20046477

Moccia, P. (1988). Preface. In J. G. Paterson & L. T. Zderad, *Humanistic nursing* (pp. iii–v). National League for Nursing.

Morrison, J. (2014). *DSM-5 made easy: The clinician's guide to diagnosis*. Guilford Press.

National Alliance on Mental Illness. (2021). *Anosognosia*. https://www.nami.org/About-Mental-Illness/Common -with-Mental-Illness/Anosognosia

National Resource Center on Psychiatric Advance Directives. (2021). *State by state info*. https://www .nrc-pad.org

O'Brien, O., Woods, M., & Palmer, C. (2001). The emancipation of nursing practice: Applying anti-psychiatry to the therapeutic community. *Australian and New Zealand Journal of Mental Health Nursing, 10,* 4.

O'Connor, N. (1993). *Paterson and Zderad: Humanistic nursing theory*. Sage.

Paterson, J. G., & Zderad, L. T. (1988). *Humanistic nursing*. National League for Nursing.

Pipher, M. (2003). *Letters to a young therapist: Stories of hope and healing*. Basic Books.

Pouncey, C. L., & Lukens, J. M. (2013). Madness versus badness: The ethical tension between the recovery movement and forensic psychiatry. In D. A. Sisti, A. L. Caplan, & H. Rimon-Greenspan (Eds.), *Applied ethics in mental health care: An interdisciplinary reader* (loc. 5060–5416). MIT Press.

Radden, J. (2002a). Notes towards a professional ethics for psychiatry. *Australian and New Zealand Journal of Psychiatry, 36,* 52–59.

Radden, J. (2002b). Psychiatric ethics. *Bioethics, 16*(5), 397–411.

Rangel, S., Hobble, W. H., Lansinger, T., Magers, J. A., & McKee, N. J. (1998). Joyce Travelbee: Human-to-human relationship model. In A. M. Tomey & M. R. Alligood (Eds.), *Nursing theorists and their work* (4th ed., pp. 364–374). Mosby.

Robbins, B. (2012). *Open letter to the DSM-5*. https://www. ipetitions.com/petition/dsm5/

Rogers, C. R. (1980). *A way of being*. Houghton Mifflin.

Rosen, A., Walter, G., Casey, D., & Hocking, B. (2000). Combating psychiatric stigma: An overview of contemporary initiatives. *Australasian Psychiatry, 8*(1), 19–26.

Schneider, M. R. (2016). Clinical and social contexts of ethical issues in mental health care. *AMA Journal of Ethics, 18*(6), 567–571.

Seedhouse, D. (2000). *Practical nursing philosophy: The universal ethical code.* John Wiley & Sons.

Shimrat, I. (2003, July/August). Freedom. *Off Our Backs, 55,* 18.

Singer, B. J. (2003). Mental illness: Rights, competence, and communication. In G. McGee (Ed.), *Pragmatic bioethics* (2nd ed., pp. 151–162). MIT Press.

Smart, D. (2003, April 7). Take action now to banish mental health prejudices. *Pulse-I-Registrar, 63*(14), 60.

Smith-Bell, M., & Winslade, W. J. (2003). Privacy, confidentiality, and privilege in psychotherapeutic relationships. In D. N. Bersoff (Ed.), *Ethical conflicts in psychology* (3rd ed., pp. 157–161). American Psychological Association.

Sokolowski, R. (1991). The fiduciary relationship and the nature of professions. In E. D. Pellegrino, R. M. Veatch, & J. P. Langan (Eds.), *Ethics, trust, and the professions: Philosophical and cultural aspects* (pp. 23–43). Georgetown University.

Travelbee, J. (1971). *Interpersonal aspects of nursing.* F. A. Davis.

U.S. Department of Health and Human Services. (1999). *Mental health: A report of the surgeon general—executive summary.*

U.S. Department of Health and Human Services. (2017). *HIPAA FAQs for professionals.* https://www.hhs.gov/hipaa/for-professionals/faq/index.html

Verhaeghe, M., & Bracke, P. (2012). Associative stigma among mental health professionals: Implications for professional and service user well-being. *Journal of Health and Social Behavior, 53*(1), 17–32. https//doi.org/10.1177/0022146512439453

Wahl, O. F. (2003). Depictions of mental illnesses in children's media. *Journal of Mental Health, 12*(3), 249–258.

Watts, J., & Priebe, S. (2002). A phenomenological account of users' experiences of assertive community treatment. *Bioethics, 16*(5), 439–454.

Westrick, S. J. (2014). *Essentials of nursing law and ethics* (2nd ed.). Jones & Bartlett Learning.

CHAPTER 11

Public Health Nursing Ethics

Karen L. Rich

OBJECTIVES

After reading this chapter, the reader should be able to do the following:

1. Distinguish a moral community from a population.
2. Apply different ethical approaches to public health nursing issues.
3. Discuss healthcare disparities and identify populations at risk.
4. Analyze ethical issues related to communicable diseases.
5. Analyze ethical issues that may arise during disasters.
6. Identify ethical issues and questions that are outcomes of the Human Genome Project.
7. Explain what it means for a nurse to be a servant leader.

▶ Introduction

In their own `way, public health nurses are contributors to the building of the world. Public health nursing "focuses on improving population health by emphasizing prevention and attending to multiple determinants of health . . . this nursing practice includes advocacy, policy development, and planning, which addresses issues of social justice" (American Public Health Association [APHA], 2013, para. 2). "Public health nursing practice is evidence-based and focuses on promotion of the health of entire populations and prevention of disease, injury, and premature death" (American Nurses Association [ANA], 2013, p. 3).

Population is the term used to describe the recipients of the health promotion and disease and disability prevention care that is the primary focus of public health nursing. In this chapter, a population is defined as a group of people who share at least one common descriptive characteristic but do not necessarily have a collective commitment to a common good. The name used to denote an aggregate within a population often is related to the common characteristics of the people who make up the population, such as *male alcoholics* or *pregnant teenagers*. People within populations may or may not interact or share in a collective dialogue.

The word **community** means different things to different people (see **BOX 11-1**).

BOX 11-1 Community

Community, a word of many connotations—a word overused until its meanings are so diffuse as to be almost useless. Yet the images it evokes, the deep longings and memories it can stir, represent something that human beings have created and recreated since time immemorial, out of our profound need for connection among ourselves and with Mother Earth.

Data from Forsey, H. (1993). Circles of strength: Community alternatives to alienation. New Society, p. 1.

A community is a group of people who have a shared interest in a common good, and members of the group have the potential to share in a collective dialogue about their common good. Membership in the community forms some part of each member's identity. The sharing in a commitment to promote the community's well-being, which transcends individual interests and goals, makes personal relationships within the community moral in nature. A **moral community** is formed by members who care about collectively alleviating the suffering and facilitating the well-being of other members of the community and who may act to do so. Individual persons may be active or inactive members of a moral community.

A moral community can be as large as the global community, whose members are generally committed to the common good and prosperity of the earth's inhabitants, or it can be as small as a community of senior nursing students at a university. The common good of a community of nursing students might be the collective concern about obtaining professional nursing licensure while maintaining individual physical and psychological well-being. The student community accomplishes its goals through the members' shared commitment to providing emotional support to members and to helping one another move toward the successful completion of the National Council Licensure Examination (NCLEX). An even smaller community

is a family that is committed to common goals beyond the individual personal goals of family members.

Members of a community may or may not share close geographic boundaries; however, if members of a community share some type of geographic boundaries, the primary moral connection among the members is typically not based solely on that geography. Nurses, patients, and other people in society are usually members of more than one community. A nurse is a member of the community of registered nurses who are collectively committed to the common good of alleviating patients' suffering and promoting patients' well-being. The same nurse also may be a member of a faith community, a member of a geographic neighborhood community that is interested in the common good and safety of the neighbors, and a member of a parent/guardian–teacher community that is committed to the common good of a population of children.

ETHICAL REFLECTION

- How has community been reflected or not been reflected in behaviors during the Covid-19 pandemic?

▶ Setting the Stage: Public Health Is Controversial

"Public health promotes and protects the health of people and the communities where they live, learn, work and play. While a doctor treats people who are sick, those of us working in public health try to prevent people from getting sick or injured in the first place. We also promote wellness by encouraging healthy behaviors" (APHA, 2021, para. 1–2).

The APHA's (2021) position is that public health is important because it "saves money, improves our quality of life, helps children thrive and reduces human suffering" (para. 5). Therefore, public health, prima facie, seems to be a noncontroversial endeavor. Unfortunately, this is not the case.

As compared to outcomes from treating and curing disease using the medical model, outcomes of public health frequently are not directly recognizable (Schneider, 2021). People who pay the greatest economic cost for public health may not be the biggest recipients of the benefits. Public health activities, regulations, and interventions sometimes interfere with the financial bottom line of some organizations; for example, regulating air pollution affects a power company's revenue, and car safety regulations affect the profit of the automobile industry. Finally, "people are often unwilling to pay short-term costs in order to obtain a long-term benefit" (Schneider, 2021, p. 16). Sexual and reproductive health and safety efforts through public health interventions sometimes raise religious and moral opposition. These are only a few of the reasons underlying controversies about public health.

Historically, public health has been associated with governmental or nonprofit (government-type) agencies. Groups that are suspicious of government interventions into the private lives of U.S. citizens and consistently scan for signs of increasing government power tend to think negatively about things connected with public health. This suspicion leads these groups to pose a slippery slope argument—if the government is given an inch of power, it may take a mile in interfering with individuals' rights to live life as they desire. This negative view of public health exploded during the Covid-19 pandemic. Government distrust was rampant regarding Covid prevention, treatment, and vaccines. Even public health statistics were disputed, and the Centers for Disease Control and Prevention (CDC) and physicians working for the federal government were heavily criticized. Unfortunately, public health experienced political divisiveness and distrust at a time when public health interventions and success were most needed.

It is true that historically public health has not always protected individuals. Government and nonprofit public health organizations have been implicated in public health ethical failures as well as success stories. A few of the many examples of public health ethical failures include the following:

- The unethical Tuskegee syphilis research conducted for 40 years under the direction of the U.S. Public Health Service (Reverby, 2012)
- The failure of the U.S. government to aggressively address the HIV outbreak when it was first identified (Shilts, 2007)
- Accusations that the United Nations' laxness in screening peacekeepers sent to the third-world country of Haiti caused the introduction of cholera after a major Haitian earthquake (Schecter, 2013)

The CDC last outlined 10 public health achievements in its May 28, 2011, *Morbidity and Mortality Weekly Report (MMWR)*. Though particular statistics included in the CDC's data might have changed, the overall information still invokes opportunities for ethical analysis and debate. Covid-19 certainly added another level of ethical controversy to these achievements. Also, keep in mind that the CDC suffered a credibility problem during the Covid pandemic. Seven of the 10 achievements from 2001 to 2010 are discussed below with commentary about current ethical implications and controversy. The ethics commentary and questions provide a good source for debate and reflection.

- Vaccine Preventable Diseases:
  - Achievements cited in the CDC's report:
    - Economic analysis indicated that vaccination of each U.S. birth cohort with the current childhood immunization schedule prevents approximately 42,000 deaths and 20 million cases of disease, with

net savings of nearly $14 billion in direct costs and $69 billion in total societal costs

- Following the introduction of the pneumococcal conjugate vaccine, an estimated 211,000 serious pneumococcal infections and 13,000 deaths were prevented during 2000 to 2008. Routine rotavirus vaccination, implemented in 2006, now prevents an estimated 40,000 to 60,000 rotavirus hospitalizations each year

- Commentary and questions regarding ethical implications and controversy:
  - Vaccines protect the people vaccinated as well as the community. This is a matter of utilitarianism, communitarianism, beneficence, nonmaleficence, and justice.
  - Vaccine hesitancy was becoming widespread even before the Covid-19 pandemic. Parents and guardians express concerns about vaccine-related autism in children. Some of the public as well as healthcare professionals, incorrectly believe the influenza vaccine causes influenza and refuse to receive the vaccination.

- There has been widespread resistance to Covid-19 vaccines, both the traditional vaccine and messenger RNA vaccines. Vaccine hesitancy with the Covid vaccine has many factors including the following:
  - Distrust of government involvement with vaccine manufacturing
  - New technology with vaccine manufacturing
  - Political and media influences and misinformation
  - Belief that vaccination undermines autonomy
  - Greater fear of undermining one's autonomy than risk of death
  - Belief that non-evidence-based prevention interventions, such as

hydroxychloroquine and ivermectin, are better than vaccines

- The cost in lives and health care due to vaccine hesitancy during the Covid pandemic has been enormous. This is a cost born by the U.S. public.
- Unvaccinated people have harmed others through spreading Covid.

Prevention and Control of Infectious Diseases:

- Achievements cited in the CDC's report:
  - 30% reduction from 2001 to 2010 in reported U.S. tuberculosis cases
  - 58% decline from 2001 to 2009 in central line–associated blood stream infections
  - Efforts to extend HIV testing, including recommendations for expanded screening of persons aged 13 to 64 years, increased the number of persons diagnosed with HIV/AIDS and reduced the proportion with late diagnoses
  - CDC predictive models and reports of suspected West Nile virus transmission through blood transfusion spurred a national investigation, leading to the rapid development and implementation of new blood donor screening

- Commentary and questions regarding ethical implications and controversy:
  - Covid-19 was first reported in 2019.
  - There are major controversies about how the Covid-19 pandemic was managed or mismanaged at all levels of the government.
  - How many lives may have been saved and how much suffering and economic losses may have been prevented if the pandemic was managed differently?
  - Did political influences overtake ethical considerations?

- People might ask "Am I my brother and sister's keeper?"
- Has autonomy been prized over beneficence? Should autonomy be prized over beneficence?

Tobacco Control:
- Achievements cited in the CDC's report:
  - Smoke-free laws
  - Decrease in total number of smokers
  - By 2010, the FDA had banned flavored cigarettes, established restrictions on youth access, and proposed larger, more effective graphic warning labels that are expected to lead to a significant increase in quit attempts.
- Commentary and questions regarding ethical implications and controversy:
  - According to the CDC's report in 2011, despite the progress, smoking still results in an economic burden, including medical costs and lost productivity, of approximately $193 billion per year.
  - How do smoke-free laws compare to mask mandates during the Covid pandemic? Is autonomy affected similarly? Are both mandates equally reasonable or unreasonable?
  - The rise of vaping as a substitute to smoking. Mixed messages in the media have placed economics over public health. How have social and other media contributed to this habit? How has strong lobbying affected regulations?

Motor Vehicle Safety:
- Achievements cited in the CDC's report:
  - From 2000 to 2009, while the number of vehicle miles traveled on the nation's roads increased by 8.5%, the death rate related to motor vehicle travel declined

from 14.9 per 100,000 population to 11.0, and the injury rate declined from 1,130 to 722
  - Behavior was improved by protective policies, including effective seat belt and child safety seat legislation
- Commentary and questions regarding ethical implications and controversy:
  - Autonomy is overridden with mandatory seatbelt and child safety seat laws. These laws protect oneself and others, i.e., they are designed to do good (beneficence) using paternalism. They also reduce healthcare costs from injuries that theoretically impact the cost of health care among the greater population. Decreasing healthcare costs for the greater population might leave more money to spend on people without good access to care.
  - Do the above laws that override autonomy to protect people differ from mask and vaccine mandates to prevent Covid infections?

Occupational Safety:
- Achievements cited in the CDC's report:
  - Following widespread dissemination and adoption of best practices by the nursing home industry, Bureau of Labor Statistics data showed a 35% decline in low back injuries in residential and nursing care employees between 2003 and 2009.
  - Because it was an earlier government achievement, occupational safety mandated by the U.S. Department of Labor, Occupational Safety and Health Administration (OSHA) was not mentioned in the CDC's report.
- Commentary and questions regarding ethical implications and controversy:
  - See **BOX 11-2**

BOX 11-2 Covid-19 Healthcare Emergency Temporary Standard (ETS)

The information in this box is taken directly from OSHA's website and links addressing the Covid ETS. Whether or not this standard remains in effect when you read this chapter, learning about this type of standard is important. As of December 27, 2021, OSHA announced "that it intends to continue to work expeditiously to issue a final standard that will protect healthcare workers from COVID-19 hazards and will do so as it also considers its broader infectious disease rulemaking" (para. 2). Note, do not confuse the healthcare ETS with those that focused on Covid-19 vaccination or testing.

On January 21, 2021, President Biden issued an Executive Order that declared that ensuring the health and safety of workers is a national priority and a moral imperative. The order directed the Occupational Safety and Health Administration (OSHA) to take action to reduce the risk that workers may contract COVID-19 in the workplace.

September [2021] Report

To assess the ongoing need for an Emergency Temporary Standard for healthcare and related industries, the Occupational Safety and Health Administration (OSHA) has reviewed the latest guidance, science and data on COVID-19 and has consulted with the Centers for Disease Control and Prevention (CDC) (through the National Institute for Occupational Safety and Health (NIOSH)). OSHA has determined that the requirements of the healthcare ETS released on June 10, 2021, remain necessary to address the grave danger of COVID-19 in health care. OSHA will continue to monitor and assess the need for changes in the healthcare ETS each month.

- The COVID-19 ETS is one standard with multiple sections.
- The ETS is aimed at protecting workers facing the highest COVID-19 hazards—those working in healthcare settings where suspected or confirmed COVID-19 patients are treated. This includes employees in hospitals, nursing homes, and assisted living facilities; emergency responders; home healthcare workers; and employees in ambulatory care facilities where suspected or confirmed COVID-19 patients are treated.
- The ETS exempts fully vaccinated workers from masking, distancing, and barrier requirements when in well- defined areas where there is no reasonable expectation that any person with suspected or confirmed COVID-19 will be present.

Questions

- Review the complete ETS or final standard for healthcare .
- Do you agree that ensuring the health and safety of workers is a moral imperative as President Biden said?
- Is the concept of a moral community relevant to the ETS or final standard?
- Explain the rationale for your answers using ethics language, theories, and approaches. Use this and other chapters in this book, as needed.

U.S. Department of Labor, Occupational Safety and Health Administration (OSHA). (n.d.) *Covid-19 emergency temporary standard (ETS)*. https://www.osha.gov/coronavirus/ets

- Childhood Lead Poisoning Prevention:
  - Achievements cited in the CDC's report:
    - Findings of the National Health and Nutrition Examination Surveys from 1976–1980 to 2003–2008 reveal a steep decline, from 88.2% to 0.9%, in the percentage of children aged 1 to 5 years with blood lead levels ≥ 10 μg/dL
    - The risks for elevated blood lead levels based on socioeconomic status and race also were reduced significantly

- ◦ The economic benefit of lowering lead levels among children by preventing lead exposure is estimated at $213 billion per year
- Commentary and questions regarding ethical implications and controversy:
  - ◦ See Ethical Reflection Box regarding the Flint Michigan water crisis.

Public Health Preparedness and Response During an Emergency, Disaster, or Pandemic:

- Achievements cited in the CDC's report:
  - ◦ From 2006 to 2010, the percentage of Laboratory Response Network labs that passed proficiency testing for bioterrorism threat agents increased from 87% to 95%.
  - ◦ The percentage of state public health laboratories correctly subtyping Escherichia coli O157:H7 and submitting the results into a national reporting system increased from 46% to 69%.
  - ◦ The percentage of state public health agencies prepared to use Strategic National Stockpile material increased from 70% to 98%.
  - ◦ During the 2009 H1N1 influenza pandemic, these improvements in the ability to develop and implement a coordinated public health response in an emergency facilitated the rapid detection and characterization of the outbreak, deployment of laboratory tests, distribution of personal protective equipment from the Strategic National Stockpile, development of a candidate vaccine virus, and widespread administration of the resulting vaccine. These public health interventions prevented an estimated 5 to 10 million cases, 30,000 hospitalizations, and 1,500 deaths.
  - ◦ The President's Emergency Plan for AIDS Relief clinics were used to rapidly deliver treatment following the 2010 cholera outbreak in Haiti.

Commentary and questions regarding ethical implications and controversy:

- The response to the 2009 H1N1 influenza pandemic has mixed reviews from people and organizations, including the Department of Health and Human Services (HHS, 2012), which published a retrospective review of preparedness and response. Below are a few areas that HHS noted that need improvement:
  - ◦ Challenges in timeliness and widely distributing surveillance data
  - ◦ The 2009 influenza pandemic raised concerns about the need for better medical surge guidelines and standards
  - ◦ There were no methods to track school and workplace absenteeism
  - ◦ There was too much variability among states in distribution of antiviral medications
  - ◦ Influenza testing capabilities for the H1N1 virus were insufficient to help control infection
  - ◦ Dependence on egg-based vaccine technology for the vaccine that affected timeliness of production
  - ◦ Projections regarding the timing of vaccine availability changed frequently and undermined trust
  - ◦ Confusion about who was eligible for the vaccine
  - ◦ Disparities in vaccination with racial and ethnic minorities receiving fewer vaccinations
  - ◦ Some of the communication with the public was not conveyed simply and clearly
- The big question is: Did lessons learned during the 2009 H1N1

pandemic improve the Covid-19 response? Some of these issues are covered later in this chapter.

Ethical Theories and Approaches to Public Health

As with all sorts of ethical considerations regarding nurses' personal and professional beliefs and behaviors, it is difficult to limit one's philosophy to just one ethical theory or approach in public health practice. At various times in different situations, a number of important ethical approaches and theories may help guide nurses' actions and the development of public health policies.

Kantian Ethics (Deontology)

Kantian ethics emphasizes that all rational persons are autonomous, ends in themselves, and worthy of dignity and respect. Kantianism is highly valued in Western medicine because of the focus on individual rights and informed consent. In the U.S. healthcare system and in Western bioethics, the choices of rational

individuals are generally respected. However, in public health, practitioners often must balance the rights of individuals with the rights of members of populations and communities. Sometimes, navigating this delicate balance can be controversial or generate dilemmas, such as considering appropriate actions when a person with a communicable disease may jeopardize the health of other people, such as with tuberculosis, meningitis, and Covid-19. This situation results in a need to balance respecting the autonomy and protecting the confidentiality of one person while trying to protect the safety and rights of other persons.

Utilitarianism (Consequentialism)

Utilitarianism is an ethical approach based on maximizing the good, happiness, or moral consequences of one's decisions and actions. Although there are variations in utilitarian theories, when utilitarianism is used in health care, the goal or intended consequence generally is to produce the greatest good for the greatest number of people. Because of the emphasis on population-focused care, utilitarianism is one of the most widely used ethical approaches in public health. The second distinguishing principle of public health nursing outlined in the ANA's (2013) *Public Health Nursing: Scope and Standards of Practice* is "the primary obligation is to achieve the greatest good for the greatest number of people or the population as a whole" (p. 8). This directive for public health nurses is a classic example of utilitarianism.

Communitarian Ethics

There is no power for change greater than a community discovering what it cares about.

—Margaret Wheatley,
Turning to One Another

The philosophy of communitarian ethics is in opposition to rights theories that promote liberal individualism (Beauchamp & Childress, 2019). **Communitarian ethics** derives from "communal values, the common good, social goals, traditional practices, and cooperative virtues" (Beauchamp & Childress, 2009, p. 356). Communitarian ethics is relevant to moral relationships in any community, and this ethical approach is particularly useful in the practice of public health nursing because of the focus on populations and communities rather than on the care of individuals.

The notion that communitarian ethics is based on the model of friendships and relationships that existed in the ancient Greek city-states as described by Aristotle was popularized in modern times by philosopher and ethicist Alasdair MacIntyre (1984) in his book *After Virtue*. Generally, in societal ethics and specifically in bioethics, the valuing and consideration of community relationships have come to mean different things to different people. Communitarian ethics as an ethical approach is distinguished because the epicenter of communitarian ethics is the community rather than any one individual (Wildes, 2000). Populations in general and moral communities in particular are the starting points for public health nursing practice.

The value of discussing and articulating an approach to communitarian ethics lies in the benefit that can be gained through illuminating and appreciating the relationships and interconnections among people that are often overlooked in everyday life. Although personal moral goals, such as the pursuit of personal well-being, are significant, the importance of forming strong communities and identifying the moral goals of communities must not be neglected if both individuals and communities are to be free to flourish.

An important distinction that legitimately can be drawn between communitarian and other popular ethical approaches, such as deontological, or rule-based, ethics, is based on communitarian ethicists' proposal that it is natural for humans to favor the people with whom they live and have frequent interactions, whereas Kantian deontologists base their ethics on an impartial stance toward the persons who experience the effects of their morally related actions. However, using a communitarian ethic and valuing partiality as a way of relating to other people does not have to exclude caring about people who are personally unknown to moral agents. Although it is often easier for people to care about and have compassion for people who are relationally closest to them, it is not unrealistic to believe that people also can develop empathy or compassion toward people who are personally unknown to them. Such behavior and expectations are, for example, an integral part of Christian and Buddhist philosophies. Accepting the notion that humans usually are more partial to people with whom they are most closely related while also believing it is possible to expand the scope of their empathy and compassion to unknown others broadens the sphere of morality in communitarian ethics.

Nussbaum (2004) suggested that people often develop an us-versus-them mentality, especially when significant ethnic and cultural differences separate them. People are able to generate sympathy, or fellow feeling, when they hear about epidemics, disasters, and wars occurring on continents far away, but it is often difficult for people to sustain their sympathy for more than a short period of time after media coverage diminishes. People tend to stop to notice the needs of other people and then soon turn back to their personal lives. According to Nussbaum, humanity will "achieve no lasting moral progress unless and until the daily unremarkable lives of people distant from us become real in the fabric of our own daily lives" (p. 958) and until people include others they do not know personally within the important sphere of their lives. Public health nurses need to expand their scope of concern to consistently include people affected by healthcare disparities, diseases, epidemics, and ethnic violence and wars all over the world, every day, not only when issues are highlighted in the media.

"All communities have some organizing vision about the meaning of life and how one ought to conduct a good life" (Wildes, 2000, p. 129). Public health nurses have an important role in bringing populations and communities together to work toward a common humanitarian good. Transforming a community from an us-versus-them mentality to one that seeks a common good is possible through education (Nussbaum, 2004): "Children [and people] at all ages must learn to recognize people in other countries as their fellows, and to sympathize with their plights. Not just their dramatic plights, in a cyclone or war, but their daily plights" (p. 959). This need for empathetic understanding also is important in one's own country, state, city, town, or neighborhood. Many people of all ages are suffering in the United States and throughout the world because they lack adequate health care, proper food, a sanitary environment, and good housing.

The education of communities often occurs through role modeling (Wildes, 2000). Members of communities learn about what is and is not accepted as moral through personal and group interactions and dialogue within their communities. Narratives are told by nurses about the lives of exemplars, such as Florence Nightingale and Lillian Wald, to illustrate moral living. By her efforts to improve social justice and health protection through environmental measures and to elevate the character of nurses, Nightingale exhibited moral concern for her local society, the nursing profession, and people remote from her local associations, such as the population of soldiers affected by the Crimean War. Likewise, Lillian Wald was an excellent role model for members of communities because of her efforts to improve social justice through her work at the Henry Street Settlement. When learning from the examples of Nightingale and Wald, communitarian-minded public health nurses are in an excellent position to educate the public and other nurses and healthcare professionals about why they should assume the role of being their brothers' and sisters' keepers.

ETHICAL REFLECTION

Have you noticed us-versus-them thinking among members of the nursing community or among members of the larger community of healthcare professionals? If so, what effect has this thinking had on relationships among members of the particular community?

FOCUS FOR DEBATE

Since the 9/11 terrorist attacks, there has been much controversy regarding "us-versus-them" thinking among U.S. citizens. Muslim Americans were targeted as being unacceptably different after 9/11. Illegal immigration at the U.S.–Mexican border brought Central American and Mexican immigrants to the forefront of this type of thinking. Covid-19, with its beginning in China, was associated with negative treatment of Asian people.

- Debate the ethical implications of "us-versus-them" thinking in any of the instances listed above.

Social Justice

Social justice is the fair distribution of benefits and burdens among members of a society. **Market justice** is based on the principle that the benefits and burdens of a society should be distributed among its members according to the members' individual efforts and abilities to pay for services. In a market justice system, money for health care tends to be invested in technology and curing diseases rather than in health promotion and disease prevention. In the United States, market justice traditionally has been the dominant model of health care (Beauchamp, 1999; Riegelman, 2010). It is unclear whether this will remain so into the future because of changes implemented through the Affordable Care Act (ACA) of 2010. However, health care is a political issue that seems to change with changing government administrations.

Major public health problems often are concentrated among a small minority of the U.S. population. For social justice to be achieved, members of U.S. society who are not directly experiencing problems, such as a lack of access to health care, low income, poor quality of housing, and malnutrition, may have to reduce their share of societal benefits and increase their share of societal burdens. Therefore, public health and social justice involve important ethical decisions about how members of societies choose to distribute their resources and provide for the well-being of their fellow citizens.

One glaring social justice versus market justice issue in U.S. healthcare discussions is the disparity in access to care. People who believe health care is a human right argue for universal healthcare coverage for U.S. citizens, that is, health care for all. Libertarians argue that health care is a privilege for people who can pay for it and is not a matter for government intervention to assure that all people have access to health insurance. Generally, children have access to health insurance through programs such as the Children's Health Insurance Program (CHIP), and the elderly have health insurance through the Medicare program. Young adults have been an underserved population. Again, establishing the right to health care has become a political football.

FOCUS FOR DEBATE

Is health care a right or a privilege?

▶ Virtue Ethics: Just Generosity

Pieper (1966) proposed "the subject of justice is the 'community'" (p. 70). Justice can be viewed in terms of which rights or resources should be accorded or distributed to persons or populations. However, there is another conception of justice that is communitarian in nature. This approach is based on virtue ethics and emphasizes the virtue of **just generosity**, which is a conception of justice highlighting human connections and not separateness (MacIntyre, 1999). Indebtedness is the hallmark of this type of justice, and although the concept of justice as a stand-alone virtue is important to public health ethics, the combination of the virtue of justice with the virtue of generosity expands the scope of justice.

People are accustomed to thinking of justice in limited terms and to separating the individual virtues of justice and generosity. Thinking and acting in terms of the comprehensive virtue of just generosity requires the use of one's moral imagination to envision what could be. Whereas justice involves giving others what they are due, generosity involves giving to people from a source that is somehow personal. Fusion of the single virtues of justice and generosity into a combined, activated virtue is important for people in facilitating the development of flourishing communities, both as large as the global community and as small as families.

Cultivation of the virtue of just generosity is based on a person's motivation to actively participate in a community-centered network of giving and receiving. Persons, including nurses, who exhibit the virtue of just generosity do not give merely in proportion to what an individual receiver or community is perceived as being due, but instead, they give to persons or communities based on the receivers' or communities' needs. The giver believes in and does more than dispassionately allocate or distribute resources. The person or group exhibiting just generosity gives from resources that in some way touch the giver personally, which may not necessarily involve giving something material or tangible but often involves what might be called giving from the heart.

In her book *Rambam's Ladder*, Salamon (2003) adapted the Jewish physician and philosopher Maimonides's (1135–1204) ladder of charity for contemporary use. Salamon's book provides a meditation on generosity and underscores that an awareness of the need for giving has become more important than ever in a post-9/11 world. Salamon's ladder of charity starts, as did Maimonides's ladder, with the bottom rung representing the least generous motivation for giving (reluctance) and progresses upward, with the top step being what Salamon proposed to be the highest form of giving, "responsibility—the gift of self-reliance" (Salamon, 2003, Introduction). All steps of the ladder can be found online. The top step of the ladder is like the Chinese proverb, if you give a man a fish, you feed him for a day; teach him to fish and he eats for a lifetime.

Public health nurses can use the ladder of charity as a gauge of the type of giving that occurs within communities while keeping their eyes focused on aiming for the top step of the ladder. Public health nurses usually do not directly give money or material resources to people; nurses' services to individuals, families, communities, and populations can be substituted for monetary or material giving in the steps of the ladder. Salamon (2003) herself recognized that monetary giving is not always the primary means of generosity. However, depending on their particular jobs, public health nurses sometimes are responsible for coordinating and distributing gifts and donations to populations.

Nurses might ask themselves whether they give begrudgingly during their work. Do they work from the motivation of a generous servant, hoping to affect the well-being of a population or community who will not know how the nurse's services have positively affected them and their health? Must individual and community recipients of the services of public health nurses directly ask for each of their specific needs to be met? Do nurses use their moral imagination and anticipate needs, reflecting and acting based on the big picture of what could be but may not be readily apparent to them unless they suspend their initial judgments? When the practice of just generosity is consistent with the top step of Maimonides's ladder, public health nurses enter into community partnerships and teach other people how to be responsible for helping themselves and their communities so that community members and, ultimately, whole communities become self-reliant whenever possible.

▶ Health Disparities

If we gloss over the difficulties that people face in their communities, we cannot hope to build a better world.

—**Helen Forsey,** Circles of Strength: Community Alternatives to Alienation, p. 50

Reprinted by permission of the author.

The U.S. healthcare system was in an exciting time of change with the ACA providing the first major attempt to decrease health disparities since the initiation of the Medicare and Medicaid programs in the Social Security Amendments of 1965. However, the ACA has been the target of political wrangling and legal fights. **Health disparities** are inequalities or differences in healthcare access and treatment that result in poor health outcomes for persons and populations. Health disparities occur because of some characteristic of the persons or population affected. Eliminating health disparities is a moral issue for public health nurses because social justice and communitarian ethics are based on building flourishing communities that support the common good of all community members.

According to nurse–anthropologist Lundberg (2005), "social and cultural factors give context and meaning to health, illness, and injury. The experience is more than that of the patient. It also reflects the worldview of the individuals helping the person in distress" (p. 152). A major concern of bioethicists is that people's health and access to health care are adversely affected in proportion to their lack of power and privilege in a society (Sherwin, 1992). It is known that wealthy people tend to have better health. Consequently, low income and the placement of people within the margins of society are key factors in the determination of public health. When any community members are suffering or in need, all people in the community are affected, even if it is in imperceptible ways. One must only think about the hypothetical net of Indra to imagine how this situation might be a reality (see earlier chapter 1).

Racial and ethnic minorities suffer serious health disparities in access to care and health outcomes. Public health nurses need to play a role in helping members of communities collectively develop the capacity to help themselves in resolving problems that lead to health disparities. This is consistent with the top step of Rambam's Ladder, as discussed above, and is reminiscent of the previously mentioned old Chinese proverb "If you give a man a fish, you feed him for a day. If you teach a man to fish, you feed him for a lifetime." This form of teaching is difficult. People who experience disparities usually find it difficult to take responsibility for their own health when forces of society prevent them from doing so. One coordinated plan to address public health disparities involves four phases or themes: community participation, community mobilization, commitment to social justice, and the leadership challenge (Berkowitz et al., 2001).

Public health nurses can support members of communities by participating in the validation of suspected problems through investigation and research and by building partnerships to collaborate on policy development. Public health nurses facilitate community mobilization by educating members of the community about health promotion and health protection measures likely to improve the lives of people in the community. Teaching people in the community about how to begin grassroots political efforts to obtain needed resources is an important advocacy role of public health nurses. Being committed

to social justice requires public health nurses to speak out about health disparities to other nurses and healthcare professionals to a wide group of community members and to politicians (see **BOX 11-3**). In helping communities increase participation, mobilize action, and expand social justice, the leadership challenge for public health nurses is to "act as a resource, consultant, facilitator, educator, advocate, and role model" (Berkowitz et al., 2001, p. 53).

A widely accepted approach to organizing communities to address health disparity and social justice problems traditionally has been based on the idea that healthcare professionals must appeal to the self-interest of the community and its members (Minkler & Pies, 2002). However, Minkler and Pies argued that this traditional approach often further divides groups of people by emphasizing the notion of individualism and separateness, which is already a divisive way of thinking in Western societies. This approach does not support a community's interest in a common good.

Minkler and Pies (2002) adapted a feminist approach to social change as an agenda for trying to eliminate disparities in the equitable distribution of community resources.

BOX 11-3 Three Parts of a Legislative Meeting

During meetings with legislators, nurses can use the following strategies to effect change:

1. Hook: Briefly explain who you are.
2. Line: Briefly explain your issue and why you care about it. Present a strong argument, a personal story, or both. Try to humanize your issue.
3. Sinker: Clearly present your specific request and try to get a commitment. It is very important to stay focused on your message and to listen attentively to feedback.

Data from Kush, C. (2004). *The one hour activist: The 15 most powerful actions you can take to fight for the issues and candidates you care about.* Jossey-Bass.

Historically, feminist philosophers and activists have approached their agenda in terms of the disparities experienced by women, but a feminist approach often can be used with other marginalized populations. This approach can be used to build a bridge that connects local community efforts to eliminate disparities with efforts to address more global social concerns. Nurses and other healthcare professionals working with community members who are involved in organizing to facilitate change might ask the following:

> (1) Does [the community's organizing effort] materially improve the lives of community members and if so, which members and how many? (2) Does [participating in the organizing process] give community members a sense of power, strength and imagination as a group and help build structures for further changes? And (3) Does the struggle . . . educate community members politically, enhancing their ability to criticize and challenge the system in the future? (Minkler & Pies, 2002, pp. 132–133)

ETHICAL REFLECTION

What is meant by the term **marginalized population**? Identify populations in your community that may be marginalized and discuss why this may be so.

▶ The Precautionary Principle

The ANA (2013) noted the **precautionary principle** is a good guide to use in supporting social justice and a populations' rights. The precautionary principle is based on the German word *vorsorgeprinzip*, which means the principle of forecaring. The word *forecaring*

conveys more than being cautious; it means people use foresight and preparation, and it is aligned with the principle of first do no harm (nonmaleficence) and the adage better safe than sorry (Science and Environmental Health Network [SEHN], 2018a). In 1998, a multinational, multiprofessional group met at the Wingspread conference, sponsored by the SEHN, to discuss using the precautionary principle as the basis of international agreements, especially those related to the environment and health. The participants at the conference developed a statement to guide actions by governmental and nongovernmental agencies. The group stated, "When an activity raises threats of harm to the environment or human health, precautionary measures should be taken even if some cause and effect relationships are not fully established scientifically" (SEHN, 2018b, para. 2).

According to SEHN (2018b), a key element of the principle is that it moves people to take anticipatory "precaution in the face of scientific uncertainty" (para. 3). Advocates of the precautionary principle contend that people should not wait until they have certain evidence from traditional science to show the causal connection among various actions or toxins and their harmful effects. Minimum standards for citing evidence of cause-and-effect relationships via traditional science are usually very high (SEHN, 2018b), and it can take a long time to gather the large amounts of evidence required. The type of science needed to support the precautionary principle has been called appropriate science, as distinguished from traditional science (Kriebel et al., 2003). Appropriate science is based on the context of the problem at hand rather than requiring scientific pursuits to be forced into a preconceived idea of necessary rigor. The principle is used to advocate for taking early action when there are appropriate suspicions that something causes harm.

People who oppose the precautionary principle believe that if science has not provided certain evidence that a particular activity or substance is harmful to humans or the environment, the activity or substance is assumed to be safe until shown otherwise. However, proponents of using the precautionary principle answer with the argument that by the time harmful causal relationships are established with certainty, much, and sometimes irreparable, damage already may have occurred (SEHN, 2018). An example cited by proponents of the precautionary principle is the harmful connection between cigarette smoking and lung cancer. People had reason to believe that smoking and lung cancer were connected long before this was admitted or demonstrated by the scientific community. Fortunately, many smokers had stopped smoking based on precautionary measures rather than waiting on scientific certainty to confirm the harmful effects.

For public health nurses to practice ethically, it is recommended in the ANA's (2013) *Public Health Nursing: Scope and Standards of Practice* that public health nurses use the precautionary principle. As a follow-up to the Wingspread conference, another community of philosophers, scientists, and environmentalists, called the Blue Mountain group, met to discuss the ethics that underlie the precautionary principle. This group's consensus was that "particular values form the basis of our survival" (Myers, 2002, p. 218). Whereas traditional science tries to separate evidence from values, the precautionary principle supports the integration of the two. The Blue Mountain group contended that humans are permeable with their environment and become the relationships they share. Values affirmed by the group were gratitude, empathy, sympathy, compassion, and humility. As members of the community of Earth, the group said they practice respect, restraint, simplicity, and humor.

The following are examples relevant to the precautionary principle, which inherently is a public health principle:

■ Even though there is traditional scientific evidence supporting the impacts of climate change, some people do not accept it. This may include health-related impacts. The precautionary principle can be used to support research or projects focused on nurses' or other people's involvement in addressing climate change issues that impact the health of populations.

■ A significant example of violating the precautionary principle occurred in the 1980s when blood bank administrators refused to warn the public that the U.S. blood supply was contaminated with HIV before there was a test to detect the virus. If something similar occurred today, nurses might study how and why this occurred, attitudes, outcomes, and population impacts.

■ When there is little traditional scientific evidence about a novel virus, decisions must be made about what type of appropriate science needs to be followed. Studies and projects can be done about how people react when traditional science is not yet available but harmful impacts are occurring.

ETHICAL REFLECTION

Some people do not believe that global warming is a matter of concern. Research information about global warming. Discuss the following as they relate to global warming:

■ Appropriate science versus traditional science
■ The precautionary principle
■ Communitarianism
■ Provision 9.4 of the ANA's (2015) *Code of Ethics for Nurses with Interpretive Statements*

Environmental Justice

Environmental justice is distributing environmental benefits and burdens in an equitable manner. The U.S. Environmental Protection Agency (EPA, 2021, September 8) more specifically defines environmental justice as "the fair treatment and meaningful involvement of all people regardless of race, color, national origin, or income, with respect to the development, implementation, and enforcement of environmental laws, regulations, and policies" (para. 1).

Meaningful involvement from this definition is outlined in **BOX 11-4**. It is the goal of the EPA for all people in the United States to have a voice in environmental policy making and to be protected from environmental hazards that affect their health and well-being.

ETHICAL REFLECTION

Visit the Healthcare Without Harm, U.S. and Canada, website (https://noharm-uscanada.org), and read some of the success stories. Which stories do you find particularly interesting? Which stories do you believe convey particularly innovative actions?

Environmental racism is a particular type of environmental injustice affecting populations of color. People of color generally

BOX 11-4 Meaningful Involvement in the Development, Implementation, and Enforcement of Environmental Laws, Regulations, and Policies

Meaningful involvement means

- People have an opportunity to participate in decisions about activities that may affect their environment and/or health;
- The public's contribution can influence the regulatory agency's decision;
- Community concerns will be considered in the decision-making process; and
- Decision makers will seek out and facilitate the involvement of those potentially affected.

Data from U.S. Environmental Protection Agency (EPA). (2021, September 22). Learn about *environmental justice*, (para. 3). https://www.epa.gov/environmentaljustice/learn-about-environmental-justice

experience a disproportionate number of environmental burdens; for example, children of color are more likely than white children to experience the effects of environmental hazards, such as exposure to lead. Bullard (as cited by the EPA, 2021, August 3) stated "whether by conscious design or institutional neglect, communities of color in urban ghettos, in rural 'poverty pockets,' or on economically impoverished Native-American reservations face some of the worst environmental devastation in the nation (para. 2)."

These environmental disparities are likely to result from power and privilege differentials within a society or community (Friis, 2007). It is interesting that it was primarily people of color who advanced the environmental justice movement in association with the 1960s civil rights movement (EPA, 2021, August 3).

ETHICAL REFLECTION

As of 2022, the people in an unincorporated part of Lowndes County, Alabama, were living without a municipal sewerage system. Because of this, vulnerable people in this pocket of the country are living with raw sewerage entering and surrounding their homes.

- Research historical and current stories about pockets of environmental injustice in the United States
- Discuss commonalities among these stories.
- Explain how nurses can use traditional ethical theories and approaches to support their advocacy for vulnerable pockets of people experiencing environmental injustice.

▶ Communicable Diseases

Public health advances in the 20th century dramatically decreased morbidity and mortality from infectious diseases in the United

States; because of this progress, national health officials began to lose interest in funding and promoting research directed at infectious disease treatment and control (CDC, 2003). However, people in government, healthcare systems, and the general public now realize that humanity's fight against infectious diseases is never ending (Markel, 2004). In her popular book about the global collapse of the public healthcare system, Garrett (2000) stated "we now live in comfortable ignorance about the health and well-being of people in faraway places. But in truth we are never very far away from the experiences of our forebears" (p. xii). Since Garrett's statement, things have continued to change. As evidenced by the Ebola virus epidemic of 2014 and, especially, the Covid pandemic beginning in 2019–2020, it is hard to remain ignorant of the health and well-being of people in faraway places and the dangerous infectious diseases that plague the human race.

Societies are still tormented by diseases that have affected the public's health since ancient times, such as tuberculosis and malaria, while novel infectious diseases loom now and in the future. "Socioeconomic, environmental and behavioral factors, as well as international travel and migration, foster and increase the spread of communicable diseases. Vaccine-preventable, foodborne, zoonotic, health care-related and communicable diseases pose significant threats to human health . . ." (World Health Organization [WHO], 2021a, para. 1). After Ebola outbreaks and the Covid pandemic, it is apparent that no one in the United States or elsewhere should feel safe from unexpected or mass casualties involving infectious diseases. Public health nurses and nurses working in other capacities have been at the epicenter of the healthcare system during the Covid pandemic. The words of the poet John Donne (1623/1962) provide a good representation of how infectious diseases that affect the global community are related to ethics in nursing:

No man is an island, entire of itself;
every man is a piece of the continent,

a part of the main. If a clod be washed away by the sea, Europe is the less, as well as if a promontory were, as well as if a manor of thy friend's or of thine own were. Any man's death diminishes me, because I am involved in mankind; and therefore never send to know for whom the bell tolls; it tolls for thee. (p. 1107)

FOCUS FOR DEBATE

Imagine a colleague telling you the state of health care and epidemic diseases in poor countries is not a moral issue. Debate whether and why your colleague is or is not correct.

In regard to health care in poor countries, Paul Farmer (2001), the late physician at Harvard Medical School who traveled to central Haiti to work at the Clinique Bone Sauveur, said "we can no longer accept whatever we are told about 'limited resources'" (p. xxvi). Healthcare professionals must challenge the often-repeated line that resources are too limited to fund programs to treat epidemics in poor countries. According to Farmer, "the wealth of the world has not dried up; it has simply become unavailable to those who need it most" (p. xxvi). He proposed that people must ask to be shown the data supporting the truth of statements that there are fewer resources for public health than there were when effective therapies were not available to treat many diseases. "Our challenge, therefore, is not merely to draw attention to the widening outcome gap, but also to attack it, to dissect it, and to work with all our capacity to reduce this gap" (p. xxvi). Healthcare professionals and the public must make it clearly known they are not willing to idly watch when the wealth of nations is being concentrated on limited populations and programs while, on a mass scale, people in other populations die of treatable diseases.

Malaria

Malaria, which means bad air, has been a problem for humans for more than 4,000 years. An interesting fact is that in 1946 the CDC itself was developed as an agency to fight malaria (CDC, 2018, November 14). Globally in 2019, there were about 229 million malaria infections and 409,000 deaths (WHO, 2021, April 1), and malaria disproportionately affects low income populations. According to the "World Malaria Report 2020" (WHO, 2020, p. 8), which covers malaria data over two decades, the following milestones have been reached in malaria control:

- 1.5 billion cases averted and 7.6 million lives saved
- Stepped-up investment in research and innovation led to the development of new disease-cutting tools, such as insecticide-treated nets, rapid diagnostic tests, and more effective medicines
- Robust political commitment in Africa
- Global malaria mortality fell by 60% over the period 2000–2019
- Twenty-one countries have eliminated malaria over the last 2 decades and, of these, 10 countries were officially certified by WHO as malaria free

Unfortunately, the 2020 report (WHO, 2020) also noted that progress has plateaued. In 2017, the WHO cautioned that malaria control was at a "crossroads" and 2020 targets probably would be missed (p. 9). Reductions of disease were missed by 37% and deaths by 22%. Covid-19 added additional hurdles to the already difficult challenges posed by malaria control measures. Malaria has been eliminated in the United States. The global plateauing of progress means that the world should not avert its eyes from malaria but should continue to forge ahead to eliminate this formidable disease in poor countries. Fortunately, as of October 2021, a malaria vaccine became available that the WHO recommended for use "among children in sub-Saharan Africa and in other regions with moderate to high *P. falciparum* malaria transmission" (para. 1). "This is a historic moment" (para. 2).

FOCUS FOR DEBATE

The use of DDT to prevent malaria has been controversial. Is it being used today to control malaria? Go to the Internet and locate both evidence that supports and contradicts the benefits of using DDT. Justify your position about this issue.

Tuberculosis

According to the WHO (2021), each year tuberculosis (TB) causes illness in 10 million people. TB is preventable and curable, which makes it horrific that 1.5 million people die every year from TB. Rates of TB are highest in lower- and middle- income countries, and this indicates it is a disease of poverty.

Since TB is airborne, its treatment is a major public health concern in terms of infected persons' infringement on the well-being of noninfected persons. Treatment for TB requires a person to take multiple drugs for an extended period, which can promote nonadherence to treatment. Nonadherence to prescribed TB therapy leads to serious negative outcomes, such as drug resistant strains. The reasons patients fail to follow their treatment regime usually relate to the same social and psychological factors that led to their infection in the first place (Beauchamp & Childress, 2009). Unfortunately, healthcare professionals have no convenient and reliable way to know who will and who will not adhere to their TB treatment plan. People infected with TB who are unable or do not choose to adhere to recommended treatment present a moral problem. Freedom and autonomy should, of course, be supported whenever possible; however, when persons infected with active TB do not voluntarily adhere to treatment, it is ethically and legally obligatory to mandate isolation because of health threats to others. This means one person's privacy and autonomy may be breached in deference to protecting the welfare of other people. The least restrictive means should be used to gain a TB-infected person's cooperation with treatment, but detention and isolation are legal and ethical, if needed, to protect the public's safety. This is a classic example of utilitarianism.

Directly observed therapy (DOT), which involves watching persons while they take their TB medications, is the best means of ensuring that affected individuals adhere to their treatment regimen. The international community has responded to the problem of the spread of TB with coordinated efforts to control it through DOT. Beauchamp and Childress (2009) presented typical arguments for and against using DOT as a routine practice in the majority of active TB cases. Because most patients with active TB adhere to their treatment plan, critics of using DOT for all patients say that to do so would be "wasteful, inefficient, and gratuitously annoying" (p. 301). Using DOT with patients who adhere to their therapy also is not the least restrictive means of treating patients. On the other hand, advocates of the widespread use of DOT contend that not using DOT risks the escalation of the number of TB cases and costs, especially regarding drug-resistant forms of the disease.

The least problematic way to address the global burden of TB is to develop public policies to address the underlying causes of TB and patient nonadherence to treatment. Priority should be given to policies that protect a person's privacy and autonomy. The ethical issue that looms large when considering adherence to treatment is "how a society ensures compliance often reflects its attitudes toward its vulnerable members" (Beauchamp & Childress,

2009, p. 301). Coercive approaches should be balanced with policies sensitive to the needs of persons with TB.

Note that the WHO's (2018) End TB Strategy includes an ethics component. The main principles of the strategy include the following (p. 1):

1. Government stewardship and accountability, with monitoring and evaluation
2. Strong coalition with civil society organizations and communities
3. Protection and promotion of human rights, ethics and equity
4. Adaptation of the strategy and targets at country level, with global collaboration

ETHICAL REFLECTION

Search the ANA's (2015) *Code of Ethics for Nurses with Interpretive Statements,* and list guidance that it provides for the nursing profession regarding people suffering from global diseases such as TB, malaria, and HIV.

HIV/AIDS

According to UNAIDS (2021), the AIDS pandemic is far from over. In fact, a 2021 UNAIDS report indicated that people with HIV are more vulnerable to Covid infections, but worldwide many of these people do not have access to the Covid vaccine. Overall, the report stated there are "knowledge and tools to prevent every single new HIV infection and avoid every AIDS-related death" but progress is being hampered by factors such as race, gender, and lack of access to health care (p. 6). UNAIDS proposed these inequalities are driving the continued AIDS pandemic. Interesting facts are provided about the unequal world for people today (see Ethical Reflection Box).

ETHICAL REFLECTION

"Normal Is an Unequal World"

Normal in the first quarter of the 21st century is a fraught vision. Normal means centibillionaires sailing giga-yachts in the Mediterranean as migrants fleeing conflict and famine drown in those very same waters. Normal means that women and girls in much of the world cannot choose whether and when to marry or start a family. Normal means being harassed, imprisoned or killed for rejecting the gender assigned to you at birth, or for choosing to spend the night or the rest of your life with a person of the same sex. Normal means that the color of your skin may determine whether a police officer serves and protects, or stands on your neck. Normal means that your sex, your gender, your race and your income level will largely determine whether you have the agency and tools needed to protect yourself from disease and stay healthy. Normal means that 680,000 people die of AIDS-related causes because more than 10 million people living with HIV— including 800,000 children—are not accessing life-saving treatment that should be cheap and easily available.

UNAIDS. (2021). *Global AIDS update 2021 confronting inequalities: Lessons for pandemic responses from 40 years of AIDS* (p. 10). https://www.unaids.org/sites/default/files/media_asset/2021-global-aids-update_en.pdf

HIV Testing

In 2006, the CDC published major revisions to its HIV testing guidelines, and the new recommendations include routine HIV testing for patients in all healthcare settings. Because basic screening for treatable conditions is a common public health secondary prevention tool, it is believed that early identification of HIV infections will lead to better health outcomes. Also, risk-based screening is less effective now because the mix of people becoming infected with HIV is changing to persons who frequently are unaware of their high-risk status— racial and ethnic minorities, people younger than 20 years of age, nonmetropolitan-area dwellers, and heterosexuals.

Major revisions in the CDC's (2006) guidelines are contained in **BOX 11-5**. The CDC's position is unchanged in its continued advocacy for voluntary, noncoerced agreement for testing; no testing without a patient's knowledge; and access to clinical care and counseling for persons whose tests are positive. However, the CDC now advocates that screening should be provided in a manner similar to other diagnostic testing without special pretest counseling. Beauchamp and Childress (2019) said that this type of opt-out rather than opt-in testing maintains persons' autonomy while increasing vital HIV testing.

Good communication is an important skill for healthcare professionals who coordinate and order HIV testing. The effectiveness of healthcare professionals' communication with patients can have a significant impact on the patients' health outcomes. For example, being clear about the difference in what it means to have a *positive* HIV test and a *negative* HIV test can be critical if a patient misunderstands the meaning of these words. This type of confusion can occur with people who have sensory deficits, such as deafness, or people who do not speak English as their first language.

People who are seronegative have no significant risks from testing; however, the psychological and social risks are significant for people who are seropositive (Beauchamp & Childress, 2001). People who are HIV positive are at a high risk psychologically for anxiety, depression, and suicide and socially, for "stigmatization, discrimination, and breaches of confidentiality" (p. 299). These common risks are sometimes compounded by a patient's cultural heritage. It is the ethical responsibility of healthcare professionals to try to minimize the risks to these individuals. Participating in counseling, community education, or social and political activism is one way public health nurses can play an important role in minimizing the risk of HIV infection among populations served and negative effects on people who undergo HIV testing.

BOX 11-5 HIV Testing Guidelines from the CDC

Major revisions from previously published guidelines are as follows:

For patients in all healthcare settings:

- HIV screening is recommended for patients in all healthcare settings after the patient is notified that testing will be performed unless the patient declines (opt-out screening).
- Persons at high risk for HIV infection should be screened for HIV at least annually.
- Separate written consent for HIV testing should not be required; general consent for medical care should be considered sufficient to encompass consent for HIV testing.
- Prevention counseling should not be required with HIV diagnostic testing or as part of HIV screening programs in healthcare settings.

For pregnant women:

- HIV screening should be included in the routine panel of prenatal screening tests for all pregnant women.
- HIV screening is recommended after the patient is notified that testing will be performed unless the patient declines (opt-out screening).
- Separate written consent for HIV testing should not be required; general consent for medical care should be considered sufficient to encompass consent for HIV testing.
- Repeat screening in the third trimester is recommended in certain jurisdictions with elevated rates of HIV infection among pregnant women.

Data from Centers for Disease Control and Prevention. (2006, September 22). *Revised recommendations for HIV testing of adults, adolescents, and pregnant women in healthcare settings.* https://www.cdc.gov/mmwr/preview/mmwrhtml/rr5514a1.htm

LEGAL PERSPECTIVE: STATE HIV TESTING LAWS

At the CDC's "State HIV Testing Laws: Consent and Counseling Requirements" website or another scholarly website, check your state's HIV testing laws, including when nonvoluntary testing is permissible.

Do you agree with your state's laws? Why or why not?

LEGAL PERSPECTIVE: HIV STATUS AND CONFIDENTIALITY

HIPAA laws generally cover confidentiality even with HIV status. However, state laws must also be consulted. See the following Q and A from the HIPAA website:

My state law provides greater privacy protections on patients' HIV information than the HIPAA Privacy Rule. Is this more protective state law preempted by the Privacy Rule?

Answer:

No. The Privacy Rule establishes a floor of Federal privacy protections and rights for individuals. If a provision of State law provides greater privacy protection than a provision of the Privacy Rule, and it is possible to comply with both the State law and the Privacy Rule (e.g., where a State law prohibits the disclosure of HIV status while the Privacy Rule permits such disclosure), there is no conflict between the State law and the Privacy Rule, and no preemption.

Further, even in the unusual case where a "more stringent" provision of a State law is "contrary" to a provision of the Privacy Rule—that is, it is impossible to comply with both the Privacy Rule and the

(continues)

Pandemics: Influenza and Covid-19

In previous editions of this book, a potential lethal influenza pandemic was discussed in depth. With the sixth book edition, people view the Covid-19 as the bigger issue in front of the world's eyes. However, influenza still warrants discussion and concern and much of the information pertaining to ethics and pandemic influenza is applicable to a pandemic coronavirus. In fact, the world's next pandemic may be caused by a novel influenza virus.

Since late 2021 and into 2022 the CDC (2022, April 28) has been surveilling H5 infected birds in the United States. As of April 28, 2022, the H5 (presumptive H5N1) virus has been found in 29 states in commercial and backyard birds and in wild birds in 34 states. On April 28, 2022, the CDC reported the first human case of this H5 virus in the United States, which was only the second human case worldwide from this group of H5 influenza viruses currently predominant. Fortunately, neither person suffered severe symptoms from their infection. "More than 880 human infections with earlier H5N1 viruses have been reported since 2003 worldwide, however, the predominant H5N1 viruses now [as of April 2022] circulating among birds globally are different from earlier H5N1 viruses" (para. 4). Gavi (2021), a vaccine alliance, reported the case-fatality rate of the earlier H5N1 infections to be about 53%.

A research article released as part of a 2021 CDC *Emerging Infectious Diseases* report stated, "The numerous global outbreaks and continuous reassortments of highly pathogenic avian influenza (HPAI) A (H5N6/H5N8) clade 2.3.4.4 viruses in birds pose a major risk to the public health" (Bui et al., 2021, p. 2619). The researchers noted at this point human transmissibility is low; but with the continuing evolution of the viruses, improved transmissibility and increased pathogenicity in humans is possible. They recommended ongoing education, vaccine production, and surveillance of these influenza viruses.

Pandemics of influenza are rare but consistently recurring events. During the 1900s, three influenza pandemics occurred—in 1918, 1957, and 1968. The 1918–1919 Spanish influenza pandemic was one of the deadliest disease events that ever occurred, with approximately 40 to 50 million people dying worldwide during the pandemic. It is frightening that as of September 20, 2021, news reports indicated the Covid pandemic had caused numbers of U.S. deaths approximately equal to those that occurred during the 1918–1919 influenza pandemic (Johnson, 2021, September 20). When a new (novel) virus, such as a strain of influenza or SARS-CoV-2, emerges and spreads rapidly among the global population, the human immune system is not prepared to combat the new infection. The lack of immunity to a novel virus can result in many deaths, just as it did in 1918 and has done with Covid-19.

Although the pandemic did not become as serious and deadly as some people feared, the WHO declared a pandemic in 2009 when a novel H1N1 influenza virus surfaced. The U.S. public closely watched the events of the pandemic unfold to see how well the government handled the crisis. After reviewing the events, the U.S. Government Accountability Office (2011) identified key issues related to the government's response to the 2009 H1N1 pandemic. The report indicated the following: (1) prior planning and funding to prepare for a potential H5N1 avian influenza threat was beneficial during the H1N1 pandemic; (2) the number of available vaccine doses did not meet the expectations set by the government, and as a result the government's credibility was hurt; (3) a mandate for a 100-dose minimum vaccine order was problematic; (4) the CDC generally was rated well in terms of communication with the public, but communication fell short with non-English-speaking people; and (5) medicines and supplies from the Strategic National Stockpile were sufficient to meet goals, but disparities were identified between the materials ordered and received, and problems were identified with long-term storage of materials. See information discussed under the "Setting the Stage: Public Health Is Controversial" section of this chapter.

One key problem expected during the 2009 pandemic and that was a problem during the Covid pandemic involves the time needed to produce a vaccine after a pandemic-type virus first appears. However, new technology used in producing the Covid-19 vaccine may have unlocked the key to creating vaccines for influenza, HIV, and malaria (Dolgin, 2021). The novel H1N1 virus first was identified in the United States on April 15, 2009, when a 10-year-old patient in California was tested as part of a clinical study (CDC, 2010). The first vaccine for the pandemic was not distributed until October 5, 2009 (Cox, 2011). This meant the public had no vaccine protection from the pandemic virus for about 6 months after the virus first appeared. Healthcare staff who work directly with people ill with the flu were also left without vaccine protection during the period from April to October. More recently, it was about one year from the beginning of the Covid outbreak at the end of 2019 to the time of vaccine availability for healthcare workers in the United States in December 2020. Fortunately, the H1N1 pandemic of 2009 was not particularly deadly; however, during a pandemic with a high case-fatality rate, such as a pandemic caused by the lethal strain of avian H5N1 influenza, the lives of healthcare workers are at risk, especially if a vaccine is unavailable.

If the lethal strain of avian H5N1 virus in Asia or any other novel and highly lethal influenza viruses, such as the ones noted in the CDC's *Emerging Infectious Diseases* report, were to mutate to the point that they become easily transmissible from human to human, nurses would face many of the same problems they have faced during the Covid-19 pandemic or maybe a worse situation. Gavi (2021) questioned whether H5N1 or H7N9 would present the world with its next pandemic.

The CDC (2007, February 15) developed a document of ethical guidelines to address a potential influenza pandemic. The points in this document also need to be analyzed for application to the Covid pandemic:

- Identification of clear overall goals for pandemic influenza (p. 2): Goals are different than in interpandemic years. During a pandemic the goal is "preserving the functioning of society" (p. 3) rather than protecting people who are at the most serious risk from being harmed by influenza, such as elders and young children.
- A commitment to transparency throughout the pandemic influenza planning and response process (p. 3): Language used in explaining reasons for decisions must be clear, the basis for decisions must be open for review, and the process must reflect a respect for persons and involved communities.
- Public engagement and involvement are essential to build public will and trust

and should be evidenced throughout the planning and response process (p. 3): The public is treated as a partner with the influenza experts. Vulnerable and marginalized people need to be included in related processes.

- Public health officials have a responsibility to maximize preparedness to minimize the need to make allocation decisions later (p. 3). Examples "include shortening the time for virus recognition or vaccine production, increasing the capacity to produce vaccines or antivirals and increasing the supplies of antivirals" (pp. 3–4).
- Sound guidelines should be based on the best available scientific evidence (p. 4): Processes and actions should be evidence based whenever possible. However, some processes and action may need to be based on evidence-informed data, which is a bit less rigorous.
- The pandemic planning process acknowledges the importance of working with and learning from preparedness efforts globally (p. 4): This guideline is not based on merely benefiting U.S. citizens, but rather on maximizing the common good of the global community.
- Balancing of individual liberty and community interests (p. 4): During a pandemic, usual individual liberties that are highly valued in our society may need to be suspended. If suspending liberties is necessary, care needs to be taken to use the least restrictive policies, to ensure "that restrictions are necessary and proportional to the need for protection" (p. 5), and to support people who are affected by the restrictions.
- Diversity in ethical decision making (p. 5): Historically, groups of people have been abused "in the name of the public good" (p. 5). During pandemic influenza, a variety of public voices must be included in planning and implementation processes.
- Fair process approach (procedural justice) (p. 5): Procedures must be well designed,

transparent, include consistent standards, and be managed by people who are impartial, neutral, and accountable so they lead to fair outcomes.

ETHICAL REFLECTION

Analyze each bullet point issue listed in the CDC's 2007 ethics plan for pandemic influenza. How were each of these issues managed during the Covid-19 pandemic? What was handled successfully and what was not handled successfully?

On July 1, 2011, the CDC published a document outlining ethical guidelines for allocating scarce ventilator resources during a severe influenza pandemic. This document was intended to be a supplement to the 2007 document addressing ethical issues surrounding the distribution of scarce resources, especially vaccines and antiviral medications, and the need for social distancing and limitations on personal liberties. Again, this document should be analyzed as it relates to any viral pandemic, such as the one occurring due to SARS-CoV-2 (Covid-19). Ethical questions arise about how to allocate mechanical ventilators "when there is a substantial extreme mismatch between patient need and available resources" (CDC, 2011, July 1, p. 7). The CDC recommended that the focus should shift "from individual patient-focused clinical care to a population-oriented public health approach intended to provide the best possible outcomes for a large cohort of critical care patients" (p. 7). After triage has begun regarding allocating mechanical ventilators, designated individuals must decide how to distribute these scarce resources.

Whereas the recommendations in the CDC's 2007 pandemic influenza document focused on giving priority to people who will keep society functioning during a pandemic, the 2011 document reflects a different philosophy for decision making about allocating scarce mechanical ventilators. People whose jobs are to keep society functioning might be kept on the job longer if they are given an effective vaccine or prophylactic antiviral drugs during a serious pandemic. Both interventions are aimed at keeping people healthy. However, people need a mechanical ventilator when they already are infected with a highly pathogenic virus. This means these persons would already be off the job. It is a key assumption of experts that serious pandemics occur in waves, separated by weeks or months with no significant disease. It is unlikely that a person with a highly pathogenic virus who needs ventilator support would be able to recover sufficiently to go back to work within any one wave of a pandemic. Therefore, there is no justifiable reason to give persons priority merely based

on their role in keeping society functioning. It was recommended that priorities need to be organized around giving ventilator resources to the people "who are most likely to recover after receiving them" (CDC, 2011, July 1, p. 9). It is worth noting that an available and effective vaccine may not be expected until the second wave of a viral pandemic.

Is there a clear answer about how to ethically distribute mechanical ventilators during a severe pandemic? The CDC staff who developed the 2011 document said no. As indicated in the document, the CDC (2011, July 1) offered, at best, only "a conceptual framework to assist the planning process" (p. 3). The scope of the document is too big to be adequately covered in this chapter, but **BOX 11-6** provides an overview of some of the principles that were discussed as possibilities for guiding ventilator allocation.

BOX 11-6 Considerations for Allocating Ventilator Support During a Major Pandemic

- Respect for persons and their autonomy: "During a severe influenza pandemic, public health mandates may override patient autonomy. Patients still must be treated with dignity and compassion" (CDC, 2011a, p. 10).
- Beneficence: Providers must balance obligations for doing good for individual patients while acting according to the good of a whole population. Individual patients need to receive palliative care, when appropriate, and should not be abandoned.
- Justice: Distribution of resources should be fair and "should not exacerbate existing disparities in health outcomes" (p. 10). Procedural justice is required.
- Maximizing net benefits: "The number of people who survive to hospital discharge" (p. 12) should be maximized. This consideration can be further broken down into maximizing the number of lives saved, maximizing years of life saved, or maximizing adjusted years of life saved. The authors of the CDC (2011a) document contended "that ethically, allocating scarce resources during a severe pandemic by only considering chances of survival to hospital discharge is insufficient because it omits other important ethical considerations" (p. 14).
- Social worth: There are two primary ways to approach a social worth criterion: broad social value and instrumental value or the multiplier effect. The determination when considering broad social value is "whether an individual's past and future contributions to society's goals merit prioritization for scarce resources" (p. 14). "Instrumental value refers to an individual's ability to carry out a specific function that is viewed as essential to prevent social disintegration or a great number of deaths" (p. 14). Proponents believe using instrumental value as a criterion for allocating resources is ethical because it achieves a multiplier effect. That is, if key people in a society are protected or saved, they will in turn save more lives through their work. This is the criterion recommended by the CDC for

(continues)

BOX 11-6 Considerations for Allocating Ventilator Support During a Major Pandemic *(continued)*

allocating vaccine doses and antiviral medications during a serious influenza pandemic. However, as mentioned previously, it is believed that using this criterion will not provide much benefit when deciding about allocating mechanical ventilators.

- The life cycle principle: Using this principle means younger people are given priority over older people. It is debatable whether using this principle is discriminatory or egalitarian.
- Fair chances versus maximization of best outcomes: This criterion supports giving ventilators to people with the best chance of survival over people who have a lower probability "but still [have a] significant chance of survival" (p. 16).
- A composite priority score: Several principles are combined into an allocation system that can be used to compute a score to assign priority.

Data from Centers for Disease Control and Prevention (CDC). (2011, July 1). *Ethical considerations for decision making regarding allocation of mechanical ventilators during a severe influenza pandemic or other public health emergency.* https://www.cdc.gov/about/advisory/pdf/VentDocument _Release.pdf

Other issues and questions that need to be considered when addressing mechanical ventilator allocation during a severe pandemic include the following (CDC, 2011, July 1):

- Who should make decisions about distributing resources?
- Should uniform criteria across geographic areas be used, or should local flexibility be the norm?
- How can public health workers engage local communities in decision making and the triage process?
- Who clarifies the roles of healthcare professionals during public health emergencies? How will nurses and physicians be protected from tort liability from their actions during an emergency?
- If, based on their work, healthcare professionals become severely ill from the flu, should they be given priority for ventilator resources because they faced additional risks by helping patients?
- What are the special needs of children?
- How will decisions be made to remove patients from a ventilator?

As per the CDC's (2011, July 1) ethics document, the roles of clinical care and triage should be separated. It was emphasized that guidelines and procedures should be in place prior to an emergency situation. A triage expert should be identified who has senior status at the institution where he or she will make decisions. The expert should be someone who is respected by the staff and has relevant clinical experience and the authority to carry out his or her decisions. A team of at least three members should be assembled to help the triage expert. The CDC committee that authored the document proposed "the presumption should be to follow uniform guidelines in the interest of fairness, consistency, and coordination of efforts" (p. 18). However, there should be enough flexibility for local changes that meet the needs of any one institution or community. Communities are more likely to be engaged in the process when messages are consistent, marginalized and vulnerable groups receive special attention, and spokespeople are chosen who are best heard by the target community.

Depending on the characteristics of the pandemic virus, children may have a high susceptibility to the virus and a greater need for ventilation resources. Because all ventilator equipment suitable for adults is not suitable for children and professionals who normally care for adults may not be comfortable caring for children, pre-pandemic activity is very important to assess and secure resources for children (CDC, 2011, July 1).

Decisions surrounding palliative care and withdrawing mechanical ventilator support from patients are likely to present significant ethical distress for physicians and nurses during a severe pandemic. Decision-making procedures should be established prior to being needed to ensure that decisions to remove patients from ventilators are ethical. Respectful and compassionate palliative care should be provided to patients with respiratory failure who do not receive mechanical ventilation or have ventilator support withdrawn based on an allocation system.

During a crisis involving a scarcity of ventilators (demand exceeding supply), elective surgeries usually are delayed, and patients whose condition is improving are weaned from ventilators. However, these strategies may not be enough. According to the CDC (2011, July 1), it may become necessary to remove patients from ventilators without obtaining consent. The following information is taken directly from the CDC's (2011, July 1) document regarding ethical care involving ventilator support during a pandemic:

> To achieve the public health goal of minimizing the number of preventable deaths during a severe pandemic emergency, states and hospitals need to address the issue of removing from ventilators patients with respiratory failure whose prognosis has significantly worsened in order to provide access to patients with a better prognosis. . . . Policies for withdrawal of patients from ventilators need to be the least restrictive possible—i.e., withdrawing of ventilation without requiring assent of patient or surrogate continues only as long as the shortage of ICU resources continues. . . . Patients who are removed from mechanical ventilation and their families

or surrogates, like patients with respiratory failure who are not placed on mechanical ventilation, should be notified this will occur, given a chance to say good-byes and complete religious rituals, and provided compassionate palliative care. (p. 21)

ETHICAL REFLECTION

As you understand what happened during the Covid-19 pandemic, were the guidelines for ventilator use from the CDC's July 1, 2011, document used as a method of triaging scarce resources? Explain.

There is so much that could be discussed about the ethical issues involved in the Covid-19 pandemic that it could fill an entire ethics book. The CDC's documents published for guiding practice during a major influenza pandemic are applicable. However, an additional discussion specifically pertaining to the Covid pandemic follows. In order to coherently organize the discussion, it is presented under the headings of a few ethical theories and approaches and some of the main bioethical principles. Documented behaviors and occurrences, reflections, and questions are included for self-reflection, debate, and analysis. The Covid pandemic has provided fertile ground for sorting out nurses' own public health ethical perspectives. It is evident that people within families, the general public, government officials, and healthcare professionals have been surprised at the widely varying positions and perspectives expressed and acted on during the pandemic. Unfortunately, media stories abound about divorces occurring and family splits happening because of the strong differences in people's positions about pandemic issues. Politics has permeated choices and positions. In the discussion below, political issues will be minimized as much as possible, but politics invariably affected the evolving story of the Covid pandemic.

The discussion of ethics during the Covid pandemic is not theoretical. Real societal scenarios unfolded that are documented for anyone to read. Questions need to be asked, and government officials at all levels, healthcare professionals, and the general public need to be able to think through these scenarios and analyze the ethics of decision making that occurred. The tools for analysis are the basic understanding of bioethical principles, theories, and approaches. The five R's approach discussed in an earlier chapter 2 also is relevant.

The words ethical dilemma (check definition in an earlier chapter 2) probably have been overused regarding the Covid pandemic. People may *feel* like there are or were dilemmas where none actually exists if an ethicist is consulted. In some cases, the dilemmas are real. The bioethical principles, theories, and approaches presented below provide good grounding regarding what is ethical in public health. Before the main presentation of issues begins, an interesting pandemic analogy is provided using a historic fire.

The Mann Gulch Fire

In the popular book *The Premonition: A Pandemic Story* (Lewis, 2021) the author discussed a lesson conveyed by the physician, Carter Mecher, who worked on pandemic plans during the Bush and Obama administrations. Mecher compared pandemics, specifically the Covid-19 pandemic, to wildfires, specifically the 1949 Mann Gulch fire in Montana. The story follows as outlined in *The Premonition*.

In 1939 the U.S. Department of Agriculture Forest Service (n.d.) began the smokejumper program. Members of this elite team parachute into fire zones with self-sufficient capabilities to fight wildfires. Fifteen men parachuted into the Mann Gulch area of Montana to fight a fire in 1949. The men thought they could control the fire fairly easily. To the right of them was a 76% steep ridge and to the left was a creek that flowed into the Missouri River. The fire was thought to be contained on the other side

of the creek. The men headed to the intersection of the creek and the river with their firefighting plans. When they arrived at the river, they found the fire had jumped the creek, and they stared at the raging grass fire in front of them. Grass fires move faster than forest fires, and this fire had a tailwind of 30 to 40 miles per hour (mph). Later analysis revealed the fire was moving at 1.2 mph when the men first encountered it; but within 10 minutes, the fire was chasing the men at 7 mph. Ten of the 15 men burned to death. Five men escaped over the ridge. Two of them died of burns within a day. The leader of the group was one of the 5 men climbing up the ridge. As he was trying to escape the rapidly advancing fire, he deliberately started another fire in front of him. He yelled to the other men to drop their equipment and follow him into the fire he started. The other men either did not hear him or thought he was crazy. The leader walked through his self-started fire as the main fire passed him on either side leaving him untouched by it. This new technique has become a fire-fighting strategy called an escape fire. Berwick, a Medicare and Medicaid administrator during the Obama administration later gave a presentation about the Mann Gulch fire. Mecher heard the talk and later applied the following lessons to the Covid-19 pandemic:

- It is too late to act by the time smoke clears. Don't wait!
- An epidemic cannot be outrun. It is too late to run by the time it is upon you.
- Drop everything that is not important and recognize what is important.
- Come up with an escape fire plan.

The iceberg theory also is a long-used analogy to explain the progression of epidemics and the dangers of what is invisible beneath the surface, that is, what is unknown. Both the Mann Gulch analogy and the iceberg analogy are both useful to present a picture of what happened as the Covid pandemic gained a foothold in the United States. Unfortunately, politics sometimes conflicted with public health practice.

Confusion also abounded among public health professionals because they were faced with a pandemic situation they had long expected but had not previously experienced.

In the discussion that follows, answer the questions asked according to the facts that actually unfolded globally, nationally, regionally, state-wide, and locally in your own state, city, or town and determine acceptable and applicable ethical standards. Do the facts of what happened reflect the ethics contained within the relevant ethical principles, theories, and approaches, and guidelines offered by the CDC for pandemics, such as influenza? Explain your evaluations with scholarly support. How many controversies can you identify? What type of biases occurred and how many examples of hypocrisy can you identify? Debate these issues with your colleagues.

Utilitarianism

Utilitarianism historically is the ethical theory of public health. An explanation of utilitarianism was provided in an earlier chapter 1 and in this chapter. As a reminder, the basic precept is to do the greatest good for the greatest number of people. Consequences matter! With infectious diseases, such as TB, meningitis, HIV, and other sexually transmitted diseases (STDs), infected people are legally and ethically prohibited from willfully endangering other people. People who do not take TB drugs as prescribed can be individually watched taking their medications through the DOT strategy or incarcerated to prevent spread of the disease. A person with infectious meningitis who refuses to be treated would not be released from a hospital to infect members of society. "As of 2021, 35 states have laws that criminalize [deliberate] HIV exposure" (CDC, 2021, September 17, para. 1). Specific HIV and STD criminalization laws can be found on the CDC's website: https://www.cdc.gov/hiv/policies/law/states/exposure.html

Which decisions, policies, and behaviors provide the greatest good for the greatest number of people during the Covid-19 pandemic? How should utilitarianism be applied during the Covid pandemic or another similar pandemic?

- Vaccine Distribution
  - Who should receive the first vaccines released for distribution in order to do the greatest good for the greatest number of people?
  - What should be the allocations plan?
  - How should the Food and Drug Administration (FDA) be factored into the release of vaccines? What role does the FDA play in vaccine availability to provide the greatest good for the U.S. population? During the Covid pandemic, the Trump administration criticized the work of the FDA in approving Covid vaccines. Was this criticism justified? Why or why not?
- Lockdowns and Social Distancing Mandates
  - When and where should lockdowns happen to provide the greatest good and minimize the greatest harm? For example, how should harm to students not being educated in their traditional school settings be balanced against lockdowns trying to protect people from infection?
  - Generally, what type of lockdowns and social distancing mandates are reasonable to provide the most good for the most people?
  - Who should decide about when and where lockdowns (shutdowns) and

LEGAL PERSPECTIVE: MANDATORY PANDEMIC BEHAVIORS

Is it constitutionally legal for the federal government to mandate vaccinations, mask wearing, and business shutdowns during a pandemic? Do federal and state legal justifications differ?

social distancing are mandatory to provide the greatest good for the greatest number of people?

Communitarianism

Communitarianism is discussed earlier in this chapter. The basic premise is that people who believe in a communitarian approach to ethics generally are willing to sacrifice some of their own autonomy or material benefits to promote the common good of their community. A community can be large or small.

- During the Covid pandemic, businesses lost revenue and individuals lost income because of lockdowns and social distancing mandates. One can analyze and evaluate how people responded to these difficult losses. Were the losses accepted as inevitable and necessary or were restrictions fought as being an overreach by governmental agencies? How should these conflicting interests be balanced? There is no doubt that the things that caused financial hardships were a part of trying to protect public health during the Covid pandemic.
- Mask wearing during the Covid pandemic was a hardship and distasteful for many people. Masks can be uncomfortable, expensive for some people, and a general nuisance to wear. However, mask wearing during an infectious pandemic promotes the common good of protecting oneself and others from infectious disease.
- Statistics show that Covid reduced the U.S. life expectancy in 2020, and this was disproportionally seen in Latino and African American populations (Andrasfay & Goldman, 2021). There was "an estimated 39% increase in the Black-White life expectancy gap" (p. 4). Historically, there is a Latino paradox because Latinos' life expectancy exceeds white life expectancy even though the Latino population as a whole, has "substantially lower education, income, wealth, and access to health care"

(p. 6). Andrasfay and Goldman proposed that these population disparities revealed the health risks of being socially and economically disadvantaged.

- Some healthcare professionals and healthcare workers as well as many people in the general U.S. population refused to be vaccinated against Covid once reliable vaccines were made available. Being vaccinated to protect oneself and others is a contribution to the common good of communities large and small. Illness and death among the unvaccinated are costly to the community in both decreasing the overall well-being of the community and economically with workforce reductions and healthcare costs.
- Though it may be debated from a political perspective, it is understood that spreading information that is not scientifically evidence-based does not promote and, in fact, harms the common good. During the pandemic, people became ill, died, and spread illness to others because of misinformation. Nurses and other healthcare professionals are taught to rely on evidence-based information in providing health care. Is there an ethical justification for healthcare professionals using prevention and treatment information that is not evidence-based?

Respect for Autonomy

The respect for autonomy, one's own autonomy and others' autonomy, is one of the biggest ethical issues and controversies that arose during the Covid pandemic. Autonomy, discussed in detail in a previous chapter 2, basically means that one's right to make personal decisions is respected. However, during a pandemic or when managing non-pandemic infectious diseases, public health professionals realize there are limits to a person's right to have autonomy respected. Consider again persons infected with TB who refuse to take their medications or untreated persons with HIV who indiscriminately have unprotected sexual relations with others without informing the others about their HIV status. For years, most parents and guardians have abided by state vaccine laws for school children. When parents and guardians avoided having their children vaccinated, repercussions such as measles outbreaks have occurred. Citizens riding in the front seat of a car wear a seatbelt if for no other reason than it is a federal law to do so. There are many other federal and state laws that people follow every day. Overriding autonomy is necessary to protect people themselves and to prevent them from harming others. One can only imagine the chaos and dangers that would ensue if autonomy was respected in every personal decision across the country and world.

■ During the Covid pandemic, some people expressed that they would rather face death than be made to receive Covid vaccinations. However, it is not a matter of persons merely choosing their own deaths. When unvaccinated people are infected with Covid, the health of other people, vaccinated and unvaccinated, can be negatively affected.

■ Surprisingly, as of July 2021, 27% of healthcare workers had refused a Covid vaccination (The Covid States Project, 2021, August). A quick tips article from the American Academy of Family Physicians (AAFP Family Practice Management (FPM) Editors, 2021) emphasized the influence healthcare professionals have on patients' decisions about vaccination. They outlined four reasons healthcare workers are reluctant to be vaccinated for Covid. The reasons are:

1. Concerns about safety and efficacy
2. A preference for trying to achieve herd immunity physiologically
3. Distrust of government and healthcare organizations
4. A desire for autonomy and personal freedom

Kantian deontology covered earlier in this chapter and in a previous chapter 2 mixes easily with the principle of autonomy. After all, Westerners' highly valuing autonomy stems from Kant's Enlightenment era ethical philosophy.

■ Consider the ANA's (2015) *Code of Ethics for Nurses with Interpretive Statements.* Review the *Code* and position statements from the ANA. Where does a nurse's duty lie? Are nurses who freely take the responsibility for caring for patients also free to choose actions that may negatively affect the health of their patients, even potentially causing their patients' death? Does a nurse's autonomy override the nurse's duty? How does a nurse's good character (see virtue ethics) fit into the reconciliation of autonomy versus a nurse's duty to patients?

■ Principles of the above scenario also can be applied to mask-wearing and social distancing.

■ The first amendment to the U.S. Constitution protects the right of free speech. However, one does not have the right to yell "fire" in a crowded theatre when this is known to be false information. The line between free speech and the illegality of spreading false information has blurred in recent times. This blurring of boundaries thrived during the Covid pandemic. Do people have a right to spread information for which there is no scientifically based evidence? For instance, spreading the incorrect information

ETHICAL REFLECTION

Visit the ANA Enterprise website: Pulse on the Nation's Nurses Covid-19 Survey Series: Covid-19 Vaccine. https://www.nursingworld.org/practice-policy/work-environment/health-safety/disaster-preparedness/coronavirus/what-you-need-to-know/covid-19-vaccine-survey/

■ What do you find to be interesting in this survey data?
■ How does the survey data compare to your own views?

that the Covid vaccine causes infertility. People are harmed by misinformation especially during times when they are being overwhelmed by information much of which they do not understand and that may be otherwise confusing.

Beneficence

The bioethical principle of beneficence in its most basic meaning represents the requirement to do good. Benevolence is its corollary virtue. Nurses are expected to do good for their patients and for other people they encounter. A nurses personal and professional character cannot be separated (ANA, 2015). Though the public is expected to do good toward others, nurses have a higher expectation to do so. Review the principle of beneficence and the related concept of supererogation in an earlier chapter 2.

- Is a nurse ethically required to work during a highly infectious and dangerous pandemic when protections such as a reliable vaccine and personal protective equipment are unavailable?
- Is the above question a matter of supererogation?
- Is there a difference for nurses in going to work and accepting an assignment caring for patients versus not arriving at all at one's workplace?
- How might these questions pertain to emergency situations other than pandemics, for example, weather or other disasters?

ETHICAL REFLECTION

Nurses may ask about their obligation to put themselves and their families at risk by working without adequate personal protection during a pandemic. The following is guidance from the ANA.

Provision 2 of the *Code of Ethics for Nurses with Interpretive Statements* (2015) states "the nurse's primary commitment is to the patient (p. 5)" but the *Code* also indicates "the nurse owes the same duty to self as to others" (p. 19). Provision 5 states "These equal obligations can conflict during pandemics. . . . During pandemics, nurses and their colleagues must decide how much care they can provide to others while also taking care of themselves."

Find out what nurses should consider when making these decisions by reviewing the ANA's document "Nurses, Ethics, and the Response to Covid-19" at https://www .nursingworld.org/~495c6c/globalassets /practiceandpolicy/work-environment/health --safety/coronavirus/nurses-ethics-and-the -response-to-the-covid-19-pandemic.pdf]

American Nurses Association (ANA). (2015). *Code of ethics for nurses with interpretive statements.*

Data from ANA Enterprise. (n.d.) Covid-19 resource center: FAQs. (Question 43). https://www.nursingworld.org/practice-policy /work-environment/health-safety/disaster-preparedness /coronavirus/faqs/#ethical

FOCUS FOR DEBATE

On July 26, 2021, the ANA published its position about mandatory Covid vaccination of nurses and all healthcare professionals:

The American Nurses Association (ANA), representing the interests of the nation's 4.2 million registered nurses, supports health care employers mandating nurses and all health care personnel to get vaccinated against COVID-19 in alignment with current recommendations for immunization by public health officials. (para. 1)

Review the concept of paternalism discussed in previous chapters 2 and 9.

Do you agree with the ANA's paternalistic position? Why or why not?

Data from ANA Enterprise. (n.d.) Covid-19 resource center: FAQs. (Question 43). https://www.nursingworld.org/practice-policy /work-environment/health-safety/disaster-preparedness/coronavirus /faqs/#ethical

Justice

In its most basic understanding, justice is the fair distribution of benefits and burdens.

Justice is believed to tie together other virtues and principles. Being just means that one's autonomy is respected in a Kantian sense. Each person is an end unto him or herself and not a means to an end. People, generally, are trusted to make their own decisions as long as their decisions do not infringe on the rights of others. Thus, people are treated fairly. Being just means that one tries to do good by being fair (beneficence or benevolence).

Fair distribution of vaccines and rationing of ventilators has been discussed. These matters have been far from being handled ideally and without procedural difficulty, but efforts have been made to acknowledge these ongoing problems and needs during pandemics. It was discussed earlier that the Covid pandemic continued to reveal disparities between the more negative impact of disease on people who are in low- to middle-income levels as compared to people in higher-income strata. As of this writing, these disparities need to be further evaluated as to why they occurred during the Covid pandemic and strategies need to be developed for preventing these disparities in the future.

Though there are a number of justice-related pandemic issues, one of the primary crises noted during the Covid pandemic was the availability of health care for non-Covid patients. Emergency departments and acute care and critical care hospital units at times were so overwhelmed with Covid patients that patients with everyday critical healthcare needs often waited hours or days for care. In some instances, people died from lack of care for conditions that in non-crisis times are treated quickly. Consider the ethical implications of people refusing vaccinations and to wear masks and how these people inundated hospitals when they became infected with Covid, especially during the Delta variant wave of the pandemic. Did the autonomy of these unvaccinated but ill individuals infringe on the rights of people who were vaccinated but experienced other conditions such as a myocardial infarction that required quick intensive care?

In concluding this section of the public health chapter, it is important to note the impact of the Covid-19 pandemic on nurses themselves. The American Association of Critical Care Nurses (AACN, 2021, September 20) began the "Hear Us Out" campaign that is aimed at spreading information about nurses' professional reality during the pandemic. The campaign urges unvaccinated Americans to be vaccinated. Unvaccinated people increase the burden on healthcare workers in ways that may drive many of them out of their jobs. The AACN reported results of a recent survey of critical care and acute care nurses they conducted around the initiation of their September 2021 campaign. The survey revealed the following data from the previous 18 months:

- 92% of nurses surveyed said they believe the pandemic depleted nurses at their hospitals and, as a result, their careers will be shorter than they intended
- 66% feel their experiences during the pandemic caused them to consider leaving nursing
- 76% say that people who had yet to be vaccinated threatened nurses' physical and mental well-being
- 67% believe taking care of patients with COVID-19 put their own families' health at risk (para. 5)

The AACN cited the organization's president as saying, "nurses leaving the profession will bring our healthcare system to its knees" (p. 6). The Covid-19 pandemic has exposed many of the ethical vulnerabilities in our public health system and society in general.

▶ Terrorism and Disasters

The terrorist attacks on September 11, 2001, and the anthrax-laced letters that followed this event highlighted the possible dangers of terrorist-related infectious diseases invading society (Farmer, 2001). Farmer proposed that

> investing in robust public health infra-structures, and in global health equity in general, remains our best means of being prepared for—and perhaps even preventing—bioterrorism. Indeed, this was the refrain of several of our best public health leaders during the taxing investigations of these [anthrax] attacks. (2001, p. xi)

Ethics-related guidance for public health nurses during any type of terrorism attack or before, during, or after natural or human-made disasters can be referred back to a variety of ethical approaches, such as social justice (fair distribution of resources), communitarian ethics (acting to facilitate the common good for communities), utilitarianism (considering actions that produce the greatest good for the greatest number of people), virtue ethics (having good character and being concerned about the common good), deontology (acting according to one's duty), and ethical principlism (applying rule-based principles, such as respect for autonomy, beneficence, nonmaleficence, and justice). During any type of disaster, public health professionals must make critical decisions about how to triage people, manage scarce resources, and protect everyday personal rights, such as the following: health care, including first aid; food and water; medications and immunizations; warmth and housing; protection from harmful environmental elements; and the individual freedom to travel and mingle with other people. Because of the major impact that public health actions can have on human suffering and well-being, the decisions made by public health professionals during disasters are inherently ethical in nature.

Generally, in terrorism and natural disasters, military triage is used rather than traditional medical or emergency room triage. Usual emergency room triage rules are focused on prioritizing patients who are the sickest or the most gravely injured, even those whose lives may not

ETHICAL REFLECTION

The American Nurses Association and government agencies have published guidelines for altered standards of care during disasters. Review some of these documents and identify ethical implications nurses may face based on these guidelines.

be salvageable. In military triage, medical need is considered, but decisions are balanced with consideration of the principle of social utility (Campbell et al., 2007). When managing emergency care in the battlefield, priority is given to soldiers who can quickly be returned to the battlefield to continue the fight. This approach to triage provides a social benefit to the whole population of soldiers in a given area. Ultimately, resources are allocated to provide the greatest benefit to the greatest number of people.

Another important element of ethics and public health care during disaster situations is trust. Members of society expect healthcare professionals, especially public health professionals, to be trustworthy and competent while carrying out their roles during disasters. "Public health agencies [and public health professionals] cannot function well in the absence of public trust" (Thomas, 2004, p. 4). People should be able to trust public health professionals to act according to the public's best interest during a disaster. Actions to achieve the common good and good outcomes for the whole community must be balanced with actions directed at caring for the needs of individuals. Each community member has a personal story, and each person's life narrative is important. Equanimity—evenness of temperament—is a good virtue for nurses to have during a disaster. Thich Nhat Hanh's story about Vietnamese boat people is relevant to ethical nursing care during disasters (see earlier chapter 8).

Although standards of nursing practice may need to be altered during a disaster situation, a nurse's ethics should not be compromised during a disaster. The point of disaster is not the time for nurses to begin pondering and sorting out their ethical philosophies. The Five Rs approach to ethical nursing practice (see earlier chapter 2) is a guide for nurses to prepare to act ethically under any sudden and stressful situation, including situations such as those that occur before, during, and after disasters. Through the ethics-focused activities of reading, reflecting, recognizing, resolving, and responding, nurses can cultivate their abilities to do moral reasoning.

Genomics

"Beginning on October 1, 1990 and completed in April 2003, the HGP gave us the ability, for the first time, to read nature's complete genetic blueprint for building a human being" (National Human Genome Research Institute, n.d., para. 1). In 2005, the Institute of Medicine (IOM) published a workshop summary titled "Implications of Genomics for Public Health." The summary highlighted that the science of genetics has produced benevolent outcomes in helping people live healthier lives, it also presents ethical, legal, and social challenges.

The goals of the HGP were as follows:

- *identify* all the approximately 20,500 genes in human DNA,
- *determine* the sequences of the 3 billion chemical base pairs that make up human DNA,
- *store* this information in databases,
- *improve* tools for data analysis,

- *transfer* related technologies to the private sector, and
- *address* the ethical, legal, and social issues (ELSI) that may arise from the project.

(U.S. Department of Energy, 2019, April 23, para. 1)

A total of 3% to 5% of the HGP budget was allocated to studying ethical, legal, and social issues (ELSI) being the world's largest bioethics program at that time (U.S. Department of Energy, 2019, March 26). Some of the ELSI identified include the fair use of information obtained from genetic testing; the maintenance of information privacy and confidentiality; stigmatization due to genetic differences among people; a number of reproductive issues, such as the impact of genetic information on reproductive decision making and reproductive rights; clinical issues, such as education and implementation of quality standards; uncertainty in regard to gene testing when multiple genes or gene–environment interactions are involved; considerations of whether behaviors occur according to free will or are determined according to genetic makeup; the safe use of genetically modified foods and microbes; and how property rights should be handled in regard to the commercialization of products. The HGP has opened a wide array of issues about which all healthcare professionals, including public health nurses, will continually need to become more familiar. However, many people in society are still not sure if the HGP has opened a Pandora's box. See **BOX 11-7** and consider current ethical questions regarding gene therapy.

BOX 11-7 Current Ethical Questions Related to Gene Therapy

- How can "good" and "bad" uses of gene therapy be distinguished?
- Who decides which traits are normal and which constitute a disability or disorder?
- Will the high costs of gene therapy make it available only to the wealthy?
- Could the widespread use of gene therapy make society less accepting of people who are different?
- Should people be allowed to use gene therapy to enhance basic human traits such as height, intelligence, or athletic ability?

U.S. National Library of Medicine. (2021). *What are the ethical issues surrounding gene therapy?* (para. 1). https://medlineplus.gov/genetics /understanding/therapy/ethics/

FOCUS FOR DEBATE

Gather reliable data and generate informed positions to answer the following questions. Engage in a debate with your colleagues about differing positions and provide examples.

Fairness in the use of genetic information by insurers, employers, courts, schools, adoption agencies, and the military, among others.

Who should have access to personal genetic information, and how will it be used?

Privacy and confidentiality of genetic information.

Who owns and controls genetic information?

Psychological impact and stigmatization due to an individual's genetic differences.

How does personal genetic information affect an individual and society's perceptions of that individual?

How does genomic information affect members of minority communities?

Reproductive issues including adequate informed consent for complex and potentially controversial procedures, use of genetic information in reproductive decision making, and reproductive rights.

Do healthcare personnel properly counsel parents and guardians about the risks and limitations of genetic technology?

How reliable and useful is fetal genetic testing?

What are the larger societal issues raised by new reproductive technologies?

Clinical issues including the education of doctors and other health service providers, patients, and the general public in genetic capabilities, scientific limitations, and social risks; and implementation of standards and quality-control measures in testing procedures.

How will genetic tests be evaluated and regulated for accuracy, reliability, and utility? (Currently, there is little regulation at the federal level.)

How do we prepare healthcare professionals for the new genetics?

How do we prepare the public to make informed choices?

How do we as a society balance current scientific limitations and social risk with long-term benefits?

Uncertainties associated with gene tests for susceptibilities and complex conditions (e.g., heart disease) linked to multiple genes and gene-environment interactions.

Should testing be performed when no treatment is available?

Should parents or guardians have the right to have their minor children tested for adult-onset diseases?

Are genetic tests reliable and interpretable by the medical community?

Conceptual and philosophical implications regarding human responsibility, free will vs genetic determinism, and concepts of health and disease.

Do people's genes make them behave in a particular way?

Can people always control their behavior?

What is considered acceptable diversity?

Where is the line between medical treatment and enhancement?

Health and environmental issues concerning genetically modified foods (GM) and microbes.

Are GM foods and other products safe to humans and the environment?

How will these technologies affect developing nations' dependence on the West?

Commercialization of products including property rights (patents, copyrights, and trade secrets) and accessibility of data and materials.

Who owns genes and other pieces of DNA?

Will patenting DNA sequences limit their accessibility and development into useful products?

U.S. Department of Energy. (2019, March 26). *Human genome project information archive: 1990–2003: ARCHIVE: Ethical, legal, and social issues.*

U.S. Department of Energy. (2019, March 26). Human genome project information archive: 1990 – 2003: ARCHIVE: Ethical, legal, and social issues. https://web.ornl.gov/sci/techresources/Human_Genome/elsi/index.shtml

Public Health Nursing: Contributing to Building the World

Because public health nursing is population focused, public health nurses often have opportunities to improve the welfare of many people. Public health nurses work with members of populations as equal partners and collaborate with a variety of people to promote and protect the public's health (ANA, 2013). Participating in service learning experiences and adopting a philosophy of servant leadership are two ways to ground nursing practice in the principles of public health nursing.

Service Learning

Service learning is "academic experiences in which students engage both in social action and in reflection on their experiences in performing that action" (Piliavin, 2003, p. 235). Service learning ideally is suited for supporting the moral development of public health nursing students. Kaye (2004) defined service learning as "a teaching method where guided or classroom learning is deepened through service to others in a process that provides structured time for reflection on the service experience and demonstration of the skills and knowledge acquired" (p. 7). Service learning is a means for students and teachers to work with community leaders and agencies in collaboratively identifying and working toward a common good. All participants, including teachers, agency administrators, and staff, learn from the students during their interactions with them while the students benefit from developing increased community awareness. In service learning, "community develops and builds through interaction, reciprocal relationships, and knowledge of people, places, organizations, governments, and systems" (p. 8).

Service usually is focused on direct or indirect services, advocacy, or research (Kaye, 2004). In direct services, person-to-person interactions occur between students and the recipients of the students' work. Direct services may be aimed at students developing a broader awareness of the needs and issues of various cultures, populations, or age groups while providing a needed service to a population, for example, providing a service to people with AIDS who are living at a specific AIDS hospice, to people who are staying at a particular homeless shelter, or to elderly persons who attend a specific day-care center. A whole community or the environment is the focus of indirect service learning interventions, such as activities aimed at helping to organize and implement a community-wide health education program about safe sex or organizing an effort to decrease pollution of a local waterway. Advocacy—which is a key role of public health nursing—combined with service learning involves creating and supporting change in communities to benefit people in the community. Advocacy includes grassroots societal and political activism, such as working to educate a city council about the unmet needs of people who are homeless in the city. Service learning provides an excellent opportunity for students to become involved in community research. Students can participate in developing and conducting surveys and gathering, analyzing, and reporting data regarding issues of public health concern.

Students' reflections on service learning experiences are an integral and defining part of service learning. It is in this area that the students' moral imaginations and the development of intelligent habits are cultivated. Reflection helps service learners to consider the big picture in working for the good of communities. Reflective experiences can be guided through activities such as journal writing or teacher-led group discussions and processing of experiences. Service learners may benefit from thinking in terms of the intersecting human narratives that exist among themselves, their community collaborators, and the recipients of their services.

ETHICAL REFLECTION

Conduct a literature review about service learning in nursing. Develop suggestions for service learning experiences that focus on each of the following: direct services, indirect services, advocacy, and research.

Servant Leadership

In the late 1960s and early 1970s, Robert Greenleaf (2002) was one of several businesspeople who developed and articulated the concept of servant leadership in management. Greenleaf developed the idea of servant leadership after reading the book *The Journey to the East* by Herman Hesse (1956). Hesse's book relates a story about a servant named Leo who is on a journey to the East with a group of men, members of a mysterious league, who are on a mission to find spiritual renewal. Leo brings the group together as a community with his spirit and songs. When Leo decides to leave the group, the small community becomes dysfunctional and disbands. Later, one of the journeymen discovers that Leo was really the head of the league that sponsored their original journey.

Leo was a noble leader who had chosen the role of a servant but whose leadership was of the utmost importance to the journeying group's sense of community. Greenleaf (2002) proposed that Hesse's story clearly exemplifies a servant leader through the portrayal of Leo. He suggested that "the great leader is seen as servant first, and that simple fact is the key to his [or her] greatness" (p. 21). In the story, even while Leo was directly in the role of the leader of his league, he viewed himself first and foremost as a servant (see **BOX 11-8**).

Servant leaders see themselves first as servants, and at some later point, they make the choice to lead while serving. People who are more concerned with leading before serving often are motivated by a desire for power or to

BOX 11-8 The Nature of Service

During a Midwestern storm of rain, hail, lightning, and thunder, my mother stopped at the grocery store and asked me to run in for a loaf of bread. As I prepared to get out of the car, I noticed little Janie running down the street. She wore her usual tattered clothes, and her bald head, the result of some condition unknown to me, was unprotected from the hail. Many of our schoolmates teased her, judging her as inferior because of her poverty and appearance. I jumped out of the car and gave her my raincoat. She put it over her head and continued running. I remember thinking, "I am here to help others." I was ten years old.

Reproduced from Trout, S. S. (1997). Born to serve: The evolution of the soul through service. Three Roses Press, p. 13.

obtain material possessions, although a strong concurrent secondary motivation to serve is possible. Greenleaf (2002) explained how to distinguish between a servant-first leader and a leader who views service as a secondary or lower priority:

> The difference manifests itself in the care taken by the servant-first [leader] to make sure that other people's highest priority needs are being served. The best test, and difficult to administer, is this: Do those served grow as persons? Do they, while being served, become healthier, wiser, freer, more autonomous, more likely themselves to become servants? And, what is the effect on the least privileged in society? Will they benefit or at least not be further deprived? (p. 27)

When thinking about servant leadership, it is important to note that the role of the servant follower is as important as that of the servant leader. If there are no servant followers, or seekers, great leaders are not recognized because there is no one with the awareness to recognize them. "If one is servant, leader or follower, one is always searching, listening, expecting that a better wheel for these times is in the making" (Greenleaf, 2002, p. 24).

Covey (2002) defined servant leadership as being consistent with moral authority and proposed that servant leaders and servant followers are, in reality, both followers because both are following the truth. Moral authority was described in terms of conscience and includes four dimensions:

1. Sacrifice is the heart of moral authority or conscience. Sacrifice involves an elevated recognition of one's small, peaceful inner voice while subduing the selfish voice of one's ego.

2. Being inspired to become involved with a cause that is worth one's commitment to it. A worthy cause inspires people to change their "question from asking what is it we want to what is being asked of us" (Covey, 2002, p. 7). One's conscience is expanded and becomes a factor of great influence in one's life.

3. The inseparableness of any ends and means. Moral leaders do not use unethical means to reach ends; as the philosopher Kant advocated for moral behavior, servant leaders always must treat others as ends in themselves, never as a means to an end.

4. The importance of relationships is enlivened through the development of conscience. "Conscience transforms passion into compassion" (Covey, 2002, p. 9). Living according to one's conscience emphasizes the reality of the interdependence of people and relationships. In relation to this fourth dimension of moral authority, Covey conveyed a story told by a nursing student, JoAnn C. Jones. On an exam, Ms. Jones's nursing instructor asked students the name of the school housekeeper. A student asked whether the question carried a point value. The instructor informed the student the question certainly did count toward the exam grade. She said, "In your careers you will meet many people—all are significant. They deserve your attention and care. Even if all you do is smile and say hello" (pp. 9–10).

ETHICAL REFLECTION

Reflect and write a narrative about why you want to be a nurse. Is your primary motivation the desire to be a servant or a leader? Has your perception of the servant/leadership role changed over time? How?

KEY POINTS

- Members of a community have a shared interest in a common good.
- Communities are moral in nature.
- The epicenter of communitarian ethics is the community rather than the individual perspective of any one person.
- There are a number of ethical theories and approaches useful in public health nursing. Nurses need to understand different ethical approaches and develop an ethical philosophy before a crisis or stressful situation arises.

(continues)

KEY POINTS *(continued)*

- It is a moral choice when people decide how they choose to distribute societal benefits and burdens among the members of communities.
- Healthcare disparities are often associated with race, ethnicity, and economic status.
- Humans will not achieve true moral progress until people perceive the suffering of others who are not personally known to them as important in their daily lives.
- Pandemics and disasters require different priority setting than happens during everyday health care. Nurses should be familiar with policies, guidelines, and ethical issues before they are faced with providing care during a pandemic or disaster.
- The Human Genome Project has generated a plethora of ethical questions that will need to be answered by members of the global community.
- Servant leaders view themselves as servants first and leaders second.

References

American Academy of Family Physicians Family Practice Management (FPM) Editors. (2021). Quick tips: Four reasons for COVID-19 vaccine hesitancy among health care workers, and ways to counter them. https://www.aafp.org/journals/fpm/blogs/inpractice/entry/countering_vaccine_hesitancy.html

American Association of Critical-Care Nurses. (2021, September 20). *Hear us out campaign reports nurses' Covid-19 reality.* https://www.newswise.com/coronavirus/hear-us-out-campaign-reports-nurses-covid-19-realities/?article_id=757605

American Nurses Association. (2007). *Public health nursing: Scope and standards of practice.*

American Nurses Association. (2013). *Public health nursing: Scope and standards of practice* (2nd ed.).

American Nurses Association. (2015). *Code of ethics for nurses with interpretive statements.*

American Nurses Association. Enterprise. (n.d.) *Covid-19 Resource Center: FAQs.* (Question 43). https://www.nursingworld.org/practice-policy/work-environment/health-safety/disaster-preparedness/coronavirus/faqs/#ethical

American Nurses Association. (2021, July 26). *ANA supports mandated Covid-19 vaccinations for nurses and all healthcare professionals.* https://www.nursingworld.org/news/news-releases/2021/ana-supports-mandated-covid-19-vaccinations-for-nurses-and-all-health-care-professionals/

American Public Health Association. (2013). *The definition and practice of public health nursing.* https://www.apha.org/-/media/Files/PDF/membergroups/PHN/NursingDefinition.ashx

American Public Health Association. (2021). *What is public health?* https://www.apha.org/what-is-public-health

Andrasfay, T., & Goldman, N. (2021). Reductions in 2020 US life expectancy due to Covid-19 and the disproportionate impact on the Black and Latino populations. *Proceedings of Sciences of the United States of America (PNAS), 118*(5), 1–6.

Beauchamp, D. (1999). Public health as social justice. In D. E. Beauchamp & B. Steinbock (Eds.), *New ethics for the public's health* (pp. 101–109). Oxford University Press.

Beauchamp, T. L., & Childress, J. F. (2001). *Principles of biomedical ethics* (5th ed.). Oxford University Press.

Beauchamp, T. L., & Childress, J. F. (2009). *Principles of biomedical ethics* (6th ed.). Oxford University Press.

Beauchamp, T. L., & Childress, J. F. (2013). *Principles of biomedical ethics* (7th ed.). Oxford University Press.

Beauchamp, T. L., & Childress, J. F. (2019). *Principles of biomedical ethics* (8th ed.). Oxford University Press.

Bui, C. H. T, Kuok, D. I. T, Yeung, H. W., Ng, K-C, Chu, D. K. W, Webby, R. J., Nichols, J. M., Peiris, J. S. M, Hui, K. P. Y, & Chan, M. C. W (2021). Risk assessment for highly pathogenic avian influenza A (H5N6/H5N8) clade 2.3.4.4 viruses. *Emerging Infectious Diseases, 27*(10), 2619–2627.

Campbell, A. T., Hart, K. D., & Norton, S. A. (2007). Legal and ethical issues in disaster response. In T. G. Veenema (Ed.), *Disaster nursing and emergency preparedness for chemical, biological, and radiological terrorism and other hazards* (2nd ed., pp. 100–116). Springer.

Centers for Disease Control and Prevention. (2003). Achievements in public health, 1900–1999: Control of infectious diseases. In P. R. Lee & C. L. Estes (Eds.), *The nation's health* (7th ed., pp. 31–37). Jones and Bartlett Publishers.

Centers for Disease Control and Prevention. (2006). *Revised recommendations for HIV testing of adults, adolescents, and pregnant women in health-care settings.* https://www.cdc.gov/mmwr/preview/mmwrhtml/rr5514a1.htm

Centers for Disease Control and Prevention. (2007, February 15). *Ethical guidelines in pandemic influenza.* https://stacks.cdc.gov/view/cdc/11431

Centers for Disease Control and Prevention. (2010). *The 2009 H1N1 pandemic: Summary highlights, April 2009-April 2010.* https://www.cdc.gov/h1n1flu/cdcresponse .htm

Centers for Disease Control and Prevention. (2011, July 1). *Ethical considerations for decision making regarding allocation of mechanical ventilators during a severe influenza pandemic or other public health emergency.* https://www.cdc.gov/about/advisory/pdf /VentDocument_Release.pdf

Centers for Disease Control and Prevention. (2011, May 20). Ten great public health achievements—United States, 2001-2010. *Morbidity and Mortality Weekly Report, 60*(19), 619–623. https://www.cdc.gov/mmwr /preview/mmwrhtml/mm6019a5.htm

Centers for Disease Control and Prevention. (2018, November 14). *The history of malaria, an ancient disease.* https://www.cdc.gov/malaria/about/history/index.html

Centers for Disease Control and Prevention. (2021, September 17). *HIV and STD criminalization laws.* https://www.cdc.gov/hiv/policies/law/states/exposure .html

Centers for Disease Control and Prevention. (2022, April 28). *U.S. case of avian influenza A (H5) virus reported.* https://www.cdc.gov/media/releases/2022 /s0428-avian-flu.html

Covey, S. (2002). Foreword. In R. K. Greenleaf (Ed.), *Servant leadership: A journey into the nature of legitimate power and greatness* (25th ed., pp. 1–13). Paulist Press.

The Covid States Project. (2021, August). *Report #62: Covid-19 vaccine attitudes among healthcare workers.* https://news.northeastern.edu/uploads/COVID19 %20CONSORTIUM%20REPORT%2062%20HCW %20August%202021.pdf

Cox, N. (2011). *Pandemic influenza vaccines: Lessons learned from the H1N1 influenza pandemic.* https://www.who .int/influenza_vaccines_plan/resources/cox.pdf

Dolgin, E. (2021). How COVID unlocked the power of RNA vaccines. *Nature,* https://www.nature.com/articles /d41586-021-00019-w

Donne, J. (1623/1962). Meditation 17. In *Norton anthology of English literature* (Vol. 1, 5th ed.). W. W. Norton.

Farmer, P. (2001). *Infections and inequalities: The modern plagues* (Updated). University of California Press.

Forsey, H. (1993). *Circles of strength: Community alternatives to alienation.* New Society.

Friis, R. H. (2007). *Essentials of environmental health.* Jones and Bartlett Publishers.

Garrett, L. (2000). *Betrayal of trust: The collapse of global public health.* Hyperion.

Gavi. (2021). *The next pandemic: H5N1 and H7N9 influenza?* https://www.gavi.org/vaccineswork/next-pandemic /h5n1-and-h7n9-influenza

Greenleaf, R. (2002). *Servant leadership: A journey into the nature of legitimate power and greatness* (25th ed.). Paulist Press.

Hesse, H. (1956). *The journey to the east.* Picador.

Institute of Medicine, Hernandez, L.M. (Ed.). (2005). *Implications of genomics for public health: Workshop summary.* https://www.ncbi.nlm.nih.gov/books/NBK 83751/pdf/Bookshelf_NBK83751.pdf

Johnson, C.K. (2021, September 20). Covid-19 has killed about as many Americans as the 1918-19 Spanish flu. *Associated Press.* https://www.usatoday.com/story/news /nation/2021/09/20/us-covid-deaths-675000-death -toll-1918-19-spanish-flu/5788623001/

Kaye, C. B. (2004). *The complete guide to service learning: Proven, practical ways to engage students in civic responsibility, academic curriculum, and social action.* Free Spirit.

Kriebel, D., Tickner, J., & Crumbley, C. (2003). *Appropriate science: Evaluating environmental risks in a sustainable world.* https://www.researchgate. net/publication/228600182_Appropriate_Science _Evaluating_Environmental_Risks_in_a_Sustainable _World

Kush, C. (2004). *The one-hour activist: The 15 most powerful actions you can take to fight for the issues and candidates you care about.* Jossey-Bass.

Lewis, M. (2021). *The premonition: A pandemic story.* W. W. Norton & Company

Lundberg, K. (2005). An anthropologist's analysis. In B. C. White & J. A. Zimbelman (Eds.), *Moral dilemmas in community health care: Cases and commentaries* (pp. 152–155). Pearson Education.

MacIntyre, A. (1984). *After virtue: A study of moral theory* (2nd ed.). University of Notre Dame.

MacIntyre, A. (1999). *Dependent rational animals: Why human beings need the virtues.* Open Court.

Markel, H. (2004). *When germs travel: Six major epidemics that have invaded America since 1900 and the fears they have unleashed.* Pantheon.

Minkler, M., & Pies, C. (2002). Ethical issues in community organization and community participation. In M. Minkler (Ed.), *Community organizing and community building for health* (pp. 120–138). Rutgers University Press.

Myers, N. (2002). The precautionary principle puts values first. *Bulletin of Science, Technology, & Society, 22*(3), 210–219.

National Human Genome Research Institute. (n.d.). *The human genome project.* https://www.genome.gov/human -genome-project

Nussbaum, M. (2004). Compassion and terror. In L. P. Pojman (Ed.), *The moral life: An introductory reader in ethics and literature* (2nd ed., pp. 937–961). Oxford University Press.

Occupational Health and Safety Administration. (2021, December 27). *Covid-19 healthcare emergency temporary standard.* https://www.osha.gov/coronavirus/ETS

Pieper, J. (1966). *The four cardinal virtues.* University of Notre Dame.

Piliavin, J. A. (2003). Doing well by doing good: Benefits for the benefactor. In C. L. M. Keyes & J. Haidt (Eds.), *Flourishing: Positive psychology and the life well-lived* (pp. 227–247). American Psychological Association.

Reverby, S. M. (2012). *Ethical failures and history lessons: The U.S. Public Health Service research studies in Tuskegee and Guatemala.* https://publichealthreviews .biomedcentral.com/articles/10.1007/BF03391665 #citeas

Riegelman, R. (2010). *Public health 101: Healthy people— healthy populations.* Jones and Bartlett Publishers.

Salamon, J. (2003). *Rambam's ladder: A meditation on generosity and why it is necessary to give.* Workman.

Schecter, A. (2013). *UN caused deadly cholera in Haiti, covered it up, lawsuit says.* https://www.today.com /news/un-caused-deadly-cholera-haiti-covered-it -lawsuit-says-8C11359464

Schneider, M. J. (2021). *Introduction to public health* (6th ed.). Jones & Bartlett Learning.

Science and Environmental Health Network. (2018a). *Precautionary principle.* https://www.sehn.org /precautionary-principle-understanding-science-in -regulation

Science and Environmental Health Network. (2018b). *The precautionary principle: A fact sheet.* https://static1 .squarespace.com/static/5ad8bb3336099bd6ed7b022a /t/5cc2107971c10bd1034f791c/1556222073401 /Precautionary+Principle+FAQs.pdf

Sherwin, S. (1992). *No longer patient: Feminist ethics and health care.* Temple University.

Shilts, R. (2007). *And the band played on: Politics, people, and the AIDS epidemic 20th anniversary edition.* Martin's Press.

Thomas, J. (2004). *Skills for the ethical practice of public health.* https://nnphi.org/wp-content/uploads/2015/08 /ph-code-of-ethics-skills-and-competencies-booklet .original.pdf

Trout, S. S. (1997). *Born to serve: The evolution of the soul through service.*: Three Roses Press.

UNAIDS. (2021). *Global AIDS update 2021 confronting inequalities: Lessons for pandemic responses from 40 years of AIDS.* https://www.unaids.org/sites/default /files/media_asset/2021-global-aids-update_en.pdf

U.S. Department of Agriculture, Forest Service. (n.d.). *History of smokejumping.* https://www.fs.usda.gov /science-technology/fire/smokejumpers/mccall

U.S. Department of Energy. (2019, March 26). *Human genome project information archive: 1990–2003: ARCHIVE: Ethical, legal, and social issues.* https://web .ornl.gov/sci/techresources/Human_Genome/elsi /index.shtml

U.S. Department of Energy. (2019, April 23). *Human genome project information archive: 1990 2003: Human genome project.* https://web.ornl.gov/sci/techresources /Human_Genome/index.shtml

U.S. Environmental Protection Agency. (2021, August 3). *Environmental justice timeline.* https://www.epa.gov/ environmentaljustice/environmental-justice-timeline

U.S. Environmental Protection Agency. (2021, September 8). *Environmental justice.* https://www.epa .gov/environmentaljustice

U.S. Environmental Protection Agency. (2021, September 22). *Learn about environmental justice.* https://www.epa.gov /environmentaljustice/learn-about-environmental-justice

U.S. Department of Health and Human Services (HHS). (2012). *An HHS retrospective on the 2009 H1N1 influenza pandemic to advance all hazards preparedness.* https:// www.phe.gov/Preparedness/mcm/h1n1-retrospective /Documents/h1n1-retrospective.pdf

U.S. Department of Health and Human Services (HHS). (2013). *Health information privacy.* https://www.hhs .gov/hipaa/for-professionals/faq/405/is-this-more -protective-state-law-preempted-by-the-privacy-rule /index.html

U.S. Department of Labor, Occupational Safety and Health Administration (OSHA). (n.d.) *About OSHA.* https:// www.osha.gov/aboutosha

U.S. Department of Labor, Occupational Safety and Health Administration (OSHA). (n.d.) *Covid-19 emergency temporary standard (ETS).* https://www .osha.gov/coronavirus/ets

U.S. Government Accountability Office. (2011). *Influenza pandemic: Lessons from the H1N1 pandemic should be incorporated into future planning.* https://www.gao .gov/assets/330/320176.pdf

Wheatley, M. (2002). *Turning to one another.* Berrett-Koehler.

Wildes, K. M. (2000). *Moral acquaintances: Methodology in bioethics.* University of Notre Dame.

World Health Organization (WHO). (2018). *The end TB strategy: Information sheet.* https://www .who.int/publications/m/item/the-end-tb-strategy -information-sheet

World Health Organization (WHO). (2020). *World malaria report 2020: 20 years of global challenges and progress.* https://www.who.int/publications/i/item/9789240015791

World Health Organization (WHO). (2021a). *Communicable diseases.* https://www.euro.who.int/en/health-topics /communicable-diseases

World Health Organization. (2021, April 1). *Malaria.* https:// www.who.int/news-room/fact-sheets/detail/malaria

World Health Organization. (2021b). *Tuberculosis.* https:// www.who.int/health-topics/tuberculosis#tab=tab_1

World Health Organization. (2021, October 6). *WHO recommends groundbreaking malaria vaccine for children at risk.* https://www.who.int/news/item/06 -10-2021-who-recommends-groundbreaking-malaria -vaccine-for-children-at-risk

CHAPTER 12

Ethics in Organizations and Leadership

Janie B. Butts

OBJECTIVES

After reading this chapter, the reader should be able to do the following:

1. Compare the definitions of organizational ethics and the ethic of an organization.
2. Discuss the significance of organizations being characterized as good citizens in the community and society.
3. Explore the ethical dimensions that shape the ethical climate and the culture of an organization.
4. Examine the definition and characteristics of organizational trust and integrity.
5. Identify the common unethical and illegal behaviors that people sometimes exhibit in organizations.
6. Discuss Jennings's seven signs of organizational ethical collapse.
7. Briefly explore the history of compliance programs and officers in healthcare organizations.
8. Contrast the types of occupational fraud and abuse.
9. Evaluate the cases presented in this chapter regarding conflicts of interest and healthcare fraud.
10. Define an ethical leader.
11. Differentiate the three types of leadership theories that are presented in this chapter.
12. Discuss the ethical challenges of a nurse leader and the ways to use power for leader success.

▶ Organizational Ethics

An **organization** is a group of two or more people with an intentional focus on accomplishing a shared set of goals that are consistent with the organization's purpose and conduct.

An organization is sometimes compared to a person because it functions as a moral agent that is held accountable for its actions. Organizational ethics focuses "on the choices of the individual *and* the organization" (Boyle et al., 2001, p. 16).

Organizational Culture and the Ethical Climate

Organizational culture refers to an organization's past and current shared assumptions, experiences, and philosophy, much like a tribe with its own language, stories, beliefs, assumptions, ceremonies, and power structures (Johnson, 2018). Daft (2004) presented several types of organizational cultures and indicated a potential for every culture to be successful (see **BOX 12-1**). No matter which culture is promoted by the organization's leaders, the culture needs to fit with its strategy and environment.

Organizational ethics is a broad concept that includes not only culture but also the processes, outcomes, and character and denotes "a way of acting, not a code of principles, . . . [that] is at the heart, pumping blood that perfuses the entire organization with a common sense of purpose and a shared set of values" (Pearson et al., 2003, p. 42). The **ethic of an organization** refers to an organization's attempt to define its mission and values, recognize values that could cause tension and seek the best solutions to resolve these tensions, and manage the operations to maintain quality and the organization's values. The ethics process serves as a mechanism for organizations to address ethical issues regarding financial, business, and management decisions. Organizations are systems, which means that an organization consists of highly integrated parts or groups to accomplish shared goals. A **complex adaptive system**, such as a healthcare organization, focuses on external relationships, which places the organization within a larger context or environment (Boyle et al., 2001).

BOX 12-1 Daft's Types of Organizational Cultures

1. Adaptability culture: The focus is on the external environment where innovation, creativity, risk taking, flexibility, and change are the key elements for success. This type of organization creates change in a proactive way in an effort to anticipate responses and problems. Examples are e-commerce companies such as Amazon.com and Buy.com, which are required to change quickly in anticipation of customers' needs.
2. Mission culture: The vision and goals are clearly focused on a high level of competitiveness and profit-making strategies. In this type of culture, executives and managers strongly communicate a strategic plan for the organization's employees and expect high productivity, performance goals, and fringe benefits for goal attainment. An example is PepsiCo.
3. Clan culture: The focus is on employee needs and the strategies employees can engage with for high performance. Key values in this culture consist of leaders taking care of their employees and making sure they have appropriate avenues to satisfaction and productivity. Responsibility and ownership are other key values in this type of culture. Rapid change occurs in this environment because of changing expectations from the external environment. One example is the MTW Corporation, which sells web-based software and provides consultation to state governments and the insurance industry.
4. Bureaucratic culture: The focus is primarily on the internal environment, where stability is a mainstay. Leaders develop and carry out scrupulous and detailed plans in a cautious and stable environment with slow-paced change. In this environment, personal engagement and involvement are not cultivated; instead, there is a high level of consistency, conformity, efficiency, and integration. Because of the inflexibility of this culture, many organizations are forced to change to a different, more adaptable culture. One successful organization with this type of culture is the Pacific Edge Software company, run by a husband-and-wife team, which thrives on order, discipline, and control.

Data from Daft, R. L. (2004). *Organizational theory and design* (8th ed., pp. 367–370). South-Western.

An **organizational citizenship** represents what society and communities expect from open systems (Johnson, 2007). The expectations are part of establishing and maintaining those external relationships, including those with suppliers, regulatory bodies, customers, allies, competitors, communities, and society as a whole. For an organization to be characterized as **being a good citizen**, it must anticipate ethical issues or conflicts in external relationships and then engage in dialogue and activities to manage those concerns. Even though the term *organizational ethics* often refers to an organization's image, people who work in the organizations are the ones who behave ethically or unethically and therefore shape the ambiance and character of the organization. Many unethical behaviors of organizations are also illegal, so sometimes, the lines between ethical and legal behaviors are blurred. Boyle et al. (2001) delineated some of these unethical or illegal behaviors in organizations: occupational fraud and abuse; conflicts of interest; greediness; covert operations; misleading services; cheating on negotiated terms; fuzzy policies; disloyalty; poor quality and services; humiliating strategies; bigotry, sexism, racism, and favoritism; suppressing freedom of speech and choice; mindlessly and routinely obeying authority; price fixing; not speaking up when ethically obligated to do so; hurting others while climbing the ladder; using or blaming others to get the job done; exaggerating advantages of a plan just to gather support; uncooperative with others; lying for the sake of the business; not taking responsibility for injurious practices; abusing organizational perks; corrupting the public process through legal means; and obstructing, stalling, dithering, and inefficiency.

The ethical climate, which plays a large role in shaping the culture, is formed by the way the organization responds to ethical issues and challenges. The **ethical climate** is defined as the organizational members' shared perceptions of their values related to how ethical decisions are made on the issues of power, trust, and human interactions (Johnson, 2018). Numerous researchers have studied the idea of an ethical climate, but Victor and Cullen (1987) were the first to discover and then reconfirm that organizations can have a combination of one or more of these five dimensions of ethical climates:

- Caring: Interested in team values and goals, well-being of others, and friendships
- Law and code: Guided by professional codes of conduct
- Rules: Strict adherence to policies and procedures
- Instrumental: Focused on self-interest and company profits
- Independence: Focused on personal moral beliefs and decision making

The instrumental climate manifests from self-interest gains and profits within organizations and poses more serious ethical problems than any of the other ethical climates (Johnson, 2007).

Organizational Integrity and Trust

Organizational integrity generally means that good and right behavior in relationships is found across the whole system (Brown, 2006). **Integrity** as a whole is equated with the following:

- Keeping consistency between what an organization does and what it says
- Maintaining mindfulness of relationships with others
- Listening and including all voices, whether disagreeable or agreeable, in everyday business practices
- Having a collective, worthwhile purpose

Most major relationships transpire within five dimensions of organizational life: cultural, interpersonal, organizational, social, and natural. Integrity and trust go hand in hand; organizations and leaders with integrity are also trustworthy.

Trust is a multifaceted virtue that serves as an umbrella over the key values in organizations. Shore (2007) stated that **organizational trust** is the essential ingredient—what he labeled the lubricant—that facilitates everyday business and interactions. People can trust other people to follow through on their work and commitments, just as people in the community can depend on organizations to uphold their words and promises. **Fiduciary relationships** hold a high value in organizations because these relationships represent a formal duty to another or others, imposed by loyalty, commitment, and organizational structure, which means that people place trust in others to carry out activities related to their position with morally good judgment.

Trust flourishes in organizations only when there is evidence of fairness. Victor and Cullen's (1987) descriptions of the cultures of caring, law and code, and rule enable the achievement of fairness and justice. Practicing the virtue of justice promotes fair distribution of resources (of any type) among the individuals within the organizations and in the external community. According to Gutmann (1995), an organization must practice and sustain two principles so the community it serves can have a sense of fairness—nondiscrimination in the moral standing of each person and nonrepression—so that each person has a deliberate voice if he or she chooses. Without those principles, an organization's trust and justice will be questioned.

The ethic of the organization defines the mission and values. Some of those values are teamwork, community, achievement, competence, knowledge, innovation, having fun, valuing diversity, and encouraging others. Organizations need to define their values operationally and, likewise, their ethical practices in writing and verbal communication. Jack Welch, past chairman and CEO of General Electric, once said, "Good business leaders create a vision, articulate the vision, passionately own the vision, and relentlessly drive it to completion" (as cited in Kovanic & Johnson, 2004, p. 101).

As evidenced in many corporate scandals, trust in organizations has been eroding for years, and now it is at an all-time low (Jennings, 2006; Shore, 2007). Healthcare organizations are similar. The rapid transformation in healthcare organizations has been a contributing factor in the erosion of trust. As organizations rapidly change to comply with regulatory standards, costs, the demands of internal and external stakeholders, and the needs of the populations they serve, the ethical questions that need to be answered have become more difficult to resolve. Abusive executive power and self-serving corporate decisions lead to unethical behaviors, which leave an air of mistrust within the organization and in the external community. Trust in organizations is an obscure concept that consists of a network of convoluted relationships, although researchers have found that trust critically matters in organizations for nurses and other healthcare personnel because of the following (Kramer & Schmalenberg, 2002; Laschinger et al., 2001):

- Trust promotes economic value within organizations.
- Trust increases strategic alliances, teamwork, and productivity.
- Nurses and other healthcare personnel experience a more positive practice environment as a result of trust.
- Nurses experience increased empowerment, autonomy, and overall job satisfaction because of organizational trust.

A violation of trust in organizations will prompt verbalizations, such as angry and sarcastic remarks by personnel, especially if trust has been previously entrenched throughout the organizational levels. A violation of trust in organizations is generally illegal and less forgivable than in a personal relationship where trust historically exists between two people.

There are logical reasons for the way people perceive organizations. Untrustworthy leaders of organizations could have been engaging covertly in unethical or illegal behaviors for a long while, and if left unchecked, it will result in the ethical collapse of the organization.

Jennings's Seven Signs of Organizational Ethical Collapse

Jennings (2006) identified seven signs of ethical collapse and detailed how organizations can conduct business ethically and sustain its core values. The signs of collapse are the same whether the organization is a for profit or nonprofit, though there is some variation in the unethical activities. The signs are as follows:

1. Pressure to maintain numbers
2. Fear and silence
3. "Young 'uns and a bigger-than-life CEO"
4. Weak board
5. Conflicts
6. Innovation like no other
7. Goodness in some areas atones for evil in others

When these signs of ethical collapse are present, Jennings indicated that an organization is in profound trouble. An explanation of each sign follows.

Pressure to Maintain Numbers

The first and earliest sign that the organization is in trouble is an obsession with maintaining numbers, as measured in quantifiable goals (Jennings, 2006). Numbers drive nonprofit and for-profit organizations.

Fear and Silence

In organizations about to collapse ethically, there is an air of fear, silence, and servility (Jennings, 2006). Organizations are on the road to ethical collapse when there is corruption and wrongdoing by administrators. Many times, administrators prefer to look for gray ethical or legal areas so they can manipulate or create confusion or vagueness in records, bookkeeping, and other areas in the hopes that they will conceal their behavior and not be caught. Even in the midst of an ethical meltdown, not many people challenge the workings of the organization for fear of being threatened, publicly shamed, dismissed, or demoted. Employees and administrators who have evidence of confusing, fuzzy bookkeeping or wrongdoing are silenced and sometimes bribed by those involved with unethical, and perhaps illegal, conduct. Fear of not fitting in or being a team player is often a reason for employees' silence.

Young 'Uns and a Bigger-than-Life CEO

The third sign of an ethical meltdown involves a CEO who is sometimes a generation or two older than the other members of the organization and is lavishly praised and held in high regard by the community and media (Jennings, 2006). To maintain this level of admiration, these CEOs surround themselves with extremely driven young people, sometimes their own sons or daughters, who vow loyalty to the CEO and the organization. The presence of a highly regarded CEO does not necessarily translate to legal and ethical problems in an organization. However, when problems do exist or employees see potential trouble coming, they or others hesitate to ask questions that could cause embarrassment to the bigger-than-life CEO. The sentiment is, "We don't ask questions."

Weak Board

A weak and inefficient institutional board of directors is the next sign of an organization on the edge of ethical collapse (Jennings, 2006). Several reasons for a weak board exist, alone or in combination. Sometimes, the board is composed of inexperienced members who are the CEO's cronies or are unwilling to confront the beloved CEO. The members may be inefficient and unreliable, such as not spending enough time prudently thinking about and interpreting issues, not attending meetings, and not fulfilling their obligations to the board. Weak board members often make decisions that are baseless and push the limits on ethical and legal matters.

Conflicts

Conflicts of interest can occur with the individual or organization or between the internal organization and the external community (Jennings, 2006). Executives or board members engaged in a conflict of interest must have used their position to benefit themselves in some way at the expense of the organization.

Innovation Like No Other

Organizations heading toward ethical collapse often have extremely high levels of innovation and achievement (Jennings, 2006). They are often successful, with unmatched performance that seems to defy the laws of gravity with unlimited gains and the philosophy that they are above the law. Organizations with rapid, extreme success continuously seek new ways of keeping the success up, no matter what tactic has to be used. Eventually, as these successful organizations face strong competitors with higher quality and, in the case of healthcare organizations, better outcomes for patients while also maintaining a healthy financial bottom line, they are at risk of failing. However, Jennings (2006) emphasized that just because an organization has innovation and extreme success does not mean it is on the verge of an ethical collapse. Some do collapse, but the collapse is linked to organizations never forming or practicing standards of ethical excellence that make up a healthy ethical climate.

Goodness in Some Areas Atones for Evil in Others

Some organizations and CEOs, especially in for-profit companies, are committed to the community, public service, and philanthropic activities, but sometimes this results in the philosophy that goodness in some areas (public philanthropy) atones for evil in others (unethical practices) (Jennings, 2006). Sometimes, nonprofit organizations, when acting as noble public servants, such as giving back to the community with an emphasis on environmentalism and human rights, also manifest the good-atoning-for-evil philosophy, but Jennings contends that goodness in some areas will not overcome the improprieties in others.

Compliance and Ethics Programs

Today, the compliance officer is one of the most sought-after roles in a healthcare organization. This officer oversees and monitors regulatory requirements and internal policies because organizations, like individuals, are at risk of being found guilty of criminal conduct, such as felonies and some types of misdemeanors. A **compliance program** (also known as a risk-management program) is designed to "prevent unlawful conduct and to promote conformity with externally imposed regulations [and] provide a second component of background for organizational ethics" (Pearson et al., 2003, p. 28). During the 1980s, compliance programs became popular as a way for healthcare organizations to satisfy the mandate for addressing ethical and legal issues, primarily with Medicare and Medicaid. Compliance programs were expanded in 1991 when officials in the U.S. Department of Justice created the U.S. Sentencing Guidelines to make consistent the sentencing process in federal courts (Pearson et al., 2003). The 2021 U.S. Sentencing Guidelines were updated in 2018 with new annotations in 2020 to reflect the rulings on compassionate release motions associated with the Covid-19 pandemic and other rulings. When the guidelines are implemented and consistently practiced as a whole, organizations are portrayed as being good citizens.

From the ethical perspective of noncompliance, the principles of autonomy, beneficence, nonmaleficence, and justice may be violated in relation to patients, healthcare professionals, and the general public. When organizational schemes have the potential to harm patients without their knowledge, autonomy is violated ethically, but also legally, in the form of the Patient Self-Determination Act of 1990. Hurting or injuring someone because of illegal or unethical schemes violates the principles of beneficence, nonmaleficence, and justice.

Compliance programs are not synonymous with ethics programs, yet organizations tend to use compliance programs as a way of addressing ethical issues (Pearson et al., 2003). These two programs, compliance and ethics, are needed and can complement each other if appropriately structured. Ethics programs focus on the values of an organization, pursuing virtue, and delivering ethical patient care, whereas compliance programs focus on obedience to legal and required details of performance and have enforcement capability. Today, compliance programs are mandatory, not optional. Some leaders of organizations, however, see compliance programs more as a vehicle for protecting themselves rather than as a means to instill important ethical values.

Occupational Fraud and Abuse

Occupational fraud and abuse is defined as "the use of one's occupation for personal enrichment through the deliberate misuse or misapplication of the employment organization's resources or assets" (Association of Certified Fraud Examiners, 2020, p. 6). Three types of occupational fraud and abuse have been identified by the Association of Certified Fraud Examiners:

- Asset misappropriations: Stealing and misusing an organization's resources, such as skimming cash receipts, falsifying expense reports, or forging company checks
- Corruption: Employees' use of their influences in a manner that violates the duty owed to the employer for personal gain, such as bribery, extortion, or a conflict of interest
- Financial fraud statement: A deliberate misstatement or omission of material information in an organization's financial report, such as documenting fictitious revenues, concealing expenditures and obligations, or reporting inflated assets

Occupational fraud and abuse have been a major priority with the Federal Bureau of Investigation (FBI, 2022) for a number of years. There are numerous schemes that fall within the aforementioned categories of occupational fraud and abuse. Covered in this section are conflicts of interest and healthcare fraud, along with the related issue of whistle-blowing.

Conflicts of Interest

Conflicts of interest, from the standpoint of ethics, are referred to as **conflicts of**

commitment. Commitment conflicts are complex because the decision to engage in a conflict of interest involves loyalties, concerns, and emotions in relationships that collide with the organizational and public interests. There are various ways that conflicts of commitment can result in an ethical violation of the organization's code of conduct. Ritvo et al. (2004) emphasized the conflict that executives experience when they feel compelled to choose job commitments over the expectations of home and family life. Often, a person's ethical obligations to fulfill job commitments can interfere with the time available for family or others; for example, should an executive who is also a father tell his superior that his daughter's out-of-town soccer game takes priority over his attendance at a critical meeting with the hospital's executive board members?

Morrison (2006) mentioned other types of ethical conflicts of commitment. One is when an individual's personal behavior conflicts with the organization's ethics, such as overindulgence of alcohol or use of other drugs. Because patient safety and competent care are critical to the viability of a healthcare organization, personal behavior outside the organization is extremely important, as is personal behavior inside the organization. Nurses, in particular, are open to scrutiny by the public and hospital officials because of standards mandated by their nursing license and direct care of patients.

Cooper (2006) framed **conflicts of interest** as legal matters; when one's self-interests or potential personal gain is incompatible with that person's professional obligations, positions, or roles, a conflict of interest will occur.

The main ethical issue involved in conflicts of interest is breach of trust to the public. Whatever activities an executive leader or board member engages in also affect the organization's public image. These types of activities present legal conflicts between the person's position of authority in an organization and self-interest or between a person's accountability toward an organization and personal profit.

Compliance officers, or others in charge of overseeing ethical and legal issues, need to develop clear policies regarding conflicts of interest and conduct formal reviews of actions. Maintaining a clear focus on behaviors within and outside the organization helps to bring impending conflicts of interest to the forefront. Just like in fraud situations, employees and the public need to have an avenue for safe reporting of potential or alleged conflicts of interest.

It is essential that executives disclose all significant facts and arrangements of any

ETHICAL REFLECTION: SAVANNAH'S ETHICAL AND LEGAL VIOLATION AT HER WORKPLACE

Savannah, a registered nurse in charge of direct patient care, attended a party the night before a scheduled 12-hour workday, overindulged in cocktails, went to bed around 3:00 a.m., and came to work the next morning at 6:45 a.m. with a hangover and alcohol still on her breath. This situation placed Savannah in ethical violation of the organization's values and the American Nurses Association (ANA) *Code of Ethics for Nurses with Interpretive Statements* (2015) as well as a legal violation of the state board of nursing. If alcohol is on a person's breath, it is still in the bloodstream, which could alter Savannah's judgment in patient care and result in unsafe patient care and treatments.

- Discuss the ethical implications of Savannah's partying before work. Please explain your rationale.
- Explore specific ethical violations in Savannah's case in terms of her personal behavior, the hospital's ethics and values, patient safety, the ANA *Code of Ethics for Nurses with Interpretive Statements*, and the state board of nursing.

- Can you think of other options that Savannah should consider other than going to work with an altered state of mind? Make a list of the pros and cons of at least two other alternatives Savannah could have chosen.
- Describe and justify how you would have handled this situation had you been Savannah. Justify your strategies by using an ethical framework: theory, approach, or principle.
- Do you believe the nursing supervisor should take action against Savannah? Why or why not? If you believe the supervisor should take action against Savannah, describe the specific options for disciplinary action based on your general knowledge of institutional and state board of nursing disciplinary protocols. For this answer, you could search the web for general institutional disciplinary protocols and your state board of nursing's disciplinary actions if you need more knowledge on this topic. Explain your rationale.
- Do you believe the supervisor should report Savannah's behavior to the state board of nursing? Why or why not? Explain your rationale.

ETHICAL REFLECTION: BETTY'S CONFLICT OF INTEREST AT HER WORKPLACE

Betty, the chief nursing executive, needed to make a decision about buying 340 new hospital beds for patient rooms. After she interviewed nurse managers at the units where the beds were going to be placed, Betty compiled her findings and decided to contact a well-known equipment company to obtain prices and a bid. No bids from other companies were obtained. The equipment company's executive salesperson, Jim, discussed options at length with her and invited her and her significant other to an upcoming all-expenses-paid, lavish junket at a five-star hotel in Hawaii to see demonstrations of the beds and experience a comprehensive sales program. Betty thought, "We badly need some relaxation and stress relief. Hawaii would be so much fun. Would it be wrong for us to go?"

- If you were Betty, what would you do? Give your rationale. Justify your answer with an ethical framework: theory, approach, or principle.
- Discuss the ethical principles at stake. What breaches are possible?
- Do you consider this situation a conflict of interest? Why or why not? Give your rationale.
- Speculate how Betty would handle this case if she believed she needed to seek advice from someone in higher authority. With whom would she discuss this issue?
- Discuss the policies that should be in place regarding this scenario.

proposed transaction to the board or another executive of higher authority (Cooper, 2006). When a board of trustees becomes aware that an executive's proposed transactions are not fully disclosed or the activities and timelines seem vague or fuzzy, the board should confront the person and allow for an explanation through deliberation; the board should then take disciplinary action toward the person if there was not a satisfactory explanation. If a board member is the one who has breached that trust, the other board members should exclude that member from meetings and deliberations until a time comes for confrontation. If money or luxury gifts are a source of the breach of trust, the state of affairs then becomes complicated. These types of breaches are difficult to prove and sometimes fall into a gray area of ethical wrongdoing. If board members cannot find solid evidence of a breach on their own, they must determine if legal fees and time are worth the effort of a trial that may never result in a conviction for that board member.

Healthcare Fraud

Healthcare fraud is defined as "an intentional deception or misrepresentation that an individual makes, knowing it to be false and that it could result in some unauthorized benefit to [self or others]" (Congressional Research Service, 2011, August 3, p. 9). After the 1990s, the U.S. Department of Health and Human Services (HHS, 2021, July) and the Department of Justice Health Care Fraud and Abuse Control Program began investigating and prosecuting abuse and fraud cases in healthcare organizations in significantly greater numbers. The criminality in healthcare organizations, especially defrauding federal government programs such as Medicare, became apparent as the percentage of cases continually increased each year.

The FBI (2022) investigates all healthcare fraud for federal, state, and local levels of government and for private insurance and other programs. A significant trend that has concerned the FBI is the willingness of medical professionals to commit schemes that risk patients' health and cause potential patient harm, some of which include unnecessary and harmful surgeries, prescriptions for dangerous drugs, and substandard care practices. High technology and computers have contributed to the increase in the number of fraudulent schemes. The effects of fraudulent schemes result in acts of malfeasance in terms of personal injury, wrongful death, and sometimes class action suits for the involved patients.

Because the U.S. population is growing older, more Medicare services are needed. This rise in Medicare usage serves as a temptation for an increased incidence of corporate-driven schemes and systematic abuse. Healthcare fraud events in 2005 were committed through various means throughout all segments of the healthcare system.

Nurses may be unknowingly involved in other similar arrangements, such as assisting with keeping the records for providers of care who are operating secret, fraudulent schemes.

In these cases, proving the innocence of involved nurses in a court of law would be difficult. One such unethical practice in which nurses could be involved, unintentionally or otherwise, is in the billing and maintenance of fraudulent records on ambulance transfers of patients. There are many cases of fraudulent billing.

Nurses can be involved in many other potentially unethical situations. Sometimes, nurse practitioners or other providers are unaware of their own acts of healthcare fraud. One instance is when they accept gifts or possibly money from pharmaceutical companies in exchange for prescribing that company's medications. Nurses' involvement in the ordering of supplies from medical suppliers and other vendors can pose similar problems.

Hospital-associated healthcare fraud is a tremendous problem in the United States. One case involved HealthSouth Corporation, whose central office is located in Birmingham, Alabama. The company is the largest provider of integrated healthcare services in the country, with numerous locations across the United States. The other case was at Eisenhower Medical Center in Rancho Mirage, California. These two cases are good examples of fraud cases that occur each year throughout the United States.

To reduce or prevent fraudulent schemes, Pearson et al. (2003) offered an exemplary list of broad, normative ethical obligations for organizations. Although these obligations refer to organizations as a whole, not the individual leaders, providers of care and corporate leaders must make an effort to uphold ethical obligations, such as engaging stakeholders in decision making and maintaining clear communication and actions to promote health and provide safe and quality patient care.

Prevention strategies are the most effective and efficient ways to deter financial loss through fraud. For example, there is a supportive website by BlueCross BlueShield (n.d.) where people can access information regarding facts, statistics, and types of fraud. To

ETHICAL REFLECTION: COMMON TYPES OF HEALTHCARE FRAUD REPORTED BY THE FBI IN 2022

Healthcare Fraud by Medical Providers

- Double billing: Multiple claims for the same service.
- Phantom billing: Billing a patient for service or supplies never received.
- Unbundling: Multiple bills submitted to the patient for the same service.
- Upcoding: The provider submits a bill using a procedure code that yields a higher payment than the code for the actual service rendered.

Healthcare Fraud by Patients and Others

- Bogus marketing: Billing for services not rendered, stealing identities, or enrolling people in a fake benefit plan by persuading people to provide personal data and information.
- Identity theft and identity swapping: Using another person's health insurance or allowing another person to use your insurance.
- Impersonating a health care professional: Providing or billing for health service or equipment with a license.

Fraud Involving Prescriptions

- Forgery: Creating or using prescriptions that are forged.
- Diversion: Selling prescription medications for or by illegal means.
- Doctor shopping: Visiting multiple providers for prescriptions of controlled substances or obtaining prescriptions from medical offices that engage in unethical practices.

Data from Federal Bureau of Investigation (FBI). (2022). *Health care fraud: Common scams and safety.* https://www.fbi.gov/scams-and-safety/common-scams-and-crimes/health-care-fraud

report a suspicious case of Medicare fraud or seek further directions on reporting, nurses or others who suspect fraud of any kind should call 1-877-327-2583 to report their observations. Most defrauded companies will never recover their monetary losses. They could be out of business literally in months, even days, if organizations do not put prevention measures in place. When organizations create a fraud prevention program, administrators or outside consultants need to assess the state of affairs within the organization. Strategies in the assessment phase include the following:

- The CEO or the board should consider hiring an external consultant to conduct the assessment.
- The current fraud risks should be assessed.

- Interviews with stakeholders should be held, which usually reveal the organization's risks for fraud.
- An independent agent should perform an internal audit.
- Benchmarks should be set for measuring best practices to prevent fraud.

Adams et al. (2006) developed a sample questionnaire for assessing risks of fraud in organizations. The questions yield quantitative and qualitative data. Executives or consultants could adapt the following questions for their organization's survey and have key people complete it:

- Have the board and members of the management team delineated specific

ETHICAL REFLECTION: TWO CASES OF HEALTHCARE FRAUD SCHEMES REPORTED IN 2005

HealthSouth Corporation, Birmingham, Alabama

HealthSouth Corporation paid the U.S. government $327 million to settle allegations of fraud against Medicare and other federally insured healthcare programs. The government alleged that the rehabilitative services of HealthSouth engaged in three healthcare fraud schemes to cheat the government. The first scheme, requiring a $170 million settlement, involved alleged false claims for outpatient physical therapy services that were not properly supported by certified plans of care, administered by licensed physical therapists, or for one-on-one therapy as the corporation represented in the billing. The second scheme, requiring a $65 million settlement, involved alleged accounting fraud that resulted in overbilling Medicare on hospital cost reports and home office cost statements. The third scheme, requiring a $92 million settlement, involved allegedly billing Medicare for a range of unallowable costs, such as luxury entertainment and travel expenses for the annual administrators' meeting at Disney World, among many other incurred expenses. The remaining $76 million settlement involved four *qui tam* lawsuits, also known as whistle-blowing lawsuits. (The term *qui tam* is an abbreviation of a Latin phrase that means "he who sues for the king as well as for himself.") **Qui tam lawsuits** are filed by private citizens who sue on behalf of the federal government by alleging fraud against those organizations that received government funding. The private citizen who filed the lawsuit receives a portion of the recovery money if the case is successful, and the government receives the major portion of recovered funds.

Eisenhower Medical Center, Rancho Mirage, California

Eisenhower Medical Center paid the U.S. government $8 million to settle allegations of overbilling federal health insurance programs. A former employee also filed a *qui tam* lawsuit. The allegation was that the healthcare financial advisers helped the hospital seek reimbursement for unallowable costs and specifically, that the advisers prepared two cost reports—an inflated one submitted to Medicare and one designed for internal use that accurately reflected the amount of reimbursement the hospital should have received.

Data from U.S. Department of Health and Human Services (HHS). (2021, July). *The Department of Health and Human Services and the Department of Justice Health Care Fraud and Abuse Control Program annual report for FY 2005.* https://oig.hhs.gov/publications/docs/hcfac/FY2020-hcfac.pdf

responsibilities relating to the oversight and management of fraud risks with the organization?

- What is the fraud risk management budget in dollars? In full-time equivalent resources?
- How frequently (e.g., every 6, 12, 24, or 36 months) is the fraud risk management strategy updated?
- Is an anonymous process available at any time for employees to use in reporting improprieties or breaches of ethics?

- Do you have a formal code of ethics or conduct for the board or senior management?
- Please list what you think are the top three fraud business risks that your organization faces. How would you assess your risk of exposure to each of these? (p. 58)

A new prevention program should be initiated or an existing one improved based on the assumptions that arise from the assessment data. Some of the necessary components of the program include an ethics educational program for all employees, a code of ethical conduct, and a hotline program. After the program is in place, ongoing monitoring and training are necessary. Nurses need to serve in key positions to spot or report healthcare fraud in hospitals, clinics, or agencies.

ETHICAL REFLECTION: ANALYSIS OF THE TWO FRAUD CASES

Please review the cases, and then refer to the exemplary ethical obligations for organizations as outlined in a previous section of this chapter.

The Two Hospital Cases

- Describe the feelings of conflict you might experience if you were working as a registered nurse in some area of either of these two organizations when the lawsuits were filed and became public knowledge.
- Make a list of the exemplary ethical obligations that these two hospitals did not uphold.
- Explain actions you would take in light of the charges against your place of employment. Give your rationale based on one ethical framework: theory, approach, or principle.

▶ Leadership Ethics

A **leader** influences a group or organization by engaging in relationships to further the shared goals of the other leaders and followers. At the center of leadership is ethics. Leaders face extreme moral demands on a daily basis while they strive to provide direction and shape the ethical climate and culture of the organization. Best said by Buzz McCoy (2007), the definition of a **successful leader** is an **ethical leader** who

> attempts to align the values of the enterprise with those of the individuals who form it, striving to facilitate a sense of deep meaning and

commitment in their work. A precondition is a heightened degree of sensitivity on the part of the leader to the values of society, the enterprise, and the individuals who constitute it. (p. 2)

Rost (1995) offered two ways of analyzing the ethical nature of leadership. The first way is related to the process and performance of leadership. To analyze the ethical perspectives of process and performance, a question needs to be answered: Is the leadership being done in a way that is ethical at the moment? To answer this question, a person needs to examine the degree and nature of the influence relationship between the leaders and the followers. For the process and performance to be regarded as ethical, people in a leader–follower relationship should be using a variety of nonforced measures to influence people and develop a collaborative agreement that reflects shared purposes. Griffith (2007) proposed that a prerequisite to analyzing the process and performance of leadership is to search for an ethical meaning in the very existence of influence relationships by answering questions such as "Is it ethical for leaders to influence the values and purposes of followers?" and "Does the influence relationship deprive the followers of their free will?" The second way of analyzing the ethical nature of leadership is to determine whether the shared and intended change in the community or organization is ethical. Important to this second analysis is to scrutinize what the community or organization is proposing. The goals must be genuinely communal and shared by everyone in the community as a whole.

Normative Leadership Theories

Leaders who are mindful of ethics motivate others to act in ethical ways. Ethics as praxis requires that leaders must first rethink their values on a personal level and then move from a personal ethics to a collective way of thinking. To lead with **ethics as praxis** means that a person clarifies, reflects on, makes sense of, practices, and embodies a leadership theory. At the foundation of normative leadership theories are the norms of ethical behavior, or how people ought to act, which originate from the classical ethical theories. Comprehending ethical theory contributes to a leader's expertise in leader and follower behaviors.

The ethical perspectives of three theories will be the focus of this section. Leadership theories selected for this section are not representative of all leadership theories, but these three—servant leadership, transformational leadership, and authentic leadership—have an emphasis in higher morality, ethical reasoning, altruism, caring, and the common good. These attributes are important for nursing leaders if they are to lead with ethics as praxis and have a greater influence on organizational outcomes.

Servant Leaders

Robert Greenleaf coined the term *servant leader* in his 1977 book *Servant Leadership*. A **servant leader** consistently makes decisions to further the good of the group of followers over any decisions that satisfy self-interests. Servant leaders engage others and search for ethically meaningful ways to make decisions. In fact, Griffith (2007) identified servant leadership as the ultimate level of ethicality. Servant leaders exemplify the values of moral sensitivity, altruism, caring, empathy, and ongoing development. The characteristics of servant leadership vary from author to author, but Johnson (2018) identified five attributes he believed as most central to servant leadership:

- Stewardship: Acting on behalf of others and being an agent of the followers
- Obligation: Taking seriously the responsibilities to the followers and the organization

- Partnership: Viewing followers as partners, not subordinates
- Emotional healing: Being empathetic and an active listener and instilling a sense of wholeness
- Elevating purpose: Striving for a high moral purpose and understanding the roles of followers and of oneself as a leader

Some people link weakness to any type of service and believe that servant leadership is an unrealistic and weak theory that does not work in many situations. However, the behavior of those being served will manifest as the measurement for the extent to which servant leaders are successful. Greenleaf (1977/2002) stated that the test of servant leader success is to evaluate whether those served grow as persons: "do they, while being served, become healthier, wiser, freer, more autonomous, more likely themselves to become servants? And, what is the effect on the least privileged in society; will they benefit, or, at least, not be further deprived?" (p. 27). With the rapid changes away from traditional leadership theories, people are moving toward servant leadership theory as a simplistic yet ideal and ethical way of being in relationships with other leaders and followers.

Transformational Leaders

Ethical obligations, relationships, and deontology are at the center of transformational leadership. James McGregor Burns (1978) distinguished transformational leaders from transactional leaders, with a **transformational leader** focusing on raising the moral benchmark on human behaviors of both leaders and followers, internalizing a sense of commitment, facilitating the higher-order needs and creativity of followers, placing importance on relationships and shared goals, and striving for follower empowerment to promote transformation. They strive for change in the culture of an organization rather than working within the status quo and are measured by the degree of transformation demonstrated by the followers.

While Bernard Bass (1995; as cited in Johnson, 2018) researched and expanded the work of Burns, he promoted the idea that a transformational leader can also exhibit transactional leadership qualities. Transactional leaders focus on the management processes and controls facilitated by the values of responsibility, fairness, and honesty, but they persuade followers to conform by exercising their power. By using an approach that is utilitarian, transactional leaders evaluate the morality of an action based on outcomes.

Through research, four components of transformational leadership were identified (Bass, 2008):

- Idealized influence: A solid ground of high morality exists with ideals of trust and authenticity.
- Inspirational motivation: The personality traits and charisma of the transformational leaders inspire followers to commit to and search for meaning in their work toward achieving shared values and goals.
- Intellectual stimulation: Transformational leaders encourage followers to think freely and be creative with ways to connect to the leader and achieve shared goals.
- Individual consideration: Individuals are boosted by the transformational leader's focus on each person as an individual who has a need for self-actualization, growth, and opportunities. The leader's mentoring and teaching enhance the continued growth and success of the followers.

Other features of transformational leaders include seeing the big picture in detailed matters, role modeling, networking, and flexibility (Taylor, 2009). There are pseudo-transformational leaders who claim they are transformational but are unethical in their relationships and actions (Bass, 1995). The unethical behaviors of pseudo-leaders result from their own self-interests and personal goals instead of the collective benefit for all. In contrast, the high moral standards of transformational leaders serve as the guiding principles in relationships and decision making.

Authentic Leaders

Servant leadership, transformational leadership, and authentic leadership have many commonalities, but a distinguishing feature of authentic leaders is that they are deeply anchored in relational transparency (honesty and openness) in their sense of self and right and wrong (Shirley, 2006). An **authentic leader** finds true identity in the self by retrieving and developing the soul; through an authentic presence, authentic leaders inspire and encourage well-being and thriving (*eudaimonia*) in their followers. Leaders with **authentic presence** are people-focused leaders who are true to themselves and deeply aware of who they are and how others perceive them. They epitomize Shakespeare's words, "This, above all: Unto thine own self be true." Being true to self translates to being powerful, and with that power, an authentic leader serves as a moral compass for, a facilitator to, and a supporter of followers striving to reach their high values and purposes. Many people say that when people encounter an authentic person, they know it because there is genuine presence. According to Irvine and Reger (2006), the eight characteristics of authentic presence are clarity, courage, integrity, service, trust, humility, compassion, and vulnerability. The advantages of authentic leaders are that they are highly effective and unite their followers; the disadvantages are that authenticity is overstated and is sometimes indistinguishable because various interpretations of the term exist (Johnson, 2018).

Leader Challenges

Transforming health care to a business-oriented model of practices caused traditional healthcare practices to undergo a violent revolution during the last couple of decades and led to mistrust of traditional health care (Donley, 2005). As a result, nurse leaders confront many ethical issues because of this aggressive healthcare environment, and when these issues are combined, they create extreme stress in nurses who are only trying to manage these challenges and stay balanced. One reason for this stress is the clash in values among people involved in decision making. In this environment, stress is evidenced in all relationships, not just in the usual difficult and uncivil relationships that nurses encounter in horizontal or vertical violence, but also in relationships that are generally more pleasant under normal circumstances.

Another reason for high stress is a toxic or destructive leader displaying unethical behaviors. Kellerman (2004) explained that people should not overlook bad leadership or link all leadership with good leadership because "it is confusing . . . misleading . . . and does a disservice" (p. 12). There are seven classifications of bad leaders, as identified by Kellerman: incompetent leaders, rigid leaders, intemperate leaders, callous leaders, corrupt leaders, insular leaders, and evil leaders. The followers' behaviors mirror the leader's behaviors.

Some of the issues that Thompson (2008), and Huston (2008) identified as what they perceived are the biggest challenges and needs that nursing faces in this intense environment, both now and in the future, are improved patient outcomes (safety, care, and quality), evidenced-based care and documentation, patient satisfaction, reimbursement and cost-cutting pressures to meet patient care expectations, retention of nurses, excellent decision-making skills and political skills, and acceptable channels for succession of nursing leaders.

Morris (2021, November 3) offered her comments and shared two nursing leaders' opinions about what the future holds for 2022 and beyond. Morris stated, "The last of the baby boomer generation will retire in 2030. This means changes in how healthcare is delivered will be necessary to meet more complex medical needs" (para. 3). Some of these trends, which will affect nurses and how they manage and deliver care, are:

- Job growth for nurses will continue to rise. For instance, job growth for advanced practice nurses through 2030 will be 45%.
- The need for home health care will increase.

- Anne Dabrow Woods (as cited in Morris, 2021, November 3) predicts that care model will experience a shift in the mode of delivery and nursing skills in hospital units posing the need for team-based crisis management and more flexibility to produce excellent patient care.
- More virtual simulation and technology for transformation of nursing schools.
- Woods (as cited in Morris, 2021, November 3) predicts that well-being of the healthcare staff and resilience for retaining nurses. Expect unwanted side effects in light of the nursing shortage—increased burnout of nurses with an increased early attrition of nurses from the profession and salary increases with high salary bidding for contingent nursing staff, such as travel nurses.
- Need for higher education demands, training, and online nursing programs.

Patsy Anderson, an expert in organizational behavior and a nurse educator, stated that nurse leaders in healthcare centers often have difficulty saying no to the demand that their nursing personnel meet or exceed the increasingly raised expectations for patient outcomes while absorbing extra work in light of streamlined organizational budgets that have less resource allocation for nursing positions (personal communication, December 5, 2018). When nurse leaders give in and accept the responsibility of doing more with less, serious issues are at stake—issues of patient satisfaction and safety, better health outcomes, and the provision of quality services to the public.

Ethical dilemmas arise because these challenges are not easily tackled in healthcare organizations. Forced overtime of nurses, increased workload, and burnout from stress and fatigue jeopardize the well-being of patients and nurses. Another consideration is whether the healthcare organization's monetary sustainability is enough to offer quality services to the public. In response to economic pressures and stakeholder concerns, CEOs often overrule nurse leader decisions to preserve quality care in favor of budget-related changes. These decisions often result in an infringement in one or more bioethical principles: autonomy, beneficence, nonmaleficence, and justice.

- Autonomy: Freedom of choice—The difficulties faced by the profession as a whole in saying no to expanded nursing responsibilities without a corresponding increase in autonomy makes it harder for nurses to maintain quality standards in practice. Fatigue and stress are associated with higher workloads, more job responsibilities, and overtime.
- Beneficence: Promote good—The increased workloads limit the ability of individual nurses and the profession as a whole to fulfill the expectations of promoting good in practice and in the care of patients.
- Nonmaleficence: Do no harm—The risk of missed or substandard care and corresponding worsening patient outcomes increase as nurses must take on larger workloads with fewer resources.
- Justice: Fairness
  - Individual nurses, and the profession as a whole, suffer injustice when job opportunities are diminished as a result of medical centers being forced to decrease services or close their doors to patients due to financial instability.
  - It is unfair to nurses when healthcare centers, whether by increasing workloads or via financial instability, limit the ability of nurses to give competent nursing care.
  - Issues of social justice are raised when patients are limited in their ability to receive services and access care that is comparable to patients in other locations.

Using Power to Achieve Leader Success

Power is defined as influence that leaders have over their followers to achieve common goals. In almost every interaction within an organization, power is used in some way. When leaders use their power in a positive way to guide and direct, followers more easily develop ethical ways to work. If leaders stay centered in ethics, they will use their power to create pragmatic solutions to achieve the organization's shared goals, even when they are faced with daily temptations to do otherwise. In 1959, French and Raven identified five bases of power. Leaders can use each power base alone or in combination with the other four bases:

- Legitimate power: Power that originates from the leader's title or position and the belief by followers that the title gives the leader a right to that power over them
- Referent power: Power that is created when followers believe the leader has admirable qualities they want to possess
- Expert power: Power that develops when followers believe the leader has expertise in the knowledge or skills related to the task or job
- Reward power: Power that develops when leaders offer followers certain rewards for completion of tasks or good behaviors combined with the belief of followers that the leader will follow through with the rewards
- Coercive power: Power that is based on the belief by followers that the leader has the ability to discipline or impose a penalty when the followers do not follow the required behaviors; leaders need to use caution in exercising this type of power

Often, power is negatively equated with evilness and corruption, as evidenced by the many past moral failures in the history of leadership. If the leader abuses power for self-interest motives and personal gain instead of following through with good intentions, the result is wrongdoing. In a letter to Mandell Creighton on April 5, 1887, Lord Acton stated, "Power tends to corrupt and absolute power corrupts absolutely." Lord Acton, an English magistrate, became a moral judge because he held the best-known men to a historical standard or precedence (Acton Institute, 2018).

It is a well-known fact that power can corrupt a person in authority and leadership is a complex, power-based relationship. Leaders must build strong, positive power bases to influence others. There are several ways for leaders to positively use power to enable success, but in this section, three ways are covered: collaboration, quality, and leadership succession planning.

Collaboration

Principled leaders use their power to make collaborative decisions for the best possible patient and organizational outcomes. For leaders to engage in **collaboration**, they must listen to new perspectives on what could be done to ensure best practices and confront difficulties within the organization. They seek open dialogue from wise people outside the organization and at all levels within the organization. A written ethical guide for leaders is the ANA (2015) *Code of Ethics for Nurses with Interpretive Statements*.

Quality

Quality means that leaders use power to strive for excellence in the delivery of care. Leaders are responsible for implementing quality throughout every process of the organization. Leaders who are ethical know that their obligation to the organization and community at large is to focus on quality at all levels, use benchmarking to denote successes and failures, and use innovations to heighten quality. Organizations can improve their image if leaders use commonsense judgments about ensuring quality and cutting waste in organizational time and spending. The ANA (2015) *Code of Ethics for Nurses with Interpretive Statements* clearly indicates the need for nursing leaders, and all nurses, to be accountable for quality in standards of care.

Leader Succession Planning

Leader succession planning is a way for leaders to allow and enable other leaders to surface within an organization so that successors have an opportunity to develop and use their leadership skills. When people emerge as leader candidates, the existing leaders need to mentor them for future succession without fear of territorial loss. Ethical leaders realize the critical nature of having leaders in the making through a strong leadership succession program for the long-term success of the organization.

Good, ethical leaders are hard to find, but when an organization finds that leader, it must invest in that leader for the sake of the organization. People often place significant value on the trustworthiness and authenticity of the leader. Nurse leaders are often confronted with moral indecision. Ethical leadership has become an essential part of organizational leadership, largely because of the past leadership failures that have occurred in big business and healthcare organizations throughout the world. These failures have led to character-driven leadership styles, such as the three leadership theories presented in this chapter. For guidance, leaders and staff nurses should refer to the ANA (2015) *Code of Ethics for Nurses with Interpretative Statements*.

KEY POINTS

An organization's relationship to its environment and the organization's interpretation of reality, truth, human nature, and human relationships represent the ethical dimensions that shape the organizational culture.

- Each organizational culture—adaptability, mission, clan, and bureaucratic—has the potential to be successful if the strategic plans that relate to the desired culture are accomplished and maintained.

- Organizational ethics is a way of acting that includes culture, processes, outcomes, and character.
- The ethical climate refers to the organizational members' shared perceptions on the values of power, trust, and interactions on how ethical decisions are made.
- Trust is the multifaceted, essential ingredient that serves as a lubricant for all operations and values in organizations. Without trust in organizations and among people, organizational values and relationships erode and crumble.
- Unethical and illegal behaviors committed by people ultimately shape the ambiance and character of the organization.
- Regulators of organizations and the government mandated the development of compliance programs to prevent unlawful behaviors and to promote conformity to regulations involving legal actions.
- Nurses are at an increased risk of participating, knowingly or unknowingly, in healthcare fraud cases. They need to develop a sharp perception for spotting dubious fraudulent cases in their workplace and report their suspicions to the fraud hotline.
- A leader whose leadership is centered in ethics influences a group or organization by engaging in relationships to further the shared goals of other leaders and the followers.
- For leaders, ethics as praxis means they reflect on, make sense of, practice, and embody a leadership theory.
- Some theories that are considered normative leadership theories include servant leadership, transformative leadership, and authentic leadership. These theories place a higher emphasis on morality, ethical reasoning, altruism, caring, and the common good.
- Leader challenges in today's healthcare system include maintaining patient safety, quality care, and satisfaction; issues of cost cutting and reimbursement for services; nurse retention; political issues; and decision-making and team-building skills.
  - Nurse leaders use their power to influence followers in a positive, ethical way.

References

Acton Institute. (2018). *Lord Acton quote archive.* https://www.acton.org/research/lord-acton-quote-archive

Adams, G. W., Campbell, D. R., Campbell, M., & Rose, M. P. (2006, January). Fraud prevention: An investment no one can afford to forego. *The CPA Journal, 76*(1), 56–59.

American Nurses Association. (2015). *Code of ethics for nurses with interpretive statements.* Author.

Association of Certified Fraud Examiners, Inc. (2020). *Report to the nations: 2020 global study on occupational fraud and abuse.* https://acfepublic.s3-us-west-2.amazonaws.com/2020-Report-to-the-Nations.pdf

Bass, B. M. (1995). The ethics of transformational leadership. In J. Ciulla (Ed.), *Ethics: The heart of leadership* (pp. 169–192). Praeger.

Bass, B. M. (with Bass, R.) (2008). *The Bass handbook of leadership: Theory, research and managerial applications* (4th ed.). Free Press.

BlueCross BlueShield. (2022). *Healthcare fraud.* https://www.bcbs.com/healthcare-fraud

Boyle, P. J., DuBose, E. R., Ellingson, S. J., Guinn, D. E., & McCurdy, D. B. (2001). *Organizational ethics in health care: Principles, cases, and practical solutions.* Jossey-Bass.

Brown, M. T. (2006). *Corporate integrity: Rethinking organizational ethics and leadership.* Cambridge University Press.

Burns, J. M. (1978). *Leadership.* Harper & Row.

Congressional Research Service. (2011, August 3). *Medicare program integrity: Activities to protect Medicare from payment errors, fraud, and abuse.* https://crsreports.congress.gov/product/pdf/RL/RL34217/18

Cooper, T. L. (2006). *The responsible administrator: An approach to ethics for the administrative role* (5th ed.). Jossey-Bass.

Daft, R. L. (2004). *Organizational theory and design* (8th ed.). South-Western.

Desio, P. (2010). *An overview of the organizational guidelines. U.S. sentencing guidelines.* http://www.ussc.gov/sites/default/files/pdf/training/organizational-guidelines/ORGOVERVIEW.pdf

Donley, R., Sr. (2005). Challenges for nursing in the 21st century. *Nursing Economics, 23*(6), 312–318.

Federal Bureau of Investigation. (2022). *Scams and safety: Health care fraud.* https://www.fbi.gov/scams-and-safety/common-scams-and-crimes/health-care-fraud

French, J. R. P., & Raven, B. (1959). The bases of social power. In D. Cartwright (Ed.), *Studies in social power* (pp. 150–167). University of Michigan Press.

Greenleaf, R. K. (1977/2002). *Servant leadership.* Paulist Press.

Griffith, S. D. (2007). *Servant leadership, ethics and the domains of leadership.* https://www.regent.edu/wp-content/uploads/2020/12/patterson_servant_leadership.pdf

Gutmann, A. (1995). The virtues of democratic self-constraint. In A. Etzioni (Ed.), *New communitarian thinking: Persons, virtues, institutions, and communities* (pp. 154–169). University of Virginia Press.

Huston, C. (2008). Preparing nurse leaders for 2020. *Journal of Nursing Management, 16,* 905–911.

Irvine, D., & Reger, J. (2006). *The authentic leader: It's about presence, not position.* DC Press.

Jennings, M. M. (2006). *The seven signs of ethical collapse: How to spot moral meltdowns in companies . . . before it's too late.* St. Martin's Press.

Johnson, G. E. (2007). *Ethics in the workplace: Tools and tactics for organizational transformation.* Sage.

Johnson, G. E. (2018). *Meeting the ethical challenges of leadership: Casting light or shadow* (6th ed.). Sage.

Kellerman, B. (2004). *Bad leadership: What it is, how it happens, and why it happens (Leadership for the common good).* Harvard Business School Press.

Kovanic, N., & Johnson, K. D. (2004). *Lies and truths: Leadership ethics in the 21st century.* Rule of Thumb.

Kramer, M., & Schmalenberg, C. (2002). Staff nurses identify essentials of magnetism. In M. McClure & A. Hinshaw (Eds.), *Magnet hospitals revisited* (pp. 25–59). American Nurses.

Laschinger, H., Shamian, J., & Thomson, D. (2001). Impact of Magnet hospital characteristics on nurses' perceptions of trust, burnout, quality of care and work satisfaction. *Nursing Economics, 19,* 209–219.

McCoy, B. H. (2007). *Living into leadership: A journal in ethics.* Stanford University Press.

Morris, G. (2021, November 3). Nursing and healthcare trends we can expect to see in 2022. *Nurse Journal.* https://nursejournal.org/articles/2022-nursing-healthcare-trends/

Morrison, E. E. (2006). *Ethics in health administration: A practical approach for decision makers.* Jones and Bartlett Publishers.

Pearson, S. D., Sabin, J. E., & Emanuel, E. J. (2003). *No margin, no mission: Health-care organizations and the quest for ethical excellence.* Oxford University Press.

Ritvo, R. A., Ohlsen, J. D., & Holland, T. P. (2004). *Ethical governance in health care: A board leadership guide for building an ethical culture.* Health Forum.

Rost, J. (1995). Leadership: A discussion about ethics. *Business Ethics Quarterly, 5*(1), 129–142.

Shirley, M. R. (2006). Authentic leaders creating healthy work environments for nursing practice. *American Journal of Critical Care, 15,* 266–267.

Shore, D. A. (2007). The (sorry) state of trust in the American healthcare enterprise. In D. A. Shore (Ed.), *The trust crisis in healthcare: Causes, consequences, and cures* (pp. 3–20). Oxford University Press.

Taylor, R. (2009). Leadership theories and the development of nurses in primary health care. *Primary Health Care, 19*(9), 40–45.

Thompson, P. A. (2008). Key challenges facing American nurse leaders. *Journal of Nursing Management, 16*(8), 912–914.

U.S. Department of Health and Human Services and U.S. Department of Justice. (2021, July). Annual Report of the Departments of Health and Human Services and Justice. *Health care fraud and abuse control program: Annual report for fiscal year 2020.* https://oig.hhs.gov/publications/docs/hcfac/FY2020-hcfac.pdf

U.S. Sentencing Commission. (2021). *Office of Public Affairs.* https://www.ussc.gov/guidelines/2021-guidelines-manual-annotated

Victor, B., & Cullen, J. B. (1987). A theory and measure of ethical climates in organizations. In W. C. Frederick (Ed.), *Research in corporate social performance and policy* (pp. 51–71). JAI Press.

Appendix A

Case Studies

Working through the following case studies is intended to be done using this book and the American Nurses Association's (2015) *Code of Ethics for Nurses with Interpretive Statements.* Researching supplemental information also may be helpful to expand learning opportunities and provide more complete answers to questions.

▶ Chapter 1

1-1: Which Patient's Needs Should Be Given First Priority?

Over several years, Suzie has been the nurse for 50-year-old Mrs. Gilmore, who has been frequently admitted to the oncology unit in the hospital where Suzie works. Suzie and Mrs. Gilmore have developed a close relationship based on trust and respect. During her current admission, Mrs. Gilmore's condition has been deteriorating, and she has elected to initiate a do not resuscitate (DNR) order. Today, she is experiencing agonal breathing and is nearing death. On several occasions, Mrs. Gilmore stated she is afraid of dying. She asked Suzie to promise to be with her when she dies if she is in the hospital and Suzie is working at the time. Mrs. Gilmore's daughter is alone with her mother in the hospital room, and the daughter is frightened. While Mrs. Gilmore progresses toward imminent death, Suzie's newly postoperative oncology patient, Mr. Statten, suddenly and unexpectedly has a grand mal seizure. Suzie just met this patient when he returned from surgery earlier in the morning. Mr. Statten's wife is hysterical. As Mr. Statten's primary nurse, Suzie goes into action caring for him and notifies his physician about the seizure. Jennifer, the nursing technician working with Suzie today, comes to Suzie to tell her that Mrs. Gilmore is about to die. The nursing technician also has a close relationship with Mrs. Gilmore and her daughter. The wheels of Suzie's mind begin to turn trying to figure out how to care for both of her patients who need special attention as well as the other three patients she is caring for today. Suzie has a high regard for Jennifer's intellectual abilities and technician skills, but Suzie knows there are limits to what can be delegated to unlicensed, assistive personnel. It is a busy day for all the staff on the unit.

Questions

Review the chapter content.

1.   What should Suzie do about caring for both her patients who need her at the same time as well as properly caring for her other three patients? What are the most ethical

actions? What are her patients' and their significant others' most important needs, especially regarding ethical nurse–patient relationships?

2.   Which approaches to ethical decision making might help Suzie best navigate this situation?

3.   Does the *Code of Ethics for Nurses with Interpretive Statements* provide guidance? Give as much support as you can from the *Code*.

1-2: Curing and Caring

Registered Nurse Rosie works on a surgical oncology unit at a teaching hospital. Dr. Hall, a surgical oncologist specializing in melanoma treatment, admits many patients who are undergoing treatment as part of his melanoma research study. Rosie and her colleagues notice that Dr. Hall continues to treat patients even after the treatment seems futile. Rosie has heard him say to patients "your tumor is shrinking; this is good news," yet she can see that many of these patients' overall conditions are deteriorating. Dr. Hall avoids allowing patients and their families to discuss realistic plans and outcomes. In fact, Rosie knows of instances in which Dr. Hall knew that patients and families wanted to discuss a do not resuscitate (DNR) order and Dr. Hall seemed to purposefully leave or avoid coming to the unit. The relationships Dr. Hall has with his patients saddens Rosie, especially when his patients die in the hospital after he has misled both them and their families.

Questions

Review the chapter content.

1.   What is the meaning of the term *futile*?

2.   Which worldviews or historical-era philosophies might be influencing Dr. Hall's behavior?

3.   How does Dr. Hall's treatment philosophy relate to Kantian deontology? Virtue ethics?

4.   Which philosophies, concepts, and/or ethical approaches might explain Rosie's feelings?

5.   What can Rosie and her colleagues do to alleviate some of their own and their patients' suffering in this situation?

6.   What guidance might Rosie glean from the *Code of Ethics for Nurses with Interpretive Statements*? Which provisions and subprovisions are relevant to Rosie's relationship with her patients and their families?

1-3: Cultural Relativism

The Armenian parents of Narek, a 4-year-old boy, bring Narek to the emergency department (ED) of Central Hospital. Narek has been suffering from a progressively worsening respiratory infection for 7 days. His parents report that they tried the Chinese alternative medicine treatment called cupping to cure his infection, but when his condition continued to worsen, they decided to bring him to the ED. Narek has a high fever, chills, and labored breathing and is severely dehydrated. Upon physical inspection, Registered Nurse Mary Sue and Dr. Thomas find round, red marks on Narek's back. He is diagnosed with pneumonia and must be admitted to the hospital. Mary Sue is appalled because Narek's parents trusted in the alternative treatment of cupping and did not seek health care for him sooner. Mary Sue talks with the ED physician about whether the parents should be reported to the county's child protection services. The physician says no. Registered Nurse Bill tells Mary Sue she should refrain from negatively judging Narek's parents because they treated their child according to their cultural tradition. Bill says he has adopted a worldview of cultural relativism and that Mary Sue should be more open minded.

Questions

Review the chapter content.

1. Do you believe cultural relativism is relevant in this case? Why or why not?
2. Do you agree with Bill or Mary Sue? Explain. If you agree with Mary Sue, how would you respond to Bill?
3. Should the ED staff report Narek's parents to child protective services? Why or why not?
4. What should the ED staff do to try to prevent a similar situation with Narek in the future?

▶ Chapter 2

2-1: Should This Patient Receive More Resources?

Mike is a 27-year-old unemployed male who developed endocarditis because of IV drug abuse, which ruined his mitral valve. He is newly postop from a mitral valve replacement paid for by Medicaid. After Mike was transferred from the ICU to a surgical unit, a friend provided him with illicit drugs that Mike injected while in the hospital, unbeknownst to the nursing and medical staff. The illicit drugs ruined Mike's new valve.

Questions/Discussion

Review the chapter content.

1. If you were the nurse manager of the surgical unit, how would you handle this situation in an ethical way? What would you say to the nursing and unlicensed staff?
2. Should Mike be given another valve paid for by Medicaid?
3. Explain your positions using ethical theories and approaches.

2-2: Would It Be Ethical to Give This Patient a Placebo?

Callie is a young nurse who just began a new job in an emergency department (ED). Mrs. James arrived at the ED complaining of left leg pain and is assigned to Callie. Mrs. James is known to the ED physicians and other nurses because of her frequent visits for back pain. Mrs. James is assessed by Callie and is then seen briefly by the ED physician. The physician walks out of Mrs. James's room and tells Callie to give the patient a saline IV push as a placebo.

Questions

Review the chapter content.

1. What philosophical perspective might the physician be using as a basis for his placebo order?
2. What should Callie do?

3.   Where might she immediately seek guidance about the physician's request?
4.   What is the ethical basis of your recommendation to Callie in this case?
5.   What, if any, guidance is provided in the *Code of Ethics for Nurses with Interpretive Statements*?

2-3: The Case of RaDonda Vaught

After reading the information about the RaDonda Vaught case in Chapter 2, answer the questions and discussion topics that follow.

Questions/Discussion:

1.   Explain how Vaught violated the principles of malpractice. What is the difference between malpractice and negligence?
2.   What was the legal basis for Vaught being prosecuted criminally?
3.   Discuss Vaught's error as it pertains to the four bioethical principles outlined by Beauchamp and Childress and discussed in chapter 2.
4.   Vaught said she became complacent with her job. Chambliss (1996; see reference Chapter 2) discussed *routinization* as it relates to nurses becoming complacent with their work. Routine helps nurses become proficient in their work, but mindless routine can be dangerous. Reread in Chapter 2 what Dewey said about habits.
     a.   Defend why mindless routinization and mindless habits are an ethical issue.
     b.   How can nurses combat mindless routinization and habits in their work?
     c.   What could you do if, based on behavioral observations, you believe one of your colleagues is approaching her work too routinely and mindlessly?
5.   Vaught said she was distracted by a trainee. Training other staff is an inevitable part of many nurses' jobs. What can nurses do to prevent such distractions when training other staff?
6.   Discuss unavoidable trust as it relates to the Vaught case.
7.   Discuss the second victim phenomenon as it relates to Vaught herself. If you worked closely with Vaught before she committed her error, what would you do after her error regarding communicating with and approaching her?
8.   Research the legal doctrine of *respondeat superior*. Is this doctrine relevant in Vaught's case? Explain.
9.   Who in addition to Vaught should be liable in the case? Civilly? Criminally?
10.   Investigate medication dispensing equipment. Should the company that manufactured the dispenser used by Vaught be held liable in the case? Why or why not? Are problems usually system problems with such devices or are they usually problems with the users?
11.   Was Vaught a scapegoat for system errors at VUMC? Support your answer.
12.   Does the Vaught case "change health care forever" as some professionals say? Explain.
13.   Does the Vaught case constitute a slippery slope? Why or why not?
14.   Many people fear the criminal prosecution of Vaught will prevent reporting of medical errors. Do you believe medical and nursing error reporting will change based on the case? Should this fear be a factor in how Vaught's case was handled?
15.   Ultimately, what do you believe should have been both the legal and professional punishment and discipline for Vaught's error?

2-4: The Case of Terri Schiavo

Gather information about the landmark Terri Schiavo case, and use it to complete the following:

1. Summarize key information and events in the case. Think about the information that would be needed by an ethics committee reviewing this case. Clearly list the specific ethical issues involved in her case.
2. Imagine you are a member of an ethics committee consulted for a decision about whether Terri's feeding tube should be removed. As a member of the ethics committee, analyze the case using the Four Topics Method. Some of the questions may require more discussion than others because of their direct relationship to the Schiavo case. Do your best to comprehensively answer the questions.
3. Summarize your committee's specific determinations based on the answers to the Four Topics Method questions and your research of the case. Speak for the committee to recommend either removing or not removing Terri's feeding tube and provide your ethics rationale.

2-5: Patient Refuses Blood

Mrs. Jones has gangrene of her left leg. Her hemoglobin slips to 6.4. She has a major infection and is diabetic. She has no spouse and no living will. Mrs. Jones decides she does not want to be resuscitated if she goes into cardiopulmonary arrest. She needs surgery, which she has agreed to, but she refuses a blood transfusion even though she is not a Jehovah's Witness. The surgeon will not perform the surgery, which is urgent, without Mrs. Jones agreeing to a blood transfusion if it becomes necessary. The attending physician questions the patient's capacity to make decisions. Mrs. Jones's children have donated blood for her, and she says she is not afraid to die.

Questions

Review the chapter content.

1. Which ethical issues and principles are involved with this case?
2. Generate questions that need to be answered to reach an ethical solution in this case.
3. Is an ethical dilemma involved in this case? Explain.
4. Should the physician refuse to treat this patient? Support your answer.
5. Should the family have a right to override the patient's decision to refuse blood? Support your answer.
6. What is the role of a nurse in this case?

Adapted from Pozgar, G. D. (2010). *Legal and ethical issues for health professionals* (2nd ed., p. 152). Jones and Bartlett Publishers.

2-6: Should the Public Be Informed?

During an Ebola outbreak in Africa, a small number of people with the disease are transferred to the United States for treatment. Because of their unfamiliarity with Ebola and the high case fatality rate, the U.S. public is scared that the disease will spread within the country. During this time, three hospitals in a large city plan to officially outfit their facilities to be designated by the Centers for Disease Control and Prevention as Ebola treatment centers. Administrators of the three hospitals do not want to notify the public that they are outfitting their hospitals to be first-priority treatment centers for Ebola. State nurse association representatives tell the state hospital association that the public should be told about the preparations. The hospital administrators fear that people will avoid their hospitals if the news is made public.

Questions

Review the chapter content.

1. Does this case fit the criteria of an ethical dilemma? Explain.
2. What is your position on this case?
3. On which ethical bases did you formulate your position?

2-7: Therapeutic Privilege

The Eto family emigrated from Japan within the past generation. Mrs. Eto, the family's widowed matriarch, is the patient of urology clinic Registered Nurse Sherry. Mrs. Eto is visiting the clinic today to obtain the results of her bladder biopsy, which is positive for low-grade cancer. The patient's physician, Dr. Marks, tells Sherry that he plans to do a cystoscopy to remove the cancer cells and he may order BCG bladder instillations as chemotherapy. Mrs. Eto's son, Mr. Eto, accompanies his mother to the appointment. Without his mother's knowledge, Mr. Eto asks Sherry to arrange for him to privately see Dr. Marks before his mother receives her results. Mr. Eto tells Sherry he wants to hear the biopsy results before his mother because he does not want her to be informed if she has cancer.

Questions

Review the chapter content.

1. What should Sherry tell Mr. Eto?
2. When Sherry tells Dr. Marks about the request, he talks with Sherry about what he should do. What should Sherry say to Dr. Marks in collaborating with him on a plan?
3. Is the use of therapeutic privilege warranted in this situation? Why or why not?
4. Which ethical theories or approaches might apply to the situation? Support your choices.

2-8: Informed Consent

Registered Nurse Jennifer works with Dr. Jones in a gastroenterology clinic. Primary care physicians in the area often refer their patients to one of the gastroenterologists at the clinic when a patient needs a colonoscopy. Prior to the day of their procedure, patients are told to come to the clinic to obtain their colonoscopy preparation instructions, including some of the laxative medications. When patients referred to Dr. Jones come to the clinic, Jennifer explains their pre-procedure instructions, but she also explains the benefits and risks of the colonoscopy and has the patient sign a colonoscopy consent form. Dr. Jones does not see these patients until they are in the outpatient surgery center procedure room and are being sedated to undergo their colonoscopy.

Questions/Discussion

Review the chapter content.

1. Should Jennifer be concerned about any ethical issues related to what is described in the case? Explain your answer.
2. Should Jennifer be concerned about any legal issues related to what is described in the case? Explain your answer.
3. Discuss what you would do if you were Jennifer.
4. List principles, concepts, and theories relative to this case.

2-9: Patient's Request for Prayer

Brenda is working the night shift at the County Hospital. Because of a tumor, Mrs. Taylor, Brenda's patient, is scheduled to have a nephrectomy in the morning. When Brenda is with Mrs. Taylor taking her vital signs at 8:00 p.m., Mrs. Taylor asks Brenda if she will pray with her. Brenda is a shy, introverted person and has never felt comfortable praying aloud with other people unless everyone is reciting the same prayer. Also, within the past year, she has been questioning her faith in God and no longer prays. Brenda considers herself agnostic.

Questions

Review the chapter content.

1. Which ethics principles, concepts, and theories might be involved in this situation?
2. Is it important for Brenda to be true to her own beliefs and preferences? Explain.
3. How should Brenda respond to Mrs. Taylor?

▶ Chapter 3

3-1: Jill Becomes Disheartened

Jill, aged 28 years, is an attractive, intelligent, and technically competent registered nurse who has worked for 5 years in a medical–surgical unit of a small hospital. Her professional colleagues like and respect her, and she habitually attempts to deliver compassionate care to her patients. Recently, she left her job and began working in the busy surgical intensive care unit (ICU) at a local county hospital. Jill changed jobs because she wanted to gain more varied nursing experience. She was very excited and enthusiastic about her new job, but shortly after Jill began working in the ICU, she began to question her career decision. Jill described the more experienced ICU nurses as being "sarcastic and rude," "destructive gossipers," "bullies," and "intentional withholders of important information and assistance" any time she asks them for help in learning ICU patient care and procedures. Jill stated, "The ICU nurses seem to be testing my resolve to stick it out" and "they want me to fail" at learning how to work in the ICU. Many of the surgeons who regularly have patients in the ICU are very demanding and act impatiently toward the ICU nursing staff. Jill stated she feels intimidated by both the ICU nursing staff and the physicians. One physician chastised her for asking what he called "a stupid question." There is an air of unhappiness among all the nurses throughout the hospital. Jill said working at this hospital is like no other situation she has been involved with since becoming a nurse.

Questions

Review the chapter content.

1. What do you believe are the underlying causes of the ICU nurses' treatment of Jill? Do you believe it is likely that Jill's treatment has anything to do with her personal characteristics? Please explain.
2. What could Jill do to try to improve her situation?
3. How will the mistreatment of Jill affect her delivery of care to her patients?
4. Do you believe the air of unhappiness among all the nursing staff members at the hospital might be directly or indirectly affecting their treatment of Jill? Could other nurses with similar bullying techniques be affecting hospital-wide patient care? Give your rationale.
5. If Jill wants to make positive changes at the hospital, what can she do?
6. Which competencies of an ethical nurse will Jill demonstrate when she proposes her plan to hospital administrators for making positive changes? Give your rationale.

3-2: Nurse Jane and the Surgeon

Ms. Bell, aged 65 years, is under the care of Registered Nurse Jane. Ms. Bell had a total hip replacement yesterday. She told Jane that her pain was intolerable, and then she groaned loudly and said, "Oh, I hurt worse than I have ever hurt before in my life. Please help me, please, please, I can't stand it anymore! Please give me something for pain now." When Jane assessed her level of pain, Ms. Bell described her pain as the highest level, 10 on a 10-point pain scale. Her blood pressure and pulse were slightly elevated as compared to her last documented vital signs. Jane proceeded to check Ms. Bell's orders but discovered something very unusual. The surgeon had ordered her IV pain medication for only every 6 hours instead of the typical 3-hour frequency for patients with 1-day postoperative hip replacements. Ms. Bell would have to wait 3 more hours for her next IV pain medication. Jane returned to Ms. Bell's room to explain her current pain order and inform her that she would call the surgeon now. By that time, Ms. Bell was crying out with pain and moving her head from side to side. Jane felt such empathy and concern for her. She briefly tried to comfort her with words and acts of kindness, but she needed to return quickly to the unit to call the surgeon for a new order. When he answered, she began informing him of her assessment of Ms. Bell and the 6-hour interval order, but he abruptly and loudly interrupted her and stated, "I meant to order that medication every 6 hours. She does not need more frequent pain medication, because of some past problems with prescription pain medications. Please do not call me unless you have critical information that needs my attention."

Jane was shocked, and many conflicting thoughts rushed through her mind. Why did he not want Ms. Bell to have more frequent pain medication, like other postoperative patients in his care? Was it really about her past use of prescription medications? Ms. Bell had a total hip replacement less than 24 hours ago and was in excruciating pain! Jane asked herself what she should do. After some reflection, she notified the nursing supervisor, who then reviewed the case and decided to call the surgeon. The supervisor stated the surgeon seemed approachable and decided to order a one-time dose of IV pain medication to relieve her immediate pain. By that time, another hour had passed, so Jane administered the medication as quickly as she could in an effort to relieve Ms. Bell's pain.

Questions

Review the chapter content.

1. In the relationship between Jane and the surgeon, what ethical issues are going on between them? To answer, explore the history and research on the nurse–physician relationship in the chapter. What bioethical principles did the surgeon violate with Jane and his patient, Ms. Bell?

2. Was Ms. Bell's history of pain medication use the real issue for the surgeon's not giving a new order? If not, what do you believe the underlying issue was? Please explain.

3. Of the ethical competencies presented in the chapter, which ones did Jane demonstrate with Ms. Bell during the process?

4. Did Jane do the right thing by calling her supervisor? What other actions, if any, should she have taken?

▷ Chapter 4

4-1: Ivy's Decision: Have an Abortion or Not?

Ivy West, aged 18 years, has a story that is very similar to other teen girls'. She used a home pregnancy test and discovered she was pregnant. She believes she is about 6 to 7 weeks pregnant. She has been sexually active with her boyfriend for about a year but often forgets to take her daily contraceptive pill. After discussing her pregnancy with her boyfriend, he told her that he could not tie himself down with a wife or child because he needed to attend college in the fall and earn a degree. His decision disturbed Ivy, and not sure what to do, she turned to her mother for support. Her mother strongly pressured her to have and raise the baby. She vowed to help Ivy raise her baby. After Ivy processed the information, she thought about the pros and cons related to having and raising the baby versus having an abortion. Although she was apprehensive, she was leaning toward an abortion, especially since the pregnancy was not that far along.

Questions

Review the chapter content.

1. Ivy considered issues related to abortion and the stage of fetal development. Would the idea of equal moral standing between the fetus and Ivy be a concern? Please defend your position with information from the chapter and other sources.

2. What are other issues Ivy needs to consider before making her decision, such as her potential love for the baby, the responsibilities to herself and the baby, giving up her baby for adoption, attending college, working, and living with financial considerations? Please explain.

4-2: Ms. Mason's Decision: Carry Her Fetus to Term or Have a Partial-Birth Abortion?

Ms. Mason, aged 34 years, was 20 weeks pregnant. She had an amniocentesis and received the prenatal genetic diagnosis of Huntington's disease for her fetus. The day after the diagnosis, the physician explained two options to Ms. Mason: (1) carry the fetus to term and give birth to the baby or (2) have a late-term abortion to terminate the pregnancy. The physician explained the procedure for the late-term abortion. The Masons were devastated by all the information and needed a few days to comprehend the situation and the options. They were conflicted between the love for their unborn baby and the decision to avoid future complications for the child and themselves. When they returned to the clinic, the Masons informed the physician and nurse they had made the difficult decision to have the partial-birth abortion. They made a decision to not have any more children, even after the physician had explained the possibility of using embryo selection (sperm sorting) if they decide in the future to have children.

Questions

Review the chapter content.

1. On the day the physician explains the options to Ms. Mason, you are the nurse, and you try to establish a genuine ethical relationship with her in an effort to convey caring and give support. What are the specific ethical competencies you will exercise for this encounter?

2. You are the nurse again on the day the Masons return with their decision to have the abortion. What are some nursing approaches you can use with the Masons on this day? Consider your own values and beliefs about abortion and partial-birth abortion, while bearing in mind the diagnosis of Huntington's disease for the fetus.

3. What factors did the Masons most likely consider before making their decision? Some factors, among others, may be the following:
   a. Whether they considered their fetus as having equal moral standing with them and other people
   b. The love they have already developed for their future baby
   c. The future care required for their very challenged child, especially when the Masons could no longer assist
   d. The financial demands for the provision of care

4. How can the Masons justify having an abortion when Huntington's disease does not usually affect people until their middle 30s, well after reaching adulthood?

5. How does each principle—autonomy, beneficence, nonmaleficence, and justice—guide this case? Based on these principles, justify your nursing strategies from your response in question 2.

▶ Chapter 5

5-1: Covid-19 Vaccination

A mother brings her 5-year-old daughter to the clinic to be evaluated for wheezing. While you are doing your initial assessment, you ask the child's mother if her daughter has received a Covid vaccine. She tells you "no." She says she does not trust the vaccine for children and does not believe Covid is dangerous for children.

Questions/Discussion

1. Elaborate on the information you would give to the child's mother and how you would address her concerns.
2. Is this situation ethical in nature? Explain your answer.

5-2: Withdraw Nutrition and Hydration?

Baby Sherman is a neonate admitted to the neonatal intensive care unit (NICU) at the county hospital where you work as the NICU nurse manager. Mrs. Sherman had an amniotic fluid embolus during her delivery, and Baby Sherman experienced anoxia. Consequently, Baby Sherman had an Apgar score of 0 at birth. The baby was resuscitated but remains unconscious. All of the baby's organs experienced hypoxic insult. Baby Sherman was placed on a ventilator, and parenteral nutrition was later initiated. Mrs. Sherman is physically very weak and experiencing grief, along with her husband, over the condition of their infant. They have two other young children, aged 2 and 5 years. Baby Sherman has been weaned from the ventilator but has remained unresponsive. Mr. and Mrs. Sherman have requested that the hospital staff discontinue their infant's nutrition and hydration. The NICU medical, nursing, and social work staff members have not previously experienced a situation quite like this one.

Questions

Review the chapter content.

1. You are meeting with the neonatologists, the NICU charge nurse, the infant's primary nurse, the hospital chaplain, and the social worker in the NICU. What do you contribute to the group's discussion regarding how you believe the staff should proceed in providing the best care for Baby Sherman and her family?
2. How do the Baby Doe rules affect this case?
3. One of the staff RNs comments, "I think the mother and father are being selfish about their request to withdraw nutrition from Baby Sherman. I think it is selfish because they don't want to be bothered with taking care of her at home." How do you address these comments?
4. Which surrogate decision-making standard should be used in this case? What, if any, influence should the interests of Baby Sherman's siblings have in decision making?
5. Caring for Baby Sherman and interacting with her family has caused a great deal of moral suffering for the NICU nursing staff. What behaviors might you expect to observe among the nursing staff? What do you do, as the nurse manager, to address this situation?
6. As would be expected, Mr. and Mrs. Sherman also are experiencing a great deal of moral suffering and grief. How would you handle your personal interactions with Mr. and Mrs. Sherman, and what would you do to help educate your staff in working with families in a situation such as this one? What do you know, or what information can you locate, about the grief parents experience when their infant is extremely impaired and a decision about withholding or withdrawing life support is being made? How would you try to help Mr. and Mrs. Sherman?
7. As the nurse manager, you contact the chairperson of the hospital ethics committee to make a referral for the Shermans' case. Role-play with a peer the roles of nurse manager

and ethics committee chairperson during the referral phone call. What information is important to discuss? What questions are important to ask? Remember, the committee chairperson has no information about the case.

5-3: Talking About Death

Mitch is a 10-year-old with leukemia, which, after considerable treatment, is now considered a terminal condition for him. In the 2 years since his diagnosis, his parents and other family members have focused on being optimistic around him and have asked his healthcare professionals to do the same. No one has discussed with Mitch the possibility that he might not survive his leukemia. Registered Nurse Teresa is Mitch's primary nurse during his current hospitalization for an infection. Teresa has developed a good relationship with Mitch and his family during previous hospitalizations. Mitch now seems depressed and uncommunicative. His family is still avoiding directly talking with Mitch about his deteriorating condition and impending death. Teresa asks Mitch's mother about the circumstances surrounding Mitch's decreased communication. His mother responds, "Do you think he knows he is dying?"

Questions

Before answering the following questions, research information regarding the psychological care of children who have terminal cancer or other terminal illnesses. What are the recommended tips for helping both the family and child sustain the greatest level of well-being during the illness and dying process?

1. What would be a compassionate response to the mother's question? Based on your research about situations such as this one, what should Teresa know about compassionate care?

2. Because the door has been opened to question what Mitch knows or does not know about his illness, what can Teresa do to help Mitch and his family maintain the greatest well-being during the dying process, which may be either rapid or slow?

▶ Chapter 6

6-1: An Adolescent Couple with HIV

Alexa was a senior in high school, aged 17 years, and had been an A student her whole school life. Her goal was to earn a bachelor's degree in science and one day attend medical school. For the past 3 years, she has dated only Robert, aged 20 years, and he was already attending a nearby university. Robert had plans to be an accountant. They are planning on marriage at some point in time, which led them to having unprotected sex on a regular basis. Alexa took oral contraceptives to prevent pregnancy, so she did not worry about becoming pregnant. However, Alexa began to get sick with intermittent flu-like signs and symptoms, such as no appetite, weight loss, nausea and diarrhea, and other mysterious symptoms. She finally went to her physician and received a diagnosis of HIV. She was shocked! She had never had sex with anyone but Robert, and to her knowledge she had not acquired HIV by other means. Robert did not look sick, and she had never doubted his faithfulness to her until now. After confronting him, she found out that he had been getting high on drugs and having risky, unprotected group sex with both genders. Although he too had been having symptoms, he had not yet been diagnosed with HIV when Alexa confronted him. He later received a diagnosis of HIV.

Questions

Review the chapter content.

1.   You are the nurse in the clinic on the day Alexa finds out she has HIV. She remains in the clinic for more than an hour with you while you try to support and console her. You have had formal HIV counseling training, so you apply your skills as you communicate with her. Several weeks later, after Alexa is more composed and has had time to think about her situation, she drops by the clinic and wants to talk with you on a more personal basis. She needs comforting. What approaches will you use with Alexa? Please explore how to use and apply the nursing ethical competencies to help Alexa. Be specific with your approaches and rationales.

2.   You realize that emotional support and possibly spiritual support are important to adolescent development. What nursing approaches could you use to offer support to Alexa? Be very specific. In doing so, encourage her to think about her life goals with or without Robert, her medical future, and her future in general. Imagine what you might say to her and do for her. Imagine a supportive conversation you might have with her.

3.   Consider an additional activity of role-playing with classmates for this or another scenario.

6-2: Hannah's Secret

Hannah, aged 13 years, overheard some of her friends in the hall at school talking about her big build and weight. Hannah was devastated! According to the family physician and her family, she was a normal weight and size for a girl her age. She looked at herself in the mirror many times, each time with more and more disgust. She began receiving harassing instant messages from people she did not recognize. These remarks by her friends bothered her so much that Hannah began thinking about how she could lose weight. She was terrified at what her classmates thought about her, and she thought of not fitting in or losing her friends. Over the course of a few days, she became so obsessed with her weight that she began visiting various Ana websites, such as Thin Intentions Forever and Ana Boot Camp. She found great comfort in knowing that many girls her age were having similar feelings about themselves. The websites and people commenting on blogs encouraged her to lose weight. Hannah first began cutting out all desserts, all milk products, and all fats from her diet. Later, she progressed to eating only green salads, tiny servings of meat, and water. She increased her exercise to at least 1 hour of full aerobics every day. She lost considerable weight. Everyone mentioned her weight loss to her, which encouraged her to continue. Not knowing Hannah's secret, her parents appeared proud of her new healthy eating pattern and exercise program, and therefore, they did not worry until later when people started commenting on her extreme weight loss and unhealthy appearance. Hannah discovered she could not stop her new eating and exercise ritual, nor did she want to. A couple of Hannah's friends discussed their concern with Hannah's mother. Her mother took her to the family physician. After the physician diagnosed her with anorexia nervosa, the nurse provided them with resources for recovery and support.

Questions

Review the content and statistics related to eating disorders, trust, and limits of confidentiality in the chapter. Then, search websites such as Ana Boot Camp and Thin Intentions, as well as those websites that provide recovery guidelines and support for anorexia nervosa.

1. Adolescents engaging in risky behaviors tend to keep it hidden from others as long as possible. As a school nurse, what strategies would you implement to monitor signs of eating disorders?
2. Explore the limits of confidentiality for an adolescent. As a school nurse, what ethical considerations would you face?
3. What online information did you discover about the recovery and support site? How would you incorporate some of the information in your strategies?

▶ Chapter 7

7-1: Medicalization of Mr. Bagley: Pills, Pills, and More Pills

One day Mr. Bagley, aged 46 years, developed an array of signs and symptoms that he believed were stemming from his heart disease, hypertension, and hyperlipidemia. He discovered his blood pressure was 85/50, which was significantly lower than usual, and he was experiencing dizziness, blurred vision, shortness of breath, weakness, and nausea. When Mr. Bagley visited his provider in a large internal medicine group, the registered nurse assessed his vital signs and evaluated his currently prescribed medications. Mr. Bagley's current electronic records revealed 18 different prescribed medications by several specialists within that medical network. Upon comparing pharmacological effects, the nurse found three medications that interacted in a harmful way. Mr. Bagley underwent testing in the next few days, but the provider concluded that polypharmacy, which means taking multiple medications concurrently for coexisting diseases and conditions, possibly led to Mr. Bagley's problems. As a result, the provider discontinued two prescriptions and adjusted the dosages of several other medications.

Questions

Review the content on medicalization and chronic disease and illness in the chapter.

1. Using one or more scholarly sources:
   a. Define the term *polypharmacy*.
   b. Discuss the magnitude of the polypharmacy problem in the United States today.
2. What ethical implications relate to providers' and nurses' overprescribing or inefficient monitoring of medications? Explore these issues in terms of the bioethical principles of autonomy, beneficence, nonmaleficence, and justice.
3. What is the meaning of chronic disease and illness? As you answer, discuss the related statistics and issues.
4. Do you believe that Mr. Bagley's care has become medicalized? Please explain.

7-2: Two Organ Recipient Candidates: Who Will Receive the Liver?

Mr. Mann's Clinical Scenario

Mr. Mann, aged 50 years, has been a longtime heavy drinker and has liver disease related to alcoholic cirrhosis. He will soon die if he does not receive a liver. He has been unemployed for years and on financial assistance. Mr. Mann has stated that after he receives his new liver, he will try very hard to quit drinking on a long-term basis but he will make no firm promises. He is not drinking now because he is committed to remaining abstinent for the required period of time before the organ transplant and during the recovery process. Mr. Mann is divorced, lives alone, and has two married sons who are not on good terms with him.

Ms. Bay's Clinical Scenario

Ms. Bay, aged 37 years, has active viral hepatitis C with end-stage liver disease (ESLD). Ms. Bay is a wife and mother of two children, aged 16 and 12 years. The family members are a close-knit family, very active, and well known in the community. Ms. Bay feels critically sick and is often confined to bed and frequently admitted to the hospital. Her medications are Olysio, interferon, and ribavirin, but because of her severely advanced disease, the medications are not as effective as they could be. She is ahead of Mr. Mann on the wait list for a liver.

Questions

Based on your knowledge of the two diseases, you know that patients diagnosed with alcoholic cirrhosis like Mr. Mann, with a new liver and medications, could have a slightly better success rate and a longer life than do some patients with advanced hepatitis C ESLD, despite the fact that recovering alcoholics may have a high recidivism rate (relapsing to old behavior). Mr. Mann is at the high end of the age range for receiving a liver transplant. On the other hand, Ms. Bay has only a marginal chance of recovery if she gets a liver transplant because her new liver drugs have not yet destroyed the hepatitis C virus; therefore, the virus will continue to circulate in the blood during and after the new liver transplant. As a result, hepatitis C will infect the new liver.

To increase your knowledge for this scenario, do the following:

- Compare the situations of the two organ recipient candidates.
- Read the material about organ transplantation in the chapter.
- Conduct a web search on the new drugs for hepatitis C and the recurrence of liver disease in some patients with liver transplants. Search for and analyze cases that are similar to those of Mr. Mann and Ms. Bay.
- Search the Organ Procurement and Transplantation Network site (http://optn.transplant.hrsa.gov/learn/about-transplantation/how-organ-allocation-works/ and http://optn.transplant.hrsa.gov/resources/ethics/) for principles of fair organ allocation, ethics, and other guidelines used by the network to make decisions about organ allocation.
  1. The information you have gathered about liver allocation and transplantation provides you with a picture, though somewhat limited, of Mr. Mann's and Ms. Bay's circumstances. Which patient would you choose? What is your rationale?

2. Based on what you read in the Organ Procurement and Transplantation Network information on organ allocation, how consistent, if at all, are the following factors with the network's allocation principles and guidelines? Please explain your answer.
   - The sickest patients: A medical entitlement method.
   - First-come, first-served: A fairness principle.
   - Social worth principle: A method of placing more value on some people than on others because of certain individual characteristics.
   - Best success rate and long-term outcome: Utilitarian–consequential perspective.
   - Proximity: Location in relation to the area of the hospital where the organ will be transplanted (immediate area, county, or region). What about the United States versus another country?

▶ Chapter 8

8-1: Whose Wishes Should Be Honored?

Mrs. Randle, a frail, 85-year-old woman who lives alone, is admitted to a geropsychiatric unit because of irritability, confusion, and increasing incontinence. Mrs. Randle's family states she was continually refusing assistance from her home health aides and became angry when her family and home care nurses tried to reason with her about these refusals. During her hospital admission, Mrs. Randle is treated for a urinary tract infection, is hydrated with intravenous fluids, and two of her medications are adjusted. She subsequently becomes calm and cooperative with the care that she receives while in the hospital. When Registered Nurse Terry and a social worker talk with Mrs. Randle about the safety risks of her living in her home alone, she states, "I am 85 years old and think I should be able to decide how I want to live the rest of my life. I'm willing to take my chances. I will die if I go to a nursing home." Mrs. Randle often is unsure about the correct day of the week when questioned, yet she knows the name of the hospital and the reason she was admitted for treatment. She often is confused about the names of the hospital staff but is able to state her own name and the names of her children. Though Mrs. Randle agrees to cooperate with home care providers, her family continues to insist that Mrs. Randle be admitted to a long-term care facility. Her family asks the psychiatrist to complete the paperwork so a judge can have the patient declared incompetent. The psychiatrist does not usually seem sincerely interested in his patients, and he has spent little time with Mrs. Randle. This psychiatrist is usually willing to comply with most families' wishes. Terry and the unit social worker disagree with the decision to declare Mrs. Randle incompetent and are in favor of allowing her to return home with home care agency support as she wishes.

Questions

Review the chapter content.

1. Based on the information provided, does it seem that Mrs. Randle has decision-making capacity? What criteria can be used as a basis for your decision? What needs to be included in a complete assessment of Mrs. Randle's decision-making capacity?
2. Does safety at home for Mrs. Randle seem feasible? If so, how might this be accomplished? If not, why not?

3. What could Terry and the social worker do to try to resolve the disagreement among the patient, her family, the doctor, and themselves?
4. Is a form of paternalism being used by any of the people involved in this case? If so, is it a form of justified paternalism? Does the approach seem ethical? Why or why not?
5. Which type of quality-of-life evaluation is most appropriate in this situation? Explain.
6. How is the issue of Mrs. Randle's dignity involved in this case?
7. How might the registered nurse and social worker enter into a discussion with Mrs. Randle about the meaning of her life? With her family? With the physician?

8-2: Acting on Questionable Practice

Registered Nurse Christine works in a large long-term care facility and is the nurse manager of Unit 2 North. A registered nurse colleague and Unit 2 West manager, Sylvia, calls Christine and asks her to come to Unit 2 West to help with a computer problem at the nurses' station. As Christine walks down the hall of Sylvia's unit, she hears a resident crying out very loudly. The cry sounds like an expression of pain. Christine enters the resident's room and notices the resident is tightly restrained to the bed and is lying in excrement. From a quick assessment, Christine believes the resident is alert and oriented. Though she has tried to convince herself otherwise, lately, Christine has been thinking that Sylvia acts strongly paternalistic with her residents and her manner is abrupt rather than compassionate. Christine has seen at least two residents begin to cry when Sylvia fusses at them.

Questions/Discussion

Review the chapter content.

1. What should Christine do about her findings?
2. What are the bases for your answers to question 1?
3. Does the *Code of Ethics for Nurses with Interpretive Statements* provide guidance in this situation? Explain.
4. Is paternalism always unethical when caring for long-term care residents? Explain.
5. Conduct a search of reliable literature about the use of restraints with elderly patients. From your search, develop an educational program for long-term care nurses and aides about using restraints with their residents.

8-3: Vulnerability and Dependence

Mr. Cooper, who is 89 years old, is homebound and lives alone. He has several children, grandchildren, and friends who visit him regularly, buy his groceries and other needed items, take him to appointments, and help him keep his home and yard tidy. Registered Nurse Jeffrey is Mr. Cooper's home health nurse. Jeffrey has been visiting Mr. Cooper periodically for 2 years. Mr. Cooper is still ambulatory with a walker, but he becomes short of breath when walking short distances. Lately, Jeffrey notices that Mr. Cooper is cursing under his breath as he walks and his demeanor generally is becoming negative and grouchy. Today, Mr. Cooper says, "I've lost my dignity, and I'm just a burden to others." Jeffrey thinks about something he learned in his ethics class: There are particular virtues that are good for elders to cultivate in order to maintain and improve well-being.

Questions/Discussion

Review the chapter content.

1. In Chapter 8, review the section about virtues needed by elders. Which of May's recommended virtues might be particularly helpful to Mr. Cooper?
2. Specifically, discuss things Jeffrey can do to help Mr. Cooper cultivate each of the virtues you specified in Question 1.

8-4: Treating Behavioral and Psychological Symptoms of Dementia (BPSD)

Registered Nurse Sally works in a long-term care facility and, sometimes, works on the dementia unit when extra help is needed. She notices that the nurses working on the dementia unit usually default to asking the nurse practitioner or physician for antipsychotic medication orders to treat BPSD. Sally attempts to stay updated on the latest evidence in geriatric care. She questions the practice of using antipsychotic medications to treat behavior exhibited by the patients with dementia.

Questions

Review the chapter content.

1. What are evidence-based practice guidelines for treating BPSD?
2. Is using or not using this evidence an ethical issue? Why or why not?
3. What are alternatives for treating BPSD?
4. What could Sally do to improve care for patients with dementia who live at the long-term care facility where she works?

8-5: Tube Feedings for a Patient with Alzheimer's Disease

Mr. Colson, an 83-year-old man with end-stage Alzheimer's disease, was admitted for an evaluation at the hospital-based geriatric psych unit where you work as a registered nurse. At the interdisciplinary conference with Mr. Colson's family, the physician discusses that Mr. Colson is progressively refusing soft foods and all liquids. He discusses the details of two options: either inserting or not inserting a feeding tube. The patient's family stated they want to consider both options and will make a decision soon. After the meeting, a newly hired registered nurse colleague tells you "I can't believe Dr. Howell discussed not inserting a feeding tube. A patient should not be allowed to starve to death! That is inhumane!"

Questions

Review the chapter content.

1. What are the evidence-based guidelines for patients like Mr. Colson?
2. Which ethics principles, concepts, and theories are pertinent to this case?
3. Is it ethical to forgo the insertion of a feeding tube in a patient with Alzheimer's disease at any stage of the disease? Justify your answer.
4. What would you say to your registered nurse colleague who believes that not inserting a feeding tube would be inhumane?

> # Chapter 9

9-1: End of Life with Mary Warning

Tom Warning, the oldest son of Mary Warning, took his mother to the emergency department (ED) after he found her disoriented and confused. Ms. Warning is a widow, aged 73 years. Tom had gone by her house on his way home from work to drop off her refilled prescriptions. The ED physician and Ms. Warning's primary provider agreed they could not rule out a stroke; therefore, they wanted to admit her for observation only. Tom thought, "This seems minor enough." He went home to rest for the night after he had signed the hospital admission papers. Ms. Warning went to a room on a medical unit. During the night, alone in her room, her stroke extended. When the registered nurse made one of her rounding visits, she found Ms. Warning breathing but unresponsive to commands and pain. She immediately called the ED physician to assess her and to maintain care until her primary physician could get there. A nurse notified Tom, who lived nearby. Ms. Warning's four other children all lived out of town.

A diagnosis of occlusive stroke was made based on the CT and MRI scans. Treatment was probably medically futile because of the degree of damage. The primary physician planned to send Ms. Warning to the intensive care unit (ICU) after informing Tom of her condition and unconscious state of mind. Given that their mother might not live, Tom and his siblings had to make decisions about whether they wanted her to be on a mechanical ventilator if it came to that. The physician explained several types of treatment options, even though the treatments most likely would not be beneficial for her. The physician thoroughly explained the poor prognosis and offered the options of withdrawing or withholding treatment. He explained to Tom that her prognosis was poor and that, if she lived, she probably would never regain consciousness.

Meanwhile, Tom frantically called all his siblings to explain their mother's condition and circumstances to them and asked them to come quickly because decisions needed to be made now regarding their mother's treatment and care. Tom was pacing back and forth with distress and fear because no one in his family had ever discussed these issues among themselves or with their mother. When all the siblings arrived the next day, they made the decision for the physician to withdraw all medications and intravenous fluids and requested no life-sustaining treatments of any kind. The physician withdrew all medications and fluids, and then wrote a do not -resuscitate (DNR) order on Ms. Warning's chart.

Questions

Review the chapter content.

1. You are the nurse caring for Ms. Warning in the ICU. Before bedtime, you maintain a journal of your daily experiences. The day you had to discontinue all of Ms. Warning's treatments, you went home to reflect and write down your feelings in an effort to express your pent-up emotions concerning the day. Imagine becoming involved in this nursing experience. If you were that nurse experiencing this event, what sights and sounds might you see, and what emotions might you feel? Please complete this question as if it were a journaling process.

2. Refer to the chapter to explore medical futility and the American Medical Association's (AMA's) recommended process used by physicians in situations like Ms. Warning's.

What is medical futility? What is the AMA's specific recommendation for declaring a patient medically futile?

3. Before the final decision to withdraw and withhold treatments, the primary physician mentioned to Tom the possibility of mechanical ventilation as a treatment for Ms. Warning at some point during the process. The family decided against this option. What is the difference between the care levels of nonmechanical-ventilation and mechanical ventilation–dependent care? What is the difference between higher-brain death, such as persistent vegetative state, and whole-brain death? What nursing ethical issues are associated with each level of care?

4. As the nurse carrying out Ms. Warning's care, what ethical competencies from Chapter 3 would you demonstrate to show your support for Tom and his siblings?

5. How could an advance directive have helped Tom's distressed state of mind when the physician presented him with options? Which one of the advance directives would have been the most suitable in Ms. Warning's case? Please explain.

6. What type of nursing care does Ms. Warning need after all treatment is withdrawn? In answering this question, explore the ethical issues that you as a nurse must face. Please explain your answer.

7. In Ms. Warning's case, the siblings came to a unified decision. However, if the siblings had not come to a consensus about a course of action for their mother, major disagreements and arguments could have ensued. Consider the nature of an equal voice for each of the siblings and how they might agree on one spokesperson. What approach could they take to channel their equal voice to one sibling spokesperson? Who would be the likely spokesperson for these siblings? Please explain.

8. Which bioethical principle and ethical theory serve as the basis for surrogate decision making in Ms. Warning's case? Please explain your justifications.

9-2: The Case of Brittany Maynard: "My Right to Die"

This case was an actual event. Brittany Maynard, aged 29 years, was married for 1 year when she was diagnosed with aggressive brain cancer, discovered she had approximately 6 months to live, and did not want her family to watch her suffering with pain during her dying process. After a long discussion with her physicians, her husband, and other family members, she decided to move from California to Oregon to take advantage of the Death with Dignity Act. She opted for physician-assisted suicide (PAS), which is a procedure that would allow her to self-administer physician-prescribed barbiturate medications to facilitate her death. She chose to die on November 1, 2014. On her Facebook page, she left a message that day:

> Goodbye to my friends and family that I love. Today is the day I have chosen to pass away with dignity in the face of my terminal illness, this terrible brain cancer that has taken so much from me . . . but would have taken so much more. The world is a beautiful place, travel has been my greatest teacher, my close friends and folks are the greatest givers. I even have a ring of support around my bed as I type. . . . Goodbye world. Spread good energy. Pay it forward.

Before her death, Brittany Maynard made a public statement on the right of terminally ill people to end their suffering quickly. She emphasized that no one but she could determine when her suffering had become intolerable, when her life had become unlivable, and at what point her dignity had faded. However, some people criticized Brittany Maynard for her decision to use PAS:

- One person commented that Brittany Maynard refused to embrace suffering in any meaningful way and, as a result, did not acknowledge human finitude and vulnerability.
- A group characterized her decision to use PAS as cheapening human life.

Adapted from Maynard, B. (2014, November 2). My right to die with dignity at 29. http://www.cnn.com/2014/10/07/opinion/maynard-assisted-suicide-cancer-dignity/

Questions

Review the content on PAS in the chapter. Then search the web for current articles and opinions about this case. Watch Brittany's YouTube video titled "Brittany Maynard Legislative Testimony" published by Compassion and Choices.

1. Describe PAS.
2. Which ethical issues arise during and after the decision to opt for PAS?
3. Which states legally allow people to choose PAS, or at least, do not prosecute cases? Look at Chapter 9 and check for updates on the internet.
4. What is your position about Brittany Maynard's decision to end her life at age 29 years? Please explore your rationale and explain.
5. On the internet, find the American Nurses Association's most recent Position Statement covering assisted suicide.
   a. Discuss/list the main points of the ANA's position.
   b. Discuss/list, in your own words, the ANA's position about nurses' participation in assisted suicide.

Chapter 10

10-1: Is There a Duty to Warn?

Kendrick is a 25-year-old man hospitalized with a paranoid delusional disorder. When Kendrick was admitted, he was very angry and vehemently verbalized that he believed his ex-mother-in-law had been spreading lies about him around town and she was responsible for getting him fired from his last job. When Kendrick's sister visited him at the hospital, he gave consent for Registered Nurse Ashley, his nurse, and his psychiatrist to talk with her about his condition. At that time, his sister stated Kendrick's ideas about his ex-mother-in-law are delusional thinking and there is no basis in fact regarding his beliefs. Kendrick's condition has improved with adjustments of his psychotropic drugs (he is no longer actively exhibiting angry and paranoid behavior), and he is being discharged today. When Ashley is talking with Kendrick today in preparation for his discharge, he tells her "I'm still not finished with my ex-mother-in-law." Ashley asks him to explain this statement, and he is evasive but answers with cryptic statements indicating threats against the woman.

Questions/Discussion

Review the chapter content.

1.   What should Ashley do before leaving Kendrick's room?
2.   Do you believe Kendrick should be discharged today? Explain the basis for your decision.
3.   What are the appropriate steps for Ashley to take after leaving Kendrick's room?
4.   Discuss ethics-related principles, precedents, and concepts relevant to this case.

10-2: Patient-Targeted Googling

Registered Nurse Randy works on an inpatient psychiatric unit. He notices that his registered nurse coworker, Colleen, has a habit of trying to entice unit colleagues to discuss patients' personal information. Randy believes Colleen's habit goes along with her general tendency to gossip about people. Randy views Colleen's behavior as unethical, but because he does not want to stir up trouble on the unit, he has not addressed his concerns with anyone, including Colleen. While he is at work today, Randy sees Colleen spending considerable time looking at her cell phone. He is irritated and tells her that she should be making rounds on her patients and spending time with them. She tells him, "I'm finding out some really interesting stuff about Mr. Carey on Facebook and from 'Googling' him online." This is the last straw for Randy.

Questions

Review the chapter content.

1.   What should Randy do first to address this situation? What should he do next?
2.   Does the *Code of Ethics for Nurses with Interpretive Statements* give Randy guidance to handle the situation?
3.   Which ethical principles, theories, approaches, and concepts are relevant to this case? Explain.

10-3: Psychiatric Advance Directives

Polly, a psychiatric mental health nurse practitioner, works at a community mental health center in your state. Tom, who was diagnosed with paranoid schizophrenia, is a 32-year-old patient at the clinic. Over time, he and Polly have developed a therapeutic relationship. Tom is gay and has been in a relationship with Gerald for 5 years. During his routine clinic visit today, Tom tells Polly he learned about something called a psychiatric advance directive (PAD). He asks Polly for more information about it to decide if this is something he wants to complete. He says he wants Gerald to be his decision maker. Polly has only superficial knowledge about PADs. She tells Tom that she will research the information and schedule an appointment with him to discuss it.

Questions/Discussion

Assume the role of Polly. Research the following points, and outline information to discuss with Tom:

1.   Basic purpose and elements of a PAD and what type of treatment can be predetermined
2.   Circumstances for completion of the document, including how to accomplish it

3. Benefits and risks of a PAD
4. Criteria for assigning a decision- making designee and whether Gerald can assume that role
5. Legal issues in your state, including whether PADs must be honored in a crisis
6. How to communicate Tom's PAD to care providers and other relevant people

▶ Chapter 11

11-1: The Case of Henrietta Lacks

Research the story of Henrietta Lacks, and answer the following questions or complete the assigned discussion points. A good source to use is http://rebeccaskloot.com/the-immortal-life/, but there are other websites with reliable information. If you are particularly interested in Henrietta's case, you may want to read the book *The Immortal Life of Henrietta Lacks* by Rebecca Skloot.

Questions/Discussion

Review the chapter content.

1. Summarize the story of Henrietta Lacks. Emphasize the key points.
2. Using any chapter from your ethics text, list as many ethical issues as you can find that are relevant to Henrietta's case. Explain the rationale for your selections.
3. Is Kant's deontology philosophy relevant to the case? Why or why not?
4. Is utilitarian philosophy relevant to the case? Why or why not?
5. Is virtue ethics relevant to the case? Why or why not?
6. Is narrative ethics relevant to the case? Why or why not? See information in your ethics text and find additional information in scholarly articles and sources.
7. Considering what happened to Henrietta and her children, where and how might a nurse have affected the story? Could a nurse have assumed the role of Rebecca Skloot?
8. Ultimately, do you believe the benefits of using HeLa cells, as they have been used, outweigh the ethical lapses that occurred? Defend your answer.
9. Does the *Code of Ethics for Nurses with Interpretive Statements* provide guidance about a situation like the one involving Henrietta Lacks?

11-2: The Case of Dr. Anna Pou and Nurse Colleagues

Research the story of Dr. Anna Pou and her nurse colleagues who worked at Memorial Hospital Medical Center in New Orleans during and after Hurricane Katrina in 2005. Answer the following questions or complete the assigned discussion points. If you are particularly interested in Dr. Pou's case, you may want to read the book *Five Days at Memorial: Life and Death in a Storm-Ravaged Hospital* by Sheri Fink.

Questions/Discussion

Review the chapter content.

1. Summarize the story of Dr. Pou and her colleagues at Memorial Medical Center during and after Hurricane Katrina. Emphasize the key points.

2. Using any chapter from your ethics text, list as many ethical issues as you can find that are relevant to this case. Explain the rationale for your selections.
3. Is Kant's deontology philosophy relevant to the case? Why or why not?
4. Is utilitarian philosophy relevant to the case? Why or why not?
5. Is virtue ethics relevant to the case? Why or why not?
6. Is narrative ethics relevant to the case? Why or why not? See information in your ethics text and find additional information in scholarly articles and sources.
7. Considering what happened in this case, where and how might a nurse have affected the story?
8. What was the defense used by Dr. Pou and her colleagues?
9. Do you believe their actions were illegal? Unethical? Defend your positions.
10. Reflect on what you would have done if you were in the shoes of Dr. Pou and her nurse colleagues. Discuss how you would think through the situation and make a decision.
11. How might the Five Rs Approach to ethical nursing practice help a nurse make decisions in similar circumstances?
12. What guidance does the *Code of Ethics for Nurses with Interpretive Statements* provide for a situation like the one at Memorial Hospital Medical Center in New Orleans during a disaster such as Hurricane Katrina?

11-3: Fair Distribution of Scarce Vaccine Resources During a Pandemic

Registered Nurse Doris is the nurse in charge of the immunization program for the health department at the county level. An influenza pandemic is occurring with a virus that has a high case fatality rate. A vaccine just became available in small quantities. Doris, in collaboration with other health department administrators, must lead her team in immunizing the public. The Centers for Disease Control and Prevention has notified all U.S. health departments that vaccinations should be prioritized according to the CDC's flu-related ethics documents during a significant flu pandemic. Doris's family members live in the city where Doris lives and works, and their statuses follow:

- Husband is an attorney; children are aged 1, 5, and 7 years; all are in good health.
- Parents are both retired; father has chronic lymphocytic leukemia; mother is in good health.
- Sister runs a day-care center for young children in her home; husband is a truck driver for Walmart; they have a 2-year-old child.
- Brother manages the housekeeping department and the department that handles hazardous waste at the county hospital; the hospital has not yet received the vaccine; wife is a manager of a grocery store.
- Sister is administrative assistant to the mayor of the largest city in the county; husband is a pharmacist at a retail pharmacy; their 10-year-old son has asthma.
- Brother owns and manages a jewelry store; wife owns and manages an upscale beauty salon; their son is aged 16 years and is in good health.

Questions

Review the chapter content.

1. Doris's family knows that she supervises the administration of flu vaccine. Someone from each family unit asks her whether their family members can receive the vaccine.

What is the most ethical response for Doris regarding each of her family members? Should any of her family receive the vaccine? Why or why not?

2. Some of the nurses who work in the immunization department ask Doris about whether they can give the vaccine to their family members. Doris decides she needs to discuss this issue with all the nurses in one meeting. What should she tell them?
3. Does Doris's situation constitute an ethical dilemma? Why or why not?
4. Which ethical theories, approaches, and concepts are relevant to Doris's decision making? Support your choices.

11-4: Vaccine Distribution During the Covid-19 Pandemic

Review how vaccine distribution unfolded during the early vaccine availability period during the Covid-19 pandemic.

Questions/Discussion

1. Did the distribution of the Covid-19 vaccine unfold as outlined in the CDC's pandemic influenza document discussed in chapter 11? Explain.
2. Detail your assessment of what was done well.
3. Detail your assessment of how distribution did not work well.

11-5: Fair Distribution of Scarce Ventilator Resources During a Pandemic

You are on a team at your large county hospital to develop policies for and supervise the triaging of patients during an influenza pandemic. Currently, a pandemic is expanding that involves an influenza virus with a high case fatality rate. The hospital's policies, based on CDC guidelines, are in place to guide triaging patients whose needs compete for scarce ventilator resources. It is your job to begin implementing an educational program for the hospital nurses to prepare them for the conditions healthcare professionals may soon face at the hospital, especially in the ICUs.

In Chapter 11, review information about ventilator allocation during an influenza pandemic, and search for expanded or updated information on the CDC's website:

- *Ethical Considerations for Decision Making Regarding Allocation of Mechanical Ventilators during a Severe Influenza Pandemic or Other Public Health Emergency* (https://www.cdc.gov/od/science/integrity/phethics/docs/Vent_Document_Final_Version.pdf)
- *Advancing Excellence & Integrity of CDC Science* (https://www.cdc.gov/od/science/index.htm)
- *Ethics Subcommittee Documents* (https://www.cdc.gov/od/science/integrity/phethics/esdocuments.htm)

Questions/Discussion

Review the chapter content.

1. Prepare an outline of the information you will cover during the educational sessions.
2. Discuss what you will tell nurses when answering questions about patient–family–healthcare provider communication during the triaging process.

3. What guidance will you give the nurses about exhibiting compassion during the triaging process?

4. You need to explain ethics theories, approaches, and concepts relevant to the triaging process. Explain what you will tell the nurses.

5. What guidance does the *Code of Ethics for Nurses with Interpretive Statements* provide for such a situation?

6. How do you prepare the nurses for the possibility that a patient may be removed from a ventilator without the patient's or family's consent?

7. List and discuss any differences you may encounter or different actions that would apply, if any, if this case involved the Covid-19 pandemic rather than an influenza pandemic.

▶ Chapter 12

12-1: Workplace Bullying

You are the chief nurse executive (CNE) in a busy regional hospital. In the past few weeks, you have heard a rumor from several employees that two experienced registered nurses (RNs) on an acute-care medical unit have been bullying three novice RNs on that same unit. The hospital policy includes a zero tolerance workplace violence section with this explicit statement on bullying behaviors: "Administrators are ethically responsible for providing a safe, nonviolent work environment, free from bullying and intimidating behaviors."

You discussed these rumors and the hospital policy with the nurse manager of that particular unit. The manager has heard bits and pieces of past instances of these two RNs bullying others, but lately she has not seen any specific behaviors. You strive to foster high ethical standards, harmony, and participatory efforts toward a common goal, which moves you to create an educational initiative on prevention of workplace bullying. You do not wish to call out the two RNs' behaviors in a public way, but you believe this policy is so important that more education on workplace violence, particularly bullying, would benefit all nursing staff. You plan to ask your nurse managers for their creative ideas on how to achieve this initiative and then engage them in the implementation and evaluation phases of the initiative.

Questions

Review the chapter content.

1. Would your immediate action be to discuss the bullying rumor with the two RNs? As you answer, try to integrate your ideas regarding the hospital policy, whether to include the nurse manager in your discussion with the two RNs, your commitment to high ethical standards and participatory efforts toward a common goal, accountability, and the fact that all you really know for sure at this point is a rumor you heard. If you say yes to a discussion with the two RNs, how might you proceed? Please explain.

2. What is the CNE's ethical leadership style? What other characteristics make up this type of leadership?

3. What planning strategies would you use to proceed with the educational initiative? Think about ways to integrate such topics as change strategies, fairness, justice, trust, respect, and job responsibilities.

12-2: Reese's Courage to Confront: Maryn's Drug Use

Registered Nurse Reese Summers is a nurse manager in a cancer unit where many patients require frequent administration of opiate pain medication. Reese began to notice that Registered Nurse Maryn was displaying suspicious behaviors that are characteristic of drug use, such as nodding off to sleep while sitting in the nurses station, dressing sloppily in dirty clothing, documenting questionable information in her patients' records, and caring for patients who moan in unrelieved pain just after they receive medication. Reese suspected the worst and became panicky just thinking about how she will manage this problem. She is afraid that she will not have the moral courage to confront Maryn. In reality, she does not know what to do, but she acknowledges to herself that some type of unpleasant confrontation will be inevitable.

Questions

Review the chapter content.

1. Why did Reese feel such anxiety? Please explore.
2. How would you characterize a person with moral courage? Based on this initial story and information in Chapters 3 and 12, does Reese fit the description of courage? Do you anticipate that Reese will complete her task of taking care of the problem? If so, how?
3. Do you think Reese's intervention on behalf of the patients who are being mistreated is an act of moral courage?
4. Why is acting courageously considered an ideal ethical competency?

Appendix B

International
Council of Nurses

THE ICN
CODE OF ETHICS
FOR NURSES

REVISED 2021

Copyright © 2021 by ICN - International Council of Nurses,
3, place Jean Marteau, 1201 Geneva, Switzerland

ISBN: 978-92-95099-94-4

TABLE OF CONTENTS

An international code of ethics for nurses was first adopted by the International Council of Nurses (ICN) in 1953. It has been revised and reaffirmed at various times since, most recently with this review and revision completed in 2021.

PURPOSE OF THE CODE

The *ICN Code of Ethics for Nurses* is a statement of the ethical **values**, responsibilities and professional accountabilities of **nurses** and nursing students[1] that defines and guides ethical nursing practice within the different roles **nurses** assume. It is not a code of conduct but can serve as a framework for ethical nursing practice and decision-making to meet professional standards set by regulatory bodies.

The *ICN Code of Ethics for Nurses* provides ethical guidance in relation to **nurses**' roles, duties, responsibilities, behaviours, professional judgement and relationships with patients, other people who are receiving nursing care or services, **co-workers** and allied professionals. The *Code* is foundational and to be built upon in combination with the laws, regulations and professional standards of countries that govern nursing practice. The **values** and obligations expressed in this *Code* apply to **nurses** in all settings, roles and domains of practice.

PREAMBLE

From the origins of organised nursing in the mid-1800s and recognising nursing care is deeply rooted in the traditions and practices of **equity** and inclusion and in the appreciation of diversity, **nurses** have consistently recognised four fundamental nursing responsibilities: to promote health, to prevent illness, to restore health, and to alleviate suffering and promote a dignified death. The need for nursing is universal.

Inherent in nursing is a respect for **human rights**, including cultural rights, the right to life and choice, the right to dignity and to be treated with respect. Nursing care is respectful of and unrestricted by considerations of age, colour, culture, ethnicity, disability or illness, gender, sexual orientation, nationality, politics, language, race, religious or spiritual beliefs, legal, economic or social status.

---

1   The practice of the nursing student needs to be in line with the *ICN Code of Ethics*. Depending on the level of education, the responsibility for the student nurse's conduct is shared between the student and her/his supervisor.

Nurses are valued and respected for their contributions to improving the health of individuals, families, communities and populations locally, nationally and globally. They coordinate services with those of other health care professionals and related groups. Nurses demonstrate values of the profession such as respect, justice, empathy, responsiveness, caring, compassion, trustworthiness and integrity.

THE ICN CODE

The *ICN Code of Ethics for Nurses* has four principal elements that provide a framework for ethical conduct: nurses and patients or other people requiring care or services, nurses and practice, nurses and the profession, and nurses and global health.

APPLYING THE ELEMENTS OF THE CODE

The charts that follow the description of each element of the *Code* are intended to assist nurses to translate the standards into action. Note that these charts present examples of the main tenets included in the elements of the *Code* and are not intended to be an exhaustive or complete list of concepts. The ethical duties and values of nursing apply to all forms of nursing services and roles: clinicians, educators, students, researchers, managers, policy makers and others. Professional associations are also guided by these duties and values. A diagram (p. 21) illustrates the relationship of the values and duties to the nursing profession.

SUGGESTIONS FOR USE
of the *ICN Code of Ethics for Nurses*

The *ICN Code of Ethics for Nurses* is a guide for action based on social **values** and needs. It will have meaning only as a living document if applied to the realities of nursing and health care in all settings in which nursing care is delivered.

To achieve its purpose the *Code* must be understood, internalised and used by **nurses** in all aspects of their work. It must be available to students and **nurses** throughout their study and work lives.

Nurses can therefore:

- Study the standards under each element of the *Code*.

- Personally reflect on what each standard means.
  Think about ways to apply **ethics** to the personal domain of nursing practice, education, research, management, leadership or policy development.

- Discuss the *Code* with **co-workers** and others.

- Use a specific example from experience to identify ethical dilemmas and standards of conduct as outlined in the *Code*. Identify ways in which the *Code* guides in the resolution of dilemmas.

- Work in groups to clarify ethical decision making and reach a consensus on standards of ethical conduct.

- Collaborate with the **National Nurses Association**, **co-workers**, and others in the continuous application of ethical standards in nursing practice, education, management, research and policy.

DISSEMINATION
of the *ICN Code of Ethics for Nurses*

To be effective the *ICN Code of Ethics for Nurses* must be familiar to **nurses**. We encourage its dissemination to schools of nursing, **nurses** in their workplace, the nursing press and other mass media. The *Code* should also be disseminated to other health professions, the general public, consumer and policy-making groups, **human rights** organisations and employers of **nurses**. NNAs are encouraged to adopt this *Code*, translating it into local language(s), or use it as a framework to support their own codes of nursing **ethics**.

4

1. NURSES AND PATIENTS OR OTHER PEOPLE REQUIRING CARE OR SERVICES[2]

1.1 <u>Nurses</u>' primary professional responsibility is to people requiring nursing care and services now or in the future, whether individuals, families, communities or populations (hereinafter referred to as either 'patients' or 'people requiring care').

1.2 <u>Nurses</u> promote an environment in which the <u>human rights</u>, <u>values</u>, customs, religious and spiritual beliefs of the individual, families and communities are acknowledged and respected by everyone. <u>Nurses</u>' rights are included under <u>human rights</u> and should be upheld and protected.

1.3 <u>Nurses</u> ensure that the individual and <u>family</u> receive understandable, accurate, sufficient and timely information in a manner appropriate to the patient's culture, linguistic, cognitive and physical needs, and psychological state on which to base consent for care and related treatment.

1.4 <u>Nurses</u> hold in confidence <u>personal information</u> and respect the <u>privacy</u>, <u>confidentiality</u> and interests of patients in the lawful collection, use, access, transmission, storage and disclosure of <u>personal information</u>.

1.5 <u>Nurses</u> respect the <u>privacy</u> and <u>confidentiality</u> of colleagues and people requiring care and uphold the integrity of the nursing profession in person and in all media, including <u>social media</u>.

1.6 <u>Nurses</u> share with society the responsibility for initiating and supporting action to meet the health and social needs of all people.

1.7 <u>Nurses</u> <u>advocate</u> for <u>equity</u> and <u>social justice</u> in resource allocation, access to health care and other social and economic services.

1.8 <u>Nurses</u> demonstrate professional <u>values</u> such as respect, justice, responsiveness, caring, compassion, empathy, trustworthiness and integrity. They support and respect the dignity and universal rights of all people, including patients, colleagues and families.

---

2 The two terms 'patients' and 'people requiring care or nursing services' are used interchangeably. The two terms refer to the patient, family, community and populations requiring nursing care and services. Practice settings span across hospital, home and community care, primary care, public health, population health, long term care, correctional care, academic institutions and government and are not limited to sectors.

1.9   <u>Nurses</u> facilitate a culture of safety in health care environments, recognising and addressing threats to people and safe care in health practices, services and settings.

1.10   <u>Nurses</u> provide <u>evidence-informed</u>, <u>person-centred care</u>, recognising and using the <u>values</u> and principles of <u>primary health care</u> and health promotion across the lifespan.

1.11   <u>Nurses</u> ensure that the use of technology and scientific advances are compatible with the safety, dignity and rights of people. In the case of artificial intelligence or devices, such as care robots or drones, <u>nurses</u> ensure that care remains <u>person-centred</u> and that such devices support and do not replace human relationships.

Applying the Elements of the *Code* #1: NURSES AND PATIENTS OR PEOPLE REQUIRING CARE OR SERVICES		
Nurses, Nurse Leaders and <u>Nurse Managers</u>	Educators and Researchers	National Nurses Associations
Provide people focused, culturally appropriate, care that respects <u>human rights</u> and is sensitive to the <u>values</u>, customs and beliefs of people without prejudice or unjust discrimination.	In curricula, include content on cultural norms, safety and <u>competence</u>, <u>ethics</u>, <u>human rights</u>, <u>equity</u>, human dignity, justice, disparities and solidarity as the basis for access to health care. Design studies to explore <u>human rights</u> issues.	Develop position statements, standards of practice and guidelines that support <u>human rights</u> and ethical standards.

Applying the Elements of the *Code* #1: NURSES AND PATIENTS OR PEOPLE REQUIRING CARE OR SERVICES		
Nurses, Nurse Leaders and Nurse Managers	**Educators and Researchers**	**National Nurses Associations**
Participate in continuing education on ethical issues, ethical reasoning and ethical conduct. Encourage open dialogue among all stakeholders.	Design curricula to encompass currently peer reviewed and published approaches to nursing ethics. Provide teaching and learning opportunities for ethical issues, ethical principles and reasoning, and ethical decision making. This includes respect for autonomy, nonmaleficence, beneficence and justice.	Establish standards for **ethics** education and provide continuing **ethics** education for **nurses**.
Ensure informed consent for nursing and/or medical care. This includes the right to choose or refuse treatments.	Educate about respect for autonomy, informed consent, **privacy** and **confidentiality**. Respect research participants' right to refuse to participate in or withdraw from studies without prejudice.	Provide guidelines for human participants in research, position statements, relevant documentation and continuing education related to informed consent for nursing and medical care.

Applying the Elements of the *Code* #1: NURSES AND PATIENTS OR PEOPLE REQUIRING CARE OR SERVICES		
Nurses, Nurse Leaders and Nurse Managers	**Educators and Researchers**	**National Nurses Associations**
Exercise professional ethical judgement in the use of information, health records and reporting systems, whether electronic or paper-based, to ensure protection of <u>human rights</u>, <u>confidentiality</u> and <u>privacy</u> in accord with patient preferences and community safety and in compliance with any relevant laws.	In curricula, include accuracy, <u>confidentiality</u> and <u>privacy</u> on the use of media, reporting and recording systems, whether images, recordings, or comments. Be familiar with the use of required reporting for extreme emergencies.	Prepare guidelines and standards of practice on appropriate use of information and reporting systems that ensure protection of <u>human rights</u>, <u>confidentiality</u>, <u>privacy</u>, and mandated reporting mechanisms for public health outbreaks or extreme emergencies.
Communicate to appropriate supervisors and/or authorities any risks, inappropriate behaviours or misuse of technologies that threaten people's safety, and provide facts supporting this. <u>Nurses</u> need to be involved when technology is developed, and observe and report risks with technology and scientific advancements.	Include in curriculum and conduct research on what constitutes safe care that respects dignity and rights and considers new technology.	Lobby governments, health organisations, medical device and pharmaceutical companies to include <u>nurses</u> during research and development of technology for patient use.

Applying the Elements of the *Code* #1: NURSES AND PATIENTS OR PEOPLE REQUIRING CARE OR SERVICES		
Nurses, Nurse Leaders and Nurse Managers	**Educators and Researchers**	**National Nurses Associations**
Meet nurses' ethical obligations and responsibilities and actively affirm the values and ideals of the profession.	In curricula, include professional values and ideals, ethical responsibilities and obligations, and ethical frameworks with worldviews. Contribute to and disseminate emphasis on ethical research guidelines. Design studies to explore human rights issues.	Express the values and ideals of nursing in their foundational documents and incorporate into national codes of ethics for nurses.
Develop and monitor safety in the workplace.	Teach and facilitate learning about attributes, risk factors and skills to ensure practice environments that are healthy, safe and sustainable for everyone in the health care setting.	Influence employers to promote healthy and safe workplaces for nurses and other health care workers. Provide guidelines that assure a safe environment and healthy communities. Advocate for clear, accessible, transparent and effective reporting procedures to protect health and safety.

2.   NURSES AND PRACTICE

2.1   <u>Nurses</u> carry personal responsibility and accountability for ethical nursing practice, and for maintaining <u>competence</u> by engaging in continuous professional development and lifelong learning.

2.2   <u>Nurses</u> maintain <u>fitness to practice</u> so as not to compromise their ability to provide quality, safe care.

2.3   <u>Nurses</u> practise within the limits of their individual <u>competence</u> and regulated or authorised scope of practice and use professional judgement when accepting and delegating responsibility.

2.4   <u>Nurses</u> value their own dignity, well-being and health. To achieve this requires positive practice environments, characterised by professional recognition, education, reflection, support structures, adequate resourcing, sound management practices and occupational health and safety.

2.5   <u>Nurses</u> maintain standards of personal conduct at all times. They reflect well on the profession and enhance its image and public confidence. In their professional role, <u>nurses</u> recognise and maintain personal relationship boundaries.

2.6   <u>Nurses</u> share their knowledge and expertise and provide feedback, mentoring and supporting the professional development of student nurses, novice nurses, colleagues and other health care providers.

2.7   <u>Nurses</u> are patient <u>advocates</u>, and they maintain a practice culture that promotes ethical behaviour and open dialogue.

2.8   <u>Nurses</u> may <u>conscientiously object</u> to participating in particular procedures or nursing or health-related research but must facilitate respectful and timely action to ensure that people receive care appropriate to their individual needs.

2.9   <u>Nurses</u> maintain a person's right to give and withdraw consent to access their personal, health and genetic information. They protect the use, <u>privacy</u> and <u>confidentiality</u> of genetic information and human genome technologies.

2.10 <u>Nurses</u> take appropriate actions to safeguard individuals, families, communities and populations when their health is endangered by a co-worker, any other person, policy, practice or misuse of technology.

2.11 <u>Nurses</u> are active participants in the promotion of patient safety. They promote ethical conduct when errors or near misses occur, speak up when patient safety is threatened, <u>advocate</u> for transparency, and work with others to reduce the potential of errors.

2.12 <u>Nurses</u> are accountable for data integrity to support and facilitate ethical standards of care.

Applying the Elements of the *Code #2:* NURSES AND PRACTICE		
Nurses, Nurse Leaders and <u>Nurse Managers</u>	Educators and Researchers	<u>National Nurses Associations</u>
Pursue professional development through reading and study. Request and participate in continuing education to enhance knowledge and skills.	Teach and facilitate learning the value and obligation of lifelong learning and **competence** to practice. Explore current concepts and innovative teaching methods for theory and practice.	Develop a range of continuing education opportunities, through journals, media, conferences and distance education, that reflects advances in nursing theory and practice.
Initiate continuing education and participate in workplace governance, systems for professional performance, appraisal and systematic renewal of licensure to practice. Monitor, promote and evaluate <u>fitness to practice</u> in nursing staff.	Conduct and disseminate research that explores links between continual learning and **competence** to practice.	Promote national policies for high quality <u>nurse</u> education and educational requirements for continued authorisation to practice.
Seek a work-life balance, ongoing personal growth, and maintain a healthy lifestyle.	Teach obligations to self as well as obligations to patients, the importance of <u>fitness to practice</u>, and using <u>evidence-informed</u> care. In curricula, include promoting resilience in the workplace.	Lobby for working environments that promote healthy lifestyle standards for <u>nurses</u>. Provide guidelines on safe and decent work conditions for <u>nurses</u>.

Applying the Elements of the *Code* #2: NURSES AND PRACTICE		
Nurses, Nurse Leaders and Nurse Managers	**Educators and Researchers**	**National Nurses Associations**
Foster interprofessional collaboration for managing conflict and tensions. Promote an environment of shared ethical values. To improve quality of care and safety, fear of reprisal must be extinguished. This will create a more open, transparent culture that embraces crucial conversations for advancing health for all.	Teach methods and skills of situational assessment and conflict management as well as the roles and values of other health care disciplines.	Inform other disciplines and the public about the roles of nurses and the values of the nursing profession. Promote a positive image of nursing. Champion work environments and conditions that are free from abuse, harassment and violence.
Develop appropriate professional relationships with patients and colleagues; exercise professional judgement and decline gifts or bribes and avoid conflicts of interest.	Maintain and teach professional boundaries and skills to safeguard them. Teach identification of and methods to avoid conflicts of interest.	Set standards for professional boundaries and establish processes for the expression of recognition and gratitude.
Assure continuity of care for the patient when exercising conscientious objection, where an action may cause harm or is morally objectionable to the nurse.	Encourage self-reflection and teach frameworks and processes of conscientious objection.	Develop standards and guidelines for refusal of participation in specific medical procedures. Include guidance on conscientious objection in national codes of ethics.

3. NURSES AND THE PROFESSION

3.1 <u>Nurses</u> assume the major leadership role in determining and implementing **evidence-informed**, acceptable standards of clinical nursing practice, management, research and education.

3.2 <u>Nurses</u> and nursing scholars are active in expanding research-based, current professional knowledge that supports **evidence-informed** practice.

3.3 <u>Nurses</u> are active in developing and sustaining a core of professional values

3.4 <u>Nurses</u>, through their professional organisations, participate in creating a positive and constructive practice environment where practice encompasses clinical care, education, research, management and leadership. This includes environments which facilitate a nurse's ability to practice to their optimal scope of practice and to deliver safe, effective and timely health care, in working conditions which are safe as well as socially and economically equitable for <u>nurses</u>.

3.5 <u>Nurses</u> contribute to positive and ethical organisational environments and challenge unethical practices and settings. Nurses collaborate with nursing colleagues, other (health) disciplines and relevant communities to engage in the ethical creation, conduct and dissemination of peer reviewed and ethically responsible research and practice development as they relate to patient care, nursing and health.

3.6 <u>Nurses</u> engage in the creation, dissemination and application of research that improves outcomes for individuals, families and communities.

3.7 <u>Nurses</u> prepare for and respond to emergencies, disasters, conflicts, epidemics, pandemics, social crises and conditions of scarce resources. The safety of those who receive care and services is a responsibility shared by individual <u>nurses</u> and the leaders of health systems and organisations. This involves assessing risks and developing, implementing and resourcing plans to mitigate these.

Applying the Elements of the *Code* #3: NURSES AND THE PROFESSION		
Nurses, Nurse Leaders and Nurse Managers	**Educators and Researchers**	**National Nurses Associations**
Collaborate with colleagues to support the conduct, dissemination and use of research related to patient care, nursing and health.	Teach research methodology, <u>ethics</u> and evaluation. Conduct, disseminate, utilise and evaluate research to study and advance nursing knowledge.	Develop position statements, guidelines, policy and standards informed by nursing research and scholarly inquiry.
Promote participation in <u>national nurses' associations</u> to create solidarity and cooperation to promote favourable socio-economic and working conditions for nurses.	Emphasise to learners the nature, function and importance of professional nursing associations and international nursing collaboration.	Communicate the importance of membership in professional nursing organisations and promote participation in <u>national nurses' associations</u>.
Practice ethical behaviours and develop strategies to deal with moral distress during emergent crises, such as pandemics or conflicts.	Prepare students for local response to global issues with a broader vision of solidarity and the common good. Include health disparities, particularly for infants, frail elderly, prisoners, economically disadvantaged, trafficked, displaced persons and refugees.	Collaborate with global organisations to address current and emergent <u>social justice</u> issues.

16

Applying the Elements of the *Code* #3: NURSES AND THE PROFESSION		
Nurses, Nurse Leaders and Nurse Managers	**Educators and Researchers**	**National Nurses Associations**
Develop guidelines for workplace issues, such as bullying, violence, sexual harassment, fatigue, safety, and local incident management. Participate in studies regarding **ethics** and ethical workplace issues in every setting.	Teach identification of unhealthy work environments and skills to develop resilient and healthy workplace communities. Conduct research on ethical workplace issues across the profession.	Influence, pressure and negotiate for fair and decent working conditions. Develop position statements and guidelines to address workplace issues.
Prepare for and respond to emergencies, disasters, conflicts, epidemics, pandemics and conditions of scarce resources.	Ensure that curricula include essential elements of caring for people and populations in high risk, challenging environments.	**Advocate** and lobby governments and health organisations to prioritise. and protect the health, safety and well-being of health care workers during a response to health emergencies.
Practice non-discrimination against colleagues from other cultures and countries regardless of nationality, race, ethnicity or language.	Teach the principles of the WHO *Code of Practice on International Recruitment of Health Personnel* to support the ethical recruitment of **nurses**.	Promote the ethical recruitment of **nurses** and work with government and licensing boards to reduce barriers to employment for migrant **nurses**.

4.   NURSES AND GLOBAL HEALTH

4.1   <u>Nurses</u> value health care as a human right, affirming the right
to universal access to health care for all.

4.2   <u>Nurses</u> uphold the dignity, freedom and worth of all human beings
and oppose all forms of exploitation, such as human trafficking
and child labour.

4.3   <u>Nurses</u> lead or contribute to sound health policy development.

4.4   <u>Nurses</u> contribute to population health and work towards
the achievement of the United Nations <u>Sustainable Development Goals</u>
(SDGs). (UN n.d.)

4.5   <u>Nurses</u> recognise the significance of the <u>social determinants of health</u>.
They contribute to, and <u>**advocate**</u> for, policies and programmes
that address them.

4.6   <u>Nurses</u> collaborate and practise to preserve, sustain and protect
the natural environment and are aware of the health consequences
of environmental degradation, e.g. climate change. They <u>**advocate**</u>
for initiatives that reduce environmentally harmful practices to promote
health and well-being.

4.7   <u>Nurses</u> collaborate with other health and social care professions
and the public to uphold principles of justice by promoting
responsibility in <u>**human rights**</u>, <u>**equity**</u> and fairness and by promoting
the public good and a healthy planet.

4.8   <u>Nurses</u> collaborate across countries to develop and maintain global
health and to ensure policies and principles for this.

Applying the Elements of the *Code* #4: NURSES AND GLOBAL HEALTH		
Nurses, Nurse Leaders and Nurse Managers	**Educators and Researchers**	**National Nurses Associations**
Participate in **human rights** efforts, such as trafficking prevention and detection, helping vulnerable populations, providing universal education, and mitigating hunger and poverty.	Ensure that curricula include **human rights**, **SDGs**, universal access to care, culturally appropriate care, civic responsibility, **equity**, and social and **environmental justice**.	Collaborate with nursing regulatory bodies, voluntary organisations, and global agencies to develop position statements and guidelines that support **human rights**, **environmental justice** and international peace.
Educate oneself and colleagues about global health, including current and emergent technologies. **Advocate** for the ethical use of technology and scientific advances compatible with safety, dignity, **privacy**, **confidentiality** and **human rights**.	Seek opportunities to evaluate the short and long-term ethical consequences of the use of diverse technologies and emerging practices, including innovative equipment, robotics, **genetics** and **genomics**, stem cell technologies and organ donation.	Contribute to legislation and policies on the ethical use of technology and scientific advances adapted to the health and social norms and context of the country.
Acquire and disseminate knowledge about the negative effects of climate change on people's health and on the planet.	Teach about the facts and consequences of climate change on health and the many opportunities to support climate health at policy and institutional levels.	Participate in the development of legislation to reduce the impact of hospitals and the health care industry on the environment and address climate changes that negatively affect the health of populations.

19

Applying the Elements of the *Code* #4: NURSES AND GLOBAL HEALTH		
Nurses, Nurse Leaders and Nurse Managers	**Educators and Researchers**	**National Nurses Associations**
Support the ethical and proficient use of <u>social media</u> and technologies to improve population health consistent with the <u>values</u> of the nursing profession.	Participate in developing, implementing and evaluating new and emerging technologies, including <u>social media</u>, for prevention initiatives, public health education, and the health and well-being of populations. Prepare curricula and engage in research in support of the UN <u>SDGs</u>.	Update knowledge and increase awareness about the UN <u>SDGs</u> for population health and actively strategize nursing's participation in achieving these goals.
Act on local and global issues that affect health, such as poverty, food security, shelter, immigration, gender, class, ethnicity, race, environmental health, dignified work, and education.	Educate about socio-political and economic issues that affect health, including gender, ethnicity, race, culture, inequality and discrimination. Research socio-political factors that contribute to individual and population health and illness.	Collaborate with other national and international nursing organisations to formulate policies and legislation that address the <u>socio-economic determinants of health</u>.
Embed the concepts of peace, peace diplomacy and peace building into everyday practice.	Educate and research for peace diplomacy and peace building in communities and globally.	Collaborate globally, nationally and regionally with governments and nursing agencies to further the ends of global peace and justice and ameliorate the causes of illness.

ICN Code of Ethics for Nurses
Professional Values

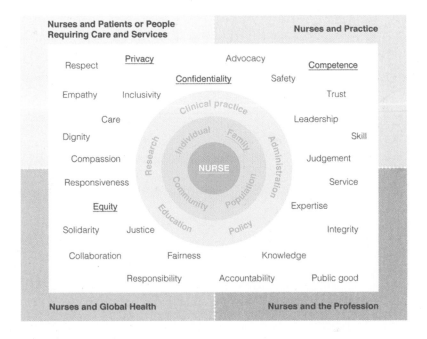

Nurses and Patients or People Requiring Care and Services

Nurses and Practice

Respect Privacy

Advocacy

Competence

Confidentiality Safety

Empathy Inclusivity

Trust

Care

Leadership

Dignity

Skill

Compassion

Judgement

Responsiveness

Service

Equity

Expertise

Solidarity Justice

Integrity

Collaboration Fairness Knowledge

Responsibility Accountability Public good

Nurses and Global Health

Nurses and the Profession

NURSE

21

GLOSSARY OF TERMS USED
in the *ICN Code of Ethics for Nurses*

Advocate	Actively supporting a right and good cause; supporting others in speaking for themselves or speaking on behalf of others who cannot speak for themselves. Advocacy is ultimately carried through with consent from the person themself.
Competence	The integrated knowledge, skills, judgement and attributes required of a nurse to practise safely and ethically in a designated role and setting.
Confidentiality	Confidentiality refers to the duty of the nurse to refrain from sharing patient information with third parties unrelated to the patient's care. Confidentiality is a limited duty, sometimes it may be overridden by law or regulation, e.g. mandated reporting of specific diseases.
Conscientious objection	Refusing to participate in required action, or seeking exemption from participation in classes of interventions (e.g. abortion, gender reassignment surgery, organ transplantation) that threaten a person's sense of moral integrity. It also includes refusal to participate in an action or intervention perceived to be inappropriate for a specific patient or it ignores the patient's wishes.
Co-workers	Nurses and other health and non-health related workers and professionals.
Environmental justice	Environmental justice seeks an equitable distribution of benefits (e.g., pure water, green spaces, clean air), and a safe and equitable distribution of burdens (e.g. toxic waste disposal, noise, factory air pollution). It includes sustainability, representative participation, and the avoidance of environmental discrimination.
Equity	Equity is an aspect of social justice. It refers to an absence of systemic disadvantages that result in health disparities for particular segments of society. Equity is essential to the full recognition of human rights.
Ethics	A branch of philosophy. Applied normative ethics is most commonly used in health care and professional ethics. It helps to determine the "ought" at the social, community or individual level. It also addresses broad social issues such as human rights, global cooperation, climate change, global pandemics, social-structural disparities.
Evidence-Informed Practice	Evidence-informed practice (EIP) is a process for making informed clinical decisions. Research evidence is integrated with clinical experience, patient values, preferences and circumstances. (Woodbury & Kuhnke 2014)

Family	A social unit composed of members connected through blood, kinship, emotional or legal relationships.
Fitness to practice	Having the skills, knowledge, health and character to do one's job safely and effectively. (UK NMC 2021)
Genetics	The study of single genes, genetic variation and heredity in organisms.
Genomics	The study of the complete set of a person's genes, the genome, to find variations that affect health, drug response, interactions among genes or with the environment.
Human rights	Human rights are inherent to all persons, regardless of nationality, sex, national or ethnic origin, colour, religion, language, or any other status. They range from the most fundamental – the right to life – to the rights to food, education, work, health, healthy living conditions, and liberty. (Adapted from OHCHR n.d.)
National Nurses Associations (NNAs)	Any professional national nursing group that clarifies, researches, educates and promotes the continued development of nurses and nursing.
Nurse	The nurse is a person who has completed a programme of basic, generalised nursing education and is authorised by the appropriate regulatory authority to practice nursing in his/her country. Basic nursing education is a formally recognised programme of study providing a broad and sound foundation in the behavioural, life and nursing sciences for the general practice of nursing, for a leadership role, and for post-basic education for specialty or advanced nursing practice. The nurse is prepared and authorised (1) to engage in the general scope of nursing practice, including the promotion of health, prevention of illness, and care of physically ill, mentally ill, and disabled people of all ages and in all healthcare and other community settings; (2) to carry out healthcare teaching; (3) to participate fully as a member of the healthcare team; (4) to supervise and train nursing and healthcare auxiliaries; and (5) to be involved in research. (ICN 1987)
Nurse manager	A nurse manager is responsible for the daily operations of a nursing unit and supervising the nursing personnel in a particular unit or department.
Personal information	Information obtained during professional contact that is private to an individual or family, and which, when disclosed, may violate the right to privacy, cause inconvenience, embarrassment, or harm to the individual or family.

Person-centred care	Valuing and respecting the characteristics, attributes and preferences of the patient, such as cultural and religious beliefs, and incorporating them into the planning and implementation of nursing care, services or programmes design.
Professional relationship	A professional relationship is an ongoing interaction between two people that observes a set of established boundaries or limits that is deemed appropriate under governing ethical standards.
Primary Health Care	Primary health care is a whole-of-society approach to health and well-being centred on the needs and preferences of individuals, families and communities. It addresses the broader determinants of health and focuses on the comprehensive and interrelated aspects of physical, mental and social health and well-being. (WHO 2019)
Privacy	Privacy is the right to freedom from intrusion into one's personal matters, information, or one's physical body.
Related groups	Other nurses, health care workers or other professionals providing service to an individual, family or community and working toward desired goals.
Self-determination	The right to have one's autonomous decisions respected. Self-determination is not absolute. It may be limited by cognitive or affective incapacity, age of majority, potential for harm to oneself or others, or the infringement of the liberty of others.
Self-reflection	The ability to evaluate one's own thoughts, plans and actions in relation to ethical responsibilities and ethical guidelines.
Social determinants of health	The conditions in which people are born, grow, live, work and age. These circumstances are shaped by the distribution of money, power and resources at global, national and local levels. The social determinants of health are mostly responsible for health inequities, i.e. the unfair and avoidable differences in health status seen within and between countries. (WHO 2020)
Social justice	Achieving equity and equality for society and the profession (ICN Strategic Plan 2019-2023). Social justice is a form of fairness requiring an impartial distribution of social goods and benefits and an equally impartial distribution of social burdens and affirms universal human rights. Social inequalities may exist only in order to benefit the least advantaged in society. Social justice applies to all persons, whether citizen or non-citizen.

Social media	Social media is an umbrella term used to describe social interaction through technology-based tools, many of which are online. This includes, but is not limited to internet forums, blogs, and networking sites such as Facebook, Twitter, Instagram and LinkedIn. (Institute of Business Ethics 2019)
Sustainable Development Goals	The Sustainable Development Goals are the blueprint to achieve a better and more sustainable future for all people. They address the global challenges we face, including those related to poverty, inequality, climate change, environmental degradation, peace and justice. The 17 Goals are all interconnected and, in order to leave no one behind, it is important that we achieve them all by 2030. (UN n.d.)
Values	Values in nursing are those ends sought by both the profession and in nurse – patient relationships. These include, for example, health, dignity, respect, compassion, equity, inclusivity. Note that some values (ends) are also obligations (actions) and attributes of character (virtues).

REFERENCES

Institute of Business Ethics (2019). The Ethical Challenges and Opportunities of Social Media Use. *Business Ethics Briefing.* 2 May 2019. Retrieved from: https://www.ibe.org.uk/resource/the-ethical-challenges-and-opportunities-of-social-media-use.html

International Council of Nurses (1987). Definition of a nurse. Available at: https://www.icn.ch/nursing-policy/nursing-definitions

Office of the High Commissioner for Human Rights (n.d.). What are human rights? Retrieved from: https://www.ohchr.org/en/issues/pages/whatarehumanrights.aspx

United Kingdom Nursing & Midwifery Council (2021). What is fitness to practice? Retrieved from: https://www.nmc.org.uk/concerns-nurses-midwives/dealing-concerns/what-is-fitness-to-practise/

United Nations (n.d.). *About the Sustainable Development Goals.* Retrieved from: https://www.un.org/sustainabledevelopment/sustainable-development-goals/

Woodbury MG & Kuhnke JL (2014). Evidence-based practice vs Evidence-informed practice. What's the Difference? *Wound Care Canada.* Vol 12, Number q, Spring 2014. Retrieved from: https://torontocentreforneonatalhealth.com/wp-content/uploads/2019/09/Article-Whatsthedifference.pdf

World Health Organization (2019). Primary Health Care Key Facts. Retrieved from https://www.who.int/news-room/fact-sheets/detail/primary-health-care

World Health Organization (2020). *Social determinants of health.* Retrieved from: https://www.who.int/gender-equity-rights/understanding/sdh-definition/en/#:~:text=Social%20determinants%20of%20health%E2%80%93The.global%2C%20national%20and%20local%20levels.

International Council of Nurses
3, Place Jean Marteau
1201 Geneva, Switzerland
+41229080100
icn@icn.ch
www.icn.ch

Appendix C

Mississippi
Advance Directive

Planning for Important Healthcare Decisions

Caring Connections
1700 Diagonal Road, Suite 625, Alexandria, VA 22314
www.caringinfo.org
800/658-8898

▶ Caring Connections

Caring Connections, a program of the National Hospice and Palliative Care Organization (NHPCO), is a national consumer engagement initiative to improve care at the end of life, supported by a grant from The Robert Wood Johnson Foundation.

Caring Connections tracks and monitors all state and federal legislation and significant court cases related to end-of-life care to ensure that our advance directives are up to date.

▶ It's About How You LIVE

It's About How You LIVE is a national community engagement campaign encouraging individuals to make informed decisions about end-of-life care and services. The campaign encourages people to:

Learn about options for end-of-life services and care

Implement plans to ensure wishes are honored

Voice decisions to family, friends and healthcare providers

Engage in personal or community efforts to improve end-of-life care

Please call the HelpLine at 800/658-8898 to learn more about the LIVE campaign, obtain free resources, or join the effort to improve community, state and national end-of-life care.

If you would like to make a contribution to help support our work, please visit www.nationalhospicefoundation.org/donate. Contributions to national hospice programs can also be made through the Combined Health Charities or the Combined Federal Campaign by choosing #11241.

Support for this program is provided by a grant from
The Robert Wood Johnson Foundation, Princeton,
New Jersey.

Your Advance Care Planning Packet

▶ Using These Materials

Before You Begin

1. Check to be sure that you have the materials for each state in which you could receive healthcare.
2. These materials include:
    *   Instructions for preparing your advance directive.
    *   Your state-specific advance directive forms, which are the pages with the gray instruction bar on the left side.

Preparing to Complete Your Advance Directive

3. Read the HIPAA Privacy Rule Summary on page 4.
4. Read all the instructions, on pages 7, as it will give you specific information about the requirements in your state.
5. Refer to the Glossary located in Appendix A if any of the terms are unclear.

Action Steps

6. You may want to photocopy these forms before you start so you will have a clean copy if you need to start over.
7. When you begin to fill out the forms, refer to the gray instruction bars - they will guide you through the process.
8. Talk with your family, friends, and physicians about your advance directive. Be sure the person you appoint to make decisions on your behalf understands your wishes.
9. Once the form is completed and signed, photocopy the form and give it to the person you have appointed to make decisions on your behalf, your family, friends, healthcare providers and/or faith leaders so that the form is available in the event of an emergency.

If you have questions or need guidance in preparing your advance directive or about what you should do with it after you have completed it, please refer to the state-specific contacts for Legal & End-of-Life Care Resources Pertaining to Healthcare Advance Directives, located in Appendix B.

▶ Summary of the HIPAA Privacy Rule

HIPAA is a federal law that gives you rights over your health information and sets rules and limits on who can look at and receive your health information.

Your Rights

You have the right to:

*   Ask to see and get a copy of your health records.
*   Have corrections added to your health information.
*   Receive a notice that tells you how your health information may be used and shared.

- Decide if you want to give your permission before your health information can be used or shared for certain purposes, such as marketing.
- Get a report on when and why your health information was shared for certain purposes.
- If you believe your rights are being denied or your health information isn't being protected, you can:
  - File a complaint with your provider or health insurer,
  - File a complaint with the U.S. Government.

You also have the right to ask your provider or health insurer questions about your rights. You can learn more about your rights, including how to file a complaint from the Web site at www.hhs.gov/ocr/hipaa/ or by calling 1-866-627-7748.

Who Must Follow this Law?

- Doctors, nurses, pharmacies, hospitals, clinics, nursing homes, and many other healthcare providers.
- Health insurance companies, HMOs, most employer group health plans.
- Certain government programs that pay for healthcare, such as Medicare and Medicaid.

What Information is Protected?

- Information your doctors, nurses, and other healthcare providers put in your medical record.
- Conversations your doctor has had about your care or treatment with nurses and other healthcare professionals.
- Information about you in your health insurer's computer system.
- Billing information about you from your clinic/healthcare provider.
- Most other health information about you, held by those who must follow this law.

Providers and health insurers who are required to follow this law must keep your information private by:

- Teaching the people who work for them how your information may and may not be used and shared,
- Taking appropriate and reasonable steps to keep your health information secure.

To make sure that your information is protected in a way that does not interfere with your healthcare, your information can be used and shared:

- For your treatment and care coordination,
- To pay doctors and hospitals for your healthcare,
- With your family, relatives, friends or others you identify who are involved with your healthcare or your healthcare bills, unless you object,
- To protect the public's health, such as reporting when the flu is in your area,
- To make required reports to the police, such as reporting gunshot wounds.

Your health information cannot be used or shared without your written permission unless this law allows it. For example, without your authorization, your provider generally cannot:

- Give your information to your employer.
- Use or share your information for marketing or advertising purposes.
- Share private notes about your mental health counseling sessions.

▶ Introduction to Your Mississippi Advance Healthcare Directive

This packet contains a legal document, the **Mississippi Advance Health-Care Directive**, that protects your right to refuse medical treatment you do not want, or to request treatment you do want, in the event you lose the ability to make decisions yourself.

1. Part 1, **Power of Attorney for Healthcare**, lets you name someone to make decisions about your healthcare—including decisions about life support—if you can no longer speak for yourself, or immediately, if you designate this on the document. The Power of Attorney for Healthcare is especially useful because it appoints someone to speak for you any time you can not or do not choose to make your own healthcare decisions, not only at the end of life.

2. Part 2, Instructions for Healthcare, functions as your living will. It lets you state your wishes about healthcare in the event that you can no longer speak for yourself and:

   a. you have an incurable or irreversible condition that will result in death within a relatively short time, or

   b. you become unconscious and, to a reasonable degree of medical certainty, will not regain consciousness, or

   c. the likely risks and burdens of treatment would outweigh the expected benefits.

3. Part 3, **Primary Physician**, is an optional section that allows you to designate your primary physician.

4. Part 4, **Certificate of Authorization for Organ Donation**, is an optional section that authorizes the donation of your organs upon death.

Note: These documents will be legally binding only if the person completing them is a competent adult who is 18 years of age or older or an emancipated minor under the age of 18 who has been married, or who has been declared by court order to be emancipated.

How do I make my Advance Healthcare Directive legal?

In order to make your Advance Healthcare Directive legally binding you have two options:

1. Sign your document in the presence of two witnesses, who must also sign the document to show that they personally know you and believe you to be of sound mind and under no duress, fraud or undue influence. Neither of your witnesses can be:
   - the person you appointed as your agent,
   - your healthcare provider, or an employee of your healthcare provider or facility.

   In addition, one of your witnesses **cannot** be:

   - related to you by blood or marriage or adoption,
   - entitled to any part of your estate either under your last will and testament or by operation of law.

   OR

2. Sign your document in the presence of a notary public.

   In addition, the signing requirements for the Certificate of Authorization for Organ Donation are separate and in addition to the signing requirements for the Advance

Healthcare Directive. If you complete the Certificate of Authorization for Organ Donation (Part 4), you must:

- Sign the Certificate (Part 4) in the presence of two (2) witnesses who, in turn, must sign the Certificate in your presence.
- If you cannot sign in person, the Certificate may be signed for you, at your direction and in your presence, and in the presence of two (2) witnesses who, in turn, must sign the Certificate in your presence.

MISSISSIPPI ADVANCE HEALTH-CARE DIRECTIVE – PAGE 1 OF 8

Explanation

You have the right to give instructions about your own health care. You also have the right to name someone else to make health care decisions for you. This form lets you do either or both of these things. It also lets you express your wishes regarding the designation of your primary physician. If you use this form, you may complete or modify all or any part of it. You are free to use a different form.

Part 1 of this form is a power of attorney for health care. Part 1 lets you name another individual as agent to make health care decisions for you if you become incapable of making your own decisions or if you want someone else to make those decisions for you now even though you are still capable. You may name an alternate agent to act for you if your first choice is not willing, able or reasonably available to make decisions for you. Unless related to you, your agent may not be an owner, operator, or employee of a residential long-term healthcare institution at which you are receiving care.

Unless the form you sign limits the authority of your agent, your agent may make all health-care decisions for you. This form has a place for you to limit the authority of your agent. You need not limit the authority of your agent if you wish to rely on your agent for all health care decisions that may have to be made. If you choose not to limit the authority of your agent, your agent will have the right to:

a.   Consent or refuse consent to any care, treatment, service, or procedure to maintain, diagnose, or otherwise affect a physical or mental condition;
b.   Select or discharge health care providers and institutions;
c.   Approve or disapprove diagnostic tests, surgical procedures, programs of medication, and orders not to resuscitate; and
d.   Direct the provision, withholding, or withdrawal of artificial nutrition and hydration and all other forms of health care.

Part 2 of this form lets you give specific instructions about any aspect of your health care. Choices are provided for you to express your wishes regarding the provision, withholding, or withdrawal of treatment to keep you alive, including the provision of artificial nutrition and hydration, as well as the provision of pain relief. Space is provided for you to add to the choices you have made or for you to write out any additional wishes.

Part 3 of this form lets you designate a physician to have primary responsibility for your health care.

Part 4 of this form lets you authorize the donation of your organs at death and declares that this decision will supersede any decision by a member of your family.

After completing this form, sign and date the form at the end and have the form witnessed by one of the two alternative methods listed below. Give a copy of the signed and completed form to your physician, to any other health care providers you may have, to any health care institution at which you are receiving care, and to any health care agents you have named. You should talk to the person you have named as agent to make sure that he or she understands your wishes and is willing to take the responsibility.

You have the right to revoke this Advance Health-Care Directive or replace this form at any time.

MISSISSIPPI ADVANCE HEALTH CARE DIRECTIVE - PAGE 2 OF 8

PART 1
POWER OF ATTORNEY FOR HEALTH CARE

(1) **DESIGNATION OF AGENT**: I designate the following individual as my agent to make health care decisions for me:

_____
(Name of individual you choose as agent)

_____
(address)   (city)   (state)   (zip code)

_____
(home phone)   (work phone)

OPTIONAL: If I revoke my agent's authority or if my agent is not willing, able, or reasonably available to make a health care decision for me, I designate as my first alternate agent:

_____
(Name of individual you choose as first alternate agent)

_____
(address)   (city)   (state)   (zip code)

_____
(home phone)   (work phone)

_____
(Name of individual you choose as second alternate agent)

_____
(address)   (city)   (state)   (zip code)

_____
(home phone)   (work phone)

MISSISSIPPI ADVANCE HEALTH CARE DIRECTIVE - PAGE 3 OF 8

ADD PERSONAL
INSTRUCTIONS
ONLY IF YOU
WANT TO LIMIT
THE POWER OF
YOUR AGENT

2) **AGENT'S AUTHORITY**: My agent is authorized to make all healthcare decisions for me, including decisions to provide, withhold, or withdraw artificial nutrition and hydration, and all other forms of health care to keep me alive, except as I state here:

_____

_____

_____

_____

(Add additional sheets if needed.)

INITIAL THE BOX
IF YOU WISH
YOUR AGENT'S
AUTHORITY
TO BECOME
EFFECTIVE
IMMEDIATELY

CROSS OUT AND
INITIAL ANY
STATEMENTS IN
PARAGRAPHS 3, 4
OR 5 THAT DO NOT
REFLECT YOUR
WISHES

(3) **WHEN AGENT'S AUTHORITY BECOMES EFFECTIVE**: My agent's authority becomes effective when my primary physician determines that I am unable to make my own health-care decisions unless I mark the following box. If I mark this box [   ], my agent's authority to make health care decisions for me takes effect immediately.

(4) **AGENT'S OBLIGATION**: My agent shall make health care decisions for me in accordance with this power of attorney for health care, any instructions I give in Part 2 of this form, and my other wishes to the extent known to my agent. To the extent my wishes are unknown, my agent shall make health care decisions for me in accordance with what my agent determines to be in my best interest. In determining my best interest, my agent shall consider my personal values to the extent known to my agent.

(5) **NOMINATION OF GUARDIAN**: If a guardian of my person needs to be appointed for me by a court, I nominate the agent designated in this form. If that agent is not willing, able, or reasonably available to act as guardian, I nominate the alternate agents whom I have named, in the order designated.

MISSISSIPPI ADVANCE HEALTH CARE DIRECTIVE - PAGE 4 OF 8

PART 2
INSTRUCTIONS FOR HEALTH CARE

If you are satisfied to allow your agent to determine what is best for you in making end-of-life decisions, you need not fill out this part of the form. If you do fill out this part of the form, you may strike any wording you do not want.

INITIAL THE PARAGRAPH THAT BEST REFLECTS YOUR WISHES REGARDING LIFE-SUPPORT MEASURES

(6) **END-OF-LIFE DECISIONS**: I direct that my health care providers and others involved in my care provide, withhold or withdraw treatment in accordance with the choice I have marked below:

[   ] (a) **Choice NOT To Prolong Life**

I do not want my life to be prolonged if (I) I have an incurable and irreversible condition that will result in my death within a relatively short time, (ii) I become unconscious and, to a reasonable degree of medical certainty, I will not regain consciousness, or (iii) the likely risks and burdens of treatment would outweigh the expected benefits, or

[   ] (b) **Choice To Prolong Life**

I want my life to be prolonged as long as possible within the limits of generally accepted health-care standards.

INITIAL THE BOX ONLY IF YOU WANT ARTIFICIAL NUTRITION AND HYDRATION REGARDLESS OF YOUR MEDICAL CONDITION

(7) **ARTIFICIAL NUTRITION AND HYDRATION**: Artificial nutrition and hydration must be provided, withheld or withdrawn in accordance with the choice I have made in paragraph (6) unless I mark the following box.

If I mark this box [   ], artificial nutrition and hydration must be provided regardless of my condition and regardless of the choice I have made in paragraph (6).

(8) **RELIEF FROM PAIN**: Except as I state in the following space, I direct that treatment for alleviation of pain or discomfort be provided at all times, even if it hastens my death:

ADDITIONAL INSTRUCTIONS (IF ANY)

(9) **OTHER WISHES**: (If you do not agree with any of the optional choices above and wish to write your own, or if you wish to add to the instructions you have given above, you may do so here.) I direct that:

(Add additional sheets if needed.)

PART 3
PRIMARY PHYSICIAN
(OPTIONAL)

PRINT THE NAME, ADDRESS AND TELEPHONE NUMBER OF YOUR PRIMARY PHYSICIAN

(10) I designate the following physician as my primary physician:

_____
(name of physician)

_____
(address)   (city)   (state)   (zip code)

_____
(phone)

OPTIONAL: If the physician I have designated above is not willing, able, or reasonably available to act as my primary physician, I designate the following physician as my primary physician:

PRINT THE NAME, ADDRESS AND TELEPHONE NUMBER OF YOUR ALTERNATE PRIMARY PHYSICIAN

_____
(name of physician)

_____
(address)   (city)   (state)   (zip code)

_____
(phone)

SIGN AND DATE THE DOCUMENT

(11) **EFFECT OF COPY**: A copy of this form has the same effect as the original.

PRINT YOUR NAME AND ADDRESS

(12) **SIGNATURES**: Sign and date the form here:

_____
(date)   (sign your name)

_____
(print your name)

_____
(address)

_____
(city)   (state)   (zip code)

MISSISSIPPI ADVANCE HEALTH CARE DIRECTIVE - PAGE 6 OF 8

PART 4
CERTIFICATE OF AUTHORIZATION FOR ORGAN DONATION
(OPTIONAL)

IF YOU DO NOT WISH TO DONATE ORGANS, DO NOT COMPLETE PART 4.

OTHERWISE, CROSS OUT AND INITIAL ANY STATEMENTS THAT **DO NOT** REFLECT YOUR WISHES.

I, the undersigned, this _____ day of _____, 20___, desire that my _____ organ(s) be made available after my demise for:

(a) Any licensed hospital, surgeon or physician, for medical education, research, advancement of medical science, therapy or transplantation to individuals;

(b) Any accredited medical school, college or university engaged in medical education or research, for therapy, educational research or medical science purposes or any accredited school of mortuary science;

(c) Any person operating a bank or storage facility for blood, arteries, eyes, pituitaries, or other human parts, for use in medical education, research, therapy or transplantation to individuals;

(e) The donee specified below, for therapy or transplantation needed by him or her, do hereby donate my _____ for said purpose to
(Name)

at _____
(Address).

I hereby authorize a licensed physician, surgeon or certified technician or the state anatomy board to remove and preserve for use my _____ for said purpose.

Witnessed this ____ day of _____ 20___.

IF YOU COMPLETE PART 4, YOU MUST SIGN THIS SECTION IN THE PRESENCE OF TWO WITNESSES WHO, IN TURN, MUST SIGN THIS SECTION IN YOUR PRESENCE.

_____
(Donor)

_____
(Address)

_____
(Telephone)

_____
(Witness #1)

_____
(Witness #2)

WITNESSING PROCEDURE FOR ADVANCE HEALTH CARE DIRECTIVE

(13) WITNESSES: This power of attorney will not be valid for making health care decisions unless it is either:

(a) signed by two (2) qualified adult witnesses who are personally known to you and who are present when you sign or acknowledge your signature: or
(b) acknowledged before a notary public in the state.

ALTERNATIVE NO. 1
WITNESS

WITNESS #1
ONE OF YOUR WITNESSES MUST AGREE WITH THIS STATEMENT HAVE YOUR WITNESS SIGN AND DATE THE DOCUMENT AND THEN PRINT THEIR NAME AND ADDRESS

I declare under penalty of perjury pursuant to Section 97-9-61, Mississippi Code of 1972, that the principal is personally known to me, that the principal signed or acknowledged this power of attorney in my presence, that the principal appears to be of sound mind and under no duress, fraud or undue influence, that I am not the person appointed as agent by this document, and that I am not a health-care provider, nor an employee of a health care provider or facility. I am not related to the principal by blood, marriage or adoption, and to the best of my knowledge, I am not entitled to any part of the estate of the principal upon the death of the principal under a will now existing or by operation of law.

_____   _____
(date).   (signature of witness)

_____
(printed name of witness)

_____
(address)

_____
(city)   (state)   (zip code)

WITNESS

WITNESS #2
ONE OF YOUR WITNESSES MUST AGREE WITH THIS STATEMENT HAVE YOUR WITNESS SIGN AND DATE THE DOCUMENT AND THEN PRINT THEIR NAME AND ADDRESS

I declare under penalty of perjury pursuant to Section 97-9-61, Mississippi Code of 1972, that the principal is personally known to me, that the principal signed or acknowledged this power of attorney in my presence, that the principal appears to be of sound mind and under no duress, fraud or undue influence, that I am not the person appointed as agent by this document, and that I am not a health care provider, nor an employee of a health care provider or facility.

_____   _____
(date)   (signature of witness)

_____
(printed name of witness)

_____
(address)

_____
(city)   (state)   (zip code)

MISSISSIPPI ADVANCE HEALTH CARE DIRECTIVE - PAGE 8 OF 8

ALTERNATIVE NO. 2

State of _____

County of _____

On this _____ day of _____, in the year _____,

before me, _____ (insert name of notary

public)

appeared _____, personally known to me (or proved to me on the basis of satisfactory evidence) to be the person whose name is subscribed to this instrument, and acknowledged that he or she executed it. I declare under the penalty of perjury that the person whose name is subscribed to this instrument appears to be of sound mind and under no duress, fraud or undue influence.

Notary Seal

_____

(Signature of Notary Public)

© 2005 National Hospice and Palliative Care Organization 2007 Revised.

Courtesy of Caring Connections
1700 Diagonal Road, Suite 625, Alexandria, VA 22314
www.caringinfo.org, 800/658-8898

You Have Filled Out Your Advance Directive, Now What?

1. Your Mississippi Advance Health-Care Directive is an important legal document. Keep the original signed document in a secure but accessible place. Do not put the original document in a safe deposit box or any other security box that would keep others from having access to it.

2. Give photocopies of the signed original to your agent and alternate agent(s), doctor(s), family, close friends, clergy and anyone else who might become involved in your healthcare. If you enter a nursing home or hospital, have photocopies of your document placed in your medical records.

3. Be sure to talk to your agent and alternate agent(s), doctor(s), clergy, family and friends about your wishes concerning medical treatment. Discuss your wishes with them often, particularly if your medical condition changes.

4. If you want to make changes to your document after it has been signed and witnessed, you should complete a new document.

5. Remember, you can always revoke one or both sections of your Mississippi Advance Health-Care Directive.

6. Be aware that your Mississippi documents will not be effective in the event of a medical emergency. Ambulance personnel are required to provide cardiopulmonary resuscitation (CPR) unless they are given a separate order that states otherwise. These orders, commonly called "non-hospital do-not-resuscitate orders," are designed for people whose poor health gives them little chance of benefiting from CPR. These orders must be signed by your physician and instruct ambulance personnel not to attempt CPR if your heart or breathing should stop.

Currently not all states have laws authorizing non-hospital do-not-resuscitate orders. We suggest you speak to your physician for more information. **Caring Connections does not distribute these forms.**

▶ **Appendix A**

Glossary

Advance directive A general term that describes two kinds of legal documents, living wills and medical powers of attorney. These documents allow a person to give instructions about future medical care should he or she be unable to participate in medical decisions due to serious illness or incapacity. Each state regulates the use of advance directives differently.

Artificial nutrition and hydration Artificial nutrition and hydration supplements or replaces ordinary eating and drinking by giving a chemically balanced mix of nutrients and fluids through a tube placed directly into the stomach, the upper intestine or a vein.

Brain death The irreversible loss of all brain function. Most states legally define death to include brain death.

Capacity In relation to end-of-life decision-making, a patient has medical decision making capacity if he or she has the ability to understand the medical problem and the risks and benefits of the available treatment options. The patient's ability to understand other unrelated concepts is not relevant. The term is frequently used interchangeably with competency but is not the same. Competency is a legal status imposed by the court.

Cardiopulmonary resuscitation Cardiopulmonary resuscitation (CPR) is a group of treatments used when someone's heart and/or breathing stops. CPR is used in an attempt to restart the heart and breathing. It may consist only of mouth-to-mouth breathing or it can include pressing on the chest to mimic the heart's function and cause blood to circulate. Electric shock and drugs also are used frequently to stimulate the heart.

Do-Not-Resuscitate (DNR) order A DNR order is a physician's written order instructing healthcare providers not to attempt cardiopulmonary resuscitation (CPR) in case of cardiac or respiratory arrest. A person with a valid DNR order will not be given CPR under these circumstances. Although the DNR order is written at the request of a person or his or her family, it must be signed by a physician to be valid. A non-hospital DNR order is written for individuals who are at home and do not want to receive CPR.

Emergency Medical Services (EMS): A group of governmental and private agencies that provide emergency care, usually to persons outside of healthcare facilities; EMS personnel generally include paramedics, first responders and other ambulance crew.

Healthcare agent: The person named in an advance directive or as permitted under state law to make healthcare decisions on behalf of a person who is no longer able to make medical decisions.

Hospice Considered to be the model for quality, compassionate care for people facing a life-limiting illness or injury, hospice and palliative care involve a team-oriented approach to expert medical care, pain management, and emotional and spiritual support expressly tailored to the person's needs and wishes. Support is provided to the persons loved ones as well.

Intubation Refers to "endotracheal intubation" the insertion of a tube through the mouth or nose into the trachea (windpipe) to create and maintain an open airway to assist breathing.

Life-sustaining treatment Treatments (medical procedures) that replace or support an essential bodily function (may also be called life support treatments). Life-sustaining treatments include cardiopulmonary resuscitation, mechanical ventilation, artificial nutrition and hydration, dialysis, and other treatments.

Living will A type of advance directive in which an individual documents his or her wishes about medical treatment should he or she be at the end of life and unable to communicate. It may also be called a "directive to physicians", "healthcare declaration," or "medical directive."

Mechanical ventilation Mechanical ventilation is used to support or replace the function of the lungs. A machine called a ventilator (or respirator) forces air into the lungs. The ventilator is attached to a tube inserted in the nose or mouth and down into the windpipe (or trachea).

Medical power of attorney A document that allows an individual to appoint someone else to make decisions about his or her medical care if he or she is unable to communicate. This type of advance directive may also be called a healthcare proxy, durable power of attorney for healthcare or appointment of a healthcare agent. The person appointed may be called a healthcare agent, surrogate, attorney-in-fact or proxy.

Palliative care A comprehensive approach to treating serious illness that focuses on the physical, psychological, spiritual, and existential needs of the patient. Its goal is to achieve the best quality of life available to the patient by relieving suffering, and controlling pain and symptoms.

Power of attorney A legal document allowing one person to act in a legal matter on another's behalf regarding to financial or real estate transactions.

Respiratory arrest: The cessation of breathing an event in which an individual stops breathing. If breathing is not restored, an individual's heart eventually will stop beating, resulting in cardiac arrest.

Surrogate decision-making Surrogate decision-making laws allow an individual or group of individuals (usually family members) to make decisions about medical treatments for a patient who has lost decision-making capacity and did not prepare an advance directive. A majority of states have passed statutes that permit surrogate decision making for patients without advance directives.

Ventilator A ventilator, also known as a respirator, is a machine that pushes air into the lungs through a tube placed in the trachea (breathing tube). Ventilators are used when a person cannot breathe on his or her own or cannot breathe effectively enough to provide adequate oxygen to the cells of the body or rid the body of carbon dioxide.

Withholding or withdrawing treatment Forgoing life-sustaining measures or discontinuing them after they have been used for a certain period of time.

Appendix B

Legal & End-of-Life Care Resources Pertaining to Healthcare Advance Directives

LEGAL SERVICES

Mississippi Department of Human Service (MDHS) is dedicated to assisting individuals over the age of 60 with low to moderate incomes with legal referrals and other services.

They also assist individuals over the age of 18 who are disabled with services and programs in their region.

Anyone over the age of 18 with a disability or over the age of 60 can get legal information and advice about most issues, including:

- Power of Attorney
- Civil Issues
- Pension Benefits
- Tenant/Landlord
- Living Wills/Trust and more
  - Must be 18 and with a disability or 60 and older
  - Free for individuals with low to moderate incomes

To locate referrals in your area:
Call toll free: 1-800-948-3090 or 1-601-359-4929

OR

Visit their website: http://www.mdhs.state.ms.us/aas.html

END-OF-LIFE SERVICES

The Mississippi Department of Human Service (MDHS) can connect individuals over the age of 60 in Mississippi with an Area Agency on Aging (AAA) in their region who can assist them with programs and services.

AAA resources and services include, but are not limited to:

- Meals
- Medical assistance
- Legal assistance
- Nutrition Programs
- Employment Programs for individuals over 55
- In Home Services
- Adult Day Care and much more

To find an AAA in your area call toll free: 1-800-948-3090

OR

Visit their website for locations and number:
http://www.mdhs.state.ms.us/aas_agcy.html

Glossary

A

Abortion The death of a fetus via either premature birth (miscarriage, or spontaneous abortion) or the intentional termination of a pregnancy.

Act utilitarians Followers of utilitarianism who believe each action in a particular circumstance should be chosen based on its likely good consequences rather than on following an inherently moral, universal rule. Compare with *rule utilitarians*.

Active euthanasia Taking purposeful steps to end a life, such as the administration of certain drugs. One reason for inducing death in this manner might be terminal illness.

Adaptation theory The idea that people adapt to the physical and social environment in which they live.

Adherence The degree to which a patient follows a healthcare professional's prescribed treatment regimen. Adherence suggests a higher level of patient involvement and agreement than compliance. See *compliance*.

Adolescent developmental process The physical, emotional, and cognitive changes that take place in children as they age; the process consists of three steps and takes place over a period of 11 years. See *early adolescence*, *middle adolescence*, and *late adolescence*.

Advance directive Written instructions for use in making medical decisions if a patient is rendered incompetent or is otherwise unable to express consent. See *living will*, *durable power of attorney*, and *psychiatric advance directive*.

Advocacy Campaigning or working in support of a cause or person; relating to nursing, trying to meet patients' needs that the patients themselves cannot meet.

Ageism Discrimination against or negative perceptions of older persons based strictly on age.

Alcohol use disorder A substance abuse problem in which alcohol has become a person's normal function of living or is to the point of causing physical, mental, social, or personal adverse effects.

Ana A popular abbreviation for anorexia nervosa, which is sometimes personified by adolescents.

Anorexia nervosa An eating disorder that is not about food but is characterized by the extremely limited or nonexistent consumption of food in relation to an intense fear of weight gain. The person equates thinness with self-worth.

Anosognosia Lack of insight into one's mental illness based on the same brain circuitry problem that causes the mental illness.

Assisted reproductive technology (ART) All types of fertility treatments in which both eggs and sperm are handled.

Authentic leader A leader who places great importance on things such as openness, honesty, and transparency in relationships with his or her followers; a deeply rooted sense of right and wrong and self-identity.

Authentic presence Being true to oneself.

Autonomy The ability to make independent decisions for oneself and to have those decisions respected by others.

B

Baby Doe rules Also known as the 1984 Child Abuse Prevention and Treatment Act Amendments. These rules prohibit discrimination based entirely on a child's handicaps.

BART behavioral intervention program The Becoming a Responsible Teen (BART) program, which is a popular theory- and evidence-based health risk prevention education program for adolescents, draws from both Bandura's social learning theory and the information–motivation–behavioral (IMB) skills model.

Battery Consists of one person *offensively touching* another person without the person's consent.

Basic dignity The respect and equality due to all human beings.

Being a good citizen Anticipating ethical dilemmas in relationships and engaging in dialogue with affected parties to resolve concerns.

Beneficence The ethical principle of doing good. See *nonmaleficence*.

Benevolence A moral trait in which a person is compelled to act on behalf of others.

Best interest standard A decision-making criterion used for patients who have never been competent and able to express their own autonomous wishes for health care (such as a child or adult mentally disabled since childhood). A surrogate decides for the patient based on the surrogate's assessment of what would provide the most benefits and fewest burdens to the patient.

Binge eating disorder An eating disorder that causes people to binge eat large amounts of food, sometimes in secret.

Bioethics A branch of ethics specifically focused on issues related to health care.

Biological view A view that a single-cell zygote does not come into being until the cell has completed the division process, at which time the entity becomes a uniquely individuated human organism.

Boundary crossings Actions that go beyond the established limits of a relationship that can cause harm to the person whose limits were not respected.

Boundary violations Actions that do not promote the best interest of another person in a relationship and pose a potential risk, harm, or exploitation to another person in a relationship.

Brain death Irreversible cessation of all functions of the entire brain, including cessation of all functions of the brain stem.

Bulimia nervosa An eating disorder that causes people either to excessively binge and purge by vomiting and taking laxatives or not to purge but to engage in other unsafe methods for losing weight, such as excessive exercise or fasting.

C

Casuistry A case-based approach to ethics.

Cardiopulmonary death A person is dead by cardiopulmonary criteria when the cessation of breathing and heartbeat is irreversible.

Categorical imperatives Kant's approach to testing whether an act is ethical. If a person cannot will (mandate) that everyone in the world should also be free to do what the person is about to do, then the act is not ethical. An example is to lie.

Chronic disease An illness that is generally characterized by multiple etiologies, a long-lasting course, and no cure; often, though, it is manageable.

Chronic illness People's perception of their quality of life and the difficulty of living with and experiencing a chronic disease.

Claim rights Also called positive rights; rights that a person can express only if another person or entity allows it to happen (either by assisting so the claim is met or by not interfering with the claim). See *liberty rights*.

Clinical wisdom The necessary combination of prudence and practical wisdom.

Collaboration Working together to achieve common goals.

Common morality Generally accepted beliefs within a community regarding normative beliefs and behavior.

Communication The act of imparting or exchanging information in meaningful, clearly understood ways.

Communitarian ethics An ethics approach emphasizing actions based on the common good of communities.

Community A group of people with a shared interest in a common good and the potential ability to engage with each other to achieve common goals.

Compassion An understanding and a recognition of suffering, along with an honest desire to alleviate said suffering.

Complex adaptive system A system, such as a healthcare organization, that focuses on external relationships, which places the organization within a larger context or environment.

Compliance An assumed agreement between a patient and a healthcare professional about a proposed treatment regimen, which is taken as an indication that the patient intends to follow the healthcare professional's plan. Compliance suggests an unequal patient–provider relationship, with the patient essentially submitting to a treatment plan with which he or she may or may not agree. See *adherence*.

Compliance program Also known as a risk-management program; an internal department at an organization charged with ensuring that the organization follows regulations and preventing unlawful conduct.

Concern A competency in which nurses feel a sense of responsibility to think about the scope of care that is important for their patients.

Concordance An approach to medication wherein a patient and a provider agree on a treatment regimen after a discussion of the patient's beliefs and wishes regarding the medication (if, when, and how a medicine is used).

Confidentiality The nondisclosure of information; preventing access to information by unapproved parties.

Conflicts of interest When individuals' personal interests and desires are at odds with their public duties or values.

Conflicts of commitment Conflicts of interest as viewed from an ethical perspective. See *conflicts of interest*.

Contentment An intermittent feeling of comfort that comes to a person as a result of practicing and following a spiritual direction.

Critical theory (also called critical social theory) An approach to ethics emphasizing the need to emancipate people in society who are subjected to the power of the hegemonic class.

Critical thinking Thinking about one's thinking.

Cultural relativism The belief that morals are inseparable from the culture in which they develop such that ideas or actions that are deemed wrong or immoral in one culture may not be viewed that way in a different culture.

Culturally sensitive care Providing care in a way that understands and respects the beliefs, values, and customs of the person receiving care.

Culture A set of values, attitudes, customs, beliefs, and so on that are shared by a particular group. Culture can be defined on the basis of race, religion, nationality, ethnicity, or other personal, geographic, or social characteristics.

D

Dead donor rule A guiding principle regarding potential organ donors that consists of two parts: (1) the donor must be declared dead before organ retrieval can begin, and (2) care or treatment must not be compromised in favor of potential organ recipients (i.e., the organ donor must not be allowed to die so organs become available).

Death The irreversible cessation of circulatory and respiratory functions and/or irreversible cessation of all functions of the brain.

Death anxiety An innate fear of death, or nonbeing.

Decisional capacity The ability to make what is generally considered to be reasonable choices.

Deontology An approach to ethics focused on judging morality based on adherence to accepted rules and duties; literally, the study of duty. Compare with *virtue ethics*.

Depression Chronic feelings of sadness, anger, or low self-esteem that interfere with daily life and prevent enjoyment in previously pleasurable activities.

Descriptive ethics A form of ethical inquiry concerned with describing and identifying rather than understanding a person's morals.

Disenfranchised grief The sorrow that results when the grieving process is not allowed or cannot be done openly; the hidden nature of the grief often results in prolonging and intensifying the process.

Distributive justice The concept of fair allocation of resources in a society.

Do not resuscitate (DNR) order A written order kept in a patient's medical record to indicate that healthcare personnel are not to perform cardiopulmonary resuscitation (CPR) or other resuscitative measures on a patient.

Doctor–nurse game A term referring to the relationship between doctors and nurses that is founded on the belief that the doctor is superior and open disagreements between nurse and doctor are to be avoided. This belief resulted in the need for nurses to be circumspect when providing guidance or suggestions to a doctor so the advice was not seen as challenging the doctor's perceived authority.

Donor card A legal document that people carry if they wish to donate their organs after their death.

Durable power of attorney A legal written directive in which a designated person can make either general or specific healthcare and medical decisions for a patient.

Duty to warn The need to disclose confidential information in instances when a clearly identifiable person is at risk of harm.

E

Early adolescence The first stage of an adolescent's development; this step takes place between the ages of 11 and 13 years and is marked by a need for experimentation and discovery (usually connected to the onset of puberty).

Eating disorder not otherwise specified (ED-NOS) An eating disorder that a care provider has not yet specified.

Effective listening When communicators in an exchange comprehend the active information and form a mutual understanding of the essence of the dialogue.

Egg donation A form of assisted reproduction in which a woman donates her eggs; the eggs are artificially inseminated with the sperm from the prospective father, and the embryos are implanted into the prospective mother's uterus.

Embryo donation A form of assisted reproduction in which a couple with successful pregnancies donates embryos (usually those remaining after in vitro fertilization treatment) to another couple.

Emergency contraception (EC) Birth control measures taken after sexual intercourse to prevent pregnancy. Emergency contraception includes RU486 (mifepristone) and Plan B (the morning-after pill).

Equanimity One of Buddhism's four immeasurable virtues; being balanced and calm.

Ethic of an organization How an organization defines its core mission and values and thinks about and implements said values.

Ethic of care An approach to ethics that emphasizes traditionally feminine traits such as love, compassion, sympathy, and concern about human well-being.

Ethical climate How an organization responds to ethical issues as determined by its members' shared values.

Ethical dilemma A ethics-laden situation in which there are two equally unfavorable choices, two equally favorable choices, or two choices that are ethically ambiguous.

Ethical leader A leader who is able to influence others through noncoercive means and works toward righteous goals.

Ethical objectivism The belief that the concepts or principles of morality are universal.

Ethical relativism The belief that differing ideas of morality among people or groups are acceptable.

Ethical subjectivism A type of ethical relativism that does not include a universal morality; rather, ethical subjectivists believe individuals create their own morality based on personal feelings.

Ethics The study of ideal human behavior and existence, focused on understanding the concepts of and distinguishing between right and wrong.

Ethics as praxis The use of theory to think about, understand, and practice moral behavior.

Eudaimonia Greek term for the state of well-being and thriving.

Euthanasia A good or painless death; the act of intentionally ending a life—often, though not always—with the goal of limiting or relieving pain and suffering.

F

Fear appeals Persuasive messages that emphasize the negative consequence of a behavior or action to frighten the target audience into not performing the action (or into choosing a healthy action instead).

Fiduciary relationships Relationships in which one party has a formal duty to uphold one's responsibilities and commitments and to act in the best interest of the other members of the relationship.

Forgiveness Always being open to others' situations and reasons for the circumstances.

Freedom The state of self-direction; not being confined or controlled by others.

Full moral standing A belief that human beings have or sentient fetuses have the potential for privileges and the capacity to reason and make autonomous decisions.

Futile Pointless or meaningless events or objects.

Futile treatments Procedures that are unlikely to provide any benefit to a patient and could, instead, cause substantial harm.

Future-like-ours argument A suggestion that, just like living human beings, a fetus has the potential to become a person with a future full-life experience and the possibility of successful self-actualization goals, a normal life span, rational decision-making abilities, and relationships.

G

Gatekeepers A suicide prevention program designed to train school nurses to recognize the warning signs of suicidal ideation and intervene as needed.

Gender selection Using genetic testing to determine the sex of embryos and then selecting for implantation only those embryos of the desired sex.

Genetic screening The use of professional counselors to discuss the potential for inheritable diseases; most often used for individuals or couples with a personal or family history of diseases caused by genetic defects.

Genuineness A lack of pretense when engaging in interpersonal relationships; credibility and honesty when interacting with others.

Gestational surrogacy A form of surrogacy in which a woman carries an embryo to which she has no genetic relationship (the embryo is created from the egg and sperm of the prospective parents).

Giver of communication An entity (such as a nurse) who is responsible for determining how, where, and what type of information is provided to a particular group.

Good death People do not allow medical care and treatment to control all their thoughts about their death; rather, they focus on the illness trajectory and the best palliative care they can receive.

H

Health disparities The differences in health outcomes that can be attributed to inequalities in healthcare delivery.

Health risk behaviors Actions and conduct that are dangerous to the health and well-being of the participants. Examples include drug and alcohol use, engaging in unsafe sex, and unhealthy eating habits.

Healthcare ethics Generally viewed as bioethics or ethics involved in any realm of health care.

Healthcare fraud The intentional misuse or misappropriation of healthcare monies or equipment for personal gain.

Hidden hurt A hurt that causes a great degree of mental stress, such as when family members or peers tease, make fun of, or bully a person because of a weight problem, poor grades in school, freckles, a big nose, other facial distortions, or other perceived shortcomings.

Higher-brain death Human death is considered the irreversible cessation of the capacity for consciousness, which implies that the person is dead even though the continual function of the brain stem regulates breathing and heartbeat (such as in a persistent vegetative state).

Honesty The quality of deliberate truthfulness and authenticity in one's actions and interactions; a lack of deception.

Horizontal violence Abuse committed by nurses toward other nurses; conflict and anger occurring among nurses as opposed to conflict coming from outside the nursing community.

I

Imaginative dramatic rehearsal Imagining an ideal scenario (such as an ideal death) to take meaning from the experience and shape how the scenario plays out in real life.

Induced abortion The result of a woman's intentional termination of a pregnancy either artificially or therapeutically and is also referred to as abortion.

Infertility The inability to conceive a child.

Informed consent Agreement to a procedure or action based on an understanding of the facts and possible consequences of said procedure or action. The three basic elements of informed consent are as follows: (1) receipt of information, (2) voluntary (unforced) agreement to the conditions presented, and (3) competency of the person or persons providing consent.

Inheritable genetic modification (IGM) Changes made to a person's genetic material that would not only affect that person but all of the person's descendants.

Integrity Honest and just behavior; maintaining consistent, ethical values in actions and relationships.

Interests view A view requiring that a being must have rights and interests at stake, which implies sentience and some degree of moral standing; those interests must matter morally to the being, and the being must be sentient enough to know what could be done to it.

Intuition test Asking if the intended action has a smell of moral wrongdoing, such as feeling not quite right, feeling wrong or uncomfortable, having an air of corruption, or making one cringe.

Involuntary euthanasia The intentional taking of one's life when the person could consent but does not, for example, in cases of capital punishment.

J

Just generosity Giving that reflects the needs of, rather than what is perceived to be owed to, the recipients.

Justice A moral concept of rightness based on fairness and equality.

Justified paternalism The belief that beneficence overrules the need to respect autonomy in cases where a patient's judgment is compromised and the planned interventions would be deemed acceptable by general consensus.

K

Kantian deontology A specific type of deontology, formulated by Immanuel Kant (1724–1804), in which the morality of an action is based on only the dutifulness of the action itself, not on the action's consequences. In Kantian deontology, the ends can never justify the means because people are an end in and of themselves and should never merely be used to attain some goal.

L

Late adolescence The third and final stage of an adolescent's development; this step takes place between the ages of 18 and 21 years and is completed by the transition from adolescence to adulthood, demonstrated by the increased importance of the future.

Late-term abortion An abortion performed in the third trimester.

Leader One who is able to influence others.

Leader succession planning Preparing and nurturing those with leadership skills and potential.

Libertarianism A theory of entitlement that suggests only those who contribute to the system should be able to receive the benefits of said system.

Liberty rights Also called negative rights. Rights a person has the freedom to express without the need for assistance from others. Freedom of speech and civil rights are examples of liberty rights. See *claim rights*.

Limits of confidentiality The situations in which patient confidentiality can be breached, usually consisting of situations in which there is potential harm to a patient or others.

Living will A formal legal document that outlines a person's desired medical care to be provided in specific circumstances; a type of advance directive.

M

Malpractice Improper or unethical conduct or unreasonable lack of skill by a nurse or other professional that results in damages.

Mandated choice The requirement that competent individuals select an option, such as in organ donation, on official documents (e.g., drivers' licenses, tax returns). This decision becomes binding unless written documentation to reverse the decision is provided.

Marginalized population Populations considered to be at the fringes of society that lack power to improve their situation in society.

Market justice The belief that benefits and burdens should be distributed based on individual abilities and contributions (i.e., wealthy people should not have to shoulder burdens because of their success).

Maternal–fetal conflict The conflict that arises when the interests of a pregnant woman (as defined by the woman) differ from the interests of the fetus (as defined by a physician).

Mechanistic approach An approach to health care associated with acting as if one is fixing a machine rather than treating a human being.

Medical futility The unacceptably low chance of physicians achieving a therapeutic benefit for the patient.

Medicalization The transformation of human social conditions into medical diagnoses so physicians then have the authority to prescribe treatments and preventive measures for the condition.

Metaethics The study of the terminology of morality (e.g., good, wrong) to understand concepts and ideas related to moral behavior.

Mia A popular abbreviation for bulimia nervosa, which is sometimes personified by adolescents.

Middle adolescence The second stage of an adolescent's development; this step takes place between the ages of 14 and 18 years and is dominated by peer influence and a need for peer acceptance and validation.

Mindfulness Being engaged and attentive in activities or roles by continuously analyzing, categorizing, and distinguishing data.

Mindlessness A state of unawareness and not focusing, similar to functioning in autopilot mode.

Moral agency The ability to make decisions that can affect the well-being of oneself or others; taking responsibility for one's own thoughts, beliefs, and actions.

Moral community A community formed by people who want to work toward promoting a sense of well-being and common good for all members of said community.

Moral courage The ability to act rightly in spite of opposition or constraints.

Moral distress The feelings of anguish or frustration when the right thing is impossible to do.

Moral imagination The use of creative thought processes, such as empathetic projection, to make moral decisions and become aware of new possibilities and answers to questions; often involves asking the question "What if?"

Moral integrity Being in possession of characteristics (such as honesty and trustworthiness) that traditionally define a person with good character; following a framework of internal, consistent values in all actions or dealings.

Moral reasoning The use of critical thinking to examine questions of right and wrong. See *reasoning*.

Moral rights Inherent, universal privileges that cannot be taken away.

Moral self-government A person's ethics, values, and direction as linked to his or her ability to make decisions that are consistent with his or her personal worldview.

Moral space The space in which people live their lives.

Moral suffering Feelings of discomfort or anguish that come from the imperfectness of life, when there is no satisfactory outcome to a situation, when it is impossible to affect change in a negative situation, or when persons choose to act in ways contrary to what they believe to be moral.

Morals Ethically derived thoughts and actions that are judged good or bad based on ethical reasoning; the goodness of how people actually behave.

Mothering person A gender-neutral term used to describe the type of mothering that would occur in a society without male domination.

N

Narrative approach to ethics Using personal stories as a means to do ethics.

Negligence Failure of a nurse to give care as a reasonably prudent and careful person would give under similar circumstances.

Nonadherence The degree to which a prescribed treatment regimen will not be followed; nonadherence can be intentional or caused by constraints outside the patient's control.

Noncompliance Not following a healthcare professional's suggested treatment regimen (i.e., not taking or incorrectly taking prescribed medications), either intentionally or otherwise.

Nonmaleficence The ethical obligation to not cause harm. See *beneficence*.

Nonvoluntary euthanasia The intentional taking of a patient's life when the patient is unable to consent to the procedure, for example, after authorization by a surrogate decision maker.

Normative ethics A form of ethical inquiry concerned with determining how humans should act and should be in terms of character.

Nursing ethics The study of moral issues related to and through the lens of nursing. Issues include those associated with the basic concepts of nursing, such as health and healing.

O

Obesity The accumulation of excess body fat.

Observer evaluation Quality-of-life judgments made by someone other than the person whose life is under consideration.

Occupational fraud and abuse The use of one's position of employment for personal gain attained via unlawful or unethical actions.

Opportunistic infections and diseases The HIV-related infections that invade the body.

Organ procurement The act of obtaining, transferring, and processing organs for transplantation through systems, organizations, or programs.

Organization A group of people who work together to attain shared goals.

Organizational citizenship The expectations that society has for open systems, specifically in terms of the relationships that organizations have with their communities.

Organizational culture An organization's common philosophy, behavior, and focus either in the past or as currently experienced.

Organizational ethics The goodness of actions, character, and purpose of an organization along with its culture.

Organizational integrity The widespread valuing of honesty and right behavior across an organization's membership.

Organizational trust The authenticity and dependability of an organization regarding its interactions with others (individuals, other organizations, society as a whole).

P

Palliative care Care that focuses on maintaining quality of life and relieving pain and suffering instead of effecting a cure.

Partial-birth abortion A nonmedical term that refers to a procedure called intact dilation and extraction (intact D&E), used to perform abortions in the third trimester. See *late-term abortion*.

Passive euthanasia Taking a life by the purposeful withdrawal or withholding of treatments or procedures used to prolong or sustain life.

Paternalism The belief that the requirement to act beneficently outweighs the need to respect a person's autonomy; the idea that people in positions of authority know what's best and it is acceptable for said authority figures to make decisions on behalf of others.

Patience Detaching from one's own agenda and outcomes and waiting on and being open to another's agenda.

Patient advocacy Working to uphold the rights and needs of patients via three core features: protecting patient autonomy, promoting patients' wishes, and effecting social justice in health care.

Persistent vegetative state A state in which a person with severe brain damage has enough automatic function to survive with constant medical intervention (e.g., can breathe without a ventilator) but does not exhibit any awareness or higher-brain function.

Personal dignity The value a community places on an individual and the individual's place in society.

Personal evaluation In quality-of-life judgments, a person's rating of the value of his or her own life.

Personal integrity Extending attention and care to one's own requisite needs.

Personhood A capacity for human beings to have complex forms of consciousness.

Phronesis A Greek term associated with the practice of wisdom or good judgment.

Physician-assisted suicide Taking one's own life via self-administration of physician-ordered drugs. Also known as physician-assisted dying.

Population A group of people who share at least one defining characteristic but do not necessarily have a shared interest in a common good. See *community*.

Potentiality view The view that a fetus, from the time of conception, possesses the potential to be a person with the same rights and protections that already-born persons appoint to themselves.

Power The ability to successfully influence the actions of others.

Praxis in nursing Ethics is embedded in practice and all activities of nursing.

Precautionary principle A guiding principle that action should be taken to prevent a future harm even if there is no conclusive scientific evidence that the future harm is inevitable.

Preimplantation genetic diagnosis (PGD) The use of genetic testing to screen embryos for multiple characteristics, including gender and potential genetic abnormalities.

Prenatal genetic diagnosis Genetic testing performed on a fetus to screen for genetic disorders prior to birth.

Presumed consent The automatic consent to a procedure or action unless the person specifically indicates the opposite. Used in some countries as the approach to organ donation (i.e., persons are assumed to agree to organ donation unless they have stated otherwise).

Prima facie "On the face of things;" accepting something as true based on face value until it is shown to be untrue.

Principlism An approach to ethics guided by fundamental bioethical directives or concepts.

PRISMS An acronym of actions central to patient advocacy: persuade, respect, intercede, safeguard, monitor, and support.

Privacy Freedom from intrusion (including keeping information inaccessible).

Privilege A legal status that protects certain individuals (such as medical professions) from having to disclose information in court proceedings; privilege is not guaranteed, and there are limits to the types of information that can be kept confidential.

Professional boundaries A set of limits that define the relationships between nurses and those with whom they interact. Boundaries establish a sense of mutual control and safe space.

Prudence The virtue of wisdom that is an extension of *phronesis*.

Psychiatric advance directive (PAD) Written instructions regarding a patient's wishes pertaining to his or her psychiatric treatment should the patient lose the ability to consent to treatment.

Pure autonomy standard Using a previously autonomous (but now incapacitated) patient's own decisions and wishes to direct care.

Q

Quality Excellence and high standards with regard to a product or service.

Qui tam **lawsuits** Also known as whistle-blower lawsuits; lawsuits filed by private citizens, on behalf of the government, against recipients of federal money that are alleged to have committed wrongdoing.

R

Rational suicide A type of voluntary, active euthanasia in which a person takes his or her own life after careful consideration and for reasons that would seem understandable to outside parties.

Reasoning The use of critical thinking to examine questions and reach sound, logical conclusions.

Required response Adults in the United States are mandated to express their wishes about organ donation.

Right to die The idea that an autonomous person has the prerogative to refuse life-saving or life-sustaining treatments.

Rule of double effect A set of criteria used to determine the ethics of a decision that involves weighing the benefit of an action (the intended, expected, positive outcome) with its possible negative but foreseeable consequences or effects. The action is considered ethical if the action in and of itself is moral, the actor intends only the positive outcome, or the good outcome greatly outweighs the possible negatives.

Rule utilitarians Followers of utilitarianism who believe there are specific rules that should be adhered to because they usually (though not necessarily always) provide the most benefit for the largest number of people. Compare with *act utilitarians*.

S

Secret drinking Hidden or underground consumption of alcohol.

Sense of harmony Remaining in contact with the reality of a situation and with others.

Sense of responsibility Knowing that people are interconnected and responsibility grows from that interconnectedness.

Sentient being A person with awareness, perception, and a capacity for feelings.

Servant leader A leader who puts the good of the group being led before his or her own personal desires or aggrandizement.

Sexual abstinence Traditionally, not engaging in sexual intercourse (specifically, penis–vagina penetrative intercourse). However, because of the variety of alternative methods for demonstrating sexual intimacy that do not involve vaginal penetration and the rise in same-sex relationships among adolescents, a new definition is necessary.

Sexual abuse Any form of unwanted sexual activity by one person on another, with perpetrators using force or making threats surrounded by apprehension and fear.

Slippery slope argument An argument based on the proposition that an action or decision can have critical, unforeseen consequences at some point in the future. In some cases, the original action or decision is morally justifiable, but the hypothetical potential outcomes are considered unethical or dangerous. Slippery slope arguments, because they deal with potential—not actual—outcomes, often are lacking in sufficient supporting evidence.

Social justice The belief in equality for all people.

Social media Internet-based applications that enable collaborative, community-based exchange of user-generated information.

Socialized power The idea that power should be used to promote the well-being of others.

Soft paternalism See *weak paternalism*.

Sperm sorting The use of genetic testing to select specific embryos for in vitro fertilization. See *preimplantation genetic diagnosis*.

Spirituality A sense of a unification of self with the world, with or without a belief in a higher power; a highly personal and important part of a person's being.

Stench test Asking if the intended action has a smell of moral wrongdoing, such as feeling not quite right, feeling wrong or uncomfortable, having an air of corruption, or making one cringe.

Stigma Individuals' personal characteristics (such as mental illness) that are associated with being dishonorable or shameful.

Substituted judgment standard Used to guide medical decisions for formerly competent patients who no longer have any decision-making capacity and based on the assumption that incompetent patients have the identical rights as competent patients to make judgments about their health care.

Successful leader A leader who works to ensure that the values of an organization align with those of its members.

Suffering A perceived undesirable inner experience that could threaten the whole existence of being, yet it is a necessary element of life, as are joy and happiness. The feeling experienced when a person is unable to achieve personal fulfillment; a negative experience that permeates the entire being.

Suffering person A tormented being whose pain can be apparent to others.

Suicidal ideation A person's preoccupation with suicide.

Suicidal tendency Behaviors, words, or actions that suggest a person is considering suicide.

Suicide The slaying of one's own life.

Surplus reproductive products The sperm, eggs, and embryos that are left after a successful pregnancy. Because in vitro fertilization has a low success rate, multiple fertilized eggs may be created but remain unused.

Surrogacy The use of a third party to carry a fetus to term.

Surrogate decision maker Also known as a proxy; an individual who is chosen to act on behalf of a patient who is incapable of making decisions. Either the patient, patient–surrogate relationship status, or the courts dictate this privilege.

T

Tall poppy syndrome Acts of horizontal violence, also labeled as *workplace bullying*, in which people are attacked or criticized because of their (perceived or actual) achievements and success.

Terminal sedation Sedating a patient into unconsciousness and then withholding life-sustaining measures until the patient dies.

Theory A fact-based explanation for how something works or why things happen a certain way.

Therapeutic privilege The right of physicians to withhold information from patients based on the potential for said information to harm the patient. Determinations of when this privilege can or should be used range from circumstances when divulging the information may lead to any negative effects to when the information potentially will lead to serious negative consequences.

Tolerance Detaching from one's own agenda and outcomes and waiting on and being open to another's agenda.

Traditional surrogacy A form of surrogacy in which the surrogate donates her eggs, which are artificially inseminated using sperm from the prospective father.

Transformational leader A leader who emphasizes improving the well-being of his or her followers by changing the culture in which they all work or live.

Trust The belief that others will not take advantage of one's vulnerabilities.

Trustworthiness Authenticity related to how dependable and accountable for one's actions a person is.

Truthfulness A lack of deception when interacting and speaking with others; when translated to *truthtelling* in the medical profession, an ethical obligation to provide accurate information combined with respecting a person's autonomy.

U

Unavoidable trust Patients' dependent need to have confidence in healthcare professionals' integrity and competence before this confidence has been earned.

Underage drinking The consumption of alcohol by persons younger than the legal drinking age (i.e., younger than 21 years old in the United States).

Uniform Determination of Death Act (UDDA) Legislation passed in 1981 by the National Conference of Commissioners on Uniform State Laws to provide a comprehensive and consistent means for determining death.

Utilitarianism An approach to ethics based on consequentialism; actions and behaviors should be judged by the usefulness of their outcomes (compare with *Kantian deontology*). Ethical behavior produces the most good or happiness and the least harm or unhappiness in a given situation.

V

Value Something that is viewed as good, meaningful, desirable, or worthwhile.

Veil of ignorance The idea that people would make impartial decisions regarding resource distribution if they were unable to know the potential impact on themselves or significant others; if a cover (veil) shielded people from seeing their place within society, this lack of knowledge (ignorance) would help them make unbiased decisions because they would not know if or how such decisions would positively or negatively affect their own situation once the veil is lifted.

Virtue ethics An approach to ethics concerned with *being* good and having moral character rather than *doing* good and following rules or focusing on duties. The normative question asked is "How should I be?" rather than "What should I do?" Compare with *deontology*.

Virtues Excellent character traits that persons develop through consistently good habits or education.

Voluntary euthanasia An autonomous patient makes the decision to end his or her life. See *physician-assisted suicide*.

W

Walking wounded Nurses who are traumatized by workplace bullying.

Weak paternalism Making decisions regarding what is best for a person when the person's ability to be autonomous (self-directing) is compromised in some way (when a person is unable to make rational decisions).

Whole-brain death or permanent brain failure Death is regarded as the irreversible cessation of all brain functions, with no electrical activity in the brain, including the brain stem.

Wholeness of character (in nursing) The recognition, integration, and expression of the values of the nursing profession and one's own moral values.

Wisdom An ethical competence that requires calculated intellectual ability, contemplation, deliberation, and efforts to achieve a worthy goal.

Withholding and withdrawing treatment The forgoing of life-sustaining treatment that the patient does not desire because of either a perceived disproportionate burden on the patient or family members or other reasons.

Workplace bullying Interpersonal conflict, harassment, intimidation, harsh criticism, sabotage, and abuse among nurses.

Wounded healers Nurses who begin to transform and transcend their wounds from workplace bullying to healing.

Index

Note: Page numbers followed by *b, f,* and *t* indicate material in boxes, figures, and tables, respectively.